The American South
and the Vietnam War

The American South
and the
Vietnam War

Belligerence,
Protest,
and Agony
in Dixie

JOSEPH A. FRY

UNIVERSITY PRESS OF KENTUCKY

Copyright © 2015 by The University Press of Kentucky

Scholarly publisher for the Commonwealth,
serving Bellarmine University, Berea College, Centre College of Kentucky, Eastern
Kentucky University, The Filson Historical Society, Georgetown College,
Kentucky Historical Society, Kentucky State University, Morehead State
University, Murray State University, Northern Kentucky University, Transylvania
University, University of Kentucky, University of Louisville, and Western
Kentucky University.
All rights reserved.

Editorial and Sales Offices: The University Press of Kentucky
663 South Limestone Street, Lexington, Kentucky 40508-4008
www.kentuckypress.com

Library of Congress Cataloging-in-Publication Data

Fry, Joseph A., 1947–
  The American South and the Vietnam War : belligerence, protest, and agony in
Dixie / Joseph A. Fry.
     pages cm. — (Studies in conflict, diplomacy, and peace)
  Includes bibliographical references and index.
  ISBN 978-0-8131-6104-4 (hardcover : alk. paper) —
  ISBN 978-0-8131-6109-9 (pdf) — ISBN 978-0-8131-6108-2 (epub)
  1. Vietnam War, 1961–1975—Southern States. 2. Vietnam War, 1961–
1975—Political aspects—Southern States. 3. Southern States—Politics and
government—20th century. 4. Public opinion—Southern States—History—20th
century. 5. Southern States—History, Military—20th century. 6. Vietnam War,
1961–1975—Influence. I. Title.
  DS559.62.S68F79 2015
  959.704'310975—dc23   2014049411

This book is printed on acid-free paper meeting
the requirements of the American National Standard
for Permanence in Paper for Printed Library Materials.
∞

Manufactured in the United States of America.

Member of the Association of
American University Presses

For Sandy

Contents

Photographs follow page 238

Abbreviations

ABM	Anti-Ballistic Missile System
AFB	air force base
ARVN	Army of the Republic of Vietnam (South Vietnam)
CIDG	Civilian Irregular Defense Group
CINCPAC	Commander in Chief, Pacific Command
CO	conscientious objection/objector
CORE	Congress of Racial Equality
DMZ	demilitarized zone
DOD	Department of Defense
DRV	Democratic Republic of Vietnam (North Vietnam)
GVN	Republic of South Vietnam
HBCU	historically black colleges and universities
JCS	Joint Chiefs of Staff
LBJ	Lyndon Baines Johnson
LZ	landing zone
MACV	Military Assistance Command, South Vietnam
NAACP	National Association for the Advancement of Colored People
NASA	National Aeronautics and Space Administration
NATO	North Atlantic Treaty Organization
NCO	noncommissioned officer
NLF	National Front for the Liberation of Vietnam
NSC-68	National Security Council Paper No. 68
NVA	North Vietnamese Army
OAS	Organization of American States
OPPLAN 34-A	Operation Plan 34-A

PCUS	Presbyterian Church in the United States
PNBC	Progressive National Baptist Convention
POW/MIA	prisoner of war/missing in action
PRC	People's Republic of China
R and R	rest and recuperation
ROTC	Reserve Officer Training Corps
SALT	Strategic Arms Limitation Treaty
SASC	Senate Armed Services Committee
SBC	Southern Baptist Convention
SCLC	Southern Christian Leadership Conference
SDS	Students for a Democratic Society
SEATO	Southeast Asia Treaty Organization
SFRC	Senate Foreign Relations Committee
SNCC	Student Nonviolent Coordinating Committee
SPIS	Senate Preparedness Investigating Subcommittee
SSOC	Southern Student Organizing Committee
UN	United Nations
USAF	United States Air Force
VC	Vietcong
VVAW	Vietnam Veterans Against the War

Introduction

Place matters in how Americans have responded to and been affected by US foreign policy. Over the past twenty-five years, scholars have cited the benefits of examining the impact of domestic regionalism on the formation and implementation of US foreign policy. In 1987 Carl N. Degler urged that the American South be viewed as "co-creator of the nation's history" rather than an "outsider" or an "obstacle" to national development; and, he declared, "What is called American foreign policy has often been heavily influenced if not molded by the South." A decade later, in 1998, Peter Trubowitz asserted, "In the final analysis, it is the realities of power inside a country, not the distribution of power in the international system, that determine the course of the nation's foreign policy." He continued, "When viewed over time and across a wide range of issues, sectional interests emerge as a powerful and consistent force shaping" US foreign policy. More recently, Paul Boyer has contended that "all diplomatic history" is "local": "Just as other fields of history are taking into account the local and grassroots sources and consequences of the processes they study, so diplomatic historians are becoming more aware of how illuminating this perspective can be."[1]

Nowhere has this dynamic of regional influence on US foreign relations been more apparent than in the American South. As residents of the most self-conscious and persistent US region from the nation's founding through at least the mid-1970s, southerners have habitually viewed US foreign relations through a distinctly regional lens grounded in a variety of shared cultural values, historical assumptions, and perceived regional interests. Over the course of American history, regional foreign policy preferences have ultimately been expressed through the political process, and regions characterized by one-party dominance have had the greatest impact on US foreign relations. Here again, the South has been conspicuous. Michael Perman has demonstrated that the one-party, politically solid South has regularly functioned not just as a region but also as a "self-conscious interest group" in domestic politics. This sectional perspective and leverage have also been brought to bear in the realm of foreign policy from the 1780s through the period of the Vietnam War.[2]

Indeed, Dixie's regional importance was graphically apparent and influential as southerners took center stage during the Vietnam conflict, the largest and most disastrous US military intervention abroad during the Cold War. President Lyndon B. Johnson and Secretary of State Dean Rusk oversaw the dramatic escalation of US military involvement from 1964 through 1968. As chairmen of the Senate and House Appropriations and Armed Services Committees, southern political leaders such as Senators Richard B. Russell and John C. Stennis and Congressmen L. Mendel Rivers and George H. Mahon shepherded essential funding bills through Congress, first under Johnson and then under his successor, Richard M. Nixon. Collectively, Dixie's senators and congressmen provided both decisive support for war appropriations and opposition to legislative attempts to hasten or compel US withdrawal from Vietnam. These strategically placed and conservative southern Democrats pressed relentlessly for more aggressive prosecution of the conflict and helped prolong the war, particularly as Democrats from other regions grew increasingly opposed to Nixon's Vietnam policies.

While serving and dying in disproportionate numbers relative to Dixie's population, southern soldiers also played formative roles. General William Westmoreland from South Carolina commanded American forces during most of the Johnson presidency and initiated the policies of search and destroy and attrition; in 1965 then–Lieutenant Colonel Harold G. "Hal" Moore, a Kentuckian, led his air cavalry troops against North Vietnamese regulars in the brutal confrontation in the Ia Drang Valley, perhaps the war's most celebrated battle; and two southerners were at the center of the My Lai massacre, the most infamous American-inflicted atrocity of the war. William L. Calley Jr. commanded the platoon responsible for killing more than five hundred unarmed women, children, and old men. Hugh C. Thompson Jr., a helicopter pilot and the "forgotten hero" of this tragic incident, dramatically confronted US soldiers while defending Vietnamese civilians. And two of Dixie's marines, Jim Webb and Gustav Hasford, wrote very different but very southern and very revealing novels based on their combat experiences in the war. Assessing the motives and experiences of these more recognizable southerners, as well as their less well-known comrades in arms, yields telling insights into the region's military tradition, prowar proclivities, devotion to honor, and demonstrative patriotism.

Majority opinion in the South, whether gauged through polling data, constituent correspondence, newspaper editorials, letters to editors, or the beliefs and attitudes of Dixie's soldiers, endorsed the prowar positions of southern legislators. Compared to Americans from other regions, southerners most often agreed that "wars are sometimes necessary to settle differences"; were least comfortable with Johnson's limited-war strategy and most in favor of going "all-out to win a military victory"; most supportive of bombing large North Vietnamese cities; most willing to pay higher taxes to finance the war; least sympathetic to proposals for a fixed withdrawal date for US troops; least willing to concede that US intervention in Vietnam had been a mistake; and most receptive to various "stab-in-the-back" explanations for the US defeat.[3]

The majority of southerners also evidenced intense dislike for student protestors. Antiwar students were a distinct minority on all American college campuses, but their status was especially pronounced in the South. Given the region's prowar proclivities and the active hostility of southern politicians, press, college administrators, and communities toward demonstrators, southern students were predictably more prowar and less activist than their peers in other regions. Despite these obstacles, hardy southern dissenters objected to the war as early as the one-thousand-person teach-in at Emory University in 1965 and mounted important protests as late as 1970, when twenty thousand students marched from the University of Texas campus to the state capitol in Austin. Examining southern students' responses to the war augments the regional perspectives gleaned from assessing Dixie's political leaders, public opinion, and soldiers.

The South's majority prowar stance derived from a host of distinctly regional values, perspectives, and interests. Staunchly conservative, most southerners readily agreed with the nation's Cold War goal of containing communism and viewed Vietnam as a crucial battleground in the worldwide conflict with the Soviet Union and the People's Republic of China. Acute concern for personal, regional, and national honor rendered southerners decidedly sympathetic to the argument that US credibility in the international arena hinged on defeating North Vietnam and the Vietcong and avoiding the humiliation of losing the war. The region's self-conscious military tradition and vocal patriotism, both central products of Dixie's Civil War experience, strongly reinforced the section's anticommunism and devotion to honor, as did the South's overwhelming commitment to a conservative, evangelical Protestantism, which made defeating atheistic communism much more than a political, strategic, or military priority. To these ideological influences, most southerners added the critical constitutional practice of granting the president broad discretionary authority in the areas of foreign policy and war making.

Economic, political, and racial calculations reinforced these southern ideological assumptions. "Fortress Dixie" had long benefited from national defense spending, and defense-related appropriations, which the Vietnam War stimulated. These fiscal benefits complemented the region's conviction that peace was best ensured by possessing superior military strength.[4] Partisan politics also colored southern attitudes on the war. Democratic loyalties were critical to Johnson's retaining the support of a majority of southern legislators who deplored his civil rights and Great Society legislation and gradual escalation of the war. By contrast, Richard Nixon's southern political strategy deemphasizing civil rights, promises to achieve "peace with honor," and ostensibly more aggressive military posture induced Dixie's conservative Democrats and a majority of the southern public to cross party lines and back the Republican president. For the majority of southerners, racial assumptions and the pursuit of traditional military victory trumped party politics.

Not all southerners were hawks. Senators J. William Fulbright, Albert Gore Sr., and John Sherman Cooper and the Reverend Martin Luther King Jr. were among the nation's most thoughtful, articulate, and influential critics of the war. Equally important, southern opposition to the war reached far beyond these political figures. Letters to the editors of southern papers and constituent correspondence to southern senators and congressmen reveal a highly discerning popular opposition to the war and a devastating critique of the conflict. The ability of these dissenters, whether prominent public figures or less well-known members of southern society, to transcend both the nation's Cold War mentality and the South's majority perception of the conflict warrants careful attention. Understanding the South's dissenting minority not only yields more inclusive insight into the region's thinking and impact on the Vietnam War but also helps clarify Dixie's majority sectional perspectives.

That Reverend King was among the most significant opponents of the war highlights the ever-present consideration of race as Dixie responded to US involvement in Vietnam. Most white southerners viewed the nonwhite Vietnamese as inferior. As Thomas McCormick has aptly observed, "People do not think one way about their national society and a different way about world society. Instead, they tend to project and internalize conceptual frameworks first articulated at home." Perceiving the Vietnamese as inferior, "as a damn little pissant country," in the words of Lyndon Johnson, yielded different inclinations. Such assumptions could produce overconfidence, even arrogance, and led LBJ and other southerners to underestimate the North Vietnamese and Vietcong, or from a more benign perspective, caused Johnson to see the South Vietnamese as needing the same assistance as the poor or minorities in America. Similar perceptions could prompt war managers such as Westmoreland to Americanize the war in response to assumed South Vietnamese military deficiencies. Or perceived South Vietnamese incompetence could discourage US involvement. Richard Russell's assessment of Asians as "devious, lazy and selfish"; unlikely to take responsibility for their own destiny; and unable to understand and adopt democracy led him to oppose American intervention.[5]

The views of black southerners complicate matters further. Like their white neighbors, African Americans agonized over the war, over the desire to serve the nation and demonstrate patriotism and the realization that blacks were more likely to be drafted, serve, and die in Vietnam. Given this reality and their objection to the disparity between stated US goals in Vietnam and the treatment of minorities at home, African Americans were more opposed to the war's escalation and more in favor of US withdrawal than white southerners. Blacks placed a priority on domestic, especially economic, and racial issues and identified with nonwhite opponents of colonial domination. These perspectives led to prominent antiwar pronouncements from groups such as the Student Nonviolent Coordinating Committee and individuals such as Julian Bond, Cassius Clay (later Muhammad Ali), and, most important, Reverend King. These pronouncements elicited criticism from those in the black community who feared opposition to the war would divert and weaken the drive for civil rights and provide ammunition for hostile southern whites who condemned King and other African American critics of the war as unpatriotic, communist sympathizers. Despite these high-profile dissenters and black dissatisfaction in the military, the majority of African Americans, like their southern white neighbors, remained supportive of the war.

Both Ali and King, the most well-known black Americans during the Vietnam War era, added a religious rationale for opposing the war. Of course, when compared to Ali's Muslim tenets, King's Baptist teachings were far more familiar to southern blacks and whites who opposed the war on the grounds that it violated their Christian beliefs. Just as religion and race could induce southerners to both support and oppose the war, Dixie's devotion to honor also cut both ways. Rather than worrying about America's international credibility and reputation, antiwar southerners contended that honor demanded the United States and its leaders admit their mistakes in becoming involved in Vietnam and right that tragic wrong with prompt US withdrawal. As the war devolved into a murderous stalemate by 1967, some southern fiscal conservatives objected to the waste of tax dollars and national resources. Pointing to the North's occupation of the South following the Civil War and to Dixie's persistent colonial economic status, Fulbright and other southern dissenters criticized the colonial nature of the US intervention and professed greater respect for the nationalistic Vietnamese opposition to outside domination. From another very southern perspective, antiwar residents of Dixie asked segregationists such as Richard Russell and J. Samuel Ervin Jr. how they would respond if another nation interfered in American racial disputes. This same sensitivity to regional dependence helped spawn southern objections to an overly powerful Cold War presidency and the dissenters' campaign for the reassertion of congressional authority in foreign policy and war making. Therefore, from religion to race, the attitudes of southerners, whether supporting or opposing the Vietnam War, were firmly rooted in regional history, values, and perceived interests.

In light of southerners' prominent roles in the Vietnam War, an examination of how the South responded to and influenced US policies speaks to an important facet of Dixie's history during the 1960s and 1970s. By assessing the region's relation to this critical episode in US foreign relations, this study addresses an aspect of the South's experience often ignored by historians of the region.[6] Focusing on the importance of domestic regionalism also moves the South from its frequent historical position on the periphery to the center of the narrative of a crucial national event. Understanding the South's influence also requires an examination of the role of Congress during the Vietnam era. Robert David Johnson has decried the lack of attention to "congressional influence . . . especially in works dealing with the Cold War"; and Johnson, William Conrad Gibbons, Robert Mann, and Andrew L. Johns have helped remedy this historiographical oversight, but only Mark David has done so from a distinctly regional perspective.[7]

Employing regionalism as a methodological approach also provides a viable mechanism for emphasizing and assessing the "internal determinants" of American foreign relations and addressing topics that have become increasingly important to the analysis of American involvement abroad. Over the past two decades, students of US foreign relations have advocated that traditional political and economic concerns be supplemented with greater attention to ideology, race and civil rights, gender, religion, and conceptions of honor and manhood. Applying regionalism as a holistic vehicle, an umbrella under which all of these domestic considerations can be incorporated, affords an inclusive methodology for assessing this broad array of relevant southern bases of Dixie's response to the Vietnam War. A careful evaluation of Dixie and the war also responds directly to recent scholarly appeals for closer appraisals of the Cold War's "impact" on "regional, local, and human levels." This appraisal elucidates not just the region's belligerence and protests but also the travails and agonies of war on the home front. By incorporating the words and stories of "regular," less prominent people as well as polling data, economic statistics, editorial opinion, and political debate, I hope to provide a more inclusive and textured understanding of the Vietnam experience within the United States. I have especially sought to gather the words and sentiments of the southern populace through an intensive reading of the correspondence southerners dispatched to their political representatives and to newspaper editors.[8]

Finally, approaching the war from the South's regional perspective yields significant insights into the conflict's nature and duration. Despite their prescient objections to a US military intervention in Southeast Asia, southern political leaders acquiesced in and even aided Johnson as he made the critical US commitments to ensuring an independent, noncommunist South Vietnam and took the nation to war by "stealth." Thereafter, conservative southern Democrats and majority southern opinion played a central role in sustaining the conflict for nearly ten years. While echoing the aggressive prowar sentiments of a decisive majority of their constituents, these conservative southern Democrats joined national Republicans in providing both Lyndon Johnson and Richard Nixon their most dependable support for the war. This bellicose coalition reinforced the aggressive inclinations of both presidents and, in turn, made it politically hazardous for either chief executive to undertake meaningful negotiations with the North Vietnamese and Vietcong. By criticizing Johnson's alleged timidity and limited-war strategy, these southern Democrats and southern Republicans such as John Tower and Strom Thurmond also helped to further domestic discord and "popular confusion" over the war. And John Stennis, one of the most prominent and influential hawks and the chair of the Preparedness Investigating Subcommittee of the Senate Armed Service Committee, led the most aggressive congressional-military attempt to force Johnson to alter the conduct of the war and pursue an all-out victory.[9]

Although the majority of southerners allied themselves with the US military in the search for a forceful military solution in Vietnam, Dixie's doves also had a significant impact on Vietnam policy. Historian John Prados has asserted that "absent pressure" from forceful dissenters, Johnson (and by extension Nixon) would have faced "*no* political pressure to counteract escalation demands," and Melvin Small has argued that these dissenters' "antiwar messages . . . eventually filtered down to the public." Senators Fulbright, Gore, and Cooper and Reverend King were among the most important dissenters applying that pressure and propagating the antiwar message. Just as Senator Stennis led the most ambitious congressional attempt to alter the conduct of the war, Fulbright held the 1966 Senate Foreign Relations Committee hearings that spurred the first sustained debate about the war's origins and the nature of the US commitment, and Cooper spearheaded efforts during the Nixon years to legislate an end to the conflict.[10]

Before undertaking this examination of the South and Vietnam, two working definitions are in order. First, we must define regionalism, which, according to Edward L. Ayers and Peter S. Onuf, has embodied "a sense of common interest and identity across an extended" if at times "indeterminate space." Regions exist only within the context of the whole and have developed at least in part as a "reaction" to other parts of the nation. Scholars such as Richard Bensel and Peter Trubowitz have located the bases of American regionalism in a section's sense of common economic interests and the associated political representation. While agreeing on the centrality of economics and politics, other students of regionalism have added cultural and ideological dimensions. Within these latter domains, shared attitudes regarding honor, race, gender, religion, or violence contribute to regional coherence. This more comprehensive conception of regional determinants will be employed in this study.[11]

Defining the South constitutes the second critical task. While acknowledging several competing definitions of the South and even the strong objections in some quarters to the idea of southern "exceptionalism" or an overemphasis on a distinctive South, I remain convinced that the presence of the economic, political, cultural, and ideological criteria discussed in this introduction continued to sustain a "South" through at least the mid-1970s. For the purposes of this book, that South will include the eleven states of the Confederacy, Alabama, Arkansas, Georgia, Florida, Louisiana, Mississippi, North Carolina, South Carolina, Tennessee, Texas, and Virginia, plus Kentucky. The latter is included on the basis of geographic proximity, long dependence on staple agriculture and low-wage industries, racial attitudes, concern for personal and national honor, vocal patriotism, devotion to a Confederate-related military tradition, and religious preferences.[12]

Employing these definitions of regionalism and the South, this book is composed of six chronological and two topical chapters. The first chronological one, which examines the South and US foreign relations from 1789 through 1973, provides the broader historical background and context for Dixie's role in the Vietnam War. Chapters 2, 3, 5, 6, and 8 trace the region's political responses and influence from 1953 through 1973, while incorporating focused sections on Vietnam and defense spending in Dixie; African Americans, civil rights, and the war; southern reactions to GI coffeehouses; country music and Vietnam; southern women as mothers and wives; the attitudes and opinions of a broad cross section of the southern public as expressed in their own words; and the war-related experiences of such exceptional southerners as Frazier Woolard, a small-town attorney from eastern North Carolina, and Jerry McCuistion, a POW wife from Montgomery, Alabama. The two topical chapters, 4 and 7, assess the experiences of southern soldiers and students. Collectively, these materials convey the historical portrait of a region whose central and at times decisive role in the Vietnam War was marked by belligerence, protest, and agony.

1

Regionalism, Southerners, and US Foreign Relations, 1789–1973

As southerners turned their attention to the American war in Vietnam in the two decades after 1953, they did so with a long history of responding to US foreign relations from a distinctly regional perspective. From the adoption of the Constitution in 1789 until at least the mid-1970s, the South was the nation's most coherent and most self-conscious region. Over this span of nearly two centuries, southerners periodically exercised a significant, even decisive, influence over policy formation and implementation, while at other times, they served as the dissenting minority in the domestic negotiation of foreign policy. Southern influence was instrumental during the Jefferson-Jackson years, the Wilson administration, and the Johnson presidency, and in the nation's decisions for war in 1812, 1846, 1917, and 1939–1941. Southerners adopted a largely oppositional posture during the 1790s and from 1865 through 1912.

The South, like other American regions, has exercised its greatest influence on US foreign policy formation during periods of one-party political dominance. In his political history of the South, Michael Perman has demonstrated convincingly that for most of the nation's first 180 years Dixie persistently sought political "unity" rather than "competition between contending parties." Only during the period from the late 1830s to the early 1850s did a viable two-party system exist, with the Whigs opposing the Jacksonian Democrats. Perman asserts that this largely solid political South functioned not just as a region but also as a "self-conscious interest group" until the mid-1970s. One-party dominance ensured repeated reelection for southern congressmen and senators. Their long and potentially more influential careers made southerners the majority congressional contingent, first with the Jeffersonians and then with the Democratic Party into the 1960s, and further augmented the South's influence within a committee system that rewarded seniority. Dixie brought this same political leverage to bear on both foreign and domestic policy.[1]

Although white southerners exercised varying degrees of influence over US foreign policy at different historical junctures and never presented a completely united sectional perspective, they acted from a consistent set of regional assumptions and interests. These concerns and objectives included the fear of being a minority section and the defense of personal and regional independence; the protection of southern racial institutions, first slavery and after 1865 segregation and black disfranchisement; the pursuit of regionally beneficial economic interests, trade policies, and defense spending; a heightened sense of honor, manhood, and patriotism; the proclamation and practice after the Civil War of an increasingly emotional and evangelical religious faith; and the advancement of partisan political goals. By the eve of US entry into Vietnam, these regional assumptions and interests led the South to favor a unilateral and often interventionist foreign policy that was aggressively anticommunist, decidedly supportive of the military and the pursuit of peace through strength, and more inclined than other American regions to solve international problems through the use of force rather than diplomacy.

Southern African Americans added another important dimension to the South's response to US foreign policy. Beginning with the Spanish-Cuban-American War of 1898, southern blacks pointedly noted the contradiction between the oppression of minorities at home and US foreign policies ostensibly devoted to the promotion of freedom and democracy abroad. Given their primary focus on domestic issues and post-1945 identification with people of color abroad, who were often seeking to escape from colonial control, African Americans were less rigidly anticommunist and less enthusiastic about US Cold War military interventions than their white neighbors.

As southerners joined other Americans in forming the new nation after 1776, they acted from an acute concern for individual, sectional, and ultimately national liberties. During the colonial period, southerners had equated political "liberty" with local control and had effectively established that control by expanding the powers of the lower houses of their colonial assemblies at the expense of British authorities. Dixie's antebellum economic development reinforced the commitment to personal and regional autonomy. From the 1600s through the Civil War, the South emphasized the production and export of staple crops rather than the development of a more diverse and sophisticated industrial or technological infrastructure. This economic system left the South in a colonial relationship with the North and Great Britain—a relationship whose irritations were intensified by the experience of coping with the burden of debt and vagaries of international markets.[2]

Racial beliefs and the institution of slavery were intrinsically tied to the South's staple agricultural economy and by extension to the determination to resist personal and regional dependence. From the 1790s until the Civil War, African American slaves constituted one-third of the South's population and provided much of the labor crucial to Dixie's agricultural prosperity. Owning slaves was widely identified with upward social mobility, and sectional well-being was tied to the institution's westward expansion. Given the centrality of slavery to the southern economy and social system, defending the peculiar institution, often via the vehicle of states' rights, commanded a high priority among southern leaders. According to Kenneth S. Greenberg, "From 1776 to 1860 the liberty white southerners celebrated always included the freedom to preserve the slavery of blacks." Indeed, slavery, the mirror of image of liberty, the "condition most cherished by Southerners," embodied a constant, graphic reminder of the dangers of dependence, oppression, and loss of freedom.[3]

For southern white men, avoiding dependence was crucial to safeguarding their honor and manhood. Southerners harbored an ardent concern for honor and its relation to demonstrated manhood, personal bravery, and devotion to family, region, and country. Antebellum southern men acted from a strong need for both a sense of self-worth and recognition of that worth by others. Real or perceived insults to one's family or region were intolerable if honor were to be properly maintained. Physical assaults and murder were more common in the South than the North, and the all-too-frequent duels most often occurred "because one antagonist cast doubt on the manliness and bearing of the other." Southern concern with "courage as a social value" and the "most efficacious means for exhibiting and defending personal, family, regional, and national honor" elevated military service to the level of planter, lawyer, or doctor among southerners. Albeit in altered forms, this southern commitment to the "ethic of honor" and the "warrior ethic" has exercised ongoing influence into the twenty-first century.[4]

These political, economic, and social experiences and assumptions rendered southerners particularly receptive to the ideology of "republicanism" with its emphasis on the maintenance of civic virtue and protection of political liberty. According to the proponents of republicanism, civic virtue existed only if citizens possessed economic, social, and political freedom, and those conditions were in turn dependent upon widespread ownership of property within an agricultural society. The more urban, more industrialized societies in Great Britain and New England, which ostensibly produced greater income disparities, impoverished factory workers, and more extreme concentrations of wealth, constituted the undesirable alternative. To avoid these social and political calamities, southerners such as Thomas Jefferson, James Madison, John Calhoun, John Tyler, and James K. Polk advocated the acquisition of new agricultural lands and markets to prolong the nation's status as an overwhelmingly agrarian republic. Working from this ideological perspective, southern republicans also argued that centralized governmental authority (unless under Dixie's direction!), standing armies, public debt, and bloated bureaucracies similarly threatened cherished liberties.[5]

With the Constitution of 1787 came a geopolitical framework that reinforced the South's republicanism and self-conscious regionalism. According to Peter Onuf, both "before and after independence, vigilant republicans sought to guard against dangerous concentrations of power." With no "great metropolis, a privileged central place," that dominated the nation's wealth and power, fears of outside oppression were "conceptualized in spatial, geographical terms." Southerners and other Americans feared that essential equality within the nation could be destroyed by "selfish politicians" promoting "the parochial concerns of one region at the expense of others." Southerners looked north for such threats after 1789 and simultaneously identified themselves and their region with legitimate unionism and national interests. It was their liberty, equality, independence, and right to own slaves that were synonymous with a correct reading of the Constitution, a healthy political economy, and a viable foreign policy. Domestic opponents and their alleged allies from abroad were all viewed as "foreigners" threatening southern, and by extension national, welfare.[6]

During the antebellum period, these ideological, racial, and economic perspectives and the resulting fear of dependence led Dixie's leaders to champion aggressive territorial and commercial expansion and to denounce obstacles, either domestic or foreign, that impeded adding land and markets. Since Great Britain, given its domination of international trade and credit and its post-1783 military occupation of US territory and overtures to Native Americans, embodied the principal foreign obstacle, Anglophobia constituted another of the South's guiding assumptions. And when Alexander Hamilton promoted a more urban, industrial, and pro-northern political economy, lobbied for a pro-British foreign policy, and organized the Federalist Party to realize these goals, southerners made partisan politics one of their ongoing foreign policy considerations. From the early 1790s through 1824, these political calculations led a decisive majority of southerners to back the Jeffersonian Republicans and their foreign policies.

Over the six decades from the ratification of the Constitution until the formation of the Confederacy, these collective southern perceptions and interests drove Dixie's responses to US foreign policy. The search for markets and their crucial connection to building a viable political economy and securing true and honorable national independence led the Jeffersonians to war with Britain in 1812. Following several futile economic attempts to coerce the British into treating the United States more equitably, Madison and his party deemed war the only way to safeguard unrestrained American commerce and thereby safeguard national honor and independence. Congressman John Clopton of Virginia characteristically declared that the British "system of aggression" reached far beyond "certain rights of commerce" and raised the "*question* . . . whether the U. States are really an independent nation." Secretary of State James Monroe agreed that since only "unconditional submission" would satisfy the British, "the only remaining alternative, was to get ready for fighting, and to begin as soon as we were ready." Southerners were only too ready to fight. Exhibiting their typical "ideas of honor and the warrior ethic," they rallied to the cause, as would subsequently be the case in 1846, 1861, 1898, 1917, 1941, 1950, and 1964–1965.[7]

Southerners also aggressively pursued landed expansion and with it the extension of slavery. Jefferson's purchase of Louisiana epitomized this facet of a Dixie-based foreign policy. Most immediately Jefferson and residents of what would become the Deep South sought to ensure use of the Mississippi, Mobile, Pearl, and Tombigbee Rivers and access to markets through the Gulf of Mexico. In addition to furthering the agrarian pursuit of export markets, the vast expanse of territory seemed to guarantee a virtually unlimited supply of land for the maintenance of personal independence and the agrarian republic. Ironically, the construction of what Jefferson called the "empire for liberty" came at the expense of both Native Americans and African American slaves. Against a backdrop of precarious national strength and sovereignty in Kentucky, Tennessee, Georgia, and what would become the states of Alabama, Louisiana, and Mississippi, the Jefferson administration encouraged migration to establish a viable "American presence"; pushed for the displacement of Indians and began the "conversion of millions of acres" of their land into "marketable real estate"; and aided in the expansion and protection of slavery. The policies toward both Native Americans and slavery came in response to demands from southern whites, who exercised strong "local" influence over national policy in these areas where "federal authority remained contested." Similar motives prompted Republican efforts to annex Florida, which was accomplished in 1819 under President James Monroe. A Mississippi editor summarized Dixie's perspective nicely. Adding Florida, he said, "rounds off our southern possessions and for ever precludes foreign emissaries from stirring up Indians to war and negroes to rebellion, whilst it gives the southern country important outlets to the sea."[8]

Significantly, Florida's annexation occurred against the backdrop of General Andrew Jackson's ruthless campaign to suppress Native Americans in the Southeast and, thereby, remove them as obstacles to the westward movement of the "Cotton Kingdom." First as a military leader and subsequently as president, Jackson seized approximately 150 million acres from the Cherokees, Chickasaws, and Choctaws; forced some forty-six thousand Native Americans to move beyond the Mississippi River; and opened the lands to Anglo ownership, settlement, and cultivation. A similar imperial dynamic ensued in Arkansas and Texas from the 1830s through the mid-1870s at the expense of the Caddos, Wichitas, Commanches, and Kiowas.[9]

Since more than twice as many Native Americans lived in the South than in the North in 1815, these southern developments set the tone for US Indian policy. White southerners justified their territorial acquisitions with the racial argument that the allegedly inferior Indian savages were incapable of using the lands productively. As with Louisiana, these new territories also fit nicely into the republican ideological construct, which required new agricultural lands for sustaining the agrarian political economy and forestalling the growth of an industrial one. And southerners were fully cognizant of the potential political gains that could come from states organized in Mississippi, Alabama, Louisiana, Arkansas, and Texas. The editor of the *Charleston Southern Patriot* asserted that northern opposition to Indian removal derived from the recognition that it would "give the Southern and Southwestern states . . . an influence in the councils of the Nation which they do not now possess, while their territory is inhabited by savages."[10]

Sectional political influence was at the heart of the debate in 1819–1820 over Missouri's entry into the Union. The controversy arose when New York congressman James Tallmadge Jr. offered amendments aimed at blocking Missouri's admission as a slave state. Northerners condemned slavery on humanitarian and moral grounds. They also objected to Dixie gaining greater political power in Congress, and, in so doing, challenged southern economic and political interests. For the first time since the American Revolution, territorial expansion threatened to come at the South's expense. If a stronger federal government could bar slavery from Missouri, might the peculiar institution be banned from the remainder of the Louisiana Purchase and the states to be formed in the wake of Indian removal? But more than Dixie's economic and political welfare was at stake. Southern honor and liberty were also imperiled. In the midst of this "rhetorical civil war," Freeman Walker of Georgia warned, "To expect such submission from the free born sons of America, upon whose birth the genius of liberty smiled, . . . 'Tis to expect from freemen the conduct of slaves." Although the crisis was resolved temporarily by the simultaneous admission of Maine as a free state and Missouri as a slave state, there followed a forty-year "imperial competition" between the North and South over control of the New West—a competition that in many ways embodied dueling foreign policies regarding slavery.[11]

Although slavery moved to the forefront of Dixie's foreign policy calculations after 1820, southerners had consistently assessed the institution's well-being while responding to diplomatic issues after 1789. Among southern objections to the Jay Treaty of 1795 was its failure to secure compensation for slaves confiscated or freed by the British during the Revolutionary War. Protecting slavery had augmented southern enthusiasm for acquiring Louisiana. Madison explained that an ongoing French presence on the nation's western border would have created "inquietude . . . in the Southern States, whose numerous slaves [had] been taught to regard the French as patrons of their cause." Stifling black slaves' aspirations for freedom also prompted Dixie's hostile response to the successful revolt in Santo Domingo (later renamed Haiti) by former black slaves against French colonial control in 1791. President George Washington found it "lamentable to see such a spirit of revolt among the Blacks" and worried that the revolt could "prove not a very pleasing or agreeable example" for bondsmen in the South. Congressman John W. Epps of Virginia stated flatly, "The Negro government should be destroyed." Yet another invidious example of free black people on Dixie's border augmented the southern quest to acquire Florida, since its annexation would eliminate the "underground railroad" that enabled runaway slaves to take refuge among the Seminoles.[12]

Both slavery and the ideology of republicanism figured prominently in the foreign policy strategies of the Jacksonian Democrats, the organizational and intellectual heirs of the Jeffersonians. These considerations were apparent in the thinking of President John Tyler (a former Jacksonian masquerading as a Whig), President James K. Polk, and other important southerners, such as John Calhoun, Abel Upsher, and Robert Walker, as they worked for the annexation of Texas in the 1840s. Fearful that an independent Texas might fall under British abolitionist influence, they argued that adding Texas to the Union as a slave state would safeguard the institution, achieve a decisive US monopoly over the growth of cotton, enhance southern influence in the US Senate, and avoid a potential obstacle to subsequent territorial and commercial expansion across adjacent areas. Jacksonians, like the Jeffersonian leaders before them, also justified aggressive landed and commercial expansion as the means to sustain the agrarian republic.[13]

Party regularity, the lure of additional markets and territory, and national honor impelled southern Democrats to back Polk and his war with Mexico (1846–1848). When the Tennessee Democrat initiated his aggressive war, southerners played a characteristically prominent role in the fighting. The South's code of honor and warrior ethic permitted no other response. The editor of the *Yazoo* (MS) *Democrat* announced that *"submission whether as regards individuals or nations provokes insult and aggression,"* and another Mississippi editor asserted that true men would be prepared "to yield up their lives as a sacrifice for their country's honor." Mississippi women agreed. Eliza Quitman, the wife of John A. Quitman, who returned a hero from the fighting, bluntly declared that she "would rather be the *widow* of a man who had fallen fighting in the battles of his country, than the *wife of a living coward.*"[14]

While opposing the annexation of Texas and criticizing the war with Mexico, southern Whigs voiced many of the foreign policy positions Dixie would adopt during the Gilded Age. Henry Clay, the Whig nominee for president in 1844, and fellow southern party members opposed the annexation of Texas, predicting that it would incite war with Mexico and lead to a dangerous concentration of federal power. Southern Whigs also warned that Texas would compete economically with older regions of the South, draw away both white and black population, and set a dangerous precedent by adding nonwhites to the body politic. When the predicted war ensued, southern Whigs such as Alexander S. Stephens of Georgia warned that the US attack on a weaker neighbor sullied national honor and America's status as a republican exemplar. Nor could these Whigs discern any constitutional basis for governing new territories as *"subject provinces."* Hostilities, they argued, promised to inflate federal spending, debt, and bureaucracy and to expand executive and military power—all of which conflicted with southern values and interests. Moreover, annexing New Mexico or California would bring a "sickening mixture" of "debased population," an "ignorant, a fanatic, a disorderly people" who would jeopardize republican government.[15]

Only an attack from outside the region caused Dixie's politicians to momentarily set aside partisan and policy differences. In August 1846 Congressman David A. Wilmot, a Pennsylvania Democrat, offered a proviso stipulating that "neither slavery nor involuntary servitude" should be allowed in any territory acquired from Mexico. As with the Missouri crisis, both the sectional balance of power and southern honor were imperiled—threats that neither southern Democrats nor Whigs could abide. John Calhoun warned that if deprived of the fruits of national expansion, the South would be left "a mere handful" of circumscribed states with their fate "entirely . . . in the hands of the non-slaveholding States." Others deemed the proviso's impugning of southern honor as distressing as its geopolitical implications. Stephens rejected this *"insult* to the South," this "expression to the world" that Dixie deserved "public censure and national odium." Francis Pickens, a Calhoun follower, agreed that the South could not accept this restriction "without *feeling* our *degradation*."[16]

Over the decade following the end of the war with Mexico in 1848 and US acquisition of New Mexico and California, the South gradually coalesced around a more united foreign policy. This occurred in response to the formation of the purely northern Republican Party in 1854–1855 and its rigid opposition to the expansion of slavery into the New West and to the South's abortive attempts during the 1850s to maintain a sectional balance by expanding into the tropics, especially to Cuba. In 1858, Senator Albert G. Brown of Mississippi left no doubt regarding southern aspirations: "I want Cuba, and I know that sooner or later we must have it. . . . I want Tamaulipas, Potosi, and one or two other Mexican states; and I want them all for the same reason—for the planting or spreading of slavery." The failure of all such efforts starkly demonstrated that the older US nationalism and foreign policy that had incorporated slavery into national expansion and thereby aided the South's effort to sustain personal and sectional independence no longer pertained. Abraham Lincoln, the newly elected Republican president, made this clear while rejecting the Crittenden Compromise of 1861 that would have extended the Missouri Compromise line of 36° 30' to the Pacific for both current and future US territories. Lincoln not only rejected any extension of slavery but also forecast with remarkable clarity the concerns of US policymakers one hundred years later regarding the deleterious effects of racial discrimination on the nation's international standing. The president elect proclaimed that "slavery deprives our republican example of its just influence in the world—[and] enables the enemies of free institutions to taunt us as hypocrites."[17]

Not surprisingly, southerners reached diametrically opposing conclusions. Conditioned to think in terms of republicanism and in agreement that foreign policy should help ensure regional and individual liberty, equality, and honor, they correctly concluded that from the South's perspective these cherished conditions were no longer safe within the Union. The South's loss of control over foreign policy and its previous sectional benefits allowed for no other conclusion. If, as Don Fehrenbacher has asserted, the federal government had demonstrated a "habitual willingness to act as an agent of slaveholders" in foreign policy, Lincoln signaled a clear end to that practice. Fittingly, Jefferson Davis, soon to become Lincoln's counterpart in the Confederacy, spoke directly to southern values and interests. By denying slavery's access to the remainder of the Louisiana Purchase, the territories acquired from Mexico, and potential acquisitions in the tropics, the northern Republicans had subverted the South's economic and political interests, but perhaps equally important its equality and honor. As early as 1851, Davis had declared that "honor was the first consideration" of Mississippians "in the face of Northern perfidy," and as the sections moved toward war a decade later, he lectured Republican senators, "Your platform . . . denies us equality . . . without which we should be degraded if we remained in the Union." Another secessionist proclaimed that the South would not "submit to the government of a foreign and hostile people," and Howell Cobb of Georgia added that "it only remains to be seen whether" southern "manhood was equal to the task" of protecting the region's "independence."[18]

As they entered the catastrophic Civil War, southerners had established a number of key foreign policy tendencies that would survive the conflict and continue to shape Dixie's postwar response to US foreign relations. Southerners had come to assess foreign policy implications from the vantage point of an embattled, minority section and to weigh national policies in terms of personal and regional independence and equality. Honor, manhood, and the warrior ethic were central to the identity and self-respect of white southerners. These white southerners also acted upon an unwavering conviction of nonwhite inferiority, whether the nonwhites were African Americans, Native Americans, or Mexicans. While endorsing, directing, or participating in the military actions that seized territory from Native Americans or Mexicans, southerners evidenced a proclivity for forceful interventions—a propensity that was temporarily suspended following the war but reappeared during the administration of Woodrow

Wilson. Finally, antebellum residents of Dixie had backed low tariffs and the aggressive pursuit of markets abroad.

In the wake of the Civil War, defeated southerners experienced the economic and political dependence and accompanying humiliation they had tirelessly sought to avoid over the previous seventy-five years. Economically, the South lacked the capital, skilled labor, technological community, and regional markets to move beyond its focus on staple agriculture and first-stage processing of agricultural and natural materials. "Like other backward economies," Edward L. Ayers has observed, "the South endured low wages, absentee ownership, and little control over national [economic] policy"—a condition that persisted until World War II. Politically, southerners first endured the North's efforts at Reconstruction and temporary loss of control and, after the mid-1870s, a clearly inferior status in the national government, whose economic policies were consistently pro-northern. Protective tariffs aided northern and eastern manufacturers while forcing the agricultural South to pay more for machinery and finished products. Currency and banking policies left southerners with insufficient supplies of money and credit. Pensions for Union veterans directed taxes collected nationally to areas above the Mason-Dixon Line and funded internal improvements disproportionately helpful to areas outside the South. These developments prompted Senator John Tyler Morgan of Alabama to complain that the Northeast held the South in colonial "vassalage"—that a "Solid North" sought to make the South into the "Ireland of the American Union."[19]

This dependent political and economic status directly influenced Dixie's postwar foreign policy perspectives. The southern Democrats, or "Redeemers," who led the successful campaign to throw off northern, Republican Reconstruction, emphasized united resistance to outside "foreign" control, states' rights and restrained federal power, fiscal conservatism, unwavering dedication to white supremacy, and a "solid" Democratic polity. Over the ensuing century, the South remained an essentially one-party region, which, combined with the seniority system in Congress, would eventually restore southern political clout on the national level. But this southern revival had to wait; and in the interim, the solid South consistently opposed Republican foreign policies. To this partisan political motive, the South added its apprehension over foreign involvements that might strengthen central governmental and military power at the expense of states' rights and local control. Activist foreign policies could necessitate greater federal spending and higher taxes and justify enhanced federal authority more capable of interfering in southern politics and race relations. The South's ever-present attention to race also disposed Dixie to oppose foreign involvements that might add nonwhites to the body politic.[20]

Collectively, these political, economic, and racial anxieties led the majority of southerners to oppose an enlarged, modernized US Navy and the annexation of Hawaii, Cuba, and the Philippines. The navy, charged Representative William C. Oates of Alabama, conflicted with the "spirit and genius" of representative government and was a GOP maneuver to spend "surplus revenue" and thereby avoid "revising the tariff and reducing taxation." While arguing against the annexation of the Philippines, Senator Hernando De Soto Money of Mississippi raised other southern fears. He decried the "steady accretion of executive power" at the expense of Congress and the growth of a "great military establishment." Both developments portended the possible "use of these same soldiers . . . in our own land." The southern rejection of Republican-sponsored initiatives often included references to Reconstruction and the region's sense of mistreatment. The *Charleston News and Courier* declared it would "go hard with [Republicans] to give up Hawaii," just as "it went hard" for them to leave the South. Other southerners asserted that insular annexations would undermine southern development by diverting northern investments abroad and that the extension of the US presence into the Pacific and East Asia would occasion conflict with other developed nations. And southerners never lost sight of race. According to the *Wilmington* (NC) *Morning Star,* Dixie had a "sufficient stock of mongrelism . . . without taking in the nut brown islanders of the South Pacific"; Senator John W. Daniel of Virginia dismissed the Philippines as a "witch's caldron," peopled by a "mess of Asiatic potage"; and James K. Vardaman of Mississippi declared Cubans "a class of people that would cause hell itself to deteriorate. . . . Of all the weak, weary and altogether worthless people that I have had the misfortune to come into contact with the Cuban is . . . the most terrifying. The American nigger is a gentleman and scholar compared with him."[21]

Despite these objections to activist foreign policies, other southern interests and values pointed toward the very interventionist inclinations that aroused Dixie's fears. Following Appomattox, southerners resumed their persistent search for markets abroad. Between 1870 and 1910, the South exported between 15 and 20 percent of its production of raw cotton and cotton textiles, coal, timber, tobacco, and iron, compared to the national and northeastern average of 5 to 6 percent. Led by Senator Morgan, southerners eagerly promoted commercial expansion and the construction of an interoceanic canal (preferably through Nicaragua) to direct trade through the Gulf of Mexico and to connect Dixie with South American and Asian markets. Morgan and other southerners also asserted that the GOP's protective tariff both impeded essential "large, free liberal commerce" in the South's agricultural goods and increased the cost of equipment for cotton and iron production. Morgan favored extending "the area of our trade throughout the world, barbarous as well as civilized," and asserted that only adequate markets were necessary to provide the "wealth and strength" needed to "build Alabama into honorable rivalry with the greatest states in the world." This emphasis on low tariffs and ample export markets remained central to the South's foreign policy perspective until the 1950s.[22]

Another, ultimately more lucrative, southern economic concern, defense spending, emerged in the late nineteenth century and also led the South toward more activist, interventionist foreign policies. War with Spain in 1898 occasioned the humble beginnings of what became an increasingly important facet of the southern economy over the subsequent century. Floridians campaigned vigorously and successfully to make Tampa the departure point for troops embarking for Cuba. Miami and Jacksonville hosted troop camps, as did the tragic Chickamauga battlefield in Tennessee. Federal funds also built defense works in numerous southern coastal cities. For example, Senator Benjamin R. Tillman secured a naval yard for Charleston, South Carolina, which together with the attached dry docks, machine shops, and other facilities brought at least $5.7 million to his state over the following twenty years. Although the spending was modest compared to future federal outlays, a prescient pattern had begun.[23]

As war loomed with Spain after 1895, southern devotion to honor, manhood, and patriotism again came to the fore. Fighting the Spanish afforded southerners an opportunity to demonstrate their devotion to the restored Union and to simultaneously affirm their manhood and honor as

worthy successors of the Confederate cause. The post–Civil War generation of southerners had been reared amid reverence for the Lost Cause,
which reinforced the South's already strong devotion to honor. According to this interpretation of the war, the South's soldiers had rallied to the
Confederate cause with remarkable enthusiasm, courage, and devotion to
duty; had followed unequaled leaders; and had been better fighters than
their northern adversaries. Only greater northern numbers and superior
equipment had overcome preeminent southern military capacity and commitment. By engaging the Spanish, true sons of Dixie could exhibit similar qualities in defense of the United States while retrospectively affirming
Confederate valor and honor. Ironically, the South's defeat in the Civil
War and subsequent efforts to devise an explanation that salvaged honor
and manhood left Dixie's men even more determined to exhibit these
traits and even more prone to demonstrative patriotism.[24]

These sentiments echoed throughout the South as war approached.
Senator Wilkinson Call from Florida pronounced that fears of material
loss could not "be allowed to . . . suppress the manhood and courage of
our people"; there could be "no prosperity in a country where there is no
sense of patriotism and national honor." Southerners relished the chance
to trumpet their patriotism. The *Lynchburg News* proclaimed representatively, "The people of the South . . . [are] as loyal to the flag of the Union
as the people of Massachusetts or Illinois," and if the United States went
to war, "the men of the South would rush to the defense of the country with as much promptness and enthusiasm as the men of any other
section."[25]

In still another prescient development that would persist through the
war in Vietnam, southern African Americans probed the inconsistencies
between the nation's stated foreign policy principles and goals and America's domestic practices. As would be their wont over the ensuing seven
decades, blacks made domestic rather than foreign policy issues their first
priority. Confronted with legal disfranchisement, segregation, and ubiq-
uitous violence across the South after 1890, numerous blacks cited atrocities, such as the 1898 murder of black Republican postmaster Frazier B.
Baker of Lake City, South Carolina, as more important than the alleged
Spanish attack on the battleship *Maine*. Black skeptics found no reason
why African Americans should fight "to bring other Negroes [in Cuba]
under the flag that has never as yet protected those who are already here."

Better this combat be left to Dixie's "brave lynchers." As they would subsequently do with European colonial subjects, African Americans identified with Hawaiians, Cubans, Puerto Ricans, and Filipinos as people of color. Booker T. Washington questioned whether the US government could do "for the millions of dark-skinned races . . . in Cuba, Porto Rico, Hawaii and the Philippine Islands that which it has not been able to do for nearly 10,000,000 negroes and Indians" already under American jurisdiction. And John Mitchell Jr., editor of the *Richmond Planet*, mocked the hypocrisy of the imperialist claim of bearing the "white man's burden" while "acquiescing in the oppression and butchery of a dark race in this country"; he urged instead that the United States "call all the missionaries home and have them work on our own people."[26]

The South's colonial and relatively depressed economic condition did not change appreciably over the first four decades of the twentieth century, and white southerners remained steadfastly opposed to federal interference with the region's racial practices. But with Woodrow Wilson's presidency, Dixie permanently modified its restrained, post–Civil War response to US foreign relations. Through support for Jefferson, Jackson, and Polk, the South had demonstrated the willingness to endorse the aggressive foreign policies directed by a southern Democrat who posed no threat to the region's racial regime, and Wilson was just such a president.

Although Wilson had been gone from the South for twenty-five years and had advanced to the White House after serving as the president of Princeton University and governor of New Jersey, he had been born in Virginia and reared in Georgia and the Carolinas. From the time he came to prominence as an author and academic in the 1880s, the South had claimed him as one of its own. During the 1912 campaign, a Georgia editor characterized him as a man "*of southern blood, of southern bone and of southern grit*"; and Wilson later contended that "a boy never gets over his boyhood, and never can change those subtle influences which have become part of him. . . . The only place in the country, the only place in the world, where nothing had to be explained to me is in the South."[27]

The new president reinforced this regional allegiance by appointing five native-born southerners to his cabinet, but the South's influence was not confined to the executive branch. When the Democrats also carried both houses of Congress in 1912, the seniority system placed southerners in key legislative leadership positions. The sons of Dixie had returned to the forefront of national politics and diplomacy for the first time since the 1840s. Edward M. House, a Texan and Wilson's confidant on foreign policy, accurately observed that the South was "clearly in the saddle, both in Congress and the Administration."[28]

This southern influence became apparent when a clear majority of southern editors and congressmen provided the essential and most reliable support for Wilson's foreign policies. Southerners voted overwhelmingly in the House and Senate for the Underwood-Simmons Tariff, the first reduction of the tariff since the Civil War. They also backed Wilson's meddlesome and ultimately futile interventions in Mexico, interventions that led to the forceful occupation of Vera Cruz, the dispatch of ten thousand US soldiers in unsuccessful pursuit of Poncho Villa, and the failed efforts to force Venustiano Carranza to adopt American-directed governmental and economic policies. Even more important, the South stood steadfastly behind Wilson's pro-British policies prior to World War I, the president's decision to hold Germany "to a strict accountability" for any harm done to Americans by submarine warfare, and the severing of diplomatic relations and call for war against Germany in April 1917. During the war, southern congressmen voted for a series of measures dramatically reducing the option of filibustering in Congress and expanding the powers of the federal government—measures that would have been unthinkable over the previous 130 years. Following the war, Dixie again rallied behind Wilson in his uncompromising fight to ratify the Treaty of Versailles and secure US membership in the League of Nations.[29]

The South's support for Wilson and its simultaneous shift toward a more assertive, interventionist foreign policy were again based on perceived regional interests and assumptions. Partisan politics and ostensible regional loyalties were fundamental. Dixie lined up behind the president it viewed as a fellow southern Democrat, another segregationist son of the South who posed no threat to Dixie's racial practices. Long out of power, southerners were convinced that Dixie had been treated unfairly during the previous fifty years of northern, Republican dominance. The South's opportunity for a more equitable share of federal assistance and patronage had arrived but depended in part on working well with Wilson. Southerners were also determined to demonstrate their ability to govern responsibly and effectively. These considerations led them to be less rigidly tied to states' rights when in the majority and occupying positions of leadership, as opposed to when they had been relegated to the minority and confronted with a Republican chief executive.[30]

Other familiar southern foreign policy concerns supplemented these political, racial, and governance matters. Dixie's ongoing commitment to commercial expansion and the pursuit of export markets led to endorsement of tariff reform and a pro-British neutrality, since Britain was the most important importer of southern products. Moreover, defense spending continued to confer distinct regional benefits. In a typical reaction, the *Montgomery Advertiser* eagerly anticipated the "immense sums to be spent" on the Camp Sheridan infantry training center, even if it were named for a despised Union officer. The federal budget expanded 2,600 percent from 1916 through 1919, and a significant portion of this increase went to defense spending in the South. Indeed, the integral connection of federal defense spending to the South's economy was firmly established during the Wilson era. The active influence of strategically placed southern legislators, the energetic solicitation by southern states and communities, and Dixie's mild climate helped to locate six of fifteen US Army camps and thirteen of sixteen National Guard cantonments in the South. For example, local Fayetteville boosters and North Carolina's congressional delegation campaigned successfully to land $17 million to construct the military's largest artillery base at Camp (later Fort) Bragg. The Newport News Shipbuilding and Drydock Company in the Hampton Roads–Norfolk area expanded its capacity via an allocation of $9.5 million and became the nation's largest naval complex. Other southern cities, such as Houston, were also permanently transformed by the war. The deepening of the Houston Ship Canal, combined with massive federal demand for cotton and oil, enabled Houston to emerge as the world's largest cotton and oil marketing and export center in the 1920s. In addition to these representative installations or projects, the war created an unprecedented demand for southern products. The US government purchased more than five hundred thousand bales of cotton for use in producing explosives, and the army consumed eight hundred thousand yards of cloth. Building army camps and wooden ships required 1.9 billion board feet of southern pine, and war-related demands afforded the southern oil industry a comparable stimulus.[31]

Honor and patriotism also remained primary southern concerns. In the midst of the Mexican involvements, Representative Pat Harrison of Mississippi declared, "As much as my people desire peace they are unwilling to see the soldiers of this nation, once torn in civil warfare, humiliated and insulted." Congressman John Walker of Georgia agreed and pronounced his support for war if it were required to defend "our flag, our uniform and our national honor," and Wilson rejected any use of American "strength" that failed to "honor the Stars and Stripes." As war with Germany approached after 1915, Wilson dismissed dissenters as "creatures of passion, disloyalty, and anarchy" and, in terms that would be echoed during the Vietnam War, warned that the nation needed to "make a unit in which no slightest line of division is visible beyond our borders." Dixie proved particularly susceptible to his appeals to patriotism and loyalty. The Reverend Randolph McKim pronounced the conflict with Germany a "holy War" and attacked pacifists as "weak-kneed, chicken-hearted, white-livered individuals." "If the pacifists' theory" were correct, he thundered, "how could Robert E. Lee have been such a saint as he was?" And Congressman W. W. Larsen of Georgia assured his colleagues that the "fires of patriotism burn bright in every [southern] home," and the South's "gallant sons can be counted upon to rally to the flag of our country with the same self-sacrificing patriotic devotion" as "those brave sons of the Confederacy who followed Gordon, Jackson, and Lee."[32]

Such full-throated proclamations of southern patriotism did not extend to the fair treatment of black soldiers. In an unfortunate precursor to southern practices during the Vietnam era, Dixie's draft boards discriminated blatantly in designating blacks for induction. Florida, Georgia, Louisiana, Mississippi, and South Carolina drafted more blacks than whites and frequently summoned black landowners while leaving landless African American workers on white properties undisturbed. Black soldiers stationed in the South regularly received scant or inappropriate clothing and equipment; seriously overcrowded barracks or incomplete, tattered tents; and inadequate, unsanitary food and water. They were also disproportionately assigned to labor details—serving in some instances almost as southern chain gangs wielding a "pick and shovel in the same state where they were previously working." In the most extreme instances, white officers in Virginia, Maryland, and Tennessee hired out black soldiers to private contractors. Such conditions and practices prompted members of the Fifteenth New York Infantry, who had been stationed at

Camp Wadsworth near Spartanburg, to remark that they had trained in "Rectum, South Carolina."[33]

Despite such treatment and even more blatant physical attacks on African American soldiers, the black press supported preparedness efforts and argued for loyal black service designed to secure racial justice and the rights of full citizenship. Even as white Alabamians anguished over a potential German-inspired black revolt and the hazards of training and arming black soldiers, African American ministers, editors, businessmen, and educators emphasized black "loyalty" and led prowar rallies, and blacks "dutifully registered" for the draft. African Americans also repeated earlier criticisms of the yawning chasm between the nation's professed foreign policy objectives and its domestic racial practices. James Weldon Johnson, who was born in Florida and educated at Atlanta University before becoming a prominent New York journalist and reformer, denounced a country that raised its "hands in horror at German 'atrocities'" while ignoring the "wholesale murder of American citizens on American soil by bloodthirsty American mobs." He also indicted Wilson, who continued "to talk . . . about bringing peace and righteousness to all nations of the earth" but had "yet to utter one word against the outraging of humanity" within America. Upon returning home and receiving receptions consistent with Wilson's racial views, African American soldiers' hopes of better treatment after the war went unfulfilled. In an experience that unfortunately previewed events during the Vietnam period, a black veteran still in uniform was characteristically reminded, "Nigger, you aren't in France no more, you're in America," as he was thrown out of a train station in Waco, Texas.[34]

Although Johnson's indictment of Wilson's and the nation's hypocrisy was telling, historians have appropriately credited the first southern-born president since Abraham Lincoln with establishing the "conceptual framework for American foreign policy in the twentieth century" and beyond. According to George C. Herring, "Wilson towers above the landscape of modern American foreign policy like no other individual, the dominant personality, the seminal figure." Michael H. Hunt has characterized Wilson's fourteen points as "the most important statement in the history of twentieth-century U.S. foreign relations," a "blueprint for U.S. leaders intent on constructing a new world order and projecting their values abroad." Wilson established this conceptual framework and his status as the dominant personality by arguing that the United States should act as the world leader and assertively participate in international affairs rather than retain a more restrained, noninterventionist posture. In fulfilling this mission to mankind, the United States was to spread democracy and capitalism, promote free trade and freedom of the seas, and oppose revolutions and disorder. Wilson further advocated disarmament and peaceful international relations, but he frequently employed force, especially when claiming to instruct nations he deemed racially inferior—such as Mexico, Haiti, the Dominican Republic, or even Russia. Significantly, the South provided Wilson's most reliable domestic support for these objectives and in the process came to favor a more interventionist, forceful, and antirevolutionary foreign policy.[35]

Two additional aspects of Wilson's approach to foreign policy amplify an understanding of the South's evolving perspective. Even before becoming president, Wilson had pronounced the executive powers in foreign policy "very absolute," a position most southerners adhered to well into the 1970s. More important, as a "believing, practicing, evangelical Christian," Wilson embodied much of the religious fervor that would play an especially important role in the South's response to the Cold War and Vietnam. Not all scholars would characterize Wilson as an "evangelical," but religion was the "primary source" of his "ideology," and his southern Presbyterian covenant theology produced essential agreement with religious conservatives, save his ostensible emphasis on collective security. Confident that God had a plan for all mortals, this son of a prominent minister and administrator in the Southern Presbyterian Church believed Americans had been chosen to be "apostles of liberty and self-government," to "show . . . the nations of the world how they should walk in the paths of liberty."[36]

In the wake of the Civil War, the South's overwhelming commitment to a conservative, evangelical Protestantism reinforced the region's martial civic religion associated with the Lost Cause and the warrior ethic. The great majority of both black and white southerners subscribed to an emotional, evangelical faith emphasizing the Bible as the "sole reference point of belief and practice"; direct, personal access to the Lord; and "morality . . . defined in individualistic . . . terms." Particularly among white southerners, these religious values led to a worldview that made sharp distinctions between good and evil and helped promote an unreserved certainty regarding public issues, including foreign policy. As Wilson contended, once issues of faith were determined, "argument is adjourned." Viewing the world from this perspective further inclined residents of Dixie to back Wilson and to agree with his belief that he and the United States had been chosen by God to reform the world, that opponents of this mission were opponents of the Almighty, and that atheists (particularly Communists) were especially dangerous adversaries. Indeed, the nation's most devoutly religious region, like its president, could meld their civic and evangelical religions to combine "religion and patriotism," to deem "patriotism in America as synonymous with obedience to the law of God."[37]

The South maintained this more assertive, interventionist perspective and its devotion to Wilson's policies and legacy through the end of World War II and in so doing came to be viewed by many observers as the nation's most internationalist region. After overwhelmingly endorsing US membership in the League of Nations, many southerners cited regional hostility as responsible for the nation's refusal to join this international organization. A former Charlotte mayor voiced this opinion: "[Henry Cabot] Lodge, the Republican Chairman of the Senate Foreign Relations Committee, and his allies, hate[d] Wilson because he is a southerner and a democrat, and was President during the greatest war this country ever had." Virginia senator Carter Glass later excoriated those responsible for the nation rejecting this opportunity for international progress. They had failed to respond "when the greatest Christian statesman of all time summoned the nations of the earth to enter into a Covenant which contained the very essence of the Sermon on the Mount and was the consummation, as far as Christians could contrive, of the sacrifice on Calvary."[38]

Consistently noting that they sought to enact the Wilsonian vision, southern congressmen voted overwhelmingly for US membership on the World Court in 1926 and 1935 and for membership in the United Nations in 1945. Following the latter vote, the *Atlanta Constitution* noted, "If among the hosts there [in the Senate] was one of that gaunt, plain, tired old Presbyterian, with his Presbyterian inflexibility and stubbornness, it would not be strange." But, neither Wilson nor Dixie was actually inclined to place the American military under international authority or to forfeit the national sovereignty that would have constituted true internationalism. To be sure, Wilson had pushed for much greater American involvement abroad, but always on US terms. He deemed US values and institutions as synonymous with correct international ones; therefore, to develop properly, other nations needed to emulate the American political and economic path. When stripped to its essentials, the president's reformist agenda was actually more unilateralist than internationalist, an inclination with which the South agreed over the ensuing six decades.[39]

This reluctance to pursue a true internationalism that entailed curbs on US freedom of action or substantive intrusion on US sovereignty was even more apparent among southerners generally. Although these inclinations became obvious after 1945, southern foreign policy preferences between the wars forecast what was to come. For example, while arguing for US membership on the World Court in 1926, Senator Claude A. Swanson of Virginia offered a reservation forbidding the court to "*entertain any request* for an advisory opinion including any dispute or question in which the United States *has or claims an interest.*" The region's unilateralist and nationalist proclivities were also apparent in southern congressmen's opposition to foreign loans or international humanitarian aid and their enthusiastic endorsement of immigration restriction during the 1920s.[40]

If the South's commitment to internationalism was dubious, its conversion to a more aggressive, interventionist, and forceful foreign policy was lasting. As the nation moved toward war after 1939, Dixie easily qualified as the nation's most interventionist, pro-Allied region. In June 1940, 70 percent of southerners endorsed aiding England even at the risk of war (compared to 54 percent in the next most aggressive region); in August 1940, 68 percent of southerners backed the destroyer-bases deal in which FDR traded overage American ships to Great Britain for strategic military locations in the Western Hemisphere (compared to 56 percent of northeasterners); and, in February 1941, 77 percent of southerners, compared to 54 percent of Americans, favored passage of the Lend-Lease Bill to funnel war materiel to Great Britain. Southern senators and congressmen acted in concert with these constituent preferences by voting overwhelmingly for legislation to make war materials more readily available to the British in 1939, for the nation's first peacetime draft in 1940, and for Lend-Lease in 1941.[41]

Senator Carter Glass attributed Dixie's foreign policy preferences to his region's "superior character and to exceptional understanding of the problem involved." Perhaps, but other more familiar, more concrete considerations were also at work. Partisan politics was again paramount as the South aligned behind another Democratic president. This partisanship led one analyst of congressional voting patterns over the entire interwar period to conclude that the "South was more Democratic than belligerent." As had become their twentieth-century practice beginning with Wilson, southerners were also inclined to grant the executive primary responsibility for the conduct of foreign relations. Representative Sam Rayburn of Texas spoke for the great majority of his regional contemporaries in the 1930s when he declared, "When the nation is in danger, you have to follow your leader. The man in the White House is the only leader this nation has." Foreign affairs, Rayburn subsequently asserted, were "definitely an Executive function." Moreover, as numerous southerners made clear over the two decades after World War I, Dixie revered Wilson and his call for international involvement and cooperation—especially if the terms of cooperation were not too clearly defined. In backing FDR, southerners could again support and help lead a cause of which they could be proud, a cause that allowed Dixie to defend democracy and American ideals rather than respond to criticism of segregating, lynching, or depriving blacks of the right to vote; poverty and sharecropping; or poorly funded educational and social services.[42]

A hardy strain of Anglophilia and the recognition that Great Britain was defending US ideals and interests reinforced the South's Democratic politics and reverence for Wilson's goals. Beginning in the late nineteenth century, prior southern hostility toward the British had begun to subside. No longer distressed at British abolitionism, potential strategic threats in the Western Hemisphere, or overt economic competition or exploitation, the South focused instead on common language and governmental ideals, mutually beneficial economic ties, and the doctrine of Anglo-Saxonism, or "the patriotism of race" and its rationale for white supremacy. In the 1930s, the South's population remained much more Anglo-Saxon in origin than residents from other regions. With many fewer German American, Italian American, and Scandinavian American constituents who opposed or were highly ambivalent about aiding Great Britain, southern congressmen were free to act on pro-British inclinations. Apprehensions over the Axis threat to the United States strengthened these inclinations. Senator Glass pronounced democracy in "mortal peril" and favored "immediate aid" for those nations defending "both our welfare and institutions." His Virginia

Senate colleague Harry F. Byrd concurred and called for "unstinted aid . . . to the gallant nation . . . which is today fighting for its very existence and for the preservation of American ideals." Interestingly, Glass's and Byrd's lofty rhetoric and rationale for defending American ideals and institutions did not go unchallenged. Citing the Byrd political machine's systematic restriction of black and poor white voting and general political participation, Jonathan Daniels, a southern reformer, declared in 1941, "Virginia . . . has a first-class claim on democracy's cradle and also on democracy's jail. . . . It's a joke, but at this time in the world's history it isn't so funny in this country as it would be perhaps in Berlin or Rome. There they could laugh and laugh."[43]

Economic considerations solidified the South's pro-Allied interventionism. As had been the case prior to World War I, the outbreak of hostilities in Asia and Europe badly disrupted Dixie's export economy. The loss of markets in Britain and continental Europe, where the bulk of the South's cotton and tobacco was sold, and the alienation of Japan, the other primary purchaser of southern cotton, were devastating. By 1940, southern exports had fallen to one-half of the 1930 total of $1.4 billion. Defeating Axis aggressors with their nationalistic economic tendencies and restoring freer-flowing commerce were judged essential to regional prosperity.

Southerners also anticipated another significant infusion of defense dollars. Voicing this assumption in 1941, Congressman Pat Harrison declared there could be "no limitation on expenditures for our defense except what the job requires," and southerners again aggressively pursued their share of the national bounty. Congressman Lyndon Johnson representatively explained his objectives to a group of Texas editors in 1943. It was "essential," he lectured, to secure defense contracts for "small Texas manufacturing plants" not only to aid the war effort but also "to bolster those firms which have been producing only for civilian needs" and to expand these operations "for normal demands of the future." By the 1940s, southerners also recognized that military spending, unlike domestic programs, seldom came with the threat of federal intrusion. Dixie's representatives understood and applauded *Business Week*'s distinction between "military" and "welfare pump priming." The former did not "alter the structure of the economy. It goes through regular channels"; the latter, by contrast, "makes new channels. . . . It creates new institutions.

It redistributes incomes." It could lead to unwelcome social and economic changes.[44]

Although military pump priming ultimately helped effect far greater social and economic changes than conservative southerners anticipated or desired, their hopes for a great stimulus in the 1940s from defense spending were realized. As had been the case in World War I, the South garnered more than its share of military bases and training centers. A salubrious climate, available space, and congressional clout once more prevailed. Of the nation's 110 new camps, more than 60 were constructed in the South. Together with the expanded or refurbished older facilities, such as Fort Benning, Georgia, which became the army's largest basic training center and home to the infantry school, these 60 new camps entailed $4 billion, or approximately 36 percent of the funds expended for military installations on the continent. Construction of the Pentagon proved far more significant. Begun in September 1941, the world's largest office complex, at more than four million square feet, graphically embodied the South's ties to the military and the broader defense establishment. Another $4.4 billion, or 17.6 percent, of national expenditures for defense industries flowed to the South. These funds benefited shipbuilding, especially at Newport News, Norfolk, Charleston, and Houston; aircraft plants, particularly in Dallas–Fort Worth and Marietta, Georgia; petroleum refineries in Louisiana and Texas; and ordnance plants in Virginia, Oklahoma, and Tennessee.[45]

Together with New Deal agricultural programs, World War II defense spending helped engender profound changes in the southern economy. Although southern agriculture became more mechanized, diversified, and productive in the three decades after 1945, it was no longer the basis of the region's economy. By 1960 only 15 percent of southerners lived on farms; by 1980 only 3 percent; and by the 1970s, soybeans, livestock, poultry, tobacco, and dairy farming occupied much greater acreage than cotton. Agriculture's decline in relative importance was offset by growth in the industrial and service sectors. Between 1940 and 1980, nonagriculture jobs increased from 7.8 million to 25.9 million, and the number of southerners working in manufacturing grew from 1.9 million to 3.4 million. Traditional industries such as textiles, coal, and steel expanded, but the bulk of this takeoff came in construction, food processing, consumer durables, and newer industries such as petrochemicals and defense-related manufacturing. Southerners also moved out of rural areas. By 1960, 58 percent of southerners had moved to cities, and by the 1980s the figure had grown to 75 percent. Even with these profound, often wrenching changes, the new Sunbelt South remained dependent, albeit less so, on the North economically. By the 1980s, it also remained the nation's poorest region, with 25 percent of the country's population and 40 percent of its poor.[46]

Far-reaching racial and political changes intensified the South's post-1945 sense of displacement and anxiety. Against a backdrop of steadily increasing restiveness and protests among southern African Americans, the erratic but growing presidential inclination to support racial reforms, liberal federal courts, and the national and international focus on civil rights, Dixie adopted a "resurgent southern sectionalism." Seeking to fend off what they viewed as radical social changes, white southerners turned to verbal pyrotechnics, legal maneuvering, token integration, political obstructionism, and violence. Indeed, race played a central role in much of the white South's movement away from the Democratic Party after World War II. As the national Democratic Party shifted leftward and displayed greater solicitude for labor and especially for blacks, the South defected from the New Deal coalition and voted increasingly Republican in presidential elections, with Richard Nixon ultimately sweeping the region in 1972. From 1952 to 1968 the proportion of southerners who considered themselves Democrats fell from two-thirds to about one-half, and by the 1980s Republicans had supplanted Democrats as Dixie's "traditional party." The dramatic changes in the South's economy, society, and politics after World War II heightened southern insecurities and intensified the region's strident, self-conscious defensiveness. These sharpened sectional perspectives in turn reinforced the South's inclination to evaluate foreign policies from a distinctive southern vantage point.[47]

The international arena confronting the nation and Dixie was as disorienting and troubling as the South's altered domestic environment. Even as southerners played a crucial role in US ratification of the UN Charter in 1945, the prospects for ongoing cooperation with the Soviet Union rapidly faded. During 1945–1946, the Soviets tightened control over Eastern Europe, probed in areas such as Iran and Manchuria, and rejected US-dominated formulas for the control of atomic energy. There followed crises in Greece, Berlin, and China from 1947 through 1949, and the United States responded with the containment policy that focused first on potential Soviet expansion toward Western Europe and ultimately was applied worldwide with the simultaneous growth of the United States' global reach and influence.

Over the two decades preceding decisive US military commitments in Vietnam, the South continued its post-1914 preference for an activist, interventionist foreign policy by providing reliable support for containment, save when national foreign policy priorities conflicted with Dixie's opposition to the Civil Rights Movement. In the process, white southerners demonstrated their proclivity for military rather than diplomatic solutions, impatience with limited war, support for the accompanying allocations for defense, aversion to arms control, growing preference for protectionism over free trade, opposition to immigration reform, and increasing disillusionment with foreign aid and the United Nations. Collectively, these responses left no doubt of Dixie's unilateralist as opposed to internationalist propensities; and, as had been true since the 1780s, these southern responses derived from clearly discernible regional attitudes and interests.

Southern blacks continued to divert from this majority sectional pattern. Far more concerned with domestic than foreign policy issues, blacks highlighted the discrepancies between the nation's declared defense of freedom abroad and the discriminatory treatment of minorities at home. This dichotomy was particularly glaring when set against the Cold War backdrop of the "free world" versus oppressive communism. African Americans were significantly less committed than whites to the rigid enforcement of containment and, instead, often placed greater importance on the struggle of people of color against colonialism.[48]

Already prone to denounce domestic social and racial reformers as communists, staunchly conservative southerners readily lined up in opposition to international communism. By August 1946, 74 percent of southerners foresaw another war within twenty-five years, and a year later, the percentage had increased to 78 percent within ten years. To counter this perceived threat from the Soviet Union, southerners provided crucial congressional leadership and votes for the Truman Doctrine's allocation to aid anticommunists in Greece and Turkey; the Marshall Plan, to help rebuild Western Europe; and the North Atlantic Treaty Organization, designed to forestall a potential Russian military attack. Even as they endorsed these key containment measures, southerners also demonstrated their fiscal conservatism. Senator J. William Fulbright from Arkansas, who was just beginning his long involvement with US foreign relations, worried appropriately, "If we undertake the support of Greece and Turkey, how and when can we stop the lavish outpouring of our resources?" Harry Byrd agreed and warned that the United States was not just committing to aid for "these two nations"; rather, "we are voting on a global policy . . . which will carry American dollars to many other foreign countries." Despite these perceptive reservations, Cold War fears and partisan support for Harry S. Truman, yet another Democratic president, kept southerners in the foreign policy fold.[49]

Dixie's religious beliefs strongly reinforced these ideological and political inclinations. According to historian William Inboden, the Cold War cannot be understood without including the "spiritual factor," the American conviction that this epic conflict embodied the "stark division . . . between those nations who believed in God and those nations who outlawed such belief." In no part of the United States was the spiritual factor more influential than the South, the nation's "Bible belt," where Dixie's religious conservatives joined their brethren nationally as the most fervent anticommunists. Southerners passionately agreed with national spokesmen who railed against the "totalitarian outlooks" that promoted "the path to Godlessness" or who viewed "the conflict between Soviet Communism and the free world . . . [as] a religious conflict . . . a struggle for the soul of modern man." Billy Graham, a Southern Baptist from North Carolina and the foremost evangelist of the era, vividly described the Cold War as a struggle with communism, which had "declared war against God, against Christ, against the Bible, and against all religion!" Convinced that communism was "master-minded by Satan himself," Graham and ministers throughout the South called on parishioners to support their churches and nation in the epic struggle between "Christian America and atheistic Russia."[50]

After 1949, when Mao Zedong and the Chinese Communist Party (CCP) seized control of China, Americans added an atheistic China to their list of adversaries. For many rural southerners their principal source of international perspective had come from the writings and speaking tours of the Protestant missionaries dispatched abroad by southern churches. Those southern Baptists, Methodists, and Presbyterians were appalled at Mao's characterization of American missionaries as practitioners of "cultural aggression" who sought "to poison the minds of the Chinese people" and shocked when the CCP expelled all US missionaries from China between 1949 and 1952.[51]

With the onset of the Cold War, calculations of regional economic benefits once again coincided with other southern foreign policy considerations. Over the quarter century after 1945, the South forged a "political alliance with the Pentagon" and vigorously pursued a hitherto undreamed of bounty from defense spending. When northerners complained that Dixie was receiving overly generous treatment, L. Mendel Rivers from South Carolina gloated, "I don't believe the Yankees will pick a fight with us again because when we get through there'll be precious few installations left north of the Mason-Dixon line." Led by Senators Richard Russell (D-GA), John C. Stennis (D-MS), and Lyndon Johnson, and Congressmen Carl Vinson (D-GA) and Rivers, southern Democrats chaired the Senate and House Armed Services Committees and tolerated virtually no reductions in Defense Department requests; in return, "fortress Dixie" became the home to seven of the nation's ten largest defense contractors. The Savannah River Plant, built in 1951–1952 in three South Carolina counties at a cost of $2 billion, was the largest US construction project to that time and employed nearly fifty thousand workers. The South's share of the nation's prime defense contracts increased from 7 percent in 1950 to 15 percent in 1960 to 25 percent in 1970. Although Dixie's portion still trailed the Northeast and West, this greater concentration of more technologically sophisticated industries helped create the Sunbelt economy. By 1968, one of fourteen income earners in the South worked directly for the Pentagon or indirectly via the payroll of a company supplying materials to the Defense Department. From 1960 through the end of the Cold War, the region's per-capita share of defense payroll payments was 40 percent higher than the national average.[52]

To direct defense spending must be added the benefits that the National Aeronautics and Space Administration (NASA) conferred on the South. In the wake of the Soviet launch of *Sputnik* in 1957, Senate Majority Leader Lyndon Johnson and Speaker of the House Sam Rayburn (D-TX) seized the issue and led the campaign to establish NASA the following year. It was hardly coincidental that the $600 million Manned Spaceflight Center (now the Johnson Space Center) was located in Houston and helped make it the Southwest's largest city. The agency also placed the launch site at Cape Canaveral, Florida, and built other important installations at New Orleans, Huntsville, Alabama, and Bay Saint Louis, Mississippi. NASA's transformative effects were evident in Brevard County, the site of Cape Canaveral. The agency's operations brought 25,000 skilled workers and their families to Brevard, and the county's population increased from 23,653 in 1950 to 230,000 in 1970. These defense dollars helped produce a more prosperous, more technologically sophisticated Sunbelt economy, but they did little for the county's poor. Brevard refused to match federal food dollars, and its annual spending on road maintenance ran more than twice the budget for welfare.[53]

Other dramatic examples of the Dixie-defense coalition illustrated this pattern of "military Keynesism." By 1958, Carl Vinson and Richard Russell could boast of fifteen defense-related enterprises, which had become Georgia's largest employer. Lockheed-Georgia, based in Marietta, operated in 55 of the state's 159 counties and was the largest industrial corporation in the Southeast. Just up the coast in South Carolina, Congressmen Rivers outdid his southern compatriots. One observer correctly characterized Rivers's district surrounding Charleston "as one of the most elaborately fortified patches of geography in the nation," and fellow southern House members jokingly warned Rivers that additional installations could cause the area to sink into the Atlantic. The warning was appropriate, since the list included an air force base; a naval station and shipyard; a US Marine Corps air station; a mine warfare center; a naval hospital; and General Electric, McDonnell-Douglas, Avco-Lycoming, and Lockheed defense operations.[54]

Ironically, as the South readily engaged in this form of "state capitalism," southerners just as readily denounced federal spending for social programs as financially irresponsible and staunchly opposed any federal intervention to promote civil rights for blacks. As early as 1956, the defense largesse was central to William Faulkner's astute observation, "Our economy is the Federal Government." Three years later, Senators Jacob Javits and Kenneth Keating of New York and Clifford Case of New Jersey proposed the Armed Services Competitive Procurement Act, designed to steer contracts away from the South. Keating complained, "Our country can't exist half rich and half broke any more than it could exist half slave and half free." Tellingly, the bill died in Russell's Senate Armed Services Committee.[55]

Southern racial attitudes also played a critical role in the region's response to Cold War foreign policy. Put bluntly, most southerners deemed nonwhites inferior whether they resided in the United States or abroad. Representatively, Senator Allen J. Ellender (D-LA) announced that he had never met "any Africans who have the capability to run their own affairs." In opposing diplomatic and military aid abroad, George Wallace was even more blunt: "All these countries with niggers in 'em have stayed the same for a thousand years." Writing in 1965, Frank E. Smith, a former liberal Mississippi congressman, whose support for civil rights and endorsement of John Kennedy in 1960 had ended his elective political career, placed this "all-encompassing racism" at the heart of Dixie's "unilateralist" views. Since productive international involvement entailed working with "black, brown, and yellow men by ignoring racial distinctions . . . anything foreign" carried "overtones of integration."[56]

This racism was apparent as leading southern segregationists, such as Senators Russell, Stennis, Ellender, Strom Thurmond (D-SC), James O. Eastland (D-MS), and Herman Talmadge (D-GA), led the opposition to Hawaii's admission as a state. Southerners proclaimed their opposition in language reminiscent of Dixie's aversion to Hawaii's annexation in the 1890s. To incorporate Hawaii with its "polyglot, mongrel crowd representing many admixtures of races" would set a dangerous precedent that could lead to admitting "Cuba . . . or Puerto Rico, or Greenland, or some European, Asian, or African country." Not only were Hawaiians and other nonwhites allegedly incapable of understanding and participating in a democratic system, but they were also described as an especially "fertile field for the Communist propagandists and agitators."[57]

The South's low opinion of nonwhites and the region's religious conservatism were apparent in Dixie's growing disillusionment with the UN. Of the original fifty-one members of the UN, only thirteen were from Asia, Africa, and the Middle East. From 1955 to 1962, this geographic distribution changed dramatically when forty-eight new Asian and African nations gained membership, giving Afro-Asian countries a sixty to fifty-three majority over nations from all other continents. As the General Assembly focused greater attention on colonialism, racism, and economic inequality, the majority of southerners dismissed the UN as another group of hostile outsider agitators; and George Wallace characteristically sounded the South's most unvarnished perspective by describing the UN as a "club for cannibals." The "anti-statist and ultrapatriotic worldview" of Dixie's evangelical Protestants reinforced their racial suspicions of a possible "regulatory world government" that might "compromise American sovereignty." Anson Gustavus Melton, a Baptist preacher from Ashland, Virginia, voiced this concern when he "opposed . . . yielding to foreign dictators" any influence over "our welfare" and asked, "Are we not in the middle of a bad fix in the so called UN?"[58]

Dixie's pessimistic racial assessment of developing nations combined with the region's fiscal conservatism and fear of economic competition to fuel the South's opposition to foreign aid. Senators Russell and Byrd warned that foreign aid left the United States susceptible to the Soviet strategy to "bleed America white," and Ellender castigated aid to even important allies such as Japan and Western Europe as unnecessary and wasteful. Southerners were most critical of aid to neutralist, less-developed nations in Asia and Africa. Intolerant of any nonaligned stand in the Cold War struggle with communism, southerners perceived no advantage in aiding potential competitors in the production of agricultural staples or low-wage industries such as textiles. Louisiana congressman Otto Passman bluntly summarized the South's perspective in 1958 when he informed a startled representative of the State Department, "Son, I don't smoke and I don't drink. My only pleasure in life is kicking the shit out of the foreign aid program of the United States."[59]

Southern racial views were also apparent in Dixie's opposition to the Immigration Act of 1965, which revised the national origins system instituted in the 1920s. The latter had set immigration quotas by country, based on the ethnic composition of the United States in 1890. This system was decisively biased toward the admission of West Europeans and virtually excluded Asians. The 1965 reform bill eliminated country-by-country quotas and set non–Western Hemisphere immigration at 170,000 persons per year. In response to pressure from Senator Sam Ervin (D-NC), a member of the critical Senate Judiciary Committee, Congress added a 120,000-person limit on immigrants from the Western Hemisphere. Southerners strongly opposed the bill's more color-blind policy. In national polls, only 40 percent of southern respondents (versus 58 percent in the East, 53 in the Midwest, and 51 in the West) agreed with replacing the older system. Senator Spessard L. Holland (D-FL) could not understand "why for the first time . . . the emerging nations of Africa" were to be placed on the same footing as "our mother countries, Britain, Germany, the Scandinavian nations, [and] France."[60]

The unilateralism and nationalism that characterized the South's perspectives on the UN, foreign aid, and immigration reform were evident in Dixie's rejection of its two-hundred-year dedication to low tariffs and liberal international commerce. The influence of free-trade advocates eroded along with the reduced importance of agriculture to the South's post–World War II economy. Champions of protectionism, representing low-wage, low-technology sectors such as Louisiana sugar producers, mountain coal companies, lumber interests, food processors, and especially textile firms and the more sophisticated chemical and petroleum industries, simultaneously gained a decisive voice. Congressman Frank Smith from Mississippi was confident that "John C. Calhoun [was] revolving in his grave" as southerners consistently voted during the 1960s and 1970s for import quotas designed to protect the domestic textile, chemical, and petroleum companies.[61]

In contrast to their change of heart regarding free trade, southerners remained wedded to the warrior ethic and a strong inclination to employ military solutions for international problems. While defending the region's customary post-1945 backing for large defense appropriations and the use of force to promote foreign policy interests, Senator Russell pointedly reminded a midwestern colleague that he would "be more military minded too if Sherman had crossed North Dakota," and the Georgia senator and other southern conservatives argued consistently that peace came only through military strength. Significantly, southerners, who considered virtually all taxes deplorable, were willing in the 1950s and 1960s to pay higher levies for enhanced military budgets. Even as the Vietnam War began to wind down in the early 1970s, southerners consistently held that defense spending should have been increased rather than reduced. These positions derived in part from the expected benefits from defense dollars, but they also reflected Dixie's preference for military over other forms of foreign aid, overt patriotism, and dedication to national military strength.[62]

The South's ambivalence toward arms control during the 1960s and 1970s embodied the region's same determination to maintain a strong military. In the early 1960s polls showed that southerners were the most pessimistic Americans concerning the possibility of peaceful coexistence with the Soviets. Southern senators were the strongest opponents of the Limited Test Ban Treaty of 1963 and the 1968 Nuclear Nonproliferation Treaty. In both instances Dixie's senators voted narrowly in favor of these pacts, which received overwhelming endorsement from the remainder of the upper house. Southern senators demonstrated similar reluctance regarding the SALT I agreement negotiated by President Richard M. Nixon in 1972. Southerners, both Democrat and Republican, voted nearly unanimously for Senator Henry M. Jackson's (D-WA) amendment specifying that any future SALT negotiations be based on the "principle of equality" and "not limit the United States to levels of intercontinental strategic forces inferior" to the Soviet Union. The South's pro-military tendencies were also evident in the vigorous support of southern senators for Anti-Ballistic Missile System (ABM) funding under both Johnson and Nixon. Voting overwhelmingly against all attempts to curtail these allocations, southerners such as Russell and Thurmond in the Senate and Robert L. Sikes (D-FL) and George H. Mahon (D-TX) in the House emphasized the Russian nuclear threat and contended that ABM capability was essential to all future negotiations with the Soviets. Their conclusions summarized the South's responses to all efforts at arms limitation: "Unilateral disarmament" in a "world of international banditry" was senseless. No "good fairy" was going to ride in on a "white horse . . . and bring disarmament and peace with a wave of her magic wand."[63]

Consistent with this support for a strong military and opposition to arms control, the South consistently backed most US military interventions after 1950, particularly in the Western Hemisphere, and railed at restraints on the nation's use of force or failure to pursue clear and decisive victories. Dixie's response to the Korean War was instructive. Southerners endorsed President Harry Truman's decision in June 1950 to send US troops to repulse North Korea's invasion across the thirty-eighth parallel that divided the two Koreas. When the People's Republic of China also dispatched troops into the struggle and President Truman opted for a limited war to contain North Korea and restore the boundary, southerners grew impatient and frustrated. Public opinion polls revealed that Dixie's residents were more willing than other Americans to attack the Chinese and North Koreans north of the thirty-eighth parallel, to launch air and naval assaults on China, and even to employ nuclear weapons. In aggressive stands that forecast their views during the Vietnam War, Senator Russell favored bombing strategic targets in China, and Senator Stennis urged Truman to pursue total victory by "hitting the enemy with everything we have until terms are met." For Stennis, "everything" included nuclear weapons. Despite these bellicose pronouncements, Russell, Stennis, Byrd, and other prominent southern conservatives emerged from the Korean experience with a much greater sense of caution regarding direct military involvement in Asia. This caution was evident as the United States moved toward intervention in Vietnam from 1954 through 1964; however, it did not extend to intervention in other regions of the world.[64]

Southerners backed President Dwight D. Eisenhower's intervention to oust a left-leaning government in Guatemala in 1954; and when polled in 1960, Dixie was the US region most willing to confront the Soviet Union over access to Berlin. Displaying the adamant anticommunism that undergirded these military proclivities, southerners were also consistently more opposed than other Americans to admitting China into the United Nations. As the 1960s got under way, southerners, with the conspicuous exception of Senator Fulbright, strongly supported President John F. Kennedy's abortive attempt to overthrow Fidel Castro with the Bay of Pigs invasion. Senator George A. Smathers of Florida and Congressman Mendel Rivers were far more representative of southern opinion than Fulbright. Smathers castigated the Cuban government as a "bloody-handed left-wing dictatorship" headed by a "tyrant and megalomaniac . . . Fuhrer Fidel," and Rivers demanded that the United States block the spread of "Communist imperialism" in the Western Hemisphere. Ignoring potential Soviet responses, the bellicose South Carolinian favored any steps necessary to "clear the trash out of our backyard."[65]

The South's preferences for staunch anticommunism, unilateral interventions, and the decisive use of force were again manifest when President Johnson dispatched twenty-two thousand US and Organization of American States (OAS) troops to the Dominican Republic in 1965. These troops prevented Juan Bosch, a former president and alleged communist with Cuban backing, from gaining power. Louisiana Senator Russell B. Long praised Johnson's timely action to block "another Cuba-type Communist takeover"; and southern congressmen voted 93–0 (with 9 others announced in favor) for a resolution endorsing unilateral action to "forestall or combat intervention, domination, control and colonization . . . by the subversive forces known as international communism." From his position as chairman of the Senate Foreign Relations Committee, Fulbright was again a conspicuous dissenter. He questioned whether there was a true communist threat and charged that Johnson had violated the OAS charter and therefore "intervened . . . unilaterally—and illegally." Fulbright's uneasiness with US interventions in less developed countries originated in part from his southern heritage. Asserting that "the very word 'Yankee' still awakens in Southern minds historical memories of defeat and humiliation," he asserted that southerners should be particularly sensitive to foreign interventions.[66]

Ironically, Fulbright's assertion applied far more accurately to black than to white southerners. Southern African Americans were noticeably less committed to a rigid anticommunist, interventionist foreign policy. Consistent with their previous priorities, blacks deemed the elimination of domestic racial discrimination far more important than combating communism abroad. In 1947 the National Association for the Advancement of Colored People (NAACP) declared, "It's not Russia that threatens the United States so much as Mississippi; not Stalin and Molotov but Bilbo and Rankin." That same year 52 percent of southern whites backed Truman Doctrine aid to Greece compared to 36 percent of southern blacks. Three years later, 52 percent of southern blacks versus 36 percent of whites would have ended the Marshall Plan. Southern blacks were less supportive of the Korean War, which they were more inclined than whites to view as a civil conflict, as opposed to a crucial front in the battle against Soviet expansion. Dixie's African Americans also identified with people of color seeking to escape colonialism abroad, and numerous black organizations closely tracked developments in India, South Africa, Liberia, and other emerging nations. By the end of the 1950s, the Reverend Martin Luther King Jr. explicitly linked the US Civil Rights Movement to anticolonial struggles abroad, and he subsequently described America's inner cities as a "system of internal colonialism." King contended that too many US military interventions derived from "racist decision making," since American leaders failed to "respect anyone who is not white." In May 1961 he identified a "revolt all over the world against colonialism, reactionary dictatorship, and systems of exploitation." With a clear focus on the evolving demand for civil rights reform, King warned that unless the United States joined the revolution, "we will be relegated to a second-class power in the world with no real moral voice to speak to the conscience of humanity."[67]

American presidents from Truman through Johnson agreed that the nation's blatant racial discrimination and violence against blacks badly compromised US foreign policy. In a typical and telling propaganda broadside at the time of the Little Rock school integration crisis in 1958, Soviet officials at the UN cited the incident in conjunction with US criticism of Russia's earlier repression in Hungary. Was it not hypocritical, they asked, for "white faced but black-souled gentlemen [to] commit their dark deeds in Arkansas, Alabama, and other Southern States, and then . . . put on white gloves and mount the rostrum in the UN General Assembly and hold forth about freedom and democracy"? Five years later, as rioters opposed the integration of the University of Mississippi, President Kennedy admonished southerners, "The eyes of the nation and all the world are upon you and all of us." And in 1964, Secretary of State Dean Rusk told an enraged Senator Strom Thurmond and his Senate Commerce Committee, "The biggest single burden we carry on our backs on our foreign policy in the 1960s is the problem of racial discrimination."[68]

Despite the South's demonstrative patriotism and stalwart support for the nation's Cold War policy of containing communism worldwide, Dixie's most powerful politicians opposed concessions on civil rights regardless of the diplomatic implications. White supremacy and segregation at home trumped anticommunism abroad. Ironically, given this clear priority, southerners regularly excoriated civil rights activists as subversives or communists. The equation of racial reformers with communism was apparent in the 1940s when Senator Russell denounced the Fair Employment Practices Committee as an "entering wedge to complete state socialism and Communism," and in 1962 when a rural Georgia sheriff exclaimed, "Some of these niggers down here would just as soon vote for Castro or Khrushchev."[69]

While eagerly engaging in this red baiting, southern political leaders made the region's priorities clear. Like the Soviets, Senator Talmadge of Georgia compared Eisenhower's use of troops in Little Rock to Soviet actions in Hungary, but he drew starkly different conclusions. Although Talmadge decried the Soviet attack, he warned, "We are now threatened with the spectacle of the President of the United States using tanks and troops in the streets of Little Rock to destroy the sovereignty of the state of Arkansas." Senator Eastland of Mississippi charged that Eisenhower sought to "destroy the social order of the South," and he was convinced that "nothing like this was ever attempted in Russia." Governor George Wallace flamboyantly reiterated these southern positions in the 1960s. Wallace dismissed the Civil Rights Movement as a communist plot, alleged that the Civil Rights Act of 1964 had been taken directly from the *Communist Manifesto,* and asserted that defenders of King and his "pro-communist friends and associates" were the "same people who told us that Castro was a 'good Democratic soul,' that Mao Tse-tung was only an 'Agrarian Reformer.'"[70]

Therefore, as the South turned its attention to Vietnam, it did so with an unwavering practice of responding to US foreign relations from an unmistakable regional perspective. Indeed, Dixie's responses to US policies abroad over the previous two centuries demonstrated that "place matters" in determining how Americans perceive and react to the nation's overseas involvements—that domestic regionalism has constituted one of the decisive "internal constellation of forces" that "shape U.S. foreign policy." By the second decade of the Cold War, the South's regional perspective included a strong emphasis on honor, manhood, overt patriotism, and the warrior ethic. Acting from this bellicose set of values, southerners championed a strong military, coveted and profited from defense spending, and opposed international efforts at arms limitations. These promilitary inclinations derived from more than bellicose values. Politically conservative and evangelically Christian southerners also adamantly opposed communist countries that advocated political revolution, the destruction of capitalism, and the demise of Christianity. When confronted with such communist threats, southerners favored unrestrained military interventions aimed at decisive victories rather than diplomatic negotiations. But the white South's commitment to the containment of communism did not extend to the willing acceptance of civil rights reforms, even if the segregation and disfranchisement of blacks compromised the sincerity of US claims to stand for freedom and liberty abroad. Unsurprisingly, when faced with pervasive racial discrimination, southern African Americans decried the hypocrisy of their white neighbors and the US government and placed far greater importance on domestic reform than on containing communism. With growing US involvement in Vietnam, these differences became even more pronounced, as did the emergence of articulate challenges to Dixie's support for the war from antiwar southern whites. Indeed, belligerence, protest, and agony would characterize the South's response to the war.[71]

2

Southerners and the Vietnam Commitment, 1953–1964

As French colonial rule in Vietnam collapsed during 1953–1954, the Eisenhower administration and Congress conducted a two-year deliberation on the proper US response. Conservative southern Democrats such as Senators Richard Russell, John Stennis, and Harry Byrd, and Lyndon Johnson, a more moderate southerner, made convincing arguments against US military intervention and played an important role in the administration's decision not to become directly involved. Ten years later, President Johnson and his southern secretary of state, Dean Rusk, presented Congress with the Gulf of Tonkin Resolution, an open-ended authorization for US military action, which became the constitutional basis for America's tragic war in Vietnam. Senators William Fulbright, chairman of the Senate Foreign Relations Committee (SFRC), and Russell, who headed the Senate Armed Services Committee (SASC), oversaw congressional approval of this US commitment to protect South Vietnam. Among other southerners endorsing the resolution were Stennis, Byrd, and A. Willis Robertson (D-VA), who had made cogent arguments against US military intervention, and Albert Gore Sr. (D-TN) and John Sherman Cooper (R-KY), who, together with Fulbright, would emerge as the most important southern senatorial critics of the war.

Over this ten-year period, a clear majority of the South's influential political figures in Washington had opposed committing US military forces to direct combat in Southeast Asia. While so doing, they developed incisive and powerful arguments in favor of restraint and against American military involvement. They also addressed, but offered less consistent opinions on, the executive's foreign policy prerogatives relative to Congress, an issue that would subsequently prompt sharp disagreement as Fulbright, Gore, and Cooper challenged Presidents Johnson's and Richard M. Nixon's assumptions on the president's war-making powers. Ultimately, in August 1964, well-established southern foreign policy proclivities, such as devotion to personal and national honor, strident anticommunism, partisan Democratic political calculations, and personal ties to fellow southerner Lyndon Johnson, led southern representatives to discard their stated preferences for caution in favor of the national commitment to support South Vietnam and oppose North Vietnam and the National Liberation Front (NLF). Southern newspapers joined Dixie's representatives in backing the president in the 1964 US commitment in Vietnam, but the southern public was more conflicted. Just as the region's most prominent senators had followed a winding and tortured road toward war, some members of the southern public argued for a robust military and American intervention, while others began as early as 1963 to offer an antiwar critique.

Vietnam had become a matter of US foreign policy concern by the early 1950s because of its ostensible significance in America's Cold War struggle with the Soviet Union (USSR) and the People's Republic of China (PRC). From the 1880s until the onset of World War II, this bedraggled, faraway land (along with Cambodia and Laos) had been a part of France's Indochina colony. After 1941, the Japanese established a protectorate over Vietnam, effectively replacing the French as the country's imperial rulers. With the defeat of the Axis powers, France sought to reestablish colonial control over Vietnam as part of a more general determination to regain great power standing. To the ultimate chagrin of both France and the United States, French forces encountered a determined nationalist resistance. Only the latest participants in a more than thousand-year tradition of resisting outside control, Ho Chi Minh and his Vietminh followers had emerged from the 1930s as the principal nationalist opposition to the French; had mounted the most effective local resistance to the Japanese; and, in the wake of the Japanese defeat, had proclaimed the independent Democratic Republic of Vietnam in early September 1945. These highly effective guerrilla fighters and proponents of an independent Vietnam might not have occasioned US concern had Ho and the Vietminh leadership not been communists.

Ho's long-standing ties with the Soviet Union and more recent associations with Mao Zedong and the Chinese Communists proved decisive as the Cold War erupted in the second half of the 1940s. As the United States responded to conflicts with the Soviets over the fate of Germany, Eastern Europe, and the Middle East by adopting measures designed to contain communism, the Truman administration steadily increased US aid to France. Ensuring French participation in the Marshall Plan to rebuild Western Europe and the North Atlantic Treaty Organization designed to defend against a possible Soviet military movement beyond Eastern Europe easily took precedence over appeals for aid from Ho and the Vietminh. Although members of the Far Eastern Section of the State Department emphasized Ho's nationalism, their arguments were dismissed as Mao and the Chinese Communists seized control in China in 1949, communist North Korea attacked the South the following year, and both the USSR and the PRC extended diplomatic recognition to Ho's government. By midcentury, Ho and the Vietminh appeared to both the Truman administration and its Republican Party critics as another Asian communist threat in a worldwide struggle pitting democracy, capitalism, and Christianity against despotism, communism, and atheism.

To this fundamental Cold War dichotomy, proponents of containment added complementary economic and strategic arguments for backing the French. Southeast Asia led the world in the production of natural rubber and was rich in oil, tin, and tungsten. Access to these materials was deemed critical not only to Americans and Europeans but, even more importantly, to Japan, which the United States envisioned as a noncommunist bulwark against China. Southeast Asia also lay astride crucial air and sea routes and was prized as the possible location for essential naval stations. When viewed in conjunction with the "loss" of China and contemporary insurgencies in Malaya, Burma, and Indonesia, a Vietminh victory threatened to undermine America's credibility and thereby embolden potential enemies, dishearten allies, and trigger communist takeovers in adjoining countries. The latter dynamic, ultimately dubbed the "domino theory" by President Dwight D. Eisenhower, was prominent in American thinking as early as 1947.[1]

All of these assumptions came together in official policies in 1950. The

United States interpreted Soviet and Chinese recognition of Ho's government as indisputable evidence that he and the Vietminh were primarily
tools of the international communist movement rather than nationalists
pursuing Vietnamese independence. In response, Washington extended
diplomatic recognition in February 1950 to a government led by Bao
Dai, the former emperor of Annam, who was a French puppet devoid of
nationalist credentials. When combined with the actions of the French,
Soviets, and Chinese, the United States helped to internationalize what
had essentially been a local war against colonial domination and to convert the struggle into a part of the larger Cold War.

In May 1950 President Truman also approved National Security
Council Paper No. 68 (NSC-68). This document depicted a worldwide
conflict instigated by the Soviet Union, which sought to "impose its absolute authority on the rest of the world." All Soviet advances had to be
stymied since "a defeat of free institutions anywhere" was considered
"a defeat everywhere." Such thinking committed the United States to a
"perimeter" defense in which all parts of the noncommunist world were
viewed as equally important and a zero-sum game in which anywhere
communists won, the United States and its allies lost. Set against contemporary developments in China and North Korea's attack in June, which
triggered the active application of containment in Asia, this foreign policy rationale seemed to raise the stakes in Vietnam to the level of those
in Europe even though this small, poor nation actually had far less economic, strategic, or ideological importance.[2]

By the summer of 1953, the United States was financing 80 percent
of French war costs. The Eisenhower administration's efforts to augment
this aid, first through a congressional appropriation and then by an inter-
governmental funds transfer, prompted considerable congressional comment. Significantly, conservative southern Democrats voiced some of the
most prescient and perceptive cautions against greater US involvement
in Vietnam. Senator Russell, the chairman of the SASC and considered
by most observers the single most powerful US senator from the mid-
1950s to the mid-1960s, minced no words while telling Assistant Secretary of State Thruston B. Morton that the United States was "pouring"
aid "down a rathole" in Vietnam. From his staunchly conservative fiscal
perspective, Russell harbored grave reservations regarding all US foreign
aid and reiterated his ongoing apprehension that the Soviet strategy was

"to bleed America white." The senator opposed the United States becoming a "world policeman" and preferred that US resources be devoted to building a strong military rather than directed toward dubious international projects.[3]

Russell's reservations about involvement in Vietnam were even more specific. As the Korean War was ending, he, like many of his contemporaries, considered the prospect of fighting another land war in Asia an anathema. In addition, Russell opposed all foreign aid to countries outside the Western Hemisphere that were either unwilling or unable to help themselves or to adopt democratic institutions. According to a close student of Russell's foreign policy views, the senator perceived Asians as "devious, lazy, and selfish" and could not envision the South Vietnamese building either a viable polity or a functional military. In an insight that matured as US involvement in Vietnam escalated, Russell's southern background afforded him a correct understanding of the Vietnamese attachment to their land and ancestors and their intense opposition to outsiders disrupting their lives and traditions. Despite these reservations, Russell demonstrated the southern tendency to defer to the executive in foreign affairs by assuring Morton he would not utter "a word of criticism," even as he declared, "We are in for something that is going to be one of the worst things this country ever got into." Over the ensuing decade, the senator maintained both this deep pessimism regarding US prospects in Vietnam and his reluctance to publicly oppose an increasingly interventionist policy.[4]

Senator Stennis, a member of the SASC and Russell protégé, was equally discerning and much more publicly vocal. Senator Stennis shared Russell's fear that the United States was becoming overcommitted internationally, that expanding US "commitments all over the world" in early 1954 could leave the nation unable to defend the "homeland" if "called upon to deliver in more than one of these places" simultaneously. While warning that Congress's foreign policy prerogatives were being eroded, the senator departed from general southern deference to the commander in chief. The United States, he contended, was "treading on dangerous ground when we commit ourselves to take action thousands of miles from home without giving Congress an opportunity to participate in the discussion."[5]

On February 9, 1954, Stennis turned pointedly to Vietnam. He first objected to the assignment of 250 US Air Force (USAF) ground person-nel to help maintain B-26 bombers given to the French for use against the Vietminh. Stennis correctly identified this seemingly insignificant action as part of a US "step by step" progression toward "war in Indo-china" and a "situation in which we may have no choice except to go there with ground forces." Were these air force troops attacked, he declared, the United States would "have to go to their aid. We could not stand back." Although these forces did not come under fire, subsequent US personnel in the war zone did, and US responses bore out Stennis's prediction.[6]

The senator elaborated on March 9, April 6, and May 11. He acknowl-edged the "loss of Southeast Asia" would "carry serious consequences," but it would be far worse "to become engaged in a long, costly, and inde-cisive war that left us without victory." While flatly rejecting a "unilateral" intervention, he also doubted that "Asiatic pacts or alliances" or "all the combined action of the so-called western free powers" would "overcome communism in southeast Asia." In explicating this position, he posed sev-eral trenchant questions: "Do they [the South Vietnamese] have a will to resist communism to the death? Are they willing to put their manpower and their resources without reservation to the task of resisting commu-nism?" In the absence of such commitments, Stennis was unwilling to move beyond "fully" equipping and training the noncommunist forces in Vietnam. The Mississippi senator concluded his compelling brief against US military involvement by adding that the "cost would inevitably prove too great for our economy" and by citing the dire prospect of a long-term occupation since the United States had remained "in every place that we have sent our armies since the beginning of World War II."[7]

Other southern Democrats echoed the Russell-Stennis views. Rus-sell Long (D-LA) agreed that the war in Vietnam could not "be won with American or French troops," that the United States could not "long preserve freedom" for those unwilling to make the requisite "sacrifices" on their own behalf. Harry Byrd was equally pessimistic. Emphasizing that the United States should not intervene militarily in Vietnam without congressional authorization, he predicted that US military involvement would leave America fighting "practically alone," would likely induce a Chinese "invasion," and would yield a "long war" in which "a military victory" was unlikely. Turning to his habitual fiscal refrain, Byrd reiter-ated that the Soviets were seeking to "weaken us both financially and militarily by trapping us into sideline wars" and asserted that US "resources" were not "unlimited."[8]

As Russell and his southern colleagues feared, additional US aid did not improve France's declining military fortunes in Vietnam. By early March 1954, fifty thousand Vietminh had laid siege to twelve thousand French soldiers manning the garrison of Dien Bien Phu in the northwest corner of Vietnam near the Laotian border. A French appeal for US military aid set off a tense round of meetings in Washington. Ultimately, President Eisenhower and Secretary of State John Foster Dulles decided against US military intervention. The Joint Chiefs of Staff (JCS), who were divided over the probable impact of American air strikes, failed to provide the president with a unified or optimistic recommendation. And Great Britain, America's key ally in Europe, rejected all overtures for a joint military response.

Congressional opposition to a unilateral US intervention also helped forestall American intervention. In addition to addressing the objections of these conservative southerners, Dulles met on April 3 with a bipartisan group of key senators and congressmen. Among those attending were Senate Minority Leader Lyndon Johnson, Russell, and Senator Earle C. Clements (D-KY). Chairman of the JCS Admiral Arthur Radford detailed the desperate French plight at Dien Bien Phu and described a possible US intervention; and Dulles warned that "if the Communists gained Indochina," they would soon conquer "all of Southeast Asia . . . along with Indonesia." To prevent this strategic calamity, Eisenhower requested a joint resolution from Congress authorizing the use of American air and naval forces.[9]

The three southern senators raised the most searching questions and objections. When Clements asked if the other members of the JCS concurred with Radford's plan for US intervention, the admiral admitted none of the other service heads agreed. Noting that the United States had provided "up to 90 percent of the men and money" to fight the North Koreans, Johnson inquired whether Secretary Dulles had secured backing from potential allies for military operations in Vietnam. After Dulles conceded that no allies were on board, LBJ and the others present made it clear that a unilateral US intervention was unacceptable. Building on Clements's and Johnson's key questions, Russell warned that air or naval actions could draw China into the war and likely lead to the use of US ground forces. Reflecting his ever-present sense of honor and his ongoing concern for commitments that exceeded US resources, an angry Russell lectured the gathering, "Once you've committed the flag, you've committed the country. There's no turning back; if you involve the American Air Force, why, you've involved the nation." It remains unclear six decades later whether Eisenhower truly wanted to intervene at Dien Bien Phu or cleverly sought political cover for a policy of abstention, but the objections of these southerners at the April 3 meeting and in other venues were important to either outcome.[10]

Given their subsequent emergence as two of the most ardent critics of the Vietnam War, it is interesting that neither Senator John Sherman Cooper nor Senator J. William Fulbright was so prominently opposed to growing US involvement. Cooper, a liberal Republican who had served as a delegate to the UN and assistant secretary of state during the Truman administration, opposed a 1953 effort in the Senate to make aid funds contingent on France agreeing to set a "target date" for granting "complete independence" to its Indochinese colonies. Cooper feared that such a condition could threaten French participation in the European Defense Community, lessen pressure on China to acquiesce in the delicate Korean War peace talks, and fatally undermine French and noncommunist Vietnamese military efforts. Explaining the latter, the Kentucky senator sought to avoid the GOP being accused of losing Vietnam as Truman and the Democrats had been maligned following the communist victory in China. Although he did not favor direct US military intervention, both political calculations and Cold War considerations muted Cooper's early responses to US efforts to assist the French.[11]

Unlike his more conservative southern colleagues, Fulbright voiced no public opposition to US military involvement in Vietnam during the 1953–1954 debate. Demonstrating an affinity for foreign affairs from his election to the House in 1941, Fulbright had moved three years later to the Senate, where he became a member of the SFRC in 1948. A Wilsonian internationalist, he had strongly favored US membership in the United Nations and endorsed containment via the Truman Doctrine and Marshall Plan. He had demonstrated far less enthusiasm for US actions in Korea, where he favored "evacuation" over an "all-out" confrontation with the PRC.[12]

During this first extended discussion of proper US policies in Vietnam, Fulbright confined his remarks to executive sessions of the SFRC, and even there he appeared less adamantly opposed to US military intervention than Stennis, Russell, Long, and Byrd. While questioning Secretary Dulles on May 12, Fulbright interpreted the secretary's remarks to mean that under certain circumstances, "we would enter into the fight on our own, that we would supply much more even than we have, even up to troops possibly," but the senator did not explicitly reject such a course. Given his subsequent objections to US involvement in Vietnam, Fulbright's 1954 sense of American objectives in Vietnam was instructive. He asserted that the United States had "often gone overboard in talking about democracy in countries such as this." What was needed instead was a "transitional period . . . with a real strong leader" who could "rally the people," since Fulbright doubted that "B-26s or any other kind of thing that we can put in" would counter "this interminable guerrilla warfare." If Bao Dai were not the needed strongman, "we ought to get another one." Fulbright was certainly ambivalent about military prospects but worried far less about supporting an authoritarian regime than he would by the mid-1960s.[13]

Regardless of their varying positions on possible US military involvement, none of these southern senators challenged the Cold War assumptions defining Vietnam's importance. This task fell to Brady P. Gentry, a World War I infantry veteran and attorney who had come to Congress in 1953 and voluntarily returned to private life in 1957. Emphasizing Ho Chi Minh and the Vietminh's nationalism and downplaying communism, Gentry argued that Ho and his followers were waging "a struggle for independence that has been going on for more than 40 years." He was aghast that the US State Department had lauded French efforts at Dien Bien Phu "as a symbol for the free world's determination to resist dictatorial aggression" and supported Bao Dai, the "French puppet ruler," who was "lolling on a beach" in Nice, France, while the "fighting was raging" in Vietnam. Voicing the lingering southern populist suspicion of the motives behind US wars, the rural Texas Democrat cited World Wars I and II and Korea as evidence that "regardless of the best intentions," US "statesmen in recent times have always" opted for war. When, Gentry asked, was "this madness . . . to end?" Did "weak and bleeding Indochina" have "to become a major battleground and suffer . . . complete devastation, a ruined economy, and a million casualties, as did Korea?" Must the

United States "forever go on waging war, perpetual war, claiming it is for peace?"[14]

Although southerners had posed searching questions and offered prescient objections to US military involvement during the 1953–1954 debate, they provided solid backing for Eisenhower when the president adopted alternative means for opposing Ho and his followers. In the wake of the French surrender at Dien Bien Phu, the Geneva Conference divided Vietnam at the seventeenth parallel, leaving Ho and the Vietminh in control of the Democratic Republic of Vietnam (DRV) in the North and the French or their successors overseeing the South. Elections were to be held in July 1956 to unite the two "regroupment zones" into one nation. Despite being a participant in the Geneva meetings, the United States refused to sign the final accord. Instead, the Eisenhower administration pledged not to "disturb" the agreements through force and endorsed the use of "free elections supervised by the United Nations" to reunite the divided country.[15]

Thereafter, the United States purposefully undermined the Geneva accords by supporting Ngo Dinh Diem as the leader of the Republic of South Vietnam (GVN) and an anticommunist alternative to Ho, by acquiescing when Diem refused to hold the 1956 elections, and by negotiating the Southeast Asia Treaty Organization (SEATO) in September 1954. SEATO was designed to block communist expansion in the region as NATO had done in Europe, but, as critics such as Fulbright and Albert Gore Sr. subsequently argued, SEATO was a weak imitation. It had no standing army, and its members were only vaguely obligated to counter "aggression" by acting according to the members' "constitutional processes." Even more problematic, South Vietnam was not a charter member of SEATO, a deficiency the United States promptly remedied by enrolling the Saigon government as a protected "protocol" state. Despite these failings and ambiguities, secretaries of state under Presidents Kennedy, Johnson, and Nixon would cite SEATO as justification for US military involvement in Vietnam.[16]

Over the remainder of the Eisenhower presidency, the United States further defied the spirit of the Geneva Conference by financing roughly 80 percent of the Republic of Vietnam's government expenses through $1.5 billion in economic aid and $500 million for the military. In early 1956, the United States established the Military Assistance and Advisory

Group to train the South Vietnamese army (ARVN), and by the end of the decade, more than fifteen hundred Americans were in Vietnam aiding Diem's regime in various civilian and military capacities. Much of this American money and military training was aimed at helping the Saigon government combat a growing insurgency in the rural South. After an initial policy of adhering to the Geneva accords and looking toward a peaceful political ascent to power in South Vietnam, the Vietminh cadre who had not gone to the North following Geneva took up arms against the Diem government after 1956. Hanoi belatedly endorsed and began to aid this struggle in 1960, when it directed the formation of the National Liberation Front (NLF), a communist-directed and -controlled popular front open to all Diem opponents. By the time Eisenhower left office, the NLF (derisively termed the Vietcong [VC] or "Vietnam Communists" by the GVN) had recruited some ten thousand fighters and controlled much of the Mekong Delta. The Second Indochina War, pitting the United States and the Republic of Vietnam against the Democratic Republic of Vietnam, NLF, and their allies, had begun.[17]

In addition to helping ratify SEATO, a majority of southern senators joined other congressmen and senators during the 1950s in approving two other congressional resolutions that paved the way for the Gulf of Tonkin Resolution and full-scale US intervention in Vietnam. Both 1950s measures extended open-ended war-making authority to President Eisenhower. The Formosa Resolution, approved in February 1955, authorized Eisenhower to employ US armed forces as "he deemed necessary" to protect Formosa and other offshore islands against "armed attack" by the PRC. Although both Senators Alben Barkley (D-KY) and Byrd correctly described the resolution as a "predated declaration of war," southerners in both houses voted overwhelmingly for the measure. More representative of Dixie's thinking were Senators Long and Strom Thurmond, who emphasized the need for national unity when confronting a communist threat. Long declared it essential to demonstrate that Congress was prepared "to stand with the President . . . and go to war with Red China"; and Thurmond argued that a resolute pronouncement would preserve peace in contrast to "weakness . . . disunity . . . or hesitation." Mendel Rivers, the bombastic congressman from Charleston, South Carolina, forecast his subsequent positions on Vietnam by voting to extend Eisenhower's "authority to use whatever is necessary, including nuclear weapons, . . . , and I hope he will start at Peking and work right down."[18]

Two years later, in January 1957, Congress approved the Middle East Resolution, empowering Eisenhower to use force if he believed it essential to assist any nation in the region "requesting assistance against armed aggression" by a communist country. As Long and Thurmond had asserted in 1955, Secretary Dulles stressed that the resolution would discourage aggression and thereby promote peace. In contrast to their response two years earlier, southern senators were far more vocal in opposing this measure. During joint sessions of the SFRC and SASC, Senator Russell bemoaned the Senate's lack of specific information on which to act. Congress was "being treated as a group of children . . . with a very low IQ" and being asked to "buy a pig-in-a-poke." Sam Ervin conceded that the president possessed the authority to commit the United States to a defensive war if the nation were attacked; but he objected to the prospect of the executive initiating an "offensive war . . . without the consent of Congress" and dreaded the prospect of "another Korea, with Russia furnishing arms, and us furnishing the boys to do the dying."[19]

While Russell and Ervin confined their criticisms to closed committee hearings, Fulbright lambasted the administration's request in a formal Senate speech on February 11. The Arkansan believed that Democrats needed to fulfill their role as an "opposition party" much more aggressively, especially as the 1960 presidential election approached. Fulbright objected to this "unprecedented delegation of authority to make wars and to spend money without restriction." To accept this open-ended resolution was equivalent to Congress "abandoning our constitutional system of checks and balances"; rather than "signing this blank check," Congress should not "even for a short time . . . abdicate its constitutional powers." Fulbright would loudly trumpet this position as he emerged as the principal southern senatorial opponent of the Vietnam War in the mid-1960s. But he did so only after a 1961 declaration that, given the Cold War "requirements of American foreign policy," Congress had "hobbled the President by too niggardly a grant of power" and after overseeing the Senate's disastrous 1964 abdication of responsibility to President Johnson in the Gulf of Tonkin Resolution. Obviously, his constitutional interpretation varied over that seven-year period according to whether he was dealing with a Republican or a Democratic president.[20]

The Senate's vote (72–19) on March 5, 1957, in favor of the Middle East Resolution reflected a far from unified southern perspective. Southern senators voted 12–11 in favor, with Fulbright not voting. Among those in favor who later raised serious question about US intervention in Vietnam were John Sherman Cooper, Albert Gore, Thruston Morton, and A. Willis Robertson. Counted in the "no" column were Harry Byrd, James Eastland, Ervin, Russell, Russell Long, and Herman Talmadge, all of whom subsequently called for a more aggressive prosecution of the war in Vietnam.[21]

As the decade ended, partisan politics helped to explain why Kentucky's two senators, Cooper and Morton, supported the president but later split with Lyndon Johnson and why Fulbright and Russell grew increasingly critical of Eisenhower but acquiesced in Kennedy's and Johnson's escalation of the Vietnam War from 1961 through 1965. In the immediate aftermath of the Korean War and in the midst of the ongoing and expensive US military presence in South Korea, numerous southerners agonized over the prospect of another land war in Asia or a "unilateral" involvement elsewhere. Fiscal considerations and a general skepticism regarding foreign aid partially prompted this response from Russell, Byrd, Ervin, Stennis, and Allen Ellender. Racial considerations also fueled these doubts. Russell, Stennis, and Ellender, for example, questioned the competence of nonwhites whom the United States sought to save from communism and raised valid questions regarding whether US aid would suffice without a sufficient anticommunist commitment from indigenous peoples such as the Vietnamese. Russell, Stennis, and Byrd also contended that the Soviets purposefully sought to draw the United States into costly, small wars and, in so doing, drain American resources and distract attention from more significant strategic interests in Europe.

Constitutional considerations also generated caution among Dixie's representatives. Southerners ranging across the ideological spectrum, from conservatives such as Russell and Ervin to the more liberal Fulbright, fretted over extending too much war-making power to President Eisenhower at the expense of Congress. At the same time, John Stennis, who had raised perceptive early warnings against US military intervention in Vietnam, contended that in the new Cold War nuclear environment the president should not be overly circumscribed when the "United States has just got to get out further and further forward . . . in world policy." To complicate this diverse southern response to Vietnam developments in the 1950s, Fulbright and Gore, who were far more supportive of foreign aid than southerners generally, had by the end of the decade begun to charge that US aid was too heavily weighted toward military rather than economic and social purposes and too often provided to autocratic governments such as that of Diem in South Vietnam. Finally, in a remarkable analysis, given the Cold War climate of the 1950s, Brady Gentry from Texas had condemned US policy for opposing Ho Chi Minh and Vietnamese nationalism and backing French imperialists and their puppet Bao Dai.[22]

These cumulative southern perspectives argued for great caution in approaching Vietnam, as fiscal, strategic, racial, ideological, and constitutional reservations weighed against anticommunism, US containment policies, the domino theory, and NSC-68's zero-sum approach and call for a perimeter defense. Over the first four years of the new decade, Dixie and the nation cast aside these cautions and moved toward the tragic war in Vietnam. As the nation made this fateful commitment, southerners played a decisive role from their positions in both the executive and legislative branches.

With the inauguration of John F. Kennedy and his persistent escalation of US involvement in Vietnam, several influential southerners remained skeptical about American intervention in Southeast Asia; however, they confined their concerns to closed hearings or private meetings. Their public silence, together with more conventional Cold War assertions from other Dixie figures, essentially reinforced JFK's policy of escalation. Subscribing to fundamental Cold War assumptions of NSC-68 and the domino theory, convinced that communist aggression had to be met resolutely, and keenly aware of the political implications of being accused of "losing" Vietnam, the young president steadily increased US aid to Vietnam. His administration greatly expanded military aid and gradually increased the number of US military personnel in South Vietnam, from 685 in January 1961 to more than 15,000 at the time of the president's assassination in November 1963.[23]

Vice President Lyndon Johnson's visit to South Vietnam helped provide the rationale for this expanded US involvement. While pursuing the Democratic presidential nomination, LBJ had referred to Kennedy as "Sonny Boy" or "Little Johnny," thinking of him as a lightweight legislator who lacked the "guts" and "wisdom" to direct US foreign policy.

But when Kennedy, who needed Johnson's political clout in Texas and the South, offered him second place on the ticket, Johnson accepted. He understood that being vice president was akin to being a "Texas steer" that had "lost his social standing in the society in which he resides," but he viewed the office as perhaps his only route to the presidency. Unlike continued service as a senator from Texas and its inescapable association with the South and the "scent of magnolias," the vice presidency provided a national office and a respite from the explosive issue of civil rights. Johnson and his staff also calculated that ten vice presidents had moved up to become president, and seven had done so upon the president's death. Seven of thirty-three, or roughly 20 percent, prompted him to explain to Clare Boothe Luce, "I'm a gamblin' man, darlin', and this is the only chance I got."[24]

Johnson delivered handsomely and secured that chance as the Democrats carried seven former Confederate states, including Texas, by a margin of fewer than fifty thousand votes. One observer noted, "Johnson helped the ticket that go-around in Alabama" because he "was still looked at as a Southerner." Once in office, that regional identification was no longer an asset, as the younger, more highly educated, primarily eastern members of the Kennedy administration viewed LBJ as an "insular southerner" and referred to him disparagingly as "Uncle Cornpone." President Kennedy recognized that he was "dealing with a very insecure, sensitive man with a huge ego" and that it was critical to "keep him happy" and occupied. One of the president's principal strategies was sending Johnson on foreign trips. While vice president, Johnson logged more than twelve thousand miles in visiting thirty-three countries on eleven trips, with one of the most important taking him to South Vietnam in 1961.[25]

With his wife, Lady Bird, and Kennedy's sister Jean Smith and her husband in tow, Johnson acquitted himself admirably in both his public and his private functions. The delegation arrived in Saigon on May 11, and Johnson promptly greeted a friendly and enthusiastic crowd by shaking hands and mingling with the people. One US observer noted that Johnson seized the opportunity for a rousing "stump speech, as though he were running for office in Vietnam." Kenneth Young, the US ambassador to Thailand, who was also in Saigon, reported that the Johnson-led American group "came, saw, and won over." As historian Mitchell Lerner has observed, Johnson's poor, rural, southern roots provided him an affinity for South Vietnamese commoners that other members of the Kennedy administration could neither achieve nor understand.[26]

Johnson also acquitted himself well in his meetings with President Diem. While following directions to praise Diem publicly, the vice president obviously exaggerated in calling the South Vietnamese leader the "Winston Churchill of Southeast Asia." Johnson's private assessment was much more accurate and restrained. He asserted that Diem had "admirable qualities, but is remote from the people, [and] is surrounded by persons less admirable and capable than he." Despite recognizing some of Diem's deficiencies, Johnson identified no viable alternative leader, and declared in typically southern terms, "Shit, Diem's the only boy we got out there"; therefore, the United States had to "decide whether to support Diem—or let Vietnam fall."[27]

In his meetings with the prickly and authoritarian South Vietnamese leader, LBJ conveyed the Kennedy administration's assurances of increased aid and military training and pressed Diem to implement economic and political reforms designed to improve his popular standing. Highly skilled at reading others, Johnson understood that Diem "was tickled as hell when I promised him forty million dollars and talked about military aid, but he turned deaf and dumb every time I talked about him speeding up and beefing up some health and welfare projects." Applying the famed Johnson treatment, LBJ "tried to get knee-to-knee and belly-to-belly so he wouldn't misunderstand me" but admitted, "I don't know if I got to him."[28]

While reporting to President Kennedy and an executive session of the SFRC, Johnson reinforced the importance of South Vietnam in the Cold War struggle and agreed with the pressing need for the United States to forestall a communist takeover. Although Thruston Morton later asserted that LBJ had been "brainwashed" by the military on this initial trip to Saigon, the vice president's conventional, procontainment, pro–domino theory, Cold War perspective should not have been surprising. Even as he and Senator Russell had staunchly opposed the use of US military forces during the 1954 crisis, Johnson had made his unqualified anticommunist position clear to his constituents. In contemporary newsletters, he had declared that the United States stood at a "crossroads" and warned that the loss of Indochina "would be disastrous to all our plans in Asia" and could lead to America being "driven out of the Pacific itself!"[29]

In entirely consistent fashion, Johnson advised Kennedy and key senators, "The basic decision in Southeast Asia is here. We must decide whether to help these countries to the best of our ability or throw in the towel in the area and pull back our defenses to San Francisco and a 'Fortress America' concept." Opting for the latter would impugn American credibility and "say to the world . . . that we don't live up to treaties and don't stand by our friends." Johnson recommended instead that the United States "move forward promptly with a major effort to help these countries defend themselves." Although Diem and other Asian leaders professed to only want US troops as trainers, LBJ was eerily prescient in noting that a decision for a "major effort" on behalf of South Vietnam "must be made in a full realization of the very heavy and continuous costs involved in terms of money, of effort and United States prestige," and that "at some point we may be faced with the further decision of whether we commit major United States forces to the area or cut our loses and withdraw." In a cruel twist of fate, Johnson would be faced with this very decision following Kennedy's death, but in the interim LBJ's trip and report contributed to the US "descent into Vietnam."[30]

As Johnson emphasized the importance of sustaining a noncommunist South Vietnam, both Fulbright and Russell remained skeptical, but neither offered viable policy alternatives. In a June 29, 1961, speech, Fulbright, who had become chairman of the SFRC in 1959 with then–Majority Leader Johnson's crucial aid, echoed the Russell mantra of avoiding unnecessary "peripheral struggles" and doubted that American military aid or actions would be decisive. While Fulbright sounded a public alarm, Senator Russell continued his persistent private opposition to US military involvement in Southeast Asia. The senator strongly approved of Kennedy's emphasis on counterguerrilla training for specified US Army and Marine units, but he deplored the prospect of deploying them to Laos or Vietnam. In February 1961 Russell advised the young president to "write . . . off" Laos and also objected when JFK seriously considered recommendations to assign US combat troops to South Vietnam in the fall of 1961.[31]

Senator Gore, who like Fulbright and Russell generally subscribed to US containment policies, had by the early 1960s begun to develop a searching critique of the escalating US involvement in South Vietnam. A personal friend and supporter of John Kennedy, Gore also confined his growing reservations to private meetings with the president and executive sessions of the SFRC. Gore's anxiety over US policies derived from a five-day trip to South Vietnam in 1959. Based on his observations and the hearings he and Senator Gale McGee (D-WY) conducted, the Tennessee liberal acknowledged that South Vietnam was on "the front line between the Communist world and the free world," but he questioned Diem's status as a key US ally. Gore criticized the 1955 referendum in which Diem received 98 percent of the vote as having "a certain Iron Curtain flavor," and he feared that US aid programs were bolstering Diem's authoritarian policies rather than promoting a country in which the South Vietnamese could "enjoy . . . benefits of a free and productive society." Influenced during the Kennedy years by the perceptive and pessimistic reports from South Vietnam by David Halberstam, a young *New York Times* reporter from Tennessee, Gore began to question US security interests in Vietnam, feared a possible war with China, and doubted that US military training efforts would succeed.[32]

Gore increasingly viewed the conflict more as a civil and colonial war for independence than as a key Cold War confrontation and asserted the United States had erred in picking up the "chips of the disintegrating French colonial empire." His anti-interventionist inclinations increased during the fall of 1963 as a US-approved coup by ARVN generals overthrew and murdered Diem and his brother, Ngo Dinh Nhu. Gore informed Secretary of Defense Robert S. McNamara that South Vietnam carried no "military importance": "I know of no strategic material that it has, I know of nothing in surplus supply there except poor people and rice. It seems to me we have no need for either." As the first of a succession of military governments succeeded Diem, Gore reiterated to Secretary of State Dean Rusk his ongoing apprehension that the "repetitive identity of the United States with military coups and repressive regimes" would tarnish the US "image . . . in many parts of the world."[33]

While southern politicians raised probing objections and signaled their discomfort with US military intervention in South Vietnam, they did so against the background of an influential economic and political reality—the South's "political alliance with the Pentagon that brought an economic bounty to the region in return for Congressional support of the Defense Department." Reliable southern support for lavish defense spending was not motivated simply by the pursuit of material gains for the region. Southern conservatives, such as Democrats Russell, Stennis,

Byrd, Ervin, McClellan, Robertson, Long, and Rivers, Republicans such as Thurmond and John Tower (R-TX), and even moderates such as LBJ and George Smathers, viewed a strong military as the key to a successful, anticommunist foreign policy. Ardent southern patriotism and concern for national honor bolstered Dixie's promilitary proclivities. Still, as had become evident as early as 1898, southerners both clearly understood the value of defense spending to the South's economic development and aggressively pursued this form of federal largesse.[34]

As the nation moved toward war in the mid-1960s, southern domination of key congressional committees provided unmistakable insight into the bureaucratic structure of the Dixie-Pentagon alliance. Southern influence in the Upper House had prompted journalist William S. White to declare in the 1950s "that the Senate might be described as the South's unending revenge upon the North for Gettysburg"; and as the second session of the Eighty-eighth Congress began in 1964, Russell was the second most senior member of the Senate Appropriations Committee, which also included Stennis, Ellender, Lister Hill, McClellan, Robertson, and Spessard Holland. Russell chaired the Department of Defense Subcommittee, Byrd oversaw Foreign Operations, and Stennis headed the Military Construction Subcommittee. Russell also chaired the Armed Services Committee, while serving alongside Byrd, Stennis, Ervin, and Thurmond; and Stennis chaired the SASC's Preparedness Investigating Subcommittee (SPIS), which monitored the Department of Defense. In the House George H. Mahon (D-TX) was second in seniority on Appropriations and chaired the Department of Defense Subcommittee, and Carl Vinson (D-GA) chaired and dominated the Armed Services Committee.[35]

Two years later, Dixie's stranglehold on defense-related appropriations was undiminished: Mendel Rivers had succeeded Vinson as chairman of House Armed Services; Mahon had become chairman of the House Appropriations Committee; Robert L. Sikes was running Appropriations' Subcommittee on Military Construction; and John Tower had been appointed to Senate Armed Services, where he became one of the most assertive and tireless champions of the military. Richard Nixon's Republican administration brought no substantive change. Russell had moved up to chairman of Senate Appropriations, Stennis had succeeded him as head of Armed Services, and the Mississippi stalwart chaired both the CIA and the SPIS subcommittees. Mahon, Sikes, and Rivers retained their leadership positions, and the latter also headed the Armed Services Investigating and CIA Subcommittees of House Armed Services.[36]

From these strategic leadership posts, powerful southern senators and congressmen provided both Johnson and Nixon unwavering aid in funding the war, while simultaneously directing defense dollars to Dixie. The southern emphasis on defense projects had been evident during the Kennedy years. Two Louisiana politicians were representative. According to a Kennedy aide, Russell Long had become "considerably agitated" at the suggested diversion of ship construction from his state to Maryland and warned that it would negatively "effect his relationship with the President." Congressman F. Edward Hebert was even more blunt when he screamed at Kennedy, "What in the hell do you think they are doing" in response to the proposed closing of the Eighth Naval District in New Orleans. To do so, Hebert continued, was equivalent to "pulling the flag down."[37]

In March 1966 Senator Russell told an Atlanta audience that he made "no apology" for taking his tin cup "and working my way to the head of the line" to secure federal funds. Rivers was equally aggressive in pursuing defense allocations. In February 1968 the *Atlanta Constitution* complained that the South Carolina congressman had "donned his admiral's cocked hat" and was about "to lead another boarding party to the Pentagon," where he would employ "heavy-handed . . . tactics" to force the construction of two nuclear-powered frigates in the Charleston navy yard. Stennis displayed similar inclinations by reminding constituents in May 1965 that "all military installations in Mississippi have my active support"; and he proudly cited the $4 million obtained for Camp Shelby, "a special project of mine" since 1959, and the funds being directed to a variety of National Guard, reserve, and active duty bases across the state. Thirty years later, the senator continued to emphasize the Mississippi-military nexus by having a staff member compute that 580,317 US military personnel had trained in the Magnolia State during the Vietnam War.[38]

John Tower compiled far more elaborate statistics for interested Texans. In November 1965 he informed readers of his constituent newsletter, "Our state supports nine key Army installations; four key Navy installations and no less that 18 major Air Force bases." Nearly 250,000 DOD personnel, civilian and military, were stationed in Texas during 1964, along with their $1.3 billion payroll; and another $1.3 billion defense dollars had come to the state via defense contracts with 1,240 Texas firms in 145 cities. Five years later, in March 1970, he assured his constituents that even though President Nixon's efforts to reduce US military involvement in Vietnam were downsizing American armed forces, none of Texas's thirty-one major military installations was being closed. As of June 30, 1970, Texas would lose only 4,600 military-related jobs, leaving the state with 243,000 DOD personnel, compared with its highest wartime figure of 271,825 at the end of FY 1969.[39]

Dixie-DOD funding ties were so blatant that they even aroused the ire of Senator Fulbright in May 1967. In a frustrated rant that American officials, manufacturers, and financiers considered Vietnam "a nice little war, not too much killing, but still a big help to the economy," the SFRC chair cited Congressman Rivers and Senator Russell specifically as backing the war in return for the stimulus defense spending brought to their states. When an indignant Rivers demanded a "complete explanation," Fulbright claimed he had been misquoted, issued a public apology, and assured Rivers he would never "say anything of this kind . . . about you" or "Senator Russell for whom I have the greatest respect and affection."[40]

Fulbright may have apologized, and neither Russell's nor Rivers's support for the war was motivated solely by the desire to direct DOD dollars to Georgia and South Carolina, but defense spending remained central to the broader southern economy during the Vietnam War. In 1971, 40 percent of the nation's US-based military personnel were stationed in the South; and Dixie produced 52 percent of DOD-contracted ships, 46 percent of its airframes, 42 percent of its petroleum products, 62 percent of its coal, and 27 percent of its ammunition. In that same year, Virginia ranked third nationally in DOD funds per capita; Texas, sixth; Georgia, tenth; Florida, eighteenth; South Carolina, nineteenth; and Alabama, twenty-first. Virginia was the third most dependent state on defense spending; Georgia, the sixth; South Carolina, the eleventh; Texas, the twelfth; and Mississippi, the seventeenth. "Southern defense dependency," which had been growing steadily since World War II, and the economic, political, and foreign policy implications were accentuated and solidified by Vietnam.[41]

Against this backdrop of ongoing southern skepticism regarding US involvement in Vietnam and the countervailing influence of defense spending as a crucial facet of Dixie's economy, the assassination of President Kennedy brought Lyndon Baines Johnson to the White House and to the post of commander in chief overseeing US foreign and military policy. Johnson inherited a rapidly deteriorating situation, as Diem's departure left a "gaping political vacuum" in South Vietnam. By late January 1964, the generals who had deposed Diem also fell victim to a coup, and continuous plots and counterplots became the political norm until Generals Nguyen Cao Ky and Nguyen Van Thieu seized power a year later. The tribulations and accompanying political chaos in Saigon were exacerbated by Hanoi's decision in late 1963 to adopt a "go for broke" military strategy in pursuit of total victory. Led by Communist Party First Secretary Le Duan, the DRV dispatched North Vietnamese Army (NVA) regulars to the South to fight alongside the Vietcong and significantly increased the flow of war materiel to equip these forces. These operations quickly yielded a series of military victories in early 1964 and revealed the strategic hamlet program, designed to isolate the Vietcong cadre and fighters from the South Vietnamese peasants, as little more than a hollow bureaucratic shell.[42]

While contemporaries and subsequent scholars have offered a staggering array of assessments of Johnson, few would disagree with Clark Clifford, who considered LBJ "the most complex man I ever met," or with Dean Acheson's contention that LBJ possessed as "many sides . . . as a kaleidoscope." As with Woodrow Wilson, the last president born in Dixie, disputes have arisen as to whether Johnson was primarily a southerner, as opposed to a westerner, southwesterner, or Texan. Part of this disagreement derives from how best to describe and locate Texas. East Texas has been aptly characterized as the "western most extension of the Deep South," and it differs dramatically from Johnson's Hill Country, west of the Pedernales River; but Texas as a state from 1876 through the 1970s, with its colonial economy, one-party Democratic politics, and discriminatory racial practices, aligned closely with the other former Confederate states.[43]

Johnson's purposeful inconsistency added to the confusion. Through much of his first two decades in Washington, LBJ described himself as a southerner and acted in ways indistinguishable from other southern politicians. He was, in the words of Senator Clinton P. Anderson (D-NM), as "southern as hominy grits," and historian William E. Leuchtenburg has observed correctly that LBJ's inclination to feel "misunderstood and abused" was typically southern. Kent Germany, another close student of the American South, has asserted that Johnson's expertise in "speaking southern," in always having an appropriate joke or story close at hand, was "a product of experiences absorbed in the rural South and West" and reflected his southern "sense of place, family, and culture." When by the mid-1950s Johnson began to eye the presidency seriously, he intentionally sought to blur this perception since he doubted that a perceived southerner could be elected to the nation's highest office. Many southerners added to the confusion by disowning Johnson when he moved to dismantle Dixie's racial order, when he became "The *Yellow* Rose of Texas," or when his initials came to represent "Let's Beat Judas." Congressman Edward Herbert cited the 1957 civil rights bill as the moment Johnson "ceased being a southerner and became a westerner."[44]

While Johnson may have veered from the southern path in domestic matters, many of his foreign policy assumptions coincided closely with important Dixie perspectives. Like other members of the "containment generation," the president was ardently anticommunist, subscribed fully to the containment policy, and believed that aggression had to be met with firm, unmistakable responses. In the absence of decisive US actions, Johnson warned a group of congressmen in early 1965, the dominos would fall. The North Vietnamese "want to take South Vietnam, and . . . Thailand, and . . . Burma, . . . Sukarno-Indonesia, [and] . . . the Philippines, [and] . . . Hawaii." Indeed, "they'd like to come right back to Seattle." Since appeasement led only to more serious confrontations, he would tolerate "no More Munichs" under his administration. Johnson was convinced the "Chinese" and the "fellas in the Kremlin" would be "taking the measure of us," and they could not be allowed to "think we're yellow." Therefore, Johnson vowed to win the war.[45]

LBJ's determination to maintain US national credibility coincided with his southern sense of honor and manhood. "Deeply immersed in the ethos of the South," Johnson repeatedly asserted that national honor was at stake in Vietnam: "If America's commitment" were "dishonored in South Vietnam," it would "be dishonored in forty other alliances." The United States had gone to war in Vietnam "because we have promises to keep. . . . To dishonor that pledge, to abandon this small and brave nation to its enemies, and to the terror that must follow, would be an unforgivable wrong." Johnson also believed his personal manhood and honor were on the line. A "profoundly insecure man," LBJ was convinced that if the United States lost in Vietnam, he would be viewed as a "coward. An unmanly man. A man without a spine." He was regularly haunted by a dream in which "thousands of people" were berating him as a "Coward! Traitor! Weakling!" If the communists prevailed, "I would be seen as a coward," and the United States "would be seen as an appeaser and we would both find it impossible to accomplish anything for anybody anywhere on the globe." Once committed to defeating Ho Chi Minh, Johnson could not admit that the cause might have been invalid or his policies flawed. Like southerners more generally, he had a limited appreciation of other nations, peoples, and cultures; "Foreigners are not like the folks I'm used to," he acknowledged. This limitation left him "culture-bound," susceptible to "clichés and stereotypes about world affairs," and unable to distinguish adequately among potential foes or to rethink the universal applicability of containment.[46]

Johnson's fear of the backlash from losing in Vietnam was not confined to the international sphere. He was also convinced that losing in Vietnam would kill his domestic reform program. Genuinely committed to social justice for all Americans, the president feared that deserting "the woman I really loved"—the Great Society—"for that bitch of a war" would result in losing "everything at home." In late 1964, he predicted correctly, "Those damn conservatives are going to sit in Congress and . . . use this war as a way of opposing my Great Society legislation. People like Stennis . . . don't want to help the poor and the Negroes. . . . They'll take the war as their weapon" and argue that "beating the Communists" was the first priority. But if fighting the war impeded domestic reform, losing it would assuredly doom those measures by provoking "an endless national debate—a mean and destructive debate" similar to the one that plagued President Truman following the victory of the communists in China in 1949. Johnson, who most feared political attacks from the right, "the great beast . . . the reactionary elements in this country," believed such a debate "would shatter my presidency, kill my administration, and damage our democracy." Or, as he phrased it less delicately, "If I don't go in now and they [southern conservatives] show later I should have, they'll . . . push Vietnam up my ass every time."[47]

When directed toward the Vietnamese, Johnson's commitment to reform further buttressed his decision for war. Grounding his reform impulse in the Social Gospel and its call for compassion, equality, social justice, and uplifting the poor, the president looked abroad through the lens of "Christian internationalism." A member of the evangelical but liberal Disciples of Christ, LBJ was "deeply religious," "devout without being doctrinaire"; therefore, his religion did not align with Dixie's dominant beliefs or practices. Still, it is significant that religion played an important role in the life of this son of the South. As Johnson proclaimed in celebrating the bicentennial of American Methodism in early 1966, he did not believe that Christian ideals should be directed "just to my own children or just to my own town or my own State or my own Nation." He was equally "concerned now with the little brown men in Southeast Asia whose freedom they are trying to preserve." Convinced "the average father and the average mother" in Asia and Africa wanted the same things for their children as American parents, the president both felt the need to help them and expected a positive response to US aid and efforts to promote democracy and economic development in South Vietnam.[48]

As the new president contemplated Vietnam policy, he agreed with Russell, Stennis, and the great majority of southerners that a strong military was essential for a viable foreign policy, that the United States could only secure "peace through strength." Throughout his political career, LBJ had consistently supported US military strength and keenly appreciated the importance of defense spending to the South's economy. His confidence in US military, technological, and economic might reinforced his determination to demonstrate American resolve. Like most Americans, he could not conceive of the world's most powerful nation losing to what he described as a "damn little pissant country." Ironically, together with this support for a strong military, Johnson harbored an uneasiness and suspicion born of his southern populism. Reflecting on information he had received at the time of the Gulf of Tonkin incident in 1964, Johnson concluded the "military had pulled a fast one on me there. I just can't fully trust the sons of bitches." This distrust and his determination to avoid a MacArthur-style challenge to civilian control of the military played an important role in his oversight of US strategy in Vietnam.[49]

Just as Johnson's attitudes toward defense policy and the military reflected his southern background, he also assumed his duties as president with the traditional southern belief that the nation's chief executive should be given broad-ranging, virtually unquestioned latitude, authority, and support in the realm of foreign policy. Johnson voiced this belief in describing his relationship with Eisenhower: "He is the only President we have, and I am going to support that President, because if I make him weaker I make America weaker." Thruston Morton, a Kentucky Republican, vouched for LBJ's adherence to this axiom. Morton recalled that during the Eisenhower years, Johnson had exhibited characteristic southern patriotism and support for the chief executive: "When the chips were down, he did nothing to negate or diminish the President's strength. . . . In fact, he tried in every way *I think* to support the flag." Johnson had supported Roosevelt, Truman, Eisenhower, and Kennedy and believed that he deserved the same backing from the American public, press, and Congress.[50]

Finally, Johnson's decision to escalate the war and his determination to proceed in Vietnam reflected his determination to become a great president, to emulate his model, Franklin Roosevelt, by passing a sweeping reform agenda at home and overseeing a victorious war abroad. Never as comfortable confronting international problems as he was exercising his virtually unparalleled domestic political skills, LBJ was convinced the media and northerners generally doubted his abilities and criticized him unfairly because of his southern background. While lamenting sarcastically the criticisms that he was "not qualified in foreign affairs like Jack Kennedy and those other experts," Johnson concluded he "was just born in the wrong part of the country." In moments of frustration, he declared, "I don't think that I will ever get credit for anything I do in foreign policy because I didn't go to Harvard." Persuaded that he faced "bigotry in the North against a southerner on questions that involve his ability to handle foreign relations," Johnson was determined to demonstrate that he was a "world statesman" rather than a "Texas provincial." Commenting on this facet of Johnson's personality, two prominent southern newspaper editors observed that LBJ had "always been hypersensitive to the demonstrable fact" of being "one of those southern politicians, who . . . travel badly, like sweet corn, being overripe by the time they reach the great cities of the nation, and offending delicate northern palates."[51]

As Johnson moved toward war in 1963 and 1964, he received significant counsel and support from another critically placed southerner, Secretary of State Dean Rusk. Unlike his boss, no one disputed Rusk's standing as a southerner. He was born into a poor, rural Georgia family in 1908 and moved to Atlanta at the age of five. From his father, who had studied to be a minister, and a pious mother, he acquired a strong Presbyterian faith. As had been true of Woodrow Wilson, this faith led him to believe that the United States was destined to promote peace and to improve the international environment by spreading democracy and social justice. By the 1960s Rusk had become an aggressive champion of civil rights for African Americans, and he projected the US reform mission abroad, confident that most people beyond the United States "want the kind of world we want." Young Dean had also imbibed Dixie's ardent patriotism and the southern reverence for the military and devotion to honor. An ROTC cadet by the age of twelve, he was proud that both of his grandfathers had fought for the Confederacy, and during World War II, he became a protégé and lifelong admirer of General George C. Marshall. After earning degrees at Davidson College in North Carolina and Oxford University, the latter as a Rhodes Scholar, Rusk served in the US Army's military intelligence branch during and after World War II. Specializing in East Asia, he moved to the State Department in 1947, to the presidency of the Rockefeller Foundation from 1952 to 1959, and became Kennedy's secretary of state in 1961.[52]

Like Johnson, Rusk was "never one of the 'Kennedy people' and never made the effort to become one." He did, however, form a close relationship with Johnson. The two southerners swapped stories about who had been poorer and which family had first acquired indoor plumbing and electricity. While still vice president, LBJ confided to his brother, "Some of the people around [Kennedy] are bastards," but not Rusk. Johnson pronounced him "a damned good man. Hard-working, bright, and loyal as a beagle. You'll never catch him working at cross purposes with his President. He's just the kind of man I'd want in my Cabinet if I were President." Acting on this assessment, Johnson kept Rusk on as head of the State Department for his five years as president, and as he and Rusk left office in 1969, LBJ's opinion had not changed. The secretary had been a "loyal, honorable, hard-working, imaginative man of conviction" who "stood by me and shared the President's load of responsibility and abuse."[53]

Johnson's comfort with Rusk was not just personal, as the secretary's foreign policy perspectives melded nicely with Johnson's. Like so many other southerners, Rusk revered Woodrow Wilson and his understanding of Wilson's promotion of international law and collective security.

Rusk believed that the United Nations and post-1945 collective security treaties embodied Wilson's vision and that world peace depended upon their functionality and defense. The Georgia Wilsonian was convinced by 1963 that there were two competing forces in the international arena: "those who want the U.N. kind of world and those who are trying to tear it down." When Rusk assessed the situation in Vietnam, he readily identified the Vietcong, North Vietnam, and the PRC as the threats to a "U.N. kind of world" defined by law, self-determination, and constitutional government. Tracing the US obligation back to the legal commitments of SEATO, he argued in traditionally southern terms that the United States had given its "pledged word" and could not be "honorable in Europe and dishonorable in Asia." "The issue," Rusk proclaimed, was "a very simple one indeed. Hanoi, with Peiping's support," refused "to leave its neighbors alone." It was "just too late in history" to allow "aggression to develop a momentum," and the US capacity "for organizing a peace" hung in the balance. Only by sustaining its "alliances" and "credibility" worldwide could the United States repulse the communist campaign of world revolution and deter those who "feel . . . they could with impunity" attack American allies. Adopting the zero-sum thinking of NSC-68, Rusk emphasized that if the United States ignored small nations like South Vietnam, "the first thing you know the periphery is the center."[54]

Neither Johnson nor Rusk moved toward war in 1964 without grave reservations. In May, Johnson told national security advisor McGeorge Bundy, "I don't think it's worth fighting for and I don't think we can get out. It's just the biggest damn mess that I ever saw. . . . What the hell is Vietnam worth to me? . . . What is it worth to this country?" LBJ conveyed similar apprehensions to Richard Russell, telling his old friend, "It's damned easy to get in a war, but it's gonna be awfully hard to extricate yourself if you get in." Like Johnson, Rusk did not rush to war thoughtlessly. He had opposed a 1961 recommendation to send US ground troops and had been uneasy about overcommitting to South Vietnamese president Diem, whom he considered a "losing horse." But when faced with the imminent collapse of South Vietnam, both men acted on their much stronger fears of the personal, domestic, and international repercussions that would accompany a Vietcong–North Vietnamese victory.[55]

Agreeing that "neutralization" of South Vietnam was just "another name for a Communist take-over," the president and secretary rejected diplomacy and opted instead for greater force in early 1964. The greater force was delivered through a covert military campaign called Operation Plan (OPLAN) 34-A, in which South Vietnamese guerrillas carried out raids against the North Vietnamese coast. US aid to South Vietnam was simultaneously increased by $50 million, and intelligence-gathering missions were flown over the North by US planes and conducted in the North China Sea by American destroyers. Unwilling to take more overt steps, such as bombing North Vietnam, especially in an American presidential election year, Johnson and his advisors began preparing a congressional resolution authorizing more aggressive measures should the proper occasion arise.[56]

Before that occasion arose in early August 1964, southerners continued to express their ambivalence over US involvement in Vietnam; but when pressed, none had clear, viable alternatives for Johnson to pursue. In a December 1963 phone conversation, Fulbright feared that Vietnam prospects were "hopeless" since the "general situation" rendered a "real victory" unlikely. Therefore, the senator advised Johnson against sending "a whole lot more men in there" or opting "to go all out." The following March the chairman of the SFRC rejected both US withdrawal and diplomatic negotiations since the US–South Vietnamese "bargaining position" was "weak" and offered "little prospect" of yielding an independent, "non-communist South Vietnam." While opposing "expansion of the conflict," Fulbright advocated "a renewed effort to bolster the capacity of the South Vietnamese to prosecute the war successfully." Three months later, on June 23, the senator reiterated the necessity of US involvement, since "we are the only power that can assure an essential degree of stability and strength in South Vietnam," and he continued to oppose negotiations.[57]

Richard Russell also conferred with President Johnson in December 1963. The Georgia senator advised his old friend "to spend whatever it takes to bring a power to government [in South Vietnam] that would ask us to go home." Recognizing this recommendation was unrealistic, Russell reiterated, "We should get out," but admitted, "I don't know any way" to do so. In a March 1964 Senate speech, he pronounced Vietnam of no "strategic, tactical, or economic value." Given the availability of "missiles and long range planes," Vietnam had "no significant value as a base for military operations." In a long phone conversation with LBJ on May 27, the senator remained exceedingly pessimistic about US prospects. The

US–South Vietnamese position was still "deteriorating"; the South Vietnamese leaders had "no sense of responsibility" or willingness to act on their own behalf; and "a major war with the Chinese" appeared likely. When Johnson pressed for concrete suggestions, Russell conceded, "I wish I could help," but "I don't know what to do." Russell may have not known how to orchestrate a withdrawal, but he explained to a constituent that his opposition to the commitment of US ground troops was unchanged: "I would rather pull out entirely, with whatever loss of face this might bring, for I am convinced that we would be bogged down in the jungle fighting the Chinese in their kind of war for the next 25 years."[58]

Although he lacked Fulbright's or Russell's close personal access to Johnson, Senator A. Willis Robertson also attempted to warn the president of the dangers of war in Vietnam. A former Virginia governor and a conservative member of the Senate Appropriations Committee, Robertson feared that Secretary of Defense McNamara was contemplating an "all-out war." On March 27, 1964, the senator advised Lawrence F. O'Brien, LBJ's special assistant, that he could see no "permanent gain" from fighting in Vietnam that "would be worth the price of the life of one Virginia boy." Like Russell, he doubted the prospects for democracy in South Vietnam since the people lacked "our capacity for self government and most of them look upon public office as an opportunity for self enrichment." Robertson predicted correctly that defeating the North Vietnamese and Vietcong would not be "either easy or cheap." By denying the people "any voice in their own government" and failing to cut "supply lines" from North Vietnam, the French had failed to suppress "far weaker" communist foes than those the United States confronted. Since the oppressive South Vietnamese government was repeating France's "political mistake," and the United States had no "definite blueprint" for blocking the flow of materiel down the Ho Chi Minh Trail, US success was unlikely.[59]

Like Robertson, Senator Allen Ellender had no close personal ties to LBJ, but he was much more direct and public in calling for a US withdrawal from Vietnam. Ellender had endorsed the early Cold War containment measures and supported a strong military, but he complained in the late 1950s that US administrators were overestimating Soviet strength and requesting military expansion on "a somewhat false assumption." Instead of dubious defense spending, he suggested that communism could be more effectively countered through exchanges of ideas, trade, and students with the Soviet Union. From this same skeptical approach, Ellender had opposed US military intervention in Vietnam in 1954, had criticized the widespread corruption in South Vietnam in 1956, and could see no compelling "commercial" or "historical ties" with the country in 1963. In March 1964 the Louisiana legislator echoed Wayne Morse's (D-OR) blunt demands that "we should get out." In May Ellender acknowledged the "difficult position . . . inherited from the French" and the narrow range of "choices," but he worried that greater US involvement would yield another Korea, in which the United States was "carrying the whole load" while its "so-called allies" were "standing on the sidelines, watching."[60]

Despite occasional bursts of southern belligerence, such as Strom Thurmond applauding ostensible news in February 1962 that "we are actually going" to take the steps necessary "to win" the war, or Thurmond joining with Senator John Tower to denounce Fulbright as an appeaser in March 1964, the overwhelming policy preference among southerners from 1954 through mid-1964 had been one of decided caution and restraint. From conservatives such as Russell, Stennis, Ervin, Byrd, Robertson, and Ellender to moderates and liberals such as Fulbright and Gore, influential southerners had consistently objected to US military intervention and had variously worried about the overcommitment of economic aid and the United States becoming injuriously identified with European imperialism. These reservations had derived from fiscal considerations; the fear of another Korea-like ground war in Asia; the US tendency to support corrupt, authoritarian regimes as anticommunist allies; the racially charged perception that the South Vietnamese were either unwilling or unable to act effectively on their own behalf or to establish a democratic polity; the contention that South Vietnam was of little strategic or economic value to the United States; and the apprehension that the United States would receive little or no aid from its major Cold War allies in a Vietnamese war. In summary, southern congressmen and senators had formulated a convincing collective brief against escalating US economic and especially military intervention in South Vietnam. But constrained by partisan politics, Cold War anticommunism, and personal ties to Johnson, they had done so primarily in private conversations with the president or executive committee sessions, especially after the Democrats regained the presidency in 1961. Only Allen Ellender, a far less influential public figure than Russell, Stennis, Fulbright, or Gore, had publicly advocated immediate withdrawal; and tragically, the far more influential skeptics put aside their incisive reservations in the face of the Gulf of Tonkin incident and heavy pressure from President Johnson and his administration.[61]

On August 2, 1964, North Vietnamese PT boats fired on the USS *Maddox*, a US destroyer cruising off the coast of North Vietnam in the South China Sea. US-sanctioned and covert OPLAN 34-A assaults by South Vietnamese gunboats on an offshore North Vietnamese island the previous night provided the crucial backdrop to these attacks on the *Maddox*. The much more powerful American ship easily fended off the smaller enemy craft, destroying one and damaging the other two. LBJ responded by continuing the *Maddox*'s intelligence-gathering mission and ordering a second US destroyer, the *C. Turner Joy*, into the area. After another round of OPLAN 34-A raids, the US commanders reported they had been attacked again on August 4. Despite significant contemporary doubts and conclusive subsequent evidence that the second incident had not occurred, Johnson and his advisors seized on the Gulf of Tonkin affair to launch retaliatory air strikes against North Vietnamese torpedo boat bases and oil storage facilities. The president also quickly dispatched the previously prepared congressional resolution to Capitol Hill authorizing broad authority for executive actions in South Vietnam.

Given the US–South Vietnamese operations directed against North Vietnam over the previous six months, the Gulf of Tonkin affair was an incident waiting to happen. President Johnson's response was as predictable as the relatively insignificant naval clash. With no improvement in the military situation over the previous six months, LBJ had been contemplating recommendations to bomb, blockade, or even invade the North. Moreover, as Rusk noted, the administration had elected to push for a congressional "resolution only when the circumstances . . . require a resolution" and would, "thereby, force congressional action." Johnson agreed. Having observed the political abuse Truman had endured for failing to obtain congressional approval before deploying troops to Korea, LBJ declared, "By God, I'm going to be damn sure those guys [Congress] are with me when we begin this thing." The president also seized on the perfect opportunity to head off Republican criticisms that he was conducting a no-win Vietnam policy of "equivocation and vacillation." His responses to the North Vietnamese attacks allowed him to distinguish himself from Senator Barry Goldwater, the hawkish GOP presidential nominee, who had advocated the possible use of nuclear weapons to halt the flow of men and materiel south from North Vietnam. As LBJ confided to an aide, he could not afford to be viewed as "vacillating or being an indecisive leader."[62]

Fulbright, the chairman of the SFRC, and Russell, who headed the SASC, played crucial roles in the passage of the Gulf of Tonkin Resolution and with it an overwhelming congressional endorsement of Johnson's retaliatory air strikes. Both were inclined to support their old southern, Democratic colleague as LBJ responded to an ostensibly overt communist challenge. That this challenge arose just four months before the presidential election reinforced their inclination. Fulbright was especially frightened by Goldwater, whom he deemed dangerously belligerent and capable of triggering a nuclear exchange with the Soviets. Fulbright and Russell accepted the administration's version of events in the Gulf of Tonkin and Johnson's assurances that he sought the resolution as a demonstration of national unity and had no intention of widening the war. The two key senators, despite their objections to Eisenhower's Middle East Resolution, also adopted the argument that a clear, united American domestic front would deter additional North Vietnamese–Vietcong aggression.

Only later would they learn that Johnson had secured their aid under false pretenses. On August 4 LBJ notified the American public that "a number of hostile" North Vietnamese vessels had launched a second round of attacks on two American destroyers. Branding these attacks "open aggression on the high seas," the president proclaimed that they would only strengthen US resolve to "carry out our full commitment to the people and to the Government of South Vietnam." Although he had ordered retaliatory air strikes, the president assured his constituents the American "response for the present will be limited and fitting." Operating from the "considered conviction . . . that firmness in the right" was "indispensable . . . for peace," Johnson assured Americans, allies, and adversaries that the United States sought "no wider war."[63]

In meetings at the White House with the congressional leadership and executive sessions of the SFRC, SASC, and House Foreign Affairs Committee, Rusk and McNamara supplemented Johnson's public statements by declaring that the North Vietnamese attacks had been "entirely unprovoked" and denying any connection between those attacks and OPLAN 34-A raids. Both assertions were patently false. Fulbright later professed no "suspicion" that he was being misled, and neither he nor Russell raised any questions in the one-hour, forty-minute combined session of the SFRC and SASC. Given their leadership positions and stature in the Upper House, either senator could have delayed the resolution and forced hearings, the absence of which Fulbright subsequently pronounced "a disaster, a tragic mistake."[64]

Fulbright and Russell also decisively influenced the Senate's floor debate and vote on the resolution. As passed on August 7, the resolution charged North Vietnam with a "deliberate and systematic campaign of aggression" against the South and of having "deliberately and repeatedly" attacked US ships in international waters. These attacks had allegedly created "a serious threat to international peace." In response to this threat, Congress supported the "determination of the President, as Commander in Chief, to take all necessary measures to repel any armed attack against the forces of the United States and to prevent further aggression." The president was further authorized "to take all necessary steps, including the use of armed force, to assist any member or protocol state [South Vietnam] of the Southeast Asia Collective Defense Treaty requesting assistance in defense of its freedom." The resolution was to remain in effect at the president's discretion, or until ended by a concurrent congressional resolution, a provision inserted at Senator Russell's request.[65]

At Johnson's behest, Fulbright introduced and managed the measure on the Senate floor. His adept and candid performance guided the resolution to passage by a vote of 88–2 but also revealed the assumptions and opposition to a wider war that provided the bases for his subsequent break with Johnson over the conflict. The SFRC chairman declared the North Vietnamese attacks "unprovoked" and pronounced Hanoi "patently guilty of military aggression and demonstrably in contempt of international law." In response, President Johnson had taken "wise and necessary action" since such "unambiguous aggression" could not "be tolerated or ignored without inviting further provocations." Fulbright recommended "prompt and overwhelming endorsement" of the resolution as a resounding message of national unity and resolve. This stance would discourage "any ambitious or reckless adventuresome spirit on the part of the North Vietnamese or the Communist Chinese" and thereby preclude "an escalation or enlargement of the war."[66]

In response to questions from Senators George McGovern (D-SD) and Ellender, Fulbright denied that the US destroyers had committed any provocative acts or coordinated with South Vietnamese boats engaged in the OPLAN 34-A raids. Both assertions were dubious but consistent with the information provided by the administration. Responding to queries from Senators Daniel B. Brewster (D-MD), Gaylord Nelson (D-WI), and John Sherman Cooper, Fulbright did not think that the resolution would "substantially alter the President's [existing] power" as commander in chief "to use whatever means" he deemed "appropriate" in Southeast Asia. Voicing a southern axiom that he challenged during the Eisenhower presidency and would soon oppose again, the Arkansas senator asserted that within the American governmental system the president "must necessarily have the dominant role, however jealous" the Senate might be of its "privileges." Given this executive authority, Fulbright saw nothing in the resolution that served as a "deterrent" or "prohibition" against Johnson escalating the war. The senator could provide "no absolute assurance that large numbers of troops" might not be dispatched. Still, he found "nothing in the resolution . . . that contemplates" altering the US mission of training and aiding the South Vietnamese as the means to avoid active US participation in a general war. And he clearly expressed his opposition to such a change, declaring it would be "unwise under any circumstances to put a large land army on the Asian continent."[67]

Senator Russell cast his great influence behind the resolution by citing the Formosa and Middle East Resolutions as clear precedents; indeed, according to the SASC chairman, the "language" granting Johnson such broad powers was "almost identical" to that extending similar authority to Eisenhower. The Georgia senator reiterated Fulbright's contention that the resolution did "not alter the constitutional separation of responsibility for the conduct of foreign relations." Rather, like the earlier declarations, the current resolution was meant to demonstrate "national solidarity and steadfastness" and "avoid any broadening of the war, or any escalation of the danger." To these arguments, Russell added the quintessential southern consideration of honor. The US "right as an independent state" to sail unmolested through "international waters" directly involved "our national honor." With its "national honor . . . at stake," the United States could not command the "respect of other nations, or . . . maintain its self respect" without an appropriate response. "Ignoring aggressive acts" led only to "much more danger . . . than pursuing a course of calculated retaliation."[68]

In addition to Fulbright and Russell, other southerners made significant contributions to the debate. Senator John Sherman Cooper's principal foreign policy staffer observed, "I think he did well because while he always asked severe question, he never went for ad hominems"; and his August 6 queries to Fulbright graphically embodied this approach. Through a series of incisive questions, Cooper provided an unsettling forecast of how Johnson would employ the resolution as the equivalent of a declaration of war. The Kentucky Republican had voiced his concern over a possible "escalation and final confrontation" with China as recently as July 1, when he endorsed a level of US troops sufficient to maintain the American "position" in South Vietnam but also urged a reconvening of the Geneva Convention of 1954 to pursue an "agreement that would recognize two separate, sovereign countries" and oppose "continued aggression" by North Vietnam. Expressing this same apprehension over an escalating war, Cooper directed his queries to Fulbright on August 6: Was Congress extending the president "advance authority to take whatever action" he deemed necessary to defend South Vietnam? Might the president use this authority to employ "force" that "could lead into war"? Could the executive utilize this authority "to attack cities and ports in North Vietnam" if he believed such actions would "prevent any further aggression against South Vietnam"? By passing the resolution, would Congress be meeting the condition under the SEATO agreement that afforded the president the "authority to do whatever he determines may be proper and necessary" to safeguard "our security in South Vietnam"? When Fulbright answered yes to all of these inquires, Cooper emphasized that the Congress and the nation "must contemplate, hoping that it will not be true, the possibility of an expanded war" in South Vietnam and even "a great war" with China. Since Cooper did not consider Southeast Asia "the chief area of interest to the United States," he urged LBJ "to work for ways, consonant with our honor and security, to avoid the great catastrophe of war." Although less shrill than Wayne Morse or Ernest Gruening (D-AK), the two most vocal critics of the resolution, Cooper had brilliantly cut to the heart of the matter and tragically forecast what was to come. Unlike Morse and Gruening, Cooper voted for the resolution.[69]

Albert Gore, who would subsequently join Fulbright and Cooper as the most prominent southern senatorial opponents of the war, agreed with the SFRC chair and Russell that "freedom of the seas must be preserved," and "aggression against our forces must be repulsed." Gore pointedly noted that he had not considered it "wise" for the United States to replace France following Dien Bien Phu, and he worried that he had not expressed publicly his "deep concern" and "critical questions" about US policy in South Vietnam in the interim. Like Cooper, Gore discerned no important interests in South Vietnam, and he pointedly agreed with Frank Church (D-ID), who consented to vote for the resolution "with a heavy heart, with a genuine concern about the future of American policy in Asia." Gore also joined with Church in expressing his "confidence," perhaps more accurately his hope, that President Johnson would "act with prudence, caution, and wisdom, and with the courage necessary for the eventualities that may come."[70]

Consistent with his established position that the United States should withdraw from South Vietnam and his well-founded suspicion that US actions had invited the North Vietnamese attacks, Allen Ellender called for the involvement of America's SEATO partners. Without their active cooperation, he worried anew about a "repetition of what happened in South Korea," where the United States had borne "over 90 percent" of the "burden." Although their reservations failed to deter the 416–0 vote in favor of the resolution in the House, two southern Republican congressmen offered compelling arguments against the measure. Eugene Siler of Kentucky had announced in June that he would run for president on the platform of serving for one day, withdrawing US forces from Vietnam, and resigning. From this antiwar perspective, he denounced the resolution as "unnecessary" and warned that it would be employed "to seal the lips of Congress against further criticism." Bruce Alger from Texas, who voted for the measure "for reasons of unity," expressed "grave reservations" over "congressional abdication of responsibility in declaring war" and feared that LBJ would not "come back to Congress . . . before involving this Nation further."[71]

Other southerners voiced no such reservations. John Stennis joined Russell in emphasizing honor. He judged that North Vietnamese actions had left the president, Congress, and the nation "no choice. . . . Our flag and our men have been fired upon. . . . Our honor, our safety, and our security are at stake." Revealing the "slightest weakness or hesitation" would invite additional aggression, but passage of the joint resolution would help to "avoid war," as had been the case with the crises of the 1950s. Thruston Morton concurred. Approval of the resolution would "avoid any miscalculation on the part of either the North Vietnamese or Chinese Communists." John Sparkman (D-AL) demonstrated the southern proclivity for deferring to executive authority in foreign policy by voting for the measure, as he had done for the Formosa and Middle East measures, because Eisenhower and Johnson "made it clear" they needed "a show of unification on the part of the country." Russell Long, George Smathers, and Strom Thurmond were more belligerent. Long advised Rusk not to squander time consulting Congress since "the less time you spend on consulting and the quicker you shoot back, the better off you are." Smathers applauded Johnson's "appropriate" military retaliation, which together with the resolution would communicate to the enemy that the United States was no "paper tiger" that could "be bluffed or bullied out of our commitments to our friends and allies." From his habitually aggressive perspective, Thurmond urged Johnson to "take all necessary measures" against the "Communist aggressors" and to discard "our purely defensive posture in favor of a 'win' policy." In a demand that he would repeat often over the ensuing eight years, the South Carolina hawk declared it "imperative that victory, not stalemate, be our objective" in Vietnam.[72]

Led by Fulbright and Russell, southerners fell in line behind their president, voting unanimously for the resolution in both houses of Congress. Anticommunism, national honor and credibility, party politics, and deference to the executive prevailed over oft-expressed, perceptive, and prescient reservations regarding the abdication of congressional war-making authority, potential escalation of the ground war, and a possible conflict with China. Southerners, like other congressmen and senators, accepted Johnson's appeal for national unity and assurances that he had no intention of widening the war. Congressman Dante B. Fascell (D-FL) recalled that the actual facts of the Gulf of Tonkin incident were far less important than the belief that the "president needed the authority. . . . So the resolution was just hammered . . . through by everybody." Cooper, one of the most astute skeptics, never claimed he had been "deceived" and fully realized the Senate was granting Johnson "the authority to send troops if he made up his mind to do so." Still, Cooper admitted, "There wasn't much thought at the time that it would happen."[73]

Willis Robertson and Fulbright were more directly critical of Johnson.

Robertson remarked privately in 1965 that Johnson had gotten "through Congress a backhanded endorsement to which no one could object" since it only requested congressional approval for the "necessary" actions "to protect" American soldiers in South Vietnam. "Who," Robertson asked, "could go on record against protecting" US troops or, "at that stage, . . . openly charge the President with leading us into war through the back-door?" Fulbright, who later professed his "lasting regret" at having "played a major role" in passing the resolution, felt badly misled and manipulated regarding both the administration's account of the naval clashes in the Gulf of Tonkin and LBJ's use of the resolution. The SFRC chairman understood that the measure reaffirmed Johnson's powers as commander in chief but "did not anticipate" the resolution "would be invoked as legal sanction for a full-scale war." Rather than consciously voting for the "'functional equivalent' of a declaration of war," he and Congress had voted "in the belief" they were "acting to *prevent* war."[74]

Johnson had no patience with Fulbright's protests. Over the ensuing four years, the president and his advisors employed the Gulf of Tonkin Resolution as the legal and political basis for escalating Vietnam into the very full-scale war Russell, Fulbright, Gore, Cooper, and Stennis had warned against. Johnson later observed, "Congress gave us this authority, to do 'Whatever may be necessary'—that's pretty far-reaching; that's 'the sky's the limit.'" In even more Johnsonian terms, the president compared the resolution to "Grandma's night shirt, it covered everything." In January 1966 a Republican senator graphically described LBJ's political use of the resolution: "He pulls it out of his pocket and shakes it at you." A frustrated Democrat agreed: "It was so damned frayed and dog-eared the last time I talked to him . . . I wanted to give him a fresh copy."[75]

Johnson had seized on the Gulf of Tonkin incident to secure the congressional resolution placing Congress on record supporting his military responses and granting him authority for virtually unlimited future actions. The North Vietnamese attacks also afforded LBJ the occasion to launch a firm but restrained military response and in so doing to distinguish his policies from those of Barry Goldwater, the GOP presidential candidate. The Arizona senator had been criticizing the president's policies as lacking focus and vigor and had advocated a "must win" strategy of "aggressive prosecution" of the war. Included in his prescribed actions was the possibility of sustained bombing of North Vietnam; and when Goldwater stumbled in discussing the potential use of nuclear weapons, Johnson and the Democrats gleefully branded him a dangerous warmonger.[76]

Privately, Johnson told *Life* reporter Hugh Sidey, "We can't let Goldwater and Red China both get the bomb at the same time. Then the shit would really hit the fan." Publicly, LBJ ominously referred to Goldwater as a "raving, ranting, demagogue" and warned that "some people have more guts than brains." Having emphasized Goldwater's alleged belligerence, Johnson successfully positioned himself as the "peace candidate." The president pledged that his administration would "continue to act to halt Communist aggression" but would temper this firmness with good judgment. "I want to be very cautious and careful," he assured a New Hampshire audience. And Oklahoma voters were told, "We don't want our boys to do the fighting for Asian boys." With Vietnam as one of the campaign's most prominent issues, LBJ's political strategy helped produce his overwhelming electoral victory, in which he carried forty-four states and 486 of 538 electoral votes.[77]

As Johnson posed as the peace candidate, his advisors were at work on a series of options for increasing military pressure on North Vietnam. By early December, these advisors (save Undersecretary of State George Ball) recommended a two-phase program. The first phase called for bombing raids against North Vietnamese infiltration routes in Laos and retaliatory strikes against North Vietnam in response to any "spectacular" Vietcong actions in the South. The second phase of "graduated military pressure" included a sustained air war against North Vietnam and a possible naval blockade. Although President Johnson deferred a decision on phase two until early 1965, by endorsing phase one on December 1, he took a critical step toward the very war he had so resolutely decried ten years before.[78]

Prior to the Gulf of Tonkin incident, the southern public, like Americans generally, had paid relatively little attention to Vietnam developments. Gallup poll interviewers in late April 1964 found that 63 percent of Americans had given Vietnam little or no attention, and 67 percent either had "no opinion" or had "not followed" US policies in this remote land. As the *Montgomery Advertiser* observed in early August, after spending more than $3 billion and losing 262 men, "a large percentage of Americans don't know where Vietnam is, another group doesn't care and the largest number, including Washington policymakers, don't know where we're going or how to get there."[79]

With the attacks on the US destroyers, southern newspapers joined Americans and the national press in backing President Johnson. In so doing, the papers voiced the same caution and restraint as a decisive majority of Dixie's legislators had expressed over the previous decade. Southern editors readily agreed that North Vietnamese actions had been "unprovoked," "deliberate and unwarranted." They also applauded the president's mature and measured response. The *New Orleans Times-Picayune* termed Johnson's actions "at once appropriate and cautious"; the *Charlotte Observer* agreed that LBJ had demonstrated the "kind of caution which is imperative . . . in the nuclear age"; and the *Dallas Morning News* was pleased that the Texas president "left no doubt that he can be firm but not rash, tough but not belligerent, courageous but not impulsive."[80]

While speculating on North Vietnam's intentions and citing China as the ultimate provocateur, southern papers adopted the Johnson-Fulbright-Russell argument that a strong, united American stand provided the most viable deterrent to communist aggression and a wider war. For the *Louisville Courier-Journal,* the "real mystery" was why obviously overmatched North Vietnamese PT boats had attacked American destroyers. Perhaps it had been "trigger-happy junior officers," or a "case of low-level goofing-off," or, more ominously, a "pretext for overt Red Chinese intervention in South Vietnam's war." The *Atlanta Constitution* concluded that the communists had "apparently . . . decided to test our resolve . . . during this presidential election year"; and the *Times-Picayune* wondered if the attacks had been "a planned one-shot probe to test U.S. reflexes in a sensitive location" or the "opening gambit in a drive to insulate coastal supply lines." Regardless of the enemy's intentions, the southern press credited Peking, rather than Hanoi, as the true source of the aggression. The *Courier-Journal* referred to the "Communists of Peking and their underlings in Hanoi"; the *Charlotte Observer* cited Mao as "the real originator of Communist aggression in southeast Asia"; and the *Dallas Morning-News* worried that "Mao and his Vietcong puppets," a group of "barbarians who have no regard for humanity and its highest aspirations," could spark a global conflagration.[81]

Southern papers also adopted the thesis that a strong, united American stand provided the most effective deterrent to communist aggression and a wider war. The *Courier-Journal* described the Gulf of Tonkin Resolution as "almost a political necessity," given Eisenhower's precedents; and the paper cited the nearly unanimous congressional vote in favor of the measure as the "best hope for peace." The *Atlanta Constitution* concurred that the resolution "demonstrated before the world the solidarity of the American government in our resistance to Communist aggression . . . and in our support of the President as commander-in-chief." Indeed, the *Charlotte Observer* was certain that the US response had dispelled "all lingering questions" of US "timidity or excessive restraint"; and the *Courier-Journal* asserted that the "convincing show of . . . national unity" would "leave no doubt" among communists "that if war is what they want, war is what they will get—a certainty that should bring even Peking's fanatics to their senses."[82]

This belligerent tone, even while arguing for caution and peace, sounded somewhat discordant but all too southern. On the eve of the Gulf of Tonkin incident, the *Atlanta Constitution* noted editorially, "Many Americans . . . are impatient with our long years of involvement in South Viet Nam without victory." If US-inflicted losses failed to persuade the "Communists to abandon their aggressions," the United States would need to "take whatever countermeasures are necessary." As Congress debated the resolution, *Constitution* publisher Ralph McGill recommended the use of nuclear weapons should China intervene militarily. China as a direct participant would rule out a "conventional war" and leave "no practical way to avoid" a nuclear attack on PRC troops and nuclear plants. Two months later, the *Richmond News Leader* returned to the issue of southern impatience with limited war and further denounced the strategic mistake of forfeiting the initiative and allowing "U.S. policy . . . to be determined by the Reds." Citing reports that the United States was "losing the war in Vietnam," the *News Leader* lamented that "limited war amounts to limited annihilation, a partial participation in . . . a total conflict."[83]

Many southerners echoed this belligerent perspective. As early as August 1963, a rural Texas newspaper editor wrote to Senator John Tower protesting the US "no-win policy in South Vietnam" and the death of American soldiers "for window-dressing purposes." Following the November 1963 coup that overthrew South Vietnamese President Ngo Dinh Diem, another Tower constituent condemned the US role in Diem's removal as the "betrayal" of an ally with a "hard anti-communist policy." In January 1964, an Alabamian urged John Sparkman to work toward changing US policies "from concessionism to 'standfirmism,' from 'rocking-chair diplomacy' to an aggressive policy which will restore this country to its rightful position in world politics, a position of undisputed leadership . . . of the entire world." A second Sparkman correspondent agreed and advocated that the United States "throw a bunch of troops in there, stomp hell out of them once & get it over with." Upon learning of the North Vietnamese actions in the Gulf of Tonkin, another Texan informed Senator Ralph Yarborough (D-TX), "If we are going to try to keep the Reds out of South East Asia, . . . then we should either turn our military forces loose and win that battle or we should get out!" Voicing the fear of another land war in Asia and preference for the use of US technology, a Macon resident asked Senator Russell, "Why not an all out war against these people? We do not feel that our servicemen should be sacrificed and slaughtered as they were in Korea."[84]

In November 1964, a mother from Humbolt, Tennessee, voiced the anguish and ambivalence that dogged southern women over the ensuing eight years. She wrote "on behalf of myself, my husband and thousands of other parents who must feel as we do." She was the mother of two sons, a twenty-one-year-old serving in the air force and a sixteen-year-old who would soon be "facing a draft or enlistment." Having seen her only brother, her husband, and her brother-in-law off to war in 1943, this Tennessee woman was no stranger to "service and war," but during World War II, the nation recognized the enemy and understood the reasons for the conflict. She could discern no such clarity in 1964, when the United States would "not even admit to being at war." Were the government to ask her sons "to give their lives for their country," she wanted "to know why and for what they died." She further demanded a vigorous prosecution of the conflict: "Either take a firm stand on foreign policy at the risk of all out war, or pull out of Viet Nam completely."[85]

For other southerners, the lack of discernible progress in South Vietnam prompted them to advocate withdrawal. Indeed, citizens from across Dixie formulated an impressive collective brief during 1963 and 1964 against US involvement in Vietnam. While traveling in Europe in December 1963, an Austin resident importuned Senator Yarborough to advocate "an end to this tragic situation, daily becoming more menacing." By following the US buildup through stories in the European press, this man had concluded that the United States was being "sucked into a debacle like that in Korea" or "worse." He dismissed American rhetoric proclaiming American "determination to defend the 'freedom' and the 'liberty' of the Far East as pure hogwash." These rights were "unknown concepts" in East Asia; and if the Vietnamese valued them, "they would have obtained them by themselves," rather than being "cajoled and prodded into action by American 'advisers.'" Another Texan asserted that by late 1963 the United States had "obviously lost the initiative" in Vietnam; therefore, as in football, the "best answer" was to "quick kick" the problem back to France.[86]

Hugh B. Hester, a retired US Army brigadier general living in North Carolina, also questioned the US ability to expand "freedom or democracy" in South Vietnam. Hester argued instead that US policies had curtailed change, incited "unrest," and yielded "totalitarian or unstable" governments in less developed countries. After supporting and "largely" financing "France's colonial war," the United States had "made war against" the Vietnamese people "through its puppets." The billions "spent in this mad venture" had led to the death of "scores of thousands of Vietnamese, thousands of French and now hundreds of U.S. citizens, and the impoverishment of a whole generation of people." The general warned correctly that the United States was headed "into a major war that no one can win, but all will lose."[87]

Writing on her lunch hour in early October 1963, a Dallas "Housewife-Secretary" penned an incisive antiwar letter to Senators Tower and Yarborough. Basing her assessment on "public" information, she objected to sending "American servicemen" and "untold millions of our tax dollars" to a country where US troops were "subjected to vilification and harassment." Nor was there hope of a positive outcome when "the people . . . refuse to let you help them," and "most" South Vietnamese "hate" their minority, Catholic "government." Better to proceed on the assumption that "the biggest debt the U.S. Government owes is to the *American* people."[88]

From around the South, opponents of US involvement in South Vietnam echoed and amplified these antiwar contentions. Attentive southerners found "no clear American interest" at stake; objected to the United States "butting into Asian affairs"; decried "losing American lives in a war which is obviously unpopular" among the South Vietnamese; worried that the conflict could expand to include other "great powers, & involve the entire world"; and feared the United States would forfeit "moral leadership in the eyes of the world." In one of the harshest indictments of American policy, an Atlanta man characterized US policies in Vietnam and Laos as "hateful and imperialistic." He rejected as an "utter distortion" the portrayal of the National Liberation Front as spearheading "an international communist conspiracy" in Southeast Asia. He emphasized instead Ho's and the NLF's nationalist credentials and their leadership of an "authentic independence movement" aimed at freeing the South Vietnamese from both "a cruel and despotic regime and from foreign domination."[89]

As the year ended, Russell and Fulbright remained apprehensive about increasing US involvement in Vietnam. In November Russell worried, "If we get in there and get messing around with those Chinese, we could be in there for the next ten years." The Georgia senator continued to think the South Vietnamese would not "help themselves"; but, as had become his wont after expressing trenchant reservations, he offered no viable alternative policy. He could not "figure . . . any way to get out without scaring the rest of the world." Fulbright was equally confounded. When Maxwell Taylor, the US ambassador to Saigon, told a December 3 meeting of the SFRC that the administration was considering escalating the war, Fulbright dismissed such steps as "futile" without "a reasonably stable government that has the support of a good solid majority of the local people." As the hearing concluded, the chairman lectured Taylor, "If you want to go to war, I don't approve of it. I don't give a damn what the provocation is. . . . I am not going to vote to send 100,000 men, or it would probably be 300,000 or 400,000."[90]

Russell's and Fulbright's persistent and profound reservations regarding US military intervention in Vietnam were representative of majority opinion among southern senators and congressmen in the critical decade from 1954 through 1964. In contrast to their interventionist inclinations in Latin America, southern political leaders expressed a host of perceptive objections to American military involvement in Southeast Asia. With the Korean War as an instructive backdrop, they variously decried another land war in Asia, warned of a confrontation with China and the lack of support from NATO allies, questioned the region's strategic importance, worried over the fiscal drain occasioned by a peripheral war, doubted South Vietnamese commitment to the struggle and ability to adopt democratic institutions, and objected to Diem's autocratic regime.

Despite these farsighted protests, southerners backed fellow southern leaders, Lyndon Johnson and Dean Rusk, in responding to the Gulf
of Tonkin incident. National honor and credibility, Democratic politics,
deference to executive authority in foreign affairs, the belief in military
strength as the ultimate key to a successful foreign policy, the region's
political alliance with the Pentagon, and the Cold War devotion to containing a communistic and atheistic foe took precedence over the years
of contrary analysis in both the White House and Congress—but not
without much soul searching and reluctance. Fulbright, Russell, Stennis, Gore, Cooper, Ellender, Eugene Siler, and Bruce Alger embodied this
complex and conflicted response, as did the southern public, many of
whom were already raising perceptive objections in 1963 and 1964 to the
growing US involvement in Vietnam. Once the nation was committed,
the South became the region most supportive of the war, but Dixie was
far from united in backing the war. Along with the South's familiar belligerence came telling protest and the same painful agony that tortured
the remainder of the nation. These differing responses became apparent
during 1965–1966 as Johnson and Rusk decided on war.

3

Southerners and the Decisions for War, 1965–1966

Lyndon Johnson had deftly employed the Gulf of Tonkin incident to secure a broad, congressional authorization for military actions in Vietnam and to establish his standing as a firm but cautious foreign policy leader. To his and the nation's chagrin, neither of these accomplishments impeded the steadily deteriorating political and military situation in South Vietnam. Building on its earlier decision to dispatch regular army units south, Hanoi continued to wage big-unit operations with both NLF and NVA fighters. In May the communist military superiority over the ARVN was graphically demonstrated at Binh Gia, north of Saigon, where two South Vietnamese battalions were decimated. Employing both this military clout and accompanying political operations, the NLF had gained control over approximately one-half of South Vietnam's territory and population. In response to Saigon's acute political instability and obvious military vulnerability, LBJ chose war, first by initiating the sustained bombing of North Vietnam in February 1965 and then by committing US ground troops to the conflict during the ensuing spring and summer. Beginning with 25,000 sorties in 1965 and 79,000 in 1966, the Rolling Thunder campaign devastated North Vietnam with 643,000 tons of bombs over the following three years. Similarly, the president's decision to dispatch some 200,000 troops in 1965 led to approximately 385,000 Americans being stationed in South Vietnam by the end of 1966 and a total of more than 530,000 by the time Johnson left office in January 1969.[1]

Southern congressmen played a decisive role in Johnson's decisions for war by facilitating his strategy of suppressing congressional and public debate as he opted for this massive military involvement and by affording Johnson crucial and dependable support in the allocation of funds to prosecute the conflict. Consistent with Dixie's belligerent tendencies, the southern public proved more supportive of the war than Americans from other regions, and important southern papers solidly endorsed the US efforts. But as the grave reservations expressed by southern senators after 1953 had foreshadowed, Dixie's response to the Vietnam War's escalation was far from unified. Indeed, by the end of 1966, Senators Fulbright, Gore, and Cooper had emerged as key congressional critics of the war; Fulbright had chaired SFRC hearings that stimulated the very public debate Johnson had sought to avoid; and that public debate in the South included a strong, but minority voice of dissent.

Although this massive military intervention in such a remote, seemingly insignificant country would have occasioned much contention, Johnson provoked even greater consternation in the South by fighting a limited war characterized by the gradual escalation of the bombing campaign against North Vietnam. His prosecution of the war was limited in several key aspects. The president never sought an official declaration of war, declined to activate the National Guard or reserves, and placed Cambodia and Laos off limits to US ground forces, thereby enabling the Vietcong and NVA to seek periodic sanctuary in these neighboring countries. LBJ and Secretary of State Rusk repeatedly emphasized that the United States sought only to preserve an independent, noncommunist South Vietnam and did not seek to destroy North Vietnam's sovereignty as a nation or to displace its communist government. Consistent with these positions, Johnson refused to invade North Vietnam and placed strict guidelines on the bombing near Hanoi and Haiphong, the North's two most populous cities. The president and Secretary of Defense McNamara further restricted bombing near the Chinese border and placed off limits Haiphong harbor, through which critical war materials flowed and where Soviet and other nations' ships were docked. As if these various limitations were not sufficient to infuriate hawkish southerners, Johnson, Rusk, and McNamara only gradually accepted the military's suggestions for bombing targets and advice to escalate the severity of the bombing. Boasting that the military could not "even bomb an outhouse without my approval," LBJ and his advisors envisioned an overall strategy designed to inflict a level of collective pain sufficient only to convince North Vietnam to end its military campaign and support for the Vietcong in the South.[2]

Johnson and Rusk's commitment to a limited war derived from several key assumptions. They feared that an overly aggressive prosecution of the conflict could draw China or the Soviet Union into the war or even escalate the fighting to the use of nuclear weapons. In July 1965, LBJ told a reporter, "There is . . . the right wing solution, which would be a nuclear solution. And, of course, we could pull out. . . . Neither of these alternatives being satisfactory, what are we to do?" Johnson then pondered the crucial question to which he never found the answer: "What will be enough and not too much?" What level of force would prevent a communist takeover of South Vietnam without provoking a larger war? Johnson also recognized correctly that conservatives such as Russell and Stennis would readily cite the costs of a full-scale war or a losing effort as justification for eliminating the Great Society social programs. As LBJ confided to Under Secretary of State George Ball, "The great black beast for us is the right wing," which would "put enormous heat on us to turn it [the war] into an Armageddon and wreck all our other programs."[3]

The president's profound suspicion of the military and determination to avoid a civilian-military confrontation added another crucial dimension to his decision to wage a limited war. This distrust led Johnson to treat advice from the Joint Chiefs of Staff (JCS), who consistently advocated troop increases and more aggressive bombing, with skepticism and at times even contempt. "The generals," he remarked, "know only two words—spend and bomb." At one point, Johnson screamed at the assembled JCS that he would not "let some military idiots talk him into World War III" and ordered them "to get the hell out of my office!" Haunted by President Truman's clash with General Douglas MacArthur, Johnson instructed General William Westmoreland, "General, I have a lot riding on you," and later, "I hope you don't pull a MacArthur on me."[4]

Fearful of pressures for overly aggressive military measures and that a "major debate on the war . . . would be the beginning of the end of the Great Society," LBJ attempted to keep "foreign policy in the wings" during 1965 and, according to one historian, took the nation to war by "stealth." Exercising "indirection and dissimulation," Johnson and his administration never announced that Rolling Thunder quickly moved from a retaliatory to a sustained bombing campaign, justified the dispatch of what promptly became offensive US ground troops as only necessary to defend American air personnel and equipment, and carefully obfuscated and understated the July 1965 decision for up to two hundred thousand ground troops and the fundamental change in policy it entailed.[5]

Preventing a major congressional debate over these decisive 1965 decisions constituted an essential facet of Johnson's stealth strategy. The president's campaign for avoiding unwanted "goddamn speeches" in Congress took several forms, all of which benefited from the fact that he worked with Democratic majorities that outnumbered the GOP by more than two to one in both houses. Johnson applied his infamous "treatment" to both individuals and groups, and his cajoling, enticing, and threatening usually worked. For example, in February he scolded and helped temporarily silence Senator George McGovern (D-SD): "Goddamn it, George, you and Fulbright and all you history teachers down there [in the Senate]. I haven't got time to fuck around with history. I've got boys on the line out there." The president also hosted a series of briefings at the White House for congressmen and their wives. Together with McNamara and Rusk, Johnson presented the administration's analysis of the Vietnam situation.[6]

Given Rusk's ongoing confrontations with his fellow southerners, Senators Fulbright and Gore, the secretary's interpretation of the war was instructive, as was his explanation of why the administration would reject all overtures for a compromise settlement of the conflict. Rusk decisively rebutted any suggestion of a "civil war" in Vietnam. The conflict had resulted instead from "external aggression" against "South Vietnam . . . directed from the North, commanded from the North, inspired by the North," in blatant violation of the Geneva "agreements of 1954." Rusk instructed the congressmen that combating this aggression, which was rooted in China's "militant brand of the world revolution . . . subscribed to by Hanoi," was critical to the US goal of "organizing . . . peace" worldwide on the bases of self-determination, peaceful change, and international law. Therefore, the United States could not appease these aggressors or "be driven out" of the region.[7]

In contrast to China's and North Vietnam's aggressive, forceful, and provocative actions, Rusk assured the congressmen that the United States had "no national appetites there, no need for bases, no desire for a permanent military presence," and no inclination "to destroy the regimes in Hanoi or in mainland China." The sole US objective was the "safety and the peace of these smaller countries." Indeed, "there could be peace almost literally tomorrow" if North Vietnam were to "abandon its effort to take over South Vietnam." In response to those congressmen such as Senators Cooper and Gore who had begun to urge negotiations, Rusk rejected any talks as "some sort of a screen" for abandoning South Vietnam or as endangering that nation's independent, noncommunist status. Like the president, Rusk also reminded the representatives and senators not to oppose a leader who was "carrying out the most solemn commitment that this nation has made over a period of ten years" since 1954. Four presidents and the previous Congress, by voting 504–2 for the Gulf of Tonkin Resolution, had placed the nation's credibility on the line while opposing aggression in Southeast Asia. Criticism of Johnson and the administration, Rusk emphasized, signaled American "disunity" and sent the wrong messages to the enemy.[8]

Secretary Rusk's response to two very southern questions also revealed much about administration thinking that ultimately alienated many residents of Dixie. On February 18, a senator asked, "I'd like to know what is necessary to win that war. I don't want to see another Korea"; and, on March 2, a second legislator asked if the administration was "willing to make the maximum effort that is necessary to solve this situation." Rusk's responses were vague and evasive. He professed no ability as a "prophet" and asserted that the administration could hardly "know . . . for certain" what victory would require since "the other side—Hanoi and Peking"— was also "helping to write that scenario." The secretary could formulate no "prescription for the next year or next month," which had not yet arrived. He was similarly obscure when asked if he expected the United States "to stay in Southeast Asia indefinitely." He declared only that the administration would sustain the US practice of upholding its "commitments all over the world." Like LBJ, the secretary of state assumed incorrectly that "there must come a point where the other side" would recognize that "we are not going to be driven out . . . by military action."[9]

Johnson's strategy for controlling public and congressional responses to the war also included a major public address at Johns Hopkins University on April 7. While situating Vietnam in the Cold War context of opposing communist aggression, he pledged, "We *will not* be defeated" or "withdraw, either openly or under the cloak of a meaningless agreement." To this promise of strength and resolve, he added his commitment to undertake "unconditional discussions" with North Vietnam in pursuit of a peace settlement. Despite this pronouncement, the administration's refusal to include the Vietcong in such talks or to accept any settlement that compromised South Vietnamese independence embodied conditions that blocked all negotiations. Still, the president's ostensible call for talks pacified many early opponents of US involvement. The same held true for Johnson's final major point—his intention to request $1 billion from Congress to help fund a development project on the Mekong River as an inducement for Hanoi to agree to US peace terms. From this southern perspective on rural development, Johnson envisioned a transformation in Southeast Asia comparable to what the Tennessee Valley Authority had done for the American Southeast and rural electrification had done for the Texas Hill Country. Americans uneasy with the growing war responded favorably to this initiative, but the North Vietnamese did not. Johnson later complained, "I keep trying to get Ho to the negotiating table. I try writing him, calling him, going through the Russians and Chinese, and all I hear back is 'Fuck you, Lyndon.'"[10]

On May 4, Johnson tightened the screws on potential congressional dissenters by requesting a supplemental appropriation of $700 million for use in the Dominican Republic and South Vietnam. The sum was relatively insignificant, but LBJ's characterization of the vote portrayed congressional action as a reendorsement of his Vietnam policies, as the passage of what Undersecretary of State William P. Bundy described as a "small-scale new Gulf of Tonkin Resolution." Johnson emphasized, "This is not a routine appropriation. For each Member of Congress who supports this request is also voting to persist in our effort to halt Communist aggression in South Vietnam." By reiterating the administration stance that "national unity" was critical to US standing "in the world," the president suggested that antiwar dissent undermined American foreign policy; and he added the powerful warning that opposing the requested appropriation betrayed American soldiers in the field: "To deny and delay this means to deny and to delay the fullest support of the American people and the American Congress to those brave men who are risking their lives for freedom in Vietnam." When Congress approved the appropriation overwhelmingly, Johnson had not only forced the legislative branch to go on record again backing the war but also officially introduced the potent argument that hindering funding for the war was equivalent to abandoning the troops.[11]

As the Johns Hopkins speech and the May 4 supplemental appropriation demonstrated, Johnson's acute political sensibilities and long congressional experience went far toward limiting debate and dissent, but he could not have kept Congress so well controlled during 1965 without the assistance of fellow southerners, particularly Fulbright and Russell. Had not the chairmen of the SFRC and SASC and Mike Mansfield (D-MT), the Democratic Senate majority leader, been unwilling to oppose the president or initiate a Senate debate on Johnson's policies through most of 1965, LBJ could not have followed his relatively low-key road to war. Despite their essential complicity in Johnson's strategy for downplaying the war domestically, neither Fulbright nor Russell had altered his grave reservations about US involvement in Vietnam. By the end of the year, both became more openly critical of Johnson's prosecution of the war and in so doing embodied evolving and conflicting southern responses to the war.

Of these two southern heavyweights, Fulbright ultimately became the more persistent and outspoken critic of the war, but his open break with Johnson did not come until after the crucial decisions for widening the war had been made. After Fulbright had become chairman of the SFRC in 1959, many observers predicted he would head the State Department with Kennedy's election the following year. Opposition to civil rights legislation doomed the Arkansas senator's prospects, and the new president turned instead to Rusk and his liberal record on race. Most of Fulbright's fellow senators would have agreed with George Smathers, who described the Arkansan as a "genuine" intellectual and one of the Senate's "truly independent thinkers." While still majority leader, Johnson had declared, "Bill's *my* Secretary of State," and explained the senator's absence from late afternoon gatherings for Scotch and conversation by observing, "He'd rather sit in his office, reading books." Contemporary legislators would also have agreed with Smathers that Fulbright could be "the most obstinate, obdurate, difficult fellow . . . you've ever seen. But . . . he was one hundred percent sincere." Not so convinced of Fulbright's sincerity, President Truman had dubbed him "an over-educated Oxford S.O.B." A former Rhodes Scholar and law professor, Fulbright readily embraced the title "professor," viewed himself as an "educator," and envisioned the SFRC as a forum for debating and elucidating major policy issues.[12]

Fulbright's distress over the war's steady escalation and his growing conviction that the war was unwinnable were evident in both his private and his public observations. The senator voiced his reservations privately in executive sessions of the SFRC and the committee's joint meetings with the SASC. In January he could see no developments warranting "escalation of the war"; in June, he asked US ambassador nominee Henry Cabot Lodge how this remote, "God-forsaken part of the world" could be deemed so "vital" to American national security; and later that month the senator decried "further escalation of the war" and declared it "clear to all reasonable Americans that a complete military victory" could come only at unacceptable costs to American resources and honor.[13]

Fulbright's tense exchanges with Secretary Rusk also marked the beginning of the SFRC chairman's ongoing confrontation with first the Johnson and then the Nixon administration over the role the Senate should play in US foreign and war policies. On January 8 Fulbright unsuccessfully sought "some reassurance" from the secretary of state that the administration would consult the SFRC and Congress before reaching any decisions to escalate the war. Rusk's only reassurance was to promise that was "something the President and [congressional] leadership will talk to each other about." When Fulbright persisted that he hoped that no such "decision" would be made without "at least feeling the pulse of this committee," Rusk agreed only to "report" his "remarks" to Johnson. After Rolling Thunder had begun without such consultation, Fulbright returned to the topic on April 30 by complaining that in passing the Gulf of Tonkin Resolution the Senate had not anticipated dispatching thousands of ground troops to Vietnam. Since Congress was "traditionally" consulted when "large numbers" of troops were sent abroad, did the administration intend "to request any further authorization or approval by the Congress"? The senator also pointedly reminded Rusk that "a lot of us [senators] have been quiet" publicly because they did "not want to embarrass the administration." While stating bluntly that the administration had no plans to seek additional congressional authorization for waging the war, the secretary of state defended the use of the Gulf of Tonkin Resolution as the legal and constitutional basis for expanding the conflict on the grounds that no one could have foreseen "last August what might be required." As had been the case with the decision to commence Rolling Thunder, Johnson essentially ignored

Congress as he opted in March and July to commit thousands of ground troops to the conflict.[14]

Although increasingly alarmed by the war's escalation and frustrated by the administration's refusal to consult meaningfully with the SFRC and Congress, Fulbright did not go into open dissent or hold hearings devoted to the war as several other senators requested. Rather, at Johnson's behest, he served as the floor manager of the president's request for $89 million, $19 million of which was to be devoted to the Mekong River Basin project. On June 7 the senator asserted that LBJ had exhibited "wisdom and vision" in seeking additional economic aid for South Vietnam development. Eight days later, in a supportive Senate speech delivered expressly at the president's request, Fulbright praised Johnson for resisting "pressures" for expanding the war "with steadfastness and statesmanship" and for remaining "committed to the goal of ending the war at the earliest possible time by negotiations without preconditions."[15]

Fulbright's reluctance to break openly with Johnson derived from multiple considerations. They had a long association that had facilitated Fulbright's rise to the chairmanship of the SFRC but also acquainted him with the personal wrath the president directed at opponents. The senator was grateful for the former and appropriately dreaded the latter. As Fulbright had noted while sparring with Rusk, he also recognized that Vietnam presented an exceedingly complex and "very difficult situation." The senator further understood the war's domestic political implications. If extensive "American casualties" were suffered, the Republicans would "talk about the 'Johnson war' the way they talked about 'Truman's war' in Korea." If the war were "settled by negotiations, they'll claim we 'lost' Vietnam the way we 'lost' China." Most important, however, Fulbright later explained, "I had supported him and we were good friends. I thought I could persuade him to change his mind."[16]

Johnson's July decision to commit massive numbers of American ground soldiers to the fray demonstrated that neither Fulbright nor other skeptics had deterred the ongoing escalation of the war. The senator's alienation from LBJ and the administration increased over the remainder of the summer as the SFRC held closed hearings on Johnson's decision in late April to send more than twenty thousand US troops into the Dominican Republic to head off an ostensible communist coup. The hearings revealed that Johnson had greatly exaggerated the communist threat and the danger to Americans in the Dominican Republic, and Fulbright's September 15 Senate speech directly challenged the necessity and wisdom of the intervention. As Randall Woods, the biographer of both Fulbright and Johnson, has observed, the president personalized the criticism and viewed Fulbright as a "traitor and a coward." LBJ had complained in February that Fulbright was a "cry baby" and that he could not "continue to kiss him every morning before breakfast"; and on the eve of the Dominican Republic speech, the president had groused to Richard Russell, "This damned idiot of a Fulbright" was going to "denounce our own . . . country and . . . government." Following his speech, Fulbright had "no more access. No more phone calls. No more warmth. No more Air Force One." When he was not invited to any official White House functions during the next year, Fulbright graphically described the isolation: "My God, I feel so alone. No one seems to give a damn. I feel at times that I am walking among the blind and deaf."[17]

Fulbright's growing opposition to the war represented an important but distinctly minority southern perspective. By the end of 1965, Richard Russell had become far more representative of Dixie's view of the conflict. As Johnson's mentor in the Senate, Russell had a much closer personal relationship with the president. The senator was a lifelong bachelor who often visited Lyndon and Lady Bird in the White House and at the LBJ Ranch, and the two men talked regularly on the phone. As chairman of the SASC, Russell, like Fulbright, had the leadership position and the personal stature to influence decisively public discussion of the war and perhaps even US policy. Throughout 1965, the Georgia senator continued to question the wisdom of US involvement both privately and publicly; but, again like Fulbright, he neither challenged Johnson directly nor called for the probing SASC hearings or congressional debate that might have compromised LBJ's relatively low-key march toward war. In early March Russell commiserated with Johnson, telling the president he "couldn't have inherited a worse mess." While accepting the Georgia Association of Broadcasters' Georgian of the Year Award on June 13, the senator emphasized that he had "never been able to see any strategic, political, or economic advantage to be gained" in Vietnam and cited leading military leaders who warned "that it would be an incredible mistake for the U.S. to engage in a full-scale land war on the Asian mainland." Despite these perceptive reservations and his persistent opposition to US intervention after the mid-1950s, an opposition he never failed to cite, Russell discerned no viable route to withdrawal: the United States had a "commitment in South Vietnam. The flag is there. U.S. honor and prestige are there. And U.S. soldiers are there." As he wrote to a constituent the following month, he saw no "honorable way we could withdraw . . . without shaking the confidence of the entire world in our pledged word." Honor, credibility, and support for the troops trumped strategic, economic, and sound military considerations.[18]

Even as Russell moved toward a more hawkish position, he continued to hope for an alternative to major escalation of the war. On July 27 he responded to Fulbright's call for a meeting in Majority Leader Mansfield's Senate office. Significantly, Russell, Fulbright, and Mansfield were joined by southerners John Sparkman and John Sherman Cooper and by Vermont Republican George Aiken. This highly respected group agreed, and Mansfield reported to Johnson, that the United States was "deeply enmeshed in a place where we ought not to be; that the situation is rapidly going out of control; and that every effort should be made to extricate ourselves." The senators also warned LBJ that the country was "backing the President on Viet Nam primarily because he" was "President, not necessarily out of any understanding or sympathy with policies on Viet Nam; beneath the support, there is deep concern and a great deal of confusion." Despite the appeal of these important senators, Johnson announced his decision to commit ground forces the following day.[19]

Appearing on the CBS TV program *Face the Nation* on August 1, Russell endorsed Johnson's troop decision as "about right for the conditions" the United States confronted in Vietnam. He also maintained his conviction that South Vietnam was of little economic or strategic value and added the telling denial that the domino theory was "necessarily" applicable to Southeast Asia and the admission that Ho Chi Minh would win a "plebiscite" conducted in South Vietnam. Still, according to Russell, the United States could not afford to lose in South Vietnam and incur the damage "to our world prestige and to our reputation for keeping our word under all conditions." In a September interview in *U.S. News and World Report,* the senator predicted the United States might require 250,000 to 300,000 troops in Vietnam and articulated what would become his ongoing plea for more aggressive bombing of antiaircraft installations near Hanoi and Haiphong and the need to "render ineffective the shipping facilities of Haiphong harbor." Russell elaborated to a constituent: it was "foolish . . . to be losing more fine young men and multi-million dollar airplanes bombing roads and bridges in *North Vietnam* to prevent the movement of materials of war when we can put the stopper in the bottle very easily by closing and blockading Haiphong." It was time to "recognize that this is a real war" and to take the proper military steps.[20]

Although less influential than Fulbright or Russell, other important southern legislators assumed prominent positions on the war during 1965. Senators Albert Gore and John Sherman Cooper joined Fulbright as the most important southern congressional skeptics. Although Gore had risen from exceedingly humble beginnings, come to Congress in 1939 and moved to the Senate in 1953 as a contemporary of Johnson, and backed the Great Society social programs, he was never close to Johnson. LBJ, who sought to dominate every personal interaction, asserted, "I want people around me who would kiss my ass on a hot summer day and say it smells like roses." Aptly described as a political "loner, a man not to be controlled," Gore rejected any such posture. As one friend observed, "Show Albert the grain, so that he can go against it." Gore's maverick instincts and proclivity for aggravating Johnson were evident when the Tennessee Democrat indignantly opposed LBJ's bid to continue presiding over the Senate Democratic Caucus after he had become vice president in January 1961. A livid Johnson responded by pointedly distinguishing "between a caucus and a cactus. In a cactus," he noted, "all the pricks are on the outside."[21]

Gore's concerns about the war reached far beyond personal friction with Johnson. The senator had questioned Southeast Asia's strategic and economic value during the Kennedy years, doubted the South Vietnamese capacity for democratic government, and worried that growing US involvement would lead to a draining ground war or confrontation with China. As the US role escalated, the diversion of funds and attention from domestic needs reinforced Gore's foreign policy anxieties. These cumulative reservations had led the senator to call publicly for negotiations in December 1964 and January 1965. In his newspaper column and newsletter to constituents, Gore reiterated this policy preference by selectively praising the portions of Johnson's Johns Hopkins speech that sought "unconditional negotiations" as opposed to US positions that demanded "unconditional surrender" by the North Vietnamese and Vietcong. Gore voted for Johnson's $700 million supplemental request in May but emphasized that he did so because it was "untenable" to send "American servicemen . . . into an area of danger" without providing them proper equipment. The senator added "emphatically" that his vote should not be "interpreted as a 100-percent endorsement" of US policy, but rather as his refusal to "deny support" to the troops.[22]

Gore was more outspokenly critical on July 28 following Johnson's ground troop announcement. While assuming in a patronizing tone that Johnson had "carefully contemplated the danger" of the United States becoming "bogged down in endless war in Asia," Gore lamented that the president had "reaffirmed" a policy that had not "worked well in any respect since 1954." To the contrary, US actions had led to a "situation in Vietnam . . . worse than it was 10 years ago; . . . worse than it was 1 year ago, or 1 month ago . . . worse today than it was 1 week ago." This mistaken policy had left the United States mired in "a war that makes little sense as it is being waged; . . . that we have scant hope of winning except at a cost which far outweighs the fruits of victory; . . . in a place and under conditions that no military man in his right mind would choose; . . . which threatens to escalate into a major power confrontation and which could easily escalate into nuclear holocaust."[23]

Cooper shared Gore's fear of a disastrous confrontation with the Soviet Union or China and joined the Tennessee senator in repeatedly calling for negotiations rather than military escalation in Vietnam. A native of rural Kentucky, Cooper was portrayed by columnist Drew Pearson as "homespun," but the senator was no hick. He had earned an undergraduate degree at Yale and attended Harvard Law School. Tall, stately, notoriously forgetful, highly respected among his peers, and viewed uneasily by the Johnson administration as a senator of great influence, Cooper brought a diverse and impressive foreign policy background to the Vietnam debate. In addition to service in Patton's Third Army during World War II, his past duties included delegate to the UN General Assembly in 1949, special assistant to Secretary of State Dean Acheson focusing on the formation of NATO in 1950, US ambassador to India in the late 1950s, and head of a JFK-appointed fact-finding mission in New Delhi and Moscow in 1961.[24]

In March Cooper urged the administration to state clearly that the United States was prepared to accept mediation by the 1954 Geneva Conferees, the UN, or another appropriate third party. While agreeing that the president could not accept US withdrawal from South Vietnam as a condition for peace talks, Cooper deemed the administration's precondition that North Vietnam stop all "intervention and aggression" equally obstructive. Both sides were in effect requiring that their adversary accept "unconditional surrender" before talks could begin, thereby leaving "war as the only arbiter." Simply to negotiate, Cooper emphasized, did not obligate the United States to accept an objectionable settlement. On May 5 he urged Johnson to pursue "a just and honorable settlement" through diplomatic talks. The United States had "nothing to lose by doing so." After all, the communists had negotiated and compromised regarding Vietnam in 1954 and Laos in 1962. The senator also stressed that "no one can foresee the end" of an expanded Vietnam conflict, which could bring war with "Communist China" or even the "horrendous" prospect of "nuclear warfare" if "Soviet Russia should intervene." A month later, the Kentucky Republican joined Fulbright in supporting Johnson's request for additional funds for South Vietnamese economic development as the only alternative to an "escalated war" or an extended US presence as a "holding force."[25]

Despite Cooper's apprehensions and insights, he had not moved beyond the larger Cold War mind-set in mid-1965. Later in June, he told the Louisville VFW that although he opposed increased "bombing against such centers as Hanoi . . . unless it became necessary" to safeguard US "national security," he also rejected American withdrawal because it "would break our commitments," "cast doubt" on US willingness to uphold other obligations, and embolden the communists to "strike against other countries." Even for the skeptical and cosmopolitan Cooper, credibility and the domino theory prevailed over doubts about Vietnam's strategic value and fears of a larger, perhaps catastrophic war.[26]

Just as Gore and Cooper joined Fulbright in raising searching questions about the war during 1965, Senators John Stennis, Russell Long, and a host of other southerners enlisted with Russell as Johnson's most stalwart Democratic supporters of the conflict. Elected to the Senate in 1947, Stennis, with Russell's and Harry Byrd's tutelage, quickly gained admission into the Senate "club," or the group of senators who exercised decisive influence over crucial institutional processes and decisions. Stennis's impressive work habits, attention to younger colleagues, and willingness to shoulder institutional burdens led others to characterize him as a "Senator's Senator." Following his appointment to the Armed Services Committee in 1951, he took an increasingly active interest in national defense and foreign relations. His influence over national defense policy grew dramatically when he became chairman in 1962 of the Preparedness Investigating Subcommittee (SPIS) of the SASC. This powerful subcommittee exercised much of the Senate's oversight of the Defense Department and was empowered to investigate all aspects of military affairs.[27]

It was fitting that Stennis reported Johnson's $700 million supplemental request from the SASC and managed the bill on the floor of the Senate. Like Russell, Stennis had harbored grave reservations over US intervention in Vietnam, but, along with his mentor, the Mississippi senator grew increasingly hawkish once the nation was committed. Echoing the basic thread of LBJ's letter to the Senate, Stennis left his colleagues virtually no alternative to supporting US soldiers in the field: "The only question" was whether the Senate was "going to give the men who we have already sent off to do jungle battle the tools with which to fight." Should the Senate "refuse to pass the joint resolution . . . by less than an overwhelming vote," it would inform "the world" the United States was "backing up" and would "soon . . . pull out." Most important, he concluded, "it would be a direct message" to American soldiers that the nation was not going to furnish them the necessary "tools of war." In announcing this stance, from which he never varied over the ensuing seven years, Stennis both reinforced the Johnson-Rusk strategy for ensuring congressional backing for the war and articulated Dixie's faithful support for the military and executive requests for defense appropriations. In the House of Representatives, George H. Mahon, Mendel Rivers, and Robert Sikes adopted identical and equally strategic positions.[28]

As Stennis's persistent objections after 1954 to direct US military intervention demonstrated, he had not adopted these hawkish perspectives thoughtlessly. In a joint session of the SFRC and SASC on April 2, 1965, the senator observed gravely that "putting those land troops in there" was "where the serious part" began. He also recognized that if Congress failed to "intervene or assert" itself in opposition to the war's escalation, it was essentially "making a decision" to enforce the president's actions. As the military situation continued to deteriorate, Stennis concluded that if the United States were "going to be effective," it would have to "take over command." He had arrived at this position, one so diametrically opposed to his 1954 perspective, because the United States had no choice but to "stand and fight," to uphold its "commitments," and to depart Vietnam in an "honorable" fashion. Still, as he warned his listeners in Meridian, Mississippi, on May 16, there was "no quick and easy solution to the Vietnam problem," and US involvement would "become even greater before we reach the end of the trial." More prophetic than he realized, Stennis, like most Americans, did not entertain the possibility that the United States might fail to impose its will on the Vietnamese.[29]

Senator Russell Long, the Democratic whip and a member of the SFRC, was more demonstrably hawkish than Russell and Stennis. The Louisiana senator asserted that the nation's communist adversaries, especially the Chinese, sought "to take over the whole world" and "would stop at nothing" in pursuing this goal. The war in Vietnam was a "pure and simple" aggression "directed from North Vietnam" and the "latest effort by the Communists to seize new lands." Rather than accept such "foreign conquest," the United States should do "whatever" was "necessary to win"—including bombing Hanoi. Were this to draw Peking or Russia into the struggle, Long favored taking "them on"; "to start running" would leave "no place to stop except at our own borders." The senator had no patience for critics of the war, the "modern day appeasers," the "handful of Senators and Congressmen and the bearded beatniks" who undermined the president and led the communists to believe that "if they can just keep the pressure on us we will collapse after a while."[30]

Even Long appeared moderate when compared to Mendel Rivers, the chair of the House Armed Services Committee. Perhaps the ultimate cold warrior, Rivers had once referred to West Point as "Tass West" and in August 1965 endorsed a potential preventive war in which nuclear weapons would be employed against China. Unless the United States was "prepared to risk the possible consequences of destroying" China's "nuclear capability," Rivers intoned, the war in Vietnam might have been fought "in vain." Rivers once admitted "the lightning of intellect" never struck "the taproot of my family tree," and this outburst regarding China's nuclear capacity prompted LBJ to observe, "The damn fool that's out here advocating bombing Peking ain't got no business being chair of a committee." A staunch proponent of air power, Rivers opposed sending US ground troops in early 1965; however, once they were dispatched, the

Charleston congressmen declared he was "prepared to do anything to protect our troops." By July, Rivers asserted what would become an increasingly prominent southern refrain. The war should be turned "over to the
military. . . . The sooner we . . . let them select the targets, . . . the sooner
we'll win." After a visit to South Vietnam in September 1965, Rivers lobbied forcefully for the bombing of Haiphong and asserted that "it would
be foolish not to use all the weapons in our arsenal" should the Chinese "be so rash" as to intervene actively in the war. As 1965 ended, the
congressman criticized Johnson's "ridiculous" ground war of attrition and
argued instead for playing the US "holecard" by bombing both Hanoi
and Haiphong.[31]

While expressing a variety of concerns, other southern Democrats fell
in line behind the war effort. Senators Allen Ellender and John McClellan worried about the volume of US aid, and Ellender and John Sparkman lamented the absence of support from major US allies; but all agreed
by the summer of 1965 that the war had to be fought and won. Ellender,
who had come to favor strategic bombing of North Vietnam, deemed the
conflict one in which the United States "cannot afford to fight and cannot
afford to quit." Willis Robertson continued to worry about the US commitment. On June 15, he recalled for the Senate his grandfather's maxim,
"The tendency of everything is to be more so." Since that had become the
pattern of American involvement in South Vietnam, he renewed his suggestion for soliciting negotiations through the UN, if only to show "the
world . . . where to place the blame" if North Vietnam refused. The Virginia senator's reservations about Vietnam had increased markedly in the
fifteen months since his attempt to warn LBJ about intervention in March
1964. Privately, Robertson suggested that "to win . . . might require"
the use of "hydrogen bombs to destroy about one-half of the Chinese
people"—a "bloodcurdling" action that would provoke international condemnation. And he further denigrated US prospects in a country that
was "utterly unstable from a political standpoint," "bitterly" divided by
a "religious conflict between Catholics and Buddhists," and devoid of
any "conception of personal freedom" or "self-government." Significantly,
Robertson also agonized over the war's fiscal implications and identified
the drain on the US gold reserves that would become acute by 1968.[32]

Herman Talmadge perceptively recognized in February that bombing
North Vietnam would not alter communist domination over the "approx-

imately 90 percent" of the villages they controlled in South Vietnam, and in July he could "see nothing to be gained by an all-out war with North Vietnam." But he also rejected withdrawal, since "all of Southeast Asia would rapidly fall under Communist control," thereby jeopardizing the American strategic position "throughout all of Asia" and dealing a "tremendous blow to American prestige" worldwide. Senator Sam Ervin acknowledged that Vietnam was "one of the most baffling problems now confronting us" but lectured a skeptical constituent that to withdraw without an acceptable settlement "would destroy the last vestige of confidence which freedom-loving people have in the United States." Representative Dante Fascell (D-FL) agreed that the United States could not afford "to be nibbled to death" and that no adversary could be allowed to doubt that Americans would "stand up, fight and die if necessary to protect what we believe in." Convinced that "peaceful coexistence" was "part of the communist arsenal," Senator George Smathers added his voice to this southern chorus.[33]

This growing phalanx of southern conservatives and their support for the war, and often for its more aggressive prosecution, carried significant implications. As Johnson feared, they began by 1965 to argue that meeting the war's escalating costs required commensurate reductions in domestic programs. Stennis voiced this argument in September. Rather than enacting "additional welfare and social programs," Congress and the president needed to "realize that the war on poverty is not the only war we are fighting." Since the Vietnam involvement would "cost many additional billions of dollars," the nation would "at some point . . . have to choose between guns and butter." Ironically, many of Johnson's most dependable southern backers of the war were also among the harshest critics of the Great Society. Their influence was not confined to this domestic political dynamic and its complications for the president. The emphasis of southern hawks on national honor, the futility of negotiating with communists, aggressive bombing, and traditional military victory both reinforced LBJ's personal inclinations and narrowed his options.[34]

The national Republican Party and the few southern Republicans in 1965 had a similar impact. While endorsing the Cold War rationale for US intervention in Vietnam, Republicans had criticized both Kennedy and Johnson for pursuing a "no-win," unfocused, and publicly obscure policy. Save the conspicuous exceptions of Senators Cooper and Jacob Javits

(R-NY), all important Republicans demanded victory and advocated the aggressive bombing of North Vietnam. In February 1965 Congressman Melvin Laird (R-WI) could have been mistaken for a southern hawk when he contended that the United States should either "pull out completely or go all out and go in to win." Among southern Republicans, Strom Thurmond, who had moved to the GOP in September 1964 in opposition to Johnson's civil rights policies, remained blatantly belligerent. Thurmond opened the year demanding that the United States deny the enemy any "sanctuaries" in Southeast Asia and later asked Ambassador Maxwell Taylor if the administration planned to "just fight a defensive action like we did in Korea" or pursue "victory." Was there a "plan to win," or would the United States settle for a "stalemate and be subject to keeping our troops over there . . . indefinitely?" John Tower was similarly strident. In January Tower declared Johnson was unwilling to "come to grips with the seriousness of the situation" in Vietnam. The Texas senator opposed the use of US ground troops but endorsed massive bombing of North Vietnam and the Ho Chi Minh trail since "continuation of the present policy means continuation of a policy that is losing the war." Although his views would change dramatically by the fall of 1967, Senator Thruston Morton (R-KY) agreed with Thurmond and Tower on the essentials of Vietnam policy. In October Morton advised a constituent that the United States should only negotiate from a military position of "relative . . . equality" with the North Vietnamese and PRC. He too dreaded the prospect of a "land war" and contended instead for "greater use of naval and air forces," including a "quarantine" like that being enforced against Cuba and a "sharp step up of activity against strategic targets in North Viet Nam."[35]

Southern newspapers overwhelmingly subscribed to Dixie's emerging, majority prowar position. The *Dallas Morning News* applauded Johnson's decisions for bombing and the dispatch of ground troops, derided the "peace-at-any price faction" in the United States, and emphasized that "worldwide confidence in America's commitment to freedom" was at stake. Only by fulfilling this commitment, the *Montgomery Advertiser* agreed, could the United States avoid looking like "the 'paper tiger' which China contends we are." The *Advertiser* editorial staff also pointedly distinguished between the Vietcong's use of "terrorism" for "subjugating" others and the US "effort . . . at knocking out installations" and "reducing" enemy military capacity. Eugene Patterson, the editor of the *Atlanta*

Constitution, endorsed LBJ's "surefooted" and appropriately firm bombing response to the clear "pattern of aggression." As Johnson made the decision for ground troops in July, the *Constitution* opined that the United States should deploy "whatever forces are necessary" since there was "nothing to do but fight them, and fight them well." From New Orleans, the *Times-Picayune* hoped Johnson's retaliatory bombing in February would head off "a major Southeastern Asia conflict" by convincing the North Vietnamese they would "be among the greatest sufferers" and showing the Chinese they were "vulnerable to punishment." When Rolling Thunder failed to restrain Hanoi or the Vietcong, the *Times-Picayune* fell in line behind the deployment of ground troops.[36]

Adopting a perspective similar to that of Senator Cooper, the *Louisville Courier-Journal* ultimately accepted the decision for war, but only after stressing the need for negotiations from February through July and with the unenthusiastic observation that the dispatch of ground troops was "a decision the nation had little choice but to support" and "pray that it is right." Editorial page editor Russell Brinly and his staff responded to the initiation of US bombing of North Vietnam in February by urging President Johnson to promptly repeat the US "preference for a negotiated settlement" and to press for UN mediation. As the administration adopted its rigid negotiating position and marched toward the "major land war on the mainland of Asia" that Cooper and the *Courier-Journal* warned against, the paper's editorials predicted that the war in Vietnam would "soon become a symbol of horror to most Americans. Only a quick victory would be acceptable," but that was beyond "the realm of possibility."[37]

The *Texas Observer,* an Austin weekly edited by Ronnie Dugger, was more unabashedly liberal than the *Courier Journal,* but not necessarily more antiwar. Dugger ran pieces applauding dissent and others clearly out of step with majority southern opinion. For example, John S. Ambler, an assistant professor of political science at Rice University, asserted that "saturation bombing from high altitude" at the cost of "numerous civilian lives" undermined the South Vietnamese government's standing with its people and that US loss of prestige would be far greater if "we fight for another decade and still are forced to withdraw." Otto Mullinax, a senior partner in a major Dallas law firm, charged the United States with subverting its "moral position in the world" by waging "aggressive undeclared war" in Vietnam. In both a fascinating debate with Republican congressman George H. W. Bush before the Junior Bar of Texas and a speech to the state convention of the Texas Liberal Democrats, Dugger criticized LBJ's bombing of North Vietnam, which had turned world opinion "against us," driven Hanoi closer to China, and harmed US relations with the Soviet Union. Fearful of land war in Asia and even a nuclear conflict, Dugger accentuated the need to pursue "peace with honor"; but he, like virtually all southern critics of the war in 1965, did not believe the United States could "unilaterally withdraw," and he offered no clear prescription for forcing or inducing North Vietnam and the Vietcong to agree to US terms for negotiations.[38]

None of these other southern papers expressed reservations equivalent to the *Courier-Journal* or *Texas Observer,* but even the more hawkish dailies sounded perceptive notes of caution. The *Advertiser* considered an Asian land war "a chilling thought" and raised "the question of whether there is any way out, except out." While rejecting "withdrawal and total defeat," Eugene Paterson acknowledged to *Atlanta Constitution* readers that "total victory" in Vietnam was a "pipedream." And the *Times-Picayune* recognized "the fighting might go on for years without a military decision" and considered US prospects bleak without a viable South Vietnamese government.[39]

Polling of the southern public revealed a similarly prowar majority. From May 1965, when systematic Gallup polling regarding Vietnam began, through the end of the year, the South, when compared to the East, Midwest, and West, was more inclined to believe that the war would be "won on the battlefield" rather than "in the minds" of the Vietnamese. Only 44 percent of southerners polled opted for the nonmilitary solution versus 50 percent of persons both nationally and from the other region (the West) least inclined to agree with this statement. Southerners were also most likely to respond "very well" (65 percent compared to the national average of 60) to the question of how US forces were performing in Vietnam, were most willing to "continue the war" alone even if the South Vietnamese stopped fighting, and were most opposed to inviting the UN to "try to work out its own formula for peace in Viet Nam." Dixie's 65 percent approval of the last question, versus 74 percent nationally and in the other least positive region (the West), revealed both the South's decided unilateralist tendencies and its disdain for the United

Nations. Reflecting the view of Dixie's public opinion leaders from Fulbright and Cooper to Russell and Stennis, southerners frequently agreed that the United States should not have become "involved with our military forces in Southeast Asia." These collective southern opinions helped make Dixie the region most dissatisfied with both LBJ's overall performance as president and his administration's "handling of the situation in Viet Nam." In May only 49 percent of southerners endorsed Johnson's work as president (versus 64 percent in the next most negative region), and the margin (47 and 63 percent, respectively) remained similar in September. Although the discrepancies were not nearly so glaring, the South was consistently three to seven percentage points less supportive of the president's war leadership during 1965.[40]

The South's established opposition to limited war and the rising demand for more aggressive bombing of North Vietnam constituted the decisive reasons for the region's negative evaluation of Johnson's performance as commander in chief. Dixie's disapproval of Johnson's domestic programs undoubtedly reinforced the negative assessment of his Vietnam leadership. From the southern perspective his most egregious misstep was to push the pace of African American "integration too fast," a policy that caused southerners to brand him a "turncoat-son-of-a-bitch." In the wake of Johnson's passage of the 1964 and 1965 civil rights bills, 61 percent of southerners expressed that opinion, as opposed to 40–45 percent of Americans nationally. Federal programs and the deficit spending associated with the Great Society intensified the South's discomfort with the Civil Rights Movement, and all of these domestic matters influenced Dixie's assessment of the administration's war policies.[41]

Southerners' letters to newspaper editors and their congressional representatives elucidated the polling data. Dixie's prowar residents continued to denounce LBJ's limited-war strategy. A Georgia physician voiced an unvarnished version of this position to Senator Russell. The United States "should go to war with an effort to *win*." To do otherwise was "being dishonest and untrue to the youth of our nation whom we are sending to their death. . . . I feel we should bomb and destroy Hanoi and Haiphong and any other military target necessary to win the war. I think we should attempt to . . . obtain unconditional surrender with all means at our command, including atomic weapons." From Savannah, the wife of a member of the USAF agreed: "If we are going to continue the war in Viet

Nam . . . then in God's name let us go in it to win." Although the couple
were newlyweds, neither dreaded the airman's assignment to Vietnam if it
would do *any good at all.*" It would be "a small price to enjoy the heritage
of freedom so painstakingly won and given to us by prior generations."
The young woman acknowledged that this assertion might sound "corny"
but assured Senator Russell, "We believe it." Indeed, she declared, "If the
Army would recognize the fact that women would make much sneakier
fighters than men . . . I would dearly love to be in the fray myself."[42]

Prowar southerners asked why the war was being run by "political
appointees rather than our trained military personnel." Some contended
that the State Department, replete with its "'No Win' policy," was in "full
charge of the Viet Nam debacle." How else to explain Johnson's "disgust-
ing and humiliating" offer of the Mekong River project as a "bribe" to
this "small Asian gangster nation . . . to stop fighting us"? Many more
southerners cited Secretary of Defense McNamara as the civilian culprit
responsible for the military's restraint. A Tupelo attorney wrote representatively to Stennis urging an "irresistible uproar" from Congress demanding McNamara's firing, and an indignant Mississippi parent informed
McNamara, "Our boys are being killed because the Civilians in Washington won't let General [Earle] Wheeler [chairman of the JCS] and his
staff fight the war."[43]

Regardless of whom they credited with overseeing the US war effort,
most southerners flatly rejected negotiations with North Vietnam or the
Vietcong. Since communists never kept their word, negotiations had
invariably left "our side . . . empty handed"; and Vietnam talks would
likely yield a coalition government that the communists would control
via "subversion, treason, and murder." Senator Gore's mail following his
renewed call for negotiations in February left no doubt of the prevailing
southern perspective. His constituents termed his statement a "degenerate
form of defeatism," condemned his proposal as "a surrender," denounced
negotiations as a species of "appeasement" worthy of Neville Chamber-
lain, and began and concluded letters with "Dear Spineless Senator" and
"Disrespectfully yours." Even Willis Robertson's far more reserved call
for negotiations elicited a charge that he was "advocating retreat" with his
"shabby display of lack of will and courage."[44]

Southern backers of the war in 1965 and 1966 included an ongoing
religious theme in their brief. A rural Tennessee woman stated the prowar

perspective succinctly: "I feel that the world situation boils down to the fact that communism is fighting Christianity." Another Gore constituent asked what could be "the basis of negotiations for a true peace in a war between the godless materialism of communism," which asserted "God was created in the imagination of man[,] and the community of God-fearing men who believe that man was created in the image of God." According to a third southerner, the United States, "as a Christian nation," needed to "face up to the fact that communism is our enemy too" and "*not* just a foreign disease." A Virginia physician traced US world leadership to "its form of government . . . based on the importance of the individual," which derived "primarily . . . from the fundamental concept of the Christian religion." Therefore, if US religious and political principles were "right and those of communism are wrong, . . . we have no choice" but to "do whatever is necessary" to prevail in Vietnam.[45]

To these arguments and opinions, prowar southerners added their condemnation of antiwar protestors. A Georgia father, whose son was serving in Vietnam, wondered "what he and his buddies think of these bastards that are burning their draft cards and being traitors to our country." Another Georgian deplored these "insignificant, but ignorant, mentally incompetent, overeducated, cowardly, or disloyal" protestors, who "sought to embarrass the National Government." Class tensions were evident when the owner of a North Carolina construction company complained to Senator Ervin that demonstrators should be "punished severely, but they are the ones who get all the breaks. They get out of serving in the military, and it seems as if they are patted on the back and treated like a first class citizen."[46]

Southern opponents of the war offered equally heartfelt rejoinders. Expressing and acting on antiwar positions was difficult in Dixie's prevailing prowar society. A rural Georgia woman in her late forties explained her apprehension to Senator Russell in October 1965. Over the previous "few months," she had waged a daily battle "to get shut of the Mask of Fear" that had prevented her from taking a "stand on an issue, which is right, regardless of how many friends, neighbors, [and] leaders" she might "offend." She had "Won" and was "now Free" to castigate Russell for his criticism of young protestors. Better the senator spend his time "erasing" the South's "UnAmerican Segregation Laws" and taking a "stand based on TRUTH" if he believed "any part of the Bible and its teachings."

Given the South's hostility toward demonstrators, another Georgian felt compelled to begin his letter lobbying for referral of Vietnam matters to the UN with the assurance that he was not "an unwashed beatnik" or "some kind of subversive. I bathe am a college graduate and have been fortunate in making well in the upper five figures for the last five years." The only "organizations" to which he belonged were "the Baptist Church and the Human Race."[47]

Like defenders of the war, Dixie's critics worried that America's NATO "allies" would offer no help, leaving the United States "to shoulder the responsibility alone." Dissenters also portrayed the conflict as a "*Civil* War," which the United States was "perpetuating and feeding," only to become aligned with the weaker side. South Vietnam's government had "no identifiable leadership," and, as the ARVN "falter[ed] or disintegrate[d]," the United States would be left fighting alone. This position could be viewed only as "imperialism," and since it served to "encourage the reunification of world Communism," it was best described as "lamentable," "stupid," and "immoral." With a nod to Korea, a second Virginian asked if the Defense Department had "any plans for occupying Indo China" if the war were actually won. Another southerner favored negotiations; but, while readily agreeing that US soldiers in the field had to be supported, he also voiced prophetic qualms to Senator Stennis. This Mississippian had "very serious doubts" about whether the American public "would support an all out war in Southeast Asia. . . . Our people are not remotely interested in having our young men sent there and sacrificed for what to them is a meaningless war."[48]

Writing to the *Louisville Courier-Journal,* W. Forrest Smith cast the US dilemma in Vietnam in a broad, provocative, and distinctly un-southern perspective. Smith cited the Truman Doctrine's pledge to confront communism worldwide as the root of the US proclivity for intervening in the affairs of other nations. This proclivity, together with US military power, left the world with a "Frankenstein on its hands" and the United States in "the embarrassing position of waging undeclared war on two small nations, neither of which had committed an unfriendly act against our nation." The United States, Smith asserted, needed to realize "we are merely one sovereign nation in a big world, with no authority . . . to tell other nations what type of government" they should adopt or "to occupy their territory, establish military bases, destroy their property or murder their people."[49]

Others, with moral qualms akin to Smith's last prohibition, objected to the war on religious grounds during the 1965–1966 period and, in so doing, demonstrated how religion in the Bible Belt could lead to diametrically opposing stands on the war. A Winston-Salem, North Carolina, resident articulated clearly how religion could lead southerners to oppose as well as support the war. "As a Christian," he declared, he did not believe that US policies were "in accordance with the will of God," and this contradiction was "more important than 'Saving Face.'" A Georgia minister asserted that President Johnson and his advisors had not "yet met Jesus Christ, in whose commandments is plainly written, thou shall not kill." Other Dixie residents were "deeply ashamed" that the United States was "killing people half a world away"; appalled that America employed "chemical warfare," which "perverts every ethic of the American Christian heritage"; aghast at "our continued ruthless and inhumane air assaults against a people who do not even have planes" for their defense; and "disturbed by our increasing propensity for playing God" with the fate of "emerging nations." Terry Bisson, a Louisville resident, expanded on the issue of "bombing . . . Vietnamese civilians." Perhaps "the murder of women and children" was "more humane with a bomb than a knife," and such "distinctions" might be "comforting to Americans," but they were far "too subtle for the dead."[50]

Among the constituents who wrote to Senator Sam Ervin opposing the war was Frazier T. Woolard, an attorney from Washington, North Carolina, a small town on Albemarle Sound. Forty-five years old in 1965 and a navy veteran who had survived Pearl Harbor and the battles of Guadalcanal and Okinawa, Woolard had attended William and Mary and graduated from Duke Law School in 1954. Consistent with his minority southern opinion on the war, Woolard represented African American clients and actively aided blacks in securing professional positions. The North Carolina attorney deemed the Vietnam intervention strategically unnecessary and pronounced it "outrageous" to send "large numbers of troops" to fight in this "unjustified conflict." His protest to Senator Ervin began an outspoken decade of opposition to the war, and the small-town lawyer's experience graphically demonstrated Dixie's majority support for the war and the potential implications for those who challenged that perspective.[51]

Woolard's antiwar inclinations were informed and reinforced by his fascinating friendship with a South Vietnamese official, whom he encountered in 1966 while seeking information on local elections under Diem and his successors. A remarkable twenty-year correspondence and friendship ensued. During those two decades, Woolard's Vietnamese friend, who had been educated at Hanoi University and the Sorbonne and was fluent in English and French, served periodically as a South Vietnamese diplomat and taught in a variety of private schools and universities. From this perspective, he afforded Woolard expert insights on Vietnamese nationalism and on governmental and popular conditions in South Vietnam. This cosmopolitan observer greatly appreciated Woolard's sympathy for the Vietnamese people. From their initial letters in the fall of 1966, he expressed his "great joy of . . . miraculously meeting a friend in the desert" who understood the "agony of our people" and had the "courage and humanity to raise" his voice. The Vietnamese diplomat thereafter complimented the North Carolina attorney as "one of the very few people" who was "really concerned about the human condition" and willing "to give of their time and of themselves to help alleviate human suffering."[52]

In addition to this correspondence, Woolard read widely on Vietnam and frequently wrote US government agencies requesting information. Among the contemporary authors he consulted were Bernard Fall, David Halberstam, Joseph Buttinger, Harold Issacs, George McTurnan Kahin, and Ellen Hammer. He also read *Ramparts, I. F. Stone's Weekly, Foreign Affairs,* the *Washington Post, New York Times, Greensboro Daily News,* and *Norfolk Virginian-Pilot.* From these materials, Woolard concluded that the United States was prosecuting an economically motivated war "to prevent a depression," and he dismissed the domino theory as "mere propaganda." He was appalled at what he considered US-induced destruction in South Vietnam and contended that the American presence had served to "suppress" rather than promote democracy. Were the Vietnamese allowed to express their political preferences, Woolard was confident they would choose Ho Chi Minh, who "despite his political flavor [was] first of all a Vietnamese nationalist whom the Vietnamese admire[d]." US policies and actions were especially troubling since the nation "itself was born in revolutionary violence" and was in no "position to regulate how other peoples establish their government." The Vietnamese and Asians more generally should be allowed "to work their own problems out themselves" since "Caucasians" only created "more animosity and hostility."[53]

As the war dragged on, Woolard became increasingly outraged at US policies. In August 1967, Woolard seized on a Johnson quote that his "administration hasn't lost its ass yet." The North Carolina firebrand informed the president that his policy of "killing . . . Asian peasants under the false propaganda of 'helping them'" was a loser and that LBJ should "consider resigning." During 1968, Woolard continued "smoking 'like a locomotive,'" in the words of his Vietnamese friend, while spending considerable time attempting to establish a link between the American Friends of Vietnam, a US pro–South Vietnam group, and the CIA. He also defended the "insistent political demonstrators" at the Democratic national convention in Chicago who had greater "justice" on their side than the "[Mayor] Daley gang." In contrast to majority southern opinion, Woolard sympathized with student dissent, which he correctly noted was part of a "worldwide phenomenon." Over the following two years, Woolard wrote directly to Walt Whitman Rostow, Johnson's former special assistant for national security affairs, and to Dean Rusk, reprimanding them for their roles in the "Vietnam war atrocity," and informed his congressman, Walter B. Jones (D-NC), that the war was "*criminal* and those who support it knowing the true nature of the war are likewise guilty." Building on this assumption, Woolard suggested the UN might form a "committee of non-aligned nations" to assess US war policies and the actions of American leaders. Although such suggestions were far too drastic for the vast majority of Woolard's contemporaries or most subsequent commentators, his charges that US tactics such as search-and-destroy ground missions and the Rolling Thunder bombing campaign killed huge numbers of North and South Vietnamese civilians have since been substantiated. Therefore, his basic insight into the war's impact on the Vietnamese people was correct.[54]

Unsurprisingly, given his antiwar views and vehement stands, Woolard became a black sheep in eastern North Carolina, and both his family and his law practice suffered. At the end of the war and after, several correspondents spoke to the ramifications of his unpopular positions. Two local North Carolina journalists wrote to Woolard in 1972. The first acknowledged that he had begun to accept substantial portions of Woolard's antiwar brief after learning about the My Lai massacre and following the trial of William Calley. Prior to those events, he had "admired" his neighbor's knowledge regarding the war, but "could not believe that you knew more than all the presidents, their cabinets and top advisors when they had all the information, much of which could not possibly have been available to you." The second journalist, Bartow Houston Jr., wrote in late 1972, expressing "great admiration" for what Woolard "had to go through" in their community and for his opposition to the war "so very, very long before I learned what it was all about." Two years later, Houston commented further on Woolard's "mostly lonely efforts to prick the conscience of the American people." He judged it "astonishing that a small-town lawyer, faced with the task of making a living, should have emerged as such an erudite authority on the Vietnam War. . . . Not only were you right, you were one of the first in this nation who were 'right.' Your cries to the mostly unhearing populous may well stand as a monument to your concern for mankind." Writing the same month as Houston, one of Woolard's unhearing neighbors told him, "I am deeply sorry for anything and everything done to you by me. Some times our mouths just say too much. I think the whole thing began about the Vietnam War. May you and God forgive me." At the time of her graduation from East Carolina University in May 1983, Suzanne Woolard, one of Frazier's twin girls, may have had the last word: "I accept you for you—one hell of an individual."[55]

Even as Frazier Woolard was beginning his lonely and courageous opposition to the Vietnam War in eastern North Carolina, a far more significant protest was brewing in the SFRC. Since May 1965, both committee staffers and members such as Jacob Javits, Frank Church, and Gore had been pressing Fulbright to hold public hearings on the war. While still hoping to convince President Johnson not to escalate the conflict, the chairman had stubbornly resisted. LBJ's July 1965 troop decisions, the flap over the Dominican Republic intervention, and Fulbright's subsequent social and official ostracism prompted the senator to begin rethinking his role in helping Johnson to suppress public debate. On January 11, 1966, Fulbright proposed public SFRC hearings, and the majority of the committee agreed on February 3.[56]

During the three-week interim that the SFRC deliberated over holding the hearings, several events solidified Fulbright's resolve and helped produce the committee decision for the sessions that directly challenged administration policies in Vietnam. On January 24, Secretary Rusk appeared before the SFRC in executive session to discuss his recent trips abroad. The secretary reiterated standard administration positions on the war, and Fulbright engaged him in a nasty personal confrontation. The chairman, who was described as "personally intolerant" of Rusk and referred privately to Rusk's "devious reasoning," questioned the secretary's understanding and representation of the Vietnam imbroglio, and the out-raged Rusk responded that he was "extremely sensitive" about the "ques-tion of credibility and integrity" and "would never lie to the press." The standoff left Fulbright even more convinced that Johnson was committed to disastrous military escalation and left a wounded Rusk wary of dealing with the SFRC.[57]

The following day, Fulbright attended a White House meeting of con-gressional leaders with the president. Addressing his reluctance to chal-lenge Johnson overtly, General Earle Wheeler once explained, "You just don't go in there and piss in the President's soup"—an admonition Ful-bright might have heeded, given his habit of doing just that. The Arkansas senator raised his familiar objections to escalating the conflict, contended that the United States was "taking the place of the French" and seeking to "reimpose colonial power," and urged LBJ to continue the suspension of bombing over North Vietnam that he had begun reluctantly on Decem-ber 24, 1965, in hopes of enticing Hanoi to negotiate. LBJ responded by pointedly ignoring Fulbright as he spoke and paying much closer atten-tion to Senator Russell's diametrically opposing message. Russell declared that the bombing "lull" had continued too long and caused unnecessary American deaths. His prescription was clear: "For God's sake, don't start the bombing halfway. Let them know they are in a war. We killed civil-ians in World War II and nobody opposed. I'd rather kill them than have American boys die. Please, Mr. President. . . . Go all the way." Accen-tuating their inclusion among the group Secretary McNamara dubbed the "heavier bombing boys," Rivers, Long, and Mahon strongly endorsed Russell's position.[58]

Fulbright and opponents of the war found Senator Stennis's January 27 address to a joint session of the Mississippi legislature even more trou-bling. As a member of the SASC and chair of the Preparedness Subcom-mittee, Stennis had particularly close ties to the US military and regularly represented Pentagon preferences. The senator voiced the dismay of most southerners by asking how the United States with its "great power" had failed to secure a "decisive and relatively quick military victory against

a small and underdeveloped country like North Vietnam and the guerrillas in South Vietnam." His answer: the administration's decision "to
fight what amounts to a holding action" and the civilian-imposed "restrictions" that prevented the military from "waging a hard-hitting and all-out
attack in North Vietnam." It was time to take the gloves off—to bomb
Haiphong and halt the "flow of men and supplies from the North to the
South." Should these "stepped-up operations" provoke "Red China to full
intervention in the war," the senator recommended that the United States
keep open the option of retaliating with "every weapon we have." Winning would also require the United States to commit additional troops,
and Stennis predicted four hundred thousand in Vietnam by the end of
1966 and perhaps as many as six hundred thousand thereafter.[59]

Stennis's projection of a possible six hundred thousand US troops
in Vietnam and his veiled proposal for using tactical nuclear weapons
against China "scare[d] the hell" out of Fulbright, who feared that the
Mississippi senator was speaking for the JCS and signaling a "gathering,
incontrollable momentum, carrying us into open conflict with China."
To a reporter Fulbright exclaimed, "For God's sake this is becoming a
major war! I assume that this is still a democracy, that the Senate has a role
to play in foreign affairs." The SFRC hearings embodied that role. The
Arkansas senator and other committee dissenters sought a public discussion about the war and its implications that would prompt the administration to slow the war's escalation and avert a possible confrontation with
China. Senator Gore was particularly blunt. Since closed sessions with
Rusk and McNamara had yielded no discernible influence on Johnson, he
deemed open, widely publicized hearings the opportunity "to go over the
head of the President to the American people, and reach him by way of
the people." By soliciting the views of witnesses and projecting their own
opinions, the skeptical majority on the SFRC mounted a direct challenge
to Lyndon Johnson and his war and provided the first true public debate
over the conflict's origins and merits. Journalist and historian David Halberstam subsequently described the proceedings as disputing the "word
of the President," and Senator Everett Dirksen (R-IL) observed, "Bill Fulbright has a lot of guts to do a thing like this." As Fulbright, Rusk, Gore,
Sparkman, and Long actively participated in the hearings, they further
demonstrated the emerging divisions in Dixie.[60]

To President Johnson's acute discomfort, the SFRC hearings were not only held in open session but also televised nationally, with the key sessions running from February 4 to February 18. To bolster their antiwar positions, Fulbright and his allies called as witnesses General James M. Gavin (ret., USA) and George F. Kennan, the former foreign service officer who had formulated the doctrine of containing communism in 1946–1947 and had subsequently served as US ambassador to the Soviet Union and Yugoslavia. The Johnson administration countered with Rusk and General Maxwell Taylor (ret., USA), who had served both as chairman of the JCS and US ambassador to South Vietnam.

Opponents of the war mounted a withering attack on the rationale for US involvement in Vietnam. They emphasized the nationalist credentials of Ho and his followers, portrayed the conflict as being as much a civil war as one of outside aggression, and argued that Vietnam was of minimal strategic importance to the United States. The dissenters asserted that US intervention in Vietnam had deflected attention from far more important relations with the USSR and China and raised the prospect of war with the latter and even the possibility of a nuclear holocaust. The antiwar critics rejected the mechanistic features of the domino theory and denied that US credibility was on trial in Vietnam. In so doing, they asserted that an outcome short of traditional victory would not decisively impair US credibility.

Together with Senators Fulbright, Frank Church, Claiborne Pell (D-RI), George Aiken (R-VT), and Wayne Morse, Albert Gore scored the administration. The Tennessee maverick regretted not having objected publicly to US-Vietnam policies "7 years ago" and contended this SFRC hearing should have been held "3 years ago." Gore denied that the United States had any SEATO-related "specific commitment" to fight a war in Vietnam, and he sought to "disassociate" himself from "any interpretation" of the Gulf of Tonkin Resolution that embodied a "declaration of war." The senator worried anew that if the United States became "bogged down" in Vietnam, the Soviet Union would be free to "work her machinations" in Berlin and Latin America; but he continued to fear most of all a nuclear war with China. Based on this threat, Gore, together with others on the committee, queried Taylor and Rusk regarding the upper "limits on [US] forces." When Taylor responded that Hanoi would "decide" this depending on its pursuit of further aggression, Gore was appalled by the assumption there were "no limits on the forces to be employed until Hanoi capitulates." It was precisely such uncontrolled escalation that could furnish the USSR troubling opportunities and lead to armed conflict with China. Given these "dangers and risks," the senator prescribed negotiations rather than escalation in pursuit of elusive credibility and a potentially pyrrhic victory.[61]

Just as Gore raised a strong antiwar voice, John Sparkman and Russell Long joined Stuart Symington (D-MO), Frank L. Lausche (D-OH), and Bourke Hickenlooper (R-IA) as prominent defenders of Johnson's Vietnam policies. Sparkman's principal contributions came in the form of careful, pointed questions put to both pro- and antiwar witnesses. To Taylor and Rusk, was the intervention in Vietnam an application of containment akin to the Truman Doctrine? Was not the conflict a case of outside aggression rather than a "civil war"? Had the United States tried "every way" possible to get to the "conference table"? Had the United States attempted "insofar as practical" to avoid damage to "villages" and "civilians"? Would losing the war have a deleterious impact on neighboring countries in Southeast Asia? As the administration witnesses responded and elaborated, Sparkman facilitated presentation of the arguments Johnson and Rusk had been making over the previous eighteen months. From Gavin, Sparkman elicited the acknowledgment that force should at least be maintained "at its present level" and that Haiphong should be bombed because of its service "as a major port of entry for military supplies"; and from Kennan he gained the concession that a "satisfactory peaceful resolution of the conflict" was "not entirely visible."[62]

Praised for knowing "how to get things done" as a legislator, Russell Long had been elected Senate Democratic whip in January and assumed the chairmanship of the Finance Committee in November. Despite his southern "corn-pone exterior," one perceptive observer recognized that the canny Long was "never more effective than when confronted by liberals who think they are smarter than he is." A "five-star hawk," the Louisiana senator played the role of a "screaming eagle" who "wrapped himself in Old Glory like a beach towel," in sharp contrast with the reserved Sparkman. Long rejected any suggestion of "rolling over and playing a dead dog" when confronted with communist aggression. If the United States instead recognized its "power" and was willing to "use it," he was convinced victory was attainable. The Louisiana senator cited SEATO and the Gulf of Tonkin Resolution as ample justification for US involvement and harbored no doubts of the domino theory's validity. The communists "planned to take over everything that borders on Red China, everything that borders on the Soviet Union, then everything that borders on everything that borders on that." Long indignantly dismissed any suggestion that the United States had acted as an "international criminal," as the communists and some senators had charged. Rather, in assertions that he also took to the floor of the Senate, the senator was convinced Americans were the "international good guy[s]" who followed the "rules of war" and were "just better and more honorable and more moral people than the Communists."[63]

In his February 16 Senate speech, Long also charged "advocates of retreat, defeat, surrender, and national dishonor" with undermining the war effort and encouraging the enemy. Had northern public figures daily voiced such doubts during the Civil War, the struggle might "have gone the other way," and the South "would have won the principles of States rights." Gore angrily rejected these attacks on his honor and patriotism. He expressed satisfaction that the hearings had "not been characterized by intemperate and flamboyant language and arm waving." Moreover, "the issue before the committee" was not "defeat, retreat, and surrender," but whether the war was to be held within "manageable" limits or expanded into "an open end commitment for total victory" and even grow into a "global" conflict. Such a threat was "far too important to be considered with catch phrases and loosely selected slogans." Unapologetic, Long retorted, "When I speak of my love for my great country, I am not embarrassed because now and then I become a little enthusiastic. I swell with pride when I see Old Glory flying from the Capitol."[64]

Although southerners such as Gore, Sparkman, and Long played revealing and important roles in the SFRC hearings, Fulbright remained the most prominent committee member, and his exchanges with Secretary Rusk provided the hearings' most dramatic moments. The SFRC chairman protested to Rusk that official discussion of US intervention had been "rather superficial" and challenged the administration "to clarify the nature" of US involvement and demonstrate that the "ultimate objective justifies the enormous sacrifice in lives and treasure." Fulbright bemoaned the spiraling cost of the war, which he estimated as $15.8 billion for FY 1966, and objected to the argument that the preservation of US credibility made continued involvement and victory essential. Since considerations of "prestige and face" were "grossly exaggerated," US policy should be based on "wisdom" rather than an elusive sense of national appearance. The essential nature of the conflict rendered Cold War credibility even less relevant, since Ho and his followers were "indigenous Vietnamese nationalists" who had begun their resistance seeking "liberation from French colonial rule." Therefore, it was an "oversimplification" to term the actions of these "nationalistic Communists . . . a clear cut aggression" by North Vietnam against "a free, independent neighboring nation."[65]

Moving beyond the US rationale for intervention in Vietnam, Fulbright questioned the administration's and its supporters' emphasis on US efforts to minimize casualties in contrast to Vietcong terrorism. In a direct challenge to America's sense of exceptionalism, the chairman asserted that war was "inherently . . . atrocious" and that all combatants used the weapons they possessed. Technologically sophisticated countries such as the United States employed modern weapons such as airplanes and artillery to kill at long range; poorer, less well-equipped people by necessity used ostensibly cruder methods such as disemboweling or beheading. The United States could not "claim any great superiority because we happen to have nuclear bombs and fire bombs and the other side doesn't." Americans, Fulbright concluded, were not "bad people," but neither were they "the only good people" because of "using weapons that we happen to have, and others don't." Fulbright was equally skeptical regarding administration claims of tirelessly pursuing an equitable, negotiated settlement. How, he asked, could bombing until North Vietnam was forced to negotiate on US terms be called anything other than demanding unconditional surrender or, as "they used to say in the Ozarks, holler 'Enough,' or say 'calf rope'"?[66]

In his six-hour appearance before the committee on February 18, Rusk offered a "dignified and staid, often laborious," and only briefly "impassioned" rejoinder to Fulbright and the SFRC dissenters. The secretary rejected any suggestion that Ho and his followers were nationalists or that the United States had intervened in a civil war. Instead, the struggle in Vietnam was the most recent battle in the larger Cold War, in which North Vietnam had committed "systematic aggression . . . against the people of South Vietnam." In addition to the fate of South Vietnam and Southeast Asia, the very structure of world peace and a world consistent with American values hung in the balance. Only by confronting aggression head on could peace be preserved. Comparing China, the ultimate source of aggression in Asia, to Hitler's Germany, Rusk contended that "an airdale [*sic*] and a great dane are different but they are both dogs." Only by upholding the solemn commitments embodied in SEATO and containing China and North Vietnam could the United States avert a threat to the entire "human race." The "pledged word of the United States" had to be taken seriously by both allies and adversaries; international observers had to understand "we . . . mean business." To date, "every resource of [US] diplomacy" had been directed toward an equitable "political solution"; but all American overtures had met only North Vietnamese intransigence. Were Hanoi "prepared to call off the aggression in the south, peace would come in a matter of hours."[67]

Like Taylor, Rusk refused to set any ceiling on US forces in Vietnam. Unless SFRC critics could forecast "exactly what the other side is going to do," how could they expect the administration to specify limits on the American commitment? Nor should there be any limits, given the post-1945 pattern of US responses to aggression. Appealing directly to the national sense of exceptionalism and the self-image of peculiarly peaceful intentions, Rusk asserted that all US Cold War actions had been defensive and in answer to "specific steps of aggression launched by the other side." The secretary was "convinced" that "no people in the world" were "more deeply peace loving than . . . the American people." Rusk also reiterated one emerging strain of the "stab-in-the-back" explanation of the lack of US progress in the war. Dissenters, such as Fulbright and Gore, were prolonging the war since the North Vietnamese would negotiate only after realizing that US "internal differences" would not "pull us out of Vietnam and let them have the country." Writing after the war, the secretary added that domestic dissent had "encouraged" the enemy "to stick it out," to believe that "American public support for the war would collapse and that they could win . . . in the United States what they couldn't win on the ground in Vietnam."[68]

Given Fulbright's and Rusk's diametrically opposing perspectives on the war and previous confrontations, the virtually inevitable clash rocked the committee room as the secretary neared the end of his six-hour inquisition. The conflict involved personality as well as policy. The Senate's foremost student of foreign policy versus the secretary of state. Rhodes scholar versus Rhodes scholar. Former football star at the University of

Arkansas versus lackluster basketball player at Davidson College. Arkansas aristocrat and transplanted Washington sophisticate versus Georgia plebian and inveterate bureaucrat who shunned Washington society. Habitual maverick versus ultimate company man. Even without fundamental differences over US policy in Vietnam, such divergent personalities would have produced personal friction that belied their usual outward civility. But Fulbright also viewed Rusk as overly rigid and lacking the creative intellect to move beyond Cold War shibboleths. As the chairman cuttingly remarked to Rusk, "I wish these things appeared as simple to me as they do to you." Rusk, a deeply religious and honorable man, resented Fulbright's ongoing suggestions that the secretary had ignored or misled the SFRC, and he believed his adversary had acted dishonorably in his responses to the war. Rusk considered Fulbright a "poor chairman" of the SFRC, and in a thinly disguised reference to his adversary, Rusk complained in his autobiography of congressmen "who supported our policy initially and later changed their minds." Their sin, he continued, was not in reversing their positions and offering a forthright explanation but in "misrepresenting what both they and the administration had actually done." The secretary, a liberal on race whose daughter married an African American man, also traced Fulbright's antiwar stance to racism, to what one historian has characterized as the secretary's belief that the senator objected to "white men" having "to spill their blood to safeguard the freedom and independence of yellow men."[69]

Fulbright touched off the personal confrontation with a fifteen-minute summary critique of Rusk's testimony and administration policies. The senator reiterated his positions on the war and called again for a sincere US commitment to negotiations. After charging that the United States had never made "crystal clear" its willingness to support and accept the outcome of an election to select a government in South Vietnam, he contended that by excluding the NLF from talks, the administration was informing the Vietcong and North Vietnamese that only their "unconditional surrender" and participation at American "mercy" would bring the United States to the table. These actions contradicted Rusk's claims to be aggressively seeking peace on all fronts. By attempting to "impose our will" unilaterally, the United States was acting like previous "great empires."[70]

Rusk responded to this frontal assault with a series of questions. Did the "Senator . . . have any doubts about the good faith and credibility of the other side?" Later, in response to Fulbright's assertion that there "must be something wrong with our diplomacy," Rusk queried, "Senator, is it just possible that there is something wrong with them?" Was the Arkansan suggesting "we should abandon the effort in South Vietnam"? Although Fulbright dismissed this accusation, he returned to the need for a "conference," which was unobtainable until "you propose reasonable terms" allowing "even the liberation front, to have an opportunity to participate in an election" whose outcome the United States was pledged to accept. Moreover, Fulbright contended, "Vietnam is their country. It is not our country." From the enemy's perspective, "we are obviously intruders" who "represent the old Western imperialism." Certainly, the senator asserted, Rusk, a fellow southerner, should understand this response to outside intrusion. Following the American Civil War in "my part of the country[,] [w]e resented it for a long time. So did yours. You can remember this feeling." After additional verbal fencing, Fulbright concluded that Vietnam was not the "kind of vital interest" that warranted further escalation and a possible "confrontation with China in a world war." To avoid such a calamity, the United States was "quite strong enough" to compromise "without losing its standing in the world."[71]

Fulbright's and the SFRC's challenge to Johnson's Vietnam policies provoked a broad range of responses. Certainly the most important reactions came from the president himself, who was enraged but undeterred in prosecuting the war. LBJ resumed the bombing of North Vietnam on January 31, remarking derisively, "I don't want to back out—and look like I am reacting to the Fulbrights." Johnson also directed the FBI to monitor the hearings with an eye to linking the dissenters' opinions to contemporary communist positions, but no such ties were detected. In an effort to overshadow the hearings and minimize their influence, the president flew to Honolulu for a hastily organized summit conference with South Vietnamese leaders. In a more direct and incisive response to the Gavin-Kennan testimony, President Johnson told assembled reporters on February 11 that he could discern no "great deal of difference "between what the dissenters were "saying and what the Government is doing." He then focused on the principal weakness in the opposition brief. His critics had presented no "real program" that "offers a clear alternative . . . to what we are doing." Johnson's fury over what an aide termed Fulbright's "sophomoric bitching" remained evident at an early May Democratic fundraiser in Washington when he greeted the audience by saying he was happy to be there "among so many friends—and some members of the Foreign Relations Committee."[72]

Although the hearings had neither restrained Johnson's ongoing escalation of the war nor produced viable, alternative policies, *Newsweek* observed correctly that the TV coverage had "lifted the dialogue out of the gray austerity of the *Congressional Record* and made it an authentic national event." The "smoldering war" between Johnson and the "peace bloc on Capitol Hill" had "escalated into a full-blown national debate"— the very development that LBJ had so adroitly sought to avoid over the previous fifteen months. The hearings also helped to make opposition to the war more respectable. No one could confuse Fulbright, Gore, Gavin, Kennan, or the SFRC with the long-haired, often disorderly protestors who marched on Washington or denounced the war on college campuses. According to Senator Claiborne Pell (D-RI), "If such a group of respectable stuffed shirts as the Senate Foreign Relations Committee could question this war, it gave other people courage to question it."[73]

National responses to the hearings and the war more generally revealed the growing disapproval of President Johnson's handling of the conflict and the mounting frustration with the lack of US progress. The president's approval rating in the Harris Poll fell from 63 percent (excellent or good) in January to 42 percent in June, with 58 percent rating him as fair or poor. From December 1965 to May 1966, the percentage of Americans committed to holding the line in Vietnam decreased from 65 to 47 percent, but the proportion of respondents favoring a more aggressive prosecution of the war against North Vietnam rose from 28 to 38 percent. According to pollster Lou Harris, "increased militancy . . . and a 'get it over with' mood" were becoming more prevalent.[74]

Dixie's response to Gallup polling yielded similar but more pronounced trends. Set against their ongoing objections to LBJ's social and civil rights programs, southerners continued to assess the president more harshly than citizens of other regions on both his overall performance as president and his "handling" of the "situation in Vietnam." For example, in February 1966, only 42 percent of southerners approved of his work as president, versus 59 percent of Americans generally and 59 percent of midwesterners, the next lowest region. In April the respective numbers were 47 percent (South), 57 percent (national), and 54 percent (Midwest). That same month, 47 percent of southerners approved Johnson's Vietnam policies, compared to 56 percent nationally and 51 percent in the Midwest. By October only 37 percent of southerners endorsed Johnson's presidential work, and 35 percent backed his management of the war.[75]

Additional polling data demonstrated that the southern populace, mirroring the positions of its most prominent public figures, remained most inclined to view the "sending of troops to fight in Vietnam" as a "mistake." But once the United States had intervened, southerners possessed the least faith in South Vietnamese political capacity, were most opposed to turning to the UN or the World Court as mediators, remained most in favor of "bombing big cities in North Vietnam," and were most inclined to believe the war would end in an "all-out victory" for the United States and South Vietnam rather than "a compromise peace settlement." The Gallup results for these last two questions were telling. Southerners were 7 percent more in favor and 10 percent less opposed to bombing North Vietnamese cities and were 5 percent more confident of all-out victory and 9 percent less likely to envision a compromised outcome than national responses. Consistent with these preferences for a military solution and their expectation of a traditional, victorious outcome, residents of Dixie were the most critical of Secretary of Defense McNamara and his oversight of the Defense Department and the war in Vietnam, most willing to rate the draft as "fair," and most willing to have their sons serve in the military versus some form of alternative service.[76]

Other southern responses were less consistent with Dixie's traditional promilitary, hawkish stances and reveal, like the public debate and constituent correspondence, that even the nation's most belligerent region was deeply conflicted over Vietnam. When asked in June whether the United States should continue the war or withdraw its troops "during the next few months," southerners were the least willing to continue: 45 percent versus, 46, 51, and 51 for the East, Midwest, and West, respectively. Similarly, the South most favored withdrawal if the South Vietnamese allies began to fight among themselves or if China sent troops into the fighting, which southerners predicted would happen.[77]

As the decisions for war and Dixie's majority prowar preferences solidified during 1966, southern papers built on the positions they had adopted in 1964 and 1965. The *Dallas Morning News* praised Johnson's pledge to "do what must be done to preserve" American ideals, asserted in July that his policies were "wrecking the Red timetable" in Vietnam, denounced antiwar protestors as "leaping leftists," and upbraided Fulbright for failing to explain how to "stop a determined aggressor without being rude to him." The equally prowar *Montgomery Advertiser* recommended providing General William Westmoreland "the men and the authority to wage a real war, not just a holding operation," and advised Americans that victory might require maintaining "a military occupation indefinitely" to secure the anticipated "victory."[78]

Publisher Ralph McGill, editor Eugene Patterson, and the *Atlanta Constitution* also remained solidly behind Johnson and the war. On January 26 the *Constitution* deemed the bombing moratorium begun on December 24, 1965, a "worthwhile risk" but anticipated and approved LBJ's decision to resume bombing at the end of the month. In early February the paper pronounced as "honorable" US efforts "to defend, with its own lives, and raise up, with its own wealth, an impoverished and embattled people from whom it wants nothing" in return. Patterson subsequently argued that LBJ's policies had "stabilized" the "military situation" despite contending with unprecedented "furor" from domestic critics who based "dissent . . . on nothing much more substantial than an endless detailing of why we were unhappy."[79]

Turning specifically to the SFRC hearings, Patterson and McGill praised Taylor and Rusk and castigated Fulbright and the other dissenters. Taylor had explained US policies "coolly, precisely, and expertly," and Rusk had displayed "scholarly sharpness" and "decisiveness," while providing a "carefully framed and reasonably stated" overview of administration assumptions and actions. By contrast, Fulbright had engaged Taylor in an irrelevant debate over Dien Bien Phu and suggested irrationally to Rusk that there had to be something "wrong" with US diplomacy. The chairman could have been "more perceptive and open minded"; too often displayed "scholarly ambiguities"; and failed to rein in the intemperate Senator Morris, who drove the discussion "to a new low." Patterson repeated administration charges that the sessions had yielded no viable alternative policies and confirmed Hanoi's expectations of US "internal division and . . . wavering purpose," thereby compromising the American "effort to wage war or to make peace."[80]

While the *Morning News, Advertiser,* and *Constitution* augmented their prowar, proadministration perspectives, the *Louisville Courier-Journal* retained its skeptical view of the war. The *Courier-Journal* endorsed Senator Cooper's call in late January for an extension of the bombing halt; and the paper worried that Johnson's subsequent resumption of bombing was a "dangerous gamble" that "reopened the door" to advocates of blockading Haiphong, bombing North Vietnamese cities, and even a nuclear exchange with China. Like Kentucky's highly respected senator, the *Courier-Journal* editorial staff continued to push for negotiations; and, like Fulbright, they favored including the Vietcong, who were "an integral part of South Viet Nam's national life." It would be "distasteful" to have to interact with "ruthless murders" but "still more bitter and more distasteful" to continue fighting a war that might be "ended by including the Viet Cong at the conference table."[81]

The *Courier-Journal*'s assessment of the SFRC hearings was also more sympathetic than the prowar southern dailies'. The paper's Washington bureau chief was impressed that Fulbright had lent his "prestige" to LBJ's "critics." The Arkansas senator had given "the foes of the President's policy all the respectability of a Southern conservative, of a former university president, of a Phi Beta Kappa, of a Rhodes scholar." In an incisive editorial, the *Courier-Journal* praised the hearings for providing "public exposure of this vital issue," for emphasizing "the right and even the duty of patriotic Americans to protest their government's policies when they believe them to be dangerously wrong," and for specifying "every good reason to get out of our entanglement in Southeast Asia." Still, the paper acknowledged the hearings' limitations: "The current debate" had "aired all the important questions, but . . . provided no real answers."[82]

As had been true during 1965, the *Texas Observer* assumed a stronger antiwar posture than any of these other southern papers. The Austin weekly featured Fort Worth congressman Jim Wright's call for LBJ to propose a UN-supervised six-week truce followed by a free election to determine which groups would govern South Vietnam and Senator Ralph Yarbrough's (D-TX) question on the Senate floor as to whether neutral nations might conclude that the United States was "stomping the tiger's tail" and "trying to lure him into a war" by "dropping bombs only one minute from Red China." The *Observer* ran a May article in which Ron Bailey, after a five-week stay in South Vietnam, concluded that the United States was losing despite "killing a lot of Viet Cong and a lot of others." To prevail in this "incredibly complex war," the United States would have "to defeat the main force enemy units, occupy every acre of countryside, and thus pave the way for political cadres to establish" a viable government—all objectives Bailey deemed unlikely.[83]

In *Observer* editorials, Ronnie Dugger and his staff charged that Johnson's "lip-service to unconditional negotiations" had "debased the language" and diminished "confidence in his sincerity and candor." The *Observer* lamented the "stark disparity between his [LBJ's] humanitarianism at home and his . . . aggressiveness in Vietnam." The president was acting on a "Texan's simplistic frontier ideas about man-to-man relationships and how to behave in a fight" and seeking to impugn dissenters "with accusations" they were "communists" and "letting down our fighting men." Only by "pulling back from the brink," by restricting the bombing and the war's escalation, and by negotiating in good faith could the president "reclaim his career and his nation from tragic disaster."[84]

The reactions of individual southerners conveyed a fuller picture of Dixie's attitudes toward the Fulbright hearings and the Johnson administration's commitment to a major war during 1966. Consistent with polling data and the positions of major southern papers, most southerners maintained their prowar stances. The hearings left one Mississippi woman in an "absolute rage." She found Fulbright's "manner in questioning" General Taylor "shocking" and came away doubting the senator's "loyalty to his country." Others denounced the SFRC chairman's "blind soft-headedness"; dismissed his comments as "the most asinine appraisal yet" by a "supposedly responsible" person; and deplored his proclivity for bias, "time wasting and quibbling." Arkansans, even many of those generally supportive of Fulbright, were equally critical. An old Arkansas friend advised Fulbright "the time to criticize" had passed unless the dissenters could "offer specific, constructive criticisms and specific remedies either to cure wholly or partially this ill-advised venture." Other Fulbright constituents agreed that Congress and the nation needed to "unite, not divide," and "pull together as a people." One far less sympathetic couple was "ashamed and humiliated" by "the image" Fulbright had presented of his "loyal patriotic" constituents; another Arkansas resident declared himself a "*voter who will oppose you until you are voted out, as all pinkos will be*"; and a Jonesboro woman suggested the senator "move to North Vietnam," where he "would really be appreciated."[85]

Albert Gore's dissent elicited equally hostile comments. A frequent and caustic correspondent informed Gore that the televised hearings had revealed "brilliance, dignity and good manners on one side, and incoherency, slovenliness and bad manners on the other." He continued, "I have been a liberal Democrat all my life. But brother am I through with you." A twenty-nine-year military veteran sympathized with "Mr. Rusk, an honest, honorable, intelligent and well oriented public servant," who had endured the SFRC "inquisition." A Mumford physician perceived "no doubt" among US soldiers regarding their "objective" of keeping Southeast Asia "out of the hands of the Communists." Among Americans, doubt existed only "in the minds of beatniks, the professional demonstrators, the civil rights leaders, the Communists, a small group of liberal democratic senators and the Committee on Foreign Relations." "Senator," he continued, "this is pretty sorry company for you to keep."[86]

Southern critics of the hearings often praised Senator Long and generally agreed with the arguments presented by Johnson, Rusk, and Taylor. The open hearings served only to "tell the whole world all of our secrets," "destroy any good image of the United States in the eyes of the world," and leave countless Americans "confused as to the correctness of our position in Vietnam." Most important, these public debates gave "aid and comfort to the enemy," furnished "fuel for Communist propaganda," and prolonged the war by "bolstering" North Vietnamese "morale."[87]

Consistent with the pattern that had emerged over the previous two years, other, primarily antiwar southerners endorsed the hearings and the arguments of the SFRC dissenters. These southern skeptics deemed the public "debate . . . essential to our understanding" of the Vietnamese situation. The American people were "entitled to hear a full and frank discussion of that war, its background and its rationale." The hearings, concluded an Arkansas voter, were "very informative and enlightening . . . one of the greatest services, if not the greatest, that the medium of television has performed." Recognizing that Fulbright and Gore were challenging both the Johnson administration and the predominant prowar sentiment in Dixie, supporters of the hearings also lauded the senators' courage. An Arkansas grandmother praised Fulbright as the state's only representative with the "guts to disagree with LBJ," and a Madison, Tennessee, dentist was pleased that Gore had "the courage" to take a stand, given "the pressure which you must face as a senator to conform."[88]

Other southerners drew on the South's historical experience and acute sensitivity to outside interference to argue against US intervention in Vietnam. One of Senator Robertson's constituents likened combating the Vietcong to extracting "all the muskrats out of Back Bay and Dismal Swamp." An Atlanta resident asked Senator Russell how, if southerners believed "that people as close as New York don't quite know enough to tell us how to run Georgia," he could assert that Washington knew "what is best" for a country "as far away" as Vietnam. A Mississippi native living in Florida wrote in a similar vein to John Stennis. "Washington office holders," he contended, had sought to impose on "each and every foreign country, and our South," a predetermined outside "way of life." Should not "we in our South," having been "in the same boat," understand why this practice has led much of the world "to detest" the United States? In a particularly southern observation, a North Carolina dove asked Senator Ervin "what we would think if a foreign country" landed "troops on our shore to settle the negro question." An Augusta, Georgia, dentist denounced Senator Russell, and by extension most other conservative southern Democrats, for "claiming you were against our initial involvement" but then supporting the war "completely." This antiwar Georgian condemned the "neat political maneuver" with which Russell sought to "disclaim responsibility" for American deaths while still appealing to the hawkish southern public.[89]

Conditioned to be among the nation's most overtly patriotic citizens, southerners worried that the Vietnam War was undermining American patriotism. In "her first letter to a senator," a veteran Georgia schoolteacher noted that during World War II, "we were asked to sacrifice and did it willingly." To her chagrin, she feared this attitude no longer prevailed: "The only people who are sacrificing are the boys who are serving in the Armed Forces and their families." Why was the nation "losing" its "patriotism"? Perhaps, she concluded, it was "because people do not believe in this war." Other southerners regretfully acknowledged this lack of national commitment. In January 1966 a Baptist minister from Jackson, Mississippi, anguished over the US failure to take more aggressive actions in Vietnam and feared that his nineteen-year-old son would soon be sent to the war. After professing complete devotion to America and its ideals and his contempt for "draft card burning," he told Stennis, "Frankly . . . I am not willing to see my son and other dad's sons go to

Viet Nam to be shot at and suffer and die for NOTHING." His deep discomfort was obvious as he ended the letter: "I hate to feel as I do. I would love to be able to give whole-hearted allegiance to everything our country is trying to do."[90]

While arguing both for and against the war, southerners objected to the costs of fighting in Vietnam and paying for the Great Society. This pervasive fiscal conservatism, together with objections to the Civil Rights Movement and outrage at Johnson's limited-war strategy, go far toward explaining the president's low polling numbers in Dixie. Both the failure "to hit" the enemy "really hard where it will hurt" and Johnson's "bankrupt give away policies" at home rankled one Georgian. Another Russell constituent denounced LBJ's "appeasement" of the communist aggressors and his "Anti-Poverty Program." An antiwar southerner expressed similar dissatisfaction over "the blundering wastefulness of the so-called 'Great Society'" but cited involvement in Vietnam as "an even greater peril." A "hard working" Memphis businessman opposed the "drain on my tax dollars" used to fight both the "Viet Nam war" and the "bogus war on poverty." And a rural Arkansas woman wanted "no part" of spending for either the Great Society or the "billions of dollars" being consumed by US involvement in Vietnam.[91]

Although less pointedly southern, the heart-rending letters from parents and grandparents fearing for their sons' and grandsons' survival afford further insight into the turmoil and distress engendered by the Vietnam War. After watching her son "board a plane in Memphis . . . and fly off to war," an Arkansas mother wrote pleadingly to her senator, "Oh, Mr. Fulbright, if there is anything you fellows up there in Washington can do to help stop this senseless war in Viet Nam, please set about doing it." The grandfather of a young man "being examined . . . for college deferment" sent a similar appeal to Senator Stennis: "Is there anything you law makers in Washington can do to terminate that war that is costing us parents . . . our sons and grandsons?" Another Arkansan wrote his friend "Bill," "If you want to see a heart breaking scene visit the Little Rock Airport any afternoon and see the dozens of boys there, many away from home for the first time—on their way to the West Coast. A lot of them so young that they have been nick named CRADLE FRUIT." A seventy-four-year-old Mississippi grandmother of seven boys, one of whom was in Vietnam, the other six soon to confront the draft, concluded the situation "makes my heart heavy."[92]

Letters from two other hardworking southern families, one solidly middle class, the other less well off, also conveyed the "soul searching" that was under way across Dixie and the nation. From Fort Smith, Arkansas, a military veteran, who worked as a railroad switchman and was married to a schoolteacher, wrote to Fulbright about his son and son-in-law, who would "soon . . . be in the service." After commending the senator on the hearings and his opposition to the war, the railroad brakeman acknowledged, "Way off down here in Arkansas may not be conducive to making foreign policy but if we are to help furnish the servicemen, then we can help formulate some of the ideas." Indeed, since "our lives depend upon" US foreign policy decisions, he and his family were entitled to "knowledge of our position in world affairs." Speaking for a "family trying to improve ourselves," he suggested Americans needed to "forget some of our competitive pride . . . and humble ourselves before our God and . . . simplify our actions by living the Golden Rule *every day*." While this man's son faced possible service in Vietnam, a Memphis father, also a veteran, confronted the reality of his son having been drafted. Having "worked at hard labor" and "raised a son and daughter" that any "citizen" who "knows them can be . . . proud of," he was "sick" to his "stomach" at the outcome: "We are poor, proud & devoted to our country and fellow man and up until now I have felt that I was very patriotic." His ultimate response echoed those of others worried about their children's safety: "I'm not a hell raiser normally, but I'm not only mad, I'm bitter."[93]

His bitterness and sorrow paled when compared to families whose relatives had died in the war. In a shaky hand a grieving Knoxville grandmother informed Senator Gore that the death of her grandson "brought home to me . . . all the horrors of war & the suffering of the many thousand[s] . . . who have lost their sons." The young soldier's aunt elaborated:

The whole family, his mother and brothers, his young wife and both families have just gone through the shock, the painful waiting for the body to arrive, and the final hours of the funeral and burial, filled with memories of a gay, mischievous boy grown to a bright and outgoing young man, about to be reunited with his wife and baby daughter for a furlough when he was killed. But even as we thought of him, we were aware of the many others, who have gone through, who are going through, who will go through a similar tragedy. And for what?[94]

This Knoxville family's sorrow graphically conveyed the mounting agony that the Vietnam War was engendering across the South and the nation. Led by its southern president and secretary of state, the United States committed to war during 1965 and 1966. As Johnson and Rusk continued to act on many of the very southern assumptions and motivations that had prompted their responses to the growing crisis in Vietnam in 1964, key southern senators, especially Fulbright and Russell, facilitated LBJ's successful effort to limit debate on the increasing US commitment to hostilities during 1965. Once Johnson had initiated the Rolling Thunder bombing campaign and dispatched thousands of US ground troops, southern senators and representatives provided the administration's crucial and most dependable Democratic support for the war. By doing so, they also reinforced LBJ and Rusk's pursuit of a military solution and refusal to negotiate seriously with Hanoi or the Vietcong or to entertain a compromise settlement. With this regional backing came constricted strategic and political options. A significant majority of southern newspapers and Dixie's public also endorsed the US commitment, while objecting to Johnson's decision to fight a limited war and remaining highly critical of the president's civil rights and social agendas. Concern for national honor and credibility, overt patriotism, virulent anticommunism and adherence to Christian tenets as opposed to ostensible Soviet and Chinese atheism, and a preference for unrestrained military actions and solutions to international problems continued to underpin Dixie's prowar stance.

The South's prowar inclinations were evident in the region's hostility toward antiwar dissidents. As Johnson committed the nation to war, Senators Fulbright, Gore, and Cooper grew increasingly restive, and the first two played a central role in the SFRC hearings, which occasioned the nation's first true public debate on the war—the very debate that Johnson had worked so hard to muffle. Polling data, the caustic indictments of these senators, the experience of Frazier Woolard in small-town North Carolina, and the felt need of antiwar southerners to affirm their patriotism and deny they were beatniks or radicals all reflected the nature of majority southern opinion. Still, by late 1965, Fulbright, Gore, and Cooper had moved beyond both the US Cold War consensus and Dixie's prowar perspective to claim their place among the most persistent and perceptive critics of the war. A hardy minority of southerners echoed their concerns and praised their courage in challenging President Johnson and their prowar neighbors and constituents. Antiwar southerners continued to assert geopolitical and religious objections to the conflict and to argue that honor required admitting the US mistake in intervening. They also voiced particularly southern criticisms. From a fiscally conservative perspective, they protested against the waste of money in this ill-advised war; and, citing the South's sensitivity to outside interference, they asked how Dixie's leaders could condone US meddling in Vietnam. But whether they backed or opposed the war, the region's leaders, public, and press continued, as they had since the 1770s, to examine the war from a distinctly southern perspective. That would also be true during 1967 as the nation debated the proper conduct of the war; and as in 1965–1966, southern leaders and concerns played prominent roles in that debate.

4

Southern Soldiers

As the South's politicians, press, and public debated the wisdom of going to war in Vietnam, southern soldiers served, died, and won Medals of Honor in Vietnam in numbers substantially exceeding Dixie's share of the nation's population. This participation reflected the region's devotion to its military tradition; intense concern for patriotism, honor, and manhood; and depressed economic conditions. Although the experiences and responses of southern warriors generally coincided with those of other American troops, they often did so in a more pronounced fashion. Similar to the South's political figures, southern soldiers repeatedly played a central role in important decisions and events and, therefore, merit attention in this account. General William Westmoreland commanded US forces from 1964 through 1968 and helped devise the military's flawed ground strategies. Lieutenant Colonel Harold G. "Hal" Moore led his air cavalry battalion against North Vietnamese regulars in the epic 1965 battle in the Ia Drang Valley, a confrontation with significant, long-term implications. National Guard troops from Moore's hometown of Bardstown, Kentucky, were among the small number of guard units that saw action in Vietnam, and they endured the war's single most costly combat losses for a guard contingent. Two southerners, Lieutenant William Calley and Warrant Officer Hugh Thompson, were key actors during the My Lai massacre, the most infamous American-inflicted atrocity of the war. And Jim Webb and Gustav Hasford, both southern marines, wrote much discussed novels based on their combat experiences.

Any examination of southern service in the war zone must include women, African Americans, and Chicanos. Women went to Vietnam voluntarily as members of the military and in nonmilitary capacities such as the Red Cross. Both their motives for going and many aspects of their experiences often resembled those of southern men. Although Dixie's black soldiers shared many of these motives and experiences, issues of race, both within the United States and during their tours of duty in Vietnam, produced more divergent involvements and responses. As was true of African Americans at home, black soldiers confronted race-related challenges and discrimination, ranging from poverty, substandard education, and all-white draft boards in the United States to combat assignments, standards of dress and appearance, and discriminatory military justice and discipline in Vietnam. Southern Chicanos, primarily from Texas and far less numerous than southern blacks, endured similar discrimination based on race, class, and lack of educational opportunity.

In his excellent book *Working-Class War,* Christian G. Appy has argued that class, rather than geography, was the most influential predictor of who would go to Vietnam and serve in combat. Eighty percent of Vietnam soldiers had no more than a high school education. Reflecting their working-class status, most had neither the inclination nor the means to pursue higher education and with it a deferment from the draft or a more favorable, noncombat assignment in the military. Appy estimates that the enlisted portion of the US forces in Vietnam was approximately "25 percent poor, 55 percent working class, and 20 percent middle class, with a statistically negligible number of wealthy." They were also young, averaging nineteen years of age versus twenty-six in World War II. Significantly, Appy asserts that "rural and small town America" may have lost more of its sons in Vietnam than inner cities or blue-collar suburbs. Appy also observes that soldiers "came from neither cities, suburbs, nor small towns but from the hundreds of places in between," such as Talladega, Alabama, with a population of around 17,500, one-fourth of whom were African Americans. With its predominantly working-class population and approximately only one-third of its men having graduated from high school, Talladega lost fifteen soldiers in Vietnam, three times the national average. By contrast, Mountain Brook, a wealthy Birmingham suburb with virtually no blacks and a high school graduation rate of 90 percent, lost none.[1]

Without disputing Appy's emphasis on class, the fact that the South remained the nation's poorest and most rural section during the 1960s and early 1970s argues for also applying a regional approach and against deemphasizing geography. Although the South had made great economic strides after 1941, Dixie's per capita income in 1960 was still only two-thirds the national average of $2,216. By 1960, 58 percent of southerners (an increase of 20 percent since 1940) lived in cities; but here again, the South lagged behind national norms. In 1960, only five of the nation's thirty largest cities were in the South, and all of them had significantly lower population densities than major urban areas in other regions. Therefore, the South's comparatively poorer, more rural young men were, even by Appy's criteria, more likely to serve and die in Vietnam. These demographic considerations, when added to the region's military tradition, exuberant patriotism, sense of duty and honor, and faith-based aversion to communism, explain why southerners went to Vietnam in numbers that significantly exceeded Dixie's proportion of the national population. The eleven states of the former Confederacy plus Kentucky provided 30 percent (884,000 of 2,926,000) of the soldiers who served in Vietnam, even though the South was home to only 22 percent of the nation's population. As noted above, southerners also died and earned Medals of Honor in similarly disproportionate numbers. Approximately 27 percent (16,437 of 58,220) of the military deaths and 28 percent (68 of 256) of Medal of Honor winners came from among the region's warriors.[2]

Diverse motivations led southern soldiers to war in Vietnam. Many were simply drafted or enlisted under the threat of the draft. For example, when faced with the draft, Dr. Timothy Lockley explained his decision to enlist in the air force: "I didn't mind serving my country but I'll be damned if I was going to die for it." Other, blue-collar youth were unmistakably "working-class" warriors who either lacked the funds for college or could see no value in the experience. Raymond Wilson from near Birmingham "knew damn well" he was going to be drafted. So he enlisted with the hope of a preferable military assignment, and "the next thing you know you end up in Vietnam." Voicing the political naïveté of so many of his contemporaries, Bob Foley recalled, "I felt like . . . your parents will fuck you over, but your *country* won't do you wrong. It [the war] must be a good cause if we're sending people over there. I felt like maybe it was a good cause. . . . I knew I didn't much want to go, but there was really no choice." With equally limited choices, poor blacks and Chicanos could see the military as a way to escape poverty and racism and perhaps find a better life. Charles Richardson minced no words: "I went to Vietnam to escape Selma." And Charles, a Mexican American whose family picked cotton in South Texas, sought to "get away," since "it didn't seem like I'd go anywhere else in my situation."[3]

Young southerners generally subscribed to the official Cold War explanation that the United States was fighting to halt North Vietnamese communist aggression and to preserve a "free, democratic . . . society" in South Vietnam. They had also imbibed the nation's "victory culture," which prompted young American men to see war and themselves in the romantic and heroic images of Audie Murphy or John Wayne triumphing over evil enemies. J. Houston Matthews, a marine from South Carolina, was "intrigued by what I thought was the glamour of war." For young men who had grown up in the nation's most vocally patriotic region, the call of duty also proved compelling. As one Tennessee army officer explained, he had come to view "this type of service as a duty and obligation" and even worried that he "might miss . . . the action." Marshall Paul from Lubbock, who served in both the airborne and special forces, declared, "Part of me just flat out wanted an adventure"; but he also sought to "experience war at the lowest, . . . grittiest level," to "prove to myself that I was a man." Another Tennessee soldier appropriately added a religious dimension: his "primary reason for fighting was to keep the country [South Vietnam] free. So that they would have the option to become Christians."[4]

Dixie's military tradition reinforced all of these motives. Max Cleland from Lithonia, Georgia, spoke for many. During World War II, his father and four uncles from both sides of the family had volunteered to fight Hitler; and Cleland "loved the idea of being a soldier"; flourished as an army ROTC cadet at Stetson University in Deland, Florida; and extended his army obligation to do his "duty" in Vietnam. Larry Gwin, a Yale graduate, also sought an ROTC commission that would lead to service in Vietnam. Gwin "went because my father had gone, and his father before him, and before that, my great grandfather, who'd fought for the Confederacy. . . . I was intrigued . . . by the . . . question of how I'd measure up in combat—a question that would not have concerned me, I'm sure, if I hadn't been aware of my father's proud service in the 'Good War.'"[5]

Prominent southern devotion to honor, manhood, patriotism, and military tradition were evident in Dixie's professional soldiers. William C. Westmoreland, a native of South Carolina and the commander of the

US Military Assistance Command, Vietnam (MACV), between 1964 and 1968, has been aptly described as coming "close to embodying the perfect image of the southern warrior." In his report on the war, Westmoreland emphasized the "appreciation and respect" he had gained in the 1930s for West Point's "code of ethics" as exemplified in its "honor system." Westmoreland also warmly endorsed Robert E. Lee's assertion that duty was the "sublimest word in our language." Following his second year at the academy, Westmoreland visited his great uncle in South Carolina. Since the cantankerous Confederate veteran had fought for Lee at Gettysburg and Appomattox, the young cadet hesitated to tell his uncle that he was attending the school that had trained "Grant and Sherman." After a long pause, Uncle White replied, "That's all right, son. Robert E. Lee and Stonewall Jackson went there too." Thirty years later, southerners retained no such ambivalence regarding the US Military Academy. As Westmoreland served as commandant of cadets in 1961, a student of the entering class of 1966 observed, "the people of rural Arkansas accorded West Pointers something close to demigod status."[6]

Certainly Lieutenant Colonel Hal Moore, the commander of US troops at Ia Drang in October–November 1965, had exhibited no such ambivalence. In 1940 Moore, then seventeen, moved from his home in Bardstown, Kentucky, to Washington, DC, to enhance his prospects for an appointment to West Point. While working in a US Senate office two years later, he secured his coveted endorsement from a Georgia, rather than Kentucky, congressman. Moore later recalled having been "raised right in the South" with "Yes Ma'am, No Ma'am," which enabled him to impress the "nice southern lady" who turned out to be the Georgia congressman's sister. Perhaps even more than Westmoreland, Moore personified the southern warrior. Rejecting the common practice among US commanders in South Vietnam of observing troop maneuvers and battles from a helicopter, Moore opted to "lead from the front." He deemed it essential "to get on the ground" with his "troops to see and hear what was happening." It was "too easy to be crisp, cool, and detached at 1,500 feet; . . . too easy to make mistakes" that were "fatal" to the soldiers "far below in the mud, the blood, and the confusion." Moore recognized but brushed aside the danger: "Any officer or any soldier for that matter, who worries that he will be hit, is a nuisance. The task and your duty come first." The colonel demonstrated these convictions when General Westmoreland summoned him to Saigon for a briefing in the midst of the fighting at Ia Drang. Moore, who had flown into the battle on the first helicopter, refused to leave his troops: "I made it very clear that this battle was not over and that my place was with my men—that I was the first man of my battalion to set foot in this terrible killing ground and I damned well intended to be the last man to leave."[7]

Numerous southerners echoed these attitudes and added others. From a military family, Richard C. Ensminger joined the marines with a belief in "God and country" and the conviction that it was his "duty to go over there and fight for my country." George Riels, a Mississippian who like Ensminger lost a leg in the war, agreed that going to Vietnam was "the patriotic thing to do." Although he had not especially wanted to go to Vietnam, Manuel Valdez, from Texas, had looked up to his father "because he had been a soldier" and was "very impressed with the pride marines seemed to take in themselves." Being from a typically southern family influenced Houston Matthews; but like so many other Americans growing up in the 1950s, he was drawn by "the glamour of war, John Wayne and all that sort of thing."[8]

A far smaller number of southerners, much to their surprise, went to war in 1968 when their reserve and guard units were activated. Prior to the communist Tet Offensive in South Vietnam in early 1968, President Johnson had consistently ignored the military's calls to activate the National Guard and reserves. He feared that doing so would undermine his efforts to minimize public and political unrest at home and to prevent direct Soviet or Chinese military involvement in Vietnam. Therefore, until April 1968, the guard and the reserves had served as refuges from the draft and service in Vietnam. This changed abruptly when Johnson responded to Tet by activating 24,500 men, some 600 of whom were members of the Kentucky National Guard, 138th Artillery, Second Howitzer Battalion, based in Louisville, Kentucky, and neighboring small towns. Jerry Janes from Bardstown, whose young men made up Battery C of the battalion, spoke for the overwhelming majority of the guardsmen when he recalled, "I just couldn't believe it. . . . In all honesty, I joined the Guard to beat the draft. I thought I could serve six months and then be home, a weekend warrior situation, . . . and possibly stay out of Vietnam." Sam Filiatreau had felt "secure in the fact that I was in the Guard unit, and I thought I was protected." Although he had not been "anti-Vietnam," Filiatreau certainly had not wanted "to go there." But once called, he "felt patriotic. I felt that it was our duty to be there." Interestingly, not all of the Kentucky guardsmen responded this positively. By 1968, after nearly 37,000 American deaths in Vietnam, little military or political progress, and widespread disaffection at home, more than one hundred of the battalion members sued to block the unit's activation and deployment to Vietnam. Although a leader in the legal challenge declared the group sought only "to present the background of why our call-up was illegal" rather than "to oppose the war in Vietnam," the objective of avoiding the fight was apparent. Their response was hardly surprising or unique.[9]

Significantly, southern women, who were not subject to the draft and, therefore, went to Vietnam by choice, echoed many of the men's perspectives. Duty, patriotism, curiosity, adventure, and the opportunity to escape domestic gender constraints beckoned. Nancy Randolph, an army nurse from Ravenscroft, Tennessee, had originally enlisted in return for the military paying for her final year of nursing school. Once on active duty as a lieutenant, she decided, "If I was . . . the true army nurse that I should be . . . , I needed to go to war just like everyone else," since "the army and soldiers needed me." She was also "curious" and drawn to the fight and the "glory" associated with being a combat nurse. Brenda Sue Castro, the daughter of an Alabama coal miner, joined the Army Nurses Corp in 1967 because she "wanted to go to Vietnam." With "American men . . . being shot and killed in a foreign country," Castro believed "American women should be there to take care of them." Becky Pietz, who went to Vietnam as a Red Cross social worker, derived her "patriotism" from her middle-class Richmond family, which traced its roots to Robert E. Lee. Like so many southern men, she was "drawn" to the military. She too had been seduced by "Audie Murphy and John Wayne movies"; "even if you're a girl," she recalled, there was the attraction of being "a hero somewhere." In grand southern tradition, she sought the approval of her father, who responded when he learned Becky was going to Vietnam, "Well, if I had a son I'd expect him to go." Karen K. Johnson, whose father had been killed in World War II, pronounced her induction into the Women's Army Corp "the proudest day of my life. . . . I was gung-ho and I was doing it for my father." Lola McGourty joined the Army Nurses Corps in 1967 after graduating from Northwestern State University to escape the boredom of Shreveport, Louisiana. Cheri Rankin, a Floridian, went to Vietnam as part of the Red Cross SRAO (Supplemental Recreation Activities Overseas) Program, more commonly known as "Donut Dollies." Rankin was specifically concerned about her marine brother, who was serving in Vietnam, but more generally sought "adventure" and an understanding of "what was going on" in Vietnam. Although Rankin sensed that the "war was wrong," she hoped to support the troops.[10]

In contrast to southern white women, Dixie's African Americans, especially the men, had dramatically fewer options. Like blacks nationally, southern blacks were far more likely than their white counterparts to be drafted, to serve in combat, and to be wounded or killed. Between 1965 and 1970, blacks constituted just over 11 percent of the nation's draft-eligible men. During that period, the percentage of African Americans drafted ranged from 13.4 to 16 (1967 and 1970) of the total number of draftees. For example, African Americans comprised 23.7 percent of the population of Shreveport, Louisiana, and 41.3 percent of the town's draftees. In 1965 black soldiers manned 20 percent of the combat slots in Vietnam, and in 1965 and 1966, they suffered 25 percent of the battle-field deaths.[11]

Class and black poverty went far toward explaining these numbers. Like the South's poor whites, southern African Americans possessed few of the resources that enabled middle- and upper-class whites to avoid the draft. For example, only 5 percent of blacks nationally went to college during the Vietnam War, and percentages were even lower in the South. Race compounded the likelihood of blacks serving in Vietnam. In 1966, African Americans comprised 1.3 percent of draft boards nationally, and six southern states (Alabama, Arkansas, Georgia, Louisiana, Mississippi, and South Carolina) had no black board members. Reform of this structural bias was halting. In 1968, three blacks were appointed to boards in Alabama, fifteen in Georgia, and thirty-five in Arkansas; but two years later South Carolina had only six black board members and Mississippi had none. Within this skewed institutional structure, some white southern draft board members were overtly and aggressively racist. Jack Helms, who headed Louisiana's largest draft board from 1957 through 1967, was a grand dragon in the Ku Klux Klan and characterized the NAACP (National Association for the Advancement of Colored People) as a "communist inspired anti-Christ, sex-perverted group of tennis short beatniks whose sole purpose is to cause strife in our beloved land." Civil rights activist Julian Bond observed, "Each draft notice begins: 'Friends and neighbors,' but none of my friends are on my local draft board." Indeed, he might have characterized the board members as enemies, as his board chairman referred to Bond as a "nigger" and admitted that he had "always regretted" that the board had "missed [drafting] him." Southern draft boards caught many other civil rights workers whose challenges to Dixie's racial practices and institutions clearly earned them induction notices.[12]

African Americans' inability to join reserve and National Guard units compounded the inequalities of the draft since access to reserve and guard units essentially served as safe alternatives for middle-class whites. Although this unfairness was true nationally, it was especially apparent in the South. As the war got under way in 1965, Alabama, with 30 percent of its population black, had fourteen African American guards. Georgia had three. Four years later Mississippi, composed of 42 percent African Americans, had enrolled one black among the state's 10,365 guard slots.[13]

Responding to these economic and racial conditions, southern blacks also went to war for diverse reasons. Commissioned and noncommissioned military careerists, much like their white contemporaries, viewed the war as a patriotic and professional obligation. Colonel Fred Cherry, who had grown up as one of eight children in rural Virginia, had joined the air force in 1951 to become a pilot. Marine sergeant major Edgar A. Huff, the first black marine to gain that rank, had been earning $1.40 per day when he joined the corps in Birmingham in 1942. Navy captain Norman A. McDaniel from Fayetteville, North Carolina, had earned his commission in ROTC at North Carolina A&T in the mid-1960s and voiced this sense of duty. Upon learning in early 1966 that he would be flying missions over North Vietnam, McDaniel "felt good, really proud to be part of it. The Communists were attempting to take over South Vietnam. I felt that we had a good cause." African American women careerists acted from similar motives. Doris I. "Lucki" Allen had graduated from Tuskegee Institute and joined the army in 1950. An intelligence specialist, Allen volunteered for Vietnam duty in 1967 because she was a "soldier" and the "country was at war." She also believed she had an "expertise that was needed . . . that my intelligence would save lives." Pinkie Houser, the youngest child of an Alabama cotton farmer, reenlisted for six years as a personnel sergeant in the army in 1968 in return for assignment to Vietnam. It was what Houser "had to do" since she did not believe she was "serving" her country adequately through her work at Fort Knox.[14]

Other, primarily younger, black enlisted men more closely represented the bulk of southern African American soldiers who served in Vietnam. Charles Strong, the son of migrant workers in Florida, was drafted when he could not raise the twenty-seven dollars needed to enroll in junior college. Strong had no clear opinion on the war but considered "two years in the service" preferable to "five years in prison." Moreover, he had a duty and an obligation, having "enjoyed a whole lot of fruits" of American society. Reginald "Malik" Edwards from Louisiana was the first person in his family to graduate from high school, but he had no money for college: "I only weighed 117 pounds, and nobody's gonna hire me. . . . So the only thing left to do was to go into the service." He chose the marines because they were "bad"; they "built men. Plus just before I went in they had all these John Wayne movies on every night."[15]

Edwards's references to building men and John Wayne were consistent with the assertion that the "U.S. military was selling manhood during the Vietnam War, and African American men were eager to buy." Lewis Lowe II, whose Alabama parents had to sign for his enlistment in the marines at the age of seventeen, acted on a similar "John Wayne complex." While admitting his naïveté and demonstrating the military's appeal to black manhood, Terry Whitmore was more blunt. He admitted to being a "dumb motherfucker" when he graduated from high school in Memphis in 1966, wondering what "Sam [would] want with me. A nobody. Just a poor-ass black on the block. Sam doesn't even know I'm alive." Whitmore promptly learned otherwise. Facing the draft, he opted for three years in the marines, "the *real* military," rather than any "cheap imitations."[16]

Bill Henry Terry Jr. from Birmingham quit high school and enlisted at the age of nineteen. Terry recognized he could not go to college and would almost certainly be drafted, but he also envisioned the military as the career through which he could support his wife and young son. Robert L. Mountain from Georgia naively left Savannah State College to realize his dream of playing trombone in the army band. He ended up in Vietnam as an army mortar man. In a declaration that could have been substituted for that of Bob Foley, the white Alabamian, Luther C. Benton III from Portsmouth, Virginia, went to Vietnam "to see what the war was all about. And I thought that if we were there, then it must be right. We have to stop Communism before it gets to America. I was just like all the other dummies."[17]

Mexican Americans in South Texas were, like African Americans, more likely to be poor, to have received substandard education, and to have little chance of going to college. They also faced discriminatory draft boards overwhelmingly composed of whites. Therefore, they too were more likely to be drafted or to enlist under threat of the draft. Most simply accepted this fate, but many did so with the hope also held by poor southern whites and blacks that the military offered the prospect of upward social mobility—a way up and out—and greater equality. Where else, asked one "cotton picker," could he have the "freedom" to tell "white people what to do"? The majority of Mexican Americans also believed, as S. B. Sanchez, a Texan, wrote from Vietnam, that the United States was a "great country" and that all Americans should be ready to "bear arms . . . to defend our freedom and heritage." Last, but certainly not least important, "warrior patriotism" was a central facet of Mexican American culture. Roy Benavidez, who was wounded in Vietnam, explained, "It was important to me to prove that I wasn't afraid of anything, much less anybody." When Douglas MacArthur Herrera challenged this ethos and refused orders for Vietnam, his father, a proud World War II veteran, was aghast, since no Herrera had ever "refused to serve his country." The elder Herrera was convinced their family would "never live it down" and would "probably have to move out of Texas to get over the embarrassment and humiliation." The impact of these economic and social conditions and Mexican American attitudes was devastating. Chicanos composed 10–12 percent of the population of Arizona, California, New Mexico, and Texas but incurred nearly 20 percent of those states' casualties in Vietnam from 1961 through 1969. The figures for Texas were even worse: 22 percent for January 1961–February 1967 and 25 percent for December 1967–March 1969.[18]

Upon their arrival in South Vietnam, southern soldiers, like their fellow American comrades, confronted a vastly different climate and culture. Despite coming from a warmer climate than most of their US counterparts, they too complained of the intense heat. Ann Powlas, an army nurse, recalled that it was "hot and humid in North Carolina" but "nothing compared" to what greeted her as she deplaned at Tan Son Nhut air base. The Vietnamese people and culture were even more foreign than the tropical climate. Although southerners had just left some of the poorest parts of the United States, they were shocked and appalled at Vietnamese living conditions and lifestyles. Again, like other Americans, southerners repeatedly commented on the stench that derived variously from mixtures of diesel fuel, animal and human waste, and cooking or rotten fish. Marine rifleman William U. Tant remembered landing at Danang on Christmas 1967: "It was hot, it stunk. I guess it was the buffalo crapping in that dirty rice paddy water. . . . And I thought, this is for real and I realized I didn't really want to be there. I wanted to be home in Alabama, pulling corn for my daddy." Ted A. Burton, an army medic from Tennessee, had a similar experience while riding in the back of a truck near Bien Hoa. Burton saw "pigs and hogs" running "through the houses," and "about the first thing" he noticed "was a woman walking along the side of the road" who "just pulled up her britches leg and went to the bathroom. It was the stinkingest place I ever experienced. It was nasty. I didn't know what to think. I . . . never knew nothing like that existed." Pinkie Houser was equally appalled to find that the poverty-stricken Vietnamese ate fried roaches, dogs, and rats.[19]

American soldiers received virtually no training for interacting with Vietnamese civilians in this exceedingly alien country and culture. To do so in the midst of a guerrilla war in which US troops had great difficulty distinguishing the Vietcong from the remainder of the population produced a range of responses. Some Americans ended up hating all Vietnamese. Houser explained, "I shouldn't hate them but again I think I have reason to because of the war." A Tennessee veteran agreed that he "hated" not just the enemy but South Vietnamese generally. He complained that while the United States "was over there fighting the damn war for them," the South Vietnamese were "lazy" and "wanted somebody to wait on 'em, take care of 'em." While he and other US troops fought the war, the apparently ungrateful South Vietnamese were "spittin' at us, throwing rocks at us." A former Florida soldier agreed that the US allies "didn't want us in Vietnam—they didn't even want their own country. They wouldn't fight for it."[20]

Other southerners, while maintaining appropriate vigilance, even distrust, toward South Vietnamese civilians, had much greater sympathy for their plight. According to one Texan, "The trouble is, no one sees the Vietnamese as people. . . . Therefore, it doesn't matter what you do to them." Lieutenant John S. Candler from Atlanta recognized "those poor people were caught in the middle." They just "wanted . . . to be left alone by us, the NVA, and the VC so they could farm their rice." Another southern officer agreed, "They didn't care who ran the government. . . . The important things in their life [were] their water buffalo, their children, and their ancestors that were buried in that area." A Tennessee trooper concluded, "They're people just like us. Wanting to live, . . . wanting to be happy."[21]

Dixie's soldiers were especially concerned about the children caught in the war zone. One officer remembered the children in an orphanage near Duc Hoa who were "so deprived and pitiful, they kinda tugged at your heartstrings." Manny Valdez used his "spare time to work with children in friendly villages. . . . They were brown-faced; they reminded me of my brothers and sisters and cousins." Southern nurses had a similar response. Eunice Splawn from Spartanburg, South Carolina, recalled that "you could lose your heart" to a wounded child, but she also warned there were others who could not be trusted. They would "absolutely rip the watch off your arm" or even "come up to you and throw a Molotov cocktail." Children, like their parents, were caught between the Vietcong and their adversaries.[22]

Southern soldiers had no such ambivalent response to the Army of the Republic of South Vietnam (ARVN). Some agreed with General Westmoreland, who believed that the South Vietnamese soldiers were "doing their best" and had "progressed to a point" in 1967 that enabled the general to "visualize a U.S. withdrawal strategy." Southerners who shared Westmoreland's assessment pronounced the ARVN "good soldiers," especially those with the "proper training," but most of Dixie's troops offered far less positive characterizations. They viewed the ARVN as noisy, undisciplined, untrustworthy, "lazy bastards" who were "not too keen on combat" and "would probably run" rather than fight. A Tennessee veteran recalled that the best allied soldiers he encountered "were the former Vietcong that worked for our side," and a marine from the Volunteer State declared that he would "as soon shoot" the ARVN as the "bad guys" since he at least knew what the latter were "gonna do." Without disagreeing with these scathing indictments, other southerners acknowledged that the young South Vietnamese soldiers had little idea what they were fighting for. All the common ARVN soldier understood was "that he was separated from his family" and likely to die for no clear cause or reason. By 1968, ARVN troops "were tired. . . . They didn't care."[23]

In contrast, southerners recognized that the Vietcong and NVA cared deeply. After watching a wounded Vietcong woman with a gunshot wound to the stomach walk off of a mountain near Danang, William Tant concluded, "If the women are this tough, how in the hell are we going to beat the men?" The North Vietnamese reminded this Memphis marine of his conception of "the old southern [Confederate] troops. . . . They was fighting for a cause they believed in and they just wasn't going to give up." Numerous other southern soldiers agreed. Louisiana lieutenant Richard A. Sones considered the NVA forces he opposed in the Plain of Reeds between Saigon and the Cambodian border to have been "patient. . . . well equipped . . . well disciplined" and prepared to "fight to the very end." He was especially impressed by the enemy soldiers who hid "by lying under water, flat on their backs, breathing through a reed." If the blast from a US air-boat blew them out of the water, "they would come up fighting." It was "the most incredible sight" Sones had ever witnessed and led him to doubt that "you could ever find another army that disciplined." Charles Strong, an army machine gunner, described an equally compelling story of an NVA soldier, "the bravest dude I had ever seen," who held out in a tunnel for two hours despite numerous shrapnel wounds. He refused to "give up. . . . This man was willing to die for what he believed in." Marine lieutenant Joe Biggers marveled similarly at a wounded enemy soldier tied to a tree so as to continue fighting to the death. These opponents were truly "hard core," willing to "do anything to win." Although less well trained and far less well equipped than the NVA, the Vietcong were elusive, skilled at camouflage and constructing booby traps, excellent marksmen, and also "terribly dedicated"—"very sneaky, . . . dirty, . . . tenacious." A Tennessee veteran added another critical consideration: "Our enemy had been practicing war for a hell of a lot longer than we had. . . . They grew up at on-the-job training. . . . Hell, you were in their back yard. . . . They knew what it was all about."[24]

Like their motivations for going to Vietnam and their impressions of their Vietnamese allies and enemies, southerners had diverse experiences in the war zone. Marine rifleman William Tant from Memphis captured this diversity perfectly when he observed, "Vietnam was not one war. It was a bunch of nasty little wars." As was true for Americans overall, southern foot soldiers experienced the most intense combat. Dixie's ground pounders repeatedly complained of a lack of sleep and exhaustion. Both officers and enlisted men reported that they regularly slept no more than four or five hours per night. Lieutenant Richard F. Timmons from Alabama was up three or four times during the night to check on his troops before rising at 4:30 A.M. for the day. Lieutenant John Robbins never turned in for the night "until everybody had a place . . . below the surface of the ground." Richard C. Ensminger, a marine forward observer, recalled that he was "fortunate to get four hours of sleep a night" and that he often became "so tired" that he "started to act by instinct alone" in a war that had "become a sort of perpetual-motion killing machine." Richard Sones, a platoon leader in the Mekong Delta, sometimes went "24 to 36 hours without even sleeping."[25]

Long, hard days were not confined to those in the field. Army nurses routinely worked twelve-hour days, six days a week, and twenty-hour days were not uncommon. During Tet 1968, Brenda Sue Castro labored for "seventy-two straight hours without a break" at the Eighth Field Hospital in Nha Trang. Even the Tennessee army officer who helped oversee food distribution to one hundred thousand soldiers from the 504th Field Depot at Cam Ranh Bay worked twelve-hour days, six and a half days per week. At both recreation centers and on trips to fire bases, the Red Cross "Donut Dollies" regularly put in ten-hour days. Regardless of duty assignment, virtually all US soldiers stationed in country, even those on the large bases, "felt under . . . threat all the time." As one officer observed, the enemy could launch mortars and rocket attacks against "our compound, even . . . the mess hall," while his unit was "having noon chow."[26]

With these long hours and the constant threat came the horrors of combat, injury, and death. Paul Aton, a Kentucky private who died in Vietnam, told his father in a July 1968 letter, "Combat isn't like it is in the movies or TV. We get dirtier. . . . When you get hit there is a lot of blood and the men fight Hard on both sides, harder in real life though. . . . When you hump you sweat . . . in the movies you don't see any sweat. Or here people don't just die like flies. They have to fight to fall and they don't give up. . . . War is hell." Other soldiers remembered wearing the "same boots, the same shirt, the same pair of pants, the same socks," during the first three months in Vietnam, or regularly spending sixty days in the field interspersed with only three days to "stand down" in the rear area.[27]

While in the field, the prospect of injury and death was ever-present. Some soldiers, like Paul Aton, did not survive. Others, such as George Watkins from Big Stone Gap, Virginia, or George Riels from Petal, Mississippi, survived but were horribly wounded. Watkins lost both eyes and both legs to a land mine, and Riels lost his left leg and was partially paralyzed after being shot. Even those who escaped such devastating injuries hardly returned unscathed. Their emotional scars could be exceedingly debilitating. Lewis Lowe, a black marine demolitions expert from Alabama, endured the incalculable stress of searching on his hands and knees for deadly booby traps and checking the internal organs of dead comrades for enemy-planted explosives. Mike Hill, a navy corpsman, recalled the "blood smell" and his stiffened, blood-soaked pants feeling like "cardboard"; and Ted Burton, an army medic who spent virtually all of his year in the field, believed "a good medic cared about his buddies and he got to them no matter what was happening." Robert Strong asked, "Can you imagine walking around policing up someone's body? . . . Maybe you find his arm here, his leg over there. Maybe you have to dig up someone's grave."[28]

Army nurses were also horrified at the injuries and deaths. A twenty-two-year-old Tennessee woman with no prior intensive care training confronted "total care patients" with "gross infections." The young soldiers were "mutilated" but still conscious. She "ended up being their nurse, their mother, their sister, their girlfriend, their wife," and the "emotional attachment . . . was just tremendous." Brenda Sue Castro was similarly appalled by the formerly "healthy, ordinary kids . . . who were being blown apart," and Pinkie Houser, a personnel officer, could not forget the terrible "smell of human flesh burning" as the limbs of American amputees were incinerated behind the hospital.[29]

Killing another human being was particularly traumatic. David Disney, a Kentucky soldier, described his first kill, a Vietcong who had gotten through the wire and was crawling toward Disney's bunker: "God Dad I didn't want to kill him, I shot the M-60 with a long burst and he fell. Dad I cried like a baby after it was all over." Our captain "shook my hand and said I did a great job. Is killing great?" Manuel Valdez refused to follow orders to "eliminate the prisoners" his squad was holding near the DMZ in 1967. Still, "bodies were scattered throughout the village. Women and children were spared, for the most part. . . . Vietnam was a very brutal war that hardened a lot of people to the value of human life." Robert Strong agreed and added that the brutality could make a soldier into "an animal" who began "to like to kill." In retrospect, Strong was appalled that he could have "walked over" an NVA body and said, "'That's one motherfucker I don't have to worry about.' . . . It made me feel good to see a human life laying down there dead."[30]

Religion was a prominent feature in the responses of many southern soldiers to these experiences. After being shot with a paralyzing round, the "first thing" George Riels did was "pray. I wasn't no saint, but I was a Christian and was saved . . . and I read the Bible almost every night. I just turned it over to God" and declared, "Lord, it's in your hands." Ben Purcell, an infantry officer captured in South Vietnam and taken to Hanoi, where he survived sixty-two months of captivity (including the repercussions of two escape attempts), endured because of the "love that I knew Anne had for me and our children, and the love that I knew Christ had for both of us." Fred Cherry, a fighter pilot and the senior African American POW, cited a similar Christian faith: "No matter how rough the tortures were, no matter how sick I became, . . . I would just pray to the Supreme Being each morning for the best mind to get through the interrogations, and then give thanks each night for makin' it through the day." For another black POW, Captain Norman Alexander McDaniel from North Carolina, the nearly seven years' captivity tested his faith. After several years of fervent prayer and continued imprisonment, he asked: "Lord, why am I here? Why do you do this to me when I've been trying to do right all this time?" Following additional prayer and reflection, McDaniel decided he might not return to the United States "in the flesh, alive." He came to understand "the children of God were not exempted from the trials and tribulations" of life. Thereafter, he decided, "if they take my mortal life, I'm still okay." Houston Matthews, whose faith led him to become an Episcopal priest following his service as a marine rifleman, also questioned "the whole idea of war and why God could let these things happen." Unlike McDaniel, he "didn't feel that God was doing something terrible to us, but rather that we were doing something terrible to each other." As with McDaniel, his faith prevailed. Following an injury in which he lost an eye and a leg, Matthews believed his "spiritual side . . . allowed the emotional and psychological sides of me to be healed."[31]

Race and racial attitudes were also integral to southern soldiers' responses to service in Vietnam. Although one Tennessee soldier declared "as far as racial discrimination, the only race that was considered inferior were the Vietnamese," the tensions among Americans were also evident. In the throes of combat, American whites and blacks generally cooperated and worked effectively together, as the mutual pursuit of survival rendered the battlefield a "place of relative equality." Away from the battlefield, their interactions were often far more tense and conflicted, especially after 1968 and Reverend King's assassination and as the war slowly wound down and many more politically radical blacks were sent to Vietnam. African Americans bridled at southern whites flying Confederate flags, the frequency of racial slurs, and, in the wake of King's death, the spectacle of anti–civil rights white soldiers donning Klan dress at Que Viet and burning crosses at Cam Ranh Bay. One black soldier declared he should fight under the "American flag" rather than having "to serve under the Confederate flag, or with it," and another believed "some stupid people are still fighting the Civil War." Black soldiers also contended with an overwhelmingly white officer corps, a military justice system that led to African Americans being more frequently charged and imprisoned, and the reality of blacks seeing combat in numbers that exceeded their proportion of the American population. Southern whites in turn complained of African American clannishness, the brothers' use of elaborate black power salutes and handshakes, blaring soul music, and posters depicting Malcolm X or black fists.[32]

Within this general framework, interesting and provocative individual relationships and reactions developed on both sides of the racial divide. Some of these interactions conformed to long-standing patterns of southern race relations. A white soldier from Louisiana informed Sergeant Allen Thomas Jr. that he would not "take orders from a nigger," and a Mississippi trooper told Thomas, "For a nigger you're a pretty good guy. If you were white we could be friends." Other interactions were more positive. Marine first lieutenant Archie "Joe" Biggers from Colorado City, Texas, found that "southerners at the first sign of a black officer being in charge of them were somewhat reluctant. But then, when they found that you know what's going on and you're trying to keep them alive, then they tried to be best damn soldier you've got." Two white southerners confirmed Biggers's perception. William Tant recalled the esteem in which he held Levi Jones, his black staff sergeant: "I probably have more respect for that man . . . than any man I've ever met in my life, which is ironic, me being from Alabama and supposed to be prejudiced." Shortly after Reverend King's assassination in March 1968, Sergeant Philip Woodall, a member of the 101st Airborne, wrote to his dad in Memphis recounting the death of his black lieutenant, Gary Scott, from Rochester, New York. Woodall confided, "He was a fine man, a good leader." While the United States mourned the death of Dr. King, Woodall would "mourn the deaths of the real leaders for peace, the people who give the real sacrifice, people like Lt. Scott."[33]

On an even more basic level of daily interaction, black and white southerners sometimes revised their racial perspectives. Robert Strong from Florida grieved when Joe, "an all right guy from Georgia," was killed. Joe "talked with that 'ol dude' accent" and came off as "a redneck, ridge runnin' cracker. But he was the nicest guy in the world." During time away from the front, Joe tended to drink and "go around the brothers and say, 'Hi there brother man.'" When the black soldiers immediately bristled, Strong intervened and assured them "Joe was all right" even though "his accent was just personal." Charlie Earl Bodiford, a marine machine gunner from Alabama who "had been brought up with that line between blacks and whites," also moved beyond his initial prejudices. Bodiford's response was stereotypical when his black squad leader came into his tent, lay down, and put his head on the Alabamian's stomach. Bodiford screamed, "What the hell is this? I'll tear your ass out of its frame. . . . I ain't your goddamn pillow." His black squad leader replied, "No problem, man," and left. Another white, who had observed the clash, suggested, "That might be the same dude who saves your ass someday." After some reflection, Bodiford agreed and recognized "there was no racial trouble in the company," that everyone "was going to eat the same C-rations . . . and we didn't have any room for trouble."[34]

This reality of no room for trouble was particularly evident to Colonel Fred V. Cherry from Virginia and Lieutenant Porter A. Halyburton from neighboring North Carolina when they were thrown together in a North Vietnamese POW camp. Halyburton, a navy navigator in a 4F4B Phantom fighter, was shot down on October 17, 1965; five days later, Cherry, the USAF pilot of an F-105, suffered the same fate. Cherry was the first African American POW. In late November, the North Vietnamese put these two American flyers together in the same cell in Cu Loc Prison in southwest Hanoi. They lived together for the next eight months. Their captors told Halyburton, "You must care for him. You must be his servant"; and Cherry believed that the Vietnamese did this purposefully, expecting to exploit the anticipated friction between the black and white soldiers, who could not "possibly get along." There were initial tensions. Cherry suspected that Halyburton was a "French spy" meant "to bleed me of information." Having encountered no black pilots or officers in the navy, Halyburton needed time to be sure that Cherry's story was genuine. After several days of trading probing questions, the two built mutual trust.[35]

Both men were in terrible condition as they began their time together. Although Halyburton had far fewer physical injuries, "the constant interrogation and indoctrination" had taken a toll, leaving him "about at the end of my rope." Cherry had endured the same regimen, but his plight was significantly worsened by the extensive injuries he had suffered while parachuting from his plane—including a broken shoulder, wrist, ankle, and ribs and extensive infections that followed a nonsterile operation.[36]

Completely contrary to North Vietnamese expectations, the two southerners proved crucial to one another's survival. Halyburton credited Cherry with turning his "life around." Upon seeing the black officer, he said to himself, "God, this guy's in a lot worse shape than I am and he's not complaining." Having been in isolation and "out of touch with other people," Halyburton had begun "to feel pretty sorry" for himself, but "taking care of Fred gave me a sense of purpose outside of my own survival." Indeed, the union was "liberating" and moved Halyburton toward the idea of a POW "brotherhood" in which the prisoners "would do anything for each other." Cherry, in turn, had no doubt that the white navigator was "responsible" for his survival. Over their eight months together, Halyburton shared his food with Cherry, used his clothes to cushion the terrible sores all over Cherry's body, took Cherry to the slop bucket, and literally washed him from head to toe. When they were separated after those eight months, Cherry endured the "most depressing evening of my life." He had "never hated to lose any body so much" in his "entire life."[37]

Although service in Vietnam fostered respect and even friendship among individual southern whites and blacks, the war experience yielded no such general transformation in southern society. Unlike in the aftermath of the two world wars, no returning black veterans were murdered while still in uniform, but they hardly returned to a suddenly more accepting South. In 1967 a white Alabamian interviewed in Vietnam declared he would "rather go into battle" with blacks "than anyone else," but he also admitted that once back home he would have virtually no interaction with African Americans. Black veterans often experienced southern responses more hostile than the absence of social interaction. After service in the infantry, Roosevelt Gore returned to live and work in his hometown of Mullins, South Carolina. When he attempted to shoot pool in the Mullins Grill, the owner informed him, "Niggers ain't allowed to come in here," and he was promptly arrested and charged with inciting a riot. Another black veteran in uniform stopped at a roadside café en route to Fort Bragg, only to be denied service at this ostensibly "private club." When he asked if that designation was a way to exclude "black people," the proprietor admitted, "OK, we don't serve niggers." An all-white VFW post in northern Kentucky refused to accept Sergeant Allen Thomas as a member, directing him instead to join a black post. Retired sergeant major Edgar Huff encountered even greater hostility after he settled in Hubert, North Carolina, near Camp Lejeune. As he, his wife, and some friends sat on the patio of the Huff house, four white marines drove by and threw white phosphorous grenades at the house and cars. A naval investigator later told Huff the attackers said they "didn't understand how a nigger could be living" in such a nice house, "sitting out there eating on a nice lawn, under the American flag" the sergeant major flew daily.[38]

Just as southerners had served in diverse capacities in Vietnam, they also had varying reactions to the war and its personal impact. Virtually all would have agreed with Ernest Peoples, a helicopter pilot from Beaumont, Texas, who concluded, "A person cannot go through a war, . . . and live with death every day and not be affected by it." Captain Rodney R. Chastant from Mobile concurred in an October 1967 letter to his parents: "As I read your letters, I am a normal person. I'm not killing people, or worried about being killed." Brenda Sue Castro asserted that the war had caused "every Vietnam nurse" she knew to grow "old before her time," and Ann Powlas, a navy nurse from North Carolina, regretted that "you never really fit in again." For Chastant, who died in battle three days after writing home, the impact was profoundly physical. Other southern warriors, such as George Watkins and George Riels, lost their sight or limbs. Still others simply lost weight. Richard C. Ensminger went to Vietnam weighing 235 pounds and returned at 175, "all solid muscle and red clay dirt." Robert L. Powell's physical transformation was comparable, 230 pounds to 170. But even for those who survived seemingly unscathed physically, the emotional toll could be far reaching.[39]

Most southerners took pride in their Vietnam service. Two army officers were representative. William D. Poynter from Arkansas considered his missions "important and vital to the U.S. Forces" and felt "very successful and proud" of his service even though the war's outcome was akin to a "bad dream." Joe N. Ballard, an African American platoon leader, was similarly chagrinned over the North Vietnamese victory but felt no "embarrassment about participating"; to the contrary, he "was quite proud to have served in Vietnam." Southern enlisted men echoed these sentiments. James Bussey from Childress, Texas, and his family members were "very proud" of his service, that he was "a soldier and a veteran"; and Manny Valdez refused to "get involved in weighing the good and bad of the war" but "was proud that I had fought for my country." Barry Campbell, a Kentucky infantry soldier, had given "110 percent the entire thirteen months and six days" and returned home with "no regrets at all, and if I had to do it again tomorrow I wouldn't even hesitate."[40]

For those who assessed the war's good and bad more closely, most would have agreed with John Candler, who opined, "Our intentions were good, . . . just as good as they've been in most other wars." George Riels concurred that the United States had intervened "for a good cause." Even Jane Hodge, a nurse from North Carolina, who conceded that being "in Vietnam might not have been right," "knew" that caring for American soldiers was entirely justified. Not all southerners agreed, and those who viewed the war less positively were often more outspoken and more vocal. Phil Woodall, a sergeant in the 101st Airborne, spoke to the war's seeming pointlessness. He wrote his dad, "The country is no gain that I can see. . . . We're fighting, dying, for a people who resent our being over here. The only firm reason I can find is paying with commie lives for U.S. lives." Lieutenant Marion Lee Kemper, a marine platoon leader, was even more derogatory in summarizing "an abortion called Operation Jackson" in September 1966: "It was 'very successful' since we managed to kill a few probably innocent civilians, found a few caves and burned a few houses, all in a driving rainstorm." A Tennessee noncom concluded that simply coming "back alive" made him "a winner." Vietnam had been "like a bad marriage. Whatever the price, just pay it," and get out. William S. Norman, a black naval officer from Virginia who served three tours, rose to the rank of lieutenant commander, and worked for Secretary of the Navy Admiral Elmo Zumwalt as a special assistant for minority affairs, asked far more probing questions by 1969 about the war's origins and the rationale for US involvement. While agreeing with US policymakers that "there was Communist aggression from the North," he deemed it "less clear" that the war was "a matter of Chinese or Soviet orchestration" as opposed to "the North and South going at it in a struggle for unification" or a "war of national liberation." Given this ambiguity regarding the role of containment in Vietnam, Norman began to doubt whether the "war was worth the American effort," the destruction, and the deaths in support of an "increasingly corrupt" South Vietnamese government.[41]

The bulk of southern soldiers, like residents of Dixie more generally, were convinced that the war could and should have been won. Donald L. Whitfield, an Alabama machine gunner, may have expressed the most unvarnished white southern perspective when he claimed, "White Americans, can't nobody whip our ass. We're the baddest son of a bitches on the face of this earth." How then was the North Vietnamese, Vietcong victory to be explained? Southern warriors, both black and white, offered an array of explanations, most of which invoked variations on the "stab-in-the-back" theme. Fred Cherry asserted that the United States should have bombed "the military targets early [in the war]. . . . The war just went the way it did because the military was not allowed to win it." William Norman agreed that the United States had fought in "a half-hearted way," and a host of southerners elaborated. Some agreed with Cherry on the need for "saturation bombing" of the North in 1965; others emphasized the "restrictions" imposed by the "politicians back in Washington" concerning not just bombing targets but also the rules for firing on the enemy or pursuing the NVA and VC into Cambodia, Laos, and North Vietnam.[42]

Southern officers found military personnel policies frustrating, even self-defeating. Richard Timmons, the CO of an infantry battalion, decried "the continuous conveyor belt of people coming and going," which inhibited training and assessing his troops. Linwood Burney agreed after serving under three battalion commanders in a year. He believed it took "two or three months . . . to understand" their orders and intentions. Timmons also criticized the higher commands for being too "damn worried about management and poor resources" and too focused on "math formulas." They needed to study "what causes soldiers to do their jobs. . . . how . . . you make those young studs hang with you whenever things fall apart."[43]

Numerous southern soldiers also joined the majority of their neighbors at home in condemning antiwar protestors and men who avoided the fight. Protestors, they believed, had weakened the war effort by helping convince the US government not to provide the necessary materials. Demonstrators who carried NVA flags or desecrated the American flag "were aiding the enemy" and "killing . . . Americans." Opponents of the war had pressured the United States "to walk out and have a no-win policy." Pete Hendricks, a North Carolina fighter pilot, considered the protestors "lesser creatures" who had "failed" to meet their responsibilities to their country. The most bitter southern warriors would have lined the "draft dodgers" and "Jane Fonda . . . up against a wall" and shot them. But, as was the case with the general southern public, some soldiers were far less harsh. Many had no strong reaction—"I don't remember having an opinion. I guess we were too scared"—or credited the demonstrators with recognizing that the war was a "wasted enterprise" the nation needed to end. Others believed that it took "a lot of guts" for dissidents to go to Canada or Sweden and potentially forfeit US citizenship and their futures. John Candler Jr. offered a thoughtful and ambivalent afterthought: "I can't fully forgive the guys who got out of it. What right did they have to decide not to go over there? On the other hand, if the war was a wasted effort, and if the American people were not behind it, you've got to wonder, are the guys who went to Canada the smart ones? . . . In retrospect they may look like they made the right moral decision because of the way we conducted the war and let it be lost."[44]

General William Westmoreland, easily the most important southern officer in the Vietnam War, agreed with Dixie's troops that American soldiers should take "unmitigated pride" in their service since "it was not they that lost the war." The conflict had not been "lost on the battlefield," and "the record of the American military services of never having lost a war [was] still intact." After Westmoreland graduated from West Point in 1936 as the class first captain, the academy's highest honor, there followed distinguished service in World War II, important associations with Generals James Gavin and Maxwell Taylor, and stints at the Pentagon and as superintendent at the US Military Academy from 1960 to 1963. He was considered one of the army's three top generals on the eve of major US military intervention in Vietnam, when Johnson and McNamara made him the MACV commander in January 1964. In addition to his exemplary record and Taylor's endorsement, Westmoreland gained favor with Johnson as a fellow southerner and with McNamara because of his organizational skills, efficiency, and Harvard Business School degree, qualities that led some to dub him the "corporate general."[45]

Westmoreland's handling of the war has elicited intense criticism, prompting one author to brand him "The General Who Lost Vietnam." According to this critique, Westmoreland used his broad discretion as commander to adopt the disastrous US attrition strategy, with its emphasis on search-and-destroy operations and body counts, and to neglect the task of training the ARVN and implementing pacification measures such as rooting out the VC infrastructure and attracting the loyalty of the rural South Vietnamese through civic action projects. While not entirely without merit, such criticisms are overly harsh. Westmoreland actually devised his basic strategies with the input and approval of the JCS and the US Pacific Command (CINCPAC) and, like the bulk of his US military contemporaries, favored the "American way of war" with its emphasis on offensive operations and the use of technology to destroy the enemy's military capacity. The general understood the need for training the South Vietnamese military and pursuing pacification and instituted these programs along with aggressive efforts to find and destroy the VC and NVA. But pacification was always a secondary, complementary strategy. In addition to his preference for aggressive, offensive operations, the general worried appropriately that the American public would not tolerate an overly long war. Repeatedly asking, "How long have we got to win the war?" he believed that pacification would require too much time and American patience. Westmoreland also fought the war with significant structural impediments. For example, he had no access to the National Guard or the US Army Reserve; could not invade North Vietnam, Cambodia, or Laos; had no authority over the ARVN; and did not have command over US air assets in Vietnam. Even more important, this focus on Westmoreland and various US strategies ignores the weakness of the South Vietnamese polity and military; the abilities and commitment of the North Vietnamese and Vietcong; and the physical, climatic, and cultural environment in which the war was fought—in short, the Vietnamese side of the equation.

Collectively, these factors rendered the war virtually unwinnable, regardless of US strategies.[46]

That said, as US commander for four years, Westmoreland cannot be absolved of all responsibility for the American debacle in Vietnam. He, like Johnson and most Americans, had too much faith in US military power and technology and the military's ability to achieve political ends through the use of force. The general also demonstrated little affinity or understanding of the Vietnamese, North or South, and their all-important cultural traits, historical experiences, aspirations, even failings. Despite his attention to pacification, nation building, and improving the ARVN, he, again like most US military leaders, believed that security had to be established in South Vietnam as a prerequisite to realizing these programs. Achieving this security for the South Vietnamese peasants reinforced his commitment to the American way of war and made search-and-destroy missions and massive use of American firepower the US military's priority. Along with this priority came the devastating impact on both US ground soldiers and civilians in North and South Vietnam, an impact that often undermined the other two strategies in the South. Through his positive, but erroneous, estimates of US progress in Vietnam, Westmoreland also helped President Johnson mislead the American public, especially during late 1967. Indeed, the general's underestimation of North Vietnamese and Vietcong strength and incorrect judgment that the principal communist threat was being directed at Khe Sanh contributed directly to American surprise and disillusionment in response to the Vietcong Tet Offensive launched in early 1968.[47]

None of these personal misjudgments appeared in Westmoreland's interpretation of the war's outcome. Instead, he laid the loss at the feet of others and demonstrated that he recognized neither limits on US power nor the importance of local circumstances. He sought to salvage his military reputation and personal honor, voiced the interpretation of much of the professional military, and expressed many of the "revisionist" arguments for how the war could and should have been won. Rather than calling for a declaration of war and instructing the American public on the gravity of the military situation and the need for sacrifice, President Johnson had downplayed the war and misled the nation. The media had also undermined the war effort. In Westmoreland's opinion, American reporters had lacked the requisite understanding of military matters and emphasized the "negative" and "sensational" aspects of the war rather than portray events accurately. These flaws led the media to misrepresent the US–South Vietnamese victory in repulsing the 1968 Tet Offensive and to devote little attention to "pacification, civic action, medical assistance, the way life went on in a generally normal way for most of the people much of the time." American protestors had further weakened the war effort. By signaling American divisions and "weakness" and a lack of national resolve, they encouraged the North Vietnamese and "helped prolong the war." And the American public more generally lacked the understanding and patience required to sustain and win a war of pacification.[48]

All of these nonmilitary facets of Westmoreland's classic "stab-in-the-back" explanation were important, but he reserved the most scathing critique for Johnson, Secretary McNamara, and other civilians in the White House and Department of Defense. Lacking respect for the military's knowledge and experience, LBJ, McNamara, and civilian bureaucrats had micromanaged the war, denied him the necessary forces, and squandered opportunities for potentially decisive strikes against the VC and North Vietnam. Overall, Johnson and his advisors had, in Westmoreland's opinion, limited the war in two crucial respects. First, the president's gradual escalation of the bombing of North Vietnam, restrictions on eligible targets, and periodic bombing halts had allowed the North Vietnamese to preserve their fighting capacity and to escape the "excruciating pain" that would have led to US-dictated negotiations. Second, by placing Cambodia, Laos, and North Vietnam off-limits for sustained ground operations, LBJ and McNamara had allowed the enemy to retain sanctuaries critical to their survival.[49]

Unlike Johnson and McNamara, who deemed the limited war necessary to avoid a potential nuclear exchange with the Soviets or ground war with China, Westmoreland harbored no such apprehensions. The Sino-Soviet split and the internal turmoil accompanying China's Cultural Revolution rendered these fears unfounded, even "paranoid." The general further asserted that he had been denied the troops needed to implement his strategic vision properly. Despite having an American force of some five hundred thousand at his disposal at the height of the war, Westmoreland lamented never having "enough troops to maintain an American, Allied, or ARVN presence everywhere all the time"—a luxury few commanders have ever possessed. In his most debatable claim, he maintained that US military progress by the fall of 1967 had left the "North Vietnamese . . . in a position of weakness" and that a desperate Hanoi had gone "for broke" in mounting the Tet Offensive in January 1968. In the wake of the unsuccessful communist campaign, Westmoreland sought additional troops to exploit "the enemy's defeat" and destroy North Vietnam's "will to continue the war." To have combined a rapid, forceful response with activation of the US Army Reserves would, Westmoreland declared, have sent an unmistakable "message" to Hanoi that the United States "intended to get the job done with dispatch." Alas, the general's troop request was blocked by the "cut and run people" in Washington. Thus, while attributing the US loss to shortcomings in the American public, press, and civilian leadership, Westmoreland accepted no personal responsibility and admitted to no errors of judgment or execution.[50]

Another southern officer has fared much better in postwar assessments. Lieutenant Colonel Harold G. "Hal" Moore from Bardstown, Kentucky, became one of the most celebrated officers from the Vietnam War, based on his stellar leadership of the Seventh Battalion of the Eleventh Cavalry during the savage battle in the Ia Drang Valley in mid-November 1965. Moore, a 1945 West Point graduate, had served in Korea and later in the 1950s had taken an active role in the development of "air mobility" while working for General James Gavin at the Pentagon. In April 1964 Moore was given the command of a battalion in the newly created Eleventh Air Assault Test Division, which evolved into the Eleventh Cavalry. Moore and Sergeant Major Basil Plumley spent the subsequent fourteen months training their troops for Vietnam with the goal of creating the "absolute best air assault infantry battalion in the world, and the proudest."[51]

When Brigadier General Richard T. Knowles, the assistant division commander of the Seventh Cavalry, called for an operation into the Ia Drang Valley to locate and attack North Vietnamese soldiers in the area, Moore's unit was selected. Indicative of the careful planning that complemented Moore's rigorous training and strict discipline, the colonel had begun reading books on Vietnam long before his deployment, and he and Plumley had carefully walked several of the battle sites in the Pleiku region, where the Vietminh had routed the French. With the mission to "find and kill the enemy," Moore personally flew over the Ia Drang Valley and designated LZ X-ray as the landing zone that would best accommodate the helicopters ferrying his roughly 450 soldiers to the battle. On November 14, 1965, Moore also rode into X-ray on the first chopper. He did so for three reasons: First, he would get a ground-level look at the LZ and could modify the flight and landing plans as needed. Second, Moore would be on the ground with his troops "to see and hear what was happening" and to gather the information necessary for his "instincts to operate correctly." Third, the colonel deemed it critical that he and Plumley accompany the first 80 US troops, who could be badly outnumbered until the remaining Americans arrived over the subsequent four hours.[52]

Moore's concern was well founded, as he and his troops confronted not the anticipated NVA regiment of approximately 1,500 but three regiments, which at times outnumbered the Americans by 12 to 1. With the buildup of US ground troops after July 1965, General Vo Nguyen Giap, the commander of the NVA, sought an opportunity to test his charges against the American forces and their imposing technology and equipment. Upon landing, Moore immediately reformulated his battle plan, sending one company west toward the massive Chu Pong mountain adjacent to the LZ to probe for the enemy and deploying a second company in a defensive posture to block a possible NVA assault. These initial decisions, which could not have been made from a helicopter overhead because of the dense vegetation, prevented the LZ from being overrun before the arrival of the other US soldiers.

After an initial period of quiet, the North Vietnamese launched what became a brutal three-day battle. Moore and his troops, with massive artillery and air support, repulsed the attack, which included human-wave assaults, NVA soldiers strapped into trees for better firing lines, incredible noise that exceeded anything Moore had experienced, blinding smoke and dust, intense heat, and extreme shortages of water. After four hours of sleep on November 13 before the operation began, Moore directed his soldiers for the next forty-eight hours without rest. Major General H. R. McMaster has asserted that Moore's preparation, intelligence, courage and composure under fire, and "adaptive" leadership were decisive. Consistent with his initial actions, Colonel Moore continued to dispatch patrols to detect enemy positions and resisted the temptation to send critically needed soldiers to aid one US platoon that had been cut off and pinned down by the North Vietnamese.[53]

Several of Moore's other decisions during the battle provide insight into McMaster's assessment and the colonel's genuine concern for his men. When medivac helicopters refused to land in the midst of the fighting, Moore personally stood up and directed the landing of Hueys coming to haul out the wounded. After the first day's fighting, Moore and Plumley walked the battalion's perimeter to check on the men and boost their morale. When General Westmoreland summoned Moore to Saigon for a report in the midst of the battle, Moore refused to leave his men. On the last morning after the battle's conclusion, Moore accompanied his men to ensure that no one was left behind or unaccounted for as they searched for the final three missing soldiers. Once safely back to base camp, Moore and Plumley ensured that their men received clean clothes and hot food; and Moore circulated among the troops, "shook every man's hand, and thanked them personally." He also sought out and thanked the artillerymen and helicopter pilots, without whom he and his battalion would not have survived.[54]

Based on the body count and the NVA's withdrawal, Moore and his troops counted the battle at X-ray a victory. According to Moore's calculations, the NVA had suffered 634 deaths, 1,215 wounded, and 6 prisoners. Seventy-nine Americans were killed, and 121 were wounded. When X-ray was combined with the one-day battle at LZ Albany on November 17, in which the NVA mauled the Second Battalion of the Seventh Cavalry, killing 151 Americans and wounding another 121, the enemy also declared victory. Significantly, of the 305 Americans killed in the Pleiku campaign in October and November 1965, of which X-ray and Albany were a part, 122 were from the American South.[55]

The two sides had drawn differing conclusions from the first battle since Dien Bien Phu in which the NVA had massed at division strength. Having confronted the NVA's training, discipline, and zeal, Moore recognized that the United States was fighting "a people who had no more give in them than the wild Scots-Irish frontier folk of Virginia and Tennessee and Kentucky and Texas" and that he and his men faced "an enemy who is going to make this a very long year." Moore and General Kinnard both perceived the difficulty of fighting an enemy who could retreat to sanctuaries in Cambodia, which the NVA regiments had done following LZ Albany. Subsequent analysts have also observed that the NVA had decided when to initiate and end the fighting, the type of initiative the enemy would maintain for the remainder of the war. In contrast, General Westmoreland concluded that the 3,561 NVA killed versus 305 US deaths, a kill ratio of 12 to 1 during the Ia Drang campaign, demonstrated the viability of his attrition strategy—that the United States could wear down the North Vietnamese and Vietcong.[56]

General Giap and his subordinates concluded the exact opposite. The North Vietnamese had purposely sought to test their troops against the United States and its obvious technological superiority. Giap and his military commanders at Ia Drang judged the battles at worst a draw, but a draw they had survived and from which they had learned important tactical lessons, such as the "Grab them by the belt buckle" approach, in which the closer NVA fighters advanced on Americans, the less effective US artillery and air support would be. The NVA also emerged convinced that they would outlast the United States in a limited war, and they were correct.[57]

Like Colonel Moore, the National Guard unit from his hometown of Bardstown, Kentucky, endured a harrowing experience in Vietnam. Activated in April 1968, the Second Battalion of the 138th Artillery shipped out to Vietnam in late October. After several weeks of in-country training and an assignment along Highway One south of Da Nang, Battery C was moved to Fire Base Tomahawk, a few miles farther south, in the spring of 1969. Described as "just a bad hill" by one of the Kentuckians, the fire base had been "cut out of the side of a giant hill." The saddle-shaped encampment was surrounded by high ground on three sides and was further compromised by a railroad tunnel at the bottom of the slope. Appropriately apprehensive, Battery C and a platoon from the 101st Airborne assigned to protect the guns dug in. The 120 artillerymen and their paratrooper protection "never stopped working on their bunkers."[58]

They also deemed a major enemy assault virtually inevitable. Voicing the group's concerns, Jerry Janes asked simply, "When will they hit us?" And Don Parrish remembered talking about "how difficult it would be to defend" Tomahawk against the NVA. They were both prescient. By early summer, Battery C, a highly skilled and efficient unit, had been weakened as some of its original members were transferred and sometimes replaced by troops with drug problems or less diligent work habits. When the expected attack did not materialize, the daily regime of "fire your missions, drink a little beer, watch movies, sleep," and fill sandbags became "routine." The troops may have become complacent. When the heat, the routine, and the lingering anxiety seemed to be taking a toll on morale, the guardsmen decided to have a cookout. Using a three-ton truck, Parrish led an expedition on June 8 to a nearby food supply depot and returned with an ample supply of pilfered hamburger patties, hot dogs, beer, and ice. That evening, on June 8, 1969, the 150 men on Fire Base Tomahawk had a barbecue, followed by the showing of a James Bond movie in the maintenance tent. The evening ended prematurely when a driving rainstorm made it impossible to hear the movie.[59]

Eleven days later, on June 19, the men returned to the maintenance facility to watch *Bonnie and Clyde,* only to be greeted by another downpour. The rainstorm not only interrupted the movie but also made it difficult to hear or see the NVA soldiers who were grouping outside the base for an attack or the virtually naked sappers who were beginning to maneuver and cut through the concertina wire around the base's perimeter. Between 150 and 180 North Vietnamese penetrated the perimeter, where they pummeled the Americans with rocket-propelled grenades, satchel charges, and AK-47s. Nine US soldiers were killed, five of them guards, and another thirty-nine Americans were wounded. While losing at least twenty-five to thirty men, the North Vietnamese destroyed three howitzer artillery guns, an ammunition storage area, five trucks, and three jeeps. Only David Collins's search for late-night chicken soup, which led him to find "gooks in the mess hall" and to alert the other Americans, and the enemy's use of the wrong color flare to summon reinforcements avoided far greater losses.[60]

The battle ended at dawn when the NVA retreated in the face of American helicopter gunships and other choppers dispatched to carry out the dead and wounded. Seeing the battlefield on June 20, Tom Raisor expressed "Disbelief, Shock, Numbness. . . . I took one look and thought we had probably lost half our men. . . . Everybody was sort of stunned, people were running around trying to identify bodies, who was wounded, where they had been taken. . . . You were just thankful you were alive." After treatment for a concussion, Raisor was given the agonizing assignment of body escort to accompany Jim Moore, who had not survived the attack, back to Bardstown. Moore's death and Battery C's losses constituted the National Guard's single deadliest battle during the Vietnam War, and southerners again played a central, if very costly, role.[61]

A southern officer was a central figure in still another illustrative battle, this time in the hotly contested A Shau Valley. Captain John D. (Dave) Blair IV arrived at the A Shau Special Forces camp, located southwest of Hue and about five miles from the Laotian border, on February 9, 1966. He and his team of eight other Americans were charged with training and conducting operations with some two hundred South Vietnamese civilian irregulars under the Civilian Irregular Defense Group (CIDGs). These operations were aimed at obstructing North Vietnamese infiltration into the South. In an area Blair remembered as "probably the most God-forsaken place on earth," the compound rested on the valley floor amid thick elephant grass and adjacent to ridge lands covered with dense jungle vegetation. A "drizzly low ceiling" made resupply and air support difficult, further compromising the site's strategic viability. Blair recalled that the camp sometimes went two or three weeks without any resupply, leaving the allied forces to eat rice balls and meat from their small herd of cattle.[62]

Although the local Vietcong presented no serious threat, Blair quickly recognized that the NVA forces were determined to destroy the special forces camp and to establish uncontested control of the valley. I Corp headquarters denied his request for reinforcements, but the CO of the Fifth Special Forces Group dispatched Captain Sam Carter and another 200 South Vietnamese CIDGs, who arrived on March 7. Blair and Carter commanded a force of 435, 17 of whom were Americans, when the NVA attacked on March 9.

Beginning at about 4:00 A.M., two NVA regiments pounded the camp with intense mortar and artillery fire, while sappers periodically attempted to breach outer defenses with bangor torpedoes and wire cutters. At dawn, the shelling stopped, and the enemy broke through the south wall of the compound. "Mass confusion and pandemonium" and virtually hand-to-hand fighting ensued. No US artillery batteries were in position to offer aid, and cloud cover hampered air support. As the battle raged on March 9, one F-4 jet crashed, and a C-74 helicopter was shot down; but air force sky raiders provided effective support, catching one NVA battalion in the open, and one helicopter was able to extract thirty of the US–South Vietnamese wounded. The US-CIDG forces survived the onslaught, but as the most intense fighting subsided in late afternoon, Blair counted only fifty troops both able and willing to fight, and they were running very low on ammunition. Even after collecting ammunition and grenades from the dead, his forces had only about twenty rounds per person and a total of ten grenades. The NVA resumed shelling the compound at dark and launched another ground assault around midnight. Blair and his troops again survived and weathered another attack the next day, when either subversion or sheer fright prompted a portion of the CIDGs to allow an NVA penetration. During the afternoon of March 10, sixteen helicopters were sent to evacuate the survivors. Blair and Carter remained behind in the compound to divert the enemy's attention and draw fire while the others moved to the landing zone. When the helicopters encountered withering fire and a portion of the CIDGs panicked and attempted to force their way onto the choppers, only sixty men were flown out of A Shau. Now Blair and Carter sought to hold out until nightfall and hoped for further relief. This "relief" came through an order to try and break out of the compound the next morning and move to a designated LZ.[63]

Achieving this tactical movement was complicated by Blair's conflict with a marine lieutenant colonel whose helicopter had been shot down. The colonel and his crew had survived, and he technically became the ranking US officer at A Shau. The marine aviator, who Blair decided was "out of his element," declared that there would be no subsequent rescue attempts and that the survivors should head overland to Thailand. Blair refused and instead moved his forces, almost all of whom were wounded, to the ridgeline overlooking the camp. The next day the marines, including the colonel, followed Blair and his men off the ridgeline and back into the valley, where the marines were extracted. The five remaining Americans and their Vietnamese charges continued to maneuver around the valley during March 11 and 12, when the last of them were lifted out. Blair and the other four US soldiers were picked up on March 12.[64]

Blair, who at one point had gone three days without sleep and two days without water and fought on despite being wounded in the initial attack, admitted to having been "naïve": "I knew a bad battle was coming and quite frankly it never crossed my mind those guys might whip us." After only 188 of the 435 (and 12 of the 17 Americans, all of whom were wounded) survived and the camp was destroyed, he readily acknowledged the enemy had prevailed. The number of estimated enemy killed was 1,000 to 1,200, but they had asserted their dominance in the A Shau Valley. In his first experience being the target of such devastating fire and facing such dire prospects, Blair had performed admirably. He concluded that after you "resign yourself" to likely dying, "you get over being afraid

. . . not that you don't try to survive." But, he continued, well-trained and disciplined soldiers, like the US Special Forces, "keep fighting, . . . in spite of the wounds, in spite of the casualties," and seek "to make it as costly as possible to the enemy." This was precisely what Captain Blair had done, and even the lost battle had positive outcomes. Blair decried "fighting set piece battles in unfavorable conditions," and an MACV assessment of the A Shau defeat agreed. No other special forces camps would be "just abandoned to their fate" without proper support and preparation.[65]

Two southerners were also at the center of the My Lai massacre, the worst American-inflicted atrocity of the Vietnam War. Second Lieutenant William L. (Rusty) Calley, who had been born and raised in Miami, Florida, commanded the First Platoon of Charlie Company, First Battalion, Twelfth Infantry Brigade of the American Division, which was responsible for killing more than five hundred unarmed women, children, and old men at My Lai 4, a hamlet in South Vietnam's Quang Nai Province, on March 16, 1968. The only member of the US military successfully prosecuted, Calley was ultimately convicted by a military court of the premeditated murder of twenty-two Vietnamese noncombatants and sentenced to life in prison. His trial from November 1970 through late March 1971, his subsequent appeals, and his ultimate pardon by President Richard M. Nixon caused great consternation in the United States generally and the South particularly.[66]

Southerners, given their majority support for the war and the military as an institution, strongly supported Calley and, like most Americans, presumed that My Lai was a terrible aberration. Several southern soldiers and recent scholarship have suggested that My Lai was not so anomalous but that US technology and overall strategies killed far more Vietnamese civilians. Terry Whitmore from Memphis recounted a fall 1967 mission in which his platoon followed their captain's orders to "level" a hamlet. The platoon burned the thatched huts and killed all the animals and people, even the children. Two southern marine forward observers spoke to the "body count" as a way of gauging progress and to the lethal impact of American technology. In a letter to the *Jackson Clarion-Ledger* Jim Waide asserted, "With our air power and artillery, we killed, maimed and rendered homeless thousands of civilians. . . . This . . . assured that the rural Vietnamese civilian population would hate us." After calling for air and artillery strikes on a South Vietnamese village, Richard Ensminger recalled that the place was "flattened . . . in less than five minutes. . . . It was a godlike display of power" that left "a burning, smoky ruin of straw and bamboo huts" with "parts of human and animal bodies scattered all around." To the issue of US technology, Ensminger added, "every marine unit in my battalion" was charged with meeting "a quota" of killed VC or NVA soldiers—"It was a meat quota. A lot of civilians who got killed were called VC." In a recent searing book entitled *Kill Anything That Moves,* Nick Turse has provided an extended and convincing investigation that confirms the experiences of these southern warriors and examines how US technology and policies such as the body count, search-and-destroy, and free fire zones led to the deaths of as many as two million Vietnamese civilians.[67]

From the shameful My Lai incident and the more general impact of the American war on Vietnamese civilians, a southerner emerged as the "forgotten hero" who conformed much more closely to the South's concern for honor and duty. Like Calley, Hugh C. (Buck) Thompson was born in 1943, but in Atlanta. He soon moved with his family to Stone Mountain, Georgia, where he was raised, went to high school, and worked on the family and neighboring farms. When Buck was seventeen, his dad accompanied him, as he had done with his older brother, to enlist in the US Navy Reserve. Both brothers were expected to serve in the military as their father had done and continued to do in the reserves. After completing his stint in the navy from 1961 to 1964, Thompson ended one unsatisfying year as a funeral director in Stone Mountain by joining the army and going to Warrant Officer School to become a helicopter pilot.[68]

On the morning of March 16, 1968, he, Larry Colburn, the door gunner, and Glenn Andreotta, the crew chief, were flying over My Lai in a small scout helicopter with the mission of drawing fire and thereby locating the enemy for attacks by Huey helicopter gunships. By 10:15 A.M., after flying over the area for more than two hours, Thompson and his crew had drawn no fire and spotted only one draft-age Vietnamese man. Instead, they saw dozens of bodies scattered around the hamlet— "infants; two-, three-, four-, and five-year olds; women; very old men; but no draft-age people whatsoever." When they observed a "ditch full of bodies," Thompson and his crew reluctantly concluded that the operation had gone terribly wrong. At approximately 11:00 A.M., Thompson landed the helicopter in an effort to aid wounded Vietnamese. His efforts yielded only a verbal confrontation with Calley in which the lieutenant made it clear that actions on the ground were his "show" and that Thompson should "mind his own business." As the chopper lifted off to resume its scout duties, Thompson, Colburn, and Andreotta were horrified to see US troops firing into the ditch and summarily executing additional unarmed Vietnamese.[69]

After another fifteen minutes in the air, Andreotta saw several members of Charlie Company chasing three Vietnamese. Thompson's immediate response was to land the helicopter again, this time between the US troops and a bunker into which the fleeing Vietnamese had crawled. As Thompson jumped out of the helicopter, he ordered Colburn to cover him and fire on the American ground troops if they "open up on me or these people." Fortunately, the other Americans backed away and did not threaten Thompson, who coaxed a total of nine terrified Vietnamese out of the bunker. He now faced a different dilemma: "I couldn't just leave them there, because there was no doubt in my mind that they would have been killed." Unable to fit them into his small helicopter, he called two members of his unit who were piloting the gunships for the morning's mission. While one Huey pilot covered them, the other made two trips to ferry the Vietnamese several miles away from My Lai. Thompson and his crew quickly lifted off after the departure of the second group of refugees, only to see movement in the ditch filled with bodies. Thompson landed a third time, and Andreotta pulled a small child covered with blood and muck from the mass of dead bodies. Thompson then flew the traumatized little girl to a close-by Catholic hospital in Quang Nai.[70]

Following the completion of the day's mission, Thompson returned to the unit's base area at LZ Dottie and reported to his platoon leader that members of Charlie Company had committed "mass murder" by "rounding . . . up" and "herding" unarmed Vietnamese into "ditches and then just shooting them." Thompson subsequently provided the same information to a colonel at the LZ Dottie command post, but his outrage and courage were soon lost in the army cover-up by the commander of the Americal Division. Only in June 1969 would Thompson be summoned to Washington, where he provided the critical eyewitness account of the massacre to the Office of the Inspector General and picked Calley out of a lineup. In the interim, Thompson had completed his tour in Vietnam in August 1968 after his copter was shot down, and he suffered a broken back. When called to Washington, he was serving as a flight instructor at Fort Rucker, Alabama.[71]

Ironically, Thompson's confrontation with Calley and members of Charlie Company led to trouble with Congressmen Mendel Rivers and F. Edward Herbert, who sought to discredit Thompson and derail the army's investigation and prosecution of Calley and others. Despite such efforts, Thompson has been aptly termed a "hero" by Colburn since the pilot was the "ranking man," the "man in charge." William Eckhardt, the military lawyer who oversaw the army's prosecution of those charged with offenses at My Lai, lauded Thompson's "moral courage" and described his actions as an example of "something good" in the midst of a day of "human tragedy," and the official US Army inquiry concluded, "If there was a hero of My Lai, he was it." Thompson proved decidedly uncomfortable with such accolades. He rejected the status of hero, responding that he was only doing his duty. In response to the question of why he took these singular actions, the humble southerner replied, "I can't answer that. There's nothing special about me. I was raised in a small town in Georgia. You don't have to be a rocket scientist to understand that what was going on wasn't right." Thompson embodied a compelling, if hardly a vocal or flamboyant, example of the South's commitment to duty and honor.[72]

The role of duty and honor in the Vietnam experience was also a central facet of novels written by two southern marines. Jim Webb both personified and celebrated the South's "warrior tradition." Although he was born in Missouri in February 1946, the son of a career air force officer, his grandfather, Robert E. Lee Webb, the family's "strong citizen-soldier military tradition," and Webb's southern Scotch-Irish ancestry firmly establish his southern roots. After graduating from the Naval Academy in 1968, he opted for a commission in the marine corps and finished first in a class of 243 in Marine Corps Officers Basic School. He then earned the Navy Cross, the Silver Star, two Bronze Star medals, and two Purple Hearts while serving as a rifle platoon leader and company commander in the An Hoa Basin west of Danang. Since leaving the marines in 1972, he has graduated from Georgetown Law School and served as counsel to the House Committee on Veterans Affairs, assistant secretary of defense, secretary of the navy, and US senator from Virginia; has traveled widely as a journalist and business consultant; and has written prodigiously.

Like so many other southerners, Webb deemed the war winnable. He cites Johnson's refusal to require competent, middle- and upper-class people to serve in the military, LBJ's failure to invade North Vietnam or to properly utilize strategic bombing, press misrepresentation of the war, and domestic protestors for the US defeat. The former marine also considered the war justifiable. He has characterized Vietnam "as probably the most moral effort we have ever made," since the United States "fought for purely ideological reasons," to contain communism. From Webb's perspective, the war's true immorality derived from America's failure to maintain its "moral and political commitment" to South Vietnam and to ensure "that those millions of people" had "the same opportunities as a culture that we have." Having served and been wounded in a war he believed had been lost unnecessarily, Webb, the veteran and southerner, was particularly disturbed by what he considered attacks on the honor of US soldiers. He had gone to Vietnam out of duty to country—"because I was a lieutenant and that was the war and I trusted my government. . . . I didn't fight in Vietnam because I thought the war was right. I fought . . . because I was a unit commander. I felt I was the best they were going to get, and that's where I belonged." To duty, Webb added honor, since "giving your life in a war is the ultimate irretrievable gift to your culture."[73]

His determination to celebrate the southern military tradition and to "restore a sense of honor to the record of servicemen in Vietnam" drove Webb's writing of his first and most acclaimed novel, *Fields of Fire,* which was published in 1978. Indeed, the southern military tradition and devotion to duty, courage, and honor define Robert E. Lee Hodges Jr., the novel's protagonist and Webb's alter ego. Hodges, descended from Scotch-Irish ancestors in the Virginia and Tennessee backcountry, belonged to a family whose forebears fought in every American war from the Revolution on, and his father died at the Battle of the Bulge during World War II. Demonstrating the unmistakable southern concern for tradition and family history, Hodges's grandmother instructed him in the family lore and the military exploits of the Hodges "Ghosts," which he was obligated to emulate. Hodges learned that "man's noblest moment is the one spent on the fields of fire" and vowed to "fight because we have always fought. It doesn't matter who."[74]

As Hodges prepared to embark for Vietnam, "he believed in God but most of all he believed in his father and the other Ghosts. God was all the way in heaven, but the Ghosts were with him everywhere he walked.

. . . If there had been no Vietnam, he would have had to invent one." The young lieutenant was destined for the marines and their demands "because endurance involved pride and pride was honor and he was nothing if he did not retain his honor." Although Hodges "did not relish facing North Vietnamese guns for a year . . . Vietnam was something to be done with, a duty. Not for Vietnam. For honor (and a whisper saying, 'for the South')." And, perhaps most of all, "for the bench seat in the town square" where he could sit and swap war stories with the honored survivors of previous American wars.[75]

Described by one of his soldiers as actually embodying the marine corps' recruiting objective of "Leaders of Men," and as a "goddamn grit" who "don't give anybody any shit and . . . don't take any shit off anybody," Hodges learned his craft well in Vietnam while always making the welfare of his men the first priority. He had no patience for "stateside shit," readily contested orders from superiors that seemed illogical or to endanger his platoon, and expressed regret that one of his men shot and missed when surprised by a dishonorable marine major who put personal advancement and medals before the grunts' well-being. As his tour progressed, Hodges believed he had secured a place among the family's ghosts, and he agreed with Snake, his bravest and most competent subordinate, who found "nobility" in the "pain, the brother-love, the sacrifice" experienced in Vietnam, none of which existed "back in the bowels of the World."[76]

Hodges's honorable behavior was not confined to the battlefield. After suffering wounds from a booby trap, he was flown to Japan to recuperate. Recovered and on his way back to Vietnam, the lieutenant was briefly quartered on Okinawa. While there, he reunited with Mitsuko, the beautiful woman to whom he made love as he awaited the final leg of his first journey to Vietnam. Hodges sought Mitsuko out, proposed, and married her after humbly asking her parents for their blessing. Despite his marriage and love for Mitsuko, Hodges declined a friendly major's offer of a safe assignment on Okinawa and returned to his unit in Vietnam. Duty called, and he missed the "purity" of his "relationship" with his comrades. Thereafter, the ever-gallant warrior and fearless leader died while attempting to save the life of Goodrich, a member of his platoon.[77]

Webb employs Goodrich, the antithesis of Hodges and the southern warrior ethic, to drive home his themes of honor, courage, and duty.

Goodrich, a Harvard dropout, had come to Vietnam, unlike his draft-dodger friends. But once there, the man the others referred to derisively as the "Senator," "Harvard shit bird," and "college Turkey," was appalled at the death and destruction, at the "complete randomness" of the war, at the senseless "futility of what they were doing," at the "killing and being killed" with no change "beyond the tragedy of the immediate event." Goodrich, who repeatedly froze during firefights, ultimately vowed "to maintain his own standards, to preserve a sense of sanity" amid chaos, and reported six of his fellow platoon members for the revenge killing of two Vietnamese prisoners. Goodrich's final battlefield failure led directly to Hodges's death and the Senator's loss of both legs.[78]

Back home in New England, Goodrich told his dad he was "*all* fucked up" both physically and mentally and that his war would "never be over." When he resumed classes at Harvard, he felt no kinship for his fellow students after "his exposure to minds unfogged by academic posturings." Nor was he drawn to his professors, who struck him as "vaporous intellectuals." Although he realized that he had never completely identified with his military comrades, he had gained a far greater respect for and understanding of them. Goodrich lectured fellow students that soldiers placed in impossible situations and directed "to kill for some goddamned amorphous reason" were acting in "utterly logical" ways. It was not "murder" or "even atrocious"; it was simply "a sad fact of life." And when invited to speak at an antiwar rally, he infuriated his audience by berating them for "PLAYING . . . GODDAMNED *GAMES*. . . . HOW MANY OF YOU ARE GOING TO GET HURT IN VIETNAM? I DIDN'T SEE ANY OF YOU IN VIETNAM. I SAW DUDES, MAN. DUDES. AND TRUCK DRIVERS AND COAL MINERS AND FARMERS. . . . WHERE WERE YOU? FLUNKING YOUR DRAFT PHYSICALS? WHAT DO YOU CARE IF IT ENDS? YOU WON'T GET HURT."[79]

Like Jim Webb, Gustav Hasford responded to his marine corps service in Vietnam from a distinctly southern perspective, but the two soldiers and authors shared little else in common. Born in November 1947, Gus Hasford grew up near Russellville in Winston County, Alabama. From this rural southern upbringing he derived a typically southern love of place and heritage. But when he looked back to the Civil War, he reveled in stories of a great-great-grandfather who had refused induction into the Confederate Army while displaying the same opposition to slavery as the majority of residents of Winston County—in short, the same "freedom-minded contrariness" that Hasford subsequently championed in his novels.[80]

Hasford dived into writing at an early age. At fourteen, he was writing stories for two local newspapers and published a piece in *Boys' Life;* at fifteen, he edited his high school paper; and at sixteen he founded and edited three issues of *Freelance,* a literary magazine that he financed with advertisements and a loan from his uncle. At eighteen, when faced with the draft, he enlisted in the marines and, based on his experience with the high school paper and *Freelance,* was made a military journalist. Following an uneventful state-side posting, Hasford requested and received assignment to Vietnam. He served in the First Marine Division Infantry Services Office outside Danang, writing puff pieces on the war and marine actions, and later in Phu Bai, where he helped cover both fighting in Hue during the 1968 Tet Offensive and the operations that broke the NVA encirclement of Khe Sanh. During his ten months of service, he was wounded once and earned the Navy Achievement Medal with a Combat V.

Hasford's postmilitary life was tumultuous. He held a variety of jobs, including security guard and editor of a porn magazine, and for a time he lived in his car while writing the twenty-three drafts of his first novel, *The Short Timers,* which was published in 1979 and became the basis for Stanley Kubrick's movie *Full Metal Jacket.* Hasford's contributions to the screenplay earned an Oscar nomination in 1988, but that same year he was convicted and served a six-month jail term for having "stolen" some ten thousand library books from across the country and the world. After all the books were returned and Hasford was freed, he published *The Phantom Blooper* (1990), but he also began to drink heavily and developed diabetes. In January 1993, at the age of forty-five, Hasford died alone in a hotel room on the Greek island of Aegina.

Just as his military service and postwar professional life differed markedly from Webb's, Hasford presented a decidedly different fictional portrayal and interpretation of America's Vietnam War. Hasford's central character and alter ego, James T. Davis, or Private Joker, was also a southerner, hailing from Russellville, Alabama. Like Hasford, Joker was a marine combat journalist, but unlike Webb and Hodges, he systematically sought to avoid responsibility and promotion and found nothing beyond the grunts' service and sacrifice honorable about US foreign policy and the war. Joker spends most of the first novel as a marine journalist, his assignment to "convince people that war is a beautiful experience," to demonstrate that "Nam is an Asian Eldorado populated by a cute, primitive but determined people. War is a noisy breakfast food . . . War can give you better checkups." His stories were "paper bullets fired into the fat black heart of Communism . . . to make the world safe for hypocrisy." Toward the end of *Short Timers,* Joker is busted from journalist to grunt; and as *The Phantom Blooper* begins, he is captured by the Vietcong and spends much of the second novel as a captive in a VC-controlled village on the Laotian border.[81]

Neither Hasford nor Joker considered the war particularly honorable or winnable. At various points, Joker declared that "a tour of duty in the military service of your country is like being put into a chain gang for the crime of patriotism"; that his country let him go "to Vietnam a military virgin, too dumb to do anything but draw fire"; and, standing over his father's grave, "I didn't want to go; I did it for you."[82] Once deployed to Vietnam, Joker decided that "getting killed over here is a waste of time," and he worried that "what you do, you become," that he was being "caught up in a constricting web of darkness"; that in "an unnecessary war, patriotism is just racism made to sound noble"; and that he was "ashamed to call myself an American. America has made me into a killer. I was not born a killer—I was *instructed.*"[83]

That he judged the war unwinnable no doubt contributed to Joker's disillusionment. He denounced the South Vietnamese as worthless allies and instructed another grunt, "Anytime you can see an Arvin you are safe from Victor Charlie." Although the South Vietnamese troops ran "like rabbits at the first sign of violence," they were neither cowardly nor stupid. They had simply been "drafted by the Saigon government, which was drafted by the lifers who drafted us," and they recognized the futility of fighting the Vietcong and North Vietnamese. By contrast, Joker respected the NVA as fellow grunts, as "brass-balled little hardasses . . . the best light infantry since the Stonewall Brigade." The VC were not "Asian mutants" like the South Vietnamese he met as a marine, "not those sad, pathetic people with a cloned culture and no self-respect, greedy and corrupt, ragged shameless beggars and whores." Rather, the Vietcong are "proud, gentle, fearless, ruthless, and painfully polite." The Americans could not defeat an enemy who had achieved the "ball-busting, monster victory" of maintaining the Ho Chi-Minh Trail against the "greatest aerial bombardment in history," an enemy who was "too real, too close to the earth."[84]

Joker, like Hasford, traced the futile US involvement in Vietnam to American moneyed interests. "Gangsters" had taken over the government and made war "a serious business" and killing the Vietnamese and others "our gross national product." This mindless foreign policy had left America "alone" in the world, under the illusion that the answer to any international problem was to "simply send in the Marines." Both during his captivity and cooperation with the Vietcong and upon his return home after being freed by American marines, Joker opted to "secede" from the "Viet Nam death trip." He had not "defected" to the communists, since communism was "boring and does not work"; rather, he had "joined the side of the people against the side of governments." He had endeavored to defend the "Confederate Dream" and its "desperate and heroic attempt to preserve from federal tyrants the liberty bequeathed to us by Thomas Jefferson and Benjamin Franklin." And in even more revealing southern commentary, Joker declared upon his return to Winston County that the "South" had been the "American Empire's first subjugated nation." As a "defeated people," residents of Dixie had been cured of their "quaint customs, quilting parties, barn raisings, and hog killings . . . and made . . . over into a homogenized replica of the North." Bereft of its culture, the South had become a "big Indian reservation populated by ex-Confederates who are bred like cattle to die in Yankee wars. In Alabama there is no circus to run off to, so we join the Marines."[85]

Webb's and Hasford's contrasting responses to the war embody some of the varied reactions of southern soldiers. Despite their general devotion to God, country, patriotism, and honor, Dixie's warriors emerged from the conflict and its agony with many of the same scars and much of the same ambivalence as other Americans. Former POW Benjamin H. Purcell may have best summarized the overall perspective of the South's troopers, a perspective endlessly repeated by Dixie's prowar majority. Purcell harbored no doubts about the war's validity. Stopping "the spread of Communism throughout Indochina" was "worthwhile, but we went at it piecemeal and with civilians making decisions on military operations." The retired army colonel deemed it "immoral to send a man into combat without a clear mission to win." Reflecting the veteran's reluctance to admit that he might have sacrificed so much for no clear gain, Purcell concluded hopefully that despite the "terrible price" paid by both the United States and the Vietnamese, the "war was not without some benefits. It raised the sensitivity of all the people of America to the horrors of war . . . and they realized that war is not a way to settle international disputes." Max Cleland's succinct appraisal, "We're losing our ass to save our face," coincided more closely with the minority of southern dissenters.[86]

Other southern soldiers were even more conflicted regarding Dixie's warrior tradition. William A. Brinkley, a Kentuckian who commanded an armor company, confessed that he "got no satisfaction out of combat. . . . It's not something that I want to do again." Rather, his "greatest satisfaction" came from "going into a fight and coming out with nobody wounded or killed." Lemos F. Fulmer Jr., a fellow armor officer from Selma, agreed, finding greater gratification in saving a "fellow soldiers' life" than in "any of my tactical successes." Black army specialist Robert Strong also made the troopers' welfare his first priority in his far more graphic and disillusioned "wish" that "the people in Washington could have walked through a hospital and seen the guys all fucked up. Seventeen-, eighteen-year-olds got casts from head to toes. . . . Dudes got legs shot off and shit, got half their faces gone." Larry Gwin, who survived the carnage of LZ Albany in November 1965 while serving as an army lieutenant and earned a Silver Star, Bronze Star, and Purple Heart, cautioned, "If anybody thinks it's good to go to war, they're crazy." Nor should people "talk about the glory of war because there is none. War sucks. . . . America's got to learn from its mistakes as well as its moments of pride, and it has got to be very careful when it chooses to send American kids to fight a war without really knowing if it's worth it." Helicopter pilot Ernest Peoples from Beaumont, Texas, who was shot down five times and had little patience for such discussions, voiced the aggrieved perspective of so many southern and US veterans by agreeing with the inscription on another vet's baseball cap: "If you ain't been there, shut the fuck up."[87]

Like Warrant Officer Peoples, southern soldiers were repeatedly at the center of the action in Vietnam. General Westmoreland had a profound influence on the war's overall direction and tenor. Other southerners, such as Dave Blair, Jim Webb, and Hugh Thompson, had an equally profound and revealing impact, but in a much smaller corner of the conflict. Even southern warriors such as Gus Haford, who did little in combat terms other than survive and observe, have augmented an understanding of Dixie's military relation to the Vietnam War. That understanding was not confined to the experiences of southern men, as Dixie's women have afforded enlightening recollections of their reasons for going to Vietnam and the travails of service there. Issues of honor, patriotism, and manhood were particularly prominent as southern men went to, fought in, and returned from the war. As might be expected, some southern soldiers met the often exaggerated regional standards of honor and courage; others, most conspicuously William Calley, failed miserably. The interaction of southern whites and African Americans serving in Vietnam furnished another regional vantage point for assessing the war—one that ran the gamut from KKK garb and Confederate flags to the forging of greater respect and life-saving support, although this respect had little impact on domestic southern race relations. Responses to the war were quite diverse, ranging from pride in service to bitterness and alienation; but the distinct majority of southern soldiers, like their neighbors, family, and political leaders, deemed the war to have been winnable. Only the misguided "stab-in-the-back" decisions of civilian leaders or the demoralizing antiwar actions of cowardly protestors and mistaken congressmen and senators had prevented the United States from employing its vastly superior power to realize a military victory. Indeed, the proper use of US military power, especially air power, was a critical component in the debate over the war's conduct in 1967.

5

Southerners and the Debate over the War's Conduct, 1967

On August 9, 1967, Senator John Stennis opened the hearings of his Senate Preparedness Investigating Subcommittee (SPIS) on the "conduct and effectiveness of the air war against North Vietnam"—hearings that would "involve the overall policy and philosophy governing and controlling the conduct of the entire war." The decisive year of 1967 was largely devoted to an "increasingly angry and divisive [national] debate" over the merits of the war's continued escalation and especially the role of bombing in the US effort. This debate left the nation increasingly disillusioned and more divided than at any time since the Civil War. By August, a Gallup Poll found that only 33 percent of respondents approved of President Johnson's handling of the war (versus 52 percent who disapproved), and only 34 percent believed the United States was making progress, compared to 56 percent who answered that American forces were "losing" or "standing still."[1]

As during the previous two years, when the Johnson administration was making the critical decisions for war, southerners—be they policymakers, congressional representatives, or the public—took an active role in this debate over how best to conduct the conflict. Together with the GOP nationally, southern hawks pressured Johnson to press for a military victory by escalating the war, particularly through more aggressive bombing of North Vietnam. In so doing, these conservative southerners and a clear majority within the region endorsed Johnson's rationale for intervention and continued to provide the most solid sectional support for the war, all the while harshly castigating the president's ostensible restraint and failure to pursue a clear strategy for victory. The high point of this southern pressure came with the SPIS hearings on the air war. Just as Fulbright and the SFRC dissenters had defied Johnson's effort to avoid a public debate over the war's rationale and the decisions leading to massive US involvement, Stennis and his hawkish cohort infuriated LBJ by engaging in the "closest thing to a real debate" over the strategy and conduct of the conflict.[2]

Although the majority of white southerners advocated this more hawkish perspective, a vocal southern minority continued to argue for deescalating the war, curtailing or even ending the bombing of North Vietnam, and pursuing a negotiated settlement. Senators Fulbright, Gore, and Cooper remained among the nation's most significant antiwar voices and were joined in September 1967 by Thruston Morton (R-KY). These prominent dissenters, together with the Reverend Martin Luther King Jr., who voiced an outspoken condemnation of the war during 1967, provided influential counterpressure against Johnson's persistent escalation of the war and in so doing elicited additional public discussion of the conflict. As had become the pattern by 1964, numerous individual southerners adopted and voiced many of the antiwar arguments.

While the debate over the war raged across the nation and within the South, the predominance of conservative, evangelical, Protestant religious beliefs also sustained Dixie's robust anticommunism and support for the war. A third dynamic, the intersection of the Civil Rights Movement and the war, was much more complicated. Among most southern whites, African American opposition to racial segregation or the war in Vietnam was objectionable, and both smacked of radical, even communist influences. Southern blacks, as well as African Americans nationally, were more divided, disagreeing over whether to oppose the war and over the impact antiwar stands had on their battle for domestic equality. These differences became apparent when the Mississippi Freedom Democratic Party, the Student Nonviolent Coordinating Committee (SNCC), the Southern Christian Leadership Conference (SCLC), and especially Reverend King denounced the war as a distraction from the campaign for domestic civil rights and unjustly burdensome for African Americans.

Despite the presence in Vietnam of 448,800 US troops at the end of 1967 (up from 385,000 the year before), the escalating monetary and human costs yielded only national frustration, mounting domestic dissent, and a military standoff. The war's monthly costs had grown to $2 billion and forced President Johnson to raise the possibility in his State of the Union address of enacting a surtax to meet war costs. Draft calls ballooned to 30,000 per month, and by the end of the year 13,500 Americans had died in Vietnam. Although this vastly enlarged US military involvement had prevented imminent North Vietnamese–Vietcong victory in mid-1965, it had produced no readily discernible progress thereafter. It had, however, elicited growing domestic antiwar protests, the most prominent to date being the fifty-thousand-strong March on the Pentagon in November.[3]

Against this backdrop, President Johnson faced unrelenting pressure over the first nine months of 1967 to expand both the air war over North Vietnam and the number of US troops in South Vietnam. The president's response led *New York Times* correspondent James Reston to declare in March, "Johnson looks more and more like a man who has decided to go for a military victory in Vietnam." In late February Johnson added fifty-three Rolling Thunder targets, approved the rebombing of several power plants, and endorsed naval bombardment of the North and the mining of selected inland waterways. While implementing these missions, the United States also attacked two North Vietnamese MiG airfields and several additional industrial targets. The president subsequently released sixteen new bombing targets in July and another twenty-nine in August. All told, Rolling Thunder sorties had increased from 79,000 in 1966 to 108,000 in 1967, and bomb tonnage had gone from 136,000 to 226,000. The number of US troops grew apace—from 385,000 at the end of 1966 to 448,800 a year later.[4]

Still, Johnson stopped short of the "all-out" war advocated by southern hawks, General Westmoreland, and the Joint Chiefs of Staff (JCS). In mid-March, the JCS requested an additional 201,000 troops for an ultimate total of 671,616; mobilization of the reserves; permission to invade Cambodia, Laos, and North Vietnam; the mining of Haiphong harbor; and the end of restrictions on bombing around Hanoi, Haiphong, and along the Chinese border. In short, they "called for mobilizing the nation to win the war." Sticking to his decision for a limited war, LBJ approved the expanded target list noted above and granted Westmoreland another 50,000 troops; but he rejected an invasion of North Vietnam or neighboring countries, unrestricted bombing of North Vietnam's two population centers, and the mining of Haiphong.[5]

Ironically, as southern hawks were poised to initiate a yearlong campaign to fundamentally alter the conduct of the war, two Dixie natives traveled to Hanoi in hopes of furthering a negotiated settlement of the conflict. Although admittedly of the "Confederate persuasion," Harry S. Ashmore and William C. Baggs were aligned more closely with Fulbright, Cooper, and Gore than with Russell, Stennis, and Tower. Both were World War II veterans and distinguished journalists—Ashmore as editor of the *Charlotte News, Arkansas Gazette,* and *Encyclopedia Britannica* and Baggs as editor of the *Miami News,* which won three Pulitzers under his direction. By the mid-1960s, these liberal Democrats were both persistent opponents of segregation and members of the board of directors of the Center for the Study of Democratic Institutions. The center, located in Santa Barbara, California, was devoted to easing Cold War tensions and promoting international peace. When Luis Quintanilla, a Mexican intellectual and former diplomat, secured an invitation for center representatives to meet with Ho Chi Minh, Ashmore and Baggs traveled to Hanoi, arriving on January 6, 1967, the same day Harrison Salisbury of the *New York Times* ended his much more visible visit.[6]

Ashmore and Baggs's observations confirmed Salisbury's assertions that US bombing had gone well beyond military and industrial targets and had destroyed entire civilian neighborhoods in Hanoi's suburbs and in other North Vietnamese towns along Route 1, the main road connecting Hanoi and Saigon. These observations became public much later when Baggs published a series of twelve articles in the *Miami News.* In the interim, the two met with State Department representatives prior to embarking for North Vietnam and agreed to make every effort to maintain the confidentiality of their journey, meetings, and impressions. The itinerant southerners claimed they clearly understood their unofficial status as "mere messengers and observers, not negotiators," and "never confused" their standing or role. Similarly, while acknowledging their "sharp" criticism of the administration's conduct of the war and their desire to see the "conflict ended," they emphasized that, unlike some "radical American peace activists," they had never "transferred their sympathies, and . . . political allegiance, to Hanoi."[7]

Operating from this perspective, Ashmore and Baggs had several meetings with Hoàng Tùng, the editor of the principal Communist Party paper and a member of the party's central committee, and a remarkably frank and informal two-hour session with Ho himself. Like numerous westerners who had met with Ho over the previous twenty-five years, these two Americans were impressed with his charm, urbanity, nationalist devotion to Vietnamese independence, commitment to a Marxist political economy, and habitual chain smoking. Upon their return to Washington, Ashmore and Baggs faithfully reported Ho's and North Vietnam's long-standing and unalterable position that there could be no negotiations until the United States unconditionally ended the bombing of the North. If the bombing ceased, Ho professed flexibility on all other issues, including the infiltration of North Vietnamese military personnel and supplies into the South, the withdrawal of US troops, and the timing and process for reunifying Vietnam.[8]

Buoyed by their sense that Ho and the North Vietnamese seemed to have met all US conditions for negotiations, save an absolute "guarantee to close the border" between the North and South to infiltration, Ashmore and Baggs returned to Washington during the week of January 15, 1967, to report on their talks. Their guarded optimism was promptly dashed when neither Rusk nor Johnson met with them. The secretary of state dismissed them as "just two more frustrated seekers of the Nobel Prize," and LBJ explained to Fulbright, "I can't talk with everybody who's been over there talking with Ho Chi Minh"—despite the fact that only two Americans had done so since the initiation of Rolling Thunder two years earlier. Although low-ranking State Department personnel were less overtly dismissive, the futility of the envoys' efforts became glaringly apparent when Johnson killed a much higher-level, potentially more promising peace overture that had been in play simultaneously with the aid of the USSR and Great Britain.[9]

Although Ashmore publicly denounced Johnson's "double-dealing" in an article published the following September, he and Baggs were back in Hanoi at the end of March 1968, when LBJ announced that he would not run for reelection and that US bombing would be confined to the most southern portions of North Vietnam. Fearful that Johnson was about to agree to General Westmoreland's requests for an additional two hundred thousand US troops, the two southerners had returned to Vietnam hoping to facilitate negotiations and head off an even larger war. Through additional meetings with Tùng, they again ascertained a useful sense of North Vietnamese perspectives and composed a joint memorandum of understanding, which the North Vietnamese viewed as their formal reply to Johnson's March 31, 1968, speech and restriction of US bombing. The unconditional cessation of US bombing of the North remained the absolute prerequisite for substantive talks, and Hanoi offered Phnom Penh, Cambodia, as the preferred site for peace talks. Despite the Dixie duo's remarkable access to high-ranking North Vietnamese officials and candid discussions, and another revelatory trip down Route 1, State Department officials exhibited even less interest in their information or opinions, and Rusk and Johnson remained off-limits. Disillusioned and embittered, Ashmore and Baggs emerged from their experience as unofficial envoys convinced that Johnson was a "thin-skinned bully," that Rusk was "preeminently the Cold Warrior," and of the validity of the "Fulbright Law": "you can't trust" the State Department. Although the likelihood of the Ashmore-Baggs efforts yielding a diplomatic breakthrough was never great, these efforts, like those of Frazier Woolard, revealed the diversity of southern opinion, even as their curt dismissal by Johnson and Rusk embodied Dixie's majority prowar perspective.[10]

While Ashmore and Baggs sought a path to negotiations, the fundamental debate over the conduct of the war continued, and southern hawks and their constituents sustained their demands for a traditional military victory. No advocate of an unfettered military effort was more important than John Stennis. By 1967, Stennis had made the war his "number one priority," and from his chairmanship of the SPIS the Mississippi senator systematically hounded Secretary of Defense McNamara, the Department of Defense (DOD), and the Johnson administration. The SPIS released three critical reports during March 1967. The most important appeared on March 27, examined "tactical air operations in Southeast Asia," and concluded predictably that the "restrictive rules of engagement in the war over North Vietnam" had been a "very significant factor in the tactical air problems in Southeast Asia." The restrictions, according to Stennis and the SPIS, had contributed to the "sacrifice of many American lives and aircraft losses extending into billions of dollars." To curtail these losses and defeat the enemy, the Johnson administration needed to adopt the "recommendations of responsible commanders to strike more meaningful military targets in North Vietnam."[11]

Stennis reiterated and elaborated this familiar message in speeches and letters to constituents. Most fundamentally, he continued to advocate following the "advice of military leaders" and doing whatever was "necessary militarily to win on the battlefield." Stennis was always in close communication with the JCS, and his declarations translated into an endorsement of the military commanders' attempt in March and April to push Johnson toward an all-out war. The SPIS chairman acknowledged the "risk" that more aggressive US actions could "provoke Red China to full intervention in the war," but he deemed this risk necessary and asserted the United States had to "be prepared to meet Red Chinese aggression . . . with whatever military might is necessary to repel it." The requisite "full national decision to win" embodied not only these military steps but also making prosecution of the war the nation's "first priority . . . very far ahead of the social welfare programs" and silencing all criticism of "our purpose or our motives."[12]

Stennis moved beyond his customary arguments in two respects. First, he worried that the United States had far too many international treaty commitments that the nation was "honor-bound to meet . . . just as we are honor-bound to follow through in Vietnam." Following the Vietnam War, the United States needed to undertake a "sober evaluation" of these commitments, determine the ones "absolutely necessary to our national security," and allocate the resources required to fulfill them. Second, the senator declared that the United States should never again become "involved in a major war by executive escalation of military intervention." He opposed any subsequent "diplomatic" war not "declared by Congress as provided for in the Constitution." Like Fulbright, Stennis had begun to rethink the traditional southern deference to the executive in foreign policy and war making.[13]

Despite these objections to Johnson's conduct of the war, Stennis remained a faithful and influential supporter of the conflict's funding from his membership on both the Senate Armed Services and Appropriations Committees. A host of other southern Democrats afforded LBJ similar backing, even as they habitually called for more aggressive tactics. Richard Russell, in his last year of significant influence before being overtaken by declining health, remained a close Johnson confidant and supporter. The Georgia senator also continued to argue for more aggressive bombing of North Vietnam and the closure of Haiphong harbor, while opposing any congressional actions designed to "cut back on the military action" in Southeast Asia. Only ongoing military pressure, he avowed, would force a Korea-like settlement, thereby saving American lives and bringing "an honorable conclusion" to the war. Although he dismissed a US invasion of North Vietnam as the "surest way to create a long period of hostilities of great magnitude in that area," Russell was unmoved by the moral objections of antiwar critics. He could see no difference between the bombing of North Vietnam and the attacks on Germany and Japan during World War II. The rising public opposition to the war reinforced his preference for an air campaign over indecisive search-and-destroy ground tactics. In early May Russell admonished Johnson, "We've just got to finish it soon because time is working against you both here and there."[14]

Mendel Rivers concurred, warning, "The war is getting very unpopular the way we are conducting it . . . the American people just don't believe in waiting and waiting." While professing to be a "staunch supporter" of the president and defending Johnson's "carefully controlled" policies designed "to avoid expansion of the war," Russell Long incongruently deplored all "off-again, on-again, Finnegan" truces and bombing halts. Agreeing with Russell and Rivers that Americans wanted "to get it over with," the Louisiana senator called for a bombing campaign to "bring the Communists to their knees." If these US actions drew the USSR and China into the war militarily, Long "would step up" the "effort and fight them too."[15]

Far less dramatic than Rivers or Long, Senators Ervin, Ellender, Sparkman, and Smathers assumed their customary places in the phalanx of prowar southerners. Decrying antiwar senators who had "contributed nothing to the settlement" of the war while giving "the enemy the impression" that the United States would tire of the effort, Sam Ervin asserted that the only viable policy was "to strike the enemy hard enough to defeat him or bring him to the conference table." Allen Ellender continued to agonize over the fiscal and human costs of the war, noting that it was necessary to pay for not only the "logistics" to sustain American troops "but also the support of their widows and children." But, like Ervin, he perceived no alternative to a more forceful bombing campaign. John Sparkman and George Smathers were more uncritical backers of the administration. Both emphasized that US involvement in Vietnam was akin to prior Cold War confrontations in Korea, Berlin, and Cuba;

that the United States could not appease communist aggressors; that US objectives were confined to realizing "a peaceful and honorable" solution; and that US withdrawal would give South Vietnam over to "terror unleashed against defenseless civilians" and shatter America's international standing. Sparkman stated approvingly that LBJ would "not surrender to extreme views" and was "conducting a responsible and careful military operation in Vietnam."[16]

Among southern Republicans, Strom Thurmond maintained his ultra-hawkish positions. "More bombing" and the closure of Haiphong were his keys to victory. The South Carolinian had no doubt the United States possessed the requisite "power," and he hoped the US public would "demand" that President Johnson "win the war." Although he agreed with Thurmond on these basic points, Senator Tower, also a member of the Armed Services Committee, had emerged by 1967 as a more prominent and thoughtful southern Republican voice on Vietnam. By the end of the year, Tower had visited Vietnam and East Asia four times in twenty-four months, and over the course of the war the Texas Republican traveled to Vietnam more often than any of his congressional colleagues. A navy veteran of World War II and former political science professor at Midwestern University in Wichita Falls, Tower had been elected in 1961 at the age of thirty-five to fill Lyndon Johnson's seat when LBJ moved to the vice presidency.[17]

During 1967, Tower built on his prior Vietnam positions. The senator expressed "100 percent" support for Johnson's "basic policy . . . to protect and guarantee the independence of South Vietnam." Indeed, the United States had no choice. As the world's "most powerful nation," America had inherited "the mantle of world leadership" and become the "first line of defense" against "communist aggression." Failure to convince the enemy on this "small front" that war was "too costly an instrument of national policy" would lead inevitably to conflict "on a broader front later . . . at a much greater cost in human life." Like Stennis, Russell, and Thurmond, Tower summarily rejected additional truces or bombing pauses. Only "unrelenting pressure on the enemy" and the "traditional American guts and determination" to wield superior power effectively would secure victory.[18]

The son and grandson of Methodist ministers and the holder of degrees from both Southwestern and Southern Methodist Universities,

Tower moved beyond other southern legislators by extensively defending the morality of US intervention in Vietnam. In a commencement speech to the first graduating class at Houston Baptist College and on numerous other occasions, he vigorously rejected all accusations of immorality associated with US involvement in Vietnam. To the contrary, the United States was championing a "transcendent moral ethic—the right of mankind to determine its own destiny within its own ethical and religious convictions." This fundamental right, together with the belief that man was "created in the image of God," was "at the heart of the Judeo-Christian ethic." Since military force was "neither morally right nor morally wrong," the US use of force for this moral purpose and America's meticulous regard for the safety of noncombatants was ethically justifiable and in blatant contrast to the Vietnamese communists' "deliberate" use of "brutality and wanton terrorism" against defenseless South Vietnamese "victims." Under these circumstances, US "failure to use military force" in this "proper place" for the "proper purpose" would be "disastrous and highly immoral."[19]

Senator Tower's conservative religious defense of US actions in Vietnam faithfully reprised the beliefs of most southerners and helps explain the region's ongoing support for the war. Aptly describing the nation's Bible Belt, a Charlotte Presbyterian minister observed, "Religion is what really makes and keeps the South a separate, solid and stable culture." A contemporary Gallup poll elucidated this observation. Southerners by margins of 9, 10, and 7 percent over the closest region, respectively, were the Americans most likely to view "organized religion" as a "relevant part" of their lives, to believe that religion could "answer all or most . . . problems," and to read the Bible regularly. Most of this southern religion was decidedly conservative—Protestant, evangelical, often fundamentalist, and solidly behind the Cold War campaign to contain and defeat atheistic communism. Most southerners viewed Vietnam as a crucial struggle in the large Cold War battle that "divided believers from nonbelievers, faith from godlessness, morality from immorality, and democracy from tyranny." Given these elemental distinctions, Vietnam and the accompanying confrontation with the Soviet Union and China were necessary and, therefore, just and moral wars. Unlike more liberal religious adherents in the North and East, most southerners were appalled at any suggestion that God was dead or that the United States might fail to defend Christianity in Southeast Asia. The southern majority just as ardently rejected the assertions by some liberal Christians that a moral equivalency existed between the United States and its communist adversaries. Good versus evil allowed for no such parity and rendered calls for disarmament or unconditional negotiations anathema. Only victory was acceptable. An indignant Tennessee resident declared, "Coexistence and peace are . . . advocated Communist policies. Coexistence . . . means our compliance to their demands; peace means our enslavement." With negotiations out of the question, "if we maintain our Christian civilization, we'll have to fight for it."[20]

Not all religious southerners arrived at these foreign policy positions. As letters to political representatives and editors demonstrated, other Dixie residents doubted that North Vietnam and the Vietcong posed a threat to the United States and, therefore, questioned whether the war was defensive and just. These antiwar southerners often contended that the United States had intervened in a Vietnamese civil war and that this intervention was at odds with the same Christian republicanism that Tower and prowar southerners cited to justify the conflict. Dixie doves also decried the massive US bombing of a small, less developed country; the chemical destruction of the environment with herbicides; and the loss of life on both sides, especially the killing of Vietnamese civilians.[21]

The attitudes of southern Presbyterians and Baptists toward the war clearly demonstrated Dixie's religious perspectives on Vietnam. The General Assembly of the Presbyterian Church in the United States (PCUS, the southern wing of the Presbyterian Church from 1861 to 1983) maintained a generally conservative and supportive stance throughout the war. This governing body did compose a series of questions about the war in 1967, indicating that its backing of US military measures was not unconditional, and the General Assembly endorsed selective conscientious objection in 1969 by a vote of 260 to 164. The crucial momentum for approving this issue turned on a speech by Paul Taylor, a Medal of Honor recipient from Alexandria, Virginia, whose son had been killed in Vietnam. Taylor beseeched his fellow commissioners to "give an honest alternative to young men other than being criminals." He recounted advising his son of his three choices: to lie about being a general conscientious objector (CO), opposed to all wars rather than just Vietnam; to be a "coward and run"; or to "join and take . . . a chance in doing something he didn't believe in." The PCUS and the nation, Taylor concluded, needed to "give a man a chance to be an honest patriot and a Christian."[22]

Although the General Assembly concurred in this instance, a 1968 poll of more than twelve hundred readers of the PCUS's *Presbyterian Survey* revealed that Taylor was far more skeptical of the war than the majority of his fellow parishioners. In response to the question of whether the United States should "immediately and unconditionally stop the bombing of North Viet Nam," 884 objected versus 231 who agreed—a margin of 79 versus 21 percent. The query as to whether the United States "should use all military strength necessary (short of nuclear weapons) to achieve victory" elicited a similar margin of 75 percent (806) in favor versus 25 percent (260) opposed. By rejecting withdrawal and endorsing aggressive military measures, southern Presbyterians agreed with their regional neighbors.[23]

Far more conspicuous in his dissent than Taylor, Dr. George Edwards, a faculty member at the Presbyterian Louisville Seminary, and his wife, Jean, embodied the minority status of religious opponents of the war. A World War II CO and a forceful proponent of civil rights, Edwards braved the epithets of hostile Kentuckians to organize peace marches, advise conscientious objectors, and even aid draft resisters and deserters as they fled to Canada. Described by Anne Braden, a fellow Louisville civil rights and peace advocate, as "the most militant pacifist you ever saw," Edwards denounced the Vietnam War as "the most obnoxious example of American Imperialism." When critics accused him of being a communist and anti-Christian, Edwards told the seminary's 1967 graduating class, "the church" and the "ministry" faced "the tests of freedom. The shrill cries of the racists, the nationalists, the birchers, and the anticommunists are raised in every corner where the Christian faith seeks its unhampered application."[24]

Had Edwards been a Southern Baptist, easily the largest denomination in Dixie, he would have experienced an even more hostile reception. Indeed, a delegate to the 1968 annual meeting of the Southern Baptist Convention (SBC) asked an antiwar Baptist student protestor, "Why don't you go on and become a Presbyterian and leave us alone?" Several polls in 1968 and 1969 yielded similar sentiments. The first found that 75 percent of 500 Baptist ministers surveyed in Florida and Louisiana deemed a US victory in Vietnam imperative, and 47 percent endorsed the use of nuclear weapons. Another poll revealed that 97 percent of Southern Baptists opposed any pause in the bombing of North Vietnam and endorsed increased US military intervention if it were needed to achieve victory. Although the SBC came to grudgingly acknowledge conscientious objection by 1972, Southern Baptists remained adamantly opposed to selective CO status.[25]

Billy Graham, the "quintessential Cold War evangelist," was the most prominent Southern Baptist supporter of the war. Graham continued to believe that communism was not only an "economic interpretation of life" but also a "religion . . . inspired, directed and motivated by the Devil himself who has declared war against God Almighty." The stakes could not have been higher, since the Cold War struggle would "end either in the death of Christianity or the death of Communism." The North Carolina minister contended that communism had to be "stopped somewhere, whether it is in Hawaii or on the West Coast," and he agreed with President Johnson that "it should be stopped in Vietnam." Graham, like Richard Russell and other prowar southerners, recognized the US intervention had become a "mess," and he harbored grave reservations about a successful outcome. Still, he had "no sympathy" for clergymen who advocated US withdrawal from Vietnam. Even if the United States confronted "an all-out war with Red China," Americans "had to clean up the mess rather than turn their backs on the South Vietnamese." Nor could he abide protestors who "so exaggerate our divisions . . . they could make Hanoi confident" of victory.[26]

Other important SBC figures echoed Graham's sentiments, often in more strident terms. Following a visit to Vietnam in 1966, Wayne Dehoney, the president of the SBC and pastor of the First Baptist Church of Jackson, Tennessee, declared, "I am returning more convinced this nation is doing the right thing." He was "encouraged by the physical aspects of the war in Vietnam but even more thrilling was the spiritual climate" in which "American youth [was] in its finest hour. They build schools, churches, and hand out candy." H. Franklin Paschall, SBC president in 1967 and 1968 and pastor of the First Baptist Church in Nashville, Tennessee, decried any effort "to have Southern Baptists join the left-leaning-liberal church groups in stabbing our Viet Nam boys in the back!" To the contrary, if "'total victory,' that is total destruction of North Vietnam," were necessary "to bring about negotiations for a just and honorable peace," he was "for it." In mid-1967, a Texan informed LBJ that he made "no apology for my patriotism" and "would be sorely disappointed if the Baptist denominations should take a position which might in any way be considered . . . unpatriotic." Other Southern Baptists left no doubt that they deemed antiwar protestors unpatriotic. Dale Cowling, pastor of the Second Baptist Church in Little Rock, declared that persons encouraging the "youth of America to rebel against military service . . . should be dealt with sternly on grounds of threatening the national security." And the editor of the *Baptist Record* in Jackson, Mississippi, deemed antiwar protest equivalent to rejecting "God, the church, moral standards, [and] patriotism."[27]

As these heartfelt opinions suggest, opposing the war within the SBC could be a lonely, professionally hazardous undertaking. Jess Moody, the pastor of the First Baptist Church of West Palm Beach, Florida, and president of Palm Beach Atlantic College, discovered this after addressing the 1969 annual conference of Southern Baptist pastors in New Orleans. While recognizing the reality and importance of the larger Cold War struggle, Moody rejected the domino theory and the assumption that North Vietnam threatened the United States. He agreed that the United States had to "stop communism" but doubted that this could be achieved "by using the techniques of communism." Could, he asked, quoting Jesus, "evil means cast out evil means? Can hate cast out hate? Can war cast out war?" In the aftermath of this speech, Moody claimed he was "never seriously considered" for another "denominational post."[28]

Moody's dissent paled compared to that of William Wallace Finlator, pastor of Pullen Memorial Baptist Church in Raleigh, North Carolina. Finlator, also an aggressive advocate of racial reform, was, like the Presbyterian George Edwards in Louisville, conspicuous as an exception to his prowar, southern church congregants. Pastor Finlator castigated the United States for reneging on its commitment to Vietnamese elections in 1956 and its pledge to "refrain from using force in that nation." These actions, together with US support for "puppet" South Vietnamese governments, were "an exposure of the moral bankruptcy of American foreign policy—all in the name of God." In 1965 the outspoken North Carolinian urged President Johnson to initiate negotiations for US withdrawal and to appeal to the UN to secure Vietnam against outside interference. In contrast to the majority of SBC clergy, Finlator encouraged and participated in antiwar protests and urged the government to recognize CO claims from persons "both inside and outside of the church." His 1971 campaign to have the SBC petition President Nixon to decriminalize draft evasion was even more radical. He called for amnesty for "the hundreds of young men who have gone to Federal jails and the thousands and thousands of others who have fled to Canada and elsewhere because their consciences refused to let them fight in a war that is now widely regarded as immoral, unwarranted, and brutal." Needless to say, the SBC rejected his resolution.[29]

Religious values also helped stimulate opposition to the war among southern African Americans. In explaining his antiwar position in 1967, Martin Luther King Jr. emphasized that the Christian gospels were meant "for all men—for communist and capitalist, for their children and ours, for black and white for revolutionary and conservative," and he declared that his ministry was "in obedience to the One who loved his enemies so fully that he died for them." Andrew Young, the executive director of the SCLC, was more succinct: the war violated the commandment "Thou shalt not kill," and "mass murder" was "no way to solve problems." Later in 1967, Young urged the nation to choose between "the cross and the flag." The African American Progressive National Baptist Convention (PNBC), the first Baptist convention to oppose the war, declared in 1965, "The Church of Jesus Christ, the PRINCE OF PEACE—must always contend militantly that *war is wrong!*" Later in 1972, the PNBC characterized the war as "immoral, murderous, and wasteful." As with Dixie's whites, religion could also prompt black support for the war. In 1963, on the eve of decisive US intervention, King himself had voiced the broader Cold War religious rationale for containment: "Communism and Christianity," he wrote, were "fundamentally incompatible"; and "a true Christian" could not "be a true Communist." The latter adhered to "ethical relativism," which justified "almost anything—love, violence, murder, lying" in pursuit of the US adversaries' "millennial end."[30]

To the extent religion influenced black opinion, these antiwar arguments appear to have been more persuasive since southern African Americans were less supportive of the war than their white neighbors. During 1966, 35 percent of blacks opposed the war; by 1969, the figure had increased to 56 percent. African Americans were consistently more in favor of withdrawal and more opposed to escalation than whites. In 1966,

16 percent of blacks favored withdrawal versus 11 percent of whites, and 33 percent of African Americans endorsed escalation compared to 48 percent of whites. By 1968, black percentages on withdrawal and escalation were 37 and 20; white preferences were 23 and 39. And in 1970 the black percentages for these categories were 57 and 10, as opposed to 37 and 29 for whites. In addition to religious and moral concerns, African American opposition derived from a priority placed on domestic, especially economic and racial, issues; an identification with nonwhite opponents of outside colonial domination; and a growing sense that blacks were being drafted, serving, and dying in Vietnam in numbers disproportionate to their place in American society.[31]

Black southerners were correct in believing that they were bearing a disproportionate burden of the fighting in Vietnam. Like African Americans nationally, southern blacks were more likely to be drafted. Between 1965 and 1970, blacks constituted about 12 percent of the nation's population. During that period, the percentage of African Americans drafted ranged from 13.4 percent (1966) to 16 percent (1967 and 1970) of the total draftees. At the height of the war, in 1967, 64 percent of eligible blacks were drafted, compared to 31 percent of eligible whites. More likely to be assigned to combat units, black soldiers were also wounded and killed more often than whites. The death rate for blacks was especially alarming in the early years of the war. From 1961 through 1965, African American deaths comprised 18.3 percent of casualties in the US Army. In 1966, the black percentage of all combat deaths rose to 22 percent before falling to 14 in 1967. For the overall span of US involvement, from January 1, 1961, through April 30, 1975, 12.6 percent of the 58,022 US deaths were African Americans. Even while dealing with the death of a loved one in Vietnam, African Americans could be graphically reminded of their place in southern society. In 1966 white elected officials in Wetumpka, Alabama, blocked the burial of Jimmie Williams, a black paratrooper, in the local public cemetery; and two years later, the family of Bill Henry Terry Jr. had to obtain a court order for him to be interred at the previously segregated Elmwood Cemetery in Birmingham, Alabama. Fort Pierce, Florida, authorities also refused to allow Pondexteur Eugene Williams's burial in the town's all-white cemetery.[32]

Although African American protests against these conditions and more general black opposition to the war reached a crescendo in 1967 with Reverend King's speech at the Riverside Church in New York City, black discontent had been mounting for several years. On August 4, 1964, in the midst of developments in the Gulf of Tonkin, Robert Moses, a Student Nonviolent Coordinating Committee (SNCC) leader, noted that President Johnson "wants to send soldiers to kill people on the other side of the world, . . . while here in Mississippi he refuses to send anyone to protect black people against murderous violence." A year later, in July 1965, members of the Mississippi Freedom Democratic Party declared, "No Mississippi Negroes should be fighting in Vietnam for the White Man's freedom, until all Negro People are free in Mississippi. . . . No one has a right to ask us to risk our lives and kill other Colored People in Santo Domingo and Vietnam, so that the White American can get richer." In January 1966, SNCC equated the death of activist Samuel Younge in Alabama to "the murder of people in Vietnam, for both Younge and the Vietnamese" were "seeking . . . rights guaranteed them by law." SNCC expressed "sympathy" for Americans "unwilling to respond" positively to the "draft" or to commit "aggression" in Vietnam. Building on African American contentions since the turn of the century, the SNCC statement highlighted the inconsistency of blacks being called upon to protect free-dom in Vietnam, "to preserve a 'democracy' which does not exist for them at home." Where, SNCC asked, "is the draft for the freedom fight in the United States?" As a Stennis constituent wrote the senator, the "cry of freedom half way around the world" could only appear dubious to blacks, "when they don't even have the freedom to listen to your speech from the galleries of the Mississippi House of Representatives."[33]

When SNCC information director Julian Bond endorsed the 1966 statement and asked if the "energy" devoted to "destroying villages thou-sands of miles away" might not be better used in "building villages here," he was barred from taking his seat in the Georgia legislature, to which he had been elected in 1965. The young legislator tellingly asked why he was not accorded the "same privilege" of criticizing LBJ as was granted white southern conservatives such as Richard Russell and James Eastland. King agreed and quickly came to his defense, warning that the nation seemed to be "approaching a dangerous totalitarian periphery where dis-sent becomes synonymous with disloyalty." The SCLC leader was "tired of the press and others trying to brainwash people" and suggested that there were "no" war-related "issues" being discussed. Building on Bond's stand for nonviolence, King asserted that the United States could only defeat communism through "moral power," by demonstrating that "democracy" was the best form of government, and by "making justice a reality for all God's children."[34]

Another, far less prominent southerner joined King in defending SNCC and Bond. From Prospect, Kentucky, Henry Wallace castigated the National Association for the Advancement of Colored People (NAACP) for failing to endorse SNCC's opposition to the war, in which "Negro soldiers, whose enemies are in the U.S., not half-way 'round the world, are killing and being killed in a much higher proportion than white soldiers." Wallace had previously deemed it "tragic in the extreme for the Negro to fight and kill and perhaps be killed for the power structure of the white man's war against colored Asians," and he lamented that the NAACP had effectively sided with the "'war hawks': The White Citizens Councils, the KKK, [and] the rest of the anti-Negro hoodlum element." Indeed, Wallace concluded, the NAACP was "fast becoming the leading Uncle Tom of the civil rights movement."[35]

In contrast to King's defense, SNCC and Bond provoked hostile responses from both whites and blacks across much of the political spectrum. By challenging US involvement in Vietnam on the grounds of morality, patriotism, and race, SNCC and the young legislator had touched on multiple raw nerves, particularly in the South. The *Louisville Courier-Journal* came closest to a sympathetic response by defending Bond's "right to speak his mind" and denouncing the Georgia legislature's "high-handed action." Georgia lieutenant governor Peter Zack Greer spoke for most of his white constituents by denouncing Bond's position as a "glaring, sad and tragic example of a total lack of patriotism." Eugene Patterson and the *Atlanta Constitution,* which had consistently supported the Civil Rights Movement, also upheld the right to "dissent" from US policy in Vietnam, but even the pro–civil rights editor was outraged. Patterson, who backed Johnson's Vietnam policies, was certain that the "SNCC outburst" did not represent the views of "a majority of Negroes in this country." SNCC, Bond, and civil rights advocates, the editor declared, only undermined their laudable domestic objective by blundering into "the thicket of foreign policy." Bond had moved beyond dissent and charged his country with "murder, deception, aggression" and was guilty of "sympathizing with and . . . even admiring" draft resisters.[36]

Whites were not the only harsh critics. The NAACP and the Urban League quickly disavowed SNCC and Bond, and in early 1966 King had yet to persuade his own SCLC to publicly oppose the war. These positions reflected the hesitation of civil rights leaders to break openly with President Johnson, who had been critical to the passage of the landmark civil rights bills of 1964 and 1965, and the black fear of distracting attention from this crucial domestic reform. African American reluctance to join antiwar critics also embodied the ongoing black dilemma over the desire to serve the nation, demonstrate patriotism, and enhance the case for more equal treatment at home, while daily confronting the disparity between America's stated foreign policy objectives and the treatment of domestic minorities.

Other southern black critics also opted decisively for the ongoing demonstration of African American patriotism and national loyalty and against linking civil rights actions and antiwar protests. In Atlanta two Morehouse College professors dismissed the SNCC position as "senseless" and destructive of the "whole civil rights movement." By mixing the issues of civil rights and the war, suggesting defiance of the draft law, and thereby addressing "highly sensitive and complex foreign policy issues that touch all Americans in . . . a raw sensitive way," SNCC endangered progress at home. Blacks had worked too long to convince Americans "that protesting and demonstrating against racial injustice" was "not treason," only to risk having such efforts squandered by rash actions. Southern black papers ranging from the Democratic *Norfolk Journal and Guide* to the Republican *Atlanta Daily World* and *Jackson Advocate* concurred. Both the *Journal and Guide* and the *Daily World* extolled the bravery and patriotism of black soldiers and expressed deep discomfort with SNCC and Bond for appearing to endorse draft resistance. Although both papers doubted that Bond would have been expelled from the Georgia House of Representatives had he been white, the *Journal and Guide* described him as "rash" and "impolitic" and dismissed his stance as unacceptable to "patriotic, law-abiding American citizens." The *Daily World* agreed and castigated any actions that conveyed the "impression" that African Americans were unwilling to bear their fair "share of responsibility" for "military service." The *Advocate* berated Bond as an "ill-advised Negro" and the "dupe" of the "most sinister [communist] forces in the world today."[37]

Muhammad Ali's refusal to be inducted into the US Army in April

1967 raised similar, very southern issues of race, religion, and patriotism. Together with Reverend King, Ali was a well-known African American, possessed a truly international presence, and became the "most visible symbol of resistance to the draft." Born Cassius Clay in Louisville, Kentucky, in 1942, the talented young boxer had represented the United States in the 1960 Olympic Games and gone on to become the heavyweight champion of the world in 1964 at the age of twenty-two. His problems with the draft and the US justice system followed soon thereafter. Ali, who converted to the Nation of Islam and changed his name in 1964, had failed the mental aptitude portion of predraft testing. As the demand for soldiers increased and standards for induction were lowered, his score left him eligible for the draft, and in February 1966, he was reclassified and notified that he would soon be called for service. The following month Ali petitioned his Louisville draft board for deferment as a conscientious objector. He based his petition on his Muslim faith and the Koran, which limited adherents to participation in defensive, holy wars. His attorney also cited the absence of blacks on his draft board. His petition was denied, and he was directed to appear in April 1967 at Houston, Texas, where he refused induction. Ali's refusal led to his conviction in June of draft evasion, carrying a five-year prison sentence and a $10,000 fine. He remained free while his case was appealed and eventually overturned by the US Supreme Court, which upheld his CO status in June 1971.[38]

Race and religion were at the heart of Ali's response to war and the draft. He emphasized, "I am a member of the Black Muslims, and we don't go to war unless they're declared by Allah himself." That the young athlete sincerely acted on principle was evident when he declined a noncombat military assignment in the US Army and the opportunity to serve safely in the National Guard. Still, sincere dedication to the Muslim faith counted for little in 1960s America, particularly in the South. Ali's racial views and connection of the war to the domestic treatment of blacks also proved inflammatory. He told a Louisville audience, "Why should they ask me and other so-called Negroes to put on a uniform and go 10,000 miles from home and drop bombs on brown people in Viet Nam while so-called Negro people in Louisville are treated like dogs and denied simple human rights?" Ali had emphasized previously that he had "no personal quarrel with those Vietcong" and subsequently asserted in 1970 that African Americans should not wage war on their "Asian brothers" since "they never lynched you, never called you nigger, never put dogs on you, never shot your leaders." For Ali, religion and race trumped patriotism.[39]

Protests by the Mississippi Freedom Democrats, SNCC, Julian Bond, and Muhammad Ali were important, but all paled in comparison to those of Reverend King, the South's and the nation's most influential African American. Although King did not devote a complete speech to the war until February 1967, he had begun expressing grave reservations as early as March 1965. Like leaders of the NAACP and Urban League, King recognized President Johnson's decisive role in the passage of the 1964 and 1965 civil rights bills and was reluctant to criticize the administration's Vietnam policies—hence the relatively muted nature of his early comments. In March 1965 he called for a negotiated settlement and judged that the war was "accomplishing nothing"; in June he recommended involving the UN in these negotiations; in July he told a meeting of the SCLC the war "must be stopped" and the Vietcong included in peace talks; and in August he expressed his concern over the daily "reports of villages destroyed and people left homeless" and of "an ever-widening war" and urged an end to US bombing of North Vietnam. Even these positions, which differed little from those of Fulbright, Gore, and Cooper, were too strident for other major civil rights leaders and King's SCLC, where Andrew Young dismissed the peace movement as a "band wagon that's playing a 'square' tune." Johnson, who, according to one staffer, rejected the idea of a "separate Negro view of foreign policy," was enraged by King's seeming lack of gratitude and loyalty and dispatched Senator Thomas Dodd (D-CT) to proclaim that King had "absolutely no competence" in international relations and had succeeded only in alienating "much of the support he previously enjoyed in Congress."[40]

If Johnson, whites generally, and more restrained African Americans were distressed at King's 1965 pronouncements, they grew more aggrieved as the SCLC leader became progressively and more outspokenly antiwar over the ensuing two years. Diverse considerations impelled Reverend King toward more shrill denunciations of the war. Linking racial considerations to some of the public figures and newspapers that objected to his addressing the war, King rejected their "assumption that foreign policy is a white man's business." He understood that the war consumed precious resources that might have been used to relieve domestic poverty and inequality. In December 1966 he lamented, "The bombs in Vietnam explode at home; they destroy the hopes and possibilities for a decent America. . . . The chaos of the cities, the persistence of poverty, the degenerating of our national prestige throughout the world are compelling arguments for achieving peace agreements." Religious and humanitarian convictions also prompted the Baptist minister to recoil from the violence, destruction, and death in Vietnam. He told his congregation at Ebenezer Baptist Church in Atlanta in February 1966 that it was "just as evil to kill Vietnamese, as it is to kill Americans, because they are God's children." In a subsequent newspaper column, King elaborated: "A war in which children are incinerated by napalm, in which soldiers die in mounting numbers while other American soldiers, according to press accounts, . . . shoot the wounded enemy as he lies upon the ground, is a war that murders the conscience." More mundane considerations also figured into King's assessment. He recognized that his previous, more restrained pronouncements had not been effective; and after passage of the two landmark civil rights bills and the subsequent splintering of the Civil Rights Movement, the SCLC leader had far less to lose politically by opposing Johnson.[41]

King articulated a full-blown antiwar stance in early 1967. In February, at a conference in Los Angeles, he made his first full public speech against the war. He situated the war as part of a larger effort designed "to turn the clock of history back and perpetuate white colonialism." This futile effort demonstrated "our paranoid anti-communism" and a "deadly Western arrogance" and further embodied "the triple events of racism, extreme materialism and militarism." To this fundamental critique of US foreign policy, King added his more specific objections to American intervention in a Vietnamese "civil war," "recalcitrant unwillingness" to halt the bombing and negotiate, the war's "nightmarish" physical casualties, and the terrifying possibility of "nuclear destructiveness."[42]

Six weeks later, on April 4, King delivered his "Beyond Vietnam" speech at the Riverside Church in New York City before an audience of three thousand. He reiterated many of the points he had made since March 1965. The war was "an enemy of the poor"; it commandeered "black young men who had been crippled by our society" and sent them "to guarantee liberties in Southeast Asia" that had been denied in "Southwest Georgia and East Harlem." Acting out of racism and "deadly western arrogance," the United States had "rejected a revolutionary government seeking self-determination" in favor of a South Vietnamese client state that was "singularly corrupt, inept and without popular support." The United States needed to acknowledge its mistakes, "atone for our sins and errors in Vietnam," and "take the initiative in bringing a halt to this tragic war." King's prescription for ending the war included an end to the bombing of North and South Vietnam, a "unilateral cease fire" to "create the atmosphere for negotiations," recognition that the National Liberation Front would "play a role in any meaningful negotiations and in any future Vietnam government," and setting a date for the withdrawal of "all foreign troops from Vietnam in accordance with the 1954 Geneva Agreement." By calling for an end to the bombing in South Vietnam, a unilateral cease-fire, and a designated date for US troop withdrawal, King had gone much further than major white southern antiwar figures. To these comparatively inflammatory recommendations, he added the argument that the pursuit of "immense profits of overseas investment" had corrupted US foreign policy, that young American men should seek CO status if they deemed "the American course in Vietnam . . . dishonorable," that the United States had become the world's "greatest purveyor of violence," and that the Vietcong and North Vietnamese had ample reason to distrust the United States.[43]

Although the SCLC had joined its leader in the antiwar column in late 1966, only SNCC and the Congress of Racial Equality agreed with his hardline stance. Both the Urban League and the NAACP quickly disassociated themselves from any combination of the civil rights and peace movements. The latter condemned such an association as "a serious tactical mistake" that aided "the cause neither of civil rights nor of peace." Other prominent African Americans, ranging from Bayard Rustin and Ralph Bunche to Jackie Robinson, voiced objections. Several southern black papers were also critical. The *Norfolk Journal and Guide* feared King's "verbal bombshell" had provided ammunition to critics of the Civil Rights Movement, divided "civil rights forces," and "damaged if not destroyed" the movement. Sounding the familiar theme that patriotic service would benefit blacks following the war, the *Dallas Post Tribune* asserted that African Americans had to "help our country fight this involved and tragic war." The far more hawkish *Atlanta Daily World* and *Jackson Advocate,* both Republican papers, were even more critical. The

Daily World objected to King taking any stand on a war in progress and denounced him for "encouraging young men to shirk the draft"; and the *Advocate* considered his pronouncements "absurd and ridiculous" and asked if "the United States should roll over and play dead" as communists "take over the world." By 1967, King's provocative denunciation of US foreign policy and the war was a minority position not just among civil rights activists but also among African Americans more generally. According to a May 1967 Harris Poll, 48 percent of blacks disagreed with his position on the war, 25 percent approved, and 27 percent had not yet decided. Significantly, like southern white opponents of the war, King could not successfully mount a persuasive antiwar brief, even among a majority of African Americans, upon whom the war fell most heavily and who were far less supportive of the conflict than whites.[44]

King may have elicited a mixed response from African Americans, but the reaction of southern whites was far more uniformly hostile. Andrew Young subsequently offered an incisive explanation for much of this reaction: "International relations in the 1960s were largely the province of an elite club of upper-class white males." This elite and most other whites were "as surprised to find a Southern black preacher with strong and sophisticated opinions on international policy" as they were "by the opinions themselves." Agreeing with arch-segregationist George Wallace, who had altered his campaign mantra from "Nigger-nigger-nigger" to "Commie-Commie-Commie," and who traced the Civil Rights Act of 1964 to the Communist Manifesto, many southerners reflexively linked King and the Civil Rights Movement to the Cold War communist threat. A Virginian asked, "Just what color does the real Reverend King represent? Black with shades of pink? Or red with shades of black?" Another resident of the Old Dominion wrote directly to King, declaring the United States had never witnessed "a bigger hate merchant and absolute hypocrite than you." One southern hawk called not just for "the use of every modern weapon at our disposal" in Vietnam but also government action to "stop completely the domestic activities of the scores of communist-supported traitors such as M. L. King, [Stokely] Carmichael, our Berkeley friends, etc." A Louisiana resident, who denounced Carmichael's "rantings and ravings," expressed even greater scorn for King for not "preaching . . . the gospel of Jesus Christ but a tirade against his own government." Noting that King had based a portion of his opposition to the war on its diversion of national attention from pressing domestic problems, a rural Georgian asked if the head of the SCLC would support the "war if it focused attention on the civil rights movement." King, he concluded, "would rather see some negro in Podunk, Iowa get his 'civil rights' than to see millions in Vietnam get their human rights." Adding another southern racial perspective, an Alabama opponent of the war called for US withdrawal by arguing that the Soviet Union and China sought to "drain us to the core," thereby making it "easy . . . for these Communists and Negroes to take over the Government."[45]

White southerners were also outraged at Muhammad Ali's initial disqualification for service and his ultimate refusal to be inducted. To a Texas couple, it seemed "indefensible" that Ali could "lack sufficient intelligence to learn to shoot firearms." Inappropriate "political influence" must have been responsible for "such an outrageous injustice to the entire country and its armed forces." Demonstrating the class resentment often directed at antiwar protestors, a Mississippian pronounced the "handling of the drafting of Cassius Clay . . . a disgrace" akin to "to others who are rich" and who avoided the war with the help of "friends or kin in very high places." Another disgruntled southerner declared that if Ali were not thrown "in jail . . . , every white person should refuse to serve, and every draft board in the United States should resign."[46]

Southern politicians were equally strident in their denunciations. Following the Supreme Court's reversal of Ali's conviction for draft evasion, several southern congressmen expressed this outrage. William F. Nichols (D-AL) derided the court's decision as "another black eye" for the US military and a "stinging rebuke to the 240,000 Americans still in Vietnam" and the 50,000 who had died there. Louisiana Democrat Joe Waggoner disparaged Ali as a "phony" who had ostensibly been exempted for "questionable religious beliefs" but must have been allowed to avoid induction "because he is black and a prizefighter." George W. Andrews (D-AL) compared Ali to Lieutenant William Calley, who had been convicted earlier in 1971 of murdering Vietnamese civilians at My Lai in 1968. Calley was "a poor little fellow" who had "volunteered and offered his life for his country," only to be convicted of murder "for carrying out orders." Ali, by contrast, had "thumbed his nose at the flag" and was "still walking the streets making millions of dollars fighting for pay, not for his country."[47]

As this national debate over the conduct of the war raged on during 1967, Senators Fulbright, Gore, and Cooper sustained their antiwar advocacy. Fulbright began the year on January 9 by assuming his customary position as the only person willing to forthrightly oppose President Johnson in a White House meeting of Democratic committee chairmen. While endorsing a resolution to cap US forces in Vietnam at 500,000 the following month, the Arkansas senator also reiterated his "regret" at not holding hearings on the Gulf of Tonkin Resolution and for uncritically accepting Johnson's assurances that no military escalations were under consideration. Portraying himself as "a simple Ozark hillbilly," Fulbright contended that since the United States had intervened "more or less casually by mistake," it would be far more honorable to admit that mistake than to "wipe off the face of the earth a small, weak, underdeveloped country." America needed "to confess its mistakes in judgment like I am willing to confess mine" and to pursue a negotiated settlement instead of an unobtainable military victory. To a constituent, he prophetically argued that a negotiated settlement was possible only if the United States halted the bombing, committed to a date for the withdrawal of its troops, and agreed to a genuine compromise. Although it would be another five years before President Nixon grudgingly accepted this prescription, Fulbright had provided the alternative policy Johnson had demanded the previous year.[48]

Amid rumors and discussions over the major escalation of the war during the spring and President Johnson's summons of General Westmoreland home for a positive public update in April, Fulbright's apprehensions mounted. On July 25, in another meeting of the Senate committee chairmen with LBJ, the senator resumed his lecturing of the president by boldly stating, "Mr. President, what you really need to do is stop the war." He continued, "The Vietnam war is a hopeless venture. Nobody likes it. . . . Vietnam is ruining our domestic and our foreign policy. I will not support it any longer." An infuriated Johnson responded, "Bill everybody doesn't have a blind spot like you do. You say don't bomb North Vietnam on just about everything. I don't have the simple solution you have." The president then played his hole card. If Fulbright and opponents of the war wanted the United States out of Vietnam, they could repeal the Gulf of Tonkin Resolution: "You can tell the troops to come home. You can tell General Westmoreland that he doesn't know what he is doing."[49]

At least a part of Johnson's angry response derived from his realization that Fulbright was right about both the war's domestic and international impact and the slight chance of gaining a military victory. LBJ also agonized over the responsibility of ordering "the flower of our youth, our finest young men, into battle." As the war ground on and the deaths and injuries mounted far beyond his expectations, "the war became a source of great personal grief." Admiral Thomas Moorer observed, "You always discussed Vietnam [with Johnson], no matter where you were"; and the president sincerely told the parents of a US soldier who had died in Vietnam that there was "no American killed or wounded in battle for whom I do not feel a sense of personal responsibility." Senator Russell eventually sought to avoid visiting his old friend in the White House because he could not bear to see Johnson crying uncontrollably over the war and US casualties. But as Johnson had confided to Lady Bird in 1965, "I can't get out. I can't finish with what I've got. So what the hell do I do?"[50]

Through the summer of 1967, the president slogged on, hoping against hope for a military breakthrough, and Fulbright continued his antiwar campaign. In addition to his Senate and public speeches and direct personal appeals to Johnson, the SFRC chairman sought to enlarge the southern antiwar contingent. Specifically, he attempted to recruit fellow southerners John Sparkman, Richard Russell, and Sam Ervin. With no chance of appealing to his more hawkish Dixie colleagues to support an end to the bombing of North Vietnam and a negotiated settlement, he turned instead to overtures designed to regain a more integral Senate role in the conduct of US foreign relations—a role that would come at the expense of the executive branch. In July Russell voiced alarm over a possible US intervention in the Congo and warned against becoming embroiled in "local rebellions and local wars" where the United States had "no stake and . . . no legal and moral commitment to intervene." Fulbright responded with his previous complaint that the executive branch had persistently committed the United States to strategic obligations without proper congressional involvement. He also proposed a Senate resolution stating that a US national commitment "necessarily and exclusively" resulted from the "affirmative action taken by the executive and legislative branches" via "a treaty, convention, or other legislative instrumentality specifically intended" to create "such a commitment." Fulbright introduced this resolution on July 31, 1967, describing it as "a conservative position which seeks to recover in some degree the constitutional role of the Senate in the making of foreign policy."[51]

Both Russell and Ervin forcefully endorsed the resolution. Russell knew of "nothing . . . more in need of clarification" than "alleged commitments of the United States all over the world"; and Ervin considered the resolution "a real, a lasting, and a most significant service to the country." The following month, Fulbright held SFRC hearings on the resolution, which provoked considerable public discussion and congressional consternation when Under Secretary of State Nicholas Katzenbach termed the Gulf of Tonkin Resolution the "functional equivalent" of a congressional declaration of war. Fulbright had "planted the seed that would flower" into subsequent congressional challenges to executive domination of Vietnam policy and US foreign policy more generally, but he once again failed to move Russell, Ervin, Sparkman, or Stennis over to the antiwar column.[52]

Despite this tactical failure, Fulbright could take solace from the ongoing antiwar advocacy of Albert Gore and John Sherman Cooper and, by late spring, the conversion of Senator Thruston Morton (R-KY), who began to bolster the arguments of this influential southern group. Gore remained particularly apprehensive that the US intervention in Vietnam could lead to a direct military clash, even a nuclear exchange with the Soviet Union or China. He emphasized to his constituents that there would be "no winner," only "losers," regardless of which nation "suffered the greatest damage" from the use of nuclear weapons. Cooper agreed. Responding on May 15 to the rumors of an imminent escalation of the war, Cooper worried such a step could foreclose "the last possibility for a peaceful settlement"—that "ever increasing bombing" could lead China and Russia into the conflict or even provoke World War III.[53]

To these familiar arguments, the senators added two contentions certain to ruffle feathers in Dixie. Gore's fellow southern Baptists no doubt agreed with his assertion that America's Judeo-Christian culture with its "noble," democratic impulses confronted "Communism, a type of materialistic religion," which had "adopted war as an instrument for its expansion." The senator's Christian constituents were equally certain to have rejected his portrayal of the United States as a coaggressor when he characterized the Cold War as a "confrontation between two aggressive cultures" with the American side being "evangelical in its zeal." Cooper was equally provocative when he likened US actions in Southeast Asia to Soviet attempts to establish a military presence in Cuba. Just as the United States viewed the USSR as "an intruder in the Western Hemisphere" and a security threat, perhaps China feared the American presence in Vietnam as "threatening its security and interests."[54]

By mid-May 1967, Fulbright's, Gore's, and Cooper's antiwar credentials were prominently established; but signs of Thurston Morton, Cooper's moderate Republican colleague from Kentucky, rethinking his hawkish position were significant from the perspective of the generally prowar Republican Party, congressional dynamics, and southern support for the war. On May 11, Morton warned that a reported streamlining of the US–South Vietnamese pacification effort might lead to a "long-term and massive American occupation . . . to secure a postwar Vietnamese Government." Twelve days later, Morton returned to the Senate floor to voice his dismay over a recent poll indicating 45 percent of Americans favored "a policy of total military victory" in Vietnam. While denouncing this "dangerous illusion," he enumerated what total military victory would entail. It required identifying and neutralizing the VC forces, who controlled "75 percent" of South Vietnam's hamlets; "destroying or driving out" North Vietnam's units in the South; demolishing Hanoi's "military installations and much of her population"; and likely facing a "total war with China." In mid-August, the senator went even further by joining Fulbright, Gore, Cooper, and Reverend King in their call for an end to the bombing of North Vietnam and a "de-escalation" of the war, leading to American "disinvolvement."[55]

As debate over how best to conduct the war extended into the summer, observers ranging from *New York Times* correspondent R. W. Apple Jr. to the keen North Vietnamese military observer General Vo Nguyen Giap pronounced the conflict a "stalemate." With no discernible progress, draft calls surpassing thirty thousand per month, and the cumulative effect of images and accounts of American suffering and death, popular support for the war declined precipitously. July polling found that 46 percent of those polled agreed with Apple and Giap that the United States was "standing still," and only 34 percent believed America was "making progress." This Gallup Poll also revealed that 41 percent of those questioned felt the United States had made a "mistake" in sending combat troops to Vietnam; by October, that percentage had increased to 47 percent, a majority of those polled. The mounting public disillusionment was also evident in Gallup's August results, which placed Johnson's approval rating for his handling of Vietnam at 33 percent (down from 41 percent in January) versus 52 percent disapproval.[56]

The South's 1967 polling responses to the war aligned with patterns established over the previous three years. Dixie remained the region least approving of Johnson's performance as president and his handling of the war. In January 38 percent of southerners consulted approved of his work as chief executive, versus 46 percent nationally and 44 percent of the next most negative region; by November, these figures were 37, 41, and 36, respectively. Dixie residents were also most critical of LBJ's handling of Vietnam. Only 32 percent approved of this facet of his foreign policy in January, and the region's positive assessment fell to 25 percent in September (versus 67 percent disapproval) and never exceeded 35 percent over the course of 1967. Even in Texas, only 45 percent of voters approved of Johnson's handling of his duties as president, versus 39 percent who disapproved. Much of his home-state response divided along party lines of Democratic endorsement and Republican and independent objection. When asked to express one thing they liked or disliked about LBJ's presidential performance, 37 percent of Texas respondents expressed "dislike" of his Vietnam policies, versus 16 percent professing "like."[57]

Most southern responses to more specific Vietnam questions confirmed the region's martial image. Dixie was the American region most in favor of going "all-out to win a military victory in Vietnam," even if that effort included using "atomic bombs." Thirty-three percent of Dixie residents endorsed this alternative, and 52 percent objected, compared to national responses of 26 and 64, respectively, and 26 and 65 for the next most warlike region (the Midwest). Southerners were also most supportive of a "military man" as the leader of the South Vietnamese government—43 percent versus the national response of 36; least in favor of a long bombing pause over North Vietnam or the offer of economic incentives to the Vietcong to induce negotiations; and most willing to pay higher taxes "to help pay for the war in Vietnam." Still, even as they endorsed an aggressive military posture, southerners, like the remainder of the nation, had clearly become disillusioned with the costs of the war. In both February and May, Dixie residents were most in agreement with the assertion that the United States had erred in sending troops to Vietnam; and in October southerners trailed only the East (37 to 41 percent) in supporting an immediate withdrawal of American troops.[58]

Letters to editors and senators amplified these poll results. Usually reflecting the national frustration with Johnson's limited-war strategy and failure to defeat a seemingly weaker opponent, the prowar arguments remained largely unchanged. An Arkansas attorney who had served in World War I declared there should be no "Marquis of Queensberry Rules in War," and a Louisiana resident railed at America's "Powder Puff War." Another Fulbright correspondent agreed that it made no sense to invest the resources required to "be the most powerful nation on earth," to "build such a power and then be afraid to use it." A North Carolinian dismissed limited war as a "farce" in which the United States annually lost "thousands of young boys" while "getting no closer to an end." "I wonder," asked a High Point, North Carolina, resident, "how a Mother and Father or wife who have lost a son or husband feel knowing their son or husband may have lived" with "the full backing of our military power."[59]

An Atlanta attorney was certain that, with the "exception of a small but loud-mouthed group of misguided pseudo-intellectuals, publicity-seekers, and plain traitors . . . Americans agree whole-heartedly" that the United States should employ "all conventional military means, to destroy any targets in North Vietnam which are directly or indirectly in support of the enemy's operations against our troops and South Vietnam." Another southerner proclaimed that it was "long past the time that the military be unmuzzled and unmanacled, and any person, politician or otherwise, who impedes their efforts" should be deemed "guilty of treason and . . . be dealt with accordingly." Nor should the unmuzzled military worry unduly about "North Viet Nam's so-called civilian population," which "fully deserves an intensive bombing to reduce their ardor for aggression." How, asked another southerner, was it "humanitarian to consider the lives of American fighting men less important than the lives of civilians in North Vietnamese cities?" A Baton Rouge father and veteran of World War II and Korea decried the "war of attrition" and the "weak guts" in the State and Defense Departments. The Johnson administration should "be told *now* that the American people are up to their ears in the liberal frightened communist vomit that says we must allow Russia and even our allies to prolong this senseless fight."[60]

Consistent with Gallup polling, one Georgia resident did not "object to paying additional taxes for the support of the war," but he added a significant caveat—only "*if* we are seriously attempting" to prevail militarily. Other essentially prowar southerners had similar reactions to President Johnson's call in 1967 for a surtax to help fund the war. A Virginian declared he was "bitterly opposed" to the proposed surtax since the nation's budget deficit resulted from "the wild, cynical, and staggering political give-away programs" rather than the war. For antiwar southerners, their aversion to taxes provided a central argument. One stated simply, "I am very unhappy about the tax money spent on the war in Vietnam."[61]

Fiscal concerns constituted only one species of the southern public's ongoing dissent. The possibility of war with China haunted the South's antiwar public as well as its most dovish senators. A Memphis resident reminded Senator Gore "that World War I started because of bluffs that were called"; and a crusty Mississippian, who had flown in both World War II and Korea, lectured Senator Stennis on the danger of a "stray bomb load" near the North Vietnam–China border. From Jackson, this former pilot described how MacArthur "misjudged the Red Chinese." Was his hawkish senator "*absolutely positive* that this increased bombing will not cause China to come to the aid of North Vietnam? If you aren't positive, it is comparable to a man trying to drive a car . . . blindfolded— he doesn't know what he is doing and shouldn't be doing it."[62]

Southern dissidents added other political and strategic reservations. A Russell constituent contended there was "no stable nation" in South Vietnam "on which to build a 'Far Eastern line of defense.'" To the contrary, the country was "plagued with utter corruption," and the South Vietnamese were "incapable of—and woefully uninterested in—democracy." Many southerners worried that the United States had become dangerously overcommitted in Southeast Asia. A Virginian linked the war's reported cost of $2 billion per month to the nation's "general protector role of world freedom" and called for a reappraisal of "the foreign policy that makes the U.S. the public defender and provider of every nation." An "eighth generation white Southerner" added an ironic twist to the issue of US overcommitment abroad. "How," she asked, "can we be presumptuous enough to tell Asiatics how to put their houses in order when our own is such a mess?" Indeed, the United States was "reaping the results of a hundred years of indignities heaped on our Negro citizens."[63]

For some southerners, US actions were so immoral they warranted comparisons to those of Nazi Germany. Was the use of "torture, gas, and civilian bombing evil *only* when it is done by Nazis or Communists?" A Korean War veteran and a self-described "patriot and productive member of the community" informed Senator Ervin, "Every day our great country resembles a bit more the Germany my family fled in the 1930s." And a staunch advocate of states' rights, who was aghast at the federal government's increasing power, equated US actions at home and abroad: "In Viet Nam and in Social Reform we are tilting with windmills. . . . You cannot wipe out poverty or nationalism—they are the only truly immortal things." Some problems simply could not be "fixed by Uncle Sam."[64]

Against this backdrop of public and political discord, Senator John Stennis led the most concerted congressional effort to force President Johnson to fundamentally alter his conduct of the conflict by scrapping his policies of gradualism and limited war in favor of unrestricted bombing of North Vietnam. Although the president had approved nearly one hundred new Rolling Thunder targets since January and granted General Westmoreland an additional fifty thousand troops in July, he had not consented to the bombing of areas closely adjacent to Hanoi or along the Chinese border, the bombing of Haiphong and mining of its harbor, or the invasion of North Vietnam and neighboring countries of Laos and Cambodia. By overseeing the SPIS hearings in August to appraise the "Air War Against North Vietnam," Stennis, together with his allies on the subcommittee, attempted to transform the conduct of the war from Johnson's policy of "defeat avoidance" into the "all-out" pursuit of victory advocated by the Joint Chiefs of Staff and their most hawkish backers. In addition to his conviction that graduated bombing pressure on North Vietnam was a flawed and failed policy, Stennis and other SPIS hawks feared that without tangible progress an increasingly frustrated and impatient American public might force the compromise settlement Fulbright, Gore, and Cooper were advocating. Stennis and Senator Stuart Symington (D-MO), both tireless boosters of the military, warned that a stalemated war could unfairly discredit US airpower, and they shared Army Chief of Staff Harold K. Johnson's uneasiness that the military leadership rather than civilian leaders and bureaucrats would "take the fall" for failure in Vietnam.[65]

The setting and tone of the Stennis hearings contrasted sharply with those directed by Fulbright the previous year. Held behind closed doors in the Old Senate Office Building in deference to security concerns, the sessions, which ran from August 9 through 25, included no bright lights, no television crews, and no cheering audiences. Nor were there tense confrontations among SPIS members, who unanimously favored a more aggressive military posture in Vietnam, or between senators and the military witnesses. To the contrary, the proceedings were rather chummy. Stennis assured US Army general Earle G. Wheeler, "This is not an adversary proceeding. . . . We are working together." Later, the senator told Admiral Thomas H. Moorer, "This is just in the family, Admiral, and I am not trying to spring any surprise question on you."[66]

Stennis's idea of working together was to afford the military commanders what *Newsweek* dubbed a "sanctuary" from which to assault the Johnson administration's strategy of gradualism and bombing restrictions. Stennis and the SPIS envisioned the military testimony as precisely the information necessary to convince the American public that the war was winnable and that aggressive bombing would force the Vietnamese communists to concede. By influencing the public, Stennis and his fellow hawks hoped to push President Johnson to abandon gradualism and adopt the shared SPIS-JCS bombing recommendations. Although the hearings were technically closed, "informed sources" provided the press with the essence of the testimony, and on August 15, Stennis began releasing the opening statement of each witness. These military-friendly dynamics, purposeful leaks, and selected news releases produced what *New York Times* reporter James Reston described as great pressure from the "old militant coalition of leading military and naval officers, Republican political leaders, and Democratic committee chairmen" and what *Newsweek* characterized as the "hawks . . . making their supreme effort."[67]

This supreme effort was clear from the hearings' organization, which was structured to discredit Secretary of Defense McNamara and by extension President Johnson and the administration's wartime leadership. The subcommittee first questioned Admiral Ulysses S. G. Sharp, the Commander in Chief, Pacific Command (CINCPAC), on August 9 and 10; General Wheeler, chairman of the JCS, on August 16; and General John P. McConnell, chief of the air force, on August 22. Their collective military brief for unrestricted bombing was then used to interrogate McNamara on August 25, after which Stennis called General Harold K. Johnson, chief of staff of the army, General Wallace M. Greene, commandant of the marine corps, and retired USAF general

Gilbert L. Meyers to rebut McNamara's positions. The SPIS issued its final report on August 31.

Senator Stennis opened the hearings on the "conduct and effectiveness of the air war against North Vietnam" on August 9 with a statement that clearly conveyed the subcommittee's objectives. Even before taking any testimony, the senator outlined his long-held personal "opinion" that "it would be a tragic and perhaps fatal mistake . . . to suspend or restrict the bombing." "Gratified" that the announcement of the hearings had apparently prompted Johnson's "step-up in the air operations . . . and increased pressure on the enemy," he hoped this pressure would "be further increased . . . and that it will hasten the end of this unhappy war." By "restricting the flow of supplies to the south," bombing had "saved the lives of many brave Americans." Therefore, to constrain Rolling Thunder would be "to throw away" America's "military advantage."[68]

Working from these key assumptions, the Mississippi hawk carefully presided over the hearings but left most of the close questioning of witnesses to others, such as Symington, Strom Thurmond, Margaret Chase Smith (R-ME), Howard C. Cannon (D-NV), Henry Jackson (D-WA), and SPIS chief counsel James T. Kendall. Still, Stennis pointedly elicited testimony from Admiral Sharp agreeing that the bombing restrictions had left many US pilots free only to attack "tree tops"; that many of their missions were "almost an act of futility" since numerous valuable targets had not been "authorized for strike"; that the graduated escalation of the bombing and target restrictions left US pilots much more vulnerable to North Vietnam's antiaircraft system; and that "any thought of stopping the bombing" was, in fact, "unthinkable." From General Wheeler, Stennis obtained the declaration that the JCS had consistently "advocated" that the United States "find a way of obstructing or stopping the flow of war making materials and other supplies" through Haiphong. As Sharp's day before the committee ended, Stennis also voiced his hopes for the proceedings. Since the public was growing increasingly restive, they needed "to know more about this war." With appropriate probombing information, many of their questions "could be explained." The "American public," he continued, would "accept anything if they understand it."[69]

Strom Thurmond, the other southerner on the SPIS, assumed a far more vocal role. Like those of Stennis and the other senators, the South Carolina Republican's views on the war were well established and consistent with majority opinion in Dixie. Thurmond voiced the essential southern perspective when he declared that despite disagreeing with LBJ's "conduct of the war," he was "backing the President in being in Vietnam" since "we cannot afford to lose Southeast Asia to the Communists." He lamented that US efforts had yielded a "stalemate" and declared wars could not be won "by fighting defensive actions." Thurmond could see no justification for sacrificing "thousands and thousands and thousands more" Americans "just to end up with a stalemate." The senator contemptuously dismissed those who disagreed as "possessed of [an] appeasing mind" and influenced by "world opinion or Communist propaganda or State Department propaganda."[70]

From this perspective, Thurmond's persistent question was, "If President Johnson gave you the authority as a military man to take the steps necessary to win this war, . . . what . . . should be done that we are not doing now?" The answer he sought and consistently received was to remove all bombing restrictions over North Vietnam and to close Haiphong harbor. For dissenters who feared China's military intervention, he confidently asserted the PRC would only intervene if the United States sent troops into North Vietnam and that Chinese leaders "must surely know" that "we could destroy their . . . ability to become a world power so far as atomic weapons are concerned."[71]

In response to such leading and unfailingly friendly questions, the first three military witnesses, Admiral Sharp and Generals Wheeler and McConnell, contended that unrestricted US airpower was "the controlling instrument of military power," which the Vietnamese communists could not "successfully oppose." All agreed with McConnell's assertion that the US bombing of North Vietnam "has been, is, and will continue to be both effective and essential." To curtail or end the bombing, Wheeler added, would be viewed by the enemy as "continuing weakness and wavering on our part." The bombing had destroyed key military and industrial targets, impeded the flow of men and materiel south, and signaled to Hanoi and the NLF that continued "aggression" would lead to "penalties of still greater severity." Without the ongoing bombing of the North, as many as eight hundred thousand additional American troops would have been required and many more US casualties incurred in South Vietnam. Only Johnson and McNamara's incremental increases in the bombing of North Vietnam after February 1965; the restrictions on striking key targets near Hanoi, Haiphong, and the Chinese border; and the failure to close Haiphong harbor had prevented US air power from decisively impacting the conflict. Sharp, Wheeler, and McConnell assured the SPIS that numerous additional targets remained to be attacked.[72]

Just as Secretary of State Rusk's testimony had been the key moment of the Fulbright hearings in 1966, Secretary of Defense McNamara's clash with the SPIS on August 25 was the highlight of the Stennis proceedings. McNamara had run afoul of the nation's military leaders and their congressional allies on the SPIS well before his dramatic confrontation with the hawkish senators. Much of the JCS's dislike of the secretary resulted from his assumption of the decision-making authority previously reserved to the service heads. They also reacted viscerally to McNamara the person. Hanson Baldwin, the *New York Times* military editor, spoke for the chiefs when he wrote, "They have little use for what they consider his intellectual arrogance, his over emphasis on cost effectiveness instead of combat effectiveness, and . . . his coldness to people." Compounding these significant irritants, McNamara fundamentally differed with the JCS over how best to fight the war. By agreeing with President Johnson on the need for gradualism and a limited war, the secretary rejected the military preferences. To this seeming disregard for the military leaders' expertise and experience, McNamara added his conclusion as early as November 1965 that the war could not be won militarily. Over the ensuing twenty-two months, the secretary had become convinced that Rolling Thunder had failed and that additional bombing would not block the flow of goods from China and the Soviet Union into North Vietnam, incapacitate Hanoi and bring the North to heel, prevent men and goods from moving south, or prove decisive in South Vietnam. In sum, as he appeared before the SPIS, the *Nation* accurately observed that McNamara differed with the JCS and by extension the promilitary subcommittee "on practically every issue."[73]

Through his opening statement and nearly five hours of withering cross-examination, the defense secretary articulated much of the analysis that has subsequently been used to explain why Rolling Thunder failed to force a seemingly weaker foe to the its knees. Although he stopped short of voicing his conviction that a negotiated, compromise settlement offered the only viable US exit from the war, his testimony pointed indisputably to that Fulbright, Gore, Cooper position. As a "predominantly agricultural" country, North Vietnam had "no real warmaking base . . . which could be destroyed by bombing." Nor was there any evidence that bombing would alter the "resolve" of the nation's leaders or lessen the "support of the . . . people." Both the nature of the war in the South, which required only a few truckloads per day of nonfood shipments, and North Vietnam's complex, resilient transportation system along the Ho Chi Minh Trail negated US efforts to stymie communist efforts in the South by bombing infiltration routes. McNamara was equally adamant that closing Haiphong would not yield victory. Were Haiphong harbor closed, the North Vietnamese would employ alternative land routes and waterways. Unwilling to stop with an explanation for the failure of US bombing to win the war, McNamara further contended that destruction of the ostensibly lucrative remaining targets cited by the chiefs would not produce a different outcome. As the secretary completed his testimony before the exasperated and infuriated SPIS, the *New Yorker* judged that he had cut "the heart out of the military case for bombing North Vietnam."[74]

Stennis and the SPIS categorically rejected such an outcome. The subcommittee promptly called its three military rebuttal witnesses, who predictably impugned all of McNamara's assertions and castigated the Johnson administration's graduated bombing strategy and target restrictions. Were US planes unleashed to begin "hitting them on the jaw" rather than "slapping them on the check," victory would follow. The SPIS then transmitted its report to the parent Senate Armed Services Committee on August 31. The subcommittee contended that while operating within the limitations imposed by Johnson and McNamara, the air war had achieved its objectives. US bombing had impeded the importation of goods into North Vietnam and their subsequent transport to the South, destroyed key military and industrial targets, and punished North Vietnam for its aggression. That these goals had not been more fully realized resulted not from the "impotence of airpower" but from "overly restrictive controls, limitations, and the doctrine of 'gradualism.'" The "cold fact" was that Johnson administration policies, which conflicted with the "best military judgment," had "not done the job" of forcing North Vietnam and the NLF to end the war on American terms. Therefore, the report continued in language that could have been lifted from a Stennis speech, "What is needed now is the hard decision to do whatever is necessary, take the risks that have to be taken, and apply the force that is required to see the job through." Rejecting any "territorial limitation" or "temporary" bombing halts, the SPIS challenged President Johnson to release all bombing targets requested by the military and argued forcefully for the need to bomb the northeast quadrant of North Vietnam, which included the Chinese buffer zone, the areas around Hanoi, and particularly Haiphong harbor. If the president refused to make this "hard decision," to fundamentally alter his conduct of the war, the subcommittee could not, "in good conscience, ask our ground forces to continue their fight in South Vietnam."[75]

The Stennis hearings and report occasioned broad public comment and much disagreement over the sessions' significance. Conservative publications applauded the subcommittee's efforts. The *National Review* declared that the SPIS had "performed a major public service" by gathering the information and publishing its conclusions. *Aviation Week*'s editor, Robert Hotz, charged that US air power had been "frittered away" and opined that the "bitter exchanges" between the SPIS and McNamara revealed the senators' "clear contempt for his credibility" and policies. More liberal press outlets reached opposing conclusions. The *Nation* noted the "serious schism" between the "military . . . on one side, and the other war-makers . . . on the other" and worried that the generals would not have "become as emphatic and venturesome before a Congressional committee" without feeling confident "the tide is running their way." On September 1, following the release of the SPIS report, the *New York Times* entitled its lead editorial, "Generals Out of Control." The paper criticized the military leaders' "insurrection" and declared the "public campaign of some of the nation's top generals for an extension of the bombing" had raised "serious issues of civilian vs. military control of defense and diplomatic policy."[76]

Although no pollsters queried the public directly concerning the Stennis hearings, Harris results from October 1967, following the release of the generals' testimony and the SPIS report, were instructive. Respondents to the question of how Johnson was handling the war answered 23 percent positive and 77 percent negative, the lowest assessment of his presidency. By December, the public also appeared to have adopted the SPIS-military brief for escalating the air war. Harris found a division of 63 to 37 percent favoring escalation over deescalation, compared to a majority endorsing deescalation in July, prior to the hearings. Also in December, respondents by a margin of 58 to 24 percent deemed it necessary "to convince the Communists they will lose if they continue the fighting," and

63 to 24 percent opposed any bombing pause to test Hanoi's willingness to negotiate. The December poll found Americans favoring the mining of Haiphong harbor by a margin of 49 to 29 percent, with 22 percent undecided. Stennis's and Dixie's aggressive positions seemed to have gained majority standing.[77]

The great bulk of John Stennis's southern correspondents during 1967 agreed with these Harris results. Frustrated by American casualties and the failure to defeat the Vietnamese communists and desperate to escape the draining stalemate, they advocated decisive blows against North Vietnam. A Virginian declared, "The American people—the vast majority at any rate—want to see *maximum* force brought to bear to win the war at *minimum* cost to our boys in the field." From Greenwood, Mississippi, came the complaint that "ordinary folks" had grown "angry . . . about our sons and husbands fighting a no-win battle." The preferred approach: "Let's forget the mistaken policy of graduated response and replace it with a policy of total response" designed to bomb North Vietnam into submission.[78]

Just as Fulbright and the SFRC dissenters faced detractors the previous year, Stennis heard from opponents of this majority southern opinion on the conduct of the war. An eighty-five-year-old Alabamian was outraged at the military's perspective. Senators such as Stennis reminded this octogenarian "of a bunch of young birds in their nests. When the mother birds return to the nest ALL OPEN THEIR MOUTHS AND GET IN POSITION TO SWALLOW AND THAT IS JUST WHAT YOU DID." Others were more succinct: "We just could be where we don't belong." Or, "Big men admit being *wrong*. . . . We are WRONG OVER THERE."[79]

The most discussed response from southern legislators to the SPIS push for a fundamental shift in the conduct of the war came from Senator Thruston Morton. The Kentucky Republican had voiced his alarm at the possible US pursuit of "total victory" in May. During August and September, the senator agonized along with the nation over how best to achieve an "honorable withdrawal" from the "two wars in Viet Nam." He believed the United States could "whip the North Vietnamese" but feared the force necessary to do so would draw "China into the picture." The second war, "a civil war in the South," was even more problematic, given the Vietcong's control of much of rural South Vietnam. Morton doubted the

United States could replace the NLF with a "loyal government . . . in each and every village." Nor did he believe that Hanoi would negotiate "while under fire" from US bombing. Since it was apparent that neither the US air war nor ground strategies were working, Morton favored confining US bombing to "supply lines," ending the attacks near "metropolitan areas," and eliminating search-and-destroy ground operations in favor of defending major population centers."[80]

In a prominent Senate speech on September 28 Morton adopted an unusual public posture by admitting he had been "wrong" in supporting the US military escalation in Vietnam. The senator bemoaned the "disastrous decline in the effectiveness of American foreign policy" over the previous three years, the "root cause" of which he traced to the "bankruptcy" of the US position in Vietnam. Unable to envision a "military solution" to the conflict, he called for "an immediate cessation of all bombing of North Vietnam," combined with aggressive "political and diplomatic action." While reiterating his prescription for changes in the US ground strategy, Morton urged the Johnson administration to pressure the South Vietnamese government to adopt reforms and to make it clear that the United States expected an "appropriate response" from North Vietnam and the NLF if America implemented "unilateral disengagement."[81]

Deeply disturbed by Morton's speech, President Johnson summoned the senator to the White House for an unsuccessful session of arm twisting. Fulbright welcomed Morton's conversion to the antiwar perspective and perceived a decisive "swing in opinion in the Senate, as well as in the country." Reporter Don Oberdorfer of the *Washington Post* agreed and cited Morton as a "political weathervane" who symbolized the "millions of American voters" who "along with many religious leaders, editorial writers and elected officials—appeared to be changing their views about the war."[82]

The reactions of Kentuckians to Morton's change of heart on the war mirrored the South's conflicted attitudes on Vietnam rather than any clear growth of antiwar sentiment. A Frankfort resident observed presciently, "It is apparent that you have no intention of running for public office again." What was less evident to this hawk was why the senator had "*sold out* to the liberals." Another critic scolded Morton for having joined the antiwar company of Martin Luther King and northern liberal Democrats such as John Galbraith, Norman Cousins, and Arthur Schlesinger

234 THE AMERICAN SOUTH AND THE VIETNAM WAR

Jr. Other Morton constituents praised his revised position on the war. They recognized that "few men" were "big enough to admit they made a mistake in judgment" and that "great courage" was required to change his "position on such an important issue." As was so often true of antiwar southerners, several hastened to assure Morton they were "loyal Americans," as opposed to "peaceniks," "radicals," "beatniks," "left-wingers," or "pinks."[83]

Responses to the SPIS hearings from congressmen and the public were instructive, but President Johnson's reaction remained decisive. LBJ was no more receptive to the SPIS debate over the nature of the war than he had been to the SFRC hearings the previous year. Following a dinner party with the president, vice president, and several other Democratic senators on September 21, Senator George McGovern described LBJ as a "confused man—literally tortured by the mess he had gotten into in Vietnam. He is restless, almost like a caged lion." Deeply disturbed by McNamara's loss of confidence in Rolling Thunder and movement toward the Fulbright, Gore, and Cooper position, Johnson was also distressed by the secretary's face-off with Stennis, the JCS, and the SPIS—a confrontation that graphically exposed the rift between the administration and its military leaders and their congressional allies. The president deplored the generals' blatant attacks on his policies and bluntly told JCS chairman Wheeler, "Your generals almost destroyed us with their testimony in the hearings," and the JCS were admonished not to "wash any more dirty linen in public." Although Johnson tilted further toward the Stennis position by releasing additional targets on September 2, he rejected the SPIS-military recommendations to bomb or mine Haiphong harbor and target all other military installations in the heavily populated northeast quadrant surrounding Hanoi and Haiphong. He also refused to invade North Vietnam, Cambodia, or Laos. In so doing he clung to his limited-war position and rejected the "all-out" alternative that would have altered fundamentally the conduct of the war. Stennis and the SPIS were no more successful than Fulbright and the SFRC in either convincing or forcing the president and his administration to adopt fundamentally new policies.[84]

Ironically, Stennis and his hearings may have hindered the outcome he sought. By seeking to discredit McNamara and the Defense Department, the Mississippi senator provided the public platform the secretary's fierce personal loyalty to Johnson kept him from adopting on his own. From that platform McNamara articulated a formidable and effective brief against unrestricted bombing of North Vietnam and the accompanying risk of war with China. *New York Times* correspondent Neil Sheehan suggested that McNamara's antibombing arguments ultimately "helped the President to hold the line against the really drastic escalation of the bombing which the generals and their political friends" were advocating.[85]

Still, Stennis and the SPIS had brought the basic divisions between the Johnson administration and the military squarely into the public eye. The JCS brief for unrestricted bombing and McNamara's rejoinder constituted the very debate over strategy that Johnson had so assiduously sought to avoid both publicly and within the administration. While making their case, Stennis, the SPIS, and the military leaders added to the "stab-in-the-back" explanation for the lack of US success in Vietnam. Whereas Rusk and other administration witnesses and supporters during the Fulbright hearings had blamed congressional dissenters, antiwar protestors, and the press for undermining the war effort and encouraging the enemy, the SPIS and the military pointed to Johnson and his civilian advisors as the principal culprits responsible for preventing US soldiers and fliers from winning the war. These hawks argued that the lack of military progress in turn prompted the decline of public support for the US effort. Given Dixie's perceptions of the war as both necessary and winnable, southerners were particularly receptive to this whole array of stab-in-the-back explanations for the lack of US military success in Vietnam.

As the year ended, southerners had continued to play a prominent role in the national debate over US involvement in Vietnam. Much of that debate in 1967 was devoted to the preferred conduct of the military campaign against North Vietnam and the NLF, and Senator John Stennis faithfully represented majority opinion in Dixie. The Mississippi senator remained committed to containing Vietnamese communism but harshly criticized President Johnson's limited-war strategy. The chair of the SPIS argued instead for the JCS preference for an "all-out" war and, along with other southern hawks such as Senators Russell, Thurmond, and Tower, pressured Johnson to adopt a far more aggressive bombing campaign against Hanoi. Like Senator Fulbright and the SFRC in 1966, Stennis and the SPIS stimulated national and, from LBJ's perspective, unwelcome debate, advanced a species of the stab-in-the-back explanation for the lack of US success, but failed to alter the administration's fundamental conduct of the war.

Through their responses to Gallup and Harris polling, letters to their political representatives, and the prowar positions of the influential Southern Baptist Convention and the Presbyterian Church of the United States, the clear majority of southerners signaled their agreement with Stennis's prescription for wining the war. Despite their vocal criticism of Johnson and his conduct of the war, southerners sustained their critical regional support for the conflict, and Dixie remained the nation's most prowar region. Without that regional support, it would have been much more difficult for Johnson to have persisted in waging an increasingly unpopular war. But even among the prowar southern majority, the war's accompanying agony was apparent. Many worried that the war's costs and lack of clear progress were damaging national patriotism. Others had come to believe that the United States had erred in sending combat troops to Vietnam and objected to paying higher taxes or allowing their sons to go off to battle unless Johnson lifted all restrictions on the conflict's prosecution.

Dixie's African Americans felt the war's agony most acutely. Long conscious of the disparity between the nation's expressed mission to bolster democracy and equality abroad and the treatment of people of color at home, black organizations and individuals such as Reverend King, Muhammad Ali, SNCC, and SCLC denounced the war in Vietnam. They asserted that African Americans were bearing an undue burden of the fighting, and the war distracted American attention from the Civil Rights Movement and the pursuit of domestic racial equality. Fearful that such protests would alienate President Johnson, impugn African American patriotism, and harm the campaign for civil rights, other blacks castigated King, Ali, Julian Bond, and SNCC. As with the South's white community, the war occasioned deep rifts and severe anguish among southern blacks; and the majority refused to openly criticize Johnson and the war. Prominent southern white proponents of civil rights dismissed black critics of US foreign policy as badly out of their element, while more hostile southerners arraigned them in far more caustic, often racist terms.

Still, King and black antiwar critics joined other opponents of the Vietnam conflict in offering trenchant criticisms of US involvement. Fulbright, Gore, and Cooper carried on despite the often-hostile responses of their constituents and congressional colleagues. Southern editors Harry

Ashmore and William Baggs, like small-town attorney Frazier Woolard, provided striking, if less well-known, examples of southerners deeply committed to ending the war. Senator Thruston Morton was the most important convert to Dixie's antiwar contingent during 1967. He joined a persistent minority who defied regional trends by registering a broad range of antiwar objections with their congressional representatives and neighbors.

Indeed, as 1967 concluded, four key southerners clearly propounded Dixie's ongoing divisions and embodied the region's prominence in the debate over the war. In an October 12 news conference Secretary Rusk reiterated his unwavering contention that any US adversary's perception that "our treaties are a bluff" could produce "catastrophic" outcomes "for all mankind." Clearly targeting domestic critics of the administration, the secretary castigated anyone who sullied the "credibility" of America's "pledged word" and thereby subjected the "nation to mortal danger." Senator Tower, just back from another trip to South Vietnam, praised the ARVN, agreed that the "only place we can lose this war . . . is in Washington," and saw "no honor in vacating solemn commitments" and no "security in . . . turning away as aggression triumphs."[86]

Senators Gore and Fulbright, two of the antiwar dissenters toward whom Rusk's and Tower's barbs were directed, pointedly disagreed with such assertions. In an extended Senate speech on October 24, Gore questioned the administration's sincerity in calling for negotiations: "If in fact we are in mortal peril in Vietnam, what is there to negotiate?" The Tennessee senator bluntly rejected Rusk's contention that either US "security" or "vital interests" were at risk there and proposed the neutralization of Vietnam as the only course through which the United States could escape the war with its "honor" intact. Six weeks later, Fulbright defended the right of dissent as "inalienable" and mocked the administration's suggestion that all critics "ought to be gratified," given Washington's "restraint in allowing us to express our views." He too dismissed Rusk's arguments regarding US credibility. Far from instilling confidence in US foreign policy and the nation's "readiness to discharge all of its prodigal commitments around the world," the war had demonstrated American inability to suppress this "war of national liberation" and raised questions over whether the American people would permit "their Government to plunge into another such costly adventure."[87]

President Lyndon B. Johnson and General William Westmoreland, a South Carolina native and US commander in Vietnam, 1964–1968, who was described as personifying the South's military tradition. Courtesy of the Library of Congress.

President Johnson visiting wounded US troops at Cam Ranh Bay. Photo by Yoichi Oka-moto. Courtesy of the Lyndon Baines Johnson Library and Museum.

President Johnson and his old friend and mentor Senator Richard Russell (D-GA), who was very critical of LBJ's military strategy in Vietnam. Photo by Yoichi Okamoto. Courtesy of the Lyndon Baines Johnson Library and Museum.

Senators John C. Stennis (D-MS) and Russell expressed perceptive reservations about US military involvement in Vietnam before becoming unwavering supporters of the war effort. John C. Stennis Collection. Courtesy of the Congressional and Political Research Center, Mississippi State University Libraries.

Senator Allen J. Ellender (D-LA) also counseled both Presidents John F. Kennedy and Johnson against US intervention in Vietnam before joining the phalanx of dependable, conservative southern Democratic backers of the conflict. Courtesy of US Senate Historical Office.

Senator Russell Long (D-LA), a member of the Senate Foreign Relations Committee and one of President Johnson's most vocal prowar backers. Photo by Yoichi Okamoto. Courtesy of the Lyndon Baines Johnson Library and Museum.

Congressman L. Mendel Rivers (D-SC), the South's most flamboyant and unrestrained hawk and a champion of US military spending, especially in his Charleston district. Courtesy of the Library of Congress.

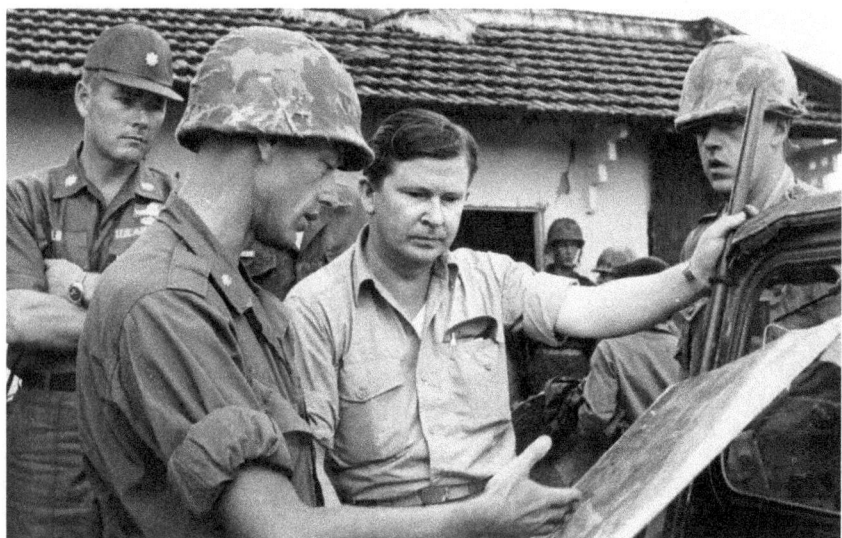

Senator John Tower (R-TX) visited Vietnam more often than any other senator or congressman. Like conservative southern Democrats, he provided both Johnson and Richard M. Nixon critical prowar support while castigating Johnson's limited-war policies. Courtesy of the US Senate Historical Office.

Secretary of State Dean Rusk and Senator J. William Fulbright (D-AR) prior to one of their many hostile exchanges during Senate Foreign Relations Committee hearings on the war. Courtesy of the Library of Congress.

Senator Albert Gore Sr. (D-TN), a member of the Senate Foreign Relations Committee, was one of the earliest and most outspoken critics of the war during both the Johnson and the Nixon years. Courtesy of the Library of Congress.

Senator John Sherman Cooper (R-KY) was one of the South's and the nation's most thoughtful and influential critics of the war. Courtesy of the Library of Congress.

Secretary Rusk testifying before the Senate Foreign Relations Committee. Courtesy of the US Senate Historical Office.

Reverend Martin Luther King Jr.'s forceful opposition to the war infuriated President Johnson and exposed significant divisions within the African American community. Courtesy of the Library of Congress.

Julian Bond, a civil rights and antiwar activist, was forced to sue to secure the seat in the Georgia legislature to which he had been elected. Courtesy of the Library of Congress.

Senator Thruston B. Morton's (R-KY) conversion to an antiwar stance in 1967 prompted extensive public comment and signified the increasing agony caused by the war in the South and nationally. Courtesy of the Library of Congress.

Senator Herman E. Talmadge (D-GA) elicited harsh criticism from a majority of his prowar constituents and hopeful praise from southern dissenters when he began to criticize President Nixon's Vietnam policies in 1970–1971. Courtesy of the Library of Congress.

Congressman F. Edward Hebert's (D-LA) direction of House Armed Services Subcommittee hearings on My Lai faithfully represented the South's majority prowar and promilitary inclinations. Courtesy of the Library of Congress.

Jerry McCuistion, an Alabamian and the wife of an American POW, was a prominent activist who helped raise the POW/MIA issue to national prominence. Courtesy of Jerry McCuistion.

6

Southerners and the Decisions to Withdraw from Vietnam, 1968–1970

During the early morning of January 30, 1968, the first day of Tet, the Vietnamese lunar New Year, the Vietcong and North Vietnamese forces attacked every important urban area and many key military installations across South Vietnam. The largest military operation of the war to that time, the Tet Offensive was the conflict's decisive turning point. Although Hanoi failed to spark a general uprising against the South Vietnamese government or to capture and retain control of any South Vietnamese cities, Tet prompted first President Johnson and then President Richard M. Nixon to opt for US withdrawal from Vietnam. As the two administrations reluctantly made decisions and initiated policies that pointed toward ultimate withdrawal, majority opinion in Dixie and key southern legislators remained doggedly supportive of US military involvement and adamantly opposed to an outcome that could be construed as a dishonorable American defeat.

This regional perspective became particularly important to President Richard M. Nixon when Democrats from other US regions abandoned the deference they had shown LBJ, a fellow party member. In a pattern that had pertained since the US decisions for war in 1965 and 1966, a vocal southern minority and several key legislators continued to question the rationale for US involvement; press for a negotiated, compromise settlement; advocate an accelerated withdrawal schedule; and demand a greater role for Congress in the conduct of US foreign and military policies. Although Senators Fulbright and Gore remained prominent Dixie doves, John Sherman Cooper assumed an increasingly important role as he and Frank Church (D-ID) cosponsored a series of important measures during the Nixon presidency designed to stop funding of the war. Other facets of the South's experience during the three years after Tet help to explicate these broad public opinions and political trends. The hostile responses of southern communities to antiwar GI coffeehouses reflected the region's prowar proclivities and intolerance of dissent. Dixie's support for the military and the war and impatience with restraints on either were similarly apparent in the section's response to the My Lai massacre and the prosecution of Lieutenant William Calley and in the failure of Senators Gore and Ralph Yarborough to gain reelection in 1970.

Upon receiving reports of the Tet Offensive and the primarily Vietcong attacks across the South, Walter Cronkite, the highly respected anchor of the CBS evening news, exclaimed, "What the hell is going on? I thought we were winning the war!" Much of the nation shared Cronkite's dismay. If the United States had been making steady progress and victory were in sight, as the Johnson administration and General Westmoreland had asserted in late 1967 in a concerted public relations campaign, how could the Vietnamese communists mount such a sustained campaign, one that even imperiled the American embassy in the heart of Saigon? This final blow to Johnson's credibility sent his public approval rating for conducting the war to a new low of 26 percent, and he soon faced challenges to his reelection from Senators Eugene McCarthy (D-MN) and Robert F. Kennedy (D-NY). The beleaguered Texan also confronted a mid-March economic crisis in which Great Society– and war-induced deficits threatened the stability of the dollar and the gold standard. As if these collective troubles were not sufficiently unsettling, the "wise men," a group of highly placed and influential advisors with whom Johnson had been consulting periodically, recommended on March 26 against increased troop levels or continued bombing of North Vietnam and in favor of US disengagement and a negotiated settlement of the war. Although Johnson feigned outrage that these "establishment bastards" had "bailed out," the president, with coaching from Secretary of Defense Clark Clifford and Secretary of State Dean Rusk, had reached similar conclusions.[1]

In the wake of Tet and its strategic and domestic fallout, Johnson rejected the military's call for an additional two hundred thousand troops and restricted the bombing of North Vietnam to the area immediately above the demilitarized zone at the seventeenth parallel. Later in October, he extended the bombing halt to all of North Vietnam. With these cumulative strategic moves, LBJ "initiated what turned out to be an irreversible process of de-escalation." At Clifford's behest, the president also launched what came to be called "Vietnamization" by seeking to shift more of the combat burden to the ARVN while linking ongoing US assistance to South Vietnamese political and military performance. In a nationally televised speech on March 31, Johnson announced his initial bombing restrictions and proclaimed his readiness to begin peace talks with North Vietnam if American "restraint" were "matched by restraint in Hanoi." He concluded this dramatic talk by declaring that he would not seek reelection in the upcoming presidential campaign.[2]

Significantly, Rusk, a fellow southerner in whom Johnson placed great trust, played a central role in convincing the president to reject a troop increase, to implement the partial bombing halt, and to pursue peace talks. The secretary and president met daily during March, and according to White House news secretary George Christian, "it was Rusk's judgment" Johnson "wanted in the end, and Rusk's judgment he followed." The same personal and regional affinities that had drawn these two southerners together during the Kennedy years remained intact as the Johnson presidency effectively ended. While pressing for the bombing restrictions, Rusk contended persuasively that they entailed no military downside. Bad weather over North Vietnam during the ensuing months would impair bombing effectiveness regardless of the bombing's geographic scope. Regarding negotiations, the secretary judged the prospects for substantive progress "bleak" but deemed the offer worth the risk, if only to demonstrate North Vietnamese insincerity.[3]

As these arguments suggested and as events over the next seven months confirmed, neither Rusk nor Johnson had suddenly been converted to the Fulbright-Gore-Cooper agenda for a negotiated, compromise end to the war. To the contrary, Johnson and Rusk's Vietnam objectives remained unchanged—mutual North Vietnamese–US troop withdrawals from South Vietnam and an independent, noncommunist South Vietnam in which the NLF had no political role. In essence, as Fulbright and Gore asserted, the president and secretary of state continued to demand that

North Vietnam and the Vietcong give up their military and political goals. LBJ made this clear by declaring he "was not about to run out on his commitments, his principles, or his friends." The United States, he emphasized, would "never . . . compromise the future of Asia at the negotiating table." Rusk, who believed the United States had won the war militarily by mid-1968, agreed completely with his president and announced that successful peace talks hinged on North Vietnamese "concessions." Despite their new strategic initiatives, the two southerners remained committed to personal and national honor and credibility and to military pressure as the key to defeating communism in Vietnam.[4]

Southern responses to Tet and subsequent 1968 developments followed well-established patterns. While often reiterating objections to Johnson's military restraint and citing the pitfalls of negotiating with communists, Dixie's hawks sustained their support for the war. Herman Talmadge asserted that the United States could not "sit idly by and watch the world swallowed up piece by piece by Communist aggression"; Sam Ervin continued to oppose any US withdrawal not accompanied by an "honorable. . . . settlement"; and John Sparkman voiced the common southern refrain that this blatant "instance of Communist aggression" should be opposed "vigorously" by bombing all military targets in North Vietnam. The ever-flamboyant Russell Long endorsed Westmoreland's troop request, reiterated the need for a naval blockade of Haiphong harbor, and reasserted his usual demand that the United States employ all "conventional force necessary to defeat the enemy." Richard Russell opposed all bombing pauses or restrictions and agreed with Long that the United States should use all its "conventional military power . . . to bring this war to an honorable conclusion."[5]

John Stennis, who would become the most important southern Democratic conservative during the Nixon presidency, agreed wholeheartedly with these hawkish perspectives. In a prominent Senate speech on February 28, 1968, and several other public appearances, Stennis remained critical of Johnson's limited-war strategy. Although Stennis declared, as had become the habit of southern hawks, that the United States should "choose between a hard-hitting war or no war at all," neither he nor other backers of the war were prepared to press for US withdrawal. To the contrary, he contended an American "pull-out" would inform US enemies worldwide that the United States "*can* be defeated" and invite "trouble for us in

every part of the world which we are . . . committed to defend." Reflec-
tive of the senator's growing conviction that US commitments abroad
had outpaced American resources, he also declared that if Asia were "to
be defended against Communism, it must be defended by Asians." Along
with this foreshadowing of what became known as the "Nixon Doctrine,"
the crusty Mississippian offered a version of Vietnamization by emphasizing that the South Vietnamese should be informed that "the American commitment" was "not . . . open-ended." The United States could
not remain in South Vietnam "indefinitely," and the South Vietnamese
should be expected "to assume and carry an increasing share of the load in
the fight for their own independence." Texas senator John Tower endorsed
this prowar argument, albeit from a partisan Republican perspective. He
pronounced Tet "a major military defeat for our enemy" and proclaimed
the war "could be ended in a reasonably short time" if Johnson abandoned
the "self-defeating policy of 'gradualism.'"[6]

Tower's fellow Republican Senator Thruston Morton also denounced
the Johnson administration, but from the Kentuckian's recently adopted
antiwar stance. On February 4, Morton accused Johnson and his advisors of "hoodwinking" the American people through their optimistic
assessments of US prospects in Vietnam. In contrast to the administration's misleading pronouncements, Tet had demonstrated that the Vietcong could "inflict terrible damage . . . at any time and any place." Given
the enemy's strength and the weakness of the "unpopular and corrupt
regime in Saigon," Morton saw "no chance of military victory in Vietnam." Negotiations and a "dramatic initiative to disengage at the earliest
. . . feasible date" constituted the preferable course for ending the war.[7]

Tower might have had Morton in mind when the Texas hawk sounded
the repeated lament of prowar figures that dissenters undermined the
national "interest" by suggesting to "the enemy . . . that we are divided
or are ready to throw in the towel." If not addressing Morton, Tower certainly was targeting Dixie's most important doves, Senators Fulbright,
Gore, and Cooper, who maintained their critique of the war during two
sets of SFRC hearings in early 1968. In the first of these hearings, held on
February 20, Secretary of Defense McNamara faced seven and one-half
hours of interrogation regarding the Gulf of Tonkin incidents of August
2 and 4, 1964. The defense secretary unyieldingly contended that the
"essential facts" were unchanged. The US destroyers had been operating

in international waters; both attacks had occurred; and the commanders of the US vessels were unaware of and "not associated" with the clandestine South Vietnamese commando raids being carried out simultaneously against North Vietnam. When Fulbright and the SFRC staff produced naval cables impugning McNamara's contentions, the North Vietnamese PT boat attacks of August 1964 no longer appeared so unprovoked, and the claims of an August 4 attack seemed spurious.[8]

Cooper, Fulbright, and Gore played important roles in these hearings, whose ostensibly closed proceedings were widely discussed in the press; further damaged Johnson's credibility; helped undermine the rationale for the war; and intensified the bitterness among Johnson, Rusk, and their fellow southerners. Cooper, who had renewed his standing call for a US bombing halt and negotiations in mid-January, carefully led McNamara through the principal administration positions. Although the senator refrained from directly disputing any of the key points, the understated Kentuckian questioned the wisdom of taking "risks" that resulted in incidents that "humiliate[d]" the United States and left it in "a position where there is danger of deeper involvement and not of our choice." Fulbright and Gore were less restrained. The SFRC chairman was convinced that Johnson, McNamara, and Rusk had intentionally misled him and the Congress into voting precipitously for the Gulf of Tonkin Resolution. Fulbright felt a "very deep responsibility" for this national misstep and considered it "very unfair" for the administration to have asked the Senate "to vote upon a resolution when the state of the evidence" was so "uncertain." Gore agreed that the American people had been "misled." Given the uncertainties surrounding the August 1964 events, the Johnson administration had "acted precipitately, inadvisably, unwisely," and "out of proportion" to the supposed "provocation."[9]

Fulbright closed the long day of charged exchanges at nearly 7:00 P.M. with the observation that under President Johnson, "the executive branch" operated as if "Congress has no function to play in foreign relations and in making war," a theme to which he returned two weeks later on the floor of the Senate. Responding specifically to press reports of the military's request for an additional two hundred thousand troops for service in Vietnam, the Arkansas dissenter declared the "Senate and the country" were "entitled to know" the administration's plans and "to have the opportunity" to offer opinions.[10]

Spurred by the newspaper accounts that Westmoreland had requested an additional two hundred thousand US troops for the war, the SFRC hearings of March 11 and 12 again concentrated on the role of the committee and Congress in formulating Vietnam policy. Secretary of State Rusk testified publicly before the SFRC for the first time since his bitter confrontation with Fulbright in February 1966. As they once again appeared on national television, the chairman assured the secretary of state that he harbored no "personal animus," that to the contrary, he had "profound respect" for Rusk's "intelligence and integrity" and "sense of duty." Pleasantries aside, Rusk knew better, and the sharp disagreements that followed during his more than ten hours of testimony demonstrated that these two centrally placed southerners remained bitter adversaries.[11]

Rusk's essential views on the war and its centrality to US international standing had not changed since 1966. North Vietnamese and Vietcong aggression had to be repulsed. US failure to fulfill its SEATO "responsibility" to preserve South Vietnam's independence as a noncommunist country would undermine US credibility, shift the international balance of power, and imperil the "peace of the world." When asked about the Gulf of Tonkin incident, the secretary echoed McNamara's prior testimony. Both attacks took place in international waters, and both were unprovoked and "unwarranted."[12]

When Fulbright, Cooper, and Gore contested virtually all facets of the secretary's brief, a Gore constituent sympathized with Rusk's plight. The "poor man" was "stuck between the intransigence of Ho Chi Minh and LBJ!" Fulbright was most direct. He rejected Rusk's "version" of the Gulf of Tonkin incident and refused to accept the Georgian's portrayal of US actions in Vietnam as "accurate." Having challenged Rusk's perception and veracity, the SFRC chairman turned to his central concern—congressional "consultation" as the administration considered whether to "enlarge the war." While repeatedly refusing to make such a commitment, Rusk asserted that Johnson had "attempted to consult with Congress more than any recent President" and complained that no secretaries of state during World War II or Korea had been forced to publicly alert the enemy to "future" US plans. As had become administration practice since 1964, he reminded his tormentor that Congress had voted overwhelmingly for the Gulf of Tonkin Resolution.[13]

These rejoinders were akin to waving a red flag before an enraged bull.

Fulbright curtly dismissed the claim of "satisfactory" and substantive consultation and asserted the SFRC could no longer accept just "anything the Administration sends down without question." Fulbright was equally emphatic regarding Rusk's reference to the Gulf of Tonkin Resolution. The senator had come to view the resolution as "null and void," like "any contract based on misrepresentation," and he was convinced the administration had used it "to prevent" the very "consultation" he sought. When the chairman asked in exasperation if Rusk were "saying in a very polite way . . . that you have no intention of consulting with this committee," Rusk essentially agreed by emphasizing that consultation was unnecessary since "the views of this committee . . . are pretty well apparent." This final exchange between the chairman of the SFRC and the secretary of state tellingly captured the deep personal hostility between them and the tension between the two branches of government they represented.[14]

Neither Cooper nor Gore garnered greater satisfaction from Rusk's responses to their queries. Apprehensive that dispatching another two hundred thousand US troops to Vietnam would markedly reduce the "possibility of . . . settlement by peaceful or political means," Cooper repeated his persistent call for meaningful negotiations. In response to Rusk's rejoinder that Hanoi would only use a US bombing halt and negotiations to gain military advantage, the Kentucky Republican emphasized that the United States needed "to take a first initiative" and test North Vietnam's "sincerity." After all, he noted, North Vietnam was not bombing the United States or South Vietnam. Agreeing with Fulbright's and Cooper's arguments, Gore termed the administration's offer to "negotiate without conditions" as "an offer to talk to anybody, any time, anywhere" if they were willing to accept a "pro-Western democracy in South Vietnam." When he was no more able than Fulbright or Cooper to elicit substantive responses from Rusk, Gore groused that the secretary had a "way of leaving things dangling."[15]

Gore, like Fulbright, had long since irritated Johnson with his "goddamn [Senate] speeches," but the Tennessee maverick ensured the president's antipathy by delivering a passionate antiwar address to the Democratic national convention in August. Unlike other convention speakers, Gore directly attacked LBJ, who in 1964 had "promised . . . that American boys would not be sent to fight in a land war in Asia." The

American people had voted for Johnson and "peace" but "got the policies of Senator Goldwater" instead. In return for twenty-five thousand American deaths, the nation had received "an erosion of the moral leadership, a demeaning entanglement with a corrupt political clique in Saigon, disillusionment, despair here at home, and a disastrous postponement of imperative programs to improve our social ills."[16]

Although the majority of southerners remained supportive of the war, they shared Gore's disillusionment with President Johnson as his presidency ended. Throughout 1968, Gallup polls found that Dixie continued to disapprove most strongly Johnson's handling of his "job as president." In January the South's approval was 11 percent less than the national average and 10 percent less than in the Midwest, the next most negative region; by December, the polling margins were essentially equivalent to the January figures, 9 and 8 percent, respectively. Much of this regional disapproval emanated from the South's ongoing perception that LBJ was "pushing integration too fast." In April 59 percent of southerners voiced this opinion, a response 20 percent greater than any other American section. Southern evaluations of the president's war policies were also unchanged, polling 8 percentage points fewer than the national average and that of the closest regional critic in January, although the Midwest and West, two more Republican regions, became equally negative over the course of the Tet Offensive.[17]

As the year began, Dixie remained the section most confident of an "all-out" US victory, with 25 percent of southerners foreseeing this outcome versus no more than 19 percent in any other region. This figure fell essentially to the national average of 10 percent following Tet. The South, by a margin of 5 percentage points fewer than the national average of 40 percent, also continued to be the region least supportive of bombing halts to induce peace negotiations. Consistent with these responses, the South was at least 9 percent less inclined than all other regions to vote for a presidential candidate pledging to begin withdrawing US troops as of January 1, 1969. Other facets of the polling in the South yielded more ambiguous results and were indicative of Dixie's and the nation's agony. For much of the year, residents of the West were more inclined to describe themselves as hawks and most likely to respond that the US commitment of ground troops to Vietnam had been a mistake. By October, the South reclaimed its position as the leading region on both issues, with the latter reflecting

Dixie's disproportionate number of war deaths and preferences for bombing and the use of technology to subdue the enemy.[18]
   Like the opinions of key southern political figures and the results of
Gallup polling, previous patterns among prominent daily papers remained
largely unchanged, a stance that contrasted with that of many metropolitan papers across the nation that came to oppose the war in 1967. Ralph
McGill, the publisher of the *Atlanta Constitution,* and Eugene Patterson,
its editor, sustained their solid support for President Johnson and his war
policies. Patterson applauded Johnson's and Senator Russell's defense of
American honor, endorsed the "U.S. obligation" to aid "formerly colonial
people" in Vietnam, and contended that Rusk in his appearance before
the SFRC had provided "the most persuasive explanation of U.S. involvement in Vietnam yet recorded." McGill castigated Senator Fulbright's
"selective morality" since he simultaneously questioned US motives and
actions in Vietnam and adopted a "racist" opposition to civil rights legislation. The *Dallas Morning News* and *Montgomery Advertiser* remained prowar. The *Morning News* recommended that the United States "persevere"
in Vietnam and sounded the common southern refrain that the enemy
should "be made to understand" that the United States would "take whatever steps are needed to end the aggression." The *Advertiser*'s observations
were less strident, while warning against overreaction to the Tet Offensive
and predicting "old Lyndon might not look so bad after all—considering
the alternatives" such as McCarthy and Kennedy. At the other end of the
spectrum, the *Louisville Courier-Journal* retained its far more moderate,
even liberal, perspective. Under its editor and publisher, Barry Bingham,
the *Courier-Journal* continued to favor negotiations, noted that Tet demonstrated the failure of US–South Vietnamese efforts at pacification and
land reform, opposed compulsory ROTC, and praised the University of
Kentucky president's "courage" in defending the right of a "leftist student" group to hold a conference on the war.[19]
   While responding to Tet, the SFRC hearings, and Johnson's March 31
speech, individual southerners articulated most of the pro- and antiwar
positions they had expressed over the previous four years. For some, Tet
pushed them into opposition to the war. A Winston-Salem resident told
Senator Ervin, "Until recent months I have 'waved the flag' and stoutly
defended our role in Viet Nam. However, I am now convinced that it has
turned out to be the greatest miscalculation in U.S. history." A Charlotte

physician agreed. This "conservative" World War II veteran had previously "felt that we would have to stay in Viet Nam until a stable government could be established" but concluded in May 1968 that Thieu's corrupt "cesspool" regime rendered that objective unobtainable. For others, Tet and its aftermath reinforced the war's importance and the necessity of a US–South Vietnamese victory. The United States had "damn well better not abandon this area to the mercies of Red China." Indeed, to sacrifice American lives in a "limited war" or by "sitting down at the peace table" with "a bunch of criminals" was "immoral." Two Georgia fathers elaborated. One deemed it "criminal" to restrict the bombing and thereby pull the "rug from under" American troops, and the second was convinced that the post–March 31 bombing cutbacks had led to his son's death in the Mekong Delta.[20]

Other southerners voiced even more peculiarly regional concerns. Cognizant of the South's disproportionate representation in the military, if not Dixie's benefits from defense spending, a Durham man feared that "northern industries" were "making money off this war, not people in North Carolina or the South," even though it was "southern boys, both white and black, who are dying there." An Atlanta resident cited more specific "facts and figures" regarding Georgians recently called to active duty—Georgia's 2.75 percent of the US population versus 7.5 percent of the troops activated. "Why," he asked, was "the South still fighting this nation's battles?" Was it "some form of martyrdom still clinging from . . . the Civil War? [or] over volunteering from the Southern states"? As residents of the nation's least prosperous region, southerners remained sensitive to the overrepresentation of poor men in Vietnam. A rural Kentuckian asserted correctly that "poor boys" were "forced to carry the burden of the national defense" simply "because they can't afford to attend college." Writing from Bethlehem, Georgia, a former sharecropper and World War II veteran offered a telling commentary on why he was "a very bitter man." He and his wife had struggled to provide their only child a "home and an Education," only to have him promptly drafted following his graduation from high school. Had he been a "man's son with money he could have gone on to school and stayed out of the army. . . . Why," he asked, "must it always be the poor man that has to fight wars? And these bearded people that burn their draft cards and cause so much trouble, why aren't they in the army?"[21]

This Georgia father's discomfort with antiwar protestors was representative of the broader southern and national concern over disorder, crime, and protestors of all stripes who were often lumped together whether they objected to the war, racial oppression, or established social and sexual mores and whether they did so peacefully or violently. A Fort Smith critic of Senator Fulbright's 1968 hearings emphasized that it was "far more important . . . to rid our Cities of crime and to make our streets a safe place" than to determine who was "responsible for the error in the Gulf of Tonkin." Other southerners were appalled that "commie inspired students mostly Negroes & Hippies" were "allowed to wreck our colleges." Was the nation going to "allow rioters and looters to destroy our cities and our right to safe streets while our boys die overseas? Will we make a national hero out of a man [Martin Luther King Jr.] who encouraged violence while he spoke of nonviolence?" Public polling confirmed these individual expressions. Sixty-five percent of southerners favored expelling students who violated laws during campus demonstrations, a figure that surpassed the next highest region by twelve points. Dixie residents were also most in favor of jailing or forcing draft resisters to serve in noncombat units.[22]

Conservative southern politicians from both parties echoed these sentiments. Senator John Tower detected a "sickness of heart . . . in all law-abiding citizens when they see their cities, their homes, their businesses go up in smoke while looters and arsonists cavort for the benefit of television." Herman Talmadge agreed that "civil disorder," which had begun "with the sit-in syndrome about 8 years ago," had led to a "rebellion against all authority, whether it emanates in the home, the church, the schools, or from legally-constituted government." While arguing for domestic unity and the mobilization of the nation "on a wartime basis," including the drastic reduction of domestic social spending, Senator Stennis cited "crime and violence in the streets" as the "most serious problem facing our government at home." The Mississippi senator, who regularly locked protestors out of his committee hearings, had asserted that antiwar dissidents were in league with the American Communist Party and that the government should "jerk" the Students for a Democratic Society "up by the roots and grind it to bits"[23]

As the 1968 presidential election approached, it was George Wallace, the former governor of Alabama notorious for his opposition to racial integration, who formed a third-party movement by capitalizing on the national discomfort with the rapidly changing social and governmental environment of the 1960s. Wallace appealed particularly to southern whites and northern ethnic voters through overtures to their racial fears, fiscal conservatism, opposition to an activist federal government, and concern over altered social and sexual mores. While fulminating against "pointy-headed intellectual morons" and liberals who could not "park their bicycles straight," he deftly tied race to social disorder by asserting it was a "sad day in the country when you can't talk about law and order" without being "called a racist." Wallace consistently linked "red-baiting" to his "anti–civil rights rhetoric," as he typically cited defenders of King and his "pro-communist friends" as defenders of Fidel Castro and Mao Zedong.[24]

The Vietnam plank of Wallace's American Independent Party and his comments on the war differed little from majority southern opinion. He sought an "honorable conclusion" to the war, preferably through "peaceful negotiations" but, if needed, via a "military" victory directed by military commanders rather than inept civilians. Wallace said nothing about nuclear weapons; but to his chagrin, his vice-presidential running mate, General Curtis Le May, declared on October 3, 1968, that he would use "anything that we could dream up—including nuclear weapons if it was necessary" to end the war. Wallace and Le May were immediately dubbed the "bombsy twins," and the campaign quickly lost momentum nationally.[25]

While maintaining an apprehensive eye on Wallace, Richard Nixon, the GOP presidential nominee, ran a shrewd campaign that included particular emphasis on the Upper South and South Carolina, where Senator Strom Thurmond provided decisive support. By making law and order his principal domestic theme, Nixon skillfully appealed to the very discontent and insecurities that Wallace had identified. To the law-and-order portion of his "southern strategy," Nixon added assurances that he would pursue minimalist enforcement of civil rights legislation and oppose forced busing to achieve racial integration of schools. Herman Talmadge later observed, "Nixon would always be a Yankee, but he was trying awfully hard to be like a Southerner." In another adroit maneuver, the formerly hawkish Nixon presented himself as far less dangerous than Wallace and Le May and their possible use of nuclear weapons but far more assertive than Hubert Humphrey, the Democratic nominee whose liberalism on race and domestic issues and association with Johnson's Vietnam policies crippled his chances in Dixie. While emphasizing that he had a "program" for an honorable peace but remaining persistently vague on its details, Nixon took advantage of the nation's and the South's war weariness. In early October polling, southerners, when asked who would "do a better job" managing the war, favored Nixon by 47 to 24 percent over Humphrey; by late October, the margin had widened to 51 to 26. In an election decided by 43.4 to 42.7 percent of the popular vote and 301 to 191 electoral votes, Nixon's performance in the South was decisive. Without carrying Florida, Kentucky, North Carolina, South Carolina, Tennessee, and Virginia, and their sixty-six electoral votes, he could not have been elected. That Wallace carried five of the remaining six southern states, all in the Deep South, left no doubt of the region's preferences on domestic issues and inclination toward a Vietnam policy likely to be more aggressive than Johnson's.[26]

Nixon's crucial southern backing was not confined to Strom Thurmond and Dixie's voters. Working with Anna Chennault, Senator John Tower, whom Chennault described as "my very good friend," helped to covertly assure South Vietnamese President Thieu that he and his nation would fare better under a Nixon administration. This assurance reinforced Thieu's refusal to sanction a full US bombing halt over North Vietnam or to participate in peace talks with Hanoi and the Vietcong. Chennault, the widow of air force general Claire L. Chennault, had long been associated with the anticommunist China Lobby and active in Republican politics. She had extensive contacts in East Asia, including the Thieu administration and its ambassador in Washington, Bui Diem. Over the course of the campaign, Chennault maintained ongoing communications with Tower and the Nixon election team. She kept the latter well informed of Thieu's intentions, especially on the eve of the election, when Johnson took the belated but potentially decisive step of halting all bombing over North Vietnam in hopes of getting peace negotiations off dead center. Although it is unlikely the canny Thieu would have agreed to participate in peace talks under any circumstances in the fall of 1968, both he and Nixon were able to move forward with a clear understanding of their mutually beneficial intentions because of the intercession primarily of Chennault, but also of Tower.[27]

Just as the South was essential to Nixon's election, Dixie provided critical support for his Vietnam policies over the ensuing five years. The backing of the majority of the southern public and conservative southern Democratic politicians became crucial after 1969 as Democrats continued to control both houses of Congress. With a Republican in the White House, a growing number of Democrats cast aside any deference they had shown to Lyndon Johnson out of party loyalty. From July 1966 through July 1973, Congress took 113 recorded votes on measures designed to curtail the war, and 94 of them came during the Nixon presidency. Nixon and his national security advisor, Henry Kissinger, did nothing to mollify this congressional opposition. To the contrary, Nixon and Kissinger believed that only the executive branch generally and the two of them specifically possessed the knowledge and perspective to formulate a viable foreign policy. On issues ranging from US actions in Thailand, Laos, and Vietnam to defense spending and anti–ballistic missile policies, Congress mounted its "first wholehearted congressional challenge to executive authority" since the early 1950s and, in so doing, exhibited a level of "assertiveness in foreign affairs" that "represented a sea change in the deference lawmakers had accorded presidents during the Cold War years."[28]

The broader southern public also played an important role in sustaining Nixon's Vietnam policies and his southern Democratic allies. Despite his contentions to the contrary, Nixon "cared deeply about public opinion" and "realized that the American public possessed a limited amount of patience when it came to Vietnam." Secretary of Defense Melvin Laird accurately described the post-1969 public sentiment on the war as a "time bomb ticking," and the administration's careful focus on public and congressional attitudes remained prominent from its inauguration in January 1969 through the US exit from the war in early 1973. This focus yielded a determinative insight by the fall of 1969—that "peace through escalation was not a viable option." Only by continuing and building upon Johnson's decisions for withdrawal through peace talks and turning the war over to the South Vietnamese could Nixon retain public support. This delicate balancing act rendered dependable backing from a strong majority of southerners crucial to the president's search for an acceptable outcome to the war from 1969 to 1973, particularly when Nixon's search threatened to widen the conflict through periodic, aggressive strikes into Cambodia and Laos and against North Vietnam.[29]

When combined with Nixon's domestic agenda, his Vietnam policies garnered majority support in Dixie. To his electoral southern strategy, the president added the nomination of two southern, but poorly qualified, judges for the Supreme Court and further appealed to majority southern opinion by condemning the "revolutionary spirit" and attempts at "insurrection" plaguing college campuses. Nixon's determination to achieve "peace with honor" and to use aggressive military actions, especially bombing, also accorded nicely with southern attitudes toward the war. Like all of his predecessors since World War II, Nixon was acutely concerned about US credibility and stressed that the United States must not act like a "pitiful, helpless giant" or, as Kissinger stated, be "humiliated" in Vietnam. To avoid such an outcome and achieve an honorable peace, which included an independent, noncommunist South Vietnam, Nixon assumed that "decisive actions" on the military front were "the only way to move negotiations off dead center." By envisioning the application of superior US military force to coerce North Vietnam and the Vietcong into accepting an American-dictated and therefore honorable peace, Nixon adopted an approach long preferred by southern hawks.[30]

The new Republican president implemented three related tactics while searching for opportunities to inflict decisive military pressure on North Vietnam: linkage, the "mad-man theory," and Vietnamization. Linkage described the Nixon-Kissinger attempt to induce the Soviet Union and China to pressure Hanoi into an acceptable settlement. Declaring privately that he knew "the fucking Commie mind," Nixon confidently expected to end the war within six months. The president boasted that he was "not going to end up like LBJ, holed up in the White House afraid to show my face on the street. I'm going to stop that war. Fast." When neither the Soviets nor the Chinese fundamentally altered their North Vietnamese policies, Nixon relied primarily on cultivating an image of "unpredictability" and on the threatened use of "excessive force." He explained to an aide, "I call it the Mad-man Theory. . . . I want the North Vietnamese to believe I've reached the point where I might do *anything* to stop the war." By informing Hanoi that Nixon had "his hand on the nuclear button," the president predicted that "Ho Chi Minh himself will be in Paris in two days begging for peace."[31]

To gain time in the United States for his policy of coercion to take effect, Nixon, pressured relentlessly by Secretary of Defense Laird, continued and greatly expanded Vietnamization, which included the progressive withdrawal of US combat forces and the shifting of responsibility for the war to South Vietnam. In theory an ever stronger, better-equipped South Vietnamese military would assume the responsibilities of the departing Americans. A brilliant domestic political strategy, Vietnamization steadily reduced US casualties and appealed to the powerful American desire to find a way out of the increasingly unpopular war while clinging to the false prospect of victory. Far "too clear-eyed" in their assessment of the Saigon regime to expect South Vietnam to progress sufficiently to ward off North Vietnam and the NLF, Nixon and Kissinger recognized that withdrawing US troops was an "implicit admission of defeat," a realization shared by many other Americans. By August 1972, Nixon admitted explicitly that South Vietnam was "never gonna survive" the US departure. Kissinger agreed and sought only a "decent interval," a period of "a year or two, after which . . . Vietnam will be a backwater," and "no one will give a damn." Hanoi proceeded with a similar calculation of winning after the US departure. If North Vietnam could survive the US military onslaught, there was little incentive to make political concessions and every expectation the NVA and NLF would prevail against ARVN forces bereft of American aid.[32]

Nixon initiated these interlocking strategies in the spring of 1969 by announcing the first troop withdrawals and by ordering the secret bombing of communist sanctuaries and supply routes in Cambodia. Both a response to North Vietnamese–Vietcong offensives in early 1969 and an alternative to resuming the bombing of North Vietnam, the Cambodian campaign was meant to signal the president's unpredictability and willingness to take aggressive measures. To Nixon and Kissinger's disgust, the bombing was quickly reported in the American press, and the attacks had no effect in Hanoi. The president also sought to implement his madman approach during the summer of 1969 by privately threatening the North Vietnamese with the "Duck Hook" operation, which envisioned the bombing of major population centers, the blockading of Haiphong, and even the possible use of tactical nuclear weapons. When these threats failed the bring Hanoi to heel, Nixon had no policy, save Vietnamization, linkage, and repeated, futile attempts to intimidate North Vietnam through other aggressive, but temporary, military actions. Ultimately, neither such actions nor the hope of Chinese or Soviet influence convinced North Vietnam to stop fighting, and Nixon and Kissinger acquiesced in a negotiated settlement, but only after conceding the long-standing US demand for a North Vietnamese troop withdrawal from the South and the assurance of an independent, noncommunist South Vietnam.[33]

Given this anomalous US strategic position, the American public's mounting war weariness, and the more assertive, Democratic-controlled Congress, southern public and congressional support was essential tò Nixon's ability to sustain US military involvement and to pursue his various policies. In polling patterns that would persist through the end of the war in early 1973, the South was the region consistently most approving of Nixon's performance as president. Dixie frequently responded most positively to his handling of Vietnam, particularly at crucial junctures such as May–June 1970, April–June 1972, and January–February 1973; and the South was always the Democratic region most solidly behind the Republican president. For example, in the midst of the US invasion of Cambodia in early May 1970, 66 percent of southerners approved of Nixon's work as president, and 59 percent endorsed his Vietnam actions, compared to national averages of 57 and 53 percent. Similarly, in June 1972, following the president's aggressive military responses to North Vietnam's Easter Offensive, southern responses on these two key questions revealed 68 and 57 percent approval and ran 7 and 4 points ahead of poll results for the nation. Nixon's civil rights policies, calls for law and order, harsh denunciation of protestors, and appeals to patriotism account for much of this support; but his pledge to achieve peace with honor and his periodically more aggressive military actions also resonated in Dixie—the region whose residents continued to be most inclined to self-identify as hawks, most convinced that war was "sometimes necessary to settle disputes," and least willing after October 1969 to acknowledge that the "U.S. made a mistake" in dispatching troops to Vietnam.[34]

Although Nixon's domestic racial and Vietnam policies garnered the support of a majority of southern whites, they alienated most African Americans. Black civil rights leaders and the black press were much more inclined to denounce the war after 1969. Reluctant to criticize LBJ's war policies and alienate the executive who had done so much to advance civil rights, black leaders and editors who had refused to join Reverend King and other dissenters during the Johnson years exhibited no such restraint regarding Nixon. Unsurprisingly, given Nixon's southern strategy and close political alliance with both Strom Thurmond and southern

Democratic segregationists, an April 1970 poll found that only 3 percent of blacks expected the new president to bolster African American interests. In a revealing example, Whitney M. Young Jr., the head of the Urban League and a sharp critic of King's anti-Vietnam stance, admitted in June 1969, "Dr. King was probably more right than I was because it is hard to separate the war from the domestic problems"; and four months later, Young sounded much like King while arguing that Vietnam had "sharpened the divisions and frustrations" at home. In 1971 the Reverend Ralph Abernathy, who had succeeded King as head the SCLC following the former's assassination in 1968, was more harsh in characterizing the conflict as "an attempt to destroy poor people of color in Southeast Asia, at the expense of black and poor at home," all in the "interest of maintaining the largest military-economic empire in history."[35]

Among southern black papers and opinion leaders, the *Atlanta Daily World* and its editor, C. A. Scott, and the *Birmingham World* provided the conspicuous exceptions to majority black criticism of Nixon and the war. Scott and his Republican paper consistently praised the president for his "wise and courageous" handling of the conflict and featured pro-Nixon columns, letters to the editor, and interviews with black residents of Atlanta. The *Birmingham World,* also a GOP paper, was equally supportive, lauding Nixon's invasion of Cambodia, criticizing end-the-war legislation as "absurd and most deplorable," and endorsing the president's bombing of North Vietnam in 1972. Indeed, these black Republican papers' perspective on the war was remarkably similar to that of the *Dallas Morning News, Montgomery Advertiser,* and *New Orleans Picayune.*[36]

Consistent with the editorial positions of these papers and their polling responses, the majority of white southerners argued that President Nixon should be given time to implement his policies. Several Arkansans made this point to Senator Fulbright. In March 1969 a Lakeview woman emphasized that it had taken "the Democrats seven years" to get the country into "the mess." A Little Rock couple concurred, declaring that "after so many dark years of being bogged down in Vietnam," Nixon had begun troop withdrawals and "made every effort . . . to reach a diplomatic accommodation with the North Vietnamese." Other Dixie residents expressly lauded Nixon's "efforts to bring the war . . . to an honorable conclusion." Prowar "tax-paying, God-loving and country-loving" southerners also echoed their established objections to negotiating with communists, calls for the use of unrestrained military force, and condemnation of dissenters as traitors for aiding the enemy.[37]

Unimpressed with South Vietnamese military capacity, other southern hawks recognized Vietnamization's inherent flaws and the ways this strategy could undermine US morale. An outraged Georgian declared, "Nixon's policy in Vietnam is one of surrender and gradual 'bugout'; nothing less than pure treason." Another Russell constituent agreed and opined, "Who ever heard of reducing forces until the battle was won? Would any of you like to be on the front lines and have your country withdrawing help from you?" How were "our young men being sent *TO* Vietnam" going to respond as others were withdrawn? Would it be "possible to maintain" their "patriotism and . . . capability" under such circumstances? A third Georgian identified the fundamental fallacy in ongoing US troop withdrawals. This "dangerous plan" might "satisfy some people" at home, but it was "unrealistic to believe that once the bulk of our forces are out of Vietnam, the enemy will not try a swift and complete take over."[38]

Southern opponents of the war disparaged the troop recalls as a ploy to "'sweeten public opinion' and slow down the . . . the growing opposition . . . to . . . a 'Futile-No Win War.'" Dixie's doves also greeted Nixon with many of their previous arguments. Vietnam was of no strategic importance; the Thieu government was oppressive and corrupt; the war was diverting precious resources better employed at home; the conflict was injuriously dividing the nation; and Congress needed to reclaim its proper role in the making and implementing of foreign policy. Critics of the war continued to offer moral and ethical objections, to contend it was "morally wrong . . . to sacrifice our young men" while seeking "ways to save face," or to proceed as if communist nations and Vietnamese peasants were "not our neighbors." In an especially emotional conclusion to a letter to Senator Ervin, a Raleigh surgeon proclaimed, "Dove am I, and proudly. Hawks are not brave, but cowards; they are not patriots but traitors; they are not smart but fools. What in God's name can be the matter with our government and with our people who tolerate this continuing murder?"[39]

Whether hawks or doves, many southerners, like Americans more generally, were exceedingly frustrated and conflicted by 1969. A Georgia bank president confessed to "feeling completely frustrated because of my own inability to do anything about this situation." From Albermarle,

North Carolina, near the home of outspoken dissenter Frazier Woolard, a physician condemned participation in the October 15, 1969, Vietnam Moratorium against the war and asserted that the United States had gone to Vietnam "for the right reason . . . to stop the expansion of Communism." While endorsing Nixon's policies, he also understood the national concern "over the apparently endless blood-letting of Americans," who were fighting for a country that could not attract the loyalty "of its own people." Therefore, he concluded, "we cannot fight this war to win . . . and should withdraw all American Troops." Like so many Americans, this southern rural doctor was strongly anticommunist, endorsed the mission in Vietnam, despised protestors, but also recognized that traditional military victory was unlikely. He was left supporting Nixon and Vietnamization, but out of resignation rather than enthusiasm.[40]

If support from the southern public was important to sustaining President Nixon's Vietnam policies, the backing of Dixie's conservative legislators was crucial. Given southern legislators' satisfaction with the president's civil rights policies, unbending anticommunism, acute concern for US honor and credibility, commitment to military strength as the basis for a viable foreign policy, clear understanding of the regional benefits of defense spending, and racially tinged doubts that South Vietnam could survive on its own, their backing of Nixon was predictable. Southern conservatives' aid for the GOP president was especially important in two areas: first, the ongoing funding of the war; and second, the fending off of efforts to set a certain date for ending US involvement in Vietnam. Key committee chairmen, such as George Mahon, Mendel Rivers, and Edward Hebert in the House and Richard Russell and especially John Stennis in the Senate, and southerners more generally helped block these antiwar measures until near the end of 1972 and thereby afforded Nixon the time to apply his various strategies.

Even as they continued to help sustain the war effort, important southern Democrats implicitly acknowledged the greatly increased antiwar sentiment by emphasizing their prior opposition to US intervention in Vietnam. For example, Stennis stressed he had "continually opposed our intervening in . . . Vietnam as far back as 1954." Sam Ervin underscored that he had "never favored the stationing" of American troops in Vietnam," but, since Nixon was "doing everything within his power to end" the war, he merited American support. Richard Russell also reminded constituents that he had "opposed initial entry" into Vietnam and also continued to advocate aggressive, strategic bombing rather than "weak-kneed and cowardly policies." Other southern Democratic hawks, such as Russell Long, reiterated their accustomed call for the United States to "fish or cut bait" by fighting to "win." Despite their collective lament that even Nixon's more aggressive military posture was insufficient, the over-whelming majority of southern Democrats extended the same deference to Nixon that they had provided his three predecessors.[41]

For southern Republicans, partisan politics reinforced their regional rationale for backing Nixon and the war. Strom Thurmond considered an independent, noncommunist South Vietnam "our only hope for defend-ing our interests" in Southeast Asia and offered his customary prescrip-tion of increased bombing as the way to achieve victory. John Tower agreed that "intensification of military pressure" was essential to ensure "an honorable, just and lasting peace" in which the South Vietnamese could "freely develop" their country. The Texas senator contended that the US "posture in Vietnam" was "the best it has been . . . since 1965"; therefore, Americans needed to "remain calm and patient" as Vietnamiza-tion progressed. Only American impatience and pressure for precipitate withdrawal could derail Nixon's policies and produce a "camouflaged sur-render." Even John Sherman Cooper, Dixie's most important Republican dove, initially lauded Nixon's policies as a "clear break" from Johnson's. Unlike LBJ, Nixon intended "to end participation in combat by United States forces," offered "realistic, definitive proposals as a basis for negotia-tion," and sought "an honorable solution to the war."[42]

Among southern hawks, John Stennis was the most influential during the Nixon years. The Mississippi Democrat assumed the chairmanship of the Senate Armed Services Committee in January 1969 as Nixon took office, a leadership position that became even more important when Stu-art Symington, a long-term defender of the military and US policies in Southeast Asia, moved to the antiwar camp. Stennis thereafter became the Senate's "number one champion of the military" and defense appropria-tions. The courtly Mississippian also continued to grant the commander in chief wide authority and latitude, particularly if that commander in chief sought to prosecute the war more aggressively than his predeces-sors. Nixon impressed the SASC chair as "conscientious and honest" in his efforts to end the war on honorable terms. Stennis solidly backed Vietnamization and Nixon's "refusal to withdraw precipitously." Based on these policy agreements and Nixon's careful cultivation of the Mississippi senator, Stennis became a confidant of the new president, who informed the SASC chairman prior to initiating the secret bombing of Cambodia in March 1969, the invasion of that country in April 1970, and the US–South Vietnamese incursion into Laos in February 1971. In the latter two instances, Stennis appears to have been the only legislator to whom Nixon gave advance notice.[43]

Although Stennis afforded Nixon indispensable backing, the Mississippi hawk's views on the war and US obligations abroad continued to evolve. In March 1969 the senator told a national television audience that the United States could not "drag on half in and half out of the war. . . . without us having to stay there ten years." Although he continued to advocate more aggressive military measures, other comments suggest that he was becoming reconciled to the fact that even under Nixon the United States would not be "going all out to win." By fall he was reemphasizing his post-Tet position that the "South Vietnamese must take over the fighting in the shortest time possible," and he essentially endorsed the enclave strategy that he had previously disparaged as overly timid. In October Stennis recommended that the United States "secure sufficient" territory "to protect" the loyal South Vietnamese and "turn the real fighting" over to the ARVN. Stennis also began the policy analysis that would lead by 1971 to his cosponsorship of the War Powers legislation designed to restrict US overcommitment abroad and to revitalize Congress's foreign policy and war-making roles. The senator was determined to avoid intervention in another limited war such as Vietnam. Future US assistance, he argued, should be limited to those situations and nations where American security was directly involved and where the people were willing to "commit *their all* to preserve *themselves.*" The United States should intervene only when prepared "to use the military forces necessary to prevail," and any decision to use such force should come "*only* after *Congress* has given its approval."[44]

The Mississippi hawk's emphasis on a reinvigorated congressional role in decisions for war and US foreign policy accorded with the views of Dixie's most prominent doves, Senators Fulbright, Gore, and Cooper. In February 1969 Fulbright had created an SFRC subcommittee chaired by Stuart Symington and charged with providing "a detailed review" of US "international military commitments . . . and their relationship to foreign policy," and later in the spring, he worried that the United States had "committed . . . to the defense of 'freedom'—very loosely defined—in almost fifty countries." With these concerns in mind, Fulbright initially hoped that Nixon's campaign promises to end the war quickly were sincere and that he might "establish a relationship" with the president and Kissinger that enabled him to have "some influence." The senator met with Nixon and Kissinger in March 1969 and urged them to restrict "military action" to the "requirements of American security" and to emphasize instead "the political approach to a settlement." When the president's more militant proclivities began to emerge, Fulbright bluntly warned Secretary Laird that the conflict would quickly become "Mr. Nixon's war." Convinced by the fall that Vietnamization was a political ploy, Fulbright rejected Senator Hugh Scott's (R-PA) call for a sixty-day moratorium on criticism of the president. The Arkansas dissenter replied that Nixon had been granted "nine months . . . , the normal period of gestation for humans to bring forth their issue," to "give birth to his plan to end the war." With no such plan in sight, the nation needed a "moratorium" on "killing" rather than on criticism.[45]

Entertaining no illusion of exercising personal influence with Nixon or Kissinger, Albert Gore never considered a moratorium on his vocal criticism of the war. In a series of Senate speeches from March through June and a letter to the *New York Times,* Gore dismissed Vietnamization as a formula for "prolonged war and indefinite involvement," rather than a road to peace. The senator's analysis and policy preferences were consistent with the unwanted advice he had imparted to President Johnson. Since "white westerners" could not win "a revolutionary political war in Asia," the United States needed to discard its persistent "self-deception" regarding potential "progress being made in the military effort" and accept limits on American power. Only by putting aside the demand for a Thieu-Ky-led, noncommunist South Vietnam and agreeing to actual "self-determination" could the United States hope to end the war. And, he concluded sharply on June 19, the war had to end because it was "immoral and . . . wrong."[46]

The revealing juxtaposition of Senators Stennis's and Fulbright's shared concern over US commitments abroad and their mutual search for a reinvigorated congressional role in foreign affairs was embodied in the Senate's passage of the National Commitments Resolution on June 25, 1969. Fulbright had introduced an earlier version of this nonbinding resolution in 1967 and brought it forward again in February 1969. The final version stated that a "national commitment" through the use or promise of US "financial resources" or "armed forces" to "assist a foreign country" required "affirmative action taken by the executive and legislative branches." Although the resolution excluded Vietnam, the *Washington Post* correctly observed that "throughout the debate, it was apparent it [the resolution] was the Senate's answer to U.S. involvement in Vietnam." It was also an effort, according to Fulbright, to restore "a proper balance" between Congress and the executive and for Congress "to reassert its own constitutional authority." While "whole-heartedly" endorsing the measure, Stennis agreed that the "primary purpose" was "to reassert the congressional responsibility in any decision to commit our Armed Forces to hostilities abroad." Despite the opposition of the Nixon administration, the resolution passed by a 70–16 vote, with all southern senators declared or voting for its passage, save Republican hawks Thurmond and Tower.[47]

Much to the consternation of Fulbright, Gore, and antiwar forces more generally, measures such as the National Commitments Resolution and even the massive Vietnam Moratorium of October 15 failed to alter Nixon's determination to avoid being the "first American president to lose a war." Described as the "largest public protest" in the nation's history and the "single most important one day demonstration of the entire war," the moratorium included at least two million participants nationwide. Moratorium activities, marked primarily by a "spirit of sadness and loss," included silent vigils, the planting of memorial flowers and trees, quiet prayers, speeches and discussions, and disciplined marches and demonstrations.[48]

Although the moratorium helped dissuade Nixon from executing the still-secret Duck Hook operation, the president skillfully countered the potential political impact of these unprecedented demonstrations with his nationally televised speech of November 3. While appealing for the patriotic support of the "great silent majority" of his "fellow Americans," the president sounded themes that were especially popular in the South. Nixon pledged to "win the peace" and reserved the right "to take strong and effective measures" to safeguard American soldiers and gain a US victory. Southerners considered peace through strength and the pursuit of victory essential foreign policy assumptions, and they were equally committed to the preservation of national honor and credibility, a concern that Nixon also addressed. Were the United States to fail, this "first defeat in our nation's history" would devastate "confidence in American leadership" and yield "more war." Only patriotism and national unity, as opposed to protest and dissent, would impress upon Hanoi the necessity to compromise. If the nation were "united against defeat," North Vietnam could not "defeat or humiliate the United States. Only Americans can do that."[49]

The president's pledge to win the war while phasing out US combat participation and reducing American casualties generated an overwhelmingly favorable public response. When combined with Vice President Spiro Agnew's vitriolic attacks on student protestors and other dissenters such as Senator Fulbright, the administration's effective intimidation of the press, and the initiation of the draft lottery in December, Nixon had gained the upper hand politically on the domestic front. But, as had been true since the 1940s, no American president could control either events in Vietnam or their ultimate impact on the US public and politics.

The president had hardly begun to savor the response to his dramatic speech when the *New York Times* published an account of the March 16, 1968, My Lai massacre, in which an American infantry unit had killed more than five hundred unarmed Vietnamese civilians, virtually all of whom were old men, women, and children. In late November the US Army announced that First Lieutenant William L. Calley Jr., the leader of the platoon responsible for the killings at My Lai, was being charged with the premeditated murder of more than one hundred of the Vietnamese who had perished in the massacre. The debate over this horrific event extended into 1971 and graphically reminded Americans of the war's ferocity, human costs, and moral implications. In March 1971 a military court convicted Calley, the only soldier successfully prosecuted for the events at My Lai, of twenty-two counts of murder and sentenced him to life in prison. President Nixon promptly directed that he be held under house arrest at Fort Benning, Georgia, rather than in a military prison. In August a military authority reduced his sentence to twenty years, and Calley ultimately served only three and one-half years of house arrest after additional judicial proceedings and a pardon from President Nixon.

The majority of Americans sympathized with Calley, but nowhere more so than in the South, where the reaction provided further evidence of Dixie's prowar, promilitary perspective. Perhaps reflecting Nixon's assertion that "most people don't give a shit whether he killed them or not," both telegrams to the White House and national polling deemed Calley's guilty verdict unfair, contended he was being made a scapegoat, and favored clemency. When compared to the remainder of the nation, southern politicians were particularly outspoken. Senator Allen Ellender from Louisiana declared that the Vietnamese villagers "got just what they deserved"; and Representative John R. Rarick, also from the Pelican State, proclaimed Calley a "true soldier and a great American" who should be granted an immediate presidential pardon. "What is war," Rarick asked, "if not premeditated murder?" Senator Ernest F. Hollings (D-SC) wondered if Calley's fate meant that all soldiers guilty of a "mistake of judgment" in the heat of battle "were going to be tried as common criminals." South Carolina congressman Mendel Rivers, the powerful chairman of the House Armed Services Committee, first doubted that "our boys would . . . do anything like that" and subsequently declared that none of the soldiers at My Lai should have been charged with crimes.[50]

Others contended that Calley was being made a scapegoat for national and institutional failings. Senator Herman Talmadge asserted the Florida soldier was "assuming the burden for the entire war, including the errors of his superiors," and the senator was "saddened to think that one could fight for his flag and then be court-martialed and convicted for apparently carrying out orders." Representative Ben B. Blackburn (R-GA) maintained that it had been a national decision "to destroy" the Vietnamese enemy. "If unconscionable acts" ensued, "the blot is upon the nation's record, and no one man should be singled out for special punishment." John Tower approved of President Nixon's pro-Calley actions and worried that the guilty verdict would "undermine morale" among US soldiers and impede future volunteers. Significantly, none of these southerners expressed outrage at the murder of unarmed Vietnamese civilians.[51]

In addition to these pro-Calley pronouncements, Alabama governor George Wallace visited the young soldier at the Fort Benning stockade and joined Governor John Bell Williams of Mississippi and Lieutenant Governor Lester Maddox of Georgia in speaking on Calley's behalf at a rally in Columbus, Georgia. Similar rallies followed in Jacksonville, Florida, and Dallas. Georgia governor Jimmy Carter proclaimed an "American Fighting Man's Day" and suggested that Georgians "honor the flag as 'Rusty' had done" while driving with their lights on for a week to demonstrate support for the American military; Governor Williams declared Mississippi was "about ready to secede from the union" in defense of Calley. The Arkansas legislature passed a resolution calling for clemency; and the Texas Senate and South Carolina legislature called for Calley's release from prison. Draft boards in Georgia and Tennessee resigned or refused to process additional inductees if Calley's verdict were upheld.[52]

The treatment of three key witnesses before a US House of Representatives subcommittee charged with investigating My Lai provided additional perspective on the South's responses to the tragedy. Appointed by House Armed Services Committee chair Rivers, Louisiana congressman F. Edward Hebert chaired the subcommittee and oversaw the hearings, which began on April 15 and concluded on June 22, 1971. First elected to Congress in 1940, the colorful Hebert referred to himself as the last of Dixie's "unreconstructed rebels," was said to have had the "most luxurious" office on Capitol Hill, and was a strong defender of southern racial practices and states' rights. As a member of the Armed Service Committee since 1941 and Rivers's successor as chair in 1971 following the latter's death, Hebert had exhibited typically strong southern patriotism and support for the military.[53]

Under the direction of the Louisiana Democrat and the subcommittee's chief counsel, John T. M. Reddan, the hearings assumed the tenor of court proceedings, during which Lieutenant Hugh Thompson, the helicopter pilot who had landed during the My Lai incident to rescue Vietnamese civilians and later reported the massacre to his superiors; his door gunner, Lawrence M. Colburn; and Ronald L. Haeberle, the army photographer who had sold pictures of the massacre to the US and foreign press, were all interrogated as if they were guilty of crimes, rather than Calley and the members of his platoon. Both Thompson and Colburn were grilled over the exact wording of military awards they had received for their actions at My Lai and whether Thompson had issued an order for Colburn to shoot American ground troops if they threatened him as he attempted to save Vietnamese civilians. Although Hebert stressed that the committee sought only to ascertain what had happened at My Lai, the interrogation of Thompson and Colburn appeared more like an effort to impugn the credibility of the men who had attempted to stop and report the atrocity. Thompson, who had become apprehensive that he was being set up for a perjury charge, often answered with qualifiers such as, "To the best of my knowledge" and "I don't remember" or took the Fifth Amendment to avoid self-incrimination. Ronald Haeberle also endured extensive questioning and comments suggesting that his principal motive for taking and selling the My Lai pictures had been personal gain and that he had sold government property belonging to the army.[54]

In assessing the work of Hebert and the subcommittee, historian Mark D. Carson notes that their treatment of Thompson "reeked of simple vindictiveness" and that the extent and manner of Haeberle's questioning "reflected the congressman's personal displeasure with those who publicly disclosed the massacre." Following the hearings, Hebert suggested that US soldiers facing criminal charges as a result of their actions at My Lai should plead temporary insanity—a recommendation that reflected both his genuine sympathy for the dilemmas facing American ground soldiers in Vietnam and his reluctance to believe that young Americans could commit such heinous crimes. His comment following Calley's conviction said much about these attitudes and his racial perspective as well. It was, he asserted, "terrible to let Cassius Clay walk the streets of America, while William Calley, who was trying to do his duty, is incarcerated."[55]

Numerous southerners shared the perspectives of Talmadge, Rivers, and Hebert and expressed these sentiments to their representatives. Three thousand constituents wrote Congressman Jim Broyhill (R-NC); 3,500 sent letters to Senator Bill Brock (R-TN); and 2,944 (97 percent opposing the conviction) contacted Senator William B. Spong Jr. (D-VA). Some Dixie residents blamed "left-wing reporters" and the "liberal news media," who sought to "discredit our own Army" in Southeast Asia. Many feared that Calley was being made a "scapegoat"; if any US soldiers were "to be tried for errors of judgment" in battle, "then surely some of our Military Brass, Pentagon officials, Senators and Representatives" should be tried for similar errors committed "in environments lacking the physical pressures of combat." Two Atlanta women declared it a "shame indeed that one person has been singled out to assume the responsibility for all the atrocities of this horrible, senseless war." An irate Texan declared, "Only a gutless, sniveling coward of a government would even think of allowing the Armed Forces and their personnel to be subjected to the debasement of trial for doing their duty in time of war."[56]

Just as they opposed the war, minority voices in the South denounced US actions at My Lai and supported Calley's conviction. For some southerners, the news and pictures detailing the massacre were the "traumatic" shock that prompted "people who had never before questioned the war . . . to not only question the morality of it all, but . . . to say let's . . . get out *now*." A Presbyterian minister pointedly informed Senator Talmadge, "It is strange how those who support law and order can be opposed to his [Calley's] conviction." Numerous southern combat veterans endorsed the outcome of Calley's trial. A former NCO who had spent fifteen months in Vietnam felt "sure," as subsequent studies have substantiated, that My Lai was "far from one isolated case," since the "general attitude of the American G.I. is to look down on the Vietnamese as a sub-human race." Another Dixie vet believed that Calley had "disgraced the uniform I wore proudly, and the nation I love and have fought for." A retired lieutenant colonel favored the prosecution of US "officers at every level of command who committed, condoned, ignored or covered up such atrocities." Other southerners asked how the United States could expect the "humane treatment of our own POW's" while condoning Calley's actions. "People who have surrendered," a Georgian emphasized, "are not to be slaughtered."[57]

Despite the national anguish occasioned by the My Lai revelations in late 1969, President Nixon had seemingly solidified public support behind his Vietnam policies. In late April the *Montgomery Advertiser* perceptively observed that Vietnamization had "been successful, at least politically"; the president's supporters were "pleased," and his antiwar critics "almost muted." But, the *Advertiser* continued, Nixon "would probably lose the advantage he has garnered from his troop withdrawal policy if he deeply involved the U.S. in Cambodia." When the president dispatched US troops into that nation on April 30, the outraged national response more than fulfilled the Alabama paper's prediction. As a facet of the mad-man strategy, the Cambodian incursion was meant to signal Nixon's toughness and unpredictability. The extension of the war to another Southeast Asian country was justified publicly on the grounds of defending a recently installed, noncommunist government in Cambodia, as necessary to eliminate immediate cross-border sanctuaries for enemy supplies and personnel, and as crucial to sustaining Vietnamization and protecting remaining US troops in South Vietnam. The two-month operation yielded some two thousand enemy dead, the destruction of eight thousand bunkers, and the capture of eighty-two hundred tons of rice and twenty-five thousand weapons. Still, enemy operations were set back by no more than six months.[58]

The public and congressional responses to Nixon's decision easily offset these military gains. More than one hundred thousand protestors descended on Washington during the first week of May, and unprecedented demonstrations erupted on college campuses, including many across the South. After four students were killed at Kent State University in Ohio and two at Jackson State College in Mississippi in confrontations with National Guard troops and police, more than two million students demonstrated, and some 450 colleges and universities experienced student strikes or closures.

Even more disturbing to President Nixon and his administration, the Cambodian operation also "provoked the most serious congressional challenge to presidential authority since the beginning of the war." Two congressional measures particularly embodied this challenge. Sponsored by John Sherman Cooper and Frank Church, the Cooper-Church Amendment to the 1971 Foreign Military Sales Bill sought to block funding for US military operations in Cambodia after June 30, 1970. The more expansive McGovern-Hatfield Amendment to the 1971 Military Procurement Authorization required the withdrawal of all US troops from Vietnam by December 31, 1971.[59]

Nixon interpreted these measures as a challenge both to the office of the presidency and to him personally. Sounding much like LBJ, he confided to Kissinger on the eve of the Cambodian incursion, "Those Senators think they can push me around, but I'll show them who's tough. The liberals are waiting to see Nixon let Cambodia go down the drain just the way Eisenhower let Cuba go down the drain." To the president's acute discomfort, the negative response to the Cambodian invasion and its aftermath was not confined to liberal legislators. Nixon's decision, and especially his failure to consult or notify in advance any senators other than John Stennis, had alienated Hugh Scott, the Republican minority leader, and conservative southern Democrats Harry F. Byrd Jr. (VA), B. Everett Jordan (NC), and Herman Talmadge. When added to the more general Democratic opposition, these potential Republican and conservative southern defections enhanced the importance of the president's support from Dixie's legislators and public. Recognizing this political reality,

Nixon told Kissinger in August, "We've got the Left where we want it now. All they've got to argue for is a bug out, and that's their problem. But when the Right starts wanting to get out, for whatever reason, that's *our* problem."[60]

Faced with this volatile political situation, Nixon moved quickly to repulse Cooper-Church. With an overall strategy of extending the Senate debate sufficiently to render the amendment meaningless, the president announced his intention to withdraw all US troops from Cambodia by June 30, the same deadline stipulated by the amendment. According to White House chief of staff H. R. Haldeman, the administration also recruited "inflammatory types to attack Senate Doves" by emphasizing their "disloyalty" and "lack of patriotism." With these aims in mind, several Republicans, including Robert Dole (R-KS) and Paul Fannin (R-KS), gladly accepted the charge to "really ram" Cooper and Church.[61]

Southern Democrats John Stennis, Sam Ervin, and Spressard Holland and Republicans John Tower and Strom Thurmond augmented the efforts of these GOP attack dogs and in the process articulated majority southern assessments of President Nixon and the war. Stennis, the member of this contingent who spoke most often against Cooper-Church, presented a comprehensive condemnation of the measure. As the only member of the Senate to have received advance notice of the US military operation, the Mississippi senator argued there were times during war when "secrecy" was essential. The SASC chairman considered Nixon "experienced and tough minded" and praised the president's "courage" in implementing "the first big thing," the first aggressive action "in a long time." Stennis backed the Cambodian invasion unreservedly since that country had long since become an "arsenal" for the enemy. To this strategic argument, Stennis added a constitutional brief for rejecting Cooper-Church. The amendment, he contended, sought to restrict inappropriately the president's authority and discretion as commander in chief. The senator could find "no precedent in all history for Congress to . . . define the perimeter of a battlefield" in the midst of a war. To do so would set an unconstitutional "precedent that would plague . . . future presidents," "repudiate" Nixon's pledge to withdraw by June 30, and indicate the US intention to "cut and run"—all of which would foster "great glee" among American "enemies."[62]

Ervin, who would come to national and international prominence as he chaired the Senate Watergate hearings during the summer of 1973, described himself as just an "old country lawyer" and was portrayed as a "genial blend of con law and corn pone" and possessed of a "down home voice that drawls from a pair of cheeky jowls that appear to be stuffed plumb full of grits." Behind this folksy exterior was a keen legal mind and a well-educated former associate justice of the North Carolina Supreme Court, who had graduated from the University of North Carolina and attended Harvard Law School following infantry service in World War I. Although Ervin was a consistent hawk on Vietnam, his opposition to government interference with "an individual's constitutional rights" led him to uphold the distribution of antiwar literature on US military bases and to oppose army surveillance of peace protestors.[63]

Ervin reinforced Stennis's arguments on May 18 in an extended Senate speech and in response to a series of leading questions from Senators Holland and Jordan. Ervin maintained that Nixon acted on sound "constitutional and legal" grounds in ordering the invasion. The Gulf of Tonkin constituted a de facto "declaration of war," and Cambodia's inability to "protect its neutrality" provided Nixon international legal sanction. As commander in chief, the president had not begun a "new war"; instead, he had prosecuted the "same war with the same enemy," which had employed Cambodia as a strategic sanctuary over the previous five years. Since the war was legally and actually in progress, Nixon had the constitutional authority as commander in chief to direct the military's "tactical operations." By asserting that Congress had the same powers, Cooper-Church sought unconstitutionally "to usurp and exercise" the "powers of the president." Holland and Tower offered similar perspectives, with the former endorsing an editorial that characterized "much of the criticism" of the Cambodian invasion as "a literal echo of the condemnation" emanating "from Moscow, Peking, and Hanoi" and the latter upholding Nixon's authority and accusing critics of "giving comfort to the enemy." Characterizing the Cambodian invasion as the "most courageous" presidential action of the Vietnam War, Thurmond warned that Senate passage of Cooper-Church would cast "Cambodia into the jaws" of "Communist expansion." While strongly backing President Nixon, these southerners aided Nixon's GOP stalwarts in forcing Cooper-Church advocates onto the defensive.[64]

Through his bipartisan work with Frank Church, Senator Cooper had moved to the forefront of antiwar legislative efforts in 1969 and 1970. This antiwar work was not the only way in which the senator had defied constituent sentiment. The liberal Republican had also demonstrated persistent political independence while opposing segregated schools and supporting federal aid to education and Medicare. Cooper's maverick political inclinations had prompted Senator Robert Taft (R-OH) to ask in the early 1950s, "Are you a Democrat or a Republican?" and a GOP Baptist in Kentucky to remark that Cooper had "a fine name but very little religion and no reliable politics at all." Still, Kentuckians appreciated his common touch, his integrity, and his genuine concern for his constituents.[65]

Cooper was initially willing to await the results of the incursion, rather than rushing to judgment, but he admitted, "I would have been happier" if Nixon "had not chosen this" operation. Acting on his long-standing fear of an expanded war involving the possible use of nuclear weapons, Cooper had joined Church in sponsoring an amendment passed in December 1969 forbidding the use of US ground troops in Laos or Thailand. This measure marked the first time since the outbreak of World War II that Congress had employed the "appropriations power" to dictate military operations; and the two senators had announced on April 12 their intention to extend this ban to Cambodia, only to have Nixon preempt the issue.[66]

This same fear of a wider war prompted Cooper and Church to sponsor their 1970 amendment. Cooper emphasized that he had supported Vietnamization because it constituted "an irreversible policy to bring our forces home." Invading Cambodia contradicted this policy. The Kentucky Republican acknowledged the president's authority to "protect our forces" through air power or temporary border crossings but contended that Nixon needed congressional approval to "engage in a major operation or war in Cambodia," where the United States had "no treaty obligations." In response to Tower and Robert Griffin (R-MI), the temperate and mannerly Cooper came as near to outrage as he could muster. He dismissed their repeated assertions that he and backers of the amendment were "trying to undermine" the president's "power to protect the troops" as "incorrect" and a "disservice" to the American people. Cooper challenged such accusations "from the bottom" of his "soul" and dismissed this debating tactic as disingenuous. If such arguments were to be employed "every time Members of the Congress believe in honesty" and acted from a sense of "duty" as legislators, Congress would be paralyzed.[67]

Fulbright and Gore sharply criticized the Cambodian operation and provided predictable support for their fellow southern dove and his amendment. Both were appalled at still another blatant executive disregard for the SFRC's and the Senate's role in foreign policy. With considerable hyperbole, Fulbright pronounced Nixon's actions, "next to the civil war, . . . the most serious constitutional crisis we've ever faced," and he pointedly asked Stennis how one of "the strongest advocates of a strict construction of the Constitution" and the Senate's "proper constitutional role" could "arrogate" to Nixon "the right" to make such "grave decisions" while ignoring Congress. Gore warned that the "pattern" of events surrounding the invasion of Cambodia was eerily reminiscent of US entry into Vietnam, a commitment made "without treaty obligations" or congressional "authorization." The senator asserted that critics of US actions in Cambodia were the true "strict constructionists" and dismissed as "deplorable" the charges by Nixon's "propaganda minions" that dissenters were "unpatriotic."[68]

When the Senate passed the Cooper-Church Amendment on June 30, the exact date that Nixon had set for the withdrawal of all US troops from Cambodia, Senator Cooper's staff admitted the measure was of largely "symbolic value." Still, what the *Washington Post* called the first congressional attempt "to limit the deployment of American troops in the course of an ongoing war" had caused great consternation in the Nixon White House and among backers of US military efforts and had built on prior attempts to reassert congressional war-making powers. The debate and the vote on Cooper-Church II also clearly demonstrated the importance of southern support for Nixon's Vietnam policies. The Senate adopted the amendment by a 57–38 vote, with Democrats voting 42 to 11 in favor and Republicans 16 to 26 against. Of the 11 Democratic "no" votes, 10 came from the South, compared to only 6 southern votes in favor. Of the 5 Dixie Republicans voting, only Cooper voted in favor. Therefore, within the 57–38 vote in favor, southerners voted 7 to 13 against. When the House tabled the amendment on July 9, southern voting was equally revealing. The tabling motion was adopted 237–153, with southern Democrats voting 67 to 8 in favor and southern Republicans agreeing 27 to 0.[69]

Southern congressional opposition to the McGovern-Hatfield Amendment was even more decisive. This "Amendment to End the War" proposed to halt all funding for the war after December 1970 and required the withdrawal of all American forces by June 30, 1971, unless Congress were to declare war in the interim. By the end of the summer, one poll found 55 percent of Americans favoring McGovern-Hatfield; but in an earlier poll, only 21 percent of southerners had endorsed setting that precise date for the US exit from Vietnam. When the Senate voted the amendment down by 39–55 on September 1, only Senators Fulbright and Ralph Yarborough voted in favor, and Yarborough was a lame duck, having lost to Lloyd M. Bentsen Jr. in the Texas Democratic primary in May. Fifteen southerners, including Cooper and Gore, voted against McGovern-Hatfield.[70]

Fulbright contended that only a "willingness to commit ourselves to a phased but total American military withdrawal . . . by a specific date" would yield a negotiated settlement. As usual, Stennis spoke for the majority of southerners when he objected to providing the enemy "the precise nature of our plans" and thereby enabling Hanoi and the NLF to "sit down and wait" for the American departure. Cooper added that Congress lacked "the authority to tell the President" to withdraw US "troops on a certain day where they might be in mutual danger"; and Gore, who was in the midst of an ultimately unsuccessful reelection campaign, explained his vote with the assertion that a "forced timetable withdrawal" would undermine the US negotiating position.[71]

Agreeing with Stennis, Ervin, and the decisive majority of southern legislators, the *Montgomery Advertiser, Dallas Morning News,* and *New Orleans Times-Picayune* applauded Nixon's actions and harshly criticized student protestors. The *Advertiser* was pleased that the president had rejected "appeasement and surrender" and maintained US "credibility." By mid-May, the paper's editors pronounced the operation "overwhelmingly" successful, thereby "heaping more shame" on the "self-righteous, pompous" campus radicals who had defamed Nixon as a "bloodthirsty warmonger." The *Morning News* agreed that President Nixon had proved to Hanoi and the American "peace-at-any-price crowd" that his pledge "to take strong and effective measures" was sincere and credible. The paper also endorsed Nixon's criticism of students at Kent State University and sided with the National Guard troops. The *Morning News* concluded, "The continued use of violence and force by one side sooner or later will provoke a violent reaction from the other side."[72]

Consistent with its prior opposition to the war, the *Louisville Courier-Journal* was much more critical of Nixon. The Kentucky paper viewed the

US movement into Cambodia as a "decisive escalation and expansion of the war" that contradicted the president's stated policy of withdrawal and demonstrated his "lack of candor." In decided contrast to majority opinion in the South and the nation, the *Courier-Journal* defended protestors and criticized Nixon and his administration for appealing to "the darkest emotions of society" and "expressing haughty contempt" for students and their concerns. Letters to the editor, which overwhelmingly supported the president and savagely attacked student protestors, reconfirmed that the paper's editorial stance on the war and related issues was, like that of Senator Cooper, a decidedly minority perspective in Kentucky and the South.[73]

In a significant development, the *Atlanta Constitution* joined the *Courier-Journal* as an important southern daily opposing the war. With Reg Murphy replacing Eugene Patterson as editor, the *Constitution* termed the Cambodian invasion "a reckless decision" and a "major escalation" of the war that broke Nixon's *"promise . . . to cool off the war, to get us out and turn it over to the South Vietnamese."* The *Constitution* also refrained from attacking student dissenters and lectured the Nixon administration that "those who call for guns and bullets to deal with student dissent are more dangerous to America and its institutions . . . than the dissenters ever could be." Despite these criticisms, the *Constitution* criticized the Cooper-Church and McGovern-Hatfield Amendments for giving "advance notice" to Hanoi that "they have won and we have lost." True Vietnamization, a "long view" that held out "hope for a solution that is realistic and honorable," was preferable to escalation or an abrupt withdrawal. Although the paper, like most southerners, still hoped for an honorable outcome, the *Constitution's* altered position was another indication that the war was taking its toll in Dixie.[74]

Southern politicians had only to read their mail to find that Stennis, Ervin, Tower, the *Montgomery Advertiser,* and the *Dallas Morning News* continued to speak for majority southern opinion. Senator Cooper's correspondence from across the South ran heavily in favor of President Nixon and the Cambodian invasion and strongly opposed to Cooper-Church and antiwar protestors. Critics of the senator and his amendment emphasized that President Nixon had "inherited" the war, was making steady progress in reducing US involvement, and deserved united American backing. A Paris, Kentucky, couple berated Cooper and cited a *Lexington*

Herald Leader poll in which 73 percent of responders backed Nixon and only 22 percent opposed the Cambodian operation. By failing to align himself with that 72 percent, Cooper had joined the "H.H. camp," or "Hanoi Helpers," and sided with the "liberals" aiding a "Communist take over" in the United States. Southern Republicans expressed "disgust" that Cooper opposed their GOP president. Was the senator "really and truly a Republican or . . . a Democrat wearing Republican clothing?" Cooper's actions so infuriated a Sarasota, Florida, resident that he dismissed the senator as "dirty rotten scum" to whom he would "love to give . . . a mouthful of knuckles." Nixon supporters had no empathy for antiwar protestors and little sympathy for the students killed at Kent State. Cooper's critics often equated his policies with those "vastly overgrown children," "STUPID COLLEGE COWARDS," and "All American Brats," who "scream, 'PEACE, PEACE,' and then bomb and burn, [and] hurl rocks and bottles," or "bearded, long haired unwashed bastards, who . . . wreck our colleges and universities."[75]

While opposing the war generally, southern supporters of the Kentucky senator and Cooper-Church especially objected to President Nixon's "unilateral decision," which "usurped" Congress's "constitutional authority," and to the president's response to "attempts at peaceful dissent . . . with armed intimidation and official violence." A Florida couple with a son in Vietnam declared, "No One MAN Should Have The Power To Commit Our Boys To Combat And Sometimes Death." They did not sanction "Looting, Burning, Or The Long Hair," but did "Approve and Support Our Young Men FOR *NOT WANTING TO Die.*" A Lexington woman, who admitted, "I voted for Nixon and Agnew, God forgive me," decried "the invasion of Cambodia" and sympathized with the student protestors: "I do believe protestors should be peaceful but, when peaceful protestors are ignored and the participants belittled and insulted, I can understand why violence has erupted." Others noted that the president's actions contradicted Vietnamization and the withdrawal of US troops and agreed with Cooper that Nixon appeared to be opting for a "military rather than a negotiated settlement."[76]

Both the arguments and the deep emotional divisions evident in the letters to Senator Cooper echoed across Dixie. Senator Fulbright, still the most prominent southern dove, was castigated as the "boob from Arkansas" who was "a professional 'aginner' . . . against just about everything except" his "campaign of assistance to the enemy." A rural Mississippian advocated the "round up" of "the Fulbrights . . . and others of the same breed" and their banishment to a "concentration camp." Antiwar southerners were often equally caustic. An irate constituent berated Senator Ervin's support for the war, Nixon's decision to invade Cambodia, and the National Guards' actions at Kent State. This Chapel Hill minister was aghast that his senator could "condone the shooting of students who were at worst throwing rocks at soldiers dressed for battle." He further accused Ervin of "aiding and abetting the murder of thousands of our young men, . . . hundreds and thousands of innocent people in Southeast Asia, . . . the destruction of this country's economy, and the final and complete loss of America's credibility, prestige, and respect abroad." Ervin was "one hell of a lousy American, and a lousy Constitutional scholar" to boot.[77]

Two other opponents of the war, a Mississippi mother and a Georgia businessman, added perspectives particularly relevant to southern attitudes on the war and foreign policy. While urging Senator Stennis to vote for Cooper-Church and asserting she did not want her young son to be sent to Vietnam, this woman was certain "that all other mothers feel the same, although some feel (have been made to feel) unpatriotic and traitorous about it and dare not admit their feelings even to themselves." The Atlanta businessman also spoke to the region's growing ambivalence about the war juxtaposed against Dixie's pervasive patriotism and intolerance of dissent. He advised Senator Talmadge that all of the "conservative business men" with whom he had spoken over the "past few months" had come to favor "getting out of Vietnam as soon as possible," although some were "reluctant to express their views publicly" out of "fear of being grouped with . . . radicals who automatically oppose anything the government is doing."[78]

Talmadge's reaction to the Cambodian operation afforded additional evidence that even some of the most hawkish southerners were tiring of the war and its agony; but the harsh responses from his Georgia constituents demonstrated the residual strength of the region's backing of Nixon and the war. Although Talmadge opposed Cooper-Church as an inappropriate restriction on the commander in chief and voted against both this measure and McGovern-Hatfield, his criticism of President Nixon provoked extensive discussion and considerable consternation in Georgia. The senator continued to favor a more aggressive prosecution of the war and was hopeful in mid-May that "moving into Cambodia" indicated the United States "at last" intended "to prosecute" the war appropriately and "destroy the Communist war effort." When the operation proved only transitory and US withdrawal remained "just a question of time," Talmadge advocated doing so "as fast as possible." Were this advice not sufficiently alarming to his militant constituents, he added that Nixon had "made a grave mistake by not consulting Congress on Cambodia."[79]

The *Atlanta Constitution* applauded Talmadge's call for a prompt ending to the war and interpreted his statements as a "major sign of the general disillusionment" over US involvement in Vietnam. Sharing the *Constitution*'s hopeful view, antiwar Georgians wrote to "congratulate" and "wholeheartedly" support their hawkish senator's partial change of heart. Even more revealing were the outraged Georgians who were "shocked" and "dismayed" at Talmadge's "shameful" censure of Nixon and at the senator's willingness to "join the Fulbrights . . . in giving comfort to the enemy." One of these constituents lectured, "We here in Georgia may be a little war weary . . . , but we are a long way from being ready to throw away (by withdrawing) what we have fought so long for and are perhaps now on the verge of winning."[80]

The failure of Senators Albert Gore and Ralph Yarborough to win reelection in 1970 provided additional evidence of the South's persistent support for the war. Close personal friends, both of these senators had received warnings from backers that their opposition to the war endangered their chances for remaining in office. As early as 1968, Yarborough's relatively muted criticism of the war prompted an old Texas friend to remind the senator he might be signing his "political death warrant"; and on the eve of the Democratic primary, another pro-Yarborough constituent predicted his "support of the Peace Movement" would "hurt the Senator." Gore had received similar admonitions that he was "committing political suicide" by joining Fulbright in "crawling into bed with the 'Eastern Liberals.'" A Memphis attorney who had backed Gore since the early 1950s reluctantly advised the senator that "the paramount importance of the war question" made "it impossible" to vote for him in 1970.[81]

These predictions proved accurate when Lloyd Bentsen defeated Yarborough in the Texas Democratic primary and Gore lost to Republican William Brock in the general election. Although Yarborough claimed in an emotional Senate speech that his defeat demonstrated "the price one risks in voting against those who make billions off this unwise, stupid war," and Texas liberal Maury Maverick Jr. suggested the Bentsen victory in part reflected the state's "sock-it-to-'em Vietnam attitude," the Democratic senator had not openly opposed the war until after Tet and was far less vocal than Fulbright, Cooper, and Gore. Still, his antiwar stance after Tet enabled Bentsen to brand him a "dove," hardly a favorable appellation in Texas. By comparison, Gore's public opposition to the war had provoked the ire of Presidents Johnson and Nixon and prompted a flood of hostile, post-1964 correspondence from his Tennessee constituents. Gore fully understood that his dissent went "against the grain of prevailing sentiment in Tennessee," where if people were shown a war, "they will fight it." Therefore, Vietnam played a much greater role in his defeat than Yarborough's.[82]

Senator Gore's opposition to the war was not the only family tie to Vietnam in 1970. Albert (Al) Gore Jr. was about to begin his tour in Vietnam as a military journalist. Following his graduation from Harvard University in May 1969, Al had bypassed an opportunity to join the National Guard and enlisted in the army in August. Part of his motivation was quite southern, part more political. Having remained registered for the draft in the small town of Carthage, Tennessee, he believed that if he did not go, another young man he had likely known for many years would be summoned. Were this the case, the younger Gore did not believe he could face his Carthage neighbors "without feeling small and guilty." He also feared that avoiding the draft and military service would further imperil his antiwar father's chances for reelection, and he often appeared with Albert at campaign rallies—sometimes in uniform. Following his dad's defeat, Al Gore served for five months in Vietnam in 1971. Although he "never claimed to have been in combat," he was one of approximately ten (of twelve hundred) members of the 1969 Harvard class to serve in Vietnam, and he traveled widely into clearly dangerous areas as a correspondent. Even though he, like Senator Gore, opposed the war, Al served honorably and later recalled feeling "more alive" in the war zone and fondly recalled the "intense and powerful" "camaraderie" established with fellow soldiers.[83]

In addition to defying majority southern opinion on the war, both Gore and Yarborough carried costly liberal political baggage. Both had voted consistently for black voting rights and most recently for the 1968

Fair Housing Act, had backed LBJ's Great Society legislation, had opposed school prayer and two of Nixon's southern nominees to the Supreme Court, and were significantly outspent by their opponents. The Nixon administration had targeted Gore. Nixon made two trips to Tennessee to campaign for Brock and funneled funds, some illegally, to bolster the GOP challenger's effort. Therefore, opposition to the war was not the only reason for Gore's and Yarborough's losses, but straying from Dixie's martial inclinations appreciably compromised their electoral prospects.

Unlike the outcome of these two elections, the South's promilitary and prowar proclivities were clearly responsible for Dixie's hostility toward GI coffeehouses. Located close to major military installations, these coffeehouses provided soldiers an environment to relax beyond military jurisdiction and became centers for antiwar activities. Although none of these Dixie soldiers who wrote to their senators from 1968 to 1970 became active in the antiwar movement within the US military, their disillusionment reflected the deteriorating morale and antiwar attitudes that permeated the coffeehouses. A combat medic informed Senator John Sparkman, "We were the fighters, the muddy and sweaty ones." This soldier was appalled at how "little" the South Vietnamese "people cared for the cause of freedom." In fact, he had "more respect for a draft dodger or war protestor than for a [South] Vietnam soldier." A marine veteran, just back from Vietnam in December 1968, agreed that the South Vietnamese would "never be able to defend their . . . homeland" or "support a democratic system." This Arkansas native lamented the costs of pursuing these "hopelessly unachievable goals." He had gone to Vietnam with "ten other Marines." Nine of them were killed, and the tenth was a "helpless paralytic. And nothing in Vietnam is changed." Still, the "worst thing" was "what we are doing *to* the Vietnamese people in the name of *our* national prestige." This soldier knew "from personal experience that more civilians are dying by far than either the NVA or Americans combined."[84]

The following year, a veteran of two combat tours, one as a member of the 101st Airborne and the second in the US Special Forces, urged Senator Talmadge to promote "every possible effort to END THIS WAR IMMEDIATELY." This ground soldier assured the senator: "I know this war. I know the mud, the heat and the rain; I know the jungle nights, the dreariness and the terror. I have seen the mountains and the valleys, the cities and the villages—on foot, from trucks and jeeps; and from helicopters and airplanes. I have talked with the people, and have shared meals with them in their homes. I have seen bodies stacked like lumber and bomb craters big enough to hold a house. I have heard my buddies shriek with pain, and have heard the loud silence when the shrieks stopped." According to this veteran, the United States was waging a futile campaign on behalf of the "venal and self-aggrandizing" Thieu government and against an enemy who "consider themselves super patriots" and "see *us* as an occupying force on *their* country."[85]

Based on such disillusionment and antiwar sentiments, the first GI coffeehouse, the UFO, was opened in late 1967 in Columbia, South Carolina, near Fort Jackson. Until it was closed under intense local pressure in January 1970, the UFO was frequented by soldiers, antiwar students from the University of South Carolina and Columbus College, and other antiwar dissenters. The UFO served "coffee, tea, soft drinks, fresh fruit, music, and anti-establishment propaganda, much of which was pointedly anti-military." The owners of neighboring businesses and local authorities charged that the UFO was also a center for the sale and consumption of illegal drugs, particularly marijuana. Other, similar coffeehouses were founded across the South—the Oleo Strut in Killeen, Texas, near Fort Hood; the GI Coffee House in El Paso, near Fort Bliss; and the Muldraugh GI coffeehouse near Fort Knox. The latter offered services similar to those at the UFO and featured "a painting of an upside-down American flag" and Mao Zedong, Che Guevara, and Black Panther posters. All of these houses were associated with underground antiwar newspapers: the *Short Times* in Columbia, *FTA* (officially, *Fun, Travel, and Adventure*) in Muldraugh, the *Gigline* in El Paso, and the *Fatigue Press* in Killeen. Such papers were "dedicated to building a movement of GIs who no longer will accept being messed over in the army and being used to mess over other people around the world." These coffeehouses also hosted touring antiwar speakers; provided organizing centers for local antiwar demonstrations, which often included off-duty soldiers; served as refuges and way stations for draftees and deserters fleeing to Canada; and afforded GI wives the opportunity to comment on women's issues and the difficulties facing military families.[86]

Given the South's overt patriotism, disdain for antiwar protestors and members of the counterculture, and dependence on defense spending, the region's aggressively negative reaction to these establishments was predictable and revealing. In the face of intense local hostility, the Muldraugh house survived for only a year. The elderly landlord refused to accept rent payments and then demanded that the coffeehouse be closed for failure to pay. When challenged by the proprietors' attorney, the eighty-one-year-old declared, "You're a Communist, the same as the rest of them." Military intelligence officers complemented this local hostility by infiltrating the coffeehouse and regularly harassing off-duty GIs.[87]

The UFO and Oleo Strut endured similar experiences. After being hounded daily by the local police, both uniformed and plainclothes, and by undercover agents from the military and the FBI, five operators of the UFO and the coffeehouse itself were indicted on January 13, 1970, for actions "detrimental to the peace, happiness, lives, safety and good morals of the people of South Carolina." Three days later the UFO was permanently closed. Held under unusually high bail and tried before an openly biased judge, who described the defendants as prone to "rebel against our form of life" and having "come to South Carolina . . . for the sole purpose of causing trouble," the five UFO defendants were convicted and sentenced to six years in prison, and the UFO was fined $10,000. After appeals, these sentences were reduced and suspended on the condition that these antiwar activists leave South Carolina immediately. The Strut outlived both the UFO and the Muldraugh houses, but only while experiencing, according to a *Texas Observer* contributor, jail time for staff members and broken windows, smoke bombs, and even a shooting courtesy of the "local shitkickers."[88]

Although the Quaker House in Fayetteville, North Carolina, outside Fort Bragg, did not exactly fit the GI coffeehouse mold, local hawks, the FBI, and military intelligence responded just as they had in Kentucky, South Carolina, and Texas. Founded in 1969 by soldiers, many of whom were Vietnam vets, and Quakers from Chapel Hill, Durham, and Greensboro, the Quaker House held religious services, distributed information regarding conscientious objection, and afforded space for soldiers who opposed the war. In the wake of the US invasion of Cambodia, local antiwar demonstrations, and a speaking appearance by Jane Fonda, arsonists burned the Quaker House on May 20, 1970. Resistance from local government and landlords prevented its reopening until October 1970, when William Carothers, a veteran, used his VA benefits to buy a house, which he donated to the Quakers. Thus, like the Strut, this antiwar center survived the events of 1970 and local southern hostility, but the travails of the operators of both establishments testify to Dixie's majority opinions on the war.[89]

These majority public and congressional opinions in support of the war afforded both Presidents Johnson and Nixon vital political space as they reluctantly made decisions leading toward US withdrawal from Vietnam. This political space was especially crucial to Nixon as Democrats from other regions were much less deferential toward the new Republican president. Responding to Nixon's southern domestic strategy, which deemphasized civil rights and accentuated law and order, and his more assertive Vietnam policy, with its declared goal of peace with honor, Dixie's residents viewed the Republican president as a kindred spirit in the areas of both race and foreign policy. Southerners indicated their approval of the president in the 1968 elections, through their letters to Dixie's editors and political leaders, and with their responses to Gallup pollsters. By vocally supporting Lieutenant Calley, attacking GI coffeehouses, and denying Senators Yarborough and Gore reelection, southerners amplified their promilitary and prowar preferences. These collective responses indicated that the South was the region most approving of Nixon's overall performance as president and his handling of Vietnam. Consistent with the majority views of their constituents, conservative southern Democratic congressmen and senators proved essential to Nixon and Kissinger's success in repulsing efforts by antiwar forces to curtail Vietnam funding or legislate an end to the war. For these southern Democrats, constitutional, racial, and war-related concerns trumped partisan politics. Acting on the same regional racial and foreign policy considerations, as well as partisan political calculations, southern Republicans, such as Senators Thurmond and Tower, also provided Nixon unwavering support.

As had been the case since 1963, a hardy antiwar minority of southerners continued to denounce the war. While helping lead a key antiwar legislative initiative, Senator Cooper remained allied with Fulbright and Gore in their persistent, if unsuccessful, battle to promote negotiations and compromise and to recapture a greater role for Congress in the making of foreign policy and war. Although the Cooper-Church Amendment targeting US operations in Cambodia did not yield immediate results, it caused great apprehension in the Nixon White House and reflected the nation's and the South's growing agony and war weariness. The latter was also evident across the southern public as the percentage of anti-war letters to Dixie's political leaders increased; as southern Democratic hawks began to emphasize their initial opposition to the commitment of US troops in Vietnam; as Senator Talmadge argued for a more rapid American withdrawal; and, most significantly, as John Stennis joined the campaign to reassert congressional foreign policy prerogatives, sought to reduce US commitments abroad, and called on the South Vietnamese to bear a greater war burden.

7

Southern College Students

As the Johnson and Nixon administrations made decisions directed toward US withdrawal from Vietnam, student opposition to the war peaked both nationally and in the South. Consistent with the attitudes of their parents, white southern students were significantly more prowar than their peers nationally. Antiwar protests on Dixie's campuses began later, were less numerous, and attracted fewer participants than those in other regions. While assessing student activism at Vanderbilt University, Paul Conkin noted that within the conservative South, even relatively mild actions appeared "radical" to Dixie's parents, college administrators, newspaper editors, and political leaders. Greg L. Michel, the historian of the Southern Student Organizing Committee (SSOC), the principal antiwar and civil rights organization for white students in the South, added that joining SSOC "required great courage" since SSOC activities "could lead to loss of friends, condemnation and rejection by one's family, and expulsion from school."[1]

African American students, for whom attending college was particularly challenging, were even less involved in the antiwar protests. In addition to weighing the same disincentives confronting white students, blacks were keenly aware of the armed attacks of white police and National Guardsmen resulting in student deaths at Jackson State College and three other black schools. Despite these obstacles, Dixie's student dissidents waged unprecedented protests against the war. In so doing, they, like student dissidents nationally, helped keep the conflict and its agonies before the American public, to restrain Johnson's and Nixon's most aggressive tendencies, and to convince national and local leaders that ending the war was essential to restoring domestic order and tranquility.

Antiwar students were a distinct minority on all American campuses, but their status was even more pronounced in the South. Given Dixie's backing of the conflict and hypersensitivity to outside criticism, southerners had little tolerance for dissenters questioning the war. The experiences of two southern students provide vivid insight into the response that most often greeted protestors. Jeff Shero, a student activist at the University of Texas, declared that joining Students for a Democratic Society (SDS) in Texas meant "breaking with your family, it meant being cut off—it was like in early Rome joining a Christian sect. . . . If you were from Texas, in SDS, you were a bad motherfucker, you couldn't go home for Christmas. . . . In most of those places it meant, '*You Goddamn Communist.*'" Or perhaps, you maniac! When David Doggett, an undergraduate at Millsaps College in Jackson, Mississippi, marched for civil rights and against the war and helped start a "Free University" off campus, the academic dean contacted Doggett's parents and suggested that he was insane and should be removed from school and sent for psychiatric treatment.[2]

The active hostility of southern political leaders, college administrators, press, and communities toward antiwar students conveyed these regional attitudes. Upon being appointed a trustee at the University of Kentucky, former governor Albert B. "Happy" Chandler, who at one point punched a student demonstrator in the face, opined, "If we can get rid of a lot of the silly, foolish professors who advocate violence on the part of the long-haired students, I think we pretty soon can correct the situation at the university." Republican governor Claude R. Kirk Jr. of Florida agreed, denouncing the October 1969 Moratorium as an "irresponsible disruption of the learning process." Voicing a similar perspective, a local South Carolina prosecutor ended a successful summation aimed at closing the UFO, an antiwar GI coffeehouse in Columbia, by citing obscenity, drug use, and opposition to the war and by singing several verses of "The Old Rugged Cross." The judge followed with a denunciation of outsider agitators who "rebel against our form of life" and "feel they have a right to be critical . . . of the other ninety-five percent of the people who have to work for a living." Senator Strom Thurmond and Congressman Mendel Rivers sponsored legislation calling for up to five years in prison and a $10,000 fine for anyone convicted of destroying a draft card or other draft-related materials.[3]

The overwhelming majority of southern papers concurred. The *Dallas Morning News* disparaged the "peacenik movement" and "leaping leftists" and admonished students at the University of Texas, Austin, that the institution's "purpose should continue to be higher education, rather than a political demonstration." The *Montgomery Advertiser* hurled similar epithets, such as "spoiled brats," "campus Jacobins," and "immature minds" favoring "appeasement and surrender," and dismissed student unrest at the University of Alabama at Tuscaloosa as "campus theater of the absurd." The *State* in Columbia, South Carolina, railed against "peaceniks, pacifists, and pinkos," and the Jackson, Mississippi, *Clarion-Ledger* suggested that when "a stink bomb was thrown among a recent gathering of beatniks and peaceniks, . . . nobody noticed any difference." In a subsequent editorial entitled "Youthful Leaders Behaved," the *Clarion-Ledger* contrasted the "noisy minority [of American students]" who attracted "entirely too much attention" compared to the "serious-minded . . . 4-H, FFA boys and girls" who were "learning to do, to think, to be courteous, to work, to worship, to lead. . . . The South is producing an excellent quota of this promising human resource. Thank God for them." Even Ralph McGill, the publisher of the more liberal *Atlanta Constitution,* questioned the judgment of "pacifist professors" and castigated "doomsayers and defeatists."[4]

The great bulk of these papers' readers found this editorial stance most congenial. In the wake of demonstrations at the University of Kentucky protesting the US invasion of Cambodia in April 1970, more than 90 percent of a *Lexington Herald Leader* poll of over one thousand people agreed with the use of the National Guard on the campus and believed that demonstrators should be expelled from the university. Letters to editors and constituent correspondence to officeholders across the South revealed a similar antipathy toward student dissidents. Southerners castigated student protestors as "raucous rabble," "hippie idiots, doped lunatics, moral and physical cowards, flag spitters, draft-card burners," "Typhoid Toms," "punks," "hoodlums," "far left reactionaries," and "Communists." Class tensions were evident as a disgruntled Tennessee resident complained that "a good portion of the people paying tuitions came by their money by honest hard work and sweat," only to have a few spoiled, privileged "rioters destroy" their education. While variously blaming "permissive parents" and "Crack-Pot" professors, other southerners recommended that authorities "quickly arrest and jail and sentence trouble makers." A retired marine veteran of the Korean War urged that in subduing the youth, who had reached a "new low in patriotism," no police be asked "to face them with blanks or to shoot high or to wound." Others echoed the need for law and order while calling for the immediate expulsion of protestors and banishment to "work camps." A Louisville mother concurred with the need for "severe punishment. . . . The kids have marched, the teachers have marched, the blacks have marched, the poor have marched, about the only ones left are the parents. The only marching left for them is to march those kids to the bathroom with a belt."[5]

Even prowar student demonstrators did not escape criticism. In January 1966 a "Draftee's Parent" doubted that the "spectacle of several hundred draft-deferred Georgia college students" rallying "in support of U.S. involvement in Vietnam" would impress American soldiers, allies, or enemies. Were these students to venture beyond the "comparative safety and comfort of Atlanta's multi-million dollar sports stadium" and march to a "Selective Service or military recruiting office and volunteer for service," their "sincerity" would have been "less open to question."[6]

This southern hostility toward student protestors was also evident among many university administrators and security personnel. Campus police at Texas A&M arrested student protestors in 1966, drove them eighty miles from College Station, and warned them not to return. That same spring, Mississippi students noted the potential consequences of opposing the war when a Greenwood church was destroyed by arson following an antiwar prayer service. In 1967 an antiwar activist was shot in Austin, Texas. The Florida State Board of Regents banned both the SSOC and SDS from all state-supported schools; the University of Texas, Austin, banished SDS from the campus; and Western Kentucky University administrators secured a restraining order to block civil rights and antiwar activist Carl Braden from speaking on campus. In the wake of the US invasion of Cambodia, the governors of South Carolina and Kentucky were two of only four chief executives nationwide declaring emergencies on their campuses; from 1967 through 1970, off-campus police and the National Guard were most often deployed in the South; and in 1972, police in Gainesville used high-pressure hoses to disperse University of Florida students protesting the US mining of Haiphong harbor. Surreptitious federal government actions reinforced the efforts of university administrators at William and Mary College, the University of Kentucky, and Georgia State University, where the CIA from 1967 to 1973 implemented Project Resistance surveillance activities, and at Louisiana State University in New Orleans from 1968 to 1971, as the FBI recruited students into Cointelpro to observe and disrupt SDS activities.[7]

Unsurprisingly, given Dixie's fundamental conservatism and regional support for the war, a clear majority of southern students were more pro-war and less activist than their peers from other regions. A survey tracing overall student protests during 1967–1968 found that 36 percent of responding southern institutions reported protests, compared to 49 percent in the Northeast, 44 percent in the Midwest, and 40 percent in the West. A May 1967 national mailing list of antiwar organizations, which were located primarily in towns or cities housing colleges, included ten in the Baltimore/Washington area; thirty in New England; thirty-four in northern California, Oregon, and Washington; but only eleven in the South. Fifty-seven percent of the 1969 freshman class at the University of Kentucky believed that student protestors should be disciplined more harshly. And following President Nixon's "silent majority" speech in November 1969, 60 percent of southern college students polled said they approved of his handling of the war, while 34 percent disapproved. These responses compared to an approval/disapproval rating of 52 and 43 percent among midwestern students and 36 and 58 percent among students in the East.[8]

In the wake of the US invasion of Cambodia and the student deaths at Kent State University and Jackson State College in May 1970 and the massive student protests on American campuses, a national Harris poll of eight hundred full-time undergraduates from fifty colleges yielded similar and revealing results. A higher proportion of southern students approved of the invasion, believed the operation would shorten the war, rated Nixon's handling of the war "excellent" or "pretty good," and favored "expanding" the war as the best course for ending the conflict. When asked to assess Nixon's performance as president, Dixie's undergraduates were significantly more supportive of the chief executive than other American students. Southerners responded with a 45 percent favorable and 55 percent negative evaluation, versus 29 favorable/71 negative for students nationally, 16/84 for both the East and the West, and 36/43 for the Midwest. Southern male students' attitudes toward the draft clearly reflected the region's military tradition. In response to the question, "If you were called up for the draft," 53 percent of southern men answered that they would "accept the draft call and serve"; 25 percent replied that they would "attempt to avoid induction, but serve if these attempts failed"; and 12 percent declared they would "leave the country" rather than be inducted. In contrast, 27 percent of eastern men declared they would accept a draft call, 33 percent of midwesterners, and 23 percent of westerners.[9]

As was true nationally, southern students responded to the Vietnam War during a time of dramatic changes in American higher education and a more general inclination of young people to question authority. As the "baby boomers," or the generation born near the end of World War II, came of age, the number of college-age students ballooned from sixteen to twenty-five million. These demographic changes were evident in the South, where enrollments increased by 75 percent from 1960 to 1965. During this time period, the University of Virginia's student body grew by 31 percent; by 1965, enrollments at the University of North Carolina, Louisiana State University, and the University of Georgia had doubled, compared to 1958; and the University of Tennessee grew by 61 percent from 1964 to 1969.[10]

Both the vast increase in the number of students and their greater concentration on college campuses created the environment for a youth culture distinguished by its music, dress, and attitudes toward drugs and sexual relations. The participants in this culture came to question their elders on a broad array of issues, ranging from the length of one's hair to economic justice, civil rights, and US foreign policy. Having gone to college at least in part to escape their parents' control, college students during the 1960s and early 1970s also resented university-imposed restrictions on their personal behavior. Acting in loco parentis, southern universities legislated on many matters. Students at church-related schools, such as Furman University, attended obligatory chapel services and often were prohibited from sporting beards or dancing. Men and especially women faced curfews, and women frequently endured dress codes. For example, as late as February 1967, University of South Carolina coeds could not wear slacks or Bermuda shorts on campus and were allowed to don tight blue jeans or sweatshirts only if covered by a coat, while women at the University of Georgia were required to wear nontransparent coats to prevent men from seeing their gym uniforms. Students at Vanderbilt University, the University of Virginia, and William and Mary protested the exclusion of women from men's dormitories. These attempts to regulate sexual conduct embodied in rules for women's dress and hours were also evident in Louisiana State University's decision to ban *Playboy* from men's dorm rooms in October 1965. Sex, dress, and church attendance were not the only areas of concern. In Tallahassee in the early 1960s, white students at Florida State University and black students at Florida A&M University could not visit one another without written permission.[11]

These personal restrictions, together with issues of race, the Civil Rights Movement, and especially the war, produced unprecedented student activism nationally and across the South. Opponents and supporters of US involvement in Vietnam acted in the midst of numerous other student protests. Students at the University of North Carolina (UNC) at Chapel Hill, Vanderbilt University, Western Kentucky University, the University of South Carolina, and Louisiana State University (LSU) decried restrictions on outside speakers. Dissidents at UNC-Chapel Hill, the University of Virginia, and LSU demanded better pay and working conditions for university service employees and marched to improve the lives of African Americans in their communities. Students at LSU criticized the university for closing the swimming pool rather than integrating it in the summer of 1964 and for refusing to integrate intercollegiate athletic teams; and University of Virginia students voted decisively in May 1970 for a student body composed of at least 20 percent African Americans. Southern students also actively objected to restrictions on their personal behavior. Indeed, on some campuses these rules engendered activism rivaling that focused on the war. A March 10, 1970, rally condemning LSU's discriminatory women's rules drew a crowd of twelve hundred, nearly twice the number who turned out for the largest on-campus protest directed at the US invasion of Cambodia and the deaths at Kent State University later in the spring.[12]

Diverse motives prompted southern students to protest the war. Both Presidents Johnson and Nixon asserted male students acted out of a desire to avoid combat. LBJ declared, "I don't give a damn about those little pinkos on the campuses; they're just waving their diapers and bellyaching because they don't want to fight." Nixon agreed that student protestors opposed the war "to keep from getting their asses shot off" rather than out of "moral conviction." Both presidents were partially correct. Beginning in 1966, the Johnson administration opted to draft undergraduate men whose grade point average fell below a C and the next year ended deferments for graduate students. These changes made the prospect of serving in Vietnam all too real for these students and their families. More ephemeral social attractions brought other students to antiwar rallies. An often-repeated boomer recollection declared, "Protesting was a great place to get laid, get high, and listen to some great rock."[13]

Self-preservation and comparatively trivial social considerations did not exhaust the bases for student opposition to the war. As one University of South Florida activist stated, "Some people were there just for the drugs and good times, but the people I knew were really not. We were committed to higher ideals." In the most general sense, antiwar students challenged the nation to live up to its professed and highest ideals, and these young people believed optimistically in the possibility of positive changes, whether in the realm of foreign policy, race relations, or women's rights. For these students the path to dissent involved both an emotional and an intellectual transformation, and the latter had often come after reading, attending lectures, discussions, and teach-ins. Steve Smith (pseudonym), a nineteen-year-old sophomore at the University of Georgia, described this process to an *Atlanta Constitution* reporter in May 1970. From a "reactionary middle-class family" in south Georgia, Smith had been a political conservative in high school; but upon arriving in Athens, he "began to read a lot and began questioning a lot of things I had never thought of before." Neither a "revolutionary" nor a proponent of violence, Smith came to favor substantive changes in American society and to oppose the "politically, morally and economically unsound" US intervention in Vietnam. After he participated in the October 1969 Moratorium opposing the war, his parents threatened to "disown" him if he continued protesting the war. During his trip home in early 1970, "the local John Birchers" had so "harassed" him and his family that he had "to pack up and leave" since he was viewed as a "Communist." Smith sadly concluded that when his parents learned that he had demonstrated against the US invasion of Cambodia, he would be unable to "go home anymore."[14]

Other southern students elaborated on their reasons and motives for opposing the war. Bentley Alexander, a lonely voice "On the Left" among LSU students in the mid-1960s, contended that US intervention in Vietnam conflicted with the nation's professed ideals and goal of self-government. He also reminded his classmates that killing people in an "impersonal" fashion with "modern weapons" was no less atrocious than deaths inflicted in a more "personal" and ostensibly more "brutal" way. Another LSU student objected to having his taxes support the war and thereby making him "indirectly responsible for the deaths of innocent people." Other students believed that the war diverted attention and resources from pressing domestic needs. A Tennessee man observed, "You couldn't fight poverty, you couldn't fight racism . . . 'cause everything was being poured into . . . this damn war over in Vietnam." An editorial writer for the *Cavalier Daily* at the University of Virginia agreed that the "Vietnam Tragedy" had forced the "most serious domestic problems—those of housing, education, job opportunities, urban development, [and] pollution control"—into the background.[15]

Some students asserted that US involvement in Vietnam was simply bad policy. A North Carolina opponent of the war declared, "We had no business in Vietnam. We had no national interest. . . . It was an unconstitutional war, it was an undeclared war, it was undemocratically decided, and it only benefitted the rich folks—the war machine, the military industrial complex." Agreeing wholeheartedly with this characterization of the war, Tom Gardner, a prominent member of SSOC and one of the foremost activists at the University of Virginia, perceived opposition to the war as integral to two more ambitious goals: first, to break all Defense Department ties to universities by eliminating ROTC and defense-related and sponsored research; and, second, "to mobilize a group of people which can effect a revolution in this country." Gardner's pursuit of revolution placed him considerably to the left of most southern student dissenters, who were politically liberal or moderate and were as likely to oppose the war simply because it was "all so senseless" as to envision radical institutional change in the United States.[16]

While subscribing to many of these sentiments, antiwar southern Vietnam veterans added an especially powerful voice to the dissenting chorus. The leaders of the University of Georgia's Vietnam Veterans Against the War chapter declared that after being "honorably discharged from active duty in Southeast Asia," they had "voluntarily enlisted" in the campaign "to end the war and to see that all Americans are brought home where they may join us in working for a just and peaceful world." Later, they urged fellow students to attend a rally in Atlanta to highlight the "suffering of the Indochinese people," the "plight of our brothers in uniform," and the misery of "American POWs." When student veterans at LSU castigated demonstrators, a former marine condemned their intolerant, "immature display of PATRIOTISM" and "False Loyalty" and argued that their service gave them no right to suppress dissent. Instead, it obligated veterans "to preserve and defend our society wherein dissent, disagreement, and protest may prevail."[17]

Although southern antiwar students acted from diverse motives and voiced numerous objections to the war, they remained a minority on even the most activist campuses, such as the University of Virginia, the University of Georgia, and the University of Texas. The majority of Dixie's students, like those nationally, were apathetic, supportive of the war, or too busy working and balancing family obligations while attending urban commuter schools or community colleges to have time for antiwar protests. For example, Greg A. Mausz, a former district president of the Florida Junior College Student Government Association, informed President Nixon that he represented "a large majority of . . . concerned students" who "do not grow our hair long, . . . do not have beards, . . . do not protest in the streets, [and] do not riot or burn down R.O.T.C. units." Similarly, the working and middle class and first-generation college students at the New Orleans branches of Southern University and Louisiana State University (LSUNO), both commuter campuses, were far more interested in "bread and butter" issues such as tuition hikes or the level of state funding for their institutions than the war. In September 1967, the editors of the LSUNO student paper explained: "In addition to the traditional playboys out for a merry old time in college, there are (and this is perhaps the largest group) students who are almost desperately eking out a stake in the economic system and seeking a means to the type of life and work they want." These students had no "inclination to risk their chances at completing the formal schooling they want so badly."[18]

On more traditional, residential southern campuses, prowar students spoke for the majority of their peers. By denouncing antiwar protestors as "dirt-balls," "hippies and dupes," "scraggly-bearded men and . . . dirty-haired girls," and "dirty-armpit Vietniks," these critics echoed the perspectives of the region's adults and daily papers. Writing from "The Right Hand Corner," in the LSU *Daily Reveille,* Mike Connelly dismissed the "peace movement" as a "gigantic fraud" directed by un-American groups, praised and supported by communists, and selectively opposed to the Vietnam War while ignoring instances of blatant communist aggression. Student supporters of the war argued that the United States had both a moral and a strategic interest in the conflict. They contended that the SEATO agreements legally justified US intervention and that the US government had made a "moral commitment" to safeguard self-government in South Vietnam. Other critics of peace activists declared that protestors demoralized American soldiers, engendered "greater inspiration" among US enemies, and thereby caused "more American and Vietnamese . . . blood [to be] spilled." Only a "united front" at home would yield "a successful peace negotiation."[19]

Prowar students also voiced the region's fervent anticommunism and forcefully propounded the accompanying strategic rationale for the war. The communist "appetite for power and control" was "insatiable," and North Vietnam and by extension the People's Republic of China were waging an aggressive war of "military conquest." In the process, the "Viet Cong murderers" had committed "atrocities" that surpassed in "scope and technique" the crimes of even the "Nazi terrorists of World War II." Since this blatant communist aggression and terrorism imperiled not just South Vietnam but all of Southeast Asia, the forceful US application of containment was imperative. Once the United States was involved, the war had to "be fought and won regardless of cost." To practice "appeasement" would forfeit a strategic region to the communists and embolden the Chinese and Soviets. Losing on this "worldwide stage for a showdown between Communism and Freedom" would destroy US credibility by reducing "us to a third-rate power in the eyes of the world and render our word valueless to all free nations." "Peace through victory" was the only acceptable path since it would "assure every potential aggressor that any encroachment . . . on the rights of others" would lead to "ultimate destruction." Achieving this victory required the unrestrained bombing of strategic and military targets in North Vietnam and perhaps even destruction of the dikes containing the Red River.[20]

Just as Vietnam veterans bolstered the antiwar cause, returning soldiers added an authoritative dimension to the prowar brief. An "outraged veteran" at the University of Virginia was appalled at what he considered "traitorous practices" by groups of "ignorant cowards" and declared he had little hope for the nation if these dissenters were "allowed to dictate policy." Another Virginia veteran emphasized the complexity of the issues and problems in Vietnam and recoiled at the thought that protestors might have a voice in whether he should be required to return to the battle: "I'm all for love and flowers and irresponsibility—but they don't" produce "decisions and leadership." An LSU vet was equally critical of peace demonstrations, which, he believed, served only to "boost" the "egos" of the marchers by thrusting them into the "limelight." These veterans urged their fellow students to stop the "foolishness" and "get behind the war."[21]

In the face of southern conservatism, student dissent emerged more slowly and proved less extensive in Dixie than nationally. As was true nationally, opposition to the war was most often spawned locally, without clear, coherent national or even regional direction. Still, the Southern Student Organizing Committee, founded in Nashville in April 1964 with a self-conscious sense of southern distinctiveness and a determination to pursue social justice without being dominated by any outside group (such as SDS), played a central role in southern student opposition to the war. After initially concentrating on civil rights, SSOC began devoting greater attention to the war in early 1966 by helping to organize the Southern Days of Protest. The high point of these early efforts came on February 12, 1966, when 500 people heard SDS leader Tom Hayden speak at Vanderbilt, 125 protestors attended an antiwar rally in Richmond, and 40 dissenters picketed a prowar Affirmation Vietnam Rally in Atlanta. Later, in May and June, SSOC members distributed protest literature at eighty Selective Service College Qualification Test Centers, where men took exams to gain deferments. In August, a fast and vigil at Nashville's War Memorial led to the arrest of 21 protestors.[22]

In an even more ambitious project, SSOC dispatched lecturers on Peace Tours to Florida in February and March 1967 and later to six other southern states during the 1967–1968 school year. The tours were a testament to the dedication and courage of Tom Gardner, David Nolan, and Nancy Hodes, the primary lecturers. Their experiences also afforded great insight into the attitudes of the majority of southern students, college administrators, and local governmental authorities. This intrepid trio gave public lectures on the Vietnam War, US relations with China, and the draft system; staffed tables for distributing antiwar literature; and spoke in classes when invited. During the Florida sojourn, they attracted considerable attention, including an interview on Larry King's radio show and a surprising amount of television coverage. However, their reception in the Sunshine State was hardly reassuring. Hodes remembered "being the object of incredible hostility" and addressing "crowds who were ready to rip us apart." After prowar students burned a Conestoga wagon adorned with Peace Tour posters in Gainesville, the SSOC travelers and a local SSOC dissenter were arrested and charged with disorderly conduct and resisting arrest at Miami-Dade Junior College, where they refused to abide by an administration-imposed five-minute time limit on talks and a ban on distributing antiwar literature.[23]

Subsequent Peace Tours to Arkansas, North Carolina, South Carolina, Tennessee, and Virginia elicited similarly discouraging reactions, ranging from apathy to hostility. Reporting on their treks through Arkansas and Virginia, Nolan complained of "contented radicals" in the former and a "cool" reception in the latter. Such responses were preferable to the Erskine College (South Carolina) student who threatened them with a loaded handgun; the mob at Appalachian State University, which destroyed their antiwar materials and pounded on their car as they hastily departed the campus; or Belmont Abbey undergraduates, who carried signs proclaiming "Commies Go Home" and "God Is A Marine."[24]

The SSOC continued its antiwar activities until its dissolution in early June 1969. Both its civil rights work and its opposition to the war had provided a crucial voice for white student dissenters and helped lay the groundwork for the most significant southern student actions against the war, in October 1969 and May 1970. Still, in January 1968 SSOC had just sixteen active chapters, with only the five at the University of Arkansas, Duke University, the University of Florida, the University of Georgia, and the University of Virginia at major schools. Like the May 1967 mailing list that cited only eleven southern antiwar centers among eighty-five nationally, the number of SSOC chapters reemphasized the relative conservatism of southern students. Moreover, the SSOC's restricted organizational reach paralleled the relatively delayed onset of student opposition to the war in the South.[25]

There were early, but exceptional, southern protests. During the fall of 1965, more than 1,000 students attended the South's first teach-in at Emory University, featuring the well-known socialist Norman Thomas and Atlanta Constitution editor Eugene Patterson; and a comparable crowd witnessed a debate between two faculty members at the University of Florida. In marked contrast, LSU's *Daily Reveille* maintained a prowar editorial stance even in the wake of the US invasion of Cambodia and the Kent State deaths; LSU antiwar protestors were physically attacked by other students in May 1967; and the largest campus demonstration prior to the October 1969 Moratorium came in November 1967, when 100 students took part in a panty raid. "Affirmation: Viet Nam," a Georgia prowar student organization, held a 20,000-person rally at Atlanta–Fulton County Stadium in February 1966, when it presented a poll ostensibly demonstrating that 96.6 percent of students consulted at forty-seven of the state's fifty colleges and universities backed Johnson's intervention in Vietnam. The University of Tennessee experienced no significant antiwar protests prior to May 1970; but 700 students rallied to support the war in October 1965; 1,000 turned out in January 1970 to see if the university president would accept a student's challenge to a "duel" via "hand-to-hand combat"; and 1,500 attended an April 1970 rally to protest freshmen women's dormitory hours. Despite SSOC's founding and its administrative headquarters being in Nashville, 77 percent of Vanderbilt students polled in November 1967 favored victory in Vietnam. Not until November 1968 did the antiwar perspective become prevalent, when 1,400 students voted for withdrawal from Vietnam, versus 534 who endorsed an increased military effort.[26]

Developments at Virginia Commonwealth University in Richmond followed a similar pattern. In both 1965 and 1966 polls, 80 percent of the students questioned endorsed US involvement; and when student sentiment began to change in early 1968, the local Committee to End the War in Vietnam could attract a crowd of only 150 for a peace vigil. In the face of pervasive prowar sentiment at the University of South Carolina, no appreciable antiwar activities occurred until late 1968, and only police intervention saved the thirty students picketing General Westmoreland's receipt of an honorary degree in May 1967 from physical attack by more than 200 hecklers. The small number of Young Liberals who had emerged by late 1966 at Florida State University regularly had their antiwar literature destroyed and were at times physically attacked by fraternity boys, athletes, and members of the Student Coalition Against Long-Haired Perverts (SCALP). In El Paso, very much a military town with Fort Bliss nearby, the first antiwar march in November 1965 drew 14 participants, 11 of whom were Texas Western University students. Only active police intervention protected these marchers from a hostile crowd of 2,000 to 2,500, who demonstrated their displeasure with eggs and tomatoes. Even at the University of Virginia, a more liberal and activist campus, the first twenty-three organized protestors confronted 300 angry prowar students in February 1966, the first teach-in held a year later drew a comparatively modest 300 participants, and the *Cavalier Daily* editors maintained a pro-war position until fall 1967.[27]

As southern student dissent grew, it adopted forms and tactics much like those practiced by antiwar students nationally, save being far less radical, violent, and destructive. When assessing the diverse southern protests, it is essential to keep Dixie's conservative context in mind. Southern students sought to sever what they considered university connections to the American war machine. They objected to mandatory ROTC on campuses, to Dow Chemical Company (the manufacturer of napalm) and the military soliciting new employees and recruits at universities, and to defense-related and -funded research at their schools. In "The Myth of Detachment," published in the October 20, 1969, *Cavalier Daily,* Tom Gardner articulated the rationale for these objections. The former SSOC national chairman rejected the assertion by a senior University of Virginia faculty member that the university was "an institution . . . properly dedicated to the promotion of studying and teaching" and should not be used as "an ideological base or a political instrument." Gardner dismissed this position as naïve, self-serving, and designed to quash dissent. How could the university be "politically and ideologically neutral," while performing "classified Department of 'Defense' research" and incorporating the Judge Advocate General (JAG) school and ROTC into the curriculum? These connections to the military amounted to "nothing less than a significant institutional commitment" to "waging . . . counter-revolutionary warfare . . . against the nationalist forces of Vietnam."[28]

Opposition arose to compulsory ROTC on virtually all southern campuses, even the more conservative ones such as LSU, and the most ardent antiwar students called for the complete expulsion of the officer training programs. SDS member Tom Falney at the University of Virginia asserted that ROTC was antithetical to a university's purposes since it promoted "blind obedience" to orders rather than critical, independent thought and conveyed instruction on "the most efficient means of killing," which was "completely nonacademic." Falney's letter generated a host of

responses asserting that ROTC was essential to the nation's defense, produced broadly educated "citizen soldiers" of whom Jefferson would have
approved, and addressed many topics other than "killing and torture."[29]

Beginning in 1966, protestors boycotted mandatory ROTC classes at
the University of Mississippi, taunted ROTC cadets with water guns at
the University of Texas, ran through the ranks and heckled the cadets
as they conducted drills at the University of Virginia, and were dragged
away by campus police after sitting down on Tulane University's air force
ROTC drill field. Antiwar students at Furman University, a small Baptist school in South Carolina, organized the Furman University Corps of
Kazoos, or "F.U.C.K.," to lampoon an ROTC parade and visiting military
officials. Dissidents at Florida State University held "antimilitary balls"
to mock the ROTC's traditional military dances. After women checked
their bras at the door for the 1971 event, they and their escorts elected a
king and queen of the ball and viewed antiwar films and Tweety Bird car-
toons. As the war ground on and student frustrations mounted, a more
violent minority of protestors sought to destroy ROTC buildings. During 1969–1970, at the height of student protests, 197 ROTC buildings
were attacked nationally. Only a small number of these attacks occurred
in the South, where students occupied ROTC buildings at the University
of Virginia and Florida State University; spray-painted antiwar slogans on
the ROTC headquarters at Mercer University; broke windows at the University of Tennessee; unsuccessfully attempted to burn ROTC facilities at
the University of Virginia, the University of North Carolina, Chapel Hill,
and the University of Georgia; and were assumed (but not proven) to have
burned the air force ROTC building at the University of Kentucky.[30]

Student opposition to defense-related activities included opposition
to the Dow Chemical Company recruiting new employees on college
campuses. Dow elicited the intense ire of antiwar students by producing and selling napalm, the jellied gasoline that the US military dropped
from planes on its enemies (and nearby civilians) in Vietnam. Here again,
efforts to disrupt recruiting occurred nationwide. By the end of 1967,
Dow recruiters had faced nearly five hundred hostile receptions, often at
otherwise quiet campuses. SSOC members at the University of Virginia
greeted Dow recruiters in December 1967 with signs proclaiming "Dow
Chemical Company, Merchants of Death," "Napalm, Crime Against
Humanity," and "Burn Baby, Burn." Eighty protestors confronted Dow

representatives at Duke University in February 1968 and subsequently demanded that the university divest its stock holdings in Dow and other "war monger" companies, such as Lockheed. Emory University antiwar students posing as Dow officials interrupted their classmates' lunch at the student cafeteria by exhibiting a wrought-iron replica of a "charred body" as evidence of napalm's "effectiveness." Demonstrations at the University of Florida in early 1968 led to the arrest of thirteen students for physically blocking the door leading to the Dow interview room. And students at both Virginia Commonwealth University and Vanderbilt focused attention on this issue by threatening to burn a puppy and thereby illustrate even more graphically napalm's devastating effects.[31]

Southern antiwar activists also engaged in diverse antidraft actions and obstructed on-campus visits by military recruiters. SSOC distributed protest literature at eighty draft testing centers, organized protests in Atlanta and Raleigh to support SSOC members who had refused induction, and conducted numerous teach-ins and draft counseling sessions around the South. University of Virginia SSOC members founded the Charlottesville Draft Counseling Group and even organized a protest by thirteen students at a local high school. In Austin, six women conducted a sit-in at the Selective Service Board headquarters and announced they opposed their "husbands, boyfriends, or sons" being made into "killers in an unjust war." Students at the University of South Florida threw water and red glitter at navy recruiters. In a much more serious incident, Florida State University officials videotaped sixty students objecting to the presence of marine recruiters and subsequently suspended twelve of the protestors for "deliberately . . . interfering with the rights of others" to enter or leave a university facility. In a variation on these antimilitary tactics, antiwar students at the University of South Carolina lent their support to dissident soldiers at nearby Fort Jackson. AWARE, the antiwar student group, hosted an on-campus "GI's United Against the War in Vietnam" press conference in February 1969, and, later in April, forty students rallied in support of eight Fort Jackson soldiers charged with disturbing the peace.[32]

Like their counterparts nationally, southern antiwar students attempted to harass speakers representing both the Johnson and the Nixon administrations. The protestors' experiences further illustrated the South's relative conservatism and demonstrated why officials identified with the war ventured into Dixie with far less trepidation than into other regions of the country. Beginning in 1964, the University of Texas SDS chapter organized annual Easter weekend peace vigils at the LBJ Ranch, where they regularly were threatened by Nazi and Ku Klux Klan antagonists. The latter, of course, cared little for President Johnson but despised the student demonstrators. When General Lewis B. Hershey, the director of the Selective Service System, spoke at LSU in April 1966, six protestors braved the rain to brandish their signs reading, "Bring Our Boys Home, We Need Them in Mississippi," and "Draft Beer not Students." In a telling commentary on the prowar temper of the campus, a 105-member band welcomed Hershey, and LSU chancellor Cecil G. Taylor and president-emeritus and retired US Army general Troy H. Middleton joined Hershey on the speakers' platform.[33]

Vice President Hubert Humphrey received an even warmer welcome a year later at the University of Georgia. Protests were so mild that the vice president, after receiving the blessing of football coach Vince Dooley, complimented the Georgia undergraduates as "the most polite students" he had met. The fifty-five dissenters who greeted Humphrey at the University of North Carolina, Chapel Hill, were not so accommodating, as they brandished signs reading, "Hubie is a murderer of Vietnamese children," and "Drop Rusk and McNamara, not napalm." University of South Carolina student protestors who objected to General Westmoreland receiving an honorary doctor of law degree also found themselves in a distinctly minority position. The thirty critics who picketed the ceremony were jeered and threatened by more than two hundred prowar students who were also outside the small chapel where the ceremony was being conducted. Police intervention prevented a violent attack on the protestors but also enabled the officers to confiscate and destroy the anti-Westmoreland signs.[34]

Members of the Nixon administration encountered similarly determined but badly outnumbered antiwar protestors. Students from the University of South Florida, Florida Presbyterian, the New College in Sarasota, and Florida State attempted collectively to picket the awarding of a doctor of humane letters degree to Secretary of Defense Melvin Laird in April 1969 but were stopped a mile from the St. Leo College campus by a combined force of one hundred police and National Guard troops. Still, a few St. Leo students managed to greet Laird upon his arrival with a sign asking, "What is so Humane About 216 G.I.s Killed last week?" Significantly, President Nixon, who had cancelled a trip to Ohio State University in 1969 as students declared "DICK . . . a four-letter word," and opted not to attend his daughter's graduation from Smith College the following year so as to avoid the inevitable protestors, accepted the Reverend Billy Graham's invitation to join him for a session of his Crusade at the University of Tennessee football stadium on May 28, 1970—in the immediate aftermath of the invasion of Cambodia and the student deaths at Kent State University and Jackson State College. The four hundred student protestors who came to denounce the war paled in comparison to the crowded stadium of Nixon partisans. The students chanted "peace, peace" when Nixon spoke and carried signs proclaiming "Thou Shall Not Kill." One dissenter accurately described the scene as "250 Lions to 90,000 Christians," and the Christians reacted very angrily, threatening to "smack" the protestors and advising one student "to stick it [a sign] up your a—."[35]

As was true nationally, the apogee of southern student protests came in 1969–1970, first with the October 15, 1969, Vietnam Moratorium Day and then with the reactions to the US invasion of Cambodia and subsequent student deaths at Kent State and Jackson State. In decided contrast to attacks on ROTC buildings or clashes with university administrators or police, the Vietnam Moratorium was envisioned by two former staffers for Senator Eugene McCarthy's 1968 presidential campaign as a day during which people stopped their regular activities—declared a moratorium— and expressed opposition to the war. By early fall, organizations were in place on at least three hundred campuses when the idea "caught on like wildfire" and spread to schools across the nation. Even more important, what had begun "as a day of student protest spilled out into the adult community" and included at least two million participants.[36]

Southern college students participated in ways much like the rest of the nation. Now eighty-nine years old, Jeanette Rankin, who was the first woman elected to the US House of Representatives and who voted against US entry into both World Wars I and II, spoke to a massive crowd at the University of Georgia; 4,500 students rallied for peace at the University of Texas, and a crowd of nearly 12,000 listened to speakers on the state capitol grounds; 1,200 University of Louisville students joined the university president in planting a "peace tree"; 44 Louisiana State University undergraduates conducted an all-night prayer vigil; in New Orleans,

200 Tulane and Loyola University students joined a crowd of 3,000 to hear antiwar speeches near City Hall; 3,000 Florida State students sang antiwar songs and chanted "Stop the War" as they joined a candlelight march around the campus on October 14; 700 Vanderbilt undergraduates attended a sermon, distributed antiwar literature in Nashville, or listened to the names of war dead being read aloud; the Black Student Association at Talladega College declared a day of protest without administration consent; Virginia Commonwealth students joined townspeople in a 2,000-strong procession reaching from the public library to the state capitol; and 1,200 Western Kentucky students attended a five-hour peace rally, which the student newspaper described as the university's "first bona fide demonstration in memory."[37]

At the University of South Carolina, antiwar students attended a memorial service for the war dead, symposia, and films but faced a competing message from the Young Republicans and YAF, who denounced the Moratorium as a "fraud" designed as an excuse to miss classes and sponsored "a positive, pro-American rally" supporting President Nixon and the war. Moratorium organizers at Louisiana State University also encountered opposition. Graves Thomas proclaimed in a *Daily Reveille* editorial entitled "Moratorium?—Hell!" that calls for immediate US withdrawal would embolden the communists in Vietnam and elsewhere and prolong the war, and YAF members derided the event. In predicting the Moratorium would attract only "a couple of hundred demonstrators" and be a "flop," Graves underestimated both the protest organizers and the depth of discontent with the war on this decidedly conservative campus. The Vietnam Moratorium Steering Committee wisely emphasized that it was not advocating immediate withdrawal; instead, the day would be devoted to "constructive and peaceful activity" and to providing an opportunity for LSU students to "show their desire for an end to the war." Operating from this decidedly moderate position, the committee garnered the endorsement of the Inter Fraternity Council and oversaw a day on which forty-four students planted crosses on the "drill field" to honor American war dead, twelve hundred attended an address at midday, and one thousand participated in a candlelight memorial service as the Moratorium ended.[38]

As Moratorium Day approached at the University of Virginia, protest organizers and the Student Council urged President Edgar Shannon to cancel classes; the YAF threatened to sue for breach of contract if classes were formally suspended; and senior faculty members openly debated the propriety of locating such a protest at the university. Shannon refused to cancel classes, but Moratorium organizers still judged their efforts a success. Senator George McGovern, a prominent critic of the war, spoke on October 10; and Professor Norman A. Graebner, a specialist on US foreign relations, denounced the war on October 14, while other faculty members led discussions in the dorms, and a candlelight march wound through the university grounds. There followed on October 15 a full day of seminars, debates, and chapel services, with fifteen hundred students gathering for a rally at noon. Reflecting the heady optimism that such activities embodied nationwide, the *Cavalier Daily* proclaimed, "The days of the military domination of United States foreign policy are numbered."[39]

Such assumptions proved unfounded as President Nixon effectively countered the Moratorium and the subsequent five-hundred-thousand-plus demonstration in Washington in mid-November 1969 with his "silent majority" speech condemning the minority of protestors and troublemakers who ostensibly endangered the nation's "future and a free society." Playing on and reinforcing the general public's hostility toward the protestors, Nixon declared, "North Vietnam cannot defeat or humiliate the United States." Only unpatriotic, disloyal Americans who undermined the war effort could "do that."[40]

The president subsequently squandered his seeming public relations coup by dispatching US troops into Cambodia and provoking "easily the most massive and shattering protest in the history of American higher education." Outraged that the president appeared to be expanding rather than contracting the war, as he had promised, students lashed out following the nationally televised announcement of his decision on April 30 and his disparaging reference the next morning to "bums" who were "blowing up campuses." As eleven northeastern student editors called for a national student strike, walkouts erupted spontaneously across the country. Student deaths at Kent State and Jackson State greatly intensified the initial student unrest. After the ROTC building was burned and sixty-nine students arrested on May 3, nervous and exhausted Ohio National Guard troops fired on Kent State students (some who had hurled bricks and insults and others who were just on their way to class). Nine were wounded and four killed. Once again, Nixon heightened student indignation by declaring that events at Kent State "should remind us all . . . that when dissent turns into violence, it invites tragedy."[41]

Nine days later, partly in response to the invasion of Cambodia and the shootings at Kent State, a group of about three hundred students at Jackson State College, an all-black school in Mississippi, threw rocks at passing cars and attempted to burn the ROTC quarters. When unrest resumed the next night, May 14, state police fired on the students. Three hundred rounds hit a dormitory, twelve students were wounded, and two young women inside the dorm were killed. The deaths at Jackson State received far less attention than those at Kent State, but the young women's fate said much about the temper of the times and further stimulated student dissent.[42]

In the immediate aftermath of the Jackson State tragedy, Turner McCullough, an African American student at the University of South Carolina (USC), spoke for black students across the South when he declared he was not "greatly shocked" at the deaths in Mississippi. Events at Jackson State were simply a "continuation of insults being thrown at black people." He also drew a pointed contrast between the use of tear gas and clubs against white students in South Carolina and the use of bullets against blacks in Mississippi. Elaborating on this racial dichotomy, McCullough asserted that black students supported the USC protests in Columbia, but "as far as active participation, we know what the University can do. You can fight it if you're white."[43]

McCullough raised two important issues regarding African American students and antiwar protests in the South. First, as was true nationally, black students participated at a lower rate than whites; second, African American students incurred greater personal risks by taking part in any form of protest. At the height of the war, in 1968, most black college students, approximately 150,000, or 61 percent, attended historically black colleges and universities (HBCUs) in the South. These students were not quiescent, but they were, compared to their white counterparts, less inclined to protest the war. Although black undergraduates certainly understood the heavier burden the war placed on young black men, African American students gave greater priority to domestic racial issues, such as the continuing segregation of public facilities, and university matters, such as calls for more black professors and black studies curricula, a greater voice in university decision making, and enhanced pay for campus service workers.[44]

Black students were also acutely aware of the deadly force directed at the protestors on HBCU campuses. A series of incidents beginning in 1967 demonstrated that police and National Guard troops were even more prone to be employed at black schools than on campuses in the South generally. Jackson State was no aberration. In May 1967 police fired three thousand rounds into a dormitory at Texas Southern University in Houston. The following year members of the South Carolina Law Enforcement Division killed three and wounded another thirty students at South Carolina State University in Orangeburg. Also in 1968, three hundred National Guards and seventy state troopers were called to Tuskegee University when the students boycotted classes to protest compulsory ROTC and locked twelve university trustees in a guest house. Possible violence was averted when a black sheriff intervened.[45]

Nineteen sixty-nine brought two similar incidents. Antiwar sentiment was a part of the motivation for student dissent at Voorhees College in Denmark, South Carolina. No shots were fired, but police invaded faculty homes in search of protestors; and in the aftermath of the demonstrations, five faculty were fired for allegedly prompting the student protestors, and seven students were convicted of rioting, looting, and arson and sentenced to eighteen months to two years of hard labor. Following protests over Vietnam and a number of local issues at North Carolina A&T University in Greensboro in May, police shot and killed one student, and in a subsequent confrontation five police and two students were wounded. Greensboro's mayor declared, "It's just like guerillas in Vietnam," and Governor Louis B. Nunn dispatched six hundred National Guards, a tank, several armed personnel carriers, an airplane, and a helicopter to the campus in what one journalist termed "the most massive armed assault ever made on an American university." Finally, in November 1972, sheriff's deputies killed two unarmed students at the Southern University Campus in Baton Rouge. As the war ended in 1973, a *Black Collegian* editorial reflected on these campus events at HBCU campuses and the lack of national indignation: "Why are we not screaming about the injustice? Good God, we are being murdered, not just on the college campus, but everywhere, with the same lack of consideration and lack of law as during the days of lynching."[46]

Violence was not confined to black campuses in the wake of the invasion of Cambodia and the deaths at Kent State and Jackson State as student opposition to the war rose to a crescendo. More than two million students demonstrated, and approximately 450 colleges and universities experienced strikes or closures. Although outbreaks of violence received disproportionate press attention, the protests were overwhelmingly peaceful, with only 5 percent involving violence and 7 percent requiring the intervention of outside police or the National Guard. Consistent with the conservatism of southern students, Dixie's university and college administrators reported the lowest number (54) and lowest percentage (20.8) of schools experiencing "incidents of campus unrest." Still, these administrators and southern governors were more likely than officials from other regions to summon off-campus police. Even as southern students demonstrated greater restraint than students nationally, the number of reported incidents of campus unrest more than doubled when compared to the 1968–1969 school year. Still, developments on southern campuses were more than sufficient to elicit vociferous condemnation from public officials, the press, and the southern public.[47]

The depth of student "frustration" and the "volatile, angry crowd" stunned a Florida State University (FSU) protestor; and the FSU chancellor, who had "never seen students so angry," spoke for university administrators nationwide. Despite this anger and potential volatility, no violence ensued at FSU. Although students occupied the ROTC building on May 5, they left peacefully when the police arrived. Over the next four days, groups of student protestors ranging from four hundred to four thousand repeatedly ringed the ROTC building. Although a few windows were broken, there were no serious altercations with the authorities. At the urging of students and faculty, classes were officially cancelled on May 8 when one thousand antiwar students marched to the state capitol to present a petition calling for an end to the war. Members of the Florida House of Representatives wearing black arm bands accepted the petition in a civil political gesture complemented by that of Governor Claude Kirk spending the entire night of May 7 on campus answering student questions. Although Kirk, a conservative Republican, did not waver in his support for President Nixon's Vietnam policies, his calming actions contrasted sharply with those of the president he defended.[48]

In terms of the number of students involved, the protestors' tactics, and the frequent use of outside police, events at FSU were generally representative of developments at southern universities. Following a candlelight memorial march by one thousand students at the University of Alabama, approximately fifty of the protestors "liberated" the snack bar at the student union. Later that evening, the students peacefully left the building at the behest of 140 state, university, and Tuscaloosa city police. Governor Albert Brewer then imposed a campus curfew and forbade campus gatherings of more than six people. After a three-day moratorium on demonstrations, a May 12 rally of three hundred students in defiance of the curfew led to fifty-seven arrests. A contingent of five hundred University of Arkansas students marched from the campus to downtown Fayetteville, where fifty-seven of them were arrested for sitting down in the street outside of the local draft board. One thousand University of Miami students attended a rally on May 7. The next day three hundred protestors blocked the entrance to the administration building but dispersed peacefully after the university president agreed to a faculty resolution for a three-day suspension of classes. Nearly one thousand dissidents also attended rallies at Emory, Eastern Kentucky, North Texas State, and the University of Texas at El Paso, the latter in marked contrast to the eleven lonely student marchers in November 1965. After a week of protests, more than one hundred Western Kentucky University students challenged an administration restraining order banning all campus demonstrations. At Tulane University, fistfights broke out between antiwar students and members of the football team and Young Americans for Freedom over whether the American flag should be lowered to half-mast in recognition of the Kent State deaths. Four to five hundred black students marched from the Shaw University campus to the Raleigh, North Carolina, city square, and Shaw president King V. Cheek sent a telegram on behalf of the faculty and students to President Nixon urging him to "hear" the student voices and to create a "less frustrating and more humane climate for free discussion" and dissent by all Americans. Dr. Cheek concluded, "The suppression of dissent on the college campuses by bayonets, live ammunition and inflammatory oratory from our national and state leaders is un-American [and] antithetical to the pursuit of truth in colleges and universities."[49]

On May 5 three thousand University of Tennessee students rallied against the war and the Kent State deaths and thereafter carried out a three-day strike. Similarly peaceful gatherings occurred at Vanderbilt, where rallies in support of the war equaled those in opposition, and at LSU, where two thousand attended a memorial for the Kent State students, but letters to the editor and the *Daily Reveille*'s editorial stance remained supportive of the war. Protestors at the University of Georgia were less orderly but hardly radical. After fifty students broke windows, forced their way into the Academic Building, and set off the sprinkler system on May 6, President Fred C. Davison addressed a crowd of three thousand. Many jeered when he agreed to optional class attendance for the next two days but rejected calls to suspend classes officially. Students confronted Davison again the next day at his home with demands that he sign a letter denouncing Nixon's decision to invade Cambodia. Davison again refused; and after the university secured a restraining order barring students from entering buildings "for any purpose" other than normal "educational and business affairs," the *Red and Black*'s headline, "protest fizzles," proved accurate. There followed a two-week student senate debate that yielded only a bland statement in response to Cambodia and Kent State and a referendum in which students opposed the Cambodian intervention by a 2,064 to 1,682 vote but endorsed Nixon's overall Vietnam policies by a vote of 1,967 to 1,809.[50]

Student actions at the Universities of Texas, Kentucky, South Carolina, and Virginia were less restrained. As had been the case during the October 1969 Moratorium, the largest number of southern students protested at the University of Texas (UT). Even before the invasion of Cambodia, 8,000 antiwar protestors marched through downtown Austin on March 18, 1970. Their failure to secure a permit from the city council resulted in thirteen arrests. In response to Cambodia and the deaths at Kent State, 2,500 to 3,000 students marched from the campus to the federal building, where they threw rocks and smoke bombs at police, who responded with tear gas and billy clubs and made five arrests. Five thousand students rallied the next day, and the UT president agreed to two days of forums, but not to the official suspension of classes. Although the university Board of Regents unanimously rejected the forums and called for "business as usual," most students honored the strike. The week of protests ended peacefully on May 8 with a massive march of 15,000 to 20,000 through downtown Austin. The Austin city council again denied a permit for the demonstration, but federal judge Jack Roberts approved the march, which was comprised of students 25 abreast stretching for twelve city blocks.[51]

Essentially quiescent before May 1970, University of Kentucky students also responded vigorously to Cambodia, Kent State, and the stationing of state police and National Guards on their campus. Five hundred students (out of more than fifteen thousand) gathered on May 1 and endorsed the impeachment of President Nixon. On May 5, in the wake of the deaths at Kent State, a like number protested in front of the university's eighteen-floor office tower, and thirty of those students forced their way into a Board of Trustees meeting, where they demanded the condemnation of events in Cambodia and at Kent State, a campus moratorium to protest these actions, and the disarming of campus police.[52]

That evening a memorial march swelled to one thousand despite verbal abuse and thrown bottles from football players and fraternity men. Tensions later rose appreciably when approximately five hundred marchers confronted one hundred riot-equipped police summoned to campus by university security authorities. The standoff ended when both police and students ran several blocks to the air force ROTC building, which burned to the ground. There followed three additional anxiety-filled days as groups of students ranging from eight hundred to fifteen hundred faced off against state police and National Guard troops (the latter brandishing fixed bayonets), who had been dispatched to the campus by Governor Louis B. Nunn after he declared a state of emergency. Although some students threw rocks and the police and guards used tear gas and billy clubs and made forty-five arrests, no serious incidents ensued in what were decidedly peaceful protests. At the end of the week, Nunn withdrew the state police and the National Guard, and the prowar *Lexington Herald Leader* ultimately conceded, "The campus was a lot more peaceful than anyone wanted to think it was."[53]

Governor Robert E. McNair also declared a state of emergency and dispatched the National Guard to the University of South Carolina in Columbia. Protests began there on May 5 when 300 students marched around the campus carrying four large black crosses inscribed with the names of the students killed at Kent State. Two days later, 150 students occupied the student center, and 37 of them were arrested after they refused to leave. When a crowd of 2,000 threatened the police escorting the arrested students, the National Guard was called to the campus, but no violence occurred. The guards returned to the campus the following Monday after students took over the principal administration building, where they broke windows, destroyed official files, and scrawled obscenities on the walls. In the process of evacuating the building, the National Guard clashed with a throng of 1,000 students; more rocks and bottles were hurled at the guards, and the students, 85 of whom were arrested, became the targets of tear gas and clubs. This clash resulted in the stationing of 600 National Guard troops, 145 state police and State Law Enforcement Division agents, and numerous local police on the campus and the imposition of a 9 P.M. to 6 A.M. campus curfew. On Tuesday, May 13, additional clashes took place between the students and the authorities and resulted in another 20 arrests.[54]

In the midst of this unprecedented student unrest at USC, Jane Fonda spoke to an audience of fifteen hundred at a park adjoining the campus. While explaining the US involvement in Vietnam as the product of American corporate economic interests and damning President Nixon, she implored South Carolina students to study events in Southeast Asia and to protest actively rather than just "go to Myrtle Beach and drink beer," but she also urged them to do so peacefully. She advocated draft resistance and specifically cited a regulation requiring draft boards to file all materials sent to them. Young men, she instructed, should employ their "imagination" and present their draft boards with items such as "surfboards, garbage cans, [and] water melons." Although Fonda's call for peaceful dissent was hardly the cause, USC protests subsided after her talk on May 14.[55]

Although not so rowdy or tense as in Kentucky or South Carolina or marked by as many participants as in Texas, student protests at the University of Virginia were revealing. The student strike stretched over a week; two attempts (albeit minor ones) were made to burn ROTC facilities; student activists sought to attach broad-ranging additional demands to the ones directly associated with Cambodia and Kent State; and President Edgar F. Shannon assumed a particularly active, sympathetic, and ultimately decisive role in the course of events. News of the deaths at Kent State spurred a largely spontaneous demonstration of 1,200 students in front of the Rotunda on May 3. From the Rotunda, the students marched to Shannon's home, where he began a dialogue with the protestors that extended over the next ten days. When 250 of the students subsequently occupied Maury Hall, which housed the navy ROTC, Shannon secured an injunction, and the students peacefully departed the next morning. On May 5, 900 to 1,000 students attended a series of lectures by faculty and students and listened to public pronouncements from a Strike Committee. The committee presented Shannon with a series of "demands" also endorsed by the Student Council. These demands called for an end to the injunction against occupying public buildings, the disarming of university police and the banning of outside police from the campus, the separation of ROTC and the JAG school from the university, the termination of all defense-related research, and Shannon's endorsement of a letter condemning the invasion of Cambodia. Employing a tactic often adopted by student protestors, the committee added demands that Shannon endorse the right of university employees to bargain collectively and strike and that the university establish and pursue a goal of 20 percent of the student body becoming African American.[56]

Matters continued to escalate on May 6 when three thousand students gathered for a noontime rally; and nine thousand listened to fiery speeches from William Kunstler and Jerry Rubin, both of whom had been scheduled to speak at University Hall, the basketball arena, long before the provocative events in Cambodia or at Kent State. Following the speeches, many students returned to Shannon's home to press him on the demands, and two thousand protestors again descended on Maury Hall, where approximately two hundred occupied the building in defiance of the injunction. With police en route, the students once more peacefully evacuated the building, but not before a mattress fire was discovered in the basement. In the second attempted arson of the evening, a fire was also set in the army ROTC storage facilities in another building.[57]

Although President Shannon did not accept any of the student demands and emphasized that the university was officially open despite the strike, he arranged for student leaders to speak with Virginia's US senators, Harry F. Byrd Jr. and William B. Spong. He also released his letter to the senators in which he declared his grave concerns over the "continued alienation of our young men and women owing largely" to the war and his "firm conviction that student views and questions on this matter" needed to be heard by policymakers. Shannon's plea for nonviolence and moderation was echoed by the editors of the *Cavalier Daily* and by several key faculty members, such as William Harbaugh from the History Department, whom students recognized as sympathetic and passionately opposed to the war. Indeed, moderate students asserted a decisive influence as the week ended by securing a student referendum on a slightly amended set of strike demands for Monday, May 11.[58]

Not even the arrest of fifty demonstrators and onlookers over the weekend altered the moderate tone and direction that had evolved. The arrests, which involved county and city police chasing students well onto the university grounds, came on Saturday night after the third night of students obstructing traffic and urging motorists to honk for peace. On Sunday, May 10, Shannon addressed another crowd of approximately 4,000, and on Monday, 4,909 of the students voting, or 68 percent (more than half of the student body), voted to continue the strike. The students also voted to prohibit university police from being armed, to bar outside police from the university, to treat women equally in terms of admission, and to pursue the goal of a student body composed of 20 percent African Americans. Significantly, students rejected steps to sever university ties with ROTC and the JAG school.[59]

As classes ended the week of May 11, so did the strike, but not before drawing the ire of conservative Virginians. The *Richmond Times Dispatch* criticized President Shannon for negotiating with "irresponsible activists" and for allegedly praising the protestors who attempted to burn Maury Hall. Republican governor Linwood Holton defended Nixon's Vietnam policies and declared that Virginia "taxpayers" were "mad" and "ready to cut off funds to state supported schools." It was "time now to get back to the books—back to classes." Shannon quickly released a statement emphasizing that the university had never been closed, that events in Charlottesville had remained peaceful, and that the letter he and five thousand members of the university community had signed and sent to President Nixon had asserted only two key points—that the president's announcement of the Cambodian invasion had been used for "personal public relations purposes" and that the Senate had not been consulted. Worried that Shannon's presidency was in jeopardy, the *Cavalier Daily* editorialized "In Defense of Shannon" and proclaimed that since he had "sided with the students at a crucial moment," the students also had "an obligation to support him." "Richmond" should "expect a fight" if the governor or legislature attempted to remove him. Neither sought to do so.[60]

In the midst of this unprecedented student revolt, President Nixon asked Alexander Heard, the chancellor of Vanderbilt University, to serve as a special advisor to the president. Heard was charged with keeping

Nixon "fully and currently informed on the thinking of the academic community and especially the young" and with recommending ways the president could stay "better advised on campus affairs." Working with James E. Cheek, the president of Howard University, who accepted a similar assignment, Heard formally agreed to serve until the end of June and submitted a final, forty-page "Heard Report" on July 16. Over this two-month period, Heard spent eleven hours in sessions with Nixon; arranged for a Harris poll of student opinion and a separate survey of May events on nearly two hundred campuses; met with numerous university officials, Vice President Spiro Agnew, and several cabinet members; and produced fifty single-spaced pages of memoranda for the president.[61]

Perhaps Nixon and his staff anticipated a set of face-saving, proadministration suggestions from the Georgia-born Heard, who had earned his BA and PhD degrees in political science from the University of North Carolina and had headed up private and conservative Vanderbilt since 1963. If so, they were decidedly disappointed. In his sessions with Nixon and the written materials, Heard emphasized that the administration faced a "*national* crisis," rather than an "aberrational outburst by the young—or simply a 'student crisis.'" The Vanderbilt chancellor admitted that before the invasion of Cambodia he and most other university administrators had deemed "only a small minority of students" deeply disaffected. His revised assessment held that Cambodia and Kent State had "triggered a vast pre-existing charge of pent up frustration and dissatisfaction." This dissatisfaction, according to the head of the Republican Ripon Society, focused not just on the war but also on "fears . . . of repression" by government; a sense that the administration was unresponsive and inattentive to domestic problems; and, perhaps most damning, a basic questioning of the validity of "the political system itself." Heard asserted that students were emerging as a separate, self-conscious "class in society," comparable to farmers, organized labor, or war veterans. As such, they warranted specific attention. Moreover, it was wrong to impugn their motives; although "often emotional and egocentric," students acted from genuine "idealism"—from "humane concern for victims of racial discrimination, for those who suffer in the urban ghettos, for the poor in Appalachia, and for those who die—under whatever flag—in Southeast Asia." Therefore, "the young may be trying to tell us things we ought to hear."[62]

Heard, and particularly Cheek, stressed that black students, the majority of whom matriculated in the South, harbored an even greater sense of alienation, repression, and suspicion. Their "frustration, anger, outrage, fears and anxieties" represented the "feelings and emotions" of a large segment of the African American community. Southern black students and faculty had come to expect "broken promises" from politicians and unfair "treatment" from "law enforcement agencies." Ironically, higher education heightened black young peoples' "intellectual grasp of the current inequities" and "how deeply embedded" they were in the "fabric of American life." To be sure, the war intensified these feelings of alienation, but an immediate end to the conflict and the draft "would not significantly reduce . . . cynicism and distrust among black college youth."[63]

Heard and Cheek recommended that President Nixon establish a far more effective "liaison with higher education" by meeting at regular intervals with broadly representative groups of students, faculty, and university presidents; by specifying a "high-level White House staff member" to focus on higher education; by employing relevant federal agencies, such as Health, Education, and Welfare, to keep a finger on the higher-education pulse; by scheduling a meeting "devoted exclusively to black students"; and by increasing his "exposure to representatives of the black community and other racial minorities." But the two university leaders warned that improved communications alone would not "soften tensions and dissipate alienation and disaffection." Only withdrawing from Vietnam and "more effectively" addressing "home difficulties" would restore student faith in the system and the administration.[64]

Nixon and his advisors responded negatively to virtually all of Heard's and Cheek's assessments and recommendations. H. R. Haldeman dismissed overtures to the "politicized" universities as futile; seeking to "appease the tribe" was bad policy. Even the "appearance of allowing students to rule this country would be a predictable disaster for our claim to moral leadership at home and abroad." Daniel P. Moynihan objected particularly to the premise that only revised foreign and domestic policies would yield more quiescent campuses. Such assertions were "a breathtaking form of political blackmail."[65]

Agreeing wholeheartedly with his staffers, Nixon released the Heard Report to the press, after which the president and his aides savaged the document. Most fundamentally, Nixon refused to accept any responsibility for student disaffection or campus disorder: "Responsibility for disruption" of university campuses resided "squarely on the shoulders of the disrupters" and "their elders in the faculty and the larger community who encourage or condone" their actions. College administrators and faculty needed "to face up" to their obligations to maintain order. The president also rejected the "cliché" that solving the nation's "social problems" would alleviate "the moral and spiritual crisis" affecting American universities. Even as his aides worked politically with many campus groups of Young Republicans and Young Americans for Freedom, Nixon reiterated the "truth" that colleges and universities needed to be "centers of teaching and learning, research and scholarship—not political instrumentalities." His aides contended that students were being heard and that there was no need for special mechanisms to gauge their opinions. Nor should students be viewed as a specific class or constituency. After all, according to Douglas L. Hallett, a Yale senior whom the aides quoted approvingly, university students were "frighteningly ignorant of the problems the country faces and the efforts . . . made to solve them."[66]

Heard responded to these criticisms with a July 25 news conference and a July 31 press release. He expressed surprise that Nixon had chosen to publish what he considered "private documents," and he stood by their contents. He applauded the "concern with public affairs manifested on campuses," asserted that he and President Cheek had fulfilled their charge to keep the president fully informed on the perspectives of the academic community, and declared that they had offered "concrete and precise" suggestions on how the White House could improve its "understanding of campus attitudes." When asked if he was "disappointed" by the administration's criticism, Heard deftly replied, "When one accepts an invitation to walk in the political forest, he must be prepared to be snagged by a few brambles."[67]

The unprecedented demonstrations in May 1970 marked the high point of both national and southern student opposition to the war. Despite Nixon's refusal to make any overtures to students, two of his Vietnam-related programs helped to defuse campus activism. Vietnamization, which ostensibly turned the war over to the South Vietnamese, steadily reduced the number of Americans serving and dying in Vietnam. Introduced in December 1969, the draft lottery made young men subject to the draft for only one year and purportedly ended favoritism based on income, education, or race. The downturn in the economy in the early

1970s reinforced the impact of these war-related influences by focusing students' attention on finding jobs and starting careers.

Exhausted and disillusioned, many student activists concluded by the early 1970s that they could not influence President Nixon or his policies. A frustrated Steve Maxner, who had been wounded in Vietnam and returned home and advocated antiwar positions at North Texas State University, captured the campus mood: the war was "winding down and the fervor and the passion just wasn't there." Over the years following Cambodia and Kent State, students contemplated the "Failure of Student Activism" and the "Current Apathy." Editorial writers at the University of Virginia and the University of Georgia concluded that "marching down the street in a black armband isn't necessarily going to end the war or racism." The Moratorium had been a "nice thing," but it had not "convinced people of different persuasions." In arguing against another student strike in January 1971, the *Cavalier Daily* warned that stopping classes would be "an empty form of protest, likely to be ignored by those to whom it is aimed and misunderstood" by officials in Richmond. Indeed, as more Americans questioned the war, they were learning the "lessons that students learned months ago"—that the nation was "engaged in a seemingly limitless war with no way to get out" that would satisfy Nixon and that "no amount of outrage" could alter this situation.[68]

This perception explained why students had become more apathetic, more "apolitical." According to Tom Crawford in Athens, University of Georgia students "just don't give a damn. Instead of marching against injustices, they go back to their rooms and listen to Neil Young while drinking Boone's Farm Apple Wine." From Charlottesville, Ted Jordan lamented, "The fighting continues there. The marching continues here, and both bring no results." To break this senseless stalemate, Americans needed to "withdraw ourselves," to follow the advice of Ken Kesey, who had decided "the only way to help end the war was to say 'Fuck it' and walk away." University of Virginia students should "do the same."[69]

Large numbers of southern protestors followed this advice. On May 4, 1971, a peace vigil at Louisiana State attracted only 200 participants; 250 marched to the state capitol the next day; and only 629 of more than 14,000 LSU students bothered to vote in a referendum on the war. The next May a meager 150 students congregated to decry President Nixon's decision to mine Haiphong harbor. This pattern was repeated across

Dixie. In February 1971 no more than 200 marched at the University of
South Carolina to protest the US-sponsored South Vietnamese invasion
of Laos, and later that month fewer than 20 attended a Student Mobilization Committee meeting. The campus climate had also changed dramatically in Athens and Charlottesville. At the University of Georgia
600 turned out for a Kent State memorial in May 1971, and a subdued
group of 270 rallied against US policies in May 1972. At the University of
Virginia, a paltry 140 participated in a candlelight peace march in April
1971, and the next month 63 percent of the students voting rejected a
spring moratorium against the war. In decided contrast, 2,500 students
protested against expanding the student body in October 1971, and former secretary of state Dean Rusk received a standing ovation following
his address in December 1972.[70]

Only the University of Florida and the University of Texas witnessed
post-1970 demonstrations remotely comparable to the responses to Cambodia, Kent State, and Jackson State. On May 9, 1972, 1,200 to 1,400
Florida protestors hurled rocks and bottles at campus, city, and state
police, who responded with an armored car, fire hoses, clubs, and tear gas.
The following day authorities controlled a crowd of 3,000 and added 200
arrests to the 170 from the previous day. In late April 1972, University
of Texas protestors broke windows in the ROTC building, occupied two
floors of the primary administrative building, and turned out between
2,000 and 3,000 to denounce President Nixon's bombing of Hanoi and
Haiphong.[71]

Ironically, as the student protests subsided, "such activism was no longer necessary. The call for peace, which a majority considered unpatriotic
as late as 1968," had become "patriotic" by 1971. The nation ultimately
accepted the antiwar students' message to leave the war, but public polling
demonstrated that student dissidents were exceedingly "unpopular messengers." In a June 1970 Gallup poll, 82 percent of Americans consulted
disapproved of "college students going on strike as a way to protest the
way things are run in this country." Some contemporary students perceptively understood the negative responses to protestors. As early as 1965, a
farsighted LSU editorial writer opined that antiwar demonstrations were
"having much the same effect on the Viet Nam War that southern race
bigotry has had on the civil rights movement—they are rallying the great
majority of the people in favor of it." In 1970 a University of Virginia

undergraduate noted astutely, "Campus activists are producing fear and outrage and reaction. They are pushing the public in the opposite political, philosophical, and social direction."[72]

Given the nation's ultimate adoption of the antiwar students' message that the United States should leave the war while simultaneously loathing the messengers, how is the influence of young protestors best explained nationally and more particularly in the South? Students have been correctly termed the "foot soldiers" of the antiwar movement: "far more college students" both nationally and in Dixie "actively protested the war than any other single group." Their sheer numbers were critical to demonstrations on and off campuses; and these demonstrations kept the war in the public eye, challenged the morality and practicality of US intervention and actions, and heightened "a general perception of national malaise and crisis that made ending the war even more urgent." Despite their denials, both Presidents Johnson and Nixon were deeply troubled by the student opposition, which together with the broader antiwar movement constituted an ongoing restraint on executive freedom of action. Although Dixie's student demonstrations were far less extensive that those in other regions, southern dissenters contributed to the antiwar movement's restraint of the presidents, helped keep the war at the forefront of public attention, and promoted the growing belief among key national policymakers and the public beyond the South that only ending the war could restore domestic tranquility and equilibrium. Indeed, the extent of student discontent in the conservative, prowar South during 1969–1970 could only have served to intensify these beliefs. The American public and the Nixon administration had come to expect student protests in Berkeley, Madison, and New York City, but not pitched battles in Columbia, South Carolina, twenty thousand marchers in Austin, or a weeklong strike in Charlottesville.[73]

Student protests contributed to US withdrawal from Vietnam. They also helped spawn the "backlash politics" that aided Richard Nixon's election as president in 1968 and 1972 and helped defeat antiwar southerners such as J. William Fulbright, Albert Gore Sr., and Ralph W. Yarborough in their bids for reelection to the US Senate. In the wake of three years of student demonstrations and urban rioting, respondents to a Gallup poll in early 1968 cited "crime and lawlessness" as the principal domestic problem and just behind Vietnam as the nation's most troubling issue.[74]

Coincidentally, two southerners, both conservatives and supporters of President Nixon and the Cambodian operation, sat down on May 11 to express their frustrations and war weariness—a fatigue, ironically, that would not only help to reelect Nixon in 1972 but also move even the South to accept a Vietnam outcome far short of a US victory the following year. From New Orleans, a Kentuckian studying law at Tulane University informed Senator Cooper he was *"sick and tired"* of the US government's "leftist direction," of "long haired bums . . . tearing our campuses and . . . our country apart," of a "world-wide communist movement" that was leading "thousands of innocent young people . . . astray," and of a US government that failed to "deal appropriately" with "those who seek to destroy" America. A Nashville woman pursued precisely the same themes in her letter to Senator Gore. This "tired American" was "tired of the discrimination against the South," of the communists who had "infiltrated" and created "unrest and riots" in American universities, of the media presenting "biased view points and facts," of "those who march for individual rights but have no tolerance for the rights" of their opponents, of the "lawlessness and crime in our country," and of the "members in Congress who are dividing our country instead of working to bring us together."[75]

This unintended aid for antiwar students' arch foe, President Nixon, illustrated the complexity of the protests' impact both nationally and in the South. While recognizing this complexity, it should be remembered that the Vietnam War provoked the most massive student protests in American and southern history. Although always a minority on college and university campuses and the proponents of a decidedly unpopular message that often elicited ridicule or outright physical attacks by prowar students and conservative political figures, these young people summoned the courage to challenge their elders and to question America's most tragic Cold War military intervention abroad. Doing so in the South, the nation's most conservative and prowar region, required particular personal resolution since it could lead to social isolation on campus, alienation from one's family and community, and even suspension or expulsion from school.

These hardy southern protestors added to the momentum to end the war, but their influence on opinion and policy had a primarily national, rather than southern application. The South remained the region most supportive of the war, least inclined to believe that intervention in Vietnam had been a mistake, and most convinced that the war had been winnable. George C. Herring, the foremost historian of American involvement in Vietnam, has sagely observed, "The conventional wisdom in the military is that the United States won every battle but lost the war. It could be said of the antiwar movement that it lost every battle but *eventually* won the war—the war for America's minds and especially for its soul." Herring's observation applies nationally, but in Dixie, antiwar students lost all the battles and the war for majority southern opinion regarding Vietnam.[76]

8

Southerners and the End of the Vietnam War, 1971–1973

In late February 1971 Reg Murphy and his editorial staff at the *Atlanta Constitution* published a perceptive analysis of President Nixon's "hard choices." The *Constitution* credited Nixon with working to "wind down" the war but worried appropriately that the president stubbornly retained the "hope of a purely military victory" and the illusion that "one more military action might permit the United States to withdraw from Vietnam on our own terms." While dismissing such hopes as "nonsense," Murphy and his staff doubted correctly that either "Congress or the American people would accept a reversal of the present policy of withdrawing troops" or condone any "major escalation" of the conflict. Therefore, as the United States moved inexorably toward the end of the war, two essential questions remained: How long would US military involvement continue, and what would be the terms of the negotiated settlement?[1]

While discerning that Nixon could maintain public and congressional support only by avoiding any sustained escalation involving US ground troops, the *Constitution* also depicted the president's narrowed options as he pursued peace with honor. GOP insiders provided Nixon a similar analysis. By April 1971, Secretary of Defense Laird warned the president that "congressional and popular U.S. support" for Asia was "more tenuous than ever"; and Pennsylvania senator Hugh Scott, the Republican minority leader, and several other moderate members of the party were convinced that without the plan for a clear "end date" for the war, they would be unable "to hold their party together on war issues." As the administration confronted a more assertive Democratic opposition and growing restiveness within the GOP, Kissinger pronounced the "pattern was clear." Senate dissidents would continue to introduce end-the-war amendments, and one might well pass, tying the administration's hands. Nixon's war troubles were not solely domestic; his military alternatives in Vietnam were also increasingly constricted. By June 1971, 239,200 US military personnel remained in South Vietnam, down from 543,400 soon after Nixon took office. Ten months later, when Hanoi launched the 1972 Easter Offensive, US forces had been reduced to 93,000, with approximately 6,000 of them combat soldiers. Given these political and military circumstances and the additional difficulties presented during 1971–1972 by the US–South Vietnamese invasion of Laos, the conviction of Lieutenant Calley, the publication of the *Pentagon Papers,* and the 1972 Easter Offensive, historian Melvin Small has concluded that President Nixon's "ability to maintain support for his policies over four years and win a landslide reelection in 1972 was a more remarkable feat than ending the war itself."[2]

As had been true since the beginning of the Nixon presidency, the South's support remained essential to Nixon's ability to ward off congressional and popular challenges until late 1972 and accomplish this feat. Over the final two years of the war, Dixie remained the American region most consistently approving of Nixon's performance as president and war leader, especially as the commander in chief attempted to implement his "mad-man" strategy. Southern congressmen and senators afforded Nixon decisive votes as he resisted congressional efforts to circumscribe and end the war. Still, even Dixie grew increasingly war weary. The South's agony was evident in the increased volume of antiwar mail to the region's political leaders; in the altered positions of southern hawks such as Herman Talmadge, John Stennis, Everett Jordan, William B. Spong Jr., and Phillip M. Landrum; in the more pessimistic assessments of the southern press; in the tone and trends of country music; and especially in the experiences and responses of southern women—the mothers, wives, sisters, and friends of Dixie's soldiers. As was true of the region, southern women exhibited belligerence and protest, but especially anguish and agony. Telling examples of these actions and emotions were exhibited by the female relatives of the Bardstown, Kentucky, reserve unit and others such as Lee Janot, Virginia Durr, Suzy Post, Seawillow Chambers, Segrid Blair, and Jerry McCuistion.

Acting in accordance with the *Atlanta Constitution*'s apprehensive analysis, President Nixon sought to "put real heat on North Vietnam" by ordering Lam Son 719, the US–South Vietnamese invasion of Laos in February 1971. Significantly, given the domestic response to the 1970 Cambodia operation, no US ground troops were involved. American participation was limited to massive air and artillery support for ARVN forces, who were driven from Laos by the NVA after six weeks of brutal combat. Despite administration claims of victory, the "Laotian operation was at best a costly draw," and the South Vietnamese army's performance graphically revealed that Vietnamization had achieved far more politically in the United States than militarily in Vietnam.[3]

By officially extending the conflict into a third Southeast Asian nation, Nixon again seemed to be contradicting his pledge to end the war. Still, the president would have been less disturbed had his war-related difficulties been confined to criticism of Lam Son 719. Even before the remnants of the ARVN force fled Laos, the Vietnam Veterans Against the War (VVAW) held its "Winter Soldier Investigation" in which veterans testified in February regarding atrocities they had witnessed or perpetrated. The VVAW followed this meeting in February with an April march on Washington, which featured dramatic testimony before the SFRC and the veterans literally throwing their medals back to the government that had ordered their service in the war. Also in April thousands more protestors trooped to Washington and San Francisco, and the next month soldiers and police jailed between seven and twelve thousand "May Day" dissidents in the Washington Coliseum and RFK Stadium. Adding to the public disillusionment and Nixon's consternation, William Calley's guilty verdict was announced on March 29; and in early June the *New York Times* began to publish the *Pentagon Papers*. Initiated by Secretary of Defense McNamara, this secret study had examined US involvement in Vietnam from 1945 to 1968 and revealed the American government's repeated acts of deception and the nation's strategic and military errors.

Public polling reflected the nation's disillusionment and exhaustion. By the end of June, Nixon's national approval rating had fallen to 48 percent, compared to a high of 69 percent in 1969. As had been true over the previous two years, the South sustained its backing of the president. But Dixie's cumulative responses demonstrated the region's discomfort, having fallen from 71 percent approval in November 1969 and 59 percent in

December 1970 to 52 percent in October 1971. That southerners, like all Americans, were tiring of the war was also apparent in their answers to the question of how Nixon was conducting the war. Here again, the South remained the nation's most positive section, but the approval rating had dropped from 68 percent in November 1969 to 43 percent in February 1971, a figure only 1 point higher than the national average. For a president and White House staff that monitored polls closely, Dixie's declining support for the war could only cause distress.[4]

Established patterns in the southern press also persisted. The *Dallas Morning News, Montgomery Advertiser,* and *New Orleans Times-Picayune* all endorsed Lam Son 719, and despite overwhelming evidence to the contrary, the *Morning News* pronounced the ARVN performance "new proof" of successful Vietnamization. The New Orleans paper applauded Nixon's move "to keep the North Vietnamese off balance and retain the diplomatic-military initiative." The *Advertiser* deemed the operation "a risk worth taking," but the Montgomery daily was far more realistic about the results, which revealed the "demonstrable inadequacy of Vietnamization" and threatened to devolve into a "disaster." The *Advertiser*'s analysis did not signal a move into the antiwar column, as the *Atlanta Constitution* had done in 1970; however, the Alabama paper did adopt an increasingly pessimistic view of Vietnamization in terms of both the ARVN's relative improvement and the loss of US negotiating leverage as American troops came home. The *Advertiser* continued to back Nixon's military moves, but its less hopeful tone coincided with Dixie's more ambivalent responses to Gallup pollsters. The *Atlanta Constitution* seconded the *Advertiser*'s negative assessment of the Laotian invasion and more generally held that Nixon was "misleading" the American public by suggesting that "American air power" could "resolve the terrible conflict in Southeast Asia." The *Louisville Courier-Journal* was equally pessimistic, asking at the beginning of the invasion how the South Vietnamese, who had been flown in by US planes and "backstopped by U.S. troops and artillery," could be expected to "hold on alone."[5]

The ongoing congressional efforts to legislate an end to the war were of more immediate concern to Nixon, and here southern support for the president and his war also held steady during 1971. Just as they had during 1970, a significant majority of southern congressmen and senators afforded the Republican president far greater backing than other Demo-

cratic regions and in so doing stymied efforts to curb executive authority and terminate the war. Still, within this pattern of persistent southern
backing of the president and his war, additional signs of Dixie's agony
were apparent.

Most key southern legislators sustained their prior positions on Nixon
and the war. As had been the case prior to the Cambodian invasion,
John Stennis was the only senator provided advance notice of the US–
South Vietnamese operation in Laos. The Senate's most important hawk
endorsed the invasion and remained "convinced . . . that President Nixon,
with his fine intelligence and courage," was doing everything possible to
end the war on "respectable, livable" terms. Like Stennis, Sam Ervin continued to question the constitutionality of legislative efforts to end the war
and doggedly backed the president. The North Carolinian opined that it
was not "intelligent strategy to advertise to an enemy that on a specified
date all American forces will cease fighting." From the other side of the
aisle, John Tower assured his Texas constituents that President Nixon's
forays into Cambodia and Laos were "designed to keep us out of 'another
Vietnam,'" while getting "us out of the one which we are presently in."
And Strom Thurmond defended the operation as essential to Vietnamization and the protection of US "troops during the period of withdrawal"
and reiterated his common refrain that dissidents voting for end-the-war
measures were undermining the president and aiding the enemy by suggesting that Nixon would "not keep his word and disengage U.S. forces
from Vietnam on a speedy but safe schedule."[6]

Although their antiwar convictions had not weakened, southern doves
were less vocal in their early 1971 protests. Their more muted dissent
resulted in part from Albert Gore's defeat in 1970 but also from John
Sherman Cooper's hospitalization for exhaustion and Fulbright's admission that he was discouraged and frustrated. By February 7, Cooper
had recovered sufficiently to appear on CBS's *Face the Nation,* where he
opposed the invasion of Laos and argued that Nixon's ongoing refusal to
seek congressional approval for his military incursions strengthened the
case for withdrawing all US troops from Vietnam. Fulbright agreed and
contended that although Nixon had adopted "different rhetoric," his policies were "for all practical purposes identical" to Johnson's. The SFRC
chairman took no prominent role in 1971 end-the-war legislative efforts,
but he did work effectively to force President Nixon to turn over copies

of the *Pentagon Papers* to Congress and afforded John Kerry, a prominent spokesman for the VVAW, a forum before the Foreign Relations Committee. Dressed in faded fatigues, the highly decorated former navy lieutenant told the committee and the nation there was "nothing in South Vietnam that threatens the United States" and any "attempt to justify the loss of one American in Vietnam, Cambodia, and Laos by linking such loss to the preservation of freedom" was "the height of criminal hypocrisy." In the dramatic conclusion of his testimony, the former riverboat commander asked, "How do you ask a man to be the last to die in Vietnam? How do you ask a man to be the last to die for a mistake?"[7]

As Cooper and Fulbright toiled away in the Senate, Dixie's two most important doves in the House waged an even more lonely antiwar campaign. Claude Pepper (D-FL), while concluding his fourteen-year tenure as a US senator in 1951, had objected that US association with France left America open to charges of "aligning ourselves with the hated imperialism of the past." Positions such as this and his calls for a less hostile approach to the Soviet Union had led to his defeat by George Smathers, who had disparaged him as "Red Pepper." After returning to Washington as a congressman in 1962, the inveterate Sunshine State liberal became a champion of health care for the elderly and by 1966 had come to oppose the Vietnam War. In a clear nod to southern bellicosity, Pepper later declared that "had Lyndon Johnson not been born in Texas, he would have been able . . . to step back and realize what that tragic conflict was doing to Indochina and America." On June 17, 1971, Pepper presented an amendment to the Defense Procurement Authorization, which, like the McGovern-Hatfield measures, sought to end war funding on June 1, 1972. Citing numerous Supreme Court cases, the Harvard-trained attorney asserted that by continuing to fund Nixon's actions, Congress was, "in the eyes of the courts, declaring or voting for a declaration of war." Pepper not only objected to Congress continuing as a "joint partner" in the "conduct" of the war but also sought to ensure that no "residual force" of Americans be left in Vietnam. Having served in or closely observed Congress over the previous thirty-five years, Pepper was certainly not surprised when his amendment failed by a 147–237 vote, with his fellow southerners opposing the measure 20–81.[8]

Nor would Pepper have been surprised that his amendment garnered a "yes" vote from only one of Texas's twenty-one Democrats in the House—Robert C. Eckhardt. Eckhardt had endorsed LBJ's Vietnam policies in his successful 1966 congressional campaign, but the Houston maverick promptly emerged as the most colorful and unrestrained southern congressional opponent of the war. Eckhardt had been named one of the "Capitol's Worst Dressed Men," and his 1920s "Southern plantation style of dress" featured wrinkled white linen or seersucker suits, brightly colored bow ties, and a Panama hat. Clothed in this conspicuous garb, the congressman regularly rode a bicycle from his Georgetown home to the Capitol, pausing only to direct obscenities at motorists or bus drivers who narrowly missed or bumped him. Only three months into his first term, Eckhardt endorsed unilateral US deescalation of the war that he believed was poisoning the "wellsprings of the Great Society" and urged a compromise settlement that accepted less than "a sovereign, separate state of South Vietnam." By 1968, he had become the only southern member of "The Group" in the House working to end the war and thereafter joined other conspicuously antiwar groups, such as Members of Congress for Peace Through Law, and made antiwar speeches at Rice University on Moratorium Day in 1969 and at Rice, Cornell, and Millsaps College during the protests against the invasion of Cambodia. Eckhardt rejected the goal of seeking peace by moving entire "villages . . . into detention camps"; by destroying Vietnam's "culture," "forests or fields"; or by creating "hundreds of thousands of refugees" and deaths. In the wake of the Laotian operation, the Houston congressman broke even more blatantly with his southern colleagues by joining an otherwise all-Yankee congressional delegation that toured the nation condemning US involvement in Vietnam.[9]

Nixon's eroding status on Capitol Hill, even among southerners, was more evident in the movement of Representative Phillip M. Landrum (D-GA) and Senators Everett Jordan (D-NC) and William Spong (D-VA) into the antiwar column. Landrum, a racial conservative and member of the House since 1953, was the type of old guard southerner that the president least expected to lose. The *National Review* deemed him the "most significant defector from the House pro-Vietnam position," since "much of the Administration's strongest support for the phased withdrawal policy . . . has come from Southern Democrats." The *Review* editors judged that the GOP could "absorb and contain the carping of liberal Republicans" but could not afford to lose southern Democratic backing.[10]

Jordan, a World War I veteran and successful textile manufacturer, had come to the Senate in 1958 and, like all his Democratic colleagues, had voted for the Gulf of Tonkin Resolution; but in 1970 and 1971 he began to vote consistently for end-the-war amendments. He termed his movement into the opposition "the hardest decision I have faced in my years in the Senate" and was promptly challenged by Sam Ervin, who asked, "Everett, have you lost your mind?"[11]

After service in World War II and the Virginia House of Delegates and Senate, Spong had defeated Byrd organization stalwart A. Willis Robertson for the Democratic nomination in 1966. Having been personally recruited to run by President Johnson, Spong espoused a prowar platform of applying "unremitting pressure in a carefully measured response" to communist "aggression" in Vietnam. The fledgling senator maintained his support for the war until 1969, when he worried that Vietnamization had forfeited the leverage necessary to bring North Vietnam to the negotiating table and came to perceive the war as "increasingly insoluble." The Cambodian invasion, which he feared was more "likely to widen rather than restrict the war," pushed him into the opposition. Spong voted for Cooper-Church but opposed McGovern-Hatfield, and following the invasion of Laos, the SFRC member and future dean of the William and Mary Law School became a central figure in Senate efforts to pass a war powers bill.[12]

Spong's conversion to an antiwar stance and support for war powers legislation was instructive, but contemporary observers were far more impressed when John Stennis introduced on May 11, 1971, his version of what would become the War Powers Act. As the Nixon administration's most important Senate ally explained his resolution, Jacob Javits (R-NY), a liberal and antiwar dissident who had previously crafted similar legislation, interrupted to proclaim that the Upper House was "witnessing a miracle" when two senators could "differ deeply" on other issues yet "come together" on this one. The Nixon administration was far less pleased. A staffer later recalled that the White House was convinced it was "in deep trouble" when war powers legislation "appeared with Stennis's name on it."[13]

The trouble was far more prospective than immediate, as Stennis had not suddenly shed his hawkish inclinations. The SASC chair emphasized that his resolution was not aimed at the current "war in Indochina" or

Nixon's policies, but rather at restoring Congress's "power to declare war" before the United States undertook subsequent military involvements. Stennis insisted that the president should have the authority to "meet certain immediate contingencies" such as the protection of American citizens or troops abroad or to prevent a hostile attack; but the use of US forces should not exceed thirty days without congressional sanction. This process, together with the more usual declaration of war, would produce "a full sense of personal commitment and personal obligation" behind any American war. The resulting national unity and commitment combined with the maintenance of a "preponderance of military strength" would, as Stennis lectured University of Mississippi students, enable the United States to avoid any war "we're not going to try to win." The senator had tired of the war, become uneasy with US overcommitment abroad, and was determined to restore congressional war-making powers; but he also retained his faith in peace through strength and the aggressive use of military power—even "gunboat diplomacy" when necessary. And, as he advised the Mississippi collegians in very southern terms, by focusing "more on honor and security" than the contemporary "spirit of the times," he could stand for American "preparedness" and the nation's "long-term interests."[14]

Southern congressional voting patterns were similarly consistent. Votes on two war-related issues set the tone for 1971 deliberations. Congress first sustained President Nixon's request to extend the draft for two years rather than one, as proposed by opponents of the war. The House rejected the one-year amendment on March 31 by a vote of 198 to 200. Southern Democrats voted 14 to 55 against the amendment, compared to other Democrats, who voted 119 to 40 in favor. Southern Republicans opposed the amendment by a 7 to 20 vote. Southern senators subsequently endorsed the two-year extension by 15 to 1 among Democrats and 2 to 1 for Republicans in an overall vote of 55 to 30. Southern congressmen were even more strongly behind the president and his refusal to provide Congress copies of the *Pentagon Papers*. Dixie's House members aligned 66–7 (Democrats) and 25–1 (Republicans) in favor of Edward Hebert's motion to table a resolution calling on Nixon to turn over the documents. Democrats outside the South voted 51–94 against the motion.[15]

During 1971, Dixie and its representatives also strongly opposed the various end-the-war legislation efforts. In Gallup polling southerners were less supportive of such proposals than residents of all other regions or Americans nationally by a 7 percent margin. On June 16 southern Democrats and Republicans voted 2–13 and 0–7 respectively against the McGovern-Hatfield amendment calling for a December 31, 1971, end to the funding of US military operations in Indochina. The amendment failed 42–55 but garnered 32 Democratic votes outside the South. When Senators Cooper and Church renewed their efforts to end the war with an amendment to the foreign aid bill that would have limited Vietnam funding to the withdrawal and protection of US troops, southern senators' 15–4 vote in opposition provided the decisive margin in a 47–44 decision to delete the amendment. Southern senators were only slightly less opposed to the Mansfield Resolution, the first antiwar measure to pass the Upper House. Proposed by Mike Mansfield, the Democratic majority leader, this nonbinding resolution declared it US policy that all American troops be withdrawn from Indochina within six months after the enactment of the 1972 foreign aid bill, contingent upon the prior release of all American POWs. The measure passed 57–38, with southern Democrats opposed 6–8 and southern Republicans 2–5. When the House voted to table the resolution by 130–101, southern Democrats were in favor by a 34–13 margin and southern Republicans by 16–1.[16]

Thereafter, southern congressmen and senators sustained these patterns established in 1970 and 1971. Dixie's representatives, both Democrats and Republicans, continued during 1972 to oppose various forms of end-the-war legislation by virtually identical votes. Even though there was little movement on these votes, the conversion of Congressman Landrum and Senators Jordan, Spong, and Talmadge to the antiwar contingent remained a potential omen of what might happen if the war extended into 1973.[17]

The war weariness and ambivalence evident in the antiwar inclinations of these southern legislators and Stennis's increased concern over US commitments abroad and congressional war powers were also apparent among Dixie's general population. Hawkish perspectives certainly persisted. Whether they judged Nixon to have done a "magnificent job" or to have sustained the "Johnson 'no win' policy," southerners continued to advocate a far more aggressive prosecution of the war than other Americans. For example, only 36 percent of southerners polled in October 1972 objected to Nixon's bombing of North Vietnam, compared to 45 percent of Americans nationally. Some of Dixie's advocates of a traditional victory respectfully asked antiwar senators such as Fulbright what his alternative policy would be for exiting "Vietnam as quickly as we can without losing our position as the number one free country in the world and without being confronted somewhere else by the communists because they believe we will retreat." Others pronounced the Arkansas senator a "chicken" rather than a dove and lectured that the United States could only avoid "Koreas and Vietnams" by demonstrating to the "Communist world . . . it cannot overrun weak nations with impunity."[18]

Peace through strength and the defense of national honor and credibility remained core assumptions in the South's worldview. Still, among southerners writing to their elected representatives, the volume and tone of their letters had clearly shifted toward an antiwar perspective. A number of Mississippians embodied this shift, but none more so than the Jackson attorney who also chaired the Selective Service Appeals Board for the Southern District of Mississippi. Based on his interactions with "many people of different backgrounds and status," this attorney advised Senator Stennis "that the rank and file of your constituents . . . are sick, disgusted and thoroughly tired of our boys being butchered in Viet Nam." He further opined that prominent "business leaders" were not providing the senator "a true picture of what our common and ordinary people here are thinking." The "real sadness is that most of the middle-of-the-road people hesitate to make their feelings known," thereby leaving the forum to "extremists." While attempting to speak for these moderate, ordinary people, this clearly tortured Mississippian had written "to keep a clear conscience" and pleaded with Stennis to "shout loud and clear that the killing of our boys has to stop."[19]

Other Stennis constituents explained how conservative southerners were coming to oppose the war. A father who had "always been in the Hawk category" but had a son about to become eligible for the draft realized that "staying in Vietnam under the present circumstances is futile." A decidedly states' rights Jackson resident whose brother was serving in the war zone decried the federal government's "promotion of hate, through social experimentation" at home and objected to the nation's similar "involvement in wars" abroad "on the pretext of this country's responsibility to police the world." "How much suffering" would "it take for these promoters of hate to realize the folly of their ways?" An "overburdened taxpayer" testified that even hawkish southerners set limits on defense spending. This Meridian resident complained that his tax dollars were "being misused" by the corrupt South Vietnamese government. Over the previous "two or three years," he had "made a complete turn-around" and come to favor a US exit from Southeast Asia "at once and I do not mean a gradual or phased withdrawal." Although a rural Alabama woman was writing to John Sparkman, she could have directed her cutting critique to other prowar southerners chairing the key Senate and House committees and playing key roles in sustaining war funding and blocking end-the-war legislation. She had only contempt for Sparkman and the other "flabby, gray-haired men" who "repeatedly advocate the millions of dollars spent in the war effort, yet fail to enact *fruitful* legislation to relieve the poverty within our own nation."[20]

The South's fundamental but declining support for the war was also apparent in country music, still an essentially "southern art form" during the period of the Vietnam War. Even as the war wound down in the early 1970s, southerners remained the principal fans and consumers of country music; and both the distinct majority of country artists and their hit songs reflected the region's "ardently patriotic militarism." The southern audience demonstrated a clear preference for songs that endorsed anticommunism, fighting and sacrificing for freedom, commitment to honor and duty, and attacks on antiwar protestors. A young Glen Campbell's experience in the summer of 1965 set the tone. After recording Buffy Saint-Marie's pacifist song "The Universal Soldier" and being harshly attacked as being "unpatriotic," a properly chastised Campbell pledged to sing only "red-blooded American" songs thereafter and declared that draft-card-burning protestors should be shot.[21]

Two 1965 Tom T. Hall compositions were representative top-forty hits. In "Hello Vietnam," recorded by Johnny Wright and rising to number one, young soldiers had answered America's "bugle call" to "save freedom in that foreign land" because the "fires we don't put out will bigger burn." The second 1965 Hall song, "What We're Fighting For," explained that the war was necessary "to keep Communism from our own door" and pointedly urged a soldier's mother to explain this to the "people marching in our streets." Several 1966 songs continued the antiprotestor theme. Stonewall Jackson's "The Minute Men Are Turning in Their Graves" asked, "What's happened to our heritage, What's happened to our pride . . . ?" and damned those who would "rather go to prison than heed our country's call," "these men who'd rather live as slaves." In "Viet Nam Blues," recorded by Dave Dudley, a soldier about to embark for Vietnam added, "I don't like dying either, But man, I ain't about to crawl." Also released in 1966, Staff Sergeant Barry Sadler's "Ballad of the Green Berets" sounded similar macho themes while selling two million records in just five weeks and more than seven million overall. The ballad praised the "Fighting Soldiers from the sky, Fearless men who jump and die," and ended with a fallen soldier's call for his son to become a member of the special forces: "Put silver wings upon his chest, Make him one of America's best."[22]

Although such prowar songs were far less prominent in 1967 and 1968, they regained popularity with Richard Nixon's election as the majority of country artists, like their southern fans, backed the president and his Vietnam policies. In 1970 Merle Haggard became Nixon's favorite country singer and the darling of prowar groups when he proclaimed in his number-one hit "Okie from Muskogee": "We don't burn our draft cards down on main street, but we like being right and being free." Haggard warned protestors, "when you're running down my country, hoss, you're walkin' on the fightin' side of me!" and directed those who "don't love" the country to "leave it." Majority southern opinion also concurred with the messages conveyed in the 1971 piece "The Battle Hymn of Lt. Calley." Consistent with Dixie's sentiments, but in blatant disregard for the events at My Lai, the singer, voicing Calley's perspective, declared he had loyally "followed all my orders and did the best I could." And the outcome was, "We took the jungle village exactly like they said, We responded to their rifle-fire with everything we had, And when the smoke had cleared away a hundred souls lay dead." All of this ostensibly courageous service was contrasted sharply with the cowardly protestors at home: "While we're fighting in the jungles, they were marching in the street, While we're dying in the rice fields, they were helping our defeat."[23]

Although they occupied a minority position akin to antiwar dissenters in the South generally, some country music artists questioned the war. Among major country stars, only Johnny Cash expressed doubt about Vietnam, defended the protestors' patriotism, and endorsed the withdrawal of US troops. In "What Is Truth," a song written for a concert on the Vanderbilt University campus in 1970, Cash countered the negative image of young protestors and asserted instead, "the ones that you're calling wild are going to be the leaders in a little while. This old world's waking to a newborn day and I solemnly swear that it'll be their way. You better help the voice of youth find 'What Is Truth.'" Following a trip to Vietnam to entertain the troops in 1971, Cash released the "Walkin' and Talkin' Viet Nam Blues" in which he concluded, "whether we belong over there or not," the US soldiers "belong over here somewhere."[24]

That these Cash hits reached the number-three and -eighteen positions on the charts indicates that although southerners remained supportive of the war, they too were growing weary of the sacrifices. Other, earlier songs had also embodied Dixie's agony. In 1966 Loretta Lynn released "Dear Uncle Sam" in which a woman's husband had dutifully answered the nation's "call" and "proudly" worn "the old red, white and blue," only to be killed, leaving her alone with "heartache." Ambivalence was also foremost in the Mel Tillis song "Ruby Don't Take Your Love to Town," recorded in 1967 by Johnny Danell and in 1969 by Kenny Rogers. The wheelchair-bound veteran in this song, who had not "started that old crazy Asian war" but had been wounded while doing his "patriotic chores," pleads with Ruby not to leave him alone at home. For Jan Howard, whose son Jimmy was killed in Vietnam, the agony reached far beyond a musical saga. Her "My Song" was based on a letter she had written to Jimmy and chronicles her maternal reflections on his happy childhood and life before being sent to Vietnam.[25]

In 1970 Skeeter Davis aimed "When You Gonna Bring Our Soldiers Home" directly at President Nixon. Voicing a woman's perspective, Davis declared, "Every mother has to worry about the son she loves, And every sweetheart has to worry too." Although Nixon did not think she should "protest" or "question" his policies, "I think I've got a right 'cause I just got word tonight, The Man I love was killed there yesterday, When you gonna bring our soldiers home"? The following year, Arlene Harden's "Congratulations, You Sure Made a Man Out of Him" was equally bitter and provided an even more frontal challenge to the South's patriotic militarism. Unlike Lynn's and Davis's songs, in which the US soldiers had died, the character in this song had returned home profoundly impaired: "I watch him just sit by the window and silently stare into space. And once when I watched him a tear trickled down on his face. I knew then and there, it's no use to pretend. Congratulations, you sure made a man out of him."[26]

As these country singers and songs suggested, southern women carried a heavy burden on the home front. Senator Olin Johnston (D-SC) had warned President Johnson in August 1964, "You are going to find in my state and in the South these mothers and people are afraid of war." Two of Senator Russell Long's constituents representatively embodied this fear. Writing in the shadow of the 1968 Tet Offensive, a Franklin, Louisiana, resident acknowledged that southern expectations would have her be a "Spartan Mother and say 'anything for my country,'" but she could not. Instead, she urged Long to help bring the war to a "fast conclusion" before her son was called to fulfill his ROTC obligation. She also impressed upon the senator that she was not a "leftist or a 'hippy,'" but rather "a D.A.R., a sorority sister of your wife and normally . . . considered quite conservative." Nearly three years later, a New Iberia women informed the hawkish Long, "I am neither a dove nor a hawk, just a mother, who sees our sons still being used as a political football, being sent to a country to be killed, crippled, mentally disturbed or taken prisoners, [and] exposed to prostitution [and] drugs." Over the course of the war, mothers' and wives' letters to their senators and congressmen not only confirmed Johnston's prediction but ran the gamut from strong antiwar protests to shrill and hawkish demands for aggressive pursuit of a decisive military victory. Indeed, prowar southern women were as outspoken as their male counterparts.[27]

Many southern women expressed their sentiments on the war more publicly. Lee Janot from Lake Charles, the mother of a navy pilot, the relative of a POW, and the host of a local television show, went to Vietnam in November 1967 carrying a letter from Senator Long to American soldiers and another seven hundred Christmas greetings for American soldiers; helped organize "Cheer Unlimited," a group dedicated to sending care packages to US soldiers from southwest Louisiana who were hospitalized in South Vietnam; and disseminated her prowar message on her TV show and through numerous public talks. Janot castigated those "who are marching in protest, those who desecrate our flag, those who burn draft cards," for thinking they were "the *only*" Americans who possessed "any morality." She called upon the "*majority of Americans*" who "*love America and the American way*" to "*speak up . . . get off the defensive*"— to get behind the war and the necessary containment of "international communism."[28]

Two like-minded women, Mrs. Marie Davis and Mrs. Ida Riddick, sisters and wives of US servicemen stationed in Southeast Asia, took to the streets in April 1967 in Raleigh, North Carolina. The objects of their wrath were the antiwar protestors who surrounded the Raleigh post office each Wednesday. Davis and Riddick punctuated their counterdemonstration with several placards proclaiming: "If you want this war to end, why do you help the enemy drag it out?" "My husband fights in Vietnam for you to stand here and help our enemies." And, taped to the stroller of Mrs. Davis's infant son, "Are you the people for whom my Daddy is fighting?"[29]

Other southern women were just as active in opposing the war. For Virginia Durr, a longtime member of the Women's International League for Peace and Freedom, opposing the Vietnam War, which she considered particularly wrongheaded, came naturally. Together with her attorney husband, Clifford, Durr was one of the South's and Alabama's foremost liberals. Having opposed the poll tax, taken a leading role in the Montgomery Bus Boycott, and famously faced down Senator James Eastland during Senate hearings, she openly applauded Fulbright's efforts, criticized Johnson and Rusk, and was delighted when the Arkansas legislature passed a resolution denouncing the war. As she confided to a friend in July 1967, "I simply will not and cannot stop speaking against the war."[30]

Suzy Post, also the wife of an attorney and a Louisville antiwar activist, was a less prominent but perhaps an even more committed opponent of the war. Thirty-five and the mother of five, Post opened her home to demonstrators, chaired the Kentucky Civil Liberties Union, and helped bring Dr. Benjamin Spock, the antiwar pediatrician, to speak in Louisville. Deeply disturbed by what she deemed the "racism and classism" of the draft, Post also baked cookies for protestors boarding buses for Washington, DC, and then castigated the FBI for dispatching agents to intimidate these groups. Post recognized that her socioeconomic status facilitated these actions: "My husband was a very successful trial lawyer so I could operate within that community with a kind of authority and legitimacy." But she also understood there were clear limits in her southern community: hence her relatively circumspect activism.[31]

Regardless of their perspectives on geopolitics or strategy or their level of activism, women in the South and across the country coped with diverse emotions and responsibilities. Certainly the war's most devastating impact came with the death of a loved one. Wives and mothers lived in constant fear of uniformed military personnel appearing in their neighborhood. One of the wives of a Bardstown, Kentucky, reservist recalled, "It was a bad time for anyone to wear a uniform here. It meant they were from Fort Knox and bringing bad news. If you heard a knock on your door, it meant someone was hurt or had been killed. . . . No one wanted to go to the door, or pick up the telephone." A Kentucky mother, who received one of these visits from a military chaplain with notification of her son's death, remembered that in "a few minutes . . . he was gone. I was in shock, I was numb, very numb. There's no way to explain to you my grief." A rural Arkansas mother's son had just turned nineteen when he was killed. She lamented, "He hadn't even become a man yet, to us he was just a young boy and we never got to finish raising him . . . and now we must put everything away, as though we never had a son." Having lost her son, a North Carolina mother awoke "every morning . . . from a fitful sleep," feeling as if she "must ward off a crushing blow." A Tennessee woman made a telling point to Senator Gore. She doubted that "many people care," as fallen Americans were made a "number," a statistic, and news reports periodically described the nation's losses as "light." She strenuously objected to such language; there were "no light casualties. Bill (my nephew) was not a light casualty. It was a great loss to our family." The wife of one of the Bardstown soldiers who fell in Vietnam told an interviewer, "When I was young, I just wanted to get a good job and a good husband, have a home and family, . . . but the war took it all away." And Patsy Collins, whose husband also died in the same Vietcong attack, emphasized the ongoing misery: "I look back and can't believe that it's been almost twenty-five years since David was killed. Even so, I remember it every day. . . . He'll always be with me, I'll never forget him." Nor was the Collins family's misery limited to David's death, as his mother, Dorothy, committed suicide soon after losing her son.[32]

Southern women also experienced a broad range of war-induced difficulties that fell far short of the devastation accompanying the death of a family member. Fayetteville, North Carolina, the home of Fort Bragg, where some two hundred thousand soldiers trained during the war, came to be known locally as "Fayettenam" and was characterized by a "carnival atmosphere" in which prostitution, drugs, and alcohol were readily available on Hay Street for the young soldiers. The widespread crime, numerous fights, and advertisements on the side of the Cellar Night Club featuring a nude woman and the caption "30 Beautiful Girls and 3 Ugly

Ones" testified vividly to the mixed blessing of massive defensive spending: "For women, downtown . . . became an unsheltered place of catcalls, harassment, and relentless pursuit. . . . While the sexworkers made a living, other women literally became a type of war refugee, leaving town as soon as they became adults and never going back."[33]

For most women, the war was far more personal and far less publicly dramatic. Together with the concern for their men's safety came loneliness and the added responsibility of running households and caring for children alone. At best these circumstances produced ambivalence, if not outright resentment. Joy James from Bardstown alternated between wondering why the family had "to sacrifice" during "the best time of our lives" and thinking her husband's service was "our role in history" and would make them "better people."[34]

Seawillow Chambers, from neighboring Tennessee, provides another telling and representative example of the war's effects. From a devoutly Baptist, politically conservative, working-class family in Alcoa, ten miles south of Knoxville, Seawillow Malone, then eighteen, married Ron Chambers just three weeks before he shipped out to Vietnam in the spring of 1967. Befitting her background and culture, she deemed it appropriate that Ron go to war. It was "part of a man's responsibility to his country. . . . If we go to war . . . the men go to battle." Since Seawillow had continued her secretarial work in Knoxville and lived at home with her parents, she had no financial problems. Emotional issues were another matter. She knew no other wives with husbands in Vietnam for support and found living at home an anomalous position suspended between her old and new worlds. Like many other military wives, she was "scared to death" for the first three months of Ron's deployment, more resigned during the middle six, and terrified again during the final three. Over much of the time, she was "more or less numb . . . just busy trying to keep busy."[35]

Meeting Ron for R and R in Hawaii was more harrowing than satisfying. Having never ridden in a taxi, flown on an airplane, or stayed in a hotel, Seawillow was terrified for much of the trip. Even the reunion was stressful. After their brief time as a married couple before Ron's deployment and the "shocks" to her "system" on the trip, she felt like she was "going to a hotel room" with a man she barely knew. In retrospect, Seawillow perceived a similar disjuncture in their entire relationship over the first year of marriage: "In the days that I grew up, you saved yourself for the man that you married. . . . So I had saved myself . . . then after three weeks time, I've got to lock all that back up and store it away for another year, and then re-open that door again. . . . It's had its effect for many, many years on me."[36]

Although a miscommunication had come close to notifying Seawillow incorrectly that Ron was missing in action, Segrid Blair from Forrest Park, Georgia, was accurately informed of her husband Dave's MIA status on March 11, 1969, after the NVA overran his special forces camp in the A Shau Valley. Captain Blair had received a delayed packet of Segrid's letters a few days before the battle, and she and other family members "kept saying, 'At least he got our letters before the attack came and knew we loved him.' Even after we thought he was dead," she continued, "I mailed a small package of smoked cheese and some candy." When the family "kept hearing on the radio that there were only four survivors," they were convinced Dave had died because Segrid was "sure he wouldn't let himself be captured."[37]

She was correct about his avoiding capture but wrong about his death. After being picked up by US forces on March 12, Dave called home from Da Nang. Segrid could not remember exactly what they said during the three-minute conversation. Both "were crying," with Segrid "telling him how glad" she was "he was alive and how much we loved him," and Dave asking about their three young sons and expressing his love for the family. The relieved and overjoyed Segrid unapologetically told an *Atlanta Constitution* reporter, "He's marvelous. You really have to see him and hear him to appreciate him. He's just marvelous. His two heroes are Stonewall Jackson and Lawrence of Arabia."[38]

Jerry McCuiston, an Alabama woman, was not nearly so fortunate in quickly learning of her husband's fate after his F-105 Thunderchief was shot down over North Vietnam in May 1967. Although Michael had ejected safely from the plane and been seen on the ground, it was six months before Jerry caught a glimpse of him in a North Vietnamese propaganda film and nearly three years before she received his first letter, establishing that he was alive and being held as a POW. Born in Birmingham in 1940, Jerry Phillips had grown up with her sister, Mary, two years her elder, in a traditional Southern Baptist household in Montgomery, where she graduated from high school. Jerry met Michael, a pilot, while he was stationed at Maxwell Air Force Base (AFB). They married and were assigned to Laughlin AFB in Del Rio, Texas, and Nellis AFB in Las Vegas, Nevada, before he left for Thailand on March 16, 1967. At the time of Michael's deployment, their son Danny was five, and Jerry was three months pregnant with their first daughter, Michele. Jerry and Danny moved back to Montgomery to be near her parents during Michael's absence.[39]

As Michael assumed his duties flying out of Thailand, Jerry set up household in the trailer they had purchased in Texas and looked forward to her husband's return after he had flown his requisite one hundred missions. Neither contemplating nor seeking fundamental changes during his absence, Jerry sought to sustain familiar surroundings and routines by arranging and decorating the trailer precisely as they had done in Texas— "right down" to placing "Michael's socks and underwear . . . exactly as he like[d] them in his dresser drawer." When parenting, managing the household, and writing daily letters to Michael failed to adequately occupy her time and thoughts, she resumed working part-time in the mornings as a hair stylist while Danny was in kindergarten. These cumulative efforts at keeping busy were only partially successful. The bulk of her conversations with adults centered on Michael, and she waited anxiously for the mail each day. The "constant dread" that she had felt when Michael left waned "in frequency, but not in intensity," over the ensuing weeks.[40]

With Michael about to go on R and R to Okinawa, Jerry and Danny traveled to Starkville, Mississippi, to visit friends. It was there, on May 8, 1967, that she received the dreaded visit from an air force colonel informing her that Michael had been shot down over North Vietnam. Fifty-three days after Michael's departure from Montgomery, the lives of all three McCustions and their families were changed permanently. Never having thought of herself as a "tough person," Jerry had "enjoyed being taken care of, and had given little thought of taking care of myself." In many ways she was "just a kid" who had never been a provider or attended to the diverse responsibilities that she now faced as a single parent. Confronting her new reality, Jerry quickly resolved that she could not "very well shrivel up and die."[41]

Like so many POW/MIA wives, she quickly found her status anomalous and lonely. Jerry felt like a "freak of society," not fitting into any accepted societal niche. She and other POW/MIA wives differed markedly from widows, divorcees, or single women: "For widows and divorcees," she told a reporter in May 1971, "the act is final—they know their husbands are either dead or no longer part of their lives. And single girls depend on themselves. . . . Besides, they don't have youngsters." The absence of a viable support system beyond her parents complicated this ill-defined position, and even this source of aid receded when Jerry's father died unexpectedly in January 1968. Since Jerry and Danny had moved back to Montgomery rather than remaining near Michael's last stateside base, there were no squadron wives with whom to socialize and commiserate. At first, neighbors and friends rallied around, but as the years passed, they avoided Jerry out of fear of saying the wrong thing or simply went on with their lives and priorities. Air force families stationed at Maxwell AFB provided some support after September 1969 through periodic child care, much-needed social interaction, help with home maintenance, and aid with business and legal matters.[42]

Although this assistance was much appreciated, Jerry frequently felt that she "was out there all alone." Caring for Danny and Michele, after her birth in October 1967, constituted her most immediate concern. Similar to the experiences of other POW/MIA wives, Jerry found explaining Michael's absence particularly challenging and heartbreaking. When Danny faced taunts from schoolmates that "Japs" had killed his father, she worked to reassure him that Michael was alive, even though she was far from sure herself. Responding when Michele, who had never met Michael, asked, "Where's my daddy?" proved even more difficult. Ultimately, there was no good way "to explain to her that he's alive, that he loves us, but he can't come home." For both Jerry and the children, Michael's absence was graphically restated every evening when all the other fathers in the neighborhood began arriving home; it was like a "horror movie," the "most difficult time of the day."[43]

Although aid from the air force families was much appreciated, Jerry's other interactions with the air force and the US government helped convert her from a "victimized spectator" into an unlikely public activist. When she first asked for the names of other POW/MIA wives in the Montgomery area, the air force refused. Similarly, when rumors surfaced of North Vietnamese torture and mistreatment of American prisoners, POW/MIA wives were instructed not to disclose anything they learned, lest they "jeopardize" their husband's well-being. This emphasis on so-called quiet diplomacy was ostensibly based on the assumption that publicity in the United States could "derail ongoing negotiations with the North Vietnamese." After seeing the mid-October 1967 propaganda film, Jerry unsuccessfully sought to have Michael's status changed from MIA to POW. She failed because US military procedure required verification from North Vietnam. Over the next year, Hanoi's repeated threats to try POWs for alleged war crimes reinforced her inclination "to speak out, not against the [US] military or establishment but on behalf of the prisoners and missing."[44]

McCuistion's first cautious step toward going public came in early 1969 with the organization of the other six POW/MIA families in the Montgomery area. This group met weekly in the home of retired USAF general Matthew K. Deichelmann and his wife, whose son had been missing since September 1968. Often over one of Mrs. Deichelmann's stout Bloody Marys, these wives and parents expressed their feelings and bolstered one another. These initial steps coincided with similar activities among POW/MIA wives nationally, especially those of Sybil Stockdale in San Diego, whose husband had been shot down and taken prisoner in September 1965. After comparing notes with Stockdale in March 1969, Jerry and her small contingent initiated public actions. They began by distributing POW/MIA bumper stickers and other flyers throughout Alabama. After financing these efforts through rummage sales and from their own funds, Jerry and her coworkers soon moved on to an aggressive public-speaking campaign.[45]

Young, attractive, and, like Stockdale, a woman of "prodigious energy and talent," McCuistion was about to become a prominent public figure. She was uneasy that she had no college degree or formal preparation for this new role but nevertheless determined to act on behalf of Michael and the other American POWs and MIAs. After her first speaking engagement before her father's American Legion post, she was soon averaging four appearances per week over the subsequent eighteen months. Through the remainder of the war, she spoke to legion posts, service clubs, chambers of commerce, high school assemblies, college groups all over the state, and each class of air force trainees at Maxwell. Her most prominent speaking appearance came before the national American Legion Convention in September 1970 in Portland, Oregon, where she shared the stage with Ross Perot before an audience of four thousand. In these talks her message was consistent and direct. Operating on the assumption that "our only weapon is public opinion, because Hanoi is sensitive to it," she prodded her listeners to "speak out." McCuistion sought to elicit a public outcry by painting a graphic picture of the mistreatment of American prisoners. Only Americans writing to Hanoi and US officials could rescue the POWs from their "hell holes." Although Americans were "hopelessly divided" over the war's merits, she urged them to unite regarding the "lives at stake in prisons in Southeast Asia."[46]

McCuistion's tireless efforts stretched well beyond this rigorous speaking schedule. She spearheaded the Concerned Citizens of Alabama Campaign in 1969, which collected five hundred thousand signatures on petitions expressing concern for the POWs. In the summer of 1969 she participated in the founding of the National League of Families of American Prisoners and Missing in Southeast Asia and thereafter served as the league's Alabama coordinator. Working through Postmaster General William M. Blount, another Alabamian, McCuistion was also instrumental in the US Post Office's issuance of a commemorative POW/MIA stamp in November 1970. Together with more than 170 other POW wives and relatives, she extended her lobbying to Geneva and Paris in May 1971. The delegation went first to Geneva, where it distributed "fact sheets" and solicited aid from delegates to an International Red Cross conference in communicating with American prisoners. The American group continued on to Paris, where its members collectively visited the embassies of forty countries and picketed outside the building in which US–North Vietnamese negotiations were taking place.[47]

The impact of American POW/MIA advocates on Hanoi, whose leaders shrewdly manipulated the POW issue to push for US withdrawal, is difficult to establish. But North Vietnam did allow much greater communication between the prisoners and their families beginning in early 1969 and released eighteen Americans during that year. This relaxing of the information embargo allowed Michael McCuistion's first letter, composed of the standard six lines, to get through in March 1970. Three years after his plane went down, Jerry finally had secured hard evidence that Michael had survived—"What a feeling."[48]

If the influence of the POW/MIA campaign on North Vietnam is difficult to gauge, the influence in the United States was more discernible. McCuistion, Stockdale, and other POW/MIA wives helped make the men's fate a major American public and political issue and a central component of the American peace talks. From 1964 through 1968, the US prisoners had received relatively little attention, as the Johnson administration sought to avoid discussion of the men's fate and the war's costs. Over the ensuing four years, the League of Families played a critical role in forcing the nation and its politicians to take notice of the men's treatment and to consolidate behind the demand for their release. In the midst of one of America's longest and most unpopular wars, Jerry McCuistion's message that the nation could still unite on behalf of the POWs and MIAs was correct and compelling. Indeed, a nation bitterly divided on virtually all other facets of the war came to agree that the release of the POWs was the central requirement for an acceptable peace.[49]

President Nixon was instrumental in making the POW/MIA issue a national priority, but his motives were far more complex than McCuistion's. She and her coworkers sought improved communications, better treatment, and ultimate freedom for the prisoners. Although the president favored these goals, he and his administration also utilized the POW/MIA issue as a powerful tool for countering the antiwar movement and a strong rationale for sustaining the US presence in Vietnam. Indeed, securing the release of the POWs increasingly became the central rationale for a war that fewer and fewer Americans and southerners could understand or justify on geopolitical or ideological grounds. Ironically, as historian Michael J. Allen has demonstrated, when Nixon lost control of this issue to Hanoi and the POW/MIA wives, securing the men's freedom became a powerful argument for ending the war. The *Norfolk Virginian Pilot,* hardly an antiwar paper, recognized the "cruel deception" in Nixon's position as early as May 1971. Rather than US troops remaining in "South Vietnam as long as there are any American prisoners of war in North Vietnam," the dynamic was "just the reverse: the American POWs will stay in North Vietnam as long as American forces are maintained in the South."[50]

While helping to produce a dramatic shift in the US attitude toward the POWs and making their release the sine quo non of any peace agreement, Jerry McCuistion had also undergone great personal changes, especially for a traditional southern woman. On November 17, 1971, Michael wrote to Jerry: "When I think of you I realize that there was nothing about you that I want changed; I am happy to know that I will find you just as I left you when I return." But the woman who met Michael at Maxwell AFB upon his return on March 7, 1973, was far different from the one who had seen him off six years earlier. Convinced that circumstances "had forced her into having a voice," Jerry "felt, thought, and did things I never thought I could." She was certain that the "women had changed more than the men," who had been trapped in a kind of time warp during a period of astounding social change in the United States. She later mused that Michael could not believe that she had addressed an audience of four thousand. In the process of organizing and representing the POW/MIA families in Alabama, she displayed enormous energy, endurance, focus, and spirit. H. Morgan Smith, chief of the Arctic, Desert, and Tropic Information Center at Maxwell, observed that the "soft-spoken southern girl" whom he had met in 1968 soon approached "no door she wouldn't knock on" in search of financial and public support for the cause. Still, despite her activist role and high public profile, Jerry "never" considered herself "anything special" and hoped her family could move on as soon as possible.[51]

A significant aspect of Jerry's personal change resulted from exposure to a wide variety of people and situations she might not have otherwise encountered. Among the most interesting of the people was Daniel "Chappie" James, the air force's first African American four-star general. McCuistion met James in 1970, when he represented the Defense Department and the Nixon administration in meetings with POW/MIA wives. The two seemed an unlikely pair—the diminutive, young, southern white woman and the 6-foot-4-inch, 250-pound black general who had fought his way up from a Pensacola, Florida, slum to become one of the Tuskegee airmen and achieve the top rank in the air force. McCuistion later recalled that James served as a "father figure," often spoke at meetings she had organized, and always called to have dinner when he was in Montgomery. She deemed his support vital during the period when it was unclear whether Michael had survived and all efforts at communication failed. James, who was invariably described in terms of courage, tenacity, and charisma, must have admired these same qualities in the woman who was working so hard on behalf of his fellow pilots.[52]

Unfortunately, the McCuistion saga had no storybook ending. Rather, it reflected another facet of the nation's and South's more general agony. Over the ensuing six years, Michael was stationed in Texas, South Carolina (where their second daughter, Lisa, was born in 1975), Virginia, Nevada, and Utah. In 1979 Jerry and Michael separated and subsequently divorced. Jerry returned to Las Vegas, where she raised Danny, Michele, and Lisa and worked in retail sales. Following his retirement from the air force in 1982, Michael settled in Texas. Just as the war had profoundly disrupted American society, politics, and foreign policy, it had played havoc with the McCuistion family—first through Michael's captivity and prolonged absence and ultimately through the burden this experience imposed on family relationships. If the war had divided her family, it had also prompted Jerry McCuistion to develop and demonstrate abilities, challenge traditional southern gender roles, and influence domestic public and political opinion in ways she could never have anticipated.

Despite the administration's adroit manipulation of the POW issue, 1971 ended with congressional momentum apparently increasing for passage of some form of end-the-war legislation. On January 25, 1972, President Nixon orchestrated another "political masterstroke" much like his silent majority speech in October 1969 by announcing that Kissinger had been engaged in a series of secret negotiations with the North Vietnamese, who, the president asserted, had rejected all reasonable compromise offers. In terms quite similar to the Mansfield Resolution, Nixon outlined the US offer to withdraw all American forces within six months after a cease-fire and the release of US POWs. In February the president augmented his case for sincerely seeking a peaceful resolution of the conflict by becoming the first sitting American president to visit China and in May by conducting a second high-profile meeting with Soviet leaders in Moscow. While neither of these summit conferences yielded the linkage and resulting pressure on Hanoi to which Nixon and Kissinger aspired, they forged new diplomatic paths and disarmed many domestic critics of the administration.[53]

But as had been true in early 1970, events in Vietnam promptly compromised Nixon's political gains. On March 30, the North Vietnamese launched a massive 120,000-troop invasion of South Vietnam designed to destroy ARVN forces, discredit Vietnamization, and perhaps prompt peace negotiations on Hanoi's terms. The Vietcong simultaneously reclaimed areas that became vulnerable as the ARVN moved to confront the NVA. With only 6,000 US combat soldiers remaining in the war zone, Nixon averted a South Vietnamese defeat by employing the most intense US air attacks of the war against both NVA forces in the South and North Vietnam's infrastructure. Declaring that the "bastards have never been bombed like they're going to be bombed this time," the president authorized the Linebacker I campaign, whose 9,315 sorties from May 10 through October 22 delivered approximately 150,000 tons of bombs, or about one-quarter of the tonnage of LBJ's three-year Rolling Thunder operation. Nixon seized the opportunity to "go for broke," to "cream 'em good," in his latest application of the mad-man strategy and its goal of dictating a favorable settlement of the conflict. Toward this end, the president also ordered the mining of Haiphong harbor and a naval blockade of North Vietnam's coast. The US actions inflicted severe damage on North Vietnam and the communist forces, but the Easter Offensive further demonstrated that Vietnamization had not yet prepared the ARVN to confront their enemies without significant US military assistance. As historian George Herring has observed, the "ferocious campaigns of the summer of 1972 merely raised the stalemate to a new level of violence."[54]

Both Washington and Hanoi responded to this grim reality by moving toward a negotiated settlement. By the eve of the 1972 presidential election, Kissinger and his North Vietnamese counterpart, Le Duc Tho, arrived at an agreement calling for the withdrawal of all US troops and the return of American POWs within sixty days of an announced cease-fire. Significantly, more than one hundred thousand North Vietnamese soldiers would be allowed to remain in South Vietnam, and the subsequent governance of the South would be determined by the National Council of Reconciliation and Concord (NCRC), composed of representatives of the Thieu government, the NLF, and third-party neutralists. When confronted with Thieu's adamant opposition to the agreement and correctly foreseeing an overwhelming victory over Democratic nominee George McGovern in the upcoming presidential election, Nixon backed away from Kissinger's work. The president also clung to the hope that one more round of US bombing might convince Hanoi to accept a settlement closer to "peace with honor" since the national security advisor's handiwork had departed in glaring fashion from the long-standing US demands for the withdrawal of all NVA troops from the South and refusal to recognize the political legitimacy of the NLF.[55]

Nixon crushed McGovern in the election, but this demonstration of electoral strength failed to provide him decisive leverage either at home or in Vietnam. Democrats retained control of both houses of Congress, where the president admitted the administration had stayed only "one step ahead of the sheriff, just missing fund cutoffs" for the war. Hanoi was even less cooperative, adamantly refusing to withdraw any of its troops from the South or to accept any change in the status of the NLF. Most important, North Vietnam continued to hold American POWs. In an effort to assuage his most hawkish domestic backers, assure Thieu of ongoing US support, break this diplomatic deadlock, and end the war before Congress reassembled in January and moved to block war funding, Nixon resumed bombing North Vietnam. The savage "Christmas bombing" from December 18 to 29, officially designated as Linebacker II, pummeled the Hanoi-Haiphong area with more than 36,000 tons of ordnance—more than the tonnage for the first three years of the Nixon presidency. This final attempt at the mad-man strategy destroyed much of the military and industrial infrastructure that proponents of strategic bombing had long lobbied to target. It also killed over three thousand civilians and wounded five hundred more, destroyed a major hospital in Hanoi, and damaged eight foreign embassies. More troubling from the US perspective, Linebacker II resulted in the loss of fifteen B-52 bombers and thirteen other aircraft, the death of ninety US crewmen, and the capture of another thirty-one.[56]

Decried as "war by tantrum" by *New York Times* writer James Reston, Linebacker II provoked shrill criticism within the United States and abroad and was "not politically sustainable." When North Vietnam, eager to escape the bombing but hardly ready to surrender, agreed to return to the bargaining table, Nixon quickly seized the overture and instructed Kissinger "that almost any settlement would be tolerable." Talks resumed in Paris on January 8, and an agreement was reached on January 13 and signed on January 27 by the United States, North Vietnam, South Vietnam, and the People's Revolutionary Government (NLF). Differing little in substance from the Kissinger-Tho agreement of the previous October, the settlement left North Vietnamese forces in the South, recognized the People's Revolutionary Government as a legitimate political entity, and left the NCRC in place. US forces were to be withdrawn and American POWs to be released within sixty days. The latter constituted the only clear US benefit from nearly three decades of involvement in Vietnam.[57]

As President Nixon and the United States struggled toward this inglorious outcome, Dixie sustained its position as the strongest regional backer of the embattled chief executive and his war. In early 1972, before

Nixon's announcement of the secret peace talks, 57 percent of southerners approved of his work as president, compared to a national average of 49 and with no other region polling greater than 48 percent. Six months later, in the midst of the US response to North Vietnam's Easter Offensive, Nixon's approval rating in the South continued to run 7–10 percentage points higher than nationally, and the region's endorsement of his Vietnam policies also exceeded other US sections. Dixie's residents were most in favor of ongoing military aid to South Vietnam and most opposed to a set date for withdrawing all American troops. These patterns persisted as the war ended in early 1973, when the South was most inclined to resume the bombing of North Vietnam if Hanoi refused to accept "reasonable" peace terms and least willing to halt war funding if no "peace settlement" were forthcoming. After Nixon and Kissinger secured this settlement with Hanoi, 67 percent of the nation registered its approval of the president's presidential performance, and 75 percent favored his Vietnam work. Consistent with polling results over the previous four years, Dixie's percentages were 73 and 82.[58]

Despite these overall polling figures, constituent correspondence continued to trend in an antiwar direction. Prowar southerners applauded Nixon's bombing of virtually all of North Vietnam and mining of Haiphong harbor in response to the Easter Offensive. They continued to argue for a "united front" and to accuse dissenters of being "traitors to the nation," cavorting with the "peace at any price boys," and siding with "YANKEE" opponents of the war who demonstrated "gutlessness" and "rank cowardice." The southern hawks praised Linebacker I and the mining of Haiphong, since "it was high time the most powerful nation . . . stopped being insulted by a pip-squeak bully." Only by aggressively prosecuting the war could the United States secure the freedom of its POWs. Washington "was not going to get them back by *begging* those damned Communists to release them."[59]

Opponents of the war, who wrote in greater numbers, emphasized three themes. By 1972, virtually no prowar southerners argued for the war on religious grounds to oppose atheism and protect Christianity; but the war's immorality remained a prominent theme among those urging US withdrawal from Vietnam. In May Senator Fulbright received letters of this tenor from a student at the Southern Baptist Theological Seminary in Louisville, a Catholic nun living at the Carmelite Monastery in

Little Rock, the chairperson of the Christian Social Concerns Committee in a Methodist Church in Conway, Arkansas, and the minister of a Presbyterian Church in Little Rock. This group collectively decried the US use of "indiscriminate violence" and feared that the nation's myriad "immoralities" had already prompted the "Lord" to begin "to judge our nation." Were there "some way to know the actual number of lives lost and land destroyed," there would be no way to "say that what we have accomplished justifies the wanton destruction." As a North Carolinian wrote Sam Ervin, "the ugly facts of the killing and destruction" could not be reconciled "with our professed Christianity and sense of lofty national purpose."[60]

To these arguments for a more ethical and moral US foreign policy, the Baptist seminarian added the need for Congress to reassert its proper role in the nation's foreign policy and war making and to curb Nixon's "insane 'gun-boat diplomacy.'" Opponents of the war also contended that increased bombing via Linebacker I and II actually impeded the release of American prisoners. Four Georgians cut to the heart of the matter. A husband and wife recognized that "Mr. Nixon appears to be using the POW issue to prolong the war" and asked if the United States would "agree to surrender their prisoners if the North Vietnamese were bombing Washington." Another Peach State couple added that it was "completely irrational" to expect Hanoi "to release our prisoners when we are daily providing them with more prisoners and killing not only their soldiers but undoubtedly plenty of civilians." As had often been the case over the past nine years, other southerners cited Dixie's history to illustrate their arguments. To engage in the "massive bombing of civilian targets" in a "poor peasant land," wrote a Talmadge constituent, was akin to the "actions of Sherman in Georgia." Still another Georgian asserted, "As Southerners we should know that the greatness of a people is not merely their ability to win, but their ability to accept defeat when defeat is inevitable."[61]

The key role of southerners in the Senate's passage of the War Powers Act in April 1973 afforded additional evidence of Dixie's war weariness. Although Senator Stennis continued to emphasize that the legislation did not apply to the war in Vietnam, and the Senate soundly defeated Fulbright's amendments to the contrary, historian Robert Mann has asserted that the Upper House's April 13, 1972, vote "marked the beginning of a new attitude in Congress toward American involvement in Vietnam." By voting 11–2 for the act, "conservative southern Democrats" had finally "acknowledged just how badly the constitutional powers and prerogatives of their institution had been eroded." The joint Javits-Stennis bill conformed closely to the Mississippi senator's earlier draft, particularly calling for the president to notify Congress immediately upon committing US troops abroad and to secure congressional sanction within thirty days. In addition to Stennis's crucial backing, William Spong from Virginia served as the Democratic floor manager for the bill, and Senators Cooper, Talmadge, and Lawton Chiles (D-FL) were vocal supporters. Talmadge, who was a cosponsor of the measure, reminded his colleagues that the decision for war was "the single most important decision . . . a nation can make" and that it was "too great for one man." Chiles declared it imperative to insure that "Congress fulfills its constitutional role in decisions of war and peace" and that "civilians" make such momentous judgments after adequate "deliberations." Stennis echoed the need to restore the "responsibilities of Congress"; but he also emphasized that going to war through "proper constitutional procedures" would help realize victory by preventing the president from undertaking "a war which the nation will not support."[62]

When the more hawkish House removed the thirty-day deadline, the War Powers Act was not adopted until November 1973, when this deadline was extended to sixty days. Southern Democratic senators voted 14–1 for the 1973 version, with Dixie's Republicans dividing 4–4. Indicative of the region's residual support for executive prerogatives and the impact of partisan politics, southern Democratic congressmen voted 44–27 in favor of the bill and southern Republicans 7–15 against, both much less supportive than other sections in an overall vote of 238–123. Significantly, the War Powers Act had not passed until all American soldiers and POWs had returned home and President Nixon was badly weakened by the Watergate scandal.[63]

Still, the Senate's action in 1972 and the threat of further congressional restrictions had influenced Nixon and Kissinger as they sought unsuccessfully to bludgeon North Vietnam into major concessions with the 1972 Christmas bombing. Fittingly, as US participation in the war ended, Fulbright spoke for southern dissenters and protestors. The SFRC chairman had castigated Linebacker I as "barbarous, inhumane, and obscene" and responded to Nixon's mining of Haiphong by sponsoring an unsuc-

cessful resolution condemning the "escalation of the war." Outraged by
Nixon's Christmas bombing, the Arkansas senator worried privately that
the president was "afflicted with some serious psychological problems."
Upon calling the SFRC into session on January 2, 1973, Fulbright assured
the press, "If some settlement is not reached by the 20th, then it is our
intention to employ legislative power to bring the war to a close."[64]

The threat of "open rebellion from both sides of the aisle" rendered
the growing restlessness of conservative southern Democrats particularly
ominous for Nixon and Kissinger as they sought a settlement with Hanoi.
The most important conservative Democrat, John Stennis, remained
representative of southern belligerence. As had been the case with Nixon's decisions to invade Cambodia and Laos, the SASC chair appears to
have received advance notice of the president's order to mine Haiphong.
Although Stennis continued to back Nixon, by December he concluded
that the United States had gone the "extra mile" and that South Vietnam
should assume primary responsibility for its fate. When Nixon and Kissinger pressured the reluctant President Thieu to accept the January 1973
deal with North Vietnam and the NLF, Stennis publicly made it "clear"
that the "Government of South Vietnam" should not "be an obstacle to
peace," and even John Tower told a CBS television audience, "If Saigon is
too stubborn and too unreasonable, we'll have to proceed independently."
Just as the Nixon White House had recognized the significance of Stennis's sponsorship of the War Powers Act, the Thieu administration could
hardly miss the importance of these warnings from two of the Senate's
most consistent and influential hawks. Like so many in Dixie, Stennis
and Tower had felt the war's agony and understood the feelings of their
constituents.[65]

Under intense US pressure and assured by Nixon that the United
States would respond forcefully if North Vietnam violated the settlement,
Thieu acquiesced. For all practical purposes, the US war in Vietnam
ended, as all American troops and prisoners returned by March. Both the
terms of the "peace" settlement and the decisive North Vietnamese–NLF
victory in April 1975 confirmed that the United States had neither won
nor secured peace with honor. As the United States exited Vietnam in
the spring of 1973, the NLF had been recognized as a legitimate political
entity in South Vietnam, and more than 150,000 NVA soldiers remained
south of the seventeenth parallel. By conceding on two of the most persis-

tent US war aims, the Nixon administration escaped from the disastrous conflict, but it also helped lay the groundwork for the ultimate communist triumph.[66]

Perhaps fittingly, Lyndon Johnson died on January 22, 1973, one day before the agreement with North Vietnam was signed, an agreement that Johnson, like Dean Rusk, would have no doubt deemed a US "surrender." In a sympathetic appraisal, the *Dallas Morning News* echoed LBJ's lament of having been "treated unfairly by a powerful minority of Eastern journalists" and noted the irony of his passing "when the peace he sought so diligently" was "imminent." Johnson's very southern provincialism, heightened concern for honor and manhood, belief in executive domination of foreign policy, and Christian determination to aid the lowly in the United States and Vietnam had contributed directly to the nation's disastrous intervention and escalation of the war, and he had embodied the nation's and the South's subsequent anguish. He had truly agonized over the fate of "his" troops and had sincerely felt a "sense of personal responsibility" for American casualties. As the war had ground on, an exasperated Johnson observed, "Vietnam is like being in a plane without a parachute when all the engines go out. If you jump, you'll probably be killed, and if you stay in you'll crash and probably burn." In short, as he had concluded more succinctly, "I can't get out. I can't finish with what I've got. So what the hell do I do?" As his health declined precipitously after 1969 and he endured exile on his beloved ranch in the Texas Hill Country, a perceptive journalist described Johnson's final years: "The most militant civil-rights advocate ever to occupy the White House, reviled by Negro militants; a Southerner scorned by Southerners as a turn-coat; a liberal despised by liberals despite the fact he achieved most of what they had sought for thirty years; a friend of education, rejected by intellectuals; a compromiser who could not compromise a war ten thousand miles away." The journalist might have added that the war and its domestic impact had been crucial to Johnson's alienation from all of these groups.[67]

Although William Fulbright, Johnson's foremost southern critic on the war, would live until 1995, Vietnam contributed directly to his political demise in 1974, when he lost by 65 to 35 percent in the Democratic primary to Dale Bumpers, Arkansas's popular young governor. As Fulbright's constituent correspondence had revealed over the previous decade, the senator's opposition to the war, charges of US imperialism, and uneasiness with US militarism blatantly defied majority opinion in Arkansas and the South. Even as Arkansas had tired of the war, too many of its citizens had also tired of Fulbright's foreign policy jeremiads and habitual dissent. The senator had been right about the war, but his caustic messages also served as a "living and breathing rebuke" to Arkansans and their southern perceptions of the Cold War and US foreign relations.[68]

As had been true for Albert Gore in Tennessee and Ralph Yarborough in Texas, opposition to the war in Vietnam was not the sole reason for Fulbright's defeat. He too had failed to maintain his political fences at home. Arkansans admired Fulbright's "honesty and integrity" and his "brilliance of intellect." They also complimented his courage for having the "guts to disagree with LBJ." But many of his constituents felt ignored. They had come to view the senator with some justification as an "Oxford-educated snob who rarely visited his home state, and who did so only grudgingly." Fulbright had lost touch with the lives and trials of many of his constituents, and he had grown bored with campaigning and could no longer muster the fire and determination to ward off an energetic and attractive young challenger. Fulbright's biographer, Randall Woods, succinctly concluded, "His head was not in the race," and the senator candidly agreed: "I rather think the decision of the voters may have been correct. I got into a rut."[69]

Although Fulbright's dissent had defied majority southern opinion and helped end his political career, most of the issues he raised have continued to be debated. Kissinger and Nixon had gained the administration's goal of a "decent interval" between America's military withdrawal and South Vietnam's fall two years later. But departing in this fashion failed to yield the national security advisor's prediction that after "a year or two . . . no one will give a damn." Much to the contrary, Vietnam, by prompting seemingly endless debate, has become the "war that never ends." Southern responses to the war and its outcome have made revealing contributions to that debate. As the *Louisville Courier-Journal* correctly observed, southerners, like Americans more generally, received the January 1973 agreement with "sighs of relief rather than cheers of jubilation." In its January 25 editorial and another three days later, entitled "What Have We Learned in Vietnam?" the *Courier-Journal* identified many of the issues voiced by southern dissenters over the previous nine years: the dubious morality of destroying Vietnam, the war's destructive effects at home, the worldwide influence of nationalism versus communism, containment's doubtful applicability in Southeast Asia, and whether the United States exited the conflict with its honor intact.[70]

While opposing the war, Senators Fulbright, Gore, and Cooper, Reverend King, and fellow southern dissenters had expressed pointed opinions on these issues. Dixie's most assertive Senate doves and even Reverend King had initially approved the US effort to contain communism, only to gradually reject that strategy in Vietnam. By the early 1960s, both Fulbright and Gore recognized that the communist threat was hardly monolithic; and applying such a concept to the Vietnam War became particularly dubious as President Nixon pursued détente with China and the Soviet Union in 1972. By the mid-1960s, the two maverick senators had also concluded that no US vital or national security interests were threatened in Vietnam. Like King, an even more outspoken dissenter, they recognized the force of nationalism in Vietnam and the developing world and the difficulty, if not futility, of attempting to combat former colonial subjects pursuing their freedom. Given these international realities, Fulbright, Gore, and King rejected containment as the cornerstone of US Cold War foreign policy. Fulbright decried the "universalized" application of containment, which had led to numerous ill-advised US commitments to aid other nations, none more catastrophic than in Vietnam, where US intervention had led to "disaster in Southeast Asia and demoralization at home." Fulbright, Gore, Cooper, and ultimately even numerous southern hawks decided that the disproportionate growth of presidential power and the erosion of Congress's role in declaring and making war had abetted the American commitment in Vietnam and the subsequent conduct of the war. Hence the need for the War Powers Act and the "maintenance of a strong and independent" congressional voice to avoid "executive dictatorship." Fulbright, Cooper, Robert Eckhardt, Claude Pepper, and particularly King and other black opponents of the war also concurred with Gore's conclusion that the national obsession with Vietnam had led to "despair here at home, and a disastrous postponement of imperative programs to improve our social ills." The SFRC chairman expressed even greater apprehension "that neither constitutional government nor democratic freedoms" could "survive indefinitely in a country chronically at war," and he found Vietnam and the associated Cold War militarism at the heart of this threat.[71]

Addressing their region's persistent concern for national and personal honor, antiwar southerners had long argued that admitting the terrible mistake of intervening in Vietnam, a point on which even many of Dixie's hawks agreed by the war's end, was the most honorable course. Although hardly a dove, Lieutenant General Hal Moore, one of Dixie's most distinguished Vietnam soldiers, provided additional perspective. Although he declared American soldiers had often been "noble, selfless, and honorable," Moore rejected the idea that Vietnam had been a "noble" war. Rather, there had "never been a noble war except in the history books and propaganda movies." Vietnam, like virtually all wars, was a "bloody, dirty, cruel, costly mistake" whose origins were "rooted in the failure of diplomacy and poor judgment [of] national leaders." Dixie's doves agreed and were also convinced that US intervention and conduct in Vietnam had been immoral. King spoke for both African American and white opponents of the war when he declared that the war "mutilates the conscience" and defiled US "principles and values"; and Fulbright advised a prowar constituent that taking the "lives of Asian peoples indiscriminately" could hardly "be considered a Christian doctrine." Concurring with such assessments, Frazier Woolard, the rural North Carolina attorney and outspoken critic of the war, deemed American policies and actions not just immoral but also criminal. By focusing on the latter, Woolard anticipated subsequent critics who have emphasized the murderous effects of US strategies and technology on North and South Vietnamese civilians.[72]

To oppose the war, prominent southern dissidents had challenged dominant Cold War American attitudes and Dixie's majority perspectives on US foreign relations and Vietnam. As noted above, considerations of both morality and honor had influenced these opponents of the war. In addition, Dixie's antiwar critics had often acquired more cosmopolitan, less provincial views through education: Fulbright at Oxford, Cooper at Yale and Harvard, Pepper at Harvard, and Spong at the University of Edinburgh; via national contacts and involvements: journalists Harry Ashmore and William Baggs through their editorial duties and association with the California-based Center for the Study of Democratic Institutions; as a result of intellectual curiosity and personal contacts: Frazier Woolard's wide reading and ongoing personal communication with a South Vietnamese diplomat; or as a function of personal experiences, particularly racial ones, and some combination of the above influences: Martin Luther King Jr.'s civil rights work, study of Gandhi's teachings, and appreciation for anticolonialism, and similar religious and racial considerations for Muhammad Ali and Julian Bond. Several of these antiwar southerners, such as Fulbright, Cooper, and Pepper, embraced Wilsonian internationalism, which they interpreted as calling for international cooperation and security, national self-determination, and the pursuit of peaceful solutions rather than the United States' unilateral, forceful interventions to impose its will abroad. Southern dissidents, such as Fulbright, Gore, Cooper, Pepper, Eckhardt, Wollard, and even William Spong, based on his opposition to the dominant Byrd organization in Virginia, were often mavericks personally or politically. Antiwar southerners, particularly Democrats Gore, Pepper, and Eckhardt and Republicans Cooper and Morton, were also frequently more liberal on domestic issues than their southern, prowar counterparts or viewed US military interventions with a skepticism worthy of their Populist-Progressive forebears. This was particularly true of Gore, Pepper, and less well-known skeptics, such as Brady Gentry from Texas. Indeed, Gore, Cooper, Fulbright, and the Vietnam veteran and subsequent antiwar novelist Gustav Hasford had all grown up in mountainous areas of the South characterized by persistent political independence and dissent. Finally, dissenters often drew on their interpretations of southern history to arrive at antiwar positions. Fulbright epitomized this process by citing the North's domination of the South during Reconstruction and his region's subsequent experience as an economic colony as injurious examples of flawed imperial policies that should not be applied in Vietnam.

The majority of southerners rejected these antiwar arguments and reached decidedly different conclusions far more consistent with longstanding regional views on US foreign relations. Even more than Americans from other regions, southerners were unwilling to accept an assessment that portrayed the nation blundering into an ill-advised war and thereafter acting in immoral or criminal ways. Instead, while adopting various stab-in-the-back explanations for the war's outcome, the bulk of southerners deemed the war both moral and winnable. Convinced of the necessity of enforcing containment against atheistic communists and upholding national honor and national commitments such as SEATO, Dixie's residents were less willing than other Americans to consider US military intervention in Vietnam a mistake. Although Stennis, Russell,

Ervin, Talmadge, and other conservative Democrats responded to the war's mounting unpopularity and Dixie's agony and war weariness by emphasizing their opposition to dispatching ground troops, their commitment to national honor and credibility precluded effective opposition to the war or its funding. Once the nation's flag had been committed, honor and the imperatives of Cold War credibility took precedence over prior mistakes or strategic calculations.

For these conservative Democrats, hawkish Republicans such as Strom Thurmond and John Tower, and the majority of their prowar constituents, the war's immorality resided in the nation's ordering its soldiers into battle without a clear mission to win, the unwillingness to employ all available conventional weapons effectively, and the shame associated with reneging on US commitments to safeguard South Vietnamese independence. Failing to win, Tower asserted, was "an even bigger mistake than getting involved in Vietnam in the first place." Just as most southerners were untroubled by the war's morality, they were not distressed that the conflict diverted attention and resources from domestic projects they deemed unnecessary and overly expensive. Although southern hawks occasionally complained that their tax dollars were being wasted in Vietnam, they far more vehemently opposed spending on the Great Society or civil rights reforms. Rather than lamenting the loss of domestic reform opportunities, prowar southerners' greatest demand on the home front was the restoration of law and order and the suppression of civil rights and antiwar protestors.[73]

In an argument that anticipated subsequent assertions that Vietnam had been a "necessary" war, Russell Long was unwilling "to admit we were wrong. At a minimum," he asserted, US actions had "delayed the Communist timetable for a decade in Southeast Asia" and allowed "the newly emerging nations a chance" to grow stronger. Time for South Vietnam, according to the *New Orleans Times-Picayune*, to secure a "'reasonable chance' for its independent survival." A bit more restrained in his claims for the possible benefits from US involvement, Stennis added that the United States could "at least hope that the fortitude we have shown and punishment we have inflicted on . . . North Vietnam—will give others some pause before they go on the road of conquest." Long also refused to concede that US honor had been sullied. The war had "ended honorably, because in the difficult hours . . . the majority" of Americans had "refused to heed a vocal minority who wanted our country to turn and run from its responsibilities." Ironically, while sounding dovish themes, Herman Talmadge articulated another argument for absolving the United States of guilt and avoiding blemishes to its honor. As Hanoi prevailed militarily in 1975, the Georgia senator contended, "no amount of American money or equipment" could have saved a nation whose people lacked "the will and the motivation to defend themselves." After the United States turned the battle over to the South Vietnamese, they lost "because their army was in disarray, their political institutions had crumbled, and their people were panic-stricken."[74]

With fewer doubts about the rationale for fighting in Vietnam and little inclination to admit the war's immorality, southern hawks were equally unwilling to accept responsibility for the war's outcome. Instead, they readily proffered various stab-in-the-back explanations for why a winnable war had been lost. Dixie's prowar politicians and public agreed with John Stennis that the US military had fought with fatal, civilian-imposed "limitations and restrictions . . . so serious that in effect we fought with one hand tied behind our backs." Blocked from bombing North Vietnam effectively, mining Haiphong harbor, or eliminating enemy sanctuaries in North Vietnam, Cambodia, and Laos, the US military "simply could not win." The *Montgomery Advertiser* agreed, "we didn't win the war—although we could have," if "winning had been our goal" and if "we had fought as we know how to fight, reducing North Vietnam to rubble." Dean Rusk, one of the primary civilians who had helped devise and implement Johnson's much-maligned limited-war strategy, offered no apologies for his "role in Vietnam"; instead, he found other culprits on whom to blame the war's loss. Dissident congressmen and antiwar protestors had encouraged Hanoi to refuse compromise and "stick it out" against a divided United States. Southern supporters of the war agreed with Rusk on this point and joined him, Stennis, Thurmond, Long, and Tower in castigating Dixie's dissidents for prolonging the war, endangering American troops, and impeding military progress. While echoing Stennis's charges of unwise civilian interference in military matters, General Westmoreland criticized the American people's injurious impatience and agreed with President Johnson's charge that the US press corps had misrepresented the war's progress and thereby eroded popular support. Thus, the majority of southerners came to terms with defeat by clinging tenaciously to the belief that the war had been both justifiable and win-nable. By adopting these perspectives, Dixie's majority "generally refused to join in the self-flagellation that became almost a national pastime as the United States backed out of Southeast Asia."[75]

Building on these assumptions, southern hawks derived lessons from the war that differed markedly from those of Dixie's doves. John Tower joined a host of southerners in castigating the gradual escalation of mili-tary force. For Russell Long, Vietnam demonstrated that once the nation decided on war, "You ought to use all the power at your command . . . because the American people were not going to stand for a long war." The *Dallas Morning News* approvingly contrasted the ostensible success of Nixon's "long ball" tactic of the "sudden dramatic strike, launched with great force," with Johnson's "gradualist methods." Led by Stennis and Tal-madge, southern conservatives concurred with dissenters that Cold War foreign policy had led to US overcommitment in places such as Vietnam and that Congress had abdicated too much of its authority over mak-ing the commitments and waging war. In January 1973 Talmadge hoped that America had "finally learned her lesson and will stop trying to be a banker, Santa Claus, and policeman for the entire world." Stennis stopped far short of questioning the basic concept of containment, but he too asserted that the United States needed to be much more selective in its application. US "manpower and resources" would not allow for aiding "every Asian nation any time it is confronted with a Communist threat."[76]

The SASC chairman also concluded that the absence of a formal dec-laration of war had undermined popular support for the military effort and impaired the nation's recognition of the Vietnam War's importance. Therefore, "U.S. military forces should be committed abroad *only* after *Congress* had given its approval." Hence his sponsorship of the War Pow-ers Act. Compared to Fulbright, Cooper, and Spong, he was relatively less interested in keeping the nation out of wars and more concerned with enhancing the nation's war-making capacity. If Congress declared war straightforwardly, the nation would be given a clear "signal" of the con-flict's significance and prompt Americans to "support their country sol-idly." But even as Stennis favored Congress reasserting its war power, he continued to adhere to the South's inclination to grant the president con-siderable "latitude" in foreign policy, "some room to maneuver and the authority to . . . use what used to be called 'gunboat diplomacy.'" The

Mississippi senator and the majority of southerners remained emblematic of the region most supportive of defense spending and peace through strength: "Peace" could "be secure," he asserted, "only if we have the military power to maintain it."[77]

Historians have contended that the US experience in Vietnam ended the nation's "victory culture" and deflated America's "Foundation Myth," along with the accompanying assumptions of national innocence, destiny, exceptionalism, and invincibility. In the midst of the war, C. Vann Woodward, the foremost contemporary historian of the South, spoke eloquently to these very issues. He cited his region's experiences with poverty, evil in the form of slavery and racial segregation, defeat in war, and colonial domination and humiliation, all of which contrasted with the nation's unparalleled success and accompanying myths of "innocence and virtue," "overwhelming sense of righteousness," and confidence in the "invincibility of American arms." Woodward hoped the South's history might inform the nation and result in a more restrained foreign policy grounded in greater empathy and understanding for the remainder of the world.[78]

Ironically, Woodward's hopes went unrealized for most southerners. Instead, the South was the American region most convinced of the war's anticommunist rationale and legitimacy, least willing to question US morality or use of massive technology and force, and most convinced that the war could and should have been won. Indeed, the sense of national invincibility, innocence, and exceptionalism that allegedly perished in the jungles of Vietnam survived most intact in Dixie. In these crucial responses to the war, as well as the South's war-related experiences and involvement over the previous two decades, place mattered greatly in Dixie's role in this disastrous US military intervention—just not in the ways Woodward would have preferred.

Therefore, placing the South, the nation's most prowar region, at the center of this analysis, rather than on the periphery, provides an additional but often underutilized methodological approach for understanding America's involvement in Vietnam. It also responds to the call for examining the local origins and impacts of America's Cold War foreign policies. In the wake of the Korean War, conservative southern Democrats had voiced perceptive objections to direct US military intervention in Vietnam; but once American troops were on the ground, they and a majority of their constituents provided both Presidents Johnson and Nixon indispensable support for the war. This support was also apparent from southern students, soldiers, and newspapers. Grounded in distinctive regional perceptions and attitudes regarding honor, patriotism, religion, race, politics, and economic interests, Dixie's prowar stance affords insight into why the United States intervened militarily, conducted combat operations for more than a decade, and had great difficulty in acknowledging defeat.

Assessing the South's crucial importance to America's involvement in Vietnam goes beyond aggregate regional responses to the war. Lyndon Johnson and Dean Rusk were key actors in the decisions for massive US military intervention and the persistent US refusal to reach a compromise settlement; Richard Russell, John Stennis, Russell Long, Sam Ervin, Mendel Rivers, Edward Hebert, George Mahon, and their conservative southern Democratic colleagues and southern Republicans such as John Tower and Strom Thurmond pressured LBJ to prosecute the war more aggressively, rendered substantive peace negotiations more difficult, assured the necessary war funding, and cast decisive votes against end-the-war legislation during the Nixon presidency; William Westmoreland oversaw the war through most of the Johnson years and devised or approved the ruinous search-and-destroy and attrition strategies and the accompanying application of devastating US technology against both the communist enemies and Vietnamese civilians. Although these and other southerners' guiding geopolitical assumptions did not differ markedly from those of prowar Americans residing in other regions, Dixie's public figures, like the bulk of their constituents, acted from concerns over personal honor, credibility, and manhood; vocal patriotism; proclivities for military service and solutions; dedication to peace through military strength; and religion-based opposition to communism that were more pronounced than those of Americans hailing from other parts of the country.

As the nation moved toward war in 1964 and 1965, politics and personality were appropriately critical in the responses of leaders from the nation's most solidly Democratic region and the section in which personal relations were so deeply valued. Despite prescient reservations among southern Democrats as ideologically diverse as Richard Russell, John Stennis, Allen Ellender, William Fulbright, John Sherman Cooper, Claude Pepper, and Albert Gore Sr., they all fell in line behind their southern Democratic president and former Senate colleague. And powerful committee chairs, such as Russell and Fulbright, refused to raise public objections to growing US involvement in part because of their long-standing personal friendship with the president.

Despite the South's consequential prowar, even bellicose, role, Dixie was far from a uniform backer of the war. Fulbright, Gore, Cooper, and King were among the most dogged critics of the war. Together with other antiwar public figures, they helped make dissent respectable while formulating and propounding powerful antiwar arguments that filtered down over time to a growing minority of the southern and American public. Their dissent helped restrain both Johnson's and Nixon's most aggressive inclinations; and they, like southern student protestors, kept the war's issues before the southern public. These public figures and other less prominent ones—such as Frazier Woolard and Suzy Post; southern antiwar papers, such as the *Louisville Courier-Journal,* the *Texas Observer,* and after 1971 the *Atlanta Constitution;* and southern citizens through their letters to editors and their political representatives—protested the war in spite of hostile responses from Dixie's prowar majority.

Protest proved an especially sensitive matter for southern African Americans, who bore a disproportionate burden of combat service and death but, along with the majority of Dixie's blacks, hoped that this service would lead to more equitable treatment at home. According to historian Daniel Lucks, Vietnam was the most divisive issue of the twentieth century in the black community. The majority of the South's African American papers remained supportive of the war during the Johnson years while clinging to hopes of ongoing racial progress at home, but southern blacks were far more skeptical of the conflict than their white neighbors. King and Muhammad Ali, America's two most well-known African Americans, graphically embodied and voiced this skepticism and, significantly, grounded their opposition to the war in racial and religious reasoning. As was true of white student protestors, King, Ali, and antiwar critics from SCLC, SNCC, and CORE prompted a harsh backlash from the majority of southern whites, a backlash that ironically contributed to Nixon's election as president and the prolonging of the war.[79]

Even as the South's belligerence and protests had important influences on the nature and course of US involvement in Vietnam, the war-related agony took its toll in Dixie. This agony was apparent among Dixie's soldiers, both black and white, who fought and died in Vietnam in numbers that significantly surpassed the region's percentage of the national population. Public polling, letters to representatives in Washington and to newspapers, the increasing themes of pain and loss in country music, and the experiences of southern mothers and wives of the region's soldiers and prospective soldiers graphically demonstrated this agony. And perhaps most important, southern Democrats such as Herman Talmadge, Everett Jordan, and even Sam Ervin and John Stennis began to waver in their support for the war or go into outright opposition, while Fulbright and Cooper remained in the forefront of congressional opposition to the conflict and were poised in January 1973 to lead yet another attempt to cut off war funding. By the end of 1972, both Nixon and Kissinger had expressed urgent concern over the possible defection of conservative southern Democrats from the prowar ranks and the likelihood that end-the-war legislation would be approved. Just as southerners had been at the center of decisions leading to US intervention in Vietnam, they remained exceedingly consequential as the war ended. Place still mattered, and the South's belligerence, protest, and agony provide instructive insights into the role of regionalism in US foreign relations and the local, even personal, experiences that accompanied America's most disastrous and divisive Cold War military intervention. In a fitting epitaph for the war, a final, disillusioned assessment that both Dixie's hawks and doves might have embraced, albeit for different reasons, a Mississippi veteran declared Vietnam was much "like the Confederacy, . . . a lost cause" with "thousands of people dying for nothing."[80]

Acknowledgments

Since aspects of this book have been in the works for more than two decades, I have accumulated numerous personal and professional debts. I am pleased to have the opportunity to acknowledge them.

Working productively in the mammoth senatorial collections and other manuscripts cited in this book would have been virtually impossible without the expert guidance of the resident archivists. From Virginia and North Carolina to Mississippi, Arkansas, and Texas, I was treated with genuine southern hospitality and consistently directed to sources I would have otherwise missed. Among those uniformly capable professionals, Sheryl B. Vogt, director of the Richard B. Russell Jr. Library for Political Research and Studies at the University of Georgia, and Kathryn Stallard, the director of Special Collections and Archives at Southwestern University, were especially helpful. They not only guided me through the Russell, Talmadge, and Tower papers but also helped me devise a viable approach for utilizing and citing constituent correspondence.

The photographs that illustrate this book were drawn from the John C. Stennis Collection housed at the Congressional and Research Center at Mississippi State University, the Prints and Photographs Division of the Library of Congress, the Lyndon Baines Johnson Library and Museum, and the US Senate Historical Office. The vast U.S. News and World Report Magazine Collection at the Library of Congress and Yoichi Okamoto's brilliant photographs at the LBJ Library were especially valuable; and Heather L. Moore, the photo historian in the Senate Historical Office, graciously met with me and suggested several excellent photographs, particularly those of Senator John Tower visiting Vietnam.

Before completing my thanks to library professionals, I must also thank my University of Nevada, Las Vegas (UNLV), colleagues in the Interlibrary Loan Office (ILL). Now headed by Richard Zwiercan, the

ILL staff secured microfilm versions of most of the southern daily papers and student papers consulted for this study and delivered numerous books with amazing speed via the LINK service.

ILL aid was only a portion of UNLV's extensive institutional support for this project. UNLV travel funds furnished variously by the History Department, the College of Liberal Arts, the University Research Grants and Fellowship Committee, and the University Travel Committee paid for trips to collections and for significant portions of the materials duplicated from those collections. A sabbatical for the Spring 2012 semester and a research fellowship from the Beverly Rogers, Carol C. Harter Black Mountain Institute for Fall 2012 (which reduced my teaching obligation to one course) afforded the requisite time for completing a viable draft of the manuscript.

As has been the case since my arrival at UNLV in 1975, the History Department provided an environment highly conducive to scholarship. My colleagues, with their emphasis on collegiality, mutual support, and teaching and research (rather than extraneous issues and petty bickering), have played a crucial role in my completing this book. Four chairs, Hal Rothman, Gene Moehring, David Wrobel, and David Tanenhaus, consistently endorsed crucial research trips and enjoyable, strategic teaching schedules. David W. helped me better understand the intellectual concept and historical persistence of domestic regionalism; and David T. perceptively read portions of the manuscript, patiently endured my commentary on the publishing process, and responded with excellent advice. He, along with College of Liberal Arts dean Chris Hudgins and university executive vice president and provost John Vallery White, also allowed me to keep my office while completing the manuscript.

A host of other historians graphically illustrate the validity of Kenny Rogers's and Dolly Parton's assertion that "you can't make old friends." Tennant S. McWilliams, one of the first scholars to explore the South and US foreign relations, has been a constant source of personal and intellectual support since he welcomed me into his home in Birmingham in 1982. John Ernst shared research materials from the David Morris Collection at East Tennessee State University. Colin Loader has not read a single word of this book, but he has improved it immensely by critiquing all of the major themes over the cheap red wine and French fries we share every Friday afternoon. Tom Wright, another treasured UNLV friend and colleague, advised me wisely in 1975 that it was imperative to have an intellectual life that stretched beyond the campus and Las Vegas and has subsequently occupied an adjacent office over the ensuing forty years. Tom plowed through the entire manuscript, offering keen substantive and editorial insights. Jeff Matthews, my highly accomplished former MA student and current holder of a named chair at the University of Puget Sound, also read the entire manuscript and once again reveled and excelled in his role as editor and critic. Anyone writing on Vietnam is exceedingly fortunate to have George Herring critique their work, but George's many kindnesses, sage advice, and valued friendship since we first met in 1980 have extended far beyond his informed and insightful assessment of this manuscript. I owe a similar personal and professional debt to Ed Crapol, who also read and commented incisively on all aspects of this project, as he has graciously done with virtually everything I have written since the mid-1980s. Since our first lunch in 1984, when he harassed me about the pink "starter" wine I ordered, our ongoing conversations about US foreign relations have had a far-reaching influence on my scholarship and teaching. Even more important, Ed has been a great friend without whom my life as a historian would have been far less rich and enjoyable.

I am also delighted to have had the opportunity to publish this book with the University Press of Kentucky (UPK). Appropriately, for a relationship that has yielded a book about Vietnam, I met Steve Wrinn, the UPK director, at a party in George and Dottie Herring's backyard. From our first discussions about this project, Steve has been unfailingly supportive and has overseen every step of the publication process in a timely and uniformly professional manner. As a part of that process, he secured two excellent, anonymous reviewers whose assessments of the manuscript were highly informed and marked by specific and most helpful questions and suggestions. Collectively, these readers and the friends noted above have markedly improved the book, and I suspect they would have had an even more positive impact had I followed all of their advice. Allison Webster, an acquisitions editor and Steve's executive assistant at UPK, has been exceedingly helpful with technical matters and has consistently kept me informed regarding all aspects of the manuscript's place in the publication queue. My interactions with Ila McEntire, the senior editing supervisor, and Mack McCormick, the publicity and rights manager, have been equally pleasant and productive. Last, but certainly not least, UPK assigned the manuscript to Carol Sickman-Garner, whose expert copyediting markedly enhanced the book's quality. Given this exceptional level of treatment, I hope *The American South and the Vietnam War* measures up to Steve's and his colleagues' enthusiasm for the project.

Finally, as has been the case over our nearly five decades together, my most profound gratitude goes to my wife, Sandy. I would like to thank her again for her unstinting love and support and for making me a better person and a better father. This love and support were most recently evident as she cheerfully endorsed my going to the office four or five days a week to complete the writing and revisions of this manuscript, all during the first six months of my ostensible retirement. In return for that forbearance and for the joy she has brought to my life over the past forty-eight years, this book is dedicated to Sandy.

Notes

Abbreviations

Note on the use of initials for identifying constituent correspondence: After conferring with several archivists regarding the privacy expectations of persons writing to public officials, I have opted to use initials for those correspondents when their identity could be easily tied to the language being quoted or when that language might prove embarrassing. In all other instances, I have included their names. I have also operated on the assumption that the sentiments being expressed were more revealing and significant than their individual identities. Should a reader require the name of a particular correspondent to check the accuracy or validity of my work, I shall be happy to provide that information.

AHEC	US Army History and Education Center
CD	*Cavalier Daily*
CQA	*Congressional Quarterly Almanac*
CR	*Congressional Record*
DR	*Daily Reville*
GOI	*Gallup Opinion Index*
RB	*Red and Black*
SFRC	Senate Foreign Relations Committee
TTU	Texas Tech University
WHCSFM	White House Central Files, Staff Member and Office Files

Introduction

1. Carl Degler, "Thesis, Antithesis, and Synthesis: The South, the North, and the Nation," *Journal of Southern History* 53 (Feb. 1987): 6, 17; Peter Trubowitz, *Defining the National Interest: Conflict and Change in American Foreign Policy* (Chicago: University of Chicago Press, 1998), 4, 12; Paul Boyer, "Foreword," in *Local Consequences of the Global Cold War*, ed. Jeffrey A. Engel (Stanford, CA: Stanford University Press, 2008), xv. For an extended discussion of the influence of domestic regionalism on US foreign policy, see Joseph A. Fry, "Place Matters: Domestic Regionalism and the Formation of American Foreign Policy," *Diplomatic History* 36 (June 2012): 451–82, with commentaries, 483–514.

2. Michael Perman, *Pursuit of Unity: A Political History of the American South* (Chapel Hill: University of North Carolina Press, 2009), 1. See also Nicol C. Rae, *Southern Democrats* (New York: Oxford University Press, 1994), 38, 65–66, 96–98; Adam J. Berinsky, *In Time of War: Understanding American Public Opinion from World War II to Iraq* (Chicago: University of Chicago Press, 2009), 7, 127.

3. *Gallup Opinion Index* (hereafter cited as *GOI*) (July 1965–Feb. 1973), cited in Joseph A. Fry, *Dixie Looks Abroad: The South and U.S. Foreign Relations, 1989–1973* (Baton Rouge: Louisiana State University Press, 2002), 269–70.

4. Bruce J. Schulman, *From Cotton Belt to Sunbelt: Federal Policy, Economic Development, and the Transformation of the South, 1938–1980* (Durham, NC: Duke University Press, 1994), 142 ("fortress Dixie").

5. Thomas J. McCormick, "Drift or Mastery? A Corporatist Synthesis for American Diplomatic History," in *The Promise of American History: Progress and Prospects*, ed. Stanley I. Kutler and Stanley N. Katz, *Reviews in American History* 10 (Dec. 1982): 326; Michael H. Hunt, *Lyndon Johnson's War: America's Cold War Crusade in Vietnam, 1945–1968* (New York: Hill and Wang, 1996), 105; Jeff Woods, *Richard Russell: Southern Nationalism and American Foreign Policy* (Lanham, MD: Roman and Littlefield, 2007), 39, 114.

6. For a bibliographical discussion of recent work by historians of the South on the region and US foreign policy, see Fry, "Place Matters," 451–52n2.

7. Robert David Johnson, "Congress and the Cold War," *Journal of Cold War Studies* 3 (Spring 2001): 76; Robert David Johnson, *Congress and the Cold War* (New York: Cambridge University Press, 2006); William Conrad Gibbons, *The U.S. Government and the Vietnam War: Executive and Legislative Relationships*, 4 vols. (Princeton, NJ: Princeton University Press, 1986–1995); Robert Mann, *A Grand Delusion: America's Descent into Vietnam* (New York: Basic Books, 2001); Andrew L. Johns, *Vietnam's Second Front: Domestic Politics, the Republican Party, and the War* (Lexington: University Press of Kentucky, 2010); Mark David Carson, "Beyond the Solid South: Southern Members of Congress and the Vietnam War" (PhD diss., Louisiana State University, 2003).

8. Robert J. McMahon, "The Study of American Foreign Relations: National History or International History?" in *Explaining the History of American Foreign Relations*, ed. Michael J. Hogan and Thomas G. Paterson (New York: Cambridge University Press, 1991), 16 ("internal determinants"); Jeffrey A. Engel and Katherine Carte Engel, "Introduction: On Writing the Local within Diplomatic History—Trends, Historiography, Purpose," in Engel, *Local Consequences of the Global Cold War*, 2–3; Mark Philip Bradley and Marilyn B. Young, eds., *Making Sense of the Vietnam War: Local, National, and Transnational Perspectives* (New York: Oxford University Press, 2008).

9. Fredrik Logevall, *Choosing War: The Lost Chance for Peace and the Escalation of War in Vietnam* (Berkeley: University of California Press, 1999), 304 ("stealth"); Sandra Scanlon, *The Pro-War Movement: Domestic Support for the Vietnam War and the Making of Modern Conservatism* (Amherst: University of Massachusetts Press, 2013), 10 ("popular confusion"); Johns, *Vietnam's Second Front*, 8, 336.

10. John Prados, *Vietnam: The History of an Unwinnable War, 1945–1975* (Law-

rence: University Press of Kansas, 2009), 167; Melvin Small, *Johnson, Nixon, and the Doves* (New Brunswick, NJ: Rutgers University Press, 1988), 157.

11. Edward L. Ayers and Peter S. Onuf, "Introduction," in *All Over the Map: Rethinking American Regions,* ed. Edward L. Ayers, Patricia Nelson Limerick, Stephen Nissenbaum, and Peter S. Onuf (Baltimore, MD: Johns Hopkins University Press, 1996), 9; Trubowitz, *Defining the National Interest,* 4; Richard Franklin Bensel, *Sectionalism and American Political Development, 1880–1980* (Madison: University of Wisconsin Press, 1984), xix, 25; David M. Wrobel, *Promised Lands: Promotion, Memory, and the Creation of the American West* (Lawrence: University Press of Kansas, 2002), 12; Clyde A. Milner II, "The View from Wisdom: Region and Identity in the Minds of Four Westerners," *Montana: The Magazine of Western History* 41 (Summer 1991): 2–17; David M. Emmons, "Constructed Province: History and the Making of the Last American West," *Western Historical Quarterly* 25 (Winter 1994): 442, 452.

12. For the ongoing vitality of regionalism, see Michael C. Steiner and David M. Wrobel, "Many Wests: Discovering a Dynamic Western Regionalism," in *Many Wests: Place, Culture, and Regional Identity,"* ed. Michael C. Steiner and David M. Wrobel (Lawrence: University Press of Kansas, 1997), 1–30; and Robert L. Dorman, *Hell of a Vision: Regionalism and the Modern American West* (Tucson: University of Arizona Press, 2012). For strong objections to the idea of southern exceptionalism or an overly distinctive South, see Laura F. Edwards, "Southern History as U.S. History," *Journal of Southern History* 75 (Aug. 2009): 533–64; and Matthew D. Lassiter and Joseph Crespino, "Introduction: The End of Southern History," in *The Myth of Southern Exceptionalism,* ed. Matthew D. Lassiter and Joseph Crespino (New York: Oxford University Press, 2010), 3–23.

1. Regionalism, Southerners, and US Foreign Relations, 1789–1973

1. Perman, *Pursuit of Unity,* 1, 45. For the importance of a region's one-party dominance in influencing foreign policy, see Edward W. Chester, *Sectionalism, Politics, and American Diplomacy* (Metuchen, NJ: Scarecrow Press, 1975), iii–vi, 274. For an extended discussion of the impact of domestic regionalism on US foreign policy, see Fry, "Place Matters." Interestingly, Perman cites the US Senate as the "heart of the South's national operations, in effect its department of foreign affairs" in competing with other American regions (*Pursuit of Unity,* 235). This builds on V. O. Key Jr., who wrote in 1949 that the Solid South employed the Democratic Party as its "instrument for the conduct of 'foreign affairs' of the Solid South with the rest of the nation." See V. O. Key Jr., with the assistance of Alexander Heard, *Southern Politics in State and Nation* (New York: Vintage Books, 1949), 315.

2. William J. Cooper Jr. and Thomas E. Terrill, *The American South: A History* (New York: McGraw Hill, 2002), 54 ("liberty"); Jack P. Greene, "The Role of the Lower Houses of Assembly in Eighteenth Century Politics," *Journal of Southern History* 27 (Nov. 1961): 451–74; T. H. Breen, *Tobacco Culture: The Mentality of the Great*

Tidewater Planters on the Eve of the Revolution (Princeton, NJ: Princeton University Press, 1985), 134. For a more extended assessment of the South and US foreign policy from 1789 through 1865, see Fry, *Dixie Looks Abroad,* 1–105.

3. Cooper and Terrill, *American South,* 92 ("From 1776"); Kenneth S. Greenberg, *Masters and Statesmen: The Political Culture of American Slavery* (Baltimore, MD: Johns Hopkins University Press, 1985), 87 ("condition").

4. Bertram Wyatt-Brown, *Southern Honor: Ethics and Behavior in the Old South* (New York: Oxford University Press, 1982), 17, 34, 191 ("courage," "efficacious means"), 360 ("antagonist"), 366–67; Bertram Wyatt-Brown, "The Ethic of Honor in National Crises: The Civil War, Vietnam, Iraq, and the Southern Factor," *Journal of the Historical Society* 5 (2005): 431–60; David Hackett Fischer, *Albion's Seed: Four British Folkways in America* (New York: Oxford University Press, 1989), 803, 843 ("warrior ethic"); Greenberg, *Masters and Statesmen,* 23–41.

5. Drew R. McCoy, *The Elusive Republic: Political Economy in Jeffersonian America* (New York: W. W. Norton, 1982); Lance Banning, *The Jeffersonian Persuasion: Evolution of a Party Ideology* (Ithaca, NY: Cornell University Press, 1978); Lacy K. Ford, "Republican Ideology in a Slave Society: The Political Economy of John C. Calhoun," *Journal of Southern History* 54 (Aug. 1988): 405–24; Cathy Matson and Peter S. Onuf, "Toward a Republican Empire: Interest and Ideology in Revolutionary America," *American Quarterly* 37 (Fall 1985): 496–531.

6. Peter S. Onuf, "Federalism, Republicanism, and the Origins of American Sectionalism," in Ayers et al., *All over the Map,* 13, 15; Peter S. Onuf, "Thomas Jefferson and the Origins of American Sectionalism" (paper presented at the Southern Historical Association Meeting, Atlanta, GA, Nov. 6, 1997), 8; Peter S. Onuf, *Jefferson's Empire: The Language of American Nationhood* (Charlottesville: University of Virginia Press, 2000), 7, 69–70, 73–75, 107. New Englanders also equated their regional perspective on foreign relations with the appropriate national one. See Paul A. Varg, *New England and Foreign Relations, 1789–1850* (Hanover, NH: University Press of New England, 1983); David C. Hendrickson, *Union, Nation, or Empire: The American Debate over International Relations, 1789–1941* (Lawrence: University Press of Kansas, 2009), 25.

7. Fry, *Dixie Looks Abroad,* 12–36; Norman K. Risjord, "1812: Conservatives, War Hawks, and the Nation's Honor," *William and Mary Quarterly,* 3rd series, 18 (Apr. 1961): 205 (Clopton); Roger Brown, *The Republic in Peril: 1812* (New York: W. W. Norton, 1971), 45–46 (Monroe); Fischer, *Albion's Seed,* 843 ("honor and warrior ethic"); J. C. A. Stagg, *Mr. Madison's War: Politics, Diplomacy, and Warfare in the Early Republic, 1783–1830* (Princeton, NJ: Princeton University Press, 1983), 78, 115.

8. Adam Rothman, *Slave Country: American Expansion and the Origins of the Deep South* (Cambridge, MA: Harvard University Press, 2005), 166 ("real estate"), 168 (Mississippi editor); John Craig Hammond, *Slavery, Freedom, and Expansion in the Early Republic* (Charlottesville: University of Virginia Press, 2007), 6 ("federal authority"), 170; John Craig Hammond and Matthew Mason, eds., *Contesting Slav-*

ery: The Politics of Bondage and Freedom in the New American Nation (Charlottesville: University of Virginia Press, 2011). For the purchase more generally, see Alexander DeConde, *This Affair of Louisiana* (New York: Scribner, 1976); McCoy, *Elusive Republic,* 195–208; Robert W. Tucker and David C. Hendrickson, *Empire of Liberty: The Statecraft of Thomas Jefferson* (New York: Oxford University Press, 1990), 87–135; Richard H. Immerman, *Empire for Liberty: A History of American Imperialism from Benjamin Franklin to Paul Wolfowitz* (Princeton, NJ: Princeton University Press, 2010). For Florida and the Spanish borderlands, see Frank Lawrence Owsley Jr. and Gene A. Smith, *Filibusters and Expansionists: Jeffersonian Manifest Destiny* (Tuscaloosa: University of Alabama Press, 1997); J. C. A. Stagg, *Borderlines and Borderlands: James Madison and the Spanish-American Frontier, 1776–1821* (New Haven, CT: Yale University Press, 2009).

9. Robert V. Remini, *Andrew Jackson and the Course of American Empire, 1767–1821* (New York: Harper and Row, 1977), 306, 331, 335; Anthony F. C. Wallace, *The Long, Bitter Trail: Andrew Jackson and the Indians* (New York: Hill and Wang, 1993); Fry, *Dixie Looks Abroad,* 45–49.

10. Arthur H. De Rosier Jr., *The Removal of the Choctaw Indians* (Knoxville: University of Tennessee Press, 1970), 109 (*Charleston Southern Patriot*); Reginald Horsman, *Race and Manifest Destiny: The Origins of American Racial Anglo-Saxonism* (Cambridge, MA: Harvard University Press, 1981), 98–116, 190–207; John Campbell, "The Seminoles, the 'Bloodhound War,' and Abolitionism, 1796–1865," *Journal of Southern History* 72 (May 2006): 272–73; Reginald Horsman, "American Indian Policy and Manifest Destiny," *University of Birmingham Historical Journal* 11 (1968): 128–40.

11. Robert Pierce Forbes, *The Missouri Compromise and Its Aftermath: Slavery and the Meaning of America* (Chapel Hill: University of North Carolina Press, 2007), 44 ("rhetorical"); Michael A. Morrison, *Slavery and the American West: The Eclipse of Manifest Destiny and the Coming of the Civil War* (Chapel Hill: University of North Carolina Press, 1997), 50 (Walker); Robert Kagan, *Dangerous Nation: America's Place in the World from Its Earliest Days to the Dawn of the Twentieth Century* (New York: Alfred A. Knopf, 2006), 223 (imperial competition); Robert E. May, "Epilogue to the Missouri Compromise: The South, the Balance of Power, and the Tropics in the 1850s," *Plantation Society* 1 (June 1979): 201–25.

12. Tim Matthewson, *A Proslavery Foreign Policy: Haitian-American Relations during the Early Republic* (Westport, CT: Praeger, 2003), 25 (Washington); Timothy M. Matthewson, "George Washington's Policy toward the Haitian Revolution," *Diplomatic History* 3 (Summer 1979): 327 (Washington); Charles C. Tansill, *The United States and Santo Domingo, 1798–1873: A Chapter in Caribbean Diplomacy* (1938; rpt., Gloucester, MA: Peter Smith, 1967), 105 (Epps); Ashli White, *Encountering Revolution: Haiti and the Making of the Early Republic* (Baltimore, MD: Johns Hopkins University Press, 2010), 142–43, 145, 163–65.

13. Thomas R. Hietala, *Manifest Design: Anxious Aggrandizement in Late Jacksonian America* (Ithaca, NY: Cornell University Press, 2003).

14. Gregory S. Hospodor, "'Bound by all the ties of honor': Southern Honor, the Mississippians, and the Mexican War," *Journal of Mississippi History* 61 (Spring 1999): 6.

15. William W. Freehling, *Secessionists at Bay, 1776–1854,* vol. 1 of *The Road to Disunion* (New York: Oxford University Press, 1990–2007), 437, 553; Douglas A. Ley, "Expansionists All? Southern Senators and American Foreign Policy, 1841–1860" (PhD diss., University of Wisconsin, 1990), 123; John H. Schroeder, *Mr. Polk's War: American Opposition and Dissent, 1846–1848* (Madison: University of Wisconsin Press, 1973), 53, 55; Morrison, *Slavery and the American West,* 74.

16. Freehling, *Secessionists at Bay,* 461 (Stephens), 462 (Calhoun); William J. Cooper Jr., *The South and the Politics of Slavery, 1828–1856* (Baton Rouge: Louisiana State University Press, 1978), 239 (Pickens).

17. Don E. Fehrenbacher, completed and edited by Ward M. McAfee, *The Slaveholding Republic: An Account of the United States Government's Relations to Slavery* (New York: Oxford University Press, 2001), 127 (Brown); William Earl Weeks, *Building the Continental Empire: American Expansion from the Revolution to the Civil War* (Chicago: Ivan R. Dee, 1996), 163 (Lincoln). For southern expansionism and the Caribbean, see Robert E. May, *The Southern Dream of a Caribbean Empire, 1854–1861* (Athens: University of Georgia Press, 1989).

18. Fehrenbacher, *Slaveholding Republic,* 111; Wyatt-Brown, "Ethic of Honor in National Crises," 433 ("honor"); Morrison, *Slavery and the American West,* 255 ("platform"), 259 ("manhood"), 260 ("foreign"); Paul Quigley, *Shifting Grounds: Nationalism and the American South, 1848–1865* (New York: Oxford University Press, 2012), 55, 58, 62, 107.

19. Edward L. Ayers, *The Promise of the New South: Life after Reconstruction* (New York: Oxford University Press, 1992), 187; Joseph A. Fry, *John Tyler Morgan and the Search for Southern Autonomy* (Knoxville: University of Tennessee Press, 1992), 47; Perman, *Pursuit of Unity,* 117–81.

20. For the South and US foreign relations from 1865 through 1912, see Fry, *Dixie Looks Abroad,* 106–38; Tennant S. McWilliams, *The New South Faces the World: Foreign Affairs and the Southern Sense of Self, 1877–1950* (Baton Rouge: Louisiana State University Press, 1988), 1–88; Marshall E. Schott, "The South and American Foreign Policy, 1894–1904: Regional Concerns during the Age of Imperialism" (PhD diss., Louisiana State University, 1995); Marshall E. Schott, "The South and American Foreign Policy, 1894–1900: New South Prophets and the Challenge of Regional Values," *Southern Studies* 4 (Fall 1993): 295–308; Patrick J. Hearden, *Independence and Empire: The New South's Cotton Mill Campaign, 1865–1901* (DeKalb: Northern Illinois University Press, 1982).

21. Thomas H. Coode, "Southern Congressmen and the American Naval Revolution, 1880–1898," *Alabama Historical Quarterly* 30 (Fall–Winter 1968): 99 (Oates); Trubowitz, *Defining the National Interest,* 51 (Oates); Leonard Schlup, "Hernando De Soto Money: War Advocate and Anti-Imperialist, 1898–1900," *Journal of Mississippi History* 60 (Winter 1998): 329, 332; McWilliams, *New South Faces the World,*

38 (*Charleston News and Courier*); Thomas J. Osborne, *"Empire Can Wait": American Opposition to Hawaiian Annexation, 1893–1898* (Kent, OH: Kent State University Press, 1981), 37 (*Wilmington Morning Star*); Edwina C. Smith, "Southerners on Empire: Southerner Senators and Imperialism, 1898–1899," *Mississippi Quarterly* 31 (Winter 1977–1978): 99 (Daniel); William F. Holmes, *The White Chief: James Kimble Vardaman* (Baton Rouge: Louisiana State University Press, 1970), 82.

22. Fry, *John Tyler Morgan*, 63, 73. In addition to the sources cited in note 21, see Daniel S. Margolies, *Henry Watterson and the New South: The Politics of Empire, Free Trade, and Globalization* (Lexington: University Press of Kentucky, 2006); and James M. Lindgren, "The Apostasy of a Southern Anti-Imperialist: Joseph Bryan, The Spanish-American War and Business Expansion," *Southern Studies* 2 (Summer 1991): 151–78.

23. William J. Schellings, "The Advent of the Spanish-American War in Florida, 1898," *Florida Historical Quarterly* 39 (Apr. 1961): 311–29; Francis Butler Simkins, *Pitchfork Ben Tillman: South Carolinian* (Baton Rouge: Louisiana State University Press, 1944), 352–53, 363, 365–68.

24. Gaines M. Foster, *Ghosts of the Confederacy: Defeat, the Lost Cause, and the Emergence of the New South, 1865–1913* (New York: Oxford University Press, 1987), 145–49; Charles R. Wilson, *Baptized in Blood: The Religion of the Lost Cause, 1865–1920* (Athens: University of Georgia Press, 1980).

25. Kristin L. Hoganson, "The 'Manly' Ideal of Politics and the Imperialist Impulse: Gender, U.S. Political Culture, and the Spanish-American and Philippine-American Wars" (PhD diss., Yale University, 1995), 146 (Call); Kristin L. Hoganson, *Fighting for American Manhood: How Gender Politics Provoked the Spanish-American and Philippine-American Wars* (New Haven, CT: Yale University Press, 1998); Richard E. Wood, "The South and Reunion, 1898," *Historian* 31 (May 1969): 416 (*Lynchburg News*).

26. Willard B. Gatewood Jr., *Black Americans and the White Man's Burden, 1898–1903* (Urbana: University of Illinois Press, 1973), 23–34, 29 ("brave lynchers"), 185 (Mitchell), 190 (Washington); Willard B. Gatewood, "A Negro Editor on Imperialism: John Mitchell, 1898–1901," *Journalism Quarterly* 49 (Spring 1972): 48. See also Lawrence S. Little, *Disciples of Liberty: The African Methodist Episcopal Church in the Age of Imperialism, 1884–1916* (Knoxville: University of Tennessee Press, 2000); and Pieto Gleijeses, "African Americans and the War against Spain," *North Carolina Historical Review* 78 (Apr. 1996): 184–214.

27. Arthur S. Link, "Woodrow Wilson: The American as Southerner," *Journal of Southern History* 36 (Feb. 1970): 4, 13. See also Anthony Gaughan, "Woodrow Wilson and the Legacy of the Civil War," *Civil War History* 43 (Sept. 1997): 225–42.

28. David M. Kennedy, *Over Here: The First World War and American Society* (New York: Oxford University Press, 1980), 95.

29. For the South and Wilson's foreign policies, see Fry, *Dixie Looks Abroad*, 139–74; Robert H. Block, "Southern Opinion of Woodrow Wilson's Foreign Policies, 1913–1917" (PhD diss., Duke University, 1967); Timothy G. McDonald,

"Southern Democratic Congressmen and the First World War, August 1914–April 1917: The Public Record of Their Support for or Opposition to Wilson's Policies" (PhD diss., University of Washington, 1962).

30. Gary Gerstle, "Race and Nation in the Thought and Politics of Woodrow Wilson," in *Reconsidering Woodrow Wilson: Progressivism, Internationalism, War, and Peace,* ed. John Milton Cooper Jr. (Baltimore, MD: Johns Hopkins University Press, 2008), 93–123.

31. Wesley Phillips Newton, "'Tenting Thoughts on the Old Camp Grounds': Alabama's Military Bases in World War I," in *The Great War in the Heart of Dixie: Alabama during World War I,* ed. Martin T. Olliff (Tuscaloosa: University of Alabama Press, 2008), 41–65, 43 ("immense"); Catherine A. Lutz, *Home Front: A Military City and the American Twentieth Century* (Boston: Beacon Press, 2001), 24, 26, 29; Henry C. Ferrell Jr., "Regional Rivalries, Congress, and MIC: The Norfolk and Charleston Navy Yards, 1913–20," in *War, Business, and American Society: Historical Perspectives on the Military-Industrial Complex,* ed. Benjamin Franklin Cooling (Port Washington, NY: Kinnikat Press, 1977), 59–72; George B. Tindall, *Emergence of the New South, 1913–1945* (Baton Rouge: Louisiana State University Press, 1967), 54–55; Richard L. Watson Jr., "Principle, Party and Constituency: The North Carolina Congressional Delegation, 1917–1919," *North Carolina Historical Review* 56 (July 1979): 307, 313–17; Bruce A. Beauboeuf, "War and Change: Houston's Economic Ascendancy during World War I," *Houston Review* 14 (1992): 89–112; James F. Fickle, "Defense Mobilization in the Southern Pine Industry: The Experience of World War I," *Journal of Forest History* 22 (Oct. 1977): 222.

32. Block, "Southern Opinion of Woodrow Wilson's Foreign Policies," 54 (Harrison), 64 (Walker), 302 (Larsen); Anthony Gaughan, "Woodrow Wilson and the Rise of Militant Interventionism in the South," *Journal of Southern History* 65 (Nov. 1999): 785–86 (Wilson); Roger E. Carey, "Woodrow Wilson's Principled Preaching on U.S. Foreign Relations, 1913–1917" (MA thesis, University of Nevada, Las Vegas, 2003), 80 (Wilson); C. R. Wilson, *Baptized in Blood,* 172 (McKim).

33. Arthur E. Barbeau and Florette Henri, *The Unknown Soldiers: Black American Troops in World War I* (Philadelphia: Temple University Press, 1974), 34–35, 90 ("shovel"), 100; Lee Kennett, "The Camp Wadsworth Affair," *South Atlantic Quarterly* 74 (Spring 1975): 210.

34. Wilson Fallin Jr., "Alabama's Black Baptist Leaders, the Progressive Era, and World War I," in Olliff, *Great War in the Heart of Dixie,* 66–80, 69 ("loyalty"); David Alsobrook, "A Call to Arms for African Americans during the Age of Jim Crow: Black Alabamians' Response to the U.S. Declaration of War in 1917," in Olliff, *Great War in the Heart of Dixie,* 81–100, 93 ("dutifully"); Jonathan S. Rosenberg, *How Far the Promised Land? World Affairs and the American Civil Rights Movement from the First World War to Vietnam* (Princeton, NJ: Princeton University Press, 2006), 35 (Johnson); Thomas Borstelmann, *The Cold War and the Color Line: American Race Relations in the Global Arena* (Cambridge, MA: Harvard University Press, 2001), 24 ("France"); William G. Jordan, *Black Newspapers and*

America's War for Democracy, 1914–1920 (Chapel Hill: University of North Carolina Press, 2001).

35. N. Gordon Levin Jr., *Woodrow Wilson and World Politics: America's Response to War and Revolution* (New York: Oxford University Press, 1968), 1 ("framework"); George C. Herring, *From Colony to Superpower: U.S. Foreign Relations since 1776* (New York: Oxford University Press, 2008), 379; Michael H. Hunt, *The American Ascendancy: How the United States Gained and Wielded Global Dominance* (Chapel Hill: University of North Carolina Press, 2007), 68.

36. Lloyd E. Ambrosius, *Wilsonianism: Woodrow Wilson and His Legacy in American Foreign Relations* (New York: Palgrave Macmillan, 2002), 34 ("very absolute"); Malcolm D. Magee, *What the World Should Be: Woodrow Wilson and the Crafting of a Faith-Based Foreign Policy* (Waco, TX: Baylor University Press, 2008), 6 ("believing"), 37; Carey, "Woodrow Wilson's Principled Preaching," 88 ("source"); Mark Benbow, *Leading Them to the Promised Land: Woodrow Wilson, Covenant Theology, and the Mexican Revolution, 1913–1915* (Kent, OH: Kent State University Press, 2010), 7–8 ("apostles of liberty"); Andrew Preston, *Sword of the Spirit, Shield of Faith: Religion in American War and Diplomacy* (New York: Knopf, 2012), 275–88.

37. Benbow, *Leading Them to the Promised Land*, 4 ("argument"); Magee, *What the World Should Be*, 37 ("religion and patriotism"); Samuel S. Hill, "Religion," in *Encyclopedia of Southern Culture*, ed. Charles Reagan Wilson and William Ferris (Chapel Hill: University of North Carolina Press, 1989), 1,269–74, 1,269 ("sole reference point"); David R. Goldfield, *Still Fighting the Civil War: The American South and Southern History* (Baton Rouge: Louisiana State University Press, 2002), 80–81, 84.

38. Ralph B. Levering, "Public Culture and Public Opinion: The League of Nations Controversy in New Jersey and North Carolina," in *The Wilson Era: Essays in Honor of Arthur S. Link*, ed. John Milton Cooper Jr. and Charles E. Neu (Arlington Heights, IL: Harlan Davidson, 1991), 185 (Charlotte mayor); Tindall, *Emergence of the New South*, 69 (Glass).

39. Elmo M. Roberds Jr., "The South and United States Foreign Policy, 1922–1952" (PhD diss., University of Chicago, 1954), 93 (*Atlanta Constitution*); Ambrosius, *Wilsonianism*, 33, 57; Lloyd E. Ambrosius, "Democracy, Peace, and World Order," in J. M. Cooper, *Reconsidering Woodrow Wilson*, 225, 227–28, 231, 239; George C. Herring and Gary R. Hess, "Regionalism and Foreign Policy: The Dying Myth of Southern Internationalism," *Southern Studies* 20 (Fall 1981): 247–77; Paul Seabury, *The Waning of Southern "Internationalism"* (Princeton, NJ: Princeton University Press, 1957). For the South and US foreign relations, 1920–1945, see Fry, *Dixie Looks Abroad*, 188–221.

40. Henry C. Ferrell Jr., *Claude A. Swanson of Virginia: A Political Biography* (Lexington: University Press of Kentucky, 1985), 171.

41. Alfred O. Hero Jr., *The Southerner and World Affairs* (Baton Rouge: Louisiana State University Press, 1965), 97–103; Fry, *Dixie Looks Abroad*, 204–7.

42. John Temple Graves, *The Fighting South* (New York: G. P. Putnam's Sons,

1943), 7 (Glass); George L. Grassmuck, *Sectional Biases in Congress on Foreign Policy* (Baltimore, MD: Johns Hopkins University Press, 1951), 152 ("more Democratic"); D. B. Hardeman and Donald C. Bacon, *Rayburn: A Biography* (Austin: Texas Monthly Press, 1987), 101, 228; Tennant S. McWilliams, "Jefferson, Wilson, and the Idea of the 'Militant' South, 1916–1945" (unpublished paper that Professor McWilliams generously shared with the author), 20–24.

43. George M. Fredrickson, *White Supremacy: A Comparative Study in American and South African History* (New York: Oxford University Press, 1981), 241 ("patriotism of race"); McWilliams, *New South Faces the World*, 90–92; Rorin M. Platt, "The Triumph of Interventionism: Virginia's Political Elite and Aid to Great Britain, 1939–1941," *Virginia Magazine of History and Biography* 100 (July 1992): 346, 353 (Glass, Byrd); Brent Tarter, *The Grandees of Government: The Origins and Persistence of Undemocratic Politics in Virginia* (Charlottesville: University of Virginia Press, 2013), 304 (Daniels).

44. Martha H. Swain, *Pat Harrison: The New Deal Years* (Jackson: University Press of Mississippi, 1978), 243; Robert Dallek, *Lone Star Rising: Lyndon Johnson and His Times, 1908–1960* (New York: Oxford University Press, 1991), 228; Schulman, *From Cotton Belt to Sunbelt*, 133 (*Business Week*).

45. Charles W. Johnson, "V for Virginia: The Commonwealth Goes to War," *Virginia Magazine of History and Biography* 100 (July 1992): 372–73; Dewey W. Grantham, *The South in Modern America: A Region at Odds* (New York: HarperCollins, 1994), 172–76; Tindall, *Emergence of the New South*, 694, 696–701; Sarah McCulloh Lemmon, *North Carolina's Role in World War II* (Raleigh, NC: State Department of Archives and History, 1964), 12, 20–23; John R. Skates Jr., "World War II as a Watershed in Mississippi History," *Journal of Mississippi History* 37 (May 1975): 131–42; Cooper and Terrill, *American South*, 667–69; Schulman, *From Cotton Belt to Sunbelt*, 92–102; Neil R. McMillen, ed., *Remaking Dixie: The Impact of World War II on the American South* (Jackson: University Press of Mississippi, 1977).

46. Numan V. Bartley, *The New South, 1945–1980* (Baton Rouge: Louisiana State University Press, 1995), 286, 444–45; Grantham, *South in Modern America*, 260–61; Cooper and Terrill, *American South*, 733–50.

47. Grantham, *South in Modern America*, 194–212, 247 ("traditional party"); Bartley, *New South*, 381–98.

48. For overviews of African Americans and US foreign relations in the postwar period, see Brenda Gale Plummer, *Rising Wind: Black Americans and U.S. Foreign Affairs, 1935–1960* (Chapel Hill: University of North Carolina Press, 1996); and Brenda Gale Plummer, *In Search of Power: African Americans in the Era of Decolonization, 1956–1974* (Cambridge, MA: Harvard University Press, 2013).

49. Randall B. Woods, *Fulbright: A Biography* (New York: Cambridge University Press, 1995), 126–27, 138; Hero, *Southerner and World Affairs*, 105; Ronald L. Heinemann, *Harry Byrd of Virginia* (Charlottesville: University of Virginia Press, 1996), 249; *Congressional Record*, 80th Cong., 1st sess. (Apr. 22, 1947), 3,793 (May 9, 1947), 4,975, 2nd sess. (Mar. 13, 1948), 2,793 (Mar. 31, 1948), 3,874–75 (here-

after cited as *CR*, Cong.:sess. [date]); Roberds, "South and United States Foreign Policy," 147–48, 155, 170–71; Irving Howards, "The Influence of Southern Senators on American Foreign Policy from 1939 to 1950" (PhD diss., University of Wisconsin, 1955), 93–94; Jeff Woods, *Black Struggle, Red Scare: Segregation and Anti-Communism in the South, 1948–1968* (Baton Rouge: Louisiana State University Press, 2004); Stephen J. Whitfield, *The Culture of the Cold War* (Baltimore, MD: Johns Hopkins University Press, 1996), 45.

50. William Inboden, *Religion and American Foreign Policy, 1945–1960: The Soul of Containment* (New York: Cambridge University Press, 2008), 4, 17, 21; Whitfield, *Culture of the Cold War,* 77, 80–81 (Graham). See also Rick L. Nutt, *Toward Peacemaking: Presbyterians in the South and National Security, 1945–1983* (Tuscaloosa: University of Alabama Press, 1994), 42–48.

51. Wayne Flynt and Gerald W. Berkley, *Taking Christianity to China: Alabama Missionaries in the Middle Kingdom, 1850–1950* (Tuscaloosa: University of Alabama Press, 1997), 13, 129–40, 320–30, 329 (Mao).

52. Schulman, *From Cotton Belt to Sunbelt,* 142 ("fortress Dixie"), 145 ("political alliance"); "Southern Militarism," *Southern Exposure* 1 (1973): 60–61; James Batten, "Why the Pentagon Pays Homage to John Cornelius Stennis," *New York Times Magazine,* Nov. 23, 1969, 163 (Rivers); David L. Carlton, "The American South and the U.S. Defense Economy: A Historical View," in *The South, the Nation, and the World: Perspectives on Southern Economic Development,* ed. David L. Carlton and Peter A. Coclanis (Charlottesville: University of Virginia Press, 2003), 160–61; Kari Frederickson, "Confronting the Garrison State: South Carolina in the Early Cold War Era," *Journal of Southern History* 72 (May 2006): 349–78; Kari Frederickson, *Cold War Dixie* (Athens: University of Georgia Press, 2013); Ann Markusen, Peter Hall, Scott Campbell, and Sabina Deitrick, *The Rise of the Gunbelt: The Military Remapping of Industrial America* (New York: Oxford University Press, 1991), 42, 47, 231–32, 239, 244–46, 251; Thomas Borstelmann, "The Cold War and the American South," in Engel, *Local Consequences of the Global Cold War,* 79–83.

53. Schulman, *From Cotton Belt to Sunbelt,* 147–49; William Barnaby Faherty, *Florida's Space Coast: The Impact of NASA on the Sunshine State* (Gainesville: University Press of Florida, 2002), xv, 15, 57, 115–16; Plummer, *In Search of Power,* 242–43.

54. Schulman, *From Cotton Belt to Sunbelt,* 109 ("military Keynesism"), 144; Will F. Huntley, "Mighty Rivers of Charleston" (PhD diss., University of South Carolina, 1993), 218–32, 237 ("most elaborately fortified patches"); R. D. Johnson, *Congress and the Cold War,* 159; Gilbert C. Fite, *Richard B. Russell Jr., Senator from Georgia* (Chapel Hill: University of North Carolina Press, 1991), 319.

55. Michael Lind, *Made in Texas: George W. Bush and the Southern Takeover of American Politics* (New York: Basic Books, 2003), 72 ("state capitalism"); Schulman, *From Cotton Belt to Sunbelt,* 135 (Faulkner), 144 (Keating); William E. Leuchtenburg, *The White House Looks South: Franklin D. Roosevelt, Harry S. Truman, Lyndon B. Johnson* (Baton Rouge: Louisiana State University Press, 2005), 409–10.

56. Thomas A. Becnel, *Senator Allen Ellender of Louisiana: A Biography* (Baton Rouge: Louisiana State University Press, 1995), 209; Dan T. Carter, *From George Wallace to Newt Gingrich: Race in the Conservative Counterrevolution, 1963–1994* (Baton Rouge: Louisiana State University Press, 1996), 7; Frank E. Smith, "Valor's Second Prize: Southern Racism and Internationalism," *South Atlantic Quarterly* 64 (Summer 1965): 299, 301, 303.

57. Ann K. Ziker, "Segregationists Confront American Empire: The Conservative White South and the Question of Hawaiian Statehood, 1947–1959," *Pacific Historical Review* 76 (Aug. 2007): 451, 455, 459–60.

58. Preston, *Sword of the Spirit, Shield of Faith*, 476; "Memorandum of Conversation," Donald Lesh and Governor George Wallace, Aug. 23, 1968, National Security File, Vietnam 7F (3), 4/68–10/68, box 102, Lyndon Baines Johnson Library and Museum, Austin, TX (hereafter cited as LBJ Library).

59. Fite, *Richard B. Russell Jr.*, 252; Becnel, *Senator Allen Ellender*, 188; Allen J. Ellender Oral History, Aug. 28, 1967, 28, John Fitzgerald Kennedy Library and Museum, Boston, MA (hereafter cited as JFK Library); Chester J. Pach and Elmo Richardson, *The Presidency of Dwight D. Eisenhower* (Lawrence: University Press of Kansas, 1991), 165 (Passman); Hero, *Southerner and World Affairs*, 203; Malcolm E. Jewell, *Senatorial Politics and Foreign Policy* (1962; rpt., Westport, CT: Greenwood Press, 1974), 24.

60. *GOI*, no. 3 (Aug. 1965), 14–15. The Gallup Poll defined the South as the eleven states of the Confederacy plus Kentucky and Oklahoma. See *Congressional Quarterly Almanac*, 89th Cong., 1st sess. (1965), 96, 462, 478–79 (quotes) (hereafter cited as *CQA*, Cong.:sess. [date]). The date in *CQA* indicates the year of coverage rather than the publication date; *CQA* page numbers containing a hyphen and *H* or *S* refer to tables of House and Senate votes collected at the end of each volume.

61. Seabury, *Waning of Southern "Internationalism,"* 23n42 (Smith); Hero, *Southerner and World Affairs*, 149–82; Alfred O. Hero Jr., "Changing Southern Attitudes toward U.S. Foreign Policy," *Southern Humanities Review* 8 (Summer 1974): 277–78.

62. Fite, *Richard B. Russell Jr.*, 353; Hero, *Southerner and World Affairs*, 101, 105; *GOI*, no. 26 (Aug. 1967), 7, no. 71 (May 1971), 23, no. 88 (Oct. 1972), 20, no. 93 (Mar. 1973), 10.

63. *CQA*, 88:1 (1963), 686, 90:1 (1967), 162–68, 4-S, 90:2 (1968), 19-S, 34-S, 457, 91:1 (1969), 13-S, 271 (quotes on ABM), 92:2 (1972), 589, 622–25, 62-S (Jackson amendment); George H. Gallup, *The Gallup Poll: Public Opinion, 1935–1971*, 3 vols. (New York: Random House, 1972), 3: 1,699, 1,837; R. B. Woods, *Fulbright*, 318–20, 519–25.

64. Hero, *Southerner and World Affairs*, 112–13, 240–41; Fite, *Richard B. Russell Jr.*, 253; Michael S. Downs, "A Matter of Conscience: John C. Stennis and the Vietnam War" (PhD diss., Mississippi State University, 1989), 15; *GOI*, no. 8 (Jan. 1966), 15, no. 17 (Oct. 1966), 16, no. 45 (Mar. 1969), 18, no. 65 (Nov. 1970), 9; Fry, *Dixie Looks Abroad*, 232–34.

65. Hero, *Southerner and World Affairs,* 125–26; Brian L. Crispell, *Testing the Limits: George Armistead Smathers and Cold War America* (Athens: University of Georgia Press, 1999), 159, 163; George A. Smathers Oral History, Oct. 24, 1989, 5–6, JFK Library; Huntley, "Mighty Rivers of Charleston," 197–99; R. B. Woods, *Fulbright,* 267–69.

66. Randall B. Woods, "Dixie's Dove: J. William Fulbright, the Vietnam War, and the American South," *Journal of Southern History* 60 (Aug. 1994): 548 ("Yankee"); *CQA,* 89:1 (1965), 517 (Fulbright and the resolution), 1,004–5; Randall B. Woods, *LBJ: Architect of American Ambition* (New York: Free Press, 2006), 622–34.

67. Borstelmann, *Cold War and the Color Line,* 77 (NAACP); James H. Cone, "Martin Luther King Jr. and the Third World," *Journal of American History* 74 (Sept. 1987): 462; Plummer, *Rising Wind,* 177, 184–85, 187, 206, 223, 296, 305 (King).

68. Michael L. Krenn, "'Unfinished Business': Segregation and U.S. Diplomacy at the 1958 World's Fair," *Diplomatic History* 20 (Fall 1999): 593 ("black-souled"); Thomas Borstelmann, "'Hedging Our Bets and Buying Time': John Kennedy and Racial Revolutions in the American South and Southern Africa," *Diplomatic History* 24 (Summer 2000): 443 (Kennedy); Paul G. Lauren, *Power and Prejudice: The Politics and Diplomacy of Racial Discrimination* (Boulder, CO: Westview Press, 1996), 244 (Rusk).

69. J. Woods, *Black Struggle, Red Scare;* J. Woods, *Richard Russell,* 31 (Russell); Borstelmann, "'Hedging Our Bets and Buying Time,'" 445 (Georgia sheriff).

70. Mary L. Dudziak, "The Little Rock Crisis and Foreign Affairs: Race, Resistance, and the Image of American Democracy," *Southern California Law Review* 70 (Sept. 1997): 1,685 (Talmadge, Eastland); Dan T. Carter, *The Politics of Rage: George Wallace, the Origins of the New Conservatism, and the Transformation of American Politics* (Baton Rouge: Louisiana State University Press, 1995), 161; Mary L. Dudziak, *Cold War Civil Rights: Race and the Image of American Democracy* (Princeton, NJ: Princeton University Press, 2002).

71. Robert J. McMahon, "Toward a Pluralist Vision: The Study of American Foreign Relations as International History and National History," in *Explaining the History of American Foreign Relations,* ed. Michael J. Hogan and Thomas G. Paterson (New York: Cambridge University Press, 2004), 37.

2. Southerners and the Vietnam Commitment, 1953–1964

1. Melvyn P. Leffler, *A Preponderance of Power: National Security, the Truman Administration, and the Cold War* (Stanford, CA: Stanford University Press, 1992), 143, 168.

2. George C. Herring, *America's Longest War: The United States and Vietnam, 1950–1975* (New York: McGraw Hill, 2014), 21 ("authority," zero-sum game). Unless otherwise noted, all Herring, *America's Longest War,* references are to the 2014 edition. For the other quotes, see John Lewis Gaddis, *Strategies of Containment: A Critical Appraisal of American National Security Policy during the Cold War* (New York: Oxford University Press, 2005), 89,

3. Gibbons, *U.S. Government and the Vietnam War*, 1: 139 ("rathole"); Fite, *Richard B. Russell Jr.*, 252 ("bleed"); Caroline F. Ziemke, "Senator Richard B. Russell and the 'Lost Cause' in Vietnam, 1954–1968," *Georgia Historical Quarterly* 72 (Spring 1988): 39 ("world policeman").

4. J. Woods, *Richard Russell*, 39, 41, 118; Gibbons, *U.S. Government and the Vietnam War*, 1: 139 ("criticism").

5. *CR*, 83:2 (Jan. 26, 1954), 789, 815–16.

6. *CR*, 83:2 (Feb. 9, 1954), 1,550–52.

7. *CR*, 83:2 (Feb. 9, 1954), 1,551 (Apr. 6, 1954), 4,681 (May 11, 1954), 6,360–61.

8. Gibbons, *U.S. Government and the Vietnam War*, 1: 258; *CR*, 83:2 (May 11, 1954), 6,361 (Long), 6,337 (Byrd).

9. Mann, *Grand Delusion*, 146.

10. Gibbons, *U.S. Government and the Vietnam War*, 1: 189–94, 93 (Johnson); Fite, *Richard B. Russell Jr.*, 358–59.

11. Mann, *Grand Delusion*, 111; *CR*, 83:1 (July 1, 1953), 7,779, 7,787 (Cooper).

12. R. B. Woods, *Fulbright*, 166 ("evacuation").

13. US Congress, Executive Sessions of the Senate Foreign Relations Committee, 83rd Cong., 2nd sess., vol. vi (Feb. 16, 1954), 143 (May 12, 1954), 274, 276, 279, http://congressional.proquest.com/congressional/docview/t29.d30.hrg-1965-for-0001?accountid=3611 (accessed Apr. 20, 2014).

14. *CR*, 83:2 (May 16, 1954), 7,193–95.

15. Prados, *Vietnam*, 35–38; Gibbons, *U.S. Government and the Vietnam War*, 1: 271–76.

16. Prados, *Vietnam*, 35–38; Gibbons, *U.S. Government and the Vietnam War*, 1: 271–76.

17. Herring, *America's Longest War*, 81–89; Marilyn B. Young, *The Vietnam Wars, 1945–1990* (New York: HarperPerennial, 1991), 61–81.

18. Gibbons, *U.S. Government and the War in Vietnam*, 1: 278 (Barkley and Byrd), 280 (Rivers); Carson, "Beyond the Solid South," 135 (Long and Thurmond). Thurmond switched to the Republican Party in 1964 following the passage of the 1964 civil rights bill.

19. Gibbons, *U.S. Government and the Vietnam War*, 1: 343; US Congress, Executive Sessions of the Senate Foreign Relations Committee Together with Joint Sessions with the Senate Armed Services Committee, 85th Cong., 1st sess., vol. ix (Jan. 2, 1957), 24 (Russell), (Feb. 12, 1957), 246, 295 (Russell), 296–97 (Ervin), http://congressional.proquest.com/congressional/docview/t29.d30.hrg-1957-for-0001?accountid=3611 (accessed Apr. 20, 2014).

20. Gibbons, *U.S. Government and the Vietnam War*, 1: 345; James M. Lindsay, *Congress and the Politics of U.S. Foreign Policy* (Baltimore, MD: Johns Hopkins Press, 1994), 27.

21. *CR*, 85:1 (Mar. 5, 1957), 3,129.

22. Gibbons, *U.S. Government in the Vietnam War*, 1: 346 (Stennis); *CR*,

85:1 (Aug. 5, 1958), 16,317–20 (Fulbright) 86: 2 (Apr. 29, 1960), 8,986–88 (Gore).

23. Prados., *Vietnam*, 65, 78–79; Herring, *America's Longest War*, 105–8.

24. Dallek, *Lone Star Rising*, 576 ("Texas steer"); Robert A. Caro, *The Years of Lyndon Johnson: The Passage of Power* (New York: Alfred A. Knopf, 2012), 95, 113–15.

25. R. B. Woods, *LBJ*, 380 ("insecure," "happy"); Leuchtenburg, *White House Looks South*, 291–92 (other quotes); Mitchell Lerner, "'A Big Tree of Peace and Justice': The Vice Presidential Travels of Lyndon Johnson," *Diplomatic History* 34 (Apr. 2010): 357–93.

26. Mann, *Grand Delusion*, 236 ("stump speech"), 238 ("won over"); Lerner, "'Big Tree of Peace and Justice,'" 391–93.

27. Gibbons, *U.S. Government and the Vietnam War*, 2: 41–42 ("Churchill"); Mann, *Grand Delusion*, 238 ("admirable qualities"); Stanley Karnow, *Vietnam: A History* (New York: Penguin Books, 1983), 214 ("only boy").

28. R. B. Woods, *LBJ*, 387.

29. *CR*, 90:1 (Sept. 28, 1967), 27,131 (Morton); Prados, *Vietnam*, 33.

30. Gibbons, *U.S. Government and the Vietnam War*, 2: 45–46; Mann, *Grand Delusion, passim.*

31. *CR*, 87:1 (June 29, 1961), 11,702–4; Gibbons, *U.S. Government and the Vietnam War*, 2: 30, 47–48; J. Woods, *Richard Russell*, 118–19.

32. Robert C. Hodges, "The Cooing of a Dove: Senator Albert Gore, Sr.'s Opposition to the War in Vietnam," *Peace and Change* 22 (Apr. 1997): 134; Albert Gore Sr., interview, Oct. 24, 1976, pp. 40–42, Southern Oral History Program, #4007, Louis Round Wilson Library, University of North Carolina at Chapel Hill.

33. Hodges, "Cooing of a Dove," 136; Kyle Longley, *Senator Albert Gore, Sr.: Tennessee Maverick* (Baton Rouge: Louisiana State University Press, 2004), 180.

34. Schulman, *From Cotton Belt to Sunbelt*, 145–46 ("alliance"); Lind, *Made in Texas*, 70–73; Leuchtenburg, *White House Looks South*, 409–10.

35. Rae, *Southern Democrats*, 38 (White); *CQA*, 88:2 (1964), 39–41, 49–50.

36. *CQA*, 89:2 (1966), 41, 50–51, 91:2 (1970), 38, 40, 49.

37. Mike Mantos to Lawrence O'Brien, Nov. 18, 1963, White House Staff Files: Lawrence O'Brien, box 19, JFK Library; F. Edward Hebert Oral History, July 15, 1969, p. 18, LBJ Library.

38. *Atlanta Constitution*, Mar. 5, 1966, Feb. 10, 1968; John C. Stennis, "Armed Forces Day Address," Meridian, MS, May 16, 1965, p. 3, Public Series, box 11, and Mary Shields, "Memorandum for the File," Jan. 8, 1986, series 37, box 25, both John C. Stennis Collection, Congressional and Political Research Center, Mississippi State University Libraries, Starkville (hereafter cited as Stennis Papers, series/box/folder [where applicable]).

39. Tower Newsletter, Nov. 21, 1965, box 973, folder 2, and "DOD Force Reductions in Texas Analyzed," Mar. 6, 1970, box 972, folder 16, both John G. Tower Papers, Special Collections, A. Frank Smith Jr. Library Center, Southwestern University, Georgetown, TX (hereafter cited as Tower Papers, box:folder).

40. J. Woods, *Fulbright,* 449; William C. Berman, *William Fulbright and the Vietnam War: The Dissent of a Political Realist* (Kent, OH: Kent State University Press, 1988), 82–83; Rivers to Fulbright, May 22, 1967, and Fulbright to Rivers, May 23, 1967, both series 48, box 52, folder 2, J. William Fulbright Papers, Special Collections, University of Arkansas Libraries, Fayetteville (hereafter cited as Fulbright Papers, box:folder; all subsequent cites are to series 48).

41. Schulman, *From Cotton Belt to Sunbelt,* 139–40, 142; "Southern Militarism," 60–93; Carlton, "American South and the U.S. Defense Economy," 151–62; Borstelmann, "Cold War and the American South," 79–83; Markusen et al., *Rise of the Gunbelt,* 42, 231–32, 239, 244–46, 251.

42. Herring, *America's Longest War,* 137–40 (quotes); Prados, *Vietnam,* 114–15.

43. George C. Herring, *LBJ and Vietnam: A Different Kind of War* (Austin: University of Texas Press, 1994), 16 (Clifford and Acheson); Lind, *Made in Texas,* 26 ("Deep South").

44. Hebert Oral History, July 15, 1969, p. 13, LBJ Library; Kent Germany, "'I'm Not Lying about That One': Manhood, LBJ, and the Politics of Speaking Southern," *Miller Center Report* 18 (Summer 2002): 32; Leuchtenburg, *White House Looks South,* 251, 288, 376 (other quotes).

45. Thomas G. Paterson, "Bearing the Burden: A Critical Look at JFK's Foreign Policy," *Virginia Quarterly Review* 54 (Spring 1978): 196 ("containment generation"); Transcript of Congressional Briefing, Feb. 16, 1965, p. 7, Congressional Briefings File, LBJ Library ("South Vietnam . . . Hawaii"); Eric F. Goldman, *The Tragedy of Lyndon Johnson* (New York: Knopf, 1969), 451 ("Munichs"); Robert Dallek, *Flawed Giant: Lyndon Johnson and His Times, 1961–1973* (New York: Oxford University Press, 1998), 100 ("Chinese"); Hunt, *Lyndon Johnson's War,* 79 ("yellow").

46. Wyatt-Brown, "Ethic of Honor in National Crises," 432, 441–42 (first three quotes); George C. Herring, "The Reluctant Warrior: Lyndon Johnson as Commander in Chief," in *Shadow on the White House: Presidents and the Vietnam War, 1945–1973,* ed. David L. Anderson (Lawrence: University of Kansas Press, 1993), 108 ("insecure man"); Doris Kearns Goodwin, *Lyndon Johnson and the American Dream* (New York: St. Martin's Griffin, 1991), 252–53 ("coward"); Waldo Heinrichs, "Lyndon B. Johnson: Change and Continuity," in *Lyndon Johnson Confronts the World: American Foreign Policy, 1963–1968,* ed. Warren I. Cohen and Nancy Bernkoff Tucker (New York: Cambridge University Press, 1994), 26 ("culture bound"); Goldman, *Tragedy of Lyndon Johnson,* 447 ("foreigners").

47. Goodwin, *Lyndon Johnson and the American Dream,* 251 ("woman"), 252 ("endless national debate"); R. B. Woods, *LBJ,* 597 ("damn conservatives"); Jeffrey Record, *The Wrong War: Why We Lost in Vietnam* (Annapolis, MD: Naval Institute Press, 1998), 9 ("great beast"); Herring, *America's Longest War,* 141 ("ass").

48. R. B. Woods, *LBJ,* 435, 385, 486–87; Preston, *Sword of the Spirit, Shield of Faith,* 505 ("devout without being doctrinaire").

49. R. B. Woods, *LBJ,* 436 ("peace through strength"); Hunt, *Lyndon Johnson's War,* 105 ("pissant"); Thomas J. Schoenbaum, *Waging Peace and War: Dean Rusk*

in the Truman, Kennedy, and Johnson Years (New York: Simon and Schuster, 1988), 431 ("sons of bitches").

50. Goldman, *Tragedy of Lyndon Johnson,* 489–90 ("only President"); Thruston B. Morton Oral History, Sept. 13, 1974, p. 10, LBJ Library; John Sparkman Oral History, Oct. 5, 1968, pp. 9–10, LBJ Library; Herring, "Reluctant Warrior," 97.

51. Lloyd C. Gardner, *Pay Any Price: Lyndon Johnson and the Wars for Vietnam* (Chicago: Ivan R. Dee, 1995), 228 ("not qualified"); Goldman, *Tragedy of Lyndon Johnson,* 490 ("Harvard"); Dallek, *Flawed Giant,* 86, 90 ("bigotry," "world statesman"); Harry S. Ashmore and William C. Baggs, *Mission to Hanoi: A Chronicle of Double-Dealing in High Places* (New York: Putnam, 1968), 174 ("sweet corn").

52. Thomas W. Zeiler, *Dean Rusk: Defending the American Mission Abroad* (Wilmington, DE: SR Books, 2000), 131 ("kind of world"); Alan K. Henrikson, "The Southern Mind in American Diplomacy," *Fletcher Forum* 13 (Summer 1989): 375–87.

53. Dean Rusk, as told to Richard Rusk, *As I Saw It* (New York: W. W. Norton, 1990), 296; Schoenbaum, *Waging Peace and War,* 411 ("good man"); Zeiler, *Dean Rusk,* 133 ("loyal").

54. Zeiler, *Dean Rusk,* 86, 313 ("U.N. kind of world"); Schoenbaum, *Waging Peace and War,* 423 ("honorable . . . and dishonorable"); Gaddis, *Strategies of Containment,* 201 ("periphery"); US Congress, Senate Committee on Foreign Relations, [Hearings on] *Supplemental Foreign Assistance: Fiscal Year 1966—Vietnam,* 89th Cong., 2nd sess. (Jan. 28–Feb. 18, 1966), 599; Dean Rusk, "Briefing for New Congressmen," Jan. 13, 1965, 2, and Dean Rusk, "Foreign Policy [News] Conference," May 22, 1967, 6, both in "Congressional Briefings on Vietnam," box 1, LBJ Library.

55. R. B. Woods, *LBJ,* 510 ("worth fighting for"); Herring, *America's Longest War,* 142 ("extricate"); Rusk, *As I Saw It,* 432.

56. Mann, *Grand Delusion,* 307.

57. Michael R. Beschloss, *Taking Charge: The Johnson White House Tapes, 1963–1964* (New York: Simon and Schuster, 1997), 88; *CR,* 88:2 (Mar. 25, 1964), 6,232 (June 23, 1964), 14,792.

58. Beschloss, *Taking Charge,* 95, 363–70; *CR,* 88:2 (Mar. 31, 1964), 6,630; Mann, *Grand Delusion,* 306; J. Woods, *Richard Russell,* 123–24; Fite, *Richard B. Russell Jr.,* 437 ("pull out").

59. Robertson to Lawrence F. O'Brien, Mar. 27, 1964, drawer 71, file 6, A. Willis Robertson Papers, Special Collections Research Center, Earl Gregg Swen Library, College of William and Mary, Williamsburg, VA (hereafter cited as Robertson Papers, drawer:file); Daniel T. Campbell, "Beyond George Ball: Doubts about American Intervention in the Vietnam Conflict, 1961–1965" (BA honors thesis, College of William and Mary, 1994), 41–47.

60. Becnel, *Senator Allen Ellender,* 202, 209, 248; *CR,* 88:2 (Mar. 4, 1964), 4,359, (May 13, 1964), 10,832.

61. *CR,* 87:2 (Feb. 21, 1962), 2,751 (Thurmond).

62. Mann, *Grand Delusion,* 345 (Rusk); R. B. Woods, *Fulbright,* 347 ("guys");

Johns, *Vietnam's Second Front,* 61 ("equivocation and vacillation"); R. B. Woods, *LBJ,* 516 ("indecisive").

63. *CR,* 88:2 (Aug. 7, 1964), 18,459.

64. Gibbons, *U.S. Government and the Vietnam War,* 2: 287, 311–13, 315.

65. *CR,* 88:2 (Aug. 7, 1964), 18,471.

66. *CR,* 88:2 (Aug. 6, 1964), 18,399, 18,400, 18,404 (Aug. 7, 1964), 18,462.

67. *CR,* 88:2 (Aug. 6, 1964), 18,403, 18,406–7 (Aug. 7, 1964), 18,462.

68. *CR,* 88:2 (Aug. 6, 1964), 18,410–11.

69. Robert Schulman, *John Sherman Cooper: The Global Kentuckian* (Lexington: University Press of Kentucky, 1976), 49–50 (staffer); *CR,* 88:2 (July 1, 1964), 15,672 (Aug. 6, 1964), 18,409, 18,417–18.

70. *CR,* 88:2 (Aug. 6, 1964), 18,416.

71. *CR,* 88:2 (Aug. 6, 1964), 18,412 (Ellender); Gibbons, *U.S. Government and the Vietnam War,* 2: 266, 308 (Siler), 310 (Alger).

72. *CR,* 88:2 (Aug. 6, 1964), 18,404 (Morton), 18,415 (Stennis), 18,420 (Thurmond), 18,432 (Sparkman), (Aug. 7, 1964), 18,461 (Smathers); Mann, *Grand Delusion,* 361 (Long).

73. Gibbons, *U.S. Government and the Vietnam War,* 2: 307–8 (Fascell); John Sherman Cooper Oral History, Aug. 9, 1993, 40, LBJ Library; Johns, *Vietnam's Second Front,* 70 (Cooper); Allen J. Ellender Oral History, July 30, 1969, p. 16, LBJ Library.

74. Robertson to James W. Green, Feb. 25, 1965, 76:21, Robertson Papers; J. William Fulbright, "The Legislator as Educator," *Foreign Affairs* 57 (Spring 1979): 725.

75. Joseph A. Fry, *Debating Vietnam: Fulbright, Stennis, and Their Senate Hearings* (Lanham, MD: Roman and Littlefield, 2006), 22; Gibbons, *U.S. Government and the Vietnam War,* 2: 334.

76. Jeffrey J. Matthews, "To Defeat a Maverick: The Goldwater Candidacy Revisited, 1963–1964," *Presidential Studies Quarterly* 27 (Fall 1997): 662–78.

77. Gardner, *Pay Any Price,* 119 ("get the bomb"), 131, 144 (NH and OK speeches); Matthews, "To Defeat a Maverick," 671 ("demagogue," "more guts"); R. B. Woods, *LBJ,* 547–49. For a more positive appraisal of Johnson's handling of Vietnam in the 1964 campaign, see Mitchell Lerner, "Vietnam and the 1964 Election: A Defense of Lyndon Johnson," *Presidential Studies Quarterly* 25 (Fall 1995): 751–66.

78. Gardner, *Pay Any Price,* 153; Herring, *America's Longest War,* 155–56.

79. Gallup, *Gallup Poll: Public Opinion,* 3: 1882; *Montgomery Advertiser,* Aug. 7, 1964.

80. *Atlanta Constitution,* Aug. 4, 1964; *New Orleans Times-Picayune,* Aug. 5, 6, 1964; *Charlotte Observer,* Aug. 6, 1964, quoted in *CR,* 88:2 (Aug. 7, 1964), 18,464; *Dallas Morning News,* Aug. 6, 1964.

81. *Louisville Courier Journal,* Aug. 4, 1964; *Atlanta Constitution,* Aug. 6, 1964; *New Orleans Time-Picayune,* Aug. 5, 1964, quoted in *CR,* 88:2 (Aug. 7, 1964), 18,462–63; *Charlotte Observer,* Aug. 6, 1964, quoted in *CR,* 88:2 (Aug. 7, 1964), 18,464; *Dallas Morning News,* Aug. 6, 1964.

82. *Louisville Courier-Journal*, Aug. 6, 9, 1964; *Atlanta Constitution*, Aug. 8, 1964; *Charlotte Observer*, Aug. 6, 1964, quoted in *CR*, 88:2 (Aug. 7, 1964), 18,464.

83. *Atlanta Constitution*, Aug. 1, 1964; Ralph McGill, "Viet Nam and Nuclear Arms," *Atlanta Constitution*, Aug. 6, 1964; *Richmond News Leader*, quoted in *Montgomery Advertiser*, Oct. 22, 1964.

84. J. C. P. to Tower, Aug. 5, 1963, 284:7, and T. E. M. to Tower, Nov. 10, 1963, 284:5, both Tower Papers; W. F. D. to John Sparkman, Jan. 23, 1964, and G. C. S. Jr. to Sparkman, May 21, 1964, both series 66A677, box 8, John J. Sparkman Papers, W. S. Hoole Special Collections Library, University of Alabama, Tuscaloosa (hereafter cited as Sparkman Papers, series:box); C. I. L. to Yarborough, July 14, 1964, box 42d675, folder: August 7, 1964, Ralph W. Yarborough Papers, Briscoe Center for American History, University of Texas, Austin (hereafter cited as Yarborough Papers, box:folder); W. F. to Richard Russell, July 2, 1964, series 16, box 41, folder 11, Richard B. Russell Jr. Papers, Richard B. Russell Library for Political Research and Studies, University of Georgia, Athens (hereafter cited as Russell Papers, box:folder; all subsequent cites are to series 16).

85. Mrs. I. J. W. to President of the United States, Nov. 1, 1964, box B32, folder 1, Albert Gore Sr. Senate Papers, Albert Gore Research Center, Middle Tennessee State University, Murfreesboro (hereafter cited as Gore Papers, box:folder).

86. F. K. F. to Yarborough, July 29, 196[4], 42d657:Aug. 9, 1964, Yarborough Papers; R. B. S. Jr. to Tower, Oct. 1, 1963, 285:4, Tower Papers; J. L. R. to Thruston Morton, Oct. 9, 1963, box 22, Thruston Morton Papers, Special Collections, Margaret I. King Library, University of Kentucky, Lexington (hereafter cited as Morton Papers).

87. Hugh B. Hester to Gore, July 29, 1964, with enclosure, "United States Aid: Helpful or Harmful?" pp. 2–3, B32:1, Gore Papers.

88. E. L. to Tower and Yarborough, Oct. 2, 1963, 284:2, Tower Papers.

89. Hiram H. Hiltz to Sam Ervin, Mar. 19, 1964, series 1, box 97, folder 4336, J. Samuel Ervin Jr. Papers, #3847, Southern Historical Collection, Louis Round Wilson Library, University of North Carolina at Chapel Hill (hereafter cited as Ervin Papers, box folder; all subsequent cites are to series 1); Aline T. Calendine to Sparkman, Apr. 29, 1964, 66A677:8, Sparkman Papers; Mrs. W. K. Zeis to Russell, Aug. 6, 1964, and Myron T. Roach to Russell, July 21, 1964, both 41:11, Russell Papers; Harry Wierson to Gore, Mar. 14, 1964, B32:1, Gore Papers.

90. R. B. Woods, *LBJ*, 597 (Russell); Mann, *Grand Delusion*, 380–81 (Russell); Carson, "Beyond the Solid South," 240 (Fulbright).

3. Southerners and the Decisions for War, 1965–1966

1. Herring, *America's Longest War*, 166, 179–80, 188; Prados, *Vietnam*, 115–16; Gregory A. Daddis, *Westmoreland's War: Reassessing American Strategy in Vietnam* (Chapel Hill: University of North Carolina Press, 2014), 60.

2. Michael S. Sherry, *In the Shadow of War: The United States since the 1930s* (New Haven, CT: Yale University Press, 1995), 254 ("outhouse").

3. Larry Berman, "Waiting for Smoking Guns: Presidential Decision-Making and the Vietnam War, 1965–1967," in *Vietnam as History: Ten Years after the Peace Accords,* ed. Peter Braestrup (Washington, DC: University Press of America, 1984), 21 ("solution"); Walter LaFeber, "Johnson, Vietnam, and Tocqueville," in Cohen and Bernkopf, *Lyndon Johnson Confronts the World,* 50 ("beast"); Goodwin, *Lyndon Johnson and the American Dream,* 282; Robert Buzzanco, *Masters of War: Military Dissent and Politics in the Vietnam Era* (New York: Cambridge University Press, 1996), 217; Rusk, *As I Saw It,* 499–500.

4. Lewis Sorley, *Honorable Warrior: General Harold K. Johnson and the Ethics of Command* (Lawrence: University Press of Kansas, 1998), 221, 223 ("spend and bomb," "military idiots"); Herring, *LBJ and Vietnam,* 25 ("MacArthur").

5. Goodwin, *Lyndon Johnson and the American Dream,* 282–83 ("major debate," "wings"); Logevall, *Choosing War,* 304 ("stealth"); Herring, *America's Longest War,* 164 ("indirection").

6. Mann, *Grand Delusion,* 11 ("goddamn speeches"); R. B. Woods, *Fulbright,* 365 ("history teachers"); Fry, *Debating Vietnam,* 25, 47n15.

7. Rusk, "Briefing for New Congressmen," Jan. 13, 1965, 3; Dean Rusk, Robert McNamara, McGeorge Bundy, Hubert Humphrey, and Lyndon Johnson, "Congressional Briefing," Feb. 16, 1965, 2–3, Congressional Briefings, 1964–1965, and Rusk, "National Foreign Policy Conference," Apr. 13, 1965, 3, 10, Rusk News Conferences, both LBJ Library.

8. Rusk, "National Foreign Policy Conference," Apr. 13, 1965, 1–2; Rusk, McNamara, and Johnson, "Congressional Reception," Mar. 2, 1965, 3, 8, Congressional Briefings, 1965, LBJ Library.

9. Rusk, Bundy, and Johnson, "Congressional Reception," Mar. 2, 1965, 6–8; Rusk, "National Foreign Policy Conference," Apr. 13, 1965, 7.

10. Gardner, *Pay Any Price,* 197 ("*will not*"); R. B. Woods, *LBJ,* 608 ("unconditional discussions"); Zeiler, *Dean Rusk,* 171–72 ("fuck you").

11. Gibbons, *U.S. Government and the Vietnam War,* 3: 242; Lyndon B. Johnson to Congress of the United States, May 4, 1965, *CR,* 89:1 (May 5, 1965), 9,492–93.

12. George A. Smathers Oral History, Aug. 1–24, 1989, p. 101, Senate Historical Office, Washington, DC; *Time Magazine,* Jan. 22, 1965, 18 (Johnson); Fry, *Debating Vietnam,* 9 ("professor"); R. B. Woods, *Fulbright,* 163 ("S.O.B."), 166; Haynes Johnson and Bernard M. Gwertzman, *Fulbright: The Dissenter* (Garden City, NY: Doubleday, 1968), 164 ("*my* Secretary of State").

13. US Congress, *Executive Sessions of the Senate Foreign Relations Committee, Together with Joint Sessions with the Senate Armed Services Committee,* 89th Cong., 1st sess., vol. xvii (Jan. 8, 1965), 103, 136 (June 11, 1965), 712, 989 (hereafter cited as *SFRC Executive Sessions,* Cong.:sess., vol. [date], page), http://congressional.proquest.com/congressional/docview/t29.d30.hrg-1965-for-0001?accountid=3611 (accessed Apr. 20, 2014); *CR,* 89:1 (June 7, 1965), 12,734–35 (June 15, 1965), 13,656.

14. *SFRC Executive Sessions,* 89:1, vol. xvii (Jan. 8, 1965), 104, 137 (Apr. 30, 1965), 467–69.

15. *CR,* 89:1 (June 7, 1965), 12,732 (June 15, 1965), 13,656.
16. *SFRC Executive Sessions,* 89:1, vol. xvii (Apr. 30, 1965), 469; Berman, *William Fulbright,* 43 (Republicans); Gibbons, *U.S. Government and the Vietnam War,* 3: 141 ("good friends").
17. R. B. Woods, *Fulbright,* 387; LBJ notation on Douglas Cater to the President, Feb. 8, 1965, in David M. Barrett, *Lyndon B. Johnson's Vietnam Papers: A Documentary Collection* (College Station: Texas A&M University Press, 1997), 112 ("cry baby"); David Halberstam, *The Powers That Be* (New York: Knopf, 1979), 502 ("no more access"); Gibbons, *U.S. Government and the Vietnam War,* 4: 41 ("so alone").
18. Carson, "Beyond the Solid South," 258 ("worse mess"); J. Woods, *Richard Russell,* 139; Russell to Mrs. E. B. Respers, July 30, 1965 (quote), and Russell to Alvin W. Neely, July 30, 1965, both 44:1, Russell Papers.
19. Mike Mansfield to the President, July 27, 1965, enclosure to Roberts S. McNamara to Lyndon Johnson, July 28, 1965, White Confidential File, box 71, LBJ Library.
20. Gibbons, *U.S. Government and the Vietnam War,* 3: 445; J. Woods, *Richard Russell,* 141; Russell to J. R. Morgan, Dec. 24, 1965, 40:3, Russell Papers.
21. Dallek, *Flawed Giant,* 160 ("kiss my ass"); Longley, *Senator Albert Gore,* 159 ("caucus"); Kyle Longley, "The Reluctant 'Volunteer': The Origins of Senator Albert A. Gore's Opposition to the Vietnam War," in *Vietnam and the American Political Tradition: The Politics of Dissent,* ed. Randall B. Woods (New York: Cambridge University Press, 2003), 228, 231 ("grain," "loner").
22. Gore, "Capitol Commentary," Apr. 12, 19, May 10, 1965, and Gore, "Washington Report," Apr. 1965, May 1965, both C44:1, Gore Papers; *CR,* 89:1 (May 5, 1965), 9,497.
23. *CR,* 89:1 (July 28, 1965), 18,571–72; Gore, "Capitol Commentary," Aug. 2, 1965, series 12: Weekly Newspaper Column, folder 1, Gore Papers.
24. Schulman, *John Sherman Cooper,* 68 (Pearson); Fredrik Logevall, "A Delicate Balance: John Sherman Cooper and the Republican Opposition to the Vietnam War," in R. B. Woods, *Vietnam and the American Political Tradition,* 237–46.
25. *CR,* 89:1 (Mar. 25, 1965), 5,934–35 (May 5, 1965), 9,498.
26. *CR,* 89:1 (June 7, 1965), 12,737; Cooper, speech to Louisville VFW, June 26, 1965, box 904, John Sherman Cooper Papers, Special Collections, Margaret I. King Library, University of Kentucky, Lexington (hereafter cited as Cooper Papers).
27. Fry, *Debating Vietnam,* 5.
28. Gibbons, *U.S. Government and the Vietnam War,* 3: 245.
29. *SFRC Executive Sessions,* 89:1, vol. xvii (Apr. 2, 1965), 398 (June 11, 1965), 679; Stennis Armed Forced Day Address, Meridian, MS, May 16, 1965, p. 6, Public Series, box 11, Stennis Papers.
30. *CR,* 89:1 (Mar. 1, 1965), 3,780, 3,824 (Mar. 4, 1965), 4,202–3; Long, press release, May 11, 1965, box 600, folder 33, Long, speech to US Chamber of Commerce, Apr. 26, 1965, box 600, folder 33, and Long, interview on *Meet the Press,* quoted in *Washington Post,* Mar. 1, 1965, box 600, folder 4, all Russell B. Long

Papers, Mss. 3700, Louisiana and Lower Mississippi Collections, Louisiana State University Libraries, Baton Rouge (hereafter cited as Long Papers, box:folder); *SFRC Executive Sessions,* 89:1, vol. xvii (June 7, 1965), 666.

31. Huntley, "Mighty Rivers of Charleston," 216, 287–88, 294–96; R. D. Johnson, *Congress and the Cold War,* 159 ("lightning of intellect").

32. Becnel, *Senator Allen Ellender,* 249; *CR,* 89:1 (June 3, 1965), 623 (Sparkman) (June 7, 1965), 12,734 (McClellan) (June 15, 1965), 13,577 (Robertson); Robertson to Davis A. Robertson, Feb. 15, 1965, 105:57, Robertson to Mrs. Edward G. Conroy, Feb. 20, 1965, 76:21, and Robertson to Robert I. Litchford, June 18, 1965, 76:22, all Robertson Papers.

33. Talmadge, "Reports from the United States Senate," Feb. 26, 1965, p. 2, July 30, 1965, p. 2, series, 2, box 277: folder 44, Herman E. Talmadge Papers, Richard B. Russell Library for Political Research and Studies, University of Georgia, Athens (hereafter cited as Talmadge Papers, series/box/folder); Ervin to Mr. and Mrs. John J. Honigmann, Feb. 25, 1965, 112:4979, and Ervin to Mrs. Julian Griggs, Apr. 14, 1965, 112:4981, both Ervin Papers; Crispell, *Testing the Limits,* 188; *CR,* 89:1 (Feb. 24, 1965), 3,442 (Fascell).

34. Stennis, speech to Pearl River Electric Power Associates, Sept. 25, 1965, p. 6, Public Series, box 11, Stennis Papers.

35. Johns, *Vietnam's Second Front,* 23, 37, 54, 57, 83 (Laird), 84 (Tower); Tower, "Weekly Report: Vietnam," Feb. 14, 1965, and Flexo #16 Letter re Vietnam, 1965, both 973:2, Tower Papers; *New York Times,* Jan. 7, 1965 (Thurmond); *SFRC Executive Sessions,* 89:1, vol. xvii (June 11, 1965), 696–97 (Thurmond); Morton to Joyce Spurlock, Oct. 26, 1965, box 19, Morton Papers.

36. *Dallas Morning News,* Feb. 9, July 19, 1965; *Montgomery Advertiser,* July 30, 1965; *Atlanta Constitution,* Feb. 10, 15, 19, July 13, 1965; *New Orleans Times-Picayune,* Feb. 16, 1965.

37. *Louisville Courier-Journal,* Feb. 18, July 21, 29, 1965.

38. *Texas Observer,* Apr. 30, 1965, July 23, 1965 (Dugger), Sept. 3, 1965, Nov. 26, 1965 (Dugger, Ambler, Mullinax).

39. *Montgomery Advertiser,* Aug. 7, Feb. 14, 1964; *Atlanta Constitution,* Feb. 19, 1965; *New Orleans Times-Picayune,* Feb. 16, 1965.

40. *GOI,* no. 1 (June 1965), n.p., no. 2 (July 1965), 3, 17, no. 3 (Aug. 1965), 3, 10–11, no. 4 (Sept. 1965), 3, 8, 12, no. 5 (Oct. 1965), 3, 13, no. 6 (Nov. 1965), 3, 10, 13.

41. *GOI,* no. 1 (June 1965), n.p., no. 3 (Aug. 1965), 13; Hodding Carter Oral History, Nov. 8, 1968, p. 17, LBJ Library ("turncoat"). For examples of resentment over LBJ's civil rights and social policies, see Miss E. Hope Frank to President Johnson, June 13, 1965, box 348, folder: 1965, June Constituent Correspondence, Leaman G. Bibson to Harry F. Byrd, Sr., June 29, 1965, box 348, folder: 1965, July Correspondence, and Henry P. Taylor to Byrd, Oct. 18, 1965, box 287, folder: 1961–65, Miscellaneous Correspondence, all Byrd Sr. Papers, Albert and Shirley Small Special Collections Library, University of Virginia, Charlottesville (hereafter cited as Byrd Sr. Papers, box:folder).

42. Mrs. R. G. H. to Russell, July 28, 1965, 40:12, and R. P. T. to Russell, Dec. 6, 1965, 40:14, both Russell Papers.

43. A. S. Johnson to Stennis, Dec. 15, 1965, 4/85/15, A Parent to Robert McNamara, Dec. 7, 1965, enclosed in W. I. Park to Stennis, Dec. 10, 1965, 4/85/18, and S. H. Long to Stennis, Dec. 10, 1965, 4/85/15, all Stennis Papers; William B. Zoellner to Russell, July 15, 1965, 41:2, and Julian K. Quattlebaum to Russell, July 23, 1965, 40:12, both Russell Papers.

44. Mr. and Mrs. John Mitchell to Stennis, Feb. 24, 1965, 4/85/14, Stennis Papers; David E. Stovall to Editor, *Louisville Courier-Journal,* Feb. 5, 1965; Robert G. Mabery to Gore, [Feb. 1965], Frank Miller to Gore, [Feb. 1965], Terrell Fugate to Gore, Feb. 5, 1965, and Mrs. Yarboro E. Sallee to Gore, Feb. 5, 1965, all A42:1, Gore Papers; J. K. McL. to Robertson, Jan. 17, 1965, 76:1, Robertson Papers.

45. William W. Sears to Gore, Feb. 10, 1965, A42:1, Mrs. Yarboro E. Sallee to Gore, Feb. 5, 1965, A42:1, and Mrs. Mary Olson to Gore, Mar. 14, 1966, B36:1, all Gore Papers; Clyde N. Swift to Fulbright, Feb. 21, 1966, 50:2, Fulbright Papers; J. McL. A. to Byrd, Dec. 17, 1965, 199:1965, Vietnam, Byrd Sr. Papers. See also Margaret C. Lukemeir to Editor, *Louisville Courier Journal,* Feb. 21, 1965.

46. W. P. K. to Russell, Oct. 17, 1965, 40:9, W. B. to Russell, Oct. 18, 1965, 40:9, and J. F. to Russell, Oct. 21, 1965, 40:9, all Russell Papers; L. A. S. to Ervin, Oct. 18, 1965, 112:4983, Ervin Papers.

47. Mrs. B. M. to Russell, Oct. 20, 1965, 40:8, and J. M. T. to Russell, July 12, 1965, 41:2, both Russell Papers.

48. J. T. G. to Harry F. Byrd Jr., Dec. 22, 1965, box 199, folder 1965: Vietnam, Harry F. Byrd Jr. Papers, Albert and Shirley Small Special Collections Library, University of Virginia, Charlottesville (hereafter cited as Byrd Jr. Papers, box:folder); R. G. to Ervin, Apr. 16, 1965, 112:4981, and R. E. C. to Ervin, Feb. 17, 1965, 112:4979, both Ervin Papers; J. D. R. to Robertson, Feb. 26, 1965, 76:1, Robertson Papers; R. G. P. to Stennis, June 21, 1965, 43/4/93, Stennis Papers.

49. W. Forrest Smith to Editor, *Louisville Courier-Journal,* July 2, 1965.

50. Hiram H. Hiltz to Ervin, Mar. 19, 1964, 97:4336, James C. Daniel to Ervin, Mar. 23, 1965, 112:4980, and Robert E. Willard to Ervin, Apr. 22, 1965, 112:4981, all Ervin Papers; Rev. Lawrence McLamb to Herman Talmadge, June 27, 1966, 37:6, Russell Papers; Ben W. Farley to Robertson, June 28, 1965, 76:2, Robertson Papers; George R. Edwards to Morton, May 23, 1965, box 19, Thruston Morton Papers, Special Collections, Margaret I. King Library, University of Kentucky, Lexington (hereafter cited as Morton Papers); Bertha Boettcher to Fulbright, Feb. 23, 1966, 47:2, Fulbright Papers; Wm. Archer Wright Jr. to Fulbright, Feb. 21, 1966, enclosed in Archer to Byrd Jr., Feb. 21, 1966, box 198: folder: Vietnam—Feb. 17–28, 1966, Byrd Jr. Papers; Terry Bisson to Editor, *Louisville Courier-Journal,* July 28, 1965.

51. Frazier T. Woolard to Ervin, Nov. 29, 1965, 112:4985, Ervin Papers; "Frazier Woolard, Pearl Harbor Survivor," in *Life on the Pamlico: Preserving North Carolina's Cultural Heritage through Oral History* (interview, Oct. 1993, published Dec. 1994),

http://circaneast.beaufortecc.edu/BCCC/article/December%201994/PDF/storyl
.pdf (accessed May 5, 2012); John M. Slade to Woolard, Nov. 18, 1974, Frazier T.
Woolard Papers, Special Collections Department, William R. Perkins Library, Duke
University, Durham, NC (hereafter cited as Woolard Papers; all of the Woolard correspondence is in one box).

52. Woolard to Nguyen Van Nhan, Oct. 24, 1966, and Nguyen Van Nhan to
Woolard, Oct. 28, 1966, Nov. 18, 23, 1966, Feb. 18, 1967, [Sept. 1967], all Woolard
Papers.

53. Woolard to Margaret Chase Smith, May 27, 1969, Woolard to Leo Cherne,
June 1, 1968, Woolard to Tran Khoa Hoc, Dec. 11, 1968, and Woolard to Nguyen
Van Nhan, Aug. 23, 1973, all Woolard Papers.

54. Woolard to "Mr. Lyndon Johnson, Temporary Occupant," Aug. 27, 1967,
Nguyen Van Nhan to Woolard, Dec. 15, 1987, Hugh B. O'Neill to Woolard, May 1,
1968, Woolard to Justice William O. Douglas, May 10, 1968, Woolard to Walt Rostow, Oct. 16, 23, Dec. 10, 1969, Woolard to Walter B. Jones, May 21, 1971, Woolard
to Dean Rusk, July 9, 1971, Woolard to Secretary General U. Thant, June 17, 1971,
and Woolard to Gerald Ford, Feb. 27, 1975, all Woolard Papers. For the lethal impact
of US actions on Vietnamese civilians, see Nick Turse, *Kill Anything That Moves: The
Real American War in Vietnam* (New York: Henry Holt and Co., 2013).

55. Nguyen Van Nhan to Woolard, July 2, 1975, [David M. Milligan] to
Woolard, July 21, 1972, [Bartow Houston Jr.] to Woolard, Dec. 17, [1974], J. M.
to Woolard, [Dec. 1974], and Suzanne Woolard to Woolard, May 12, 1983, all
Woolard Papers.

56. Fry, *Debating Vietnam*, 26–27.

57. Bill Moyers Memorandum for the President, Feb. 21, 1966, Office of the
President File, "William Fulbright," LBJ Library; Fulbright to W. R. Stephens, Mar.
15, 1966, 50:2, Fulbright Papers; R. B. Woods, *Fulbright*, 398.

58. Melvin Small, *Johnson, Nixon, and the Doves* (New Brunswick, NJ: Rutgers
University Press, 1988), 154 (Wheeler); "Meeting with Congressional Leadership on
the Resumption of Bombing," Jan. 25, 1966, Meeting Notes File, LBJ Library; Gibbons, *U.S. Government and the Vietnam War*, 4: 146–47, 155 (McNamara).

59. Stennis, speech to Joint Session of the Mississippi State Legislature, Jan. 27,
1966, 3, 5, 8–9, Public Series, 12/1, Stennis Papers; Stennis to Fulbright, Feb. 10,
1966, and Fulbright to Stennis, Feb. 12, 1966, both 50:2, Fulbright Papers.

60. Bill Moyers Memorandum for the President, Feb. 21, 1966; Eric Seva-
reid, "Why Our Foreign Policy Is Failing: An Exclusive Interview with Senator
Fulbright," *Look*, May 3, 1966, 25; US Congress, Senate Committee on Foreign
Relations, [Hearings on] *Supplemental Foreign Assistance: Fiscal Year 1966—Vietnam*, 89th Cong., 2nd sess., Jan. 28–Feb. 18, 1966 (Washington, DC: Government
Printing Office, 1966), 409–10 (Gore) (hereafter cited as Fulbright Hearings); Halberstam, *Powers That Be*, 492, 497; *Newsweek*, Feb. 21, 1966, 30 (Dirksen).

61. Fulbright Hearings, 51, 53, 347, 412, 524, 605, 608.

62. Fulbright Hearings, 239, 382, 446–47, 503, 506, 582.

63. Fulbright Hearings, 463, 516–17, 551, 598–99; *CR*, 89:2 (Feb. 16, 1966), 3041; Robert Mann, *Legacy to Power: Senator Russell Long of Louisiana* (New York: Paragon House, 1992), 245, 331 (descriptions of Long).

64. *CR*, 89:2 (Feb. 16, 1966), 3,041–42.

65. Fulbright Hearings, 43–44, 61, 289–90, 650–51.

66. Fulbright Hearings, 498–99, 544–46.

67. *New York Times*, Feb. 19, 1966; Fry, *Debating Vietnam*, 65; Fulbright Hearings, 570, 572, 596, 599, 612, 628.

68. Fulbright Hearings, 592, 608, 629–31; Rusk, *As I Saw It*, 472, 493.

69. Fulbright Hearings, 582; Carl M. Marcy Oral History, Sept. 14–Nov. 16, 1983, p. 130 ("poor chairman"), Senate Historical Office, copy in LBJ Library; Rusk, *As I Saw It*, 494; R. B. Woods, "Dixie's Dove," 536–38.

70. Fulbright Hearings, 652, 662.

71. Fulbright Hearings, 661–62, 666, 669.

72. Mann, *Grand Delusion*, 483 ("Fulbrights"); *New York Times*, Feb. 12, 1966 (news conference); Gibbons, *U.S. Government and the War in Vietnam*, 4: 309–10 ("among friends").

73. *Newsweek*, Feb. 28, 1966, 17; Gibbons, *U.S. Government and the War in Vietnam*, 4: 249 (Pell).

74. Gibbons, *U.S. Government and the War in Vietnam*, 4: 250–51, 336–37; Berman, *William Fulbright*, 60–61.

75. *GOI*, no. 8 (Jan. 1966), 3, no. 11 (Apr. 1966), 3–4, no. 14 (July 1966), 17, no. 16 (Sept. 1966), 18, no. 17 (Oct. 1966), 3–4.

76. *GOI*, no. 9 (Feb. 1966), 6–7, no. 10 (Mar. 1966), 7, 16–17, no. 12 (May 1966), 6, 9, no. 13 (June 1966), 7, 11–13, no. 16 (Sept. 1966), 8, 10, no. 18 (Nov.–Dec. 1966), 11.

77. *GOI*, no. 10 (Mar. 1966), 10, no. 12 (May 1966), 8, no. 13 (June 1966), 6, no. 14 (July 1966,) 6.

78. *Dallas Morning News*, Jan. 11, 14, July 1, 3, 1966; *Montgomery Advertiser*, Jan. 8, 1966; *New Orleans Times-Picayune*, Jan. 22, 1966.

79. *Atlanta Constitution*, Jan. 22, Feb. 8, 21, 1966.

80. *Atlanta Constitution*, Feb. 18, 19, 22, 25, Mar. 15, 1966.

81. *Louisville Courier-Journal*, Jan. 25, Feb. 2, 22, 1966.

82. *Louisville Courier-Journal*, Feb. 6, 13, 1966.

83. *Texas Observer*, Mar. 18, 1966 (Yarborough), May 13, 1966.

84. *Texas Observer*, July 8, Nov. 25, Dec. 9, 1966.

85. Mrs. F. H. D. to Stennis, Feb. 18, 1966, 4/8/17, and Mrs. R. L. W. to Stennis, Feb. 22, 1966, 4/85/17, both Stennis Papers; Mr. and Mrs. E. A. E. to Byrd Jr., Jan. 19, 1966, 198:Vietnam, Feb. 17–28, Byrd Jr. Papers; Mrs. B. W. J. to Russell, Feb. 22, 1966, 38:10, Russell Papers; O. F. to Fulbright, May 9, 1966, 48:1, P. B. M. to Fulbright, Feb. 9, 1966, 49:3, Mrs. H. A. to Fulbright, [Feb. 1966], 44:1; J. E. J. to Fulbright, Feb. 15, 1966, 48:4, and Mr. and Mrs. J. T. M. to Fulbright, Feb. 22, 1966, 49:3, all Fulbright Papers; J. W. H. to Fulbright, Feb. 22, 1966, 38:11, Russell Papers.

86. A. S. W. Jr. to Gore, Feb. 3, 1966, A42:1, C. H. B to Gore, Jan. 30, 1966, B36:2, and V. A. to Gore, Feb. 22, 1966, B36:1, all Gore Papers.

87. Rush Boyce to Fulbright, Feb. 4, 17, 1966, 47:3, Bernard B. Bailey to Fulbright, Feb. 8, 1966, 47:2, Paul B. Maynard to Fulbright, Feb. 9, 1966, 49:3, Mr. and Mrs. J. T. Mace to Fulbright, Feb. 15, 1966, 49:3, and Lewis Hoke to Fulbright, Feb. 15, 1966, 48: 3, all Fulbright Papers; John P. Cone Jr. to Byrd Jr., Feb. 15, 1966, 198:Vietnam, Feb. 17–28, 1966, Byrd Jr. Papers; Mrs. Robert L. Wood to Stennis, Feb. 17, 1966, 4/85/17, Stennis Papers.

88. Dr. and Mrs. J. S. Adamson to Fulbright, Feb. 18, 1966, 47:1, Lee R. McEwen to Fulbright, [Apr. 11, 1966], 49:1, Mrs. Jess Baskins to Fulbright, [Feb. 1966], 47:2, and Joshua K. Shepherd to Fulbright, May 23, 1966, 50:1, all Fulbright Papers; Daniel T. and Maria Young to Ervin, [Feb. 1966], 129:5697, Ervin Papers; Alvin R. L. Dohme to Fulbright, Feb. 15, 1966, and James T. Schollarert to Byrd Jr., Feb. 14, 1966, both 198:Vietnam, Feb. 17–28, 1966, Byrd Jr. Papers; Sam C. Love to Gore, [Feb. 1966], A42:1, and John T. Williams to Gore, Feb. 21, 1966, B36:1, both Gore Papers.

89. D. A. R. to Robertson, Feb. 10, 1965, 76:1, Robertson Papers; Mrs. A. W. G. to Russell, Feb. 20, 1966, 38:11, and Dr. J. C. H. to Russell, Mar. 28, 1966, 38:8, both Russell Papers; T. P. to Ervin, July 23, 1965, 112:4983, Ervin Papers; J. E. P. to Stennis, [Feb. 1966], 4/85/17, Stennis Papers.

90. Mrs. E. A. to Russell, May 13, 1966, 37:11, Russell Papers; W. G. W. to Stennis, Jan. 26, 1966, 4/85/16, Stennis Papers.

91. Coleman Wages to Russell, Jan. 22, 1966, 39:7, A. P. Francis to Russell, Apr. 16, 1966, 38:4, and Corbett H. Thigpen to Russell, Apr. 28, 1966, 38:4, all Russell Papers; Billy D. McFarland to Gore, Feb. 4, 1966, A42:1, Gore Papers; Mrs. B. H. Abernathy to Fulbright, Feb. 15, 1966, 47:1, Fulbright Papers.

92. Mrs. I. H. to Fulbright, Oct. 19, 1966, 48:3, and F. G. B. to Fulbright, Jan. 28, 1966, 47:3, both Fulbright Papers; V. D. to Stennis, May 17, 196[6], 48/12/32, Stennis Papers.

93. J. W. P. to Fulbright, Feb. 7, 1966, 49:5, Fulbright Papers; T. H. to Gore, [Mar. 1966], B36:1, Gore Papers.

94. Mrs. P. M. H. to Gore, Aug. 16, 1966, and A. I. H. to Gore, Aug. 16, 1966, C21:1, Gore Papers.

4. Southern Soldiers

1. Christian G. Appy, *Working-Class War: American Combat Soldiers and Vietnam* (Chapel Hill: University of North Carolina Press, 1993), 14–15, 25, 27.

2. William J. Cooper Jr. and Thomas E. Terrill, *The American South: A History*, vol. 2, 4th ed. (Lanham, MD: Rowman and Littlefield, 2009), 790; James C. Cobb, *The South and America since World War II* (New York: Oxford University Press, 2011), 65; Grantham, *South in Modern America*, 261; US Census Bureau, "Population of the 100 Largest Urban Places, 1960," June 15, 1998, http:www.census.gov/

population/www/documentation/twps00271/tab19.txt (accessed July 12, 2011); US Census Bureau, "Population of the 100 Largest Urban Places, 1970," June 15, 1998, http:www.census.gov/population/www/documentation/twps00271/tab20txt (accessed July 12, 2011); James R. Wilson, ed., *Landing Zones: Southern Veterans Remember Vietnam* (Durham, NC: Duke University Press, 1990), xi–xii; "Data on Vietnam Era Veterans . . . Veterans Administration . . . September 1981," p. 7, Government Document Call No.: VA 1.2:V 672/2/981; "Statistical Information about Fatal Casualties of the Vietnam War," pp. 3–5, https://www.archives.gov/research/military/Vietnam-war/casualty-statistics.html (accessed May 27, 2014); US Census Bureau "US Population by State from 1900," www.demographia.com/db-state1900.htm (accessed May 27, 2014); "Medal of Honor Roll by State," www.homeofheroes.com/moh/states/_states.html (accessed May 27, 2014).

3. Dr. Timothy Lockley, interview, Feb. 11, 17, 2003, p. 6, Oral History Project, Vietnam Archive, Texas Tech University (hereafter cited as Vietnam Archive, TTU); Appy, *Working-Class War,* 46 (Wilson), 72 (Foley); Myra MacPherson, *Long Time Passing: Vietnam and the Haunted Generation* (New York: Signet Books, 1984), 269 (Richardson); Lea Ybarra, ed., *Vietnam Veteranos: Chicanos Recall the War* (Austin: University of Texas Press, 2004), 40 (Charles).

4. William J. Brinker, ed., *A Time for Looking Back: Putnam County Veterans, Their Families, and the Vietnam War* (Cookeville: Tennessee Technological University, 1990), 58–59; Tom Engelhardt, *The End of Victory Culture: Cold War America and the Disillusioning of a Generation,* rev. ed. (Amherst: University of Massachusetts Press, 2007); J. Houston Matthews, interview, in J. R. Wilson, *Landing Zones,* 101; Marshall Paul, interview, Feb. 3, 1990, pp. 3–4, 9, Vietnam Archive, TTU.

5. Max Cleland, *Heart of a Patriot: How I Found the Courage to Survive Vietnam, Walter Reed and Karl Rove* (New York: Simon and Schuster, 2009), 17, 33, 58; Larry Gwin, *Baptism: A Vietnam Memoir* (New York: Presidio Press, 1999), 11–12.

6. Owen W. Gilman, *Vietnam and the Southern Imagination* (Jackson: University Press of Mississippi, 1992), 25 ("perfect image"); William C. Westmoreland, *A Soldier Reports* (New York: Dell, 1976), 12–14. See also William C. Westmoreland, interview, in J. R. Wilson, *Landing Zones,* 11–21; Westmoreland, "Vietnam in Perspective," in *Vietnam: Four American Perspectives,* ed. Patrick J. Hearden (West Lafayette, IN: Purdue University Press, 1990), 39–57; Rick Atkinson, *The Long Grey Line: The American Journey of West Point's Class of 1966* (New York: Houghton Mifflin, 1989), 35 ("demigod status").

7. General Hal Moore, interview, Oct. 25, 2000, p. 4, Vietnam Archive, TTU; H. R. McMaster, "Adaptive Leadership: Harold G. 'Hal' Moore," in *The Art of Command: Military Leadership from George Washington to Colin Powell,* ed. Harry S. Laver and Jeffrey J. Matthews (Lexington: University Press of Kentucky, 2008) 211–12, 218–19; Harold G. Moore and Joseph L. Galloway, *We Were Soldiers Once . . . and Young: Ia Drang—The Battle That Changed the War in Vietnam* (New York: HarperPerennial, 1993), 217.

8. Richard C. Ensminger, interview, in J. R. Wilson, *Landing Zones,* 28;

George D. Riels, interview, in J. R. Wilson, *Landing Zones,* 111; Manuel T. Valdez, interview, in J. R. Wilson, *Landing Zones,* 46; Matthews, interview, in J. R. Wilson, *Landing Zones,* 101.

9. Jim Wilson, *The Sons of Bardstown: 25 Years of Vietnam in an American Town* (New York: Crown, 1994), 42–43, 55–56 (Janes, Filiatreau); Anthony A. McIntire, "The Kentucky National Guard in Vietnam: The Story of Bardstown's Battery C at War," *Register of the Kentucky Historical Society* 90 (Spring 1992): 153–54 (leader of legal challenge); Appy, *Working-Class War,* 37–38; Lawrence M. Baskin and William A. Strauss, *Chance and Circumstance: The Draft, the War, and the Vietnam Generation* (New York: Alfred A. Knopf, 1978), 48–52.

10. William J. Brinker, "Nancy Randolph, Army Nurse: 'Ten Thousand Patients in Nine Months [and] All Downhill since Then,'" in *The Human Tradition in the Vietnam Era,* ed. David L. Anderson (Wilmington, DE: SR Books, 2000), 116–17; Brenda Sue Castro, interview in J. R. Wilson, *Landing Zones,* 87–88; Becky Pietz, interview in *In the Combat Zone: An Oral History of American Women in Vietnam, 1966–1975,* ed. Kathryn Marshall (Boston: Penguin Books, 1987), 103; Karen K. Johnson, interview, in J. R. Wilson, *Landing Zones,* 243; Cheri Rankin, interview, in Marshall, *In the Combat Zone,* 62–63; Heather Marie Stur, *Beyond Combat: Women and Gender in the Vietnam Era* (New York: Cambridge University Press, 2011), 127.

11. James E. Westheider, *The African American Experience in Vietnam: Brothers in Arms* (Lanham, MD: Rowman and Littlefield, 2008), 23, 44, 47; Peter B. Levy, "Blacks and the Vietnam War," in *Legacy: The Vietnam War in the American Imagination,* ed. D. Michael Shafer (Boston: Beacon Press, 1990), 211; Herman Graham III, *The Brothers' Vietnam War: Black Power, Manhood, and the Military Experience* (Gainesville: University Press of Florida, 2003), 17.

12. Westheider, *African American Experience in Vietnam,* 27–29; James Westheider, *Fighting on Two Fronts: African Americans and the Vietnam War* (New York: New York University Press, 1997), 24–25, 28; Lawrence Allen Eldridge, *Chronicles of a Two-Front War: Civil Rights and Vietnam in the African American Press* (Columbia: University of Missouri Press, 2011), 51 (Bond).

13. Westheider, *African American Experience in Vietnam,* 34–35; Westheider, *Fighting on Two Fronts,* 28. Over the course of the war, focused Pentagon policies brought these casualty figures essentially into line with the African American proportion of the US population.

14. Fred V. Cherry, interview, in *Bloods: Black Veterans of the Vietnam War: An Oral History,* ed. Wallace Terry (New York: Ballantine Books, 1985), 267–69; Edgar A. Huff, interview, in Terry, *Bloods,* 144; Norman A. McDaniel, interview, in Terry, *Bloods,* 131; Doris I. "Lucki" Allen, interview, in *A Piece of My Heart: The Stories of 26 Women Who Served in Vietnam,* ed. Keith Walker (New York: Presidio Press, 1986), 309; Doris I. "Lucki" Allen, interview, May 11, June 7, 2004, p. 64, Vietnam Archive, TTU; Pinkie Houser, interview, in Marshall, *In the Combat Zone,* 37.

15. Charles Strong, interview, in Terry, *Bloods,* 54–55; Reginald Edwards, interview, in Terry, *Bloods,* 4.

16. Graham, *Brothers' Vietnam War*, 15 ("selling manhood"); Macpherson, *Long Time Passing*, 253 (Lowe); Terry Whitmore, as told to Richard Weber, *Memphis Nam Sweden* (Garden City, NY: Double Day Company, 1971), 37–38.

17. David L. Anderson, "Bill Henry Terry Jr., Killed in Action: An African American's Journey from Alabama to Vietnam and Back," in D. L. Anderson, *Human Tradition in the Vietnam Era*, 137; Robert L. Mountain, interview, in Terry, *Bloods*, 174; Luther C. Benton III, interview, in Terry, *Bloods*, 63.

18. Ybarra, *Vietnam Veteranos*, 40 ("cotton picker"); Lorena Oropeza, *Rasa Si Guerra No? Chicano Protest and Patriotism during the Viet Nam War Era* (Berkeley: University of California Press, 2005), 58, 63 (Sanchez), 78; George Mariscal, ed., *Aztlan and Viet Nam: Chicano and Chicana Experiences of the War* (Berkeley: University of California Press, 1999), 29 (Herrera), 31 (Benavidez), 32 ("warrior patriotism"). For Mexican American casualties, see Ralph Guzman, "Mexican American Casualties in Vietnam," *La Raza* 1 (2012): 12–17; Ybarra, *Vietnam Veteranos*, 5; Charley Trujillo, ed., *Soldados: Chicanos in Viet Nam* (San Jose, CA: Chusma House Publications, 1990), vii–viii.

19. Ann Powlas, interview, in Marshall, *In the Combat Zone*, 118; Houser, interview, in Marshall, *In the Combat Zone*, 41, 49; William U. Tant, interview, in J. R. Wilson, *Landing Zones*, 119; Ted A. Burton, interview, in J. R. Wilson, *Landing Zones*, 71.

20. Houser, interview, in Marshall, *In the Combat Zone*, 41; Brinker, *Time for Looking Back*, 50 (Tennessee veteran); Leo Spooner Jr., interview, in J. R. Wilson, *Landing Zones*, 230.

21. Kyle Longley, *Grunts: The American Combat Soldiers in Vietnam* (Armonk, NY: M. E. Sharpe, 2008), 80 (Texan); Candler, interview, in J. R. Wilson, *Landing Zones*, 152; Brinker, *Time for Looking Back*, 52 (Tennessee trooper), 53 (southern officer).

22. Brinker, *Time for Looking Back*, 54 (officer); Valdez, interview, in J. R. Wilson, *Landing Zones*, 51; Eunice Splawn, interview, in Marshall, *In the Combat Zone*, 97.

23. Westmoreland, *Soldier Reports*, 129, 328; Brinker, *Time for Looking Back*, 41–43; Whitmore, *Memphis Nam Sweden*, 55; Allen, interview, May 11, June 7, 2004, p. 88, Vietnam Archive, TTU.

24. Tant, interview, in J. R. Wilson, *Landing Zones*, 126; Richard A. Sones, interview, n.d., pp. 16–18, Vietnam Oral History Project, U.S. Army History and Education Center, Carlisle, PA (hereafter cited as AHEC, Carlisle); Strong, interview, in Terry, *Bloods*, 61; Archie "Joe" Biggers, interview, in Terry, *Bloods*, 109–10; Joe N. Ballard, interview, Apr. 11, 1985, p. 21, AHEC, Carlisle; Paul E. Blackwell, interview, Nov. 19, 1983, pp. 21–22, AHEC, Carlisle; Lemos L. Fulmer Jr., interview, 1983, no day or month, pp. 55–56, AHEC, Carlisle; Brinker, *Time for Looking Back*, 12, 25; Donald Davis, interview, Mar. 6, 2003, pp. 27–28, Vietnam Archive, TTU.

25. Tant, interview, in J. R. Wilson, *Landing Zones*, 128; Richard F. Timmons, interview, 1984, no day or month, AHEC, Carlisle, 45; John E. Robbins, interview,

n.d., AHEC, Carlisle, 22; Ensminger, interview, in J. R. Wilson, *Landing Zones*, 30; Sones, interview, AHEC, Carlisle, 50.

26. Castro, interview, in J. R. Wilson, *Landing Zones*, 96; Brinker, *Time for Looking Back*, 12, 25; Stur, *Beyond Combat*, 76.

27. Yvonne Honeycutt Baldwin and John Ernst, "In the Valley: The Combat Infantryman and the Vietnam War," in *The War That Never Ends: New Perspectives on the Vietnam War*, ed. David L. Anderson and John Ernst (Lexington: University Press of Kentucky, 2007), 326; Spooner, interview, in J. R. Wilson, *Landing Zones*, 227; Brinker, *Time for Looking Back*, 19.

28. George Watkins, interview, in Christian G. Appy, *Patriots: The Vietnam War Remembered from All Sides* (New York: Viking, 2003), 21–25; Mike Hill, interview, in Ron Steinman, ed., *The Soldiers' Story: Vietnam in Their Own Words* (New York: Barnes and Noble, 2000), 117; Burton, interview, in J. R. Wilson, *Landing Zones*, 72; Strong, interview, in Terry, *Bloods*, 55.

29. Brinker, "Nancy Randolph, Army Nurse," 121; Brinker, *Time for Looking Back*, 16; Castro, interview, in J. R. Wilson, *Landing Zones*, 97; Houser, interview, in Marshall, *In the Combat Zone*, 40.

30. Baldwin and Ernst, "In the Valley," 328; Valdez, interview, in J. R. Wilson, *Landing Zones*, 50; Strong, interview, in Terry, *Bloods*, 54.

31. Riels, interview, in J. R. Wilson, *Landing Zones*, 113; Benjamin H. Purcell, interview, in J. R. Wilson, *Landing Zones*, 144; Matthews, interview, in J. R. Wilson, *Landing Zones*, 105, 108; Cherry, interview, in Terry, *Bloods*, 285–86; McDaniel, interview, in Terry, *Bloods*, 141–42.

32. Brinker, *Time for Looking Back*, 71 ("racial discrimination"); Graham, *Brothers' Vietnam War*, 45 ("relative equality"), 65; Westheider, *African American Experience in Vietnam*, 52–85; Eldridge, *Chronicles of a Two-Front War*, 196 (soldier quotes); Lockley, interview, Feb. 11, 17, 2003, pp. 61–62, Vietnam Archive, TTU.

33. James E. Westheider, "Sgt. Allen Thomas Jr.: A Black Soldier in Vietnam," in *Portraits of African American Life since 1865*, ed. Nina Mjagkij (Wilmington, DE: SR Books, 2003), 229; Biggers, interview, in Terry, *Bloods*, 111; Tant, interview, in J. R. Wilson, *Landing Zones*, 121; Phillip Woodall to Dad, Apr. 5, 1968, in Bernard Edelman, ed., *Dear America: Letters Home from Vietnam* (New York: W. W. Norton, 1985), 197.

34. Strong, interview, in Terry, *Bloods*, 57; Charlie Earl Bodiford, interview, in J. R. Wilson, *Landing Zones*, 197.

35. Porter A. Halyburton, interview, in Appy, *Patriots* (New York: Viking, 2003), 224; Cherry, interview, in Terry, *Bloods*, 275.

36. Halyburton, interview, in Appy, *Patriots*, 224.

37. Halyburton, interview, in Appy, *Patriots*, 224–25; Cherry, interview, in Terry, *Bloods*, 280.

38. Eldridge, *Chronicles of a Two-Front War*, 189–90 (Alabamian); Gore, interview, in J. R. Wilson, *Landing Zones*, 85; Ponchitta Pierce and Peter Bailey, "The Returning Vet," *Ebony* 23 (Aug. 1968): 147 ("private club"); Westheider, "Sgt. Allen Thomas Jr.," 234; Huff, interview, in Terry, *Bloods*, 152–53.

39. S. Ernest Peoples, interview, in J. R. Wilson, *Landing Zones*, 190; Rodney R. Chastant to Mom and Dad, Oct. 19, 1967, in Edelman, *Dear America*, 211; Ensminger, interview, in J. R. Wilson, *Landing Zones*, 27; Castro, interview, in J. R. Wilson, *Landing Zones*, 100; Robert L. Powell, interview, Mar. 26, 1984, p. 46, AHEC, Carlisle; Powlas, interview, in Marshall, *In the Combat Zone*, 125.

40. William D. Poynter, interview, May 13, 1983, p. 33, AHEC, Carlisle; Ballard, interview, Apr. 11, 1985, p. 63, AHEC, Carlisle; James Bussey, interview, Nov. 11, 2002, p. 57, Vietnam Archive, TTU; Valdez, interview in J. R. Wilson, *Landing Zones*, 52; Barry Campbell, interview, quoted in Baldwin and Ernst, "In the Valley," 330.

41. Candler, interview, in J. R. Wilson, *Landing Zones*, 154; Riels, interview in J. R. Wilson, *Landing Zones*, 116; Jane Hodge, interview, in Walker, *Piece of My Heart*, 275; Woodall to Dad, Apr. 5, 1968, in Edelman, *Dear America*, 214; Marion Lee Kemper to Mom, Dad, . . . , Sept. 2, 1966 in Edelman, *Dear America*, 61–62; Brinker, *Time for Looking Back*, 23; William S. Norman, interview, in Terry, *Bloods*, 195.

42. Donald L. Whitfield, interview, in J. R. Wilson, *Landing Zones*, 207; James M. Addison, interview, in J. R. Wilson, *Landing Zones*, 44; Cherry, interview, in Terry, *Bloods*, 290; Norman, interview, in Terry, *Bloods*, 195; Brinker, *Time for Looking Back*, 20; Sones, interview, p. 18, AHEC, Carlisle.

43. Timmons, interview, 1984, no day or month, pp. 43, 50, AHEC, Carlisle; Linwood Burney, interview, May 20, 1985, p. 45, AHEC, Carlisle.

44. Brinker, *Time for Looking Back*, 74–75, 77; Garland C. "Pete" Hendricks, interview, in J. R. Wilson, *Landing Zones*, 233, 240; Candler, interview, in J. R. Wilson, *Landing Zones*, 155; Lockley, interview, Feb. 11, 17, 2003, p. 76, Vietnam Archive, TTU.

45. Westmoreland, *Soldier Reports*, 547; David Halberstam, *The Best and the Brightest* (Greenwich, CT: Fawcett Publications, 1972), 679 ("corporate general," LBJ's affinity for another southerner).

46. Russell F. Weigley, *The American Way of War: A History of United States Military Strategy and Policy* (New York: Macmillan Publishing, 1973), xix, xx, xxi–xxii, 464–67; Benjamin Buley, *The New American Way of War: Military Culture and the Political Utility of Force* (London: Routledge, 2008), 1–2, 7, 36 ("how long"). See Lewis Sorley, *Westmoreland: The General Who Lost Vietnam* (Boston: Houghton Mifflin Harcourt, 2011), *passim*, for the critique. See Daddis, *Westmoreland's War*, for the more positive appraisal, esp. 9, 178–79, 183, for suggestions that the war may not have been winnable. See also Prados, *Vietnam;* and Herring, *America's Longest War*, 379–80, for this interpretation.

47. Daddis, *Westmoreland's War*, 14, 35, 84, 179, 181; Halberstam, *Best and the Brightest*, 668.

48. Westmoreland, *Soldier Reports*, 82, 547–48, 555–56, 561, 565. For a summary of the revisionist perspectives, see Gary R. Hess, *Vietnam: Explaining America's Lost War* (New York: Blackwell Publishing, 2009).

49. Westmoreland, *Soldier Reports,* 154, 210, 255.

50. Westmoreland, *Soldier Reports,* 163, 170, 189, 408, 466–67, 469, 543.

51. Moore and Galloway, *We Were Soldiers,* 25.

52. Moore and Galloway, *We Were Soldiers,* 40–41, 46.

53. McMaster, "Adaptive Leadership," 209–29.

54. Moore and Galloway, *We Were Soldiers,* 238.

55. Moore and Galloway, *We Were Soldiers,* i–x, 233–34, 366.

56. Harold G. Moore and Joseph L. Galloway, *We Are Soldiers Still: A Journey Back to the Battlefields of Vietnam* (New York: HarperCollins, 2008), 26 ("enemy"); Moore and Galloway, *We Were Soldiers,* 207, 399, 402, 406; Daddis, *Westmoreland's War,* 98.

57. Moore and Galloway, *We Are Soldiers Still,* 36–37.

58. J. Wilson, *Sons of Bardstown,* 90, 93, 124.

59. J. Wilson, *Sons of Bardstown,* 93–94.

60. J. Wilson, *Sons of Bardstown,* 105; McIntire, "Kentucky National Guard in Vietnam," 154, 158.

61. J. Wilson, *Sons of Bardstown,* 158.

62. John D. Blair IV, interview, 1983, no day, no month, 28–29, AHEC, Carlisle.

63. John D. Blair IV, interview, 1983, no day, no month, 37.

64. John D. Blair IV, interview, 1983, no day, no month, 67.

65. John D. Blair IV, interview, 1983, no day, no month, 45, 54, 76. See chapter 8 for the response of Segrid Blair to reports of this battle and her husband's MIA status.

66. See chapter 6 for more extended coverage of the South's response to My Lai and the Calley trial.

67. Whitmore, *Memphis Nam Sweden,* 61–65; Lorenzo M. Crowell, "The Lesson and Ghosts of Vietnam," in *Looking Back on the Vietnam War: A Perspective on the Decisions, Combat, and Legacies,* ed. William Head and Lawrence E. Grinter (Westport, CT: Greenwood Press, 1993), 233 (Waide); Ensminger, interview, in J. R. Wilson, *Landing Zones,* 30; Turse, *Kill Anything That Moves,* 12, *passim.*

68. Trent Angers, *The Forgotten Hero of My Lai: The Hugh Thompson Story* (Lafayette, LA: Acadian House Publishing, 1999).

69. Hugh Thompson, oral statement, in David L. Anderson, ed., *Facing My Lai: Moving Beyond the Massacre* (Lawrence: University Press of Kansas, 1998), 28; Anders, *Hugh Thompson Story,* 117, 120.

70. Anders, *Hugh Thompson Story,* 124; Thompson, oral statement, in D. L. Anderson, *Facing My Lai,* 30.

71. Thompson, oral statement, in D. L. Anderson, *Facing My Lai,* 31.

72. Anders, *Hugh Thompson Story,* 39; William Eckhardt, oral statement, in D. L. Anderson, *Facing My Lai,* 41; Thompson, oral statement, in D. L. Anderson, *Facing My Lai,* 50. Thompson was subsequently recognized for his actions. Following his retirement from the military in 1983, he received the Soldiers Medal for risking "personal hazard or danger" in 1998 and spoke to students at the US Military, Naval, and Air Force academies regarding military ethics.

73. Gilman, *Vietnam and the Southern Imagination*, 29; "Senator Jim Webb," http://webb.senate.gov/aboutjim/index.cfm (accessed Sept. 5, 2011); MacPherson, *Long Time Passing*, 632–46 (quotes at 634–35, 641, 643).

74. Gilman, *Vietnam and the Southern Imagination*, 29; James Webb, *Fields of Fire* (New York: Bantam Books, 1979), 25.

75. Webb, *Fields of Fire*, 29, 33–35.

76. Webb, *Fields of Fire*, 110, 238, 333.

77. Webb, *Fields of Fire*, 295.

78. Webb, *Fields of Fire*, 198–99, 242, 252.

79. Webb, *Fields of Fire*, 392–93, 402, 404, 407, 409.

80. Matthew Samuel Ross, "An Examination of the Life and Work of Gustav Hasford" (MA thesis, University of Nevada, Las Vegas, 2010), 3; Matthew Samuel Ross, "Haunted by the Ghosts of Pickett's Charge: Echoes of the Civil War in Two Novels by Unreconstructed Veterans of the Vietnam War," forthcoming in *Southern Cultures*. The following overview of Hasford's life is taken from Ross's excellent thesis and article and from Gilman, *Vietnam and the Southern Imagination*, 127–37.

81. Gustav Hasford, *The Short-Timers* (New York: Harper & Row, 1979), 38, 50.

82. Hasford, *The Phantom Blooper* (New York: Bantam Books, 1990), 200, 240–41.

83. Hasford, *Short-Timers*, 112, 138; Hasford, *Phantom Blooper*, 189.

84. Hasford, *Short-Timers*, 69; Hasford, *Phantom Blooper*, 38, 63, 91, 103.

85. Hasford, *Short-Timers*, 70; Hasford, *Phantom Blooper*, 190, 196, 215–17, 220–21.

86. Purcell, interview, in J. R. Wilson, *Landing Zones*, 146; Cleland, *Heart of a Patriot*, 114.

87. William A. Brinkley, interview, Apr. 12, 1985, p. 35, AHEC, Carlisle; Strong, interview, in Terry, *Bloods*, 54; Gwin, interview, in Steinman, *Soldiers' Story*, 60–61; Fulmer, interview, 1983, no day or month, p. 78, AHEC, Carlisle; Peoples, interview, in J. R. Wilson, *Landing Zones*, 190.

5. Southerners and the Debate over the War's Conduct, 1967

1. US Congress, Senate Preparedness Investigating Subcommittee of the Senate Armed Services Committee, [Hearings on] *Air War against North Vietnam*, 90th Cong., 1st sess., Aug. 9–29, 1967 (Washington, DC: Government Printing Office, 1967), 2 (hereafter cited as Stennis Hearings); *GOI*, no. 26 (Aug. 1967), 2, 4.

2. Herring, *LBJ and Vietnam*, 54.

3. Herring, *America's Longest War*, 178, 194, 198, 220; Prados, *Vietnam*, 181–82.

4. Prados, *Vietnam*, 184 (Reston); Gibbons, *U.S. Government and the Vietnam War*, 4: 566–67; Fry, *Debating Vietnam*, 98, 102; Herring, *America's Longest War*, 179.

5. Herring, *LBJ and Vietnam*, 52–53 ("mobilizing the nation"); Prados, *Viet-*

nam, 183–84; Mark Clodfelter, *The Limits of Air Power: The American Bombing of North Vietnam* (New York: Free Press, 1989), 108.

6. Ashmore and Baggs, *Mission to Hanoi*, 174.

7. Ashmore and Baggs, *Mission to Hanoi*, 10–11.

8. Ashmore and Baggs, *Mission to Hanoi*, 43, 45, 50.

9. Ashmore and Baggs, *Mission to Hanoi*, 57, 65, 84.

10. Ashmore and Baggs, *Mission to Hanoi*, 80, 182, 189.

11. Stennis to H. W. Pittman, Aug. 2, 1967, 43/68/11, and SPIS, news release, Mar. 27, 1967, 43/46/3, both Stennis Papers.

12. Stennis to Jane M. Danzy, Mar. 21, 1967, 4/68/11, Stennis to Mrs. Hughie Burcham, Mar. 21, 1967, 4/68/11, Stennis to Wallace Kimbrough, Sept. 1, 1967, 4/68/11, and Stennis, speech to Student Conference, University of Southern Mississippi, Hattiesburg, Apr. 7, 1967, 3–5, Public Series, box 13, all Stennis Papers.

13. Stennis, speech to Student Conference, University of Southern Mississippi, Apr. 7, 1967, 3–5.

14. *CR*, 90:1 (Feb. 28, 1967), 4,717, 4,723; J. Woods, *Richard Russell*, 150; Russell to Robert T. Thomason, Feb. 15, 1967, 36:2, Russell Papers.

15. Fry, *Debating Vietnam*, 94; *CR*, 90:1 (July 10, 1967), 18,227 (Rivers); Long, speech to National Association of Secondary Materials Industries, Miami, FL, Apr. 18, 1967, 11, 603:34, Long, "Of Brainwashing Republicans and the Politics of Vietnam," remarks in Congress, Sept. 26, 1967, 604:43, *Shreveport Times*, Jan. 16, 1967, 102:13, and Long, speech to Shreveport Chamber of Commerce, Mar. 28, 1967, 2, 603:34, all Long Papers.

16. Ervin to Robert L. Scott, Jan. 2, 1967, 150:6578, and Ervin to John M. Fletcher, Sept. 1, 1967, 150:6589, both Ervin Papers; Becnel, *Senator Allen Ellender*, 250; *CR*, 90:1 (Oct. 2, 1967), 27,454 (Smathers); *CR*, 90:1 (Apr. 11, 1967), 69A4119:6, "Foreign Relations," Sparkman Papers.

17. *CR*, 90:1 (Oct. 2, 1967), 27,452–53 (Thurmond).

18. Tower, remarks before the Texas State Legislature, Feb. 28, 1967, 2–3, 19:5, and Tower, speech to the Texas Cotton Growers Association, Houston, Mar. 17, 1967, 2, 4–5, 9, 19:5, both Tower Papers.

19. Tower, "The Morality of Vietnam," speech at Houston Baptist College, May 29, 1967, 5, 13, and Tower, news release, Dec. 7, 1967, 1, both 973:8, Tower Papers.

20. John Egerton, *The Americanization of Dixie: The Southernization of America* (New York: Harpers Magazine Press, 1974), 197 (minister); *GOI*, no. 70 (Apr. 1971), 49, 52–53; Preston, *Sword of the Spirit, Shield of Faith*, 420 ("divided"), 455, 499 (Tennessee resident). For a revealing example of this southern religious perspective, see the postwar campaign for Kentucky's Vietnam War memorial in Patrick Hagopian, *The Vietnam War in American Memory: Veterans, Memorials, and the Politics of Healing* (Amherst: University of Massachusetts Press, 2009), 231, 249, 252–54.

21. Michael B. Friedland, *Lift Up Your Voice like a Trumpet: White Clergy and the Civil Rights and Antiwar Movements, 1954–1973* (Chapel Hill: University of North Carolina Press, 1998), 168, 173; Preston, *Sword of the Spirit, Shield of Faith*, 520–28;

David J. Settje, *Faith and War: How Christians Debated the Cold and Vietnam Wars* (New York: New York University Press, 2011), 7, 61–65, 71–78.

22. Nutt, *Toward Peacemaking*, 74–78 (Taylor on 77–78).

23. Nutt, *Toward Peacemaking*, 125–27.

24. John Ernst and Yvonne Baldwin, "The Not So Silent Minority: Louisville's Antiwar Movement, 1966–1975," *Journal of Southern History* 78 (Feb. 2007): 109–12 (Braden on 111); Nutt, *Toward Peacemaking*, 80 (Edwards).

25. Gregory D. Tomlin, "Hawks and Doves: Southern Baptist Responses to Military Intervention in Southeast Asia, 1965–1973" (PhD diss., Southwestern Baptist Theological Seminary, 2003), 6–7, 144 (quote); Preston, *Sword of the Spirit, Shield of Faith*, 533; Settje, *Faith and War*, 68–69.

26. Steven P. Miller, *Billy Graham and the Rise of the Republican South* (Philadelphia: University of Pennsylvania Press, 2009), 22 ("evangelist"); Tomlin, "Hawks and Doves," 24, 118; Preston, *Sword of the Spirit, Shield of Faith*, 534; Friedland, *Lift Up Your Voice like a Trumpet*, 157.

27. Tomlin, "Hawks and Doves," 64–65, 77, 84, 125, 127; Settje, *Faith and War*, 69.

28. Tomlin, "Hawks and Doves," 159–61.

29. Tomlin, "Hawks and Doves," 123, 129–30, 186, 245–46.

30. Tomlin, "Hawks and Doves," 51, 223 (PNBC); Thomas J. Noer, "Martin Luther King, Jr. and the Cold War," *Peace and Change* 22 (Apr. 1997): 112; Henry E. Darby and Margaret N. Rowley, "King on Vietnam and Beyond," *Phylon* 17 (Sept. 1986): 44; Andrew J. DeRoche, *Andrew Young: Civil Rights Ambassador* (Wilmington, DE: SR Books, 2003), 33, 35.

31. Plumer, *Rising Wind*, 318; William L. Lunch and Peter W. Sperlich, "American Public Opinion and the War in Vietnam," *Western Political Quarterly* 32 (Mar. 1979): 36. These are national figures.

32. Westheider, *Fighting on Two Fronts*, 20–21; Westheider, *African American Experience in Vietnam*, 23; Herbert Shapiro, "The Vietnam War and the American Civil Rights Movement," *Journal of Ethnic Studies* 16 (Winter 1989): 136; D. L. Anderson, "Bill Henry Terry Jr.," 135–51; Eldridge, *Chronicles of a Two-Front War*, 71.

33. Eldridge, *Chronicles of a Two-Front War*, 3 (Moses); Daniel S. Lucks, *Selma to Saigon: The Civil Rights Movement and the Vietnam War* (Lexington: University Press of Kentucky, 2014), 98 (Mississippi Freedom Democratic Party); SNCC Statement on Vietnam, Jan. 6, 1966, reel 20, box 173, Student Nonviolent Coordinating Committee Papers, 1959–1973, microfilm copy, Library of Congress (hereafter cited as SNCC Papers); J. W. to Stennis, Feb. 2, 1966, 4/85/16, Stennis Papers.

34. Clyde Taylor, ed., *Vietnam and Black Americans: An Anthology of Protest and Resistance* (Garden City, NY: Anchor Books, 1973), 110 (Bond), 259; Bond, statement in unidentified newspaper clipping, reel 20, box 176, and King Statement, SNCC Press Conference, Jan. 8, 1965, reel 20, box 173, both SNCC Papers; Adam Fairclough, "Martin Luther King, Jr. and the War in Vietnam," *Phylon* 45 (Mar.

406 Notes to Pages 210–217

1984): 26; Shapiro, "Vietnam War and the American Civil Rights Movement,"
125–29.

35. Henry Wallace to Lucille Black, Dec. 11, 1965, Wallace to Roy Wilkins, Jan. 13, 1966, and Wallace to John A. Morsell, Jan. 17, 1966, all Group III, box A328, Records of the National Association for the Advancement of Colored People, Manuscripts Division, Library of Congress.

36. *Louisville Courier-Journal*, Jan. 12, 1966; Lucks, *Selma to Saigon*, 116 (Greer); *Atlanta Constitution*, Jan. 13, 14, 15, 1966. In an interesting exchange of letters the following year, Andrew Young defended King and the SCLC's opposition to the war while congratulating Patterson on winning the Pulitzer Prize. Patterson, in turn, maintained his support for Johnson and the war but declared, "The good thing about this country is that even friends are free to fall out." See Young to Patterson, May 3, 1967, and Patterson to Young, June 5, 1967, both Records of the Southern Christian Leadership Conference, 1954–1970, part II, reel 10, microfilm copy, Manuscripts Division, Library of Congress (hereafter cited as SCLC Records).

37. Arthur C. Banks Jr. and Finley C. Campbell to Editor, *Atlanta Constitution*, Jan. 13, 1966; *Norfolk Journal and Guide*, Jan. 22, Feb. 5, 1966; *Atlanta Daily World*, Jan. 8, Feb. 2, 1966; *Jackson Advocate*, Jan. 29, 1966. See also *Birmingham World*, Feb. 9, 1966.

38. Eldridge, *Chronicles of a Two-Front War*, 57 ("visible symbol"); Westheider, *African American Experience in Vietnam*, 30–31; Graham, *Brothers' Vietnam War*, 66–89; Thomas Hauser, *The Lost Legacy of Muhammad Ali* (Wilmington, DE: Sport Classic Publishing, 2005).

39. Graham, *Brothers' Vietnam War*, 72–73; Ernst and Baldwin, "Not So Silent Minority," 129.

40. Shapiro, "Vietnam War and the American Civil Rights Movement," 121–22; Fairclough, "Martin Luther King, Jr. and the War in Vietnam," 24–25; Lucks, *Selma to Saigon*, 156; Plummer, *In Search of Power*, 152 (staffer).

41. Shapiro, "Vietnam War and the American Civil Rights Movement," 129–30; Lucks, *Selma to Saigon*, 188.

42. Thomas J. Noer, "Martin Luther King, Jr. and the Cold War," *Peace and Change* 22 (Apr. 1997): 123; Shapiro, "Vietnam War and the American Civil Rights Movement," 131; Martin Luther King Jr., "The Casualties of the War in Vietnam," speech before the National Institute, Beverly Hills, CA, Feb. 25, 1967, part IV, reel 25, SCLC Records.

43. Taylor, *Vietnam and Black Americans*, 81–82, 85–86, 91–92; Lucks, *Selma to Saigon*, 193–96.

44. Eldridge, *Chronicles of a Two-Front War*, 105–6, 111; Shapiro, "Vietnam War and the American Civil Rights Movement," 134–35; Noer, "Martin Luther King Jr. and the Cold War," 126; Fairclough, "Martin Luther King, Jr. and the War in Vietnam," 34; Borstelmann, *Cold War and the Color Line*, 210; Lucks, *Selma to Saigon*, 218–19, 228; *Jackson Advocate*, Apr. 8, 1967.

45. DeRoche, *Andrew Young*, 34–35; Carter, *Politics of Rage*, 328 (Wallace); J.

Woods, *Black Struggle, Red Scare;* Thomas Noer, "Segregationists and the World: The Foreign Policy of the White Resistance," in *Window on Freedom: Race, Civil Rights, and Foreign Affairs, 1945–1988,* ed. Brenda Gayle Plummer (Chapel Hill: University of North Carolina Press, 2003), 141–52; Wilson M. Epperson to Editor, *Richmond News-Leader,* [Sept. 1965], part I, reel 13, and "A dear, dear friend" to Martin Luther King, Aug. 5, 1965, part I, reel 12, both SCLC Records; J. E. H. to Sparkman, May 25, 1967, and Mrs. M. C. W. to Sparkman, Aug. 23, 1967, both 69A4119:6, "Foreign Relations," Sparkman Papers; B. D. to Long, Apr. 22, 1967, 102:9, Long Papers; J. W. H. to Russell, Apr. 19, 1967, 35:5, Russell Papers.

46. Mr. and Mrs. J. M. S. to Tower, Jan. 30, 1966, 318:6, and J. S. B. to Tower, Apr. 29, 1967, 327:1, both Tower Papers; L. M. C. to Stennis, Apr. 30, 1967, 4/68/11, Stennis Papers.

47. Hauser, *Lost Legacy of Muhammad Ali,* 41–42.

48. Gibbons, *U.S. Government and the Vietnam War,* 4: 548; *CR,* 90:1 (Feb. 28, 1967), 4,715–16, 4,724, 4,726–27; Fulbright to Paul Foster, May 13, 1967, 51:5, Fulbright to Jewell W. Massey, Aug. 23, 1967, 52:6, and Fulbright to Ronnie Dugger, Dec. 16, 1966, 47:6, all Fulbright Papers.

49. Meeting of the President with Senate Committee Chairman, July 25, 1967, in Barrett, *Lyndon B. Johnson's Vietnam Papers,* 451–53.

50. Herring, *LBJ and Vietnam,* 1, 19.

51. *CR,* 90:1 (Feb. 28, 1967), 4,715, 4,721; R. B. Woods, *Fulbright,* 442–43, 456; Fite, *Richard B. Russell Jr.,* 451; Gibbons, *U.S. Government and the Vietnam War,* 4: 810–11.

52. R. B. Woods, *Fulbright,* 456, 458; Gibbons, *U.S. Government and the Vietnam War,* 4: 813.

53. Gore, "Capitol Commentary," June 12, 1967, C44:1 (1967), Gore Papers; *CR,* 90:1 (May 15, 1967), box 570, Cooper Papers.

54. Gore, "Capitol Commentary," Mar. 27, 1967, C44:1 (1967), Gore Papers; *CR,* 90:1 (May 15, 1967), box 570, Cooper Papers.

55. *CR,* 90:1 (May 11, 1967), 12,494, (May 23, 1967), 13,534–35; *Louisville Times,* Aug. 14, 1967, box 22, Morton Papers.

56. *New York Times,* Aug. 7, 1967; Gibbons, *U.S. Government and the Vietnam War,* 4: 840; Herring, *America's Longest War,* 220; Andrew J. Huebner, *The Warrior Image: Soldiers in American Culture from the Second World War to the Vietnam Era* (Chapel Hill: University of North Carolina Press, 2008), 188, 194; *GOI,* no. 19 (Jan. 1967), 4, no. 26 (Aug. 1967), 3–5, no. 27 (Sept. 1967), 4, and no. 29 (Nov. 1967), 4.

57. *GOI,* no. 19 (Jan. 1967), 3–4, no. 28 (Oct. 1967), 2, and no. 30 (Dec. 1967), 1; Louis, Bowles, and Grace, Inc., "The Climate of Opinion in Texas Politics as of November 1967," xii–xiii, 884:1, Tower Papers.

58. *GOI,* no. 21 (Mar. 1967), 5–6, no. 24 (June 1967), 5, 7, no. 26 (Aug. 1967), 4, 7, no. 28 (Oct. 1967), 18, and no. 29 (Nov. 1967), 3–4, 8, 16–18.

59. W. H. B. to Fulbright, Aug. 10, 1967, 51:2, and G. A. G. to Fulbright, Aug.

10, 1967, 51:6, both Fulbright Papers; F. H. B. to Long, Jan. 15, 1967, 102:8, Long Papers; J. E. E. Jr. to L. H. Fountain, Jan. 16, 1967, and C. M. I. to Ervin, Jan. 16, 1967, both 150:6578, Ervin Papers.

60. W. B. P. to Talmadge, Jan. 27, 1967, 36:3, Russell Papers; D. M. S. to Harry F. Byrd Jr., Sept. 6, 1967, 197:Vietnam, Sept. 1–10, 1967, Byrd Jr. Papers; M. A. G. to Stennis, Jan. 1, 1967, 4/68/11, and J. K. P. to Stennis, Jan. 2, 1967, 43/95/Vietnam Miscellaneous, 1967, both Stennis Papers.

61. W. B. P. to Herman Talmadge, Jan. 27, 1968, 36:3, Russell Papers; L. D. K. M. to Byrd Jr., Aug. 22, 1967, and G. M. L. to Byrd Jr., Aug. 21, 1967, both 197:Vietnam, Aug. 21–25, 1967, Byrd Jr. Papers; R. DeB. to Gore, Apr. 25, 1967, C23:1, Gore Papers.

62. V. J. R. to Gore, May 5, 1967, C23:3, Gore Papers; W. K. to Stennis, Aug. 22, 1967, 4/68/11, Stennis Papers.

63. J. H. G. to Russell, Dec. 15, 1967, 33:11, Russell Papers; R. G. L. to Byrd Jr., May 25, 1967, 197:Vietnam, Mar.–July 20, 1967, Byrd Jr. Papers; Sue Spencer to Congressmen and Senators, July 25, 1967, 69A419:6, Foreign Relations, Sparkman Papers.

64. L. S. and J. R. S. to Ervin, Feb. 2, 1967, 150: 6579, H. M. to Ervin, Mar. 9, 1967, 150:6581, and R. A. to Ervin, Sept. 8, 1967, 150:6589, all Ervin Papers.

65. Fry, *Debating Vietnam*, 88, 102; Record, *Wrong War*, 174 ("defeat avoidance"); Stuart Symington to Stennis, Aug. 14, 15, 1967, 43/4/93, Stennis Papers; Symington to Howard C. Cannon, Aug. 14, 1967, 90th Cong., box 12, folder 187, Howard C. Cannon Papers, Special Collections, University of Nevada, Las Vegas; Buzzanco, *Masters of War*, 300.

66. Stennis Hearings, 244; Fry, *Debating Vietnam*, 102–3.

67. For the press and informed sources, see Neil Sheehan's articles in the *New York Times*, Aug. 10, 17, 1967; *Newsweek*, Sept. 11, 1967, 20–21; *New York Times*, Aug. 11, 1967 (Reston).

68. Stennis Hearings, 2–3.

69. Stennis Hearings, 29, 71, 110, 121, 130, 205.

70. Stennis Hearings, 58, 92, 466–67, 500.

71. Stennis Hearings, 252, 295, 426, 465.

72. Stennis Hearings, 149, 201, 205; Fry, *Debating Vietnam*, 104–9; Joseph A. Fry, "To Negotiate or Bomb: Congressional Prescriptions for Withdrawing U.S. Troops from Vietnam," *Diplomatic History* 34 (June 2010): 522–23.

73. Fry, *Debating Vietnam*, 118–22; *New York Times*, Dec. 5, 1967; *Nation*, May 29, 1967, 675.

74. Stennis Hearings, 276, 279, 307; *New Yorker*, Sept. 16, 1967, 37–38; Fry, *Debating Vietnam*, 123–29; Herring, *LBJ and Vietnam*, 55.

75. Stennis Hearings, 504; Fry, *Debating Vietnam*, 129–34; US Congress, Senate Preparedness Investigating Subcommittee of the Senate Armed Services Committee, *Summary Report on Hearings on Air War against North Vietnam*, 90th Cong., 1st sess., Aug. 31, 1967 (Washington, DC: Government Printing Office, 1967), 2, 7–9.

76. *National Review,* Sept. 19, 1967, 1,001; *Aviation Week and Space Technology,* Sept. 11, 1967, 21, and Oct. 16, 1967, 21; *Nation,* Sept. 18, 1967, 228; *New York Times,* Sept. 1, 1967.

77. Gibbons, *U.S Government and the Vietnam War,* 4: 900–901.

78. John K. McLean to Stennis, Jan. 5, 1967, Gay Broome to Stennis, May 7, 1967, 43/95/Vietnam Miscellaneous, and E. A. Nichols to Stennis, Apr. 19, 1967, 4/68/11, all Stennis Papers.

79. C. C. Wood to Stennis, May 2, 1967, 43/95/2, Stennis Papers; E. A. Bates to Stennis, July 11, 1967, Donald Nunnery to Stennis, Sept. 1, 1967, and Buddy Graves to Stennis, July 15, 1967, all 4/68/11, Stennis Papers.

80. Morton to James S. Templeton, Aug. 22, 1967, Morton to Robert Hubbard, Aug. 24, 1967, and Morton to Raymond Guinn, Sept. 12, 1967, all box 19, Morton Papers.

81. *CR,* 90:1 (Sept. 28, 1967), 27,130–31.

82. Fulbright to Mrs. Joseph W. Schwartz, Aug. 29, 1967, 55:3, Fulbright Papers; Johns, *Vietnam's Second Front,* 176 (Oberdorfer).

83. Walter Leet Jr. to Morton, Jan. 24, 1967, and Raymond Sory to Morton, Sept. 28, 1967, both box 19, Morton Papers; Robert E. and Sylvia Burkhart to Morton, July 25, 1967, Willa Stringfield to Morton, Aug. 14, 1967, Harold Wahking to Morton, Aug. 14, 1967, Kenneth McKean to Morton, Aug. 15, 1967, C. R. Kaplan to Morton, Aug. 17, 1967, and Charles R. Gruenberger to Morton, Sept. 26, 1967, all box 22, Morton Papers.

84. Gibbons, *U.S. Government and the Vietnam War,* 4: 848 (McGovern); Notes of the President's Meeting with Rusk, McNamara . . . Wheeler, Oct. 23, 1967, in Barrett, *Lyndon B. Johnson's Vietnam Papers,* 509; Fry, *Debating Vietnam,* 139–40.

85. Neil Sheehan, "You Don't Know Where Johnson Ends and McNamara Begins," *New York Times Magazine,* Oct. 22, 1967, 127.

86. *New York Times,* Oct. 13, 1967 (Rusk); Tower, press release, Dec. 7, 1967, 973:8, Tower Papers.

87. *CR,* 90:1 (Oct. 24, 1967), 29,801–3 (Dec. 8, 1967), 35,559–60.

6. Southerners and the Decisions to Withdraw from Vietnam, 1968–1970

1. David F. Schmitz, *The Tet Offensive: Politics, War, and Public Opinion* (Lanham, MD: Rowman and Littlefield Publishers, 2005), 99 (Cronkite); Herring, *America's Longest War,* 257 (bastards); R. B. Woods, *LBJ,* 830.

2. Herring, *America's Longest War,* 257 ("restraint"), 274 ("de-escalation"); Prados, *Vietnam,* 261–62.

3. Schoenbaum, *Waging Peace and War,* 469–70 (Christian), 274; Herring, *America's Longest War,* 247 ("bleak").

4. George C. Herring, *America's Longest War: The United States and Vietnam, 1950–1975* (Boston: McGraw Hill, 2002), 255.

5. Talmadge, "Reports from the United States Senate," May 1, 1968, 2/256/15, Talmadge Papers; Ervin to Janie Sprinkle, Feb. 15, 1968, 169:7502, Ervin Papers; Sparkman to Ollie Franklin Myers, May 24, 1968, 70A4063:5, Sparkman Papers; Long to James W. Parker, Sept. 24, 1968, 108:34, and Transcript of Long Radio and Television Interview with Louisiana Broadcast Network, Mar. 16–17, 1968, 606:38, both Long Papers; Russell to Charles F. Heard, Mar. 14, 1968, 32:12, and Russell to Sherry McEachern, Mar. 7, 1969, 31:6, both Russell Papers.

6. Downs, "Matter of Conscience," 100, 106; *CR,* 90:2 (Feb. 28, 1968), 4,490; Stennis to Dr. Hans H. Behner, Mar. 27, 1968, 4/68/9, and Stennis, speech to Military Order of the World Wars, Memphis, TN, Oct. 25, 1968, 1, 4, Public Series, 5/26, both Stennis Papers; Tower, news release, Feb. 10–11, 1968, 25:15, and news release, Mar. 1, 1968, 22:1, both Tower Papers.

7. Morton, press releases, Feb. 4, Apr. 2, 1968, box 2, Morton Papers.

8. *CR,* 90:2 (Mar. 7, 1968), 5,651; US Congress, Senate Committee on Foreign Relations, "[Hearings on] The Gulf of Tonkin, the 1964 Incidents," 90th Cong., 2nd sess., Feb. 20, 1968 (Washington, DC: Government Printing Office, 1968), 1, 8–9, 30 (hereafter cited as SFRC, "Gulf of Tonkin" Hearings); R. B. Woods, *Fulbright,* 474–79; Mann, *Grand Delusion,* 579–80.

9. SFRC, "Gulf of Tonkin" Hearings, 79–80; 88–91, 102; *Baltimore Sun,* Jan. 14, 1968, box 603, Cooper Papers.

10. SFRC, "Gulf of Tonkin" Hearings, 109–10; *CR,* 90:2 (Mar. 7, 1968), 5,646.

11. US Congress, Senate Committee on Foreign Relations, [Hearings on] "Foreign Assistance Act of 1968, Part I—Vietnam," 90th Cong., 2nd sess., Mar. 11–12, 1968 (Washington, DC: Government Printing Office, 1968), 1 (hereafter cited as SFRC, "Foreign Assistance Act of 1968" Hearings).

12. SFRC, "Foreign Assistance Act of 1968" Hearings, 16–17.

13. SFRC, "Foreign Assistance Act of 1968" Hearings, 13, 46, 1,345–36; B. S. K. to Gore, Mar. 13, 1968, A47:3, Gore Papers.

14. SFRC, "Foreign Assistance Act of 1968" Hearings, 133–35, 138–39; *CR,* 90:2 (Mar. 7, 1968), 5,645.

15. SFRC, "Foreign Assistance Act of 1968" Hearings, 79, 103, 105, 258.

16. Mann, *Grand Delusion,* 11 (Senate speeches); Hodges, "Cooing of a Dove," 144.

17. *GOI,* no. 31 (Jan. 1968), 2–3, no. 32 (Feb. 1968), 2–3, 18, no. 33 (Mar. 1968), 2–3, no. 34 (Apr. 1968), 2–3, no. 35 (May 1968), 2–3, no. 40 (Oct. 1968), 5, and no. 42 (Dec. 1968), 2.

18. *GOI,* no. 32 (Feb. 1968), p. 18, no. 33 (Mar. 1968), 6, 8, no. 34 (Apr. 1968), 15–17, no. 35 (May 1968), 20–22, no. 38 (Aug. 1968), 2, 7, no. 39 (Sept. 1968), 3, no. 40 (Oct. 1968), 24–25, no. 41 (Nov. 1968), 7, and no. 42 (Dec. 1968), 2.

19. *Atlanta Constitution,* Feb. 7, 8, Mar. 12, 15, 1968; *Dallas Morning News,* Feb. 14, 16, 1968; *Montgomery Advertiser,* Feb. 1, 9, Apr. 2, 1968; *Louisville Courier-Journal,* Feb. 1, 3, 8, 16, Mar. 13, 25, 1968; Herring, *America's Longest War,* 222.

20. H. G. to Ervin, Mar. 18, 1968, 169:7507, and A. D. T. to Ervin, May 23,

1968, 169:7512, both Ervin Papers; Henry L. Lewis to Stennis, Mar. 12, 1968, with enclosure, "Open Letter to the Senate Foreign Relations Committee," 43/96/2, Stennis Papers; E. D. M. to Henry E. Niles, Mar. 28, 1968, 32:8, D. D. S. to Russell, Oct. 16, 1968, 32:2, and F. A. C. to Russell, Nov. 12, 1968, 32:1, all Russell Papers; Mrs. J. R. to Sparkman, Jan. 30, 1968, 70A4063:5, Sparkman Papers.

21. A. J. H. to Ervin, Feb. 1, 1968, 169:7502, Ervin Papers; Daniel Justice to Editor, *Atlanta Constitution,* Feb. 7, 1968; Mrs. Paul E. Miller to Editor, *Louisville Courier Journal,* Mar. 9, 1968; W. L. W. to Russell, Jan. 15, 1968, 33:7, Russell Papers.

22. L. M. D. to Fulbright, Jan. 26, 1968, 54:4, Fulbright Papers; T. A. C. to Russell, Apr. 26, 1968, 32:2, and A. C. H. Jr. to Russell, June 9, 1969, 30:11, both Russell Papers; *GOI,* no. 48 (June 1969), 11, no. 60 (June 1970), 13.

23. Excerpts from Tower, speech to Midwest Regional Conference of the Associated Credit Bureaus of America, Apr. 26, 1968, 22:11, Tower Papers; Talmadge, "Reports from the United States Senate," Apr. 10, 1968, 2/256/12, Talmadge Papers; Stennis, speech to Coast Guard Section of Reserve Officers Association, Fort Myers, VA, Feb. 21, 1968, 5, and Stennis, speech to VFW Convention, Jackson, MS, June 22, 1968, 5, 9, both Public Series, 15/12, Stennis Papers; Downs, "Matter of Conscience," 69, 96.

24. Carter, *From George Wallace to Newt Gingrich,* 14, 18; Walter LaFeber, *The Deadly Bet: LBJ, Vietnam and the 1968 Election* (Lanham, MD: Rowman and Littlefield, 2005), 138; Carter, *Politics of Rage,* 161, 305.

25. LaFeber, *Deadly Bet,* 141, 143; Johns, *Vietnam's Second Front,* 196–97.

26. Herman E. Talmadge, with Mark Royden Winchell, *Talmadge: A Political Legacy, A Politician's Life: A Memoir* (Atlanta: Peachtree Publishers, 1987), 250–51; LaFeber, *Deadly Bet,* 103–13; J. C. Cobb, *South and America since World War II,* 13–32; Johns, *Vietnam's Second Front,* 195–236; *GOI,* no. 40 (Oct. 1968), 23, no. 41 (Nov. 1968), 7.

27. Catherine Forslund, *Anna Chennault: Informal Diplomacy and Asian Relations* (Wilmington, DE: SR Books, 2002), 51–81; Johns, *Vietnam's Second Front,* 221–31; Anna Chennault to Tran Thien Khiem, Mar. 25, 1969, 974:7, Tower Papers.

28. George C. Herring, "The Executive, Congress, and the Vietnam War," in *Congress and United States Foreign Policy: Controlling the Use of Force in the Nuclear Age,* ed. Michael Barnart (Albany: State University of New York Press, 1987), 181; Robert Schulzinger, "Richard Nixon, Congress, and the War in Vietnam, 1969–1974," in R. B. Woods, *Vietnam and the American Political Tradition,* 283; R. D. Johnson, *Congress and the Cold War,* 143; Alton Frye and Jack Sullivan, "Congress and Vietnam: The Fruits of Anguish," in *To Advise and Consent: The United States, Congress and Foreign Policy in the Twentieth Century,* ed. Joel Silbey, 2 vols. (Brooklyn, NY: Carlson Publishers, 1991), 2: 336.

29. Johns, *Vietnam's Second Front,* 242, 245; Small, *Johnson, Nixon, and the Doves,* 197.

30. J. C. Cobb, *South and America since World War II,* 136–38; Prados, *Viet-*

nam, 299–302; Melvin Small, *The Presidency of Richard Nixon* (Lawrence: University Press of Kansas, 1999), 65; Jeffrey Kimball, *Nixon's Vietnam War* (Lawrence: University Press of Kansas, 1998), 212; Henry Kissinger, *White House Years* (Boston: Little, Brown, 1979), 229.

31. Small, *Presidency of Richard Nixon,* 67; Kimball, *Nixon's Vietnam War,* 78 ("Commie mind"); H. R. Haldeman, with Joseph DiMona, *The Ends of Power* (New York: Times Books, 1978), 83 ("Mad-man Theory").

32. Thomas Borstelmann, *The 1970s: A New Global History from Civil Rights to Economic Inequality* (Princeton, NJ: Princeton University Press, 2012), 23 ("too clear-eyed," "defeat"); Thomas Alan Schwartz, "'Henry, . . . Winning an Election Is Terribly Important': Partisan Politics in the History of U.S. Foreign Relations," *Diplomatic History* 33 (Apr. 2009): 174.

33. Herring, *America's Longest War,* 277–96; Kimball, *Nixon's Vietnam War, passim;* Prados, *Vietnam,* 288–517.

34. *GOI,* 1969–1973, *passim,* no. 52 (Oct. 1969), 14, no. 56 (Feb. 1970), 2, no. 60 (June 1970), 1–2, 4–5, no. 69 (Mar. 1971), 12, no. 84 (June 1972), 3–4. See also surveys of Texas public opinion, Dec. 1969, June 1970, 883:3, and Mar. 1971, 883:4, all Tower Papers.

35. Eldridge, *Chronicles of a Two-Front War,* 166, 172, 176; Lucks, *Selma to Saigon,* 234.

36. *Atlanta Daily World,* May 3, 7, 8, 10, 14, 17, 1970, consulted via the Black Studies Center, published by ProQuest in collaboration with the New York Public Library, http://ezproxy.library.unlv.edu/login?url=http://bsc.chadwyck.con (accessed Feb. 27, 2014) (hereafter cited as *Atlanta Daily World*); *Birmingham World,* Oct. 12, 1968, May 6, 16, 23, 1970, July 8, 1972.

37. Mrs. J. P. J. to Fulbright, Mar. 26, 1969, 56:7, and R. H. and M. B. S. to Fulbright, May 10, 1970, 66:2, both Fulbright Papers; T. J. Morris to Talmadge, Nov. 11, 1969, 11/74/4, Talmadge Papers; Rev. G. Wright Dole to Ervin, Oct. 10, 1969, 188:8439, and Mrs. Jerry H. Parrish to Ervin, Oct. 17, 1969, 188:8442, both Ervin Papers; Clarence McKasson to Tower, Oct. 22, 1969, 378:3, Tower Papers; Perry Hudson to Russell, Apr. 4, 1969, 31:14, Russell Papers.

38. Robert F. Morgan to John Stennis, Sept. 18, 1970, 28:4, Leroy Guinn to Russell, Aug. 10, 1969, 30:9, D. C. Ruff to Russell, Sept. 16, 1969, 30:7, and Frank Alessi to Russell, Nov. 15, 1969, 29:11, all Russell Papers. For the South's estimate of South Vietnamese military capacity, see *GOI,* no. 43 (Jan. 1969), 9.

39. Al S. James Jr. to Richard Nixon, Aug. 12, 1969, 30:9, Russell Papers; Rabbi Efraim M. Rosenzweig to Ervin, Oct. 14, 1969, 188:8438, Dr. A. T. H. to Ervin, Mar. 25, 1969, 188:8437, and Douglas Mock to Ervin, Oct. 15, 1969, 188:8449, all Ervin Papers; Ben Cashion to Fulbright, Oct. 7, 1969, 56:3, Fulbright Papers; Bill Maxwell to Tower, Nov. 8, 1969, 378:1, Tower Papers.

40. W. R. H. to Russell, Oct. 24, 1969, 30:3, Russell Papers; Dr. J. S. G. Jr., to Ervin, Oct. 16, 1969, 188:8438, Ervin Papers.

41. Stennis to Alice Faye Murphee, June 25, 1970, 31/11/72, and Stennis to

Steve Rogers, Nov. 19, 1971, 31/11/49, both Stennis Papers; Ervin to North Carolina Committee of Concerned Americans, July 1, 1969, 188:8435, and Ervin to Jim Davidson, Oct. 24, 1969, 188:8441, both Ervin Papers; Russell to Mrs. Adolphe J. Michel, Mar. 5, 1969, 31:6, and Russell to Mr. and Mrs. V. E. Dial, Apr. 14, 1969, 31:4, both Russell Papers; transcript, Long's appearance on CBS, *Face the Nation*, Nov. 2, 1969, 18, 608:80, Long Papers.

42. Johns, *Vietnam's Second Front*, 240 (Thurmond), 259 (Cooper); Tower, "Vietnam Situation" Report, Feb. 22–23, 1969, Tower, news release, Apr. 14, 1969, and Tower, news release, Oct. 1, 1969, all 974:6, Tower Papers; Robert F. Maddox, "John Sherman Cooper and the Vietnam War," *Journal of the West Virginia Historical Association* 11 (1987): 66–67.

43. Downs, "Matter of Conscience," 106 ("number one champion"), 120; Stennis, Floor Statement Regarding Vietnam, May 14, 1970, 2, 4/61/7, and Stennis, speech to National Guard Association, Jackson, MS, Sept. 17, 1970, 8, both Public Series, 18/13, Stennis Papers. Russell and Rivers were also informed of the bombing of Cambodia. See Scanlon, *Pro-War Movement*, 103.

44. Transcript of Stennis's appearance on CBS, *Face the Nation*, Mar. 9, 1969, 15, and Stennis, speech to East Mississippi Electric Power Association, Oct. 25, 1969, 10–13, both Public Series, 17/10, Stennis Papers.

45. Berman, *William Fulbright*, 105, 109, 115; R. B. Woods, *Fulbright*, 533; Mann, *Grand Delusion*, 628, 639.

46. *CR*, 91:1 (Mar. 20, 1969), 6,966–67 (May 8, 1969), 11,827 (June 17, 1969), 16,127 (June 19, 1969), 16,576.

47. R. B. Woods, *Fulbright*, 513; *CR*, 91:1 (June 25, 1969), 17,241–42, 17,244–45; *CQA*, 91:1 (1969), 178.

48. Small, *Presidency of Richard Nixon*, 183; Small, *Johnson, Nixon, and the Doves*, 74; Charles DeBenedetti, with Charles Chatfield, *An American Ordeal: The Antiwar Movement of the Vietnam Era* (Syracuse, NY: Syracuse University Press, 1990), 255–57.

49. Johns, *Vietnam's Second Front*, 271–72; Mann, *Grand Delusion*, 643–45.

50. Hagopian, *Vietnam War in American Memory*, 62 (Nixon); Claude Cookman, "An American Atrocity: The My Lai Massacre Concretized in a Victim's Face," *Journal of American History* 94 (June 2007): 160–61 (Rivers); Becnel, *Senator Allen Ellender*, 261; *CQA*, 91:1 (1969), 853 (Hollings), 92:1 (1971), 267 (Rarick).

51. *CQA*, 92:1 (1971), 744 (Talmadge, Blackburn); Tower, Weekly News Report, Apr. 10–11, 1971, 26:2, Tower Papers.

52. Michael R. Belknap, *The Vietnam War on Trial: The My Lai Massacre and the Court Martial of Lieutenant Calley* (Lawrence: University Press of Kansas, 2002), 192 (Williams); Hagopian, *Vietnam War in American Memory*, 60 (Carter); David Frum, *How We Got Here: The 70's: The Decade That Brought You Modern Life (for Better or Worse)* (New York: Basic Books, 2000), 84–85.

53. Mark D. Carson, "F. Edward Hebert and the Congressional Investigation of the My Lai Massacre" (MA thesis, University of New Orleans, 1993), 2–7; Mark

D. Carson, "F. Edward Hebert and the Congressional Investigation of the My Lai Massacre," *Louisiana History* 37 (Winter 1996): 61–64, 67–68, 62n7 ("unreconstructed rebels").

54. US Congress, House Committee on Armed Services Investigating Subcommittee of the House Armed Services Committee, [Hearings on] "Investigation of the My Lai Incident," 91st Cong., 2nd sess., Apr. 15–17, 23–24, 27–30, May 8–9, 12–13, June 9–10, 22, 1970 (Washington, DC: Government Printing Office, 1976), 204–17, 219, 223, 226–41, 251–61, 270–73, 475–88, 840–48.

55. Carson, "F. Edward Hebert" (*Louisiana History*), 73, 76–77.

56. Belknap, *Vietnam War on Trial*, 196; N. M. P. to Talmadge, Dec. 1969, 11/78/2, H. A. to Talmadge, Apr. 19, 1971, and G. H. and B. A. B. to Talmadge, Apr. 20, 1971, 11/118/3, all Talmadge Papers; M. F. to Tower, Apr. 1, 1971, 383:4, Tower Papers.

57. H. B. P. Jr. to Ervin, May 7, 1971, 243:10214, Ervin Papers; W. B. K. to Talmadge, Apr. 2, 1971, G. P. S. Jr. to Talmadge, Apr. 3, 1971, J. S. P. to Talmadge, Apr. 4, 1971, and R. A. C. to Talmadge, Apr. 8, 1971, 11/115/3, all Talmadge Papers; B. F. S. to Talmadge, Apr. 13, 1971, and Mrs. R. Y. to Talmadge, Apr. 16, 1971, both 11/118/6, Talmadge Papers. For the compelling argument that My Lai was not an aberration, see Turse, *Kill Anything That Moves*.

58. *Montgomery Advertiser*, Apr. 22, 25, 1970; Prados, *Vietnam*, 365; Herring, *America's Longest War*, 300.

59. Herring, *America's Longest War*, 301.

60. William Shawcross, *Sideshow: Kissinger, Nixon, and the Destruction of Cambodia* (New York: Simon and Schuster, 1979), 134–35 ("down the drain"); Johns, *Vietnam's Second Front*, 288 ("the Right"). Although Harry Byrd Jr., a lifelong Democrat, declared himself an Independent in 1971, he continued to caucus with the Democrats in the Senate. Therefore, I have counted him as a Democrat in calculating southern votes. See Tarter, *Grandees of Government*, 360.

61. R. D. Johnson, *Congress and the Cold War*, 165; Johns, *Vietnam's Second Front*, 284.

62. *CR*, 91:2 (Apr. 30, 1970), 13,562 (May 14, 1970), 15,553 (May 15, 1970), 15,719–20, 15,723, 15731 (June 3, 1970), 18,127–28.

63. Karl E. Campbell, *Senator Sam Ervin, Last of the Founding Fathers* (Chapel Hill: University of North Carolina Press, 2007), 4, 7, 9.

64. *CR*, 91:2 (May 18, 1970), 15,927 (May 21, 1970), 16,533; Scanlon, *Pro-War Movement*, 134, 138.

65. Schulman, *John Sherman Cooper*, 37, 57.

66. Johns, *Vietnam's Second Front*, 283 (Cooper); R. D. Johnson, *Congress and the Cold War*, 164.

67. *CR*, 91:2 (May 15, 1970), 15,723–25 (May 21, 1970), 16,532–33 (May 26, 1970), 17,066; *CQA*, 91:2 (1970), 46-S.

68. R. D. Johnson, *Congress and the Cold War*, 165 ("civil war"); *CR*, 91:2 (May 1, 1970), 13,833 (May 14, 1970), 15,562–63 (May 15, 1970), 15,727.

69. R. D. Johnson, *Congress and the Cold War,* 167 ("symbolic value"); Logevall, "John Sherman Cooper," 256 (*Washington Post*); *CQA,* 91:2 (1970), 33-S, 42–43-H.

70. Mann, *Grand Delusion,* 670; *GOI,* no. 61 (July 1970), 5; *CQA,* 91:2 (1970), 46-S.

71. R. B. Woods, *Fulbright,* 579; *CR,* 91:2 (Aug. 25, 1970), 29,938 (Cooper) (Aug. 31, 1970), 30,474 (Stennis); Maddox, "John Sherman Cooper and the Vietnam War," 68.

72. *Montgomery Advertiser,* May 2, 12, 14, 15, 1970; *Dallas Morning News,* May 5, 6, 14, 1970; *New Orleans Times-Picayune,* May 6, 12, 1970.

73. *Louisville Courier-Journal,* May 2, 6, 9, 21, 1970.

74. *Atlanta Constitution,* May 2, 5, 17, 1970.

75. Mr. and Mrs. R. C. to Cooper, May 9, 1970, box 459, Anonymous to Cooper, May 12, 1970, box 459, Donald S. Cann to Cooper, May 14, 1970, box 454, Rev. D. M. Hart to Cooper, May 15, 1970, box 468; Maurice D. Ingle to Cooper, May 26, 1970, box 455, G. E. Bowman to Cooper, May 31, 1970, box 454, Mrs. Gerald Adkins, June 6, 1970, box 467, Mrs. William E. Arnold to Cooper, June 29, 1970, box 454, and Mrs. Margaret S. Burr to Cooper, June 30, 1970, box 467, all Cooper Papers.

76. Mary McCallaway to Cooper, May 5, 1970, box 461, Dr. and Mrs. W. C. G. to Cooper, May 9, 1970, Lucienne Boswell to Cooper, May 10, 1970, Elizabeth A. Bridgeman to Cooper, May 11, 1970, box 456, and Mr. and Mrs. Raymond L. Short to Cooper and Frank Church, May 27, 1970, box 454, all Cooper Papers.

77. F. C. W. to Stennis, Apr. 27, 1970, and N. W. C. Jr. to Stennis, May 12, 1970, both 53/3/130, Stennis Papers; A. C. McG. to Fulbright, June 24, 1970, 60:5, Fulbright Papers; Rev. K. A. G. to Ervin, June 18, 1970, 212:9262, Ervin Papers.

78. M. H. to Stennis, May 15, 1970, 53/3/136, Stennis Papers; T. P. R. to Talmadge, June 12, 1970, 11/103/1, Talmadge Papers.

79. Talmadge, "Reports from the United States Senate," May 14, 1970, 2/240/16, and July 1970, 2/240/8, both Talmadge Papers.

80. *Atlanta Constitution,* June 10, 1970; Jack D. Aiken to Talmadge, May 5, 1970, 11/98/6, J. R. Eason to Talmadge, May 5, 1970, 11/98/6, L. R. Sams to Talmadge, June 8, 1970, 11/102/96, Ken Schmidt to Talmadge, June 9, 1970, and Doug Slagle to Talmadge, June 12, 1970, 11/103/1, all Talmadge Papers.

81. Patrick L. Cox, *Ralph W. Yarborough, the People's Senator* (Austin: University of Texas Press, 2002), 242; A. R. E. to Ben Musselshite, Apr. 30, 1970, 3W149: File 5/5/70, Yarborough Papers; H. C. S. to Gore, May 1, 1970, B47:1, and H. L. to Gore, May 22, 1970, B47:7, both Gore Papers.

82. *Texas Observer,* May 15, Sept. 14, 1970; Longley, *Senator Albert Gore,* 235.

83. Melinda Henneberger, "For Gore, Army Years Mixed Vietnam and Family Politics," *New York Times,* July 11, 2000, http://partners.nytimes.com/library/politics/camp/07100wh-gore.html; Longley, *Senator Albert Gore,* 220–21.

84. A. O. J. to Sparkman, Sept. 17, 1968, 70A4063:5, Sparkman Papers; R. L. W. to Fulbright, Dec. 8, 1968, 57:6, Fulbright Papers.

85. S. F. McP. to Talmadge, May 12, 1970, 11/98/4, Talmadge Papers.

86. William Shepard McAninch, "The UFO," *South Carolina Law Review* 46 (1994–1995): 363; Ernst and Baldwin, "Not So Silent Minority," 114, 116; Davie Cortright, *Soldiers in Revolt: The American Military Today* (Garden City, NY: Anchor Press, 1975), 53–56; Stur, *Beyond Combat,* 192–95; Reynolds Steward Kiefer, "Dissent in the Desert" (MA thesis, University of Texas, El Paso, 1997), 127–38, 152.

87. Ernst and Baldwin, "Not So Silent Minority," 116.

88. McAninch, "UFO," 365, 375; *Texas Observer,* Nov. 19, 1971.

89. Lutz, *Home Front,* 14

7. Southern College Students

1. Paul K. Conkin, *Gone with the Ivy: A Biography of Vanderbilt University* (Knoxville: University of Tennessee Press, 1985), 613; Gregg L. Michel, *Struggle for a Better South: The Southern Student Organizing Committee, 1964–1969* (New York: Palgrave MacMillan, 2004), 3.

2. Kenneth J. Heineman, *Campus Wars: The Peace Movement at American State Universities in the Vietnam Era* (New York: New York University Press, 1993), 82 (Shero); Stephen Flynn Young, "The *Kudzu:* Sixties Generation Revolt—Even in Mississippi," *Southern Quarterly* 34 (Spring 1996): 122–27.

3. Mitchell K. Hall, "'A Crack in Time': The Response of Students at the University of Kentucky to the Tragedy at Kent State, May 1970," *Register of the Kentucky Historical Society* 83 (Winter 1985): 39; Stephen Eugene Parr, "The Forgotten Radicals: The New Left in the Deep South: Florida State University, 1960–1972" (PhD diss., Florida State University, 2000), 218; McAninch, "UFO," 375; Terry H. Anderson, *The Movement and the Sixties: Protest in America from Greensboro to Wounded Knee* (New York: Oxford University Press, 1995), 139–40.

4. *Dallas Morning News,* Jan. 11, 1966, May 13, 1970; *Montgomery Advertiser,* Apr. 13, May 12, 15, 23, 1970; *Atlanta Constitution,* Mar. 15, 1966; McAninch, "UFO," 370 (*State*); Young, "*Kudzu,*" 130–31 (*Clarion-Ledger*).

5. Hall, "'Crack in Time,'" 62; W. C. Moffett to Editor, *Louisville Courier Journal,* Feb. 11, 1965; Sue B. Gibson to Editor, *Louisville Courier Journal,* Feb. 10, 1968; H. C. Mooningham to Editor, *Louisville Courier Journal,* May 9, 1970; Louis Bahr Sr. to Editor, *Louisville Courier Journal,* May 12, 1970; Charles Ryle to Editor, *Louisville Courier Journal,* May 12, 1970; Jerry Arnold to Editor, *Louisville Courier Journal,* May 12, 1970; Mary E. French to Editor, *Louisville Courier Journal,* May 16, 1970; Marion Brainard to President Nixon, [Feb. 1969], Human Rights, box 27, file "Beginning 3/20/69," and D. L. Rosenau Jr. to President Nixon, June 29, 1970, box 28, [folder 1 of 2], both White House Central Files, Nixon Presidential Materials Project, National Archives and Records Administration II, College Park, Maryland (hereafter cited as Nixon Project [these materials have since been moved to the Nixon Presidential Library in Yorba Linda, CA]); Bruce Farr to Albert Gore, May 7, 1970, Kenneth N. Gould to Gore, May 7, 1970, and Homer E. Russell to Gore, May 9, 1970, all

B47:8, Gore Papers. Similar letters to the editor or to political figures can be found in virtually all southern newspapers or manuscript collections of political figures.

6. "A Draftee's Parent" to Editor, *Atlanta Constitution*, Jan. 17, 1966.

7. DeBenedetti and Chatfield, *American Ordeal*, 152, 186; Tom Wells, *The War Within: America's Battle over Vietnam* (Berkeley: University of California Press, 1994), 70, 543; Parr, "Forgotten Radicals," 242; Lowell H. Harrison, *Western Kentucky University* (Lexington: University Press of Kentucky, 1987), 234; Urban Research Corporation, *On Strike . . . Shut It Down! A Report on the First National Student Strike in U.S. History, May 1970*, xiv, White House Central Files, Staff Members and Office Files (hereafter cited as WHCSFM), H. R. Haldeman, box 284, Nixon Project; Urban Institute, *Survey of Campus Incidents as Interpreted by College Presidents, Faculty Chairmen and Student Body Presidents* (Oct. 1970), 9, 13, WHCSFM, Robert Finch, box 27, "Scranton Commission," Nixon Project; David S. McCarthy, "'The Sun Never Sets on the Activities of the CIA': Project Resistance at William and Mary," *Intelligence and National Security* 28 (Oct. 2013): 611–33 http://dx.doi.org/10.1080/02684527.2012.6992912 (accessed Nov. 17, 2014); Gregory Duhe, "The FBI and Students for a Democratic Society at the University of New Orleans, 1968–1971," *Journal of the Louisiana Historical Society* 63 (Winter 2002): 53–74.

8. Durand Long and Julian Foster, "Levels of Protest," in *Protest! Student Activism in America*, ed. Julian Foster and Durand Long (New York: Morrow, 1970), 83; Mailing List of Organizations Opposing the War in Vietnam—May 1967, part IV, reel 26, SNCC Papers; Hall, "'Crack in Time,'" 40; *GOI*, no. 55 (Jan. 1970), 16.

9. Lou Harris and Associates, "A Survey of the Attitudes of College Students" (June 1970), 11, 14, 17, 21, 26, 51, WHCSFM, Robert French, box 25, "Heard Report" [1 of 2], Nixon Project.

10. Michel, *Struggle for a Better South*, 17; Ruth Anne Thompson, "'A Taste of Student Power': Protest at the University of Tennessee, 1964–1970," *Tennessee Historical Quarterly* 57 (Spring–Summer 1998): 84.

11. Alfred Sandlin Reid, *Furman University: Toward A New Identity, 1925–1975* (Durham, NC: Duke University Press, 1976), 213, 217; *Gamecock* (University of South Carolina student newspaper), Feb. 10, 1967; Thomas G. Dyer, *The University of Georgia: A Bicentennial History, 1785–1985* (Athens: University of Georgia Press, 1985), 345–46; Conkin, *Gone with the Ivy*, 615–16; *Cavalier Daily* (University of Virginia student newspaper, hereafter cited as *CD*), Mar. 17, 1966, Sept. 22, 1967; *Daily Reville* (Louisiana State University student newspaper, hereafter cited as *DR*), Oct. 12, 1965; Parr, "Forgotten Radicals," 72; McCarthy, "'Sun Never Sets on the Activities of the CIA,'" 11–15.

12. William A. Link, *William Friday: Power, Purpose, and American Higher Education* (Chapel Hill: University of North Carolina Press, 1995), 128, 138–39, 149, 151; Conkin, *Gone with the Ivy*, 616, 625; Harrison, *Western Kentucky University*, 234; *CD*, Apr. 1, 1965, Mar. 17, 1966, Feb. 18, 19, 1969, May 11, 12, 1970; *DR*, Mar. 30, 1966, Mar. 10, May 6, 7, 1970.

13. LaFeber, "Johnson, Vietnam, and Toqueville," 50; Melvin Small, *Antiwarriors: The Vietnam War and the Battle for America's Hearts and Minds* (Wilmington, DE: SR Books, 2002), 102 (Nixon); MacPherson, *Long Time Passing,* 39 ("get laid").

14. Todd V. Scofield, "History and a Slice of Social Justice: The Anti–Vietnam War Movement in Tampa and USF: 1965–1970" (MA thesis, University of South Florida, 1988), 18; *Atlanta Constitution,* May 11, 1970.

15. *DR,* Feb. 18, Sept. 9, Oct. 27, Nov. 3, 1965, Mar. 3, 1967; Michel, *Struggle for a Better South,* 110; *CD,* Oct. 3, 1967.

16. Gregg L. Michel, "'We'll Take Our Stand': The Southern Student Organizing Committee and the Radicalization of White Southern Students, 1964–1969" (PhD diss., University of Virginia, 1999), 415; *CD,* Oct. 29, 1969, May 6, 1970, Mar. 23, 1971.

17. *Red and Black* (University of Georgia student newspaper, hereafter cited as *RB*), Nov. 2, 19, 1971; Daniel J. Campbell to Editor, *DR,* May 5, 1967.

18. Greg A. Mausz to President Nixon, May 28, 1970, White House Central Files, Human Rights, file 8/1/70–8/13/70, box 29, Nixon Project; Jeffrey H. Turner, "Student Power, Black Power, Class Power: Race, Class, and Student Activism on Two Commuter Campuses," *Gulf South Historical Review* 16 (Fall 2000): 59.

19. Donald Laing to Editor, *CD,* Oct. 20, 1967; Roger Young to Editor, *CD,* Oct. 10, 1969; *DR,* Feb. 2, 10, 1966, Apr. 25, 1968; Brian Altobello to Editor, *Gamecock,* May 10, 1967; *Gamecock,* Oct. 15, 1969.

20. Jim Haw to Editor, *DR,* Oct. 29, 1965; *DR,* Mar. 4, June 29, 1965, May 5, 1968; Dana McGuinness to Editor, *CD,* Oct. 5, 1967; *Gamecock,* Oct. 17, 1969.

21. G. Robert Jones to Editor, *CD,* Oct. 20, 1967; Donald Laing to Editor, *CD,* Oct. 20, 1967; Roger Young to Editor, *CD,* Oct. 17, 1969; Donald C. Miller to Editor, *DR,* Oct. 5, 1967.

22. Michel, "'We'll Take Our Stand,'" 260–62, 337–39.

23. Michel, *Struggle for a Better South,* 148–50.

24. Michel, *Struggle for a Better South,* 151–52; Michel, "'We'll Take Our Stand,'" 409.

25. "Summary of Executive Committee Meeting," SSOC *Worklist Mailing,* Feb. 14, 1968, David Morris Collection, box 2, folder 24, Sherrod Library, East Tennessee State University, Johnson City (hereafter cited as Morris Collection). I would like to thank John Ernst for sharing these materials from the Morris Collection with me.

26. *DR,* May 3, Nov. 3, 1967; Jeffrey A. Turner, *Sitting In and Speaking Out: Student Movements in the American South, 1960–1970* (Athens: University of Georgia Press, 2010), 231–32; Thompson, "'Taste of Student Power,'" 84, 87–89; Conkin, *Gone with the Ivy,* 625–26.

27. Virginius Dabney, *Virginia Commonwealth University: A Sesquicentennial History* (Charlottesville: University of Virginia Press, 1987), 233–34; *Gamecock,* May 5, 19, 1967; Parr, "Forgotten Radicals," 120; *CD,* Feb. 15, 1966, Feb. 17, 1967; Kiefer, "Dissent in the Desert," 40–50.

28. *CD,* Oct. 20, 1969. For similar arguments by protestors at Duke University

and the University of North Carolina, Chapel Hill, see Turner, *Sitting In and Speaking Out*, 246–47, 254–55.

29. Tom Falney to Editor, *CD*, Oct. 18, 1968; David Bebzien to Editor, Paul C. Hvidding to Editor, Lawrence Burman to Editor, and Lawrence D. Smith to Editor, all *CD*, Oct. 22, 1968.

30. Michel, "'We'll Take Our Stand,'" 480; Parr, "Forgotten Radicals," 225; Stephen H. Wheeler, "'Hell No—We Won't Go, Ya'll': Southern Student Opposition to the Vietnam War," in *The Vietnam War on Campus: Other Voices, More Distant Drums*, ed. Marc Jason Gilbert (Westport, CT: Praeger, 2001), 154; *Daily Texan* (University of Texas, Austin, student newspaper), Apr. 1972; Hall, "'Crack in Time,'" 50; Urban Research Corporation, *On Strike*, 28; Turner, *Sitting In and Speaking Out*, 261–62.

31. *CD*, Dec. 6, 1967; "Dow in the South," SSOC, *Worklist Mailing*, Feb. 19, 1968, [2–3], box 2, folder 24, Morris Collection; Dabney, *Virginia Commonwealth University*, 233–34.

32. Michel, *Struggle for a Better South*, 143–48; *CD*, Sept. 25, 1968; Douglas C. Rossinow, *The Politics of Authenticity: Liberalism, Christianity, and the New Left in America* (New York: Columbia University Press, 1998), 215; Scofield, "History and a Slice of Social Justice," 161; Parr, "Forgotten Radicals," 296–98; *Gamecock*, Feb. 18, Apr. 29, 1969.

33. Rossinow, *Politics of Authenticity*, 214; *DR*, Apr. 20, 22, 1966.

34. Turner, *Sitting In and Speaking Out*, 241; *RB*, Apr. 18, 1967; *Gamecock*, Apr. 28, May 5, 1967.

35. Scofield, "History and a Slice of Social Justice," 94–96; Joseph A. Fry, "Unpopular Messengers: Student Opposition to the Vietnam War," in D. L. Anderson and Ernst, *War That Never Ends*, 227; Thompson, "'Taste of Student Power,'" 89–92.

36. Nancy Zaroulis and Gerald Sullivan, *Who Spoke Up? American Protest against the War in Vietnam, 1963–1975* (Garden City, NY: Doubleday, 1984), 265, 269 (quotes); Small, *Johnson, Nixon, and the Doves*, 183; DeBenedetti and Chatfield, *American Ordeal*, 255.

37. *RB*, Oct. 16, 1969; *Daily Texan*, Oct. 16, 1969; *Louisville Courier Journal*, Oct. 16, 1969; *DR*, Oct. 16, 1969; Thomas N. Naquin, "The Big Muddy and the Bayou State: Louisiana's Political and Public Reaction to the Vietnam War" (MA thesis, University of Louisiana at Lafayette, 2005), 76–77; Parr, "Forgotten Radicals," 217; Conkin, *Gone with the Ivy*, 626–27; Henry N. Drewry and Humphrey Doermann, *Stand and Prosper: Private Black Colleges and Their Students* (Princeton, NJ: Princeton University Press, 2001), 154; Dabney, *Virginia Commonwealth University*, 237; Harrison, *Western Kentucky University*, 233.

38. *Gamecock*, Oct. 15, 17, 1969; *DR*, Oct. 7, 8, 14, 16, 17, 1969.

39. *CD*, Sept. 26, Oct. 1, 3, 7, 9, 10, 14, 15, 16 (quote), 1969.

40. T. Anderson, *Movement and the Sixties*, 331; Kimball, *Nixon's Vietnam War*, 174.

41. DeBenedetti and Chatfield, *American Ordeal,* 280; Zaroulis and Sullivan, *Who Spoke Up?* 319; Kimball, *Nixon's Vietnam War,* 216.

42. Tim Spofford, *Lynch Street: The May 1970 Slayings at Jackson State College* (Kent OH: Kent State University Press, 1988).

43. *Gamecock,* May 18, 1970.

44. Martha Biondi, *The Black Revolution on Campus* (Berkeley: University of California Press, 2012), 32, 142, 155, 158, 165; Ibram H. Rogers, *The Black Campus Movement: Black Students and the Racial Reconstruction of Higher Education* (New York: Palgrave MacMillan, 2012), 112–13.

45. Biondi, *Black Revolution on Campus,* 31–32, 39–40; Rogers, *Black Campus Movement,* 130–31.

46. Biondi, *Black Revolution on Campus,* 157–60, 159 ("armed assault"), 163–67, 171–72 (*Black Collegian*); Rogers, *Black Campus Movement,* 139 (mayor). Mexican American students were also comparatively disinclined to demonstrate against the war. They reflected the strong patriotic sentiments in the Mexican American community and the students' giving priority to domestic issues. See Orpenza, *Rasa Si Guerra No!* 58, 77; Kiefer, "Dissent in the Desert," 142.

47. Urban Institute, *Survey of Campus Incidents,* 7–8.

48. Parr, "Forgotten Radicals," 269–74.

49. Urban Research Corporation, *On Strike,* 6–7, 27–28, 42, 45–47, 87, 106; Dr. King V. Cheek to President Nixon, May 8, 1970, White House Central Files, Human Rights, box 32, file 6/19/70–12/31/70, Nixon Project; Kiefer, "Dissent in the Desert," 156–57.

50. Conkin, *Gone with the Ivy,* 628–29; *DR,* May 6, 7, 8, 10, 14, 1970; *RB,* May 7, 12, 21, 26, 1970.

51. *Daily Texan,* Mar. 19, May 6, 1970; Urban Research Corporation, *On Strike,* 107–8.

52. Hall, "'Crack in Time,'" 36–45, 39.

53. Hall, "'Crack in Time,'" 46–63, 63 (quote).

54. Urban Research Corporation, *On Strike,* 104–5; *Gamecock,* May 13, 14, 1970.

55. *Gamecock,* May 15, 1970.

56. *CD,* May 5, 6, 7, 1970.

57. *CD,* May 7, 1970.

58. *CD,* May 7, 8, 11, 1970.

59. *CD,* May 12, 1970.

60. *CD,* May 13, 14, 15, 1970.

61. "Statement by Alexander Heard," July 23, 1970, 1–3, 7–11, WHCFSM, Finch, box 25, "Heard Report," Nixon Project.

62. Heard to Nixon, June 19, 1970, 2–5, 7–8, WHCFSM, Finch, box 25, "Heard Report," Nixon Project; Heard to Nixon, July 6, 1970, 3, WHCFSM, Finch, box 26, "The Scranton Commission," Nixon Project.

63. James E. Cheek to Nixon, July 22, 1970, 33–36 (part of Heard to Nixon,

July 22, 1970), WHCFSM, Finch, box 26, "The Scranton Commission," Nixon Project.

64. Heard to Nixon, July 6, 1970, 4–6, and Heard to Nixon, July 16, 1970, 3, both WHCFSM, Finch, box 26, "The Scranton Commission," Nixon Project.

65. H. R. Haldeman to Finch et al., July 23, 1970, 1, 3, 7, and Daniel P. Moynihan to Nixon, Aug. 4, 1970, 3, both WHCFSM, Finch, box 25, "Heard Report" (2 of 2), Nixon Project.

66. *New York Times,* July 31, 1970; Nixon to William W. Scranton, Dec. 10, 1970, 1–3, WHCFSM, Finch, box 26, "President's Commission on Campus Unrest—Response," Nixon Project.

67. "Statement by Alexander Heard," July 31, 1970, 1, 3, and "Heard Press Conference," July 25, 1970, 12, 20, both WHCFSM, Finch, box 25, "Heard Report" (2 of 2), Nixon Project.

68. *RB,* Nov. 11, 1971; *CD,* Oct. 14, 15, 1970, Jan. 10, 1971.

69. Steve Maxner, interview, Apr. 23, 2001, 83, Vietnam Archive, TTU; *DR,* Nov. 11, 1971; Ted Jordan to Editor, *CD,* Mar. 1, 1967.

70. *DR,* May 5, 6, 7, 1971, May 9, 1972; *Gamecock,* Feb. 12, 1971; *RB,* May 6, 12, 1971; *CD,* Apr. 22, May 4, Oct. 20, 1971, Dec. 8, 1972.

71. Parr, "Forgotten Radicals," 344; *Daily Texan,* Apr. 21, 22, 24, 1972.

72. T. Anderson, *Movement and the Sixties,* 380 (first quote); Fry, "Unpopular Messengers," 237–40; Rhodi Jeffreys-Jones, *Peace Now! American Society and the Ending of the Vietnam War* (New Haven, CT: Yale University Press, 1999), 88; *DR,* Oct. 27, 1965; *CD,* Oct. 14, 1970.

73. Small, *Antiwarriors,* 85 ("foot soldiers"); David Farber, *The Age of Great Dreams: America in the 1960s* (New York: Hill and Wang, 1994), 160 ("national malaise"); Kimball, *Nixon's Vietnam War,* 220.

74. Jeffreys-Jones, *Peace Now!* 80–81; LaFeber, *Deadly Bet,* 33–34 ("crime and lawlessness"); Kenneth Heineman, "The Silent Majority Speaks: Antiwar Protest and Backlash, 1965–1972," *Peace and Change* 17 (Oct. 1992): 402–33.

75. D. B. to Cooper, May 11, 1970, box 461, Cooper Papers; S. S. Matthews to Gore, May 11, [1970], B47:8, 1970, Gore Papers.

76. T. Anderson, *Movement and the Sixties,* 418 (Herring); Fry, *Dixie Looks Abroad,* 292–93.

8. Southerners and the End of the Vietnam War, 1971–1973

1. *Atlanta Constitution,* Feb. 26, 1971.

2. Johns, *Vietnam's Second Front,* 295; Kissinger, *White House Years,* 513; Small, *Presidency of Richard Nixon,* 69.

3. Prados, *Vietnam,* 407 (Nixon); Herring, *America's Longest War,* 305 ("costly draw"); Robert Cody Phillips, "Operation Lamson 719: The Laotian Invasion during the War in Vietnam" (MA thesis, University of Nevada, Las Vegas, 1979).

4. *GOI,* no. 54 (Dec. 1969), 1–2, no. 67 (Jan. 1971), 1, no. 71 (May 1971), 2, no. 72 (June 1971), 1, no. 77 (Nov. 1971), 1.

5. *Dallas Morning News,* Feb. 11, 1971; *New Orleans Times-Picayune,* Feb. 19, 1971; *Montgomery Advertiser,* Feb. 24, 1971; *Atlanta Constitution,* Feb. 26, 1971; *Louisville Courier-Journal,* Feb. 6, 1971.

6. *CR,* 92:1 (May 11, 1971), 14,336 (Stennis); Tower, "Situation Report on Southeast Asia," Feb. 6–7, 1971, 25:14, Tower Papers; Ervin to T. O. Youngblood, June 16, 1971, 243:1021, Ervin Papers; *CQA,* 92:1 (1971), 285 (Thurmond); Scanlon, *Pro-War Movement,* 155 (Thurmond).

7. Carson, "Beyond the Solid South," 429 (Cooper); Fulbright to John Martin, Aug. 6, 1970, 61:4, Fulbright Papers; R. B. Woods, *Fulbright,* 595, 599 (Kerry); Mann, *Grand Delusion,* 680 (Kerry).

8. Mann, *Grand Delusion,* 86; *CR,* 92:1 (June 17, 1971), 20, 588–89; Claude Denson Pepper, with Hayes Gorey, *Pepper: Eyewitness to a Century* (San Diego: Harcourt Brace Jovanovich, 1987), 197–202, 286 (on LBJ).

9. Gary A. Keith, *Eckhardt: There Once Was a Congressman from Texas* (Austin: University of Texas Press, 2007), 208, 218–19, 222–23.

10. Johns, *Vietnam's Second Front,* 296.

11. Ben F. Bulla, *Textiles and Politics: The Life of B. Everett Jordan: From Saxapahaw to the United States Senate* (Durham, NC: Carolina Academic Press, 1992), 284, 293, 295.

12. Spong, speech to American Legion Post 67, Suffolk, VA, May 10, 1966, 3, box 2, folder: 1966 March–June, "The Spong Report," July 1969, 2, box 34, folder 1969–1972, Spong, Senate speech, June 30, 1970, box 12, folder 1971, Spong to Frank E. Sullivan, May 22, 1970, box 34, folder 1970, and "Chronology of Developments in Cambodia and of Senator Spong's Position," box 23, folder 1970, all William B. Spong Jr. Papers, Albert and Shirley Small Special Collections Library, University of Virginia, Charlottesville.

13. *CR,* 92:1 (May 11, 1971), 14,337 (Javitts); Downs, "Matter of Conscience," 131.

14. *CR,* 92:1 (May 11, 1971), 14,333–35; Stennis, speech, University of Mississippi Honors Day, May 5, 1971, 8–9, Public Series, 19/21, Stennis Papers; John C. Stennis and J. William Fulbright, *The Role of Congress in Foreign Policy: Rational Debate Seminars* (Washington, DC: American Enterprise Institute for Public Policy Research, 1971), 96.

15. *CQA,* 92:1 (1971), 70–71, 9–10-H, 38–39-H, 12-S.

16. *GOI,* no. 69 (Mar. 1971), 11, no. 74 (Aug. 1971), 23; *CQA,* 92:1 (1971), 72–73, 15-S, 37-S, 42-S.

17. *CQA,* 92:2 (1972), 38–39, 44-S, 71-S, 24–25-H.

18. *GOI,* no. 88 (Oct. 1972), 20; Vertrees Young to Long, Mar. 15, 1971, 134:1, Long Papers; John Hargett to Richard Nixon, Sept. 8, 1971, 329-77-141:33, Sparkman Papers; L. B. Booker to Fulbright, Mar. 17, 1971, and Caroline Brendel to Fulbright, Mar. 3, 1971, both 62:1, Fulbright Papers.

19. F. S. B. to Stennis, Apr. 13, 1971, 31/11/49, Stennis Papers.

20. C. R. J. to Stennis, Jan. 16, 1971, D. E. M. to Stennis, Sept. 15, 1971, and J. L. P. to Stennis, Sept. 15, 1971, all 31/11/49, Stennis Papers; W. I. M. to Sparkman, June 18, 1971, 329-77-141:33, Sparkman Papers.

21. Milton McLaurin, "Country Music and the Vietnam War," in *Perspectives on the American South: An Annual Review of Society, Politics, and Culture,* ed. James C. Cobb and Charles R. Wilson (New York: Gordon and Breach Science Publishers, 1985), 146; Jens Lund, "Country Music Goes to War: Songs for the Red-Blooded American," *Popular Music and Society* 1, no. 4 (1972): 214; Lee Andresen, *Battle Notes: Music of the Vietnam War* (Superior, WI: Savage Press, 2000), 70.

22. McLaurin, "Country Music and the Vietnam War," 149, 151; Lund, "Country Music Goes to War," 215, 217–18, 220; Ray Pratt, "'There Must Be Some Way Outta Here!' The Vietnam War in American Popular Music," in *The Vietnam War: Its History, Literature, and Music,* ed. Kenton J. Clymer (El Paso: Texas Western Press, 1998), 171.

23. McLaurin, "Country Music and the Vietnam War," 153–54; Andresen, *Battle Notes,* 71; Lund, "Country Music Goes to War," 224.

24. McLaurin, "Country Music and the Vietnam War," 153–54; Andresen, *Battle Notes,* 75–76.

25. McLaurin, "Country Music and the Vietnam War," 151; "Dear Uncle Sam Lyrics," www.metrolyrics.com/dear-unclesam-lyrics-loretta-lynn-html (accessed May 13, 2013); Andresen, *Battle Notes,* 83.

26. McLaurin, "Country Music and the Vietnam War," 154–55; "Lyrics to When You Gonna Bring our Soldiers Home?" by Skeeter Davis, www.mp3lyrics .org/s/skeeter-avis/when-you (accessed May 30, 2013); David James, "The Vietnam War and American Music," *Social Text* 23 (Autumn–Winter 1989): 122–43.

27. R. B. Woods, *LBJ,* 516; K. C. H. to Long, Feb. 5, 1968, 108:34, and Mrs. C. R. to Long, Dec. 28, 1970, 123:4, both Long Papers.

28. Lee Janot to Long, Dec. 15, 1967, Janot, "A Long Overdue Letter to U.S. Servicemen in Viet Nam—from the Silent Millions Back Home in America," *Lake Charles American Press,* Nov. 13, 1967, and unidentified newspaper clipping, n.d., all 59:37, Long Papers.

29. Jesse Helms, "SREAL-TV Viewpoint Editorial," Apr. 21, 1967, 150:6583, Ervin Papers.

30. Durr to Jessica Mitford, July 5, 1967, in Patricia Sullivan, ed., *Freedom Writer: Virginia Foster Durr, Letters from the Civil Rights Years* (New York: Routledge, 2003), 389; Hollinger F. Bernard, ed., *Outside the Magic Circle: The Autobiography of Virginia Foster Durr* (University: University of Alabama Press, 1985).

31. Ernst and Baldwin, "Not So Silent Minority," 117, 119.

32. J. Wilson, *Sons of Bardstown,* 148, 154, 171, 181–82; Mrs. W. P. G. to Russell, Aug. 6, 1969, 30:8, Russell Papers (NC mother); M. D. to Gore, Feb. 28, 1970, B47:1, Gore Papers; McIntire, "Kentucky National Guard in Vietnam," 150, 158.

33. Lutz, *Home Front,* 134, 136–37.

34. J. Wilson, *Sons of Bardstown,* 67–68.

424 Notes to Pages 340–346

35. William J. Brinker, "Seawillow Chambers: Soldier's Wife," in D. L. Anderson, *Human Tradition in the Vietnam Era,* 100, 103, 106.

36. Brinker, "Seawillow Chambers," 106, 110.

37. *Atlanta Constitution,* Mar. 18, 1969. For Captain Blair's experience, see chapter 4 in this book, treating southern soldiers.

38. *Atlanta Constitution,* Mar. 18, 1969.

39. Joseph A. Fry, "Jerry McCuistion: POW Wife and Public Activist," in *The Human Tradition in America since 1945,* ed. David L. Anderson (Wilmington, DE: SR Books,,2003), 95–112.

40. Jerry McCuistion, untitled manuscript, 2, 9, 14–15, 18 (hereafter cited as McCuistion mss.), and *Oregon Journal,* Sept. 2, 1970, all in McCuistion files (courtesy of Jerry McCuistion); Michael J. Allen, *Until the Last Man Comes Home: POWs, MIAs, and the Unending Vietnam War* (Chapel Hill: University of North Carolina Press, 2009), 25.

41. McCuistion mss., 20–29; Jerry McCuistion, interview with the author, Nov. 8, 1999.

42. Clemmer L. Slaton, "For Hope Springs Eternal," *Airmen* 15 (May 1971): 45; McCuistion, interview with the author, Oct. 25, 1999.

43. McCuistion, interviews, Oct. 25, Nov. 8, 1999; Slaton, "For Hope Springs Eternal," 45–46.

44. McCuistion mss., 36–38, 41; McCuistion, interview, Oct. 25, 1999; Natasha Zaretsky, "Women and the Vietnam War," in *Vietnam War Era: People and Perspectives,* ed., Mitchell K. Hall (Santa Barbara, CA: ABC-CLIO, 2009), 126–29, 126 ("quiet diplomacy").

45. Fry, "Jerry McCuistion," 102–3.

46. McCuistion, interview, Nov. 8, 1999; *Birmingham Post-Herald,* July 4, Oct. 11, 1970; McCuistion, speech to the Montgomery Lions Club (taped recording), 1970, McCuistion files; Fry, "Jerry McCuistion," 103–4. For Stockdale and the POW/MIA wives more generally, see Allen, *Until the Last Man Comes Home,* 27 (quote), 28, 44; Jim Stockdale and Sybil Stockdale, *In Love and War: The Story of a Family's Ordeal and Sacrifice during the Vietnam Years* (Annapolis, MD: Naval Institute Press, 1990).

47. Fry, "Jerry McCuistion," 104–6; *Greenville Advocate,* Nov. 1970, McCuistion files.

48. *Birmingham News,* Oct. 11, 1970, McCuistion files; Allen, *Until the Last Man Comes Home,* 17, 22, 31.

49. Fry, "Jerry McCuisiton," 106–7; Elliott Gruner, *Prisoners of Culture: Representing the Vietnam P.O.W.* (New Brunswick, NJ: Rutgers University Press, 1993).

50. Allen, *Until the Last Man Comes Home,* 16, 29–31, 33, 36, 49–56, 60–62, 52 (*Virginian Pilot*); Kimball, *Nixon's Vietnam War,* 166–69, 233–34; Joan Hoff Wilson, *Nixon Reconsidered* (New York: Basic Books, 1994), 223–24. Another southerner, Congressman Gillespie V. ("Sonny") Montgomery (D-MS), was the most aggressive congressional proponent of the argument that living Americans were being held prisoner in Southeast Asia after April 1973. After chairing a select House

committee in 1975 that concluded the contrary, Montgomery was savagely attacked by leaders in the National League of Families and compared to Jane Fonda. See H. Bruce Franklin, *M.I.A. or Mythmaking in America* (Brooklyn, NY: Lawrence Hill Books, 1992), 14–15, 87, 130–31.

51. Michael McCuistion to Jerry McCuistion, Nov. 17, 1971, McCuistion files; McCuistion, interviews, Oct. 25, Nov. 8, 1999.

52. McCuistion, interview, Oct. 25, 1999.

53. Mann, *Grand Delusion*, 693.

54. Kimball, *Nixon's Vietnam War*, 303, 315; Scanlon, *Pro-War Movement*, 297; Herring, *America's Longest War*, 318.

55. Kimball, *Nixon's Vietnam War*, 323–48.

56. Prados, *Vietnam*, 509 ("sheriff"); Kimball, *Nixon's Vietnam War*, 364–65; Herring, *America's Longest War*, 326–27; Scanlon, *Pro-War Movement*, 315.

57. Kimball, *Nixon's Vietnam War*, 366 ("war by tantrum"); Prados, *Vietnam*, 513 ("not politically sustainable"); Herring, *America's Longest War*, 328 ("tolerable").

58. *GOI*, no. 79 (Jan. 1972), 5, no. 84 (June 1972), 3–4, no. 85 (July 1972), 3, no. 86 (Aug. 1972), 20–21, no. 92 (Feb. 1973), 2–3, 12–13, no. 93 (Mar. 1973), 3.

59. George Mitchell to Talmadge, [Apr. 1972], 11/136/3, Mrs. W. T. Brightwell to Richard Nixon, Apr. 18, 1972, 11/136/3, Thomas G. Gilchrist to Richard Nixon, May 8, 1972, 8/244/6, Fred L. Young to Talmadge, May 10, 1972, 8/244/5, and George Mitchell to Talmadge, May 13, 1972, 11/139/5, all Talmadge Papers; Ira E. Blackwood to Fulbright, Apr. 16, 1972, 64:1, and R. L. Brown to Fulbright, Apr. 18, 1972, 64:1, both Fulbright Papers.

60. Sister M. J. B. to Fulbright, May 1, 1972, 64:1, M. D. G. to Fulbright, May 4, 1972, 64:3; G. B. to Fulbright, May 9, 1972, 64:1, and W. S. McL. to Richard Nixon, May 11, 1972, 64:5, all Fulbright Papers; D. and V. H. to Ervin, Dec. 25, 1972, 299:12260, Ervin Papers.

61. G. B. to Fulbright, May 9, 1972, 64:1, Fulbright Papers; J. A. and E. A. F. to Talmadge, Apr. 11, 1972, 2/207/11, H. T. C. to Talmadge, Apr. 24, 1972, 11/137/2; Mr. and Mrs. J. E. S. to Talmadge, May 9, 1972, 11/139/5, and E. T. L. to Talmadge, Dec. 29, 1972, 11/144/2, all Talmadge Papers.

62. Mann, *Grand* Delusion, 698; *CQA*, 92:2 (1972), 845, 847–48, 22-S, 68–69-H.

63. *CQA*, 93:1 (1973), 76-S, 120–21-H.

64. Mann, *Grand Delusion*, 701; Berman, *William Fulbright*, 153, 166; R. B. Woods, *Fulbright*, 624–26.

65. Kimball, *Nixon's Vietnam War*, 348 ("open rebellion"); Downs, "Matter of Conscience," 143, 145, 153; transcript, CBS, *Face the Nation*, Dec. 3, 1972, 2, 25:14, Tower Papers.

66. Kimball, *Nixon's Vietnam War*, 370.

67. Rusk, *As I Saw It*, 491; Herring, *LBJ and Vietnam*, 17, 19; Herring, "Lyndon Johnson as Commander and Chief," 91; Lloyd Gardner, "America's War in Vietnam: The End of Exceptionalism?" in Shafer, *Legacy*, 22; R. B. Woods, *LBJ*, 881.

68. R. B. Woods, *Fulbright,* 656.

69. Dr. J. N. to Fulbright, Dec. 2, 1969, 57:2, and Mrs. J. B. to Fulbright, [Feb. 1966], 47:2, both Fulbright Papers; *New York Times,* Feb. 10, 1995 ("rut"); R. B. Woods, *Fulbright,* 654, 671.

70. Schwartz, "'Henry, . . . Winning an Election Is Terribly Important,'" 174; D. L. Anderson and Ernst, *War That Never Ends,* especially George C. Herring, "The War That Never Seems to Go Away," 335–49; *Louisville Courier-Journal,* Jan. 25, 28, 1973.

71. R. B. Woods, *Fulbright,* 612; Stennis and Fulbright, *Role of Congress in Foreign Policy,* 62, 67, 71; Fulbright to George T. Weigart, Aug. 15, 1968, 45:1, Fulbright Papers; Hodges, "Cooing of a Dove," 144.

72. Moore and Galloway, *We Are Soldiers Still,* 108, 188; Eldridge, *Chronicles of a Two-Front War,* 95 (King); Fulbright to Wyth Duke, Oct. 28, 1968, 56:4, Fulbright Papers. For a recent and compelling confirmation of Woolard's charges, see Turse, *Kill Anything That Moves.*

73. Scanlon, *Pro-War Movement,* 332.

74. Long, speech to the 55th Annual American Legion Department Convention, Baton Rouge, June 30, 1973, 612:50, Long Papers; *New Orleans Times-Picayune,* Apr. 7, 1973; Stennis, speech to Columbus, MS, Chamber of Commerce, Dec. 12, 1972, 3, Public Series, 22/32, Stennis Papers; Talmadge to Lisa Young, May 6, 1975, and Talmadge to Harold A. Porter, June 2, 1975, both 8/117/1, Talmadge Papers; Michael Lind, *Vietnam: The Necessary War: A Reinterpretation of America's Most Disastrous Military Conflict* (New York: Free Press, 2002).

75. Stennis, Statement on Vietnam, n.d., 4/61/5, Stennis Papers; *Montgomery Advertiser,* Dec. 6, 1972, Jan. 21, 1973; Rusk, *As I Saw It,* 492–93; Westmoreland, *Soldier Reports,* 199, 427; Schmitz, *Tet Offensive,* 159; Gaines M. Foster, "Coming to Terms with Defeat: Post-Vietnam America and the Post–Civil War South," *Virginia Quarterly Review* 66 (Winter 1990): 17–35; James C. Cobb, *Redefining Southern Culture: Mind and Identity in the Modern South* (Athens: University of Georgia Press, 1999), 83 ("self-flagellation"); Robert J. McMahon, "Contested Memory: The Vietnam War and American Society, 1975–2001," *Diplomatic History* 26 (Spring 2002): 159–84.

76. Tower to Dr. Hobart Bennett, Mar. 2, 1968, 366:9, Tower Papers; Long, TV interview, May 2, 1975, 1–2, 617:2, Long Papers; *Dallas Morning-News,* Jan. 17, 1973; Talmadge to Ralph Westbrook, Jan. 30, 1973, 8/179/2, Talmadge Papers; Stennis, address to National Security Seminar, Jackson, MS, Jan. 11, 1971, 4, Public Series, 19/3, Stennis Papers.

77. Stennis and Fulbright, *Role of Congress in Foreign Policy,* 9, 96; Stennis, speech, University of Mississippi Honors Day, May 5, 1971, 9, Public Series, 21/19, and Stennis, speech, East Mississippi Electric Power Association, Oct. 25, 1969, 12, Public Series, 17/10, both Stennis Papers.

78. Engelhardt, *End of Victory Culture,* 14–15; William W. Cobb Jr., *The American Foundation Myth in Vietnam: Reigning Paradigms and Raining Bombs* (Lanham,

MD: University Press of America, 1998); C. Vann Woodward, *The Burden of Southern History* (New York: New American Library, 1968), 135–36, 148, 151, 160–61.

79. Lucks, *Selma to Saigon,* 253.

80. Lockley, interview, Feb. 11, 17, 2003, 83, Vietnam Archive, TTU.

Bibliographic Essay

The following essay discusses the principal sources on which this book is based. Please see the endnotes for a listing of all materials consulted, full details on the location of manuscript collections, and complete publication information for books. I have drawn on these manuscript collections for the views of important southern politicians and their constituents: the Harry F. Byrd Sr., Harry F. Byrd Jr., and William B. Spong Jr. Papers (Albert and Shirley Small Special Collections, University of Virginia); the A. Willis Robertson and William Tuck Papers (Special Collections Research Center, Earl Gregg Swen Library, College of William and Mary); the J. Samuel Ervin Jr. Papers (Southern Historical Collection, Louis Round Wilson Library, University of North Carolina at Chapel Hill); the John Sherman Cooper and Thruston B. Morton Papers (Special Collections, Margaret I. King Library, University of Kentucky); the Albert Gore Sr. Senate Papers (Albert Gore Research Center, Middle Tennessee State University); the Richard B. Russell Jr. and Herman E. Talmadge Papers (Richard B. Russell Library for Political Research and Studies, University of Georgia); the J. William Fulbright Papers (Special Collections, University of Arkansas); the John C. Stennis Collection (Congressional and Political Research Center, Mississippi State University Libraries); the Russell B. Long Papers (Louisiana and Lower Mississippi Collection, Louisiana State University); the John J. Sparkman Papers (W. S. Hoole Special Collections Library, University of Alabama, Tuscaloosa); the John G. Tower Papers (Special Collections, A. Frank Smith Jr. Library Center, Southwestern University); and the Ralph W. Yarborough Papers (Briscoe Center for American History, University of Texas, Austin). The papers of the fascinating Frazier Woolard are housed in the Special Collections Department, William R. Perkins Library, Duke University, and Jerry McCuistion graciously shared her personal papers with me. I have drawn more selectively on manuscripts and oral histories in the John F. Kennedy and Lyndon B. Johnson presidential libraries and the Nixon Project (then housed in National Archives II and since moved to the Nixon presidential library). I have utilized the *Congressional Record,* the *Congressional Quarterly Almanac,* and key congressional committee hearings and reports, especially from the Senate Foreign Relations Committee, the Senate Armed Services Committee (SASC), and the Senate Preparedness Investigating Subcommittee of the SASC.

The *Gallup Opinion Index,* which traced regional responses to a variety of relevant Vietnam War–related issues from mid-1965 through 1973, provided an invaluable, broad overview of southern public opinion and attitudes. To better understand these collective, numerical materials, I have read and collected copies of more than fifteen hundred constituent letters drawn from the manuscript collections cited above. This correspondence provides a rich and largely untapped window on how the southern public responded to the war. I have supplemented these polls and constituent letters with editorials and letters to the editor from the *Atlanta Constitution,* the *Dallas Morning News,* the *Louisville Courier-Journal,* the *Montgomery Advertiser,* the *New Orleans Times-Picayune,* the *Texas Observer,* and the *Atlanta Daily World,* the *Birmingham World,* and the *Norfolk Journal and Guide* (all African American weeklies).

I have relied especially on George C. Herring, *America's Longest War: The United States and Vietnam, 1950–1975,* 5th ed. (2014), and John Prados, *Vietnam: The History of an Unwinnable War, 1945–1975* (2009), for general accounts of American involvement in Vietnam. Overviews providing historical context for the South's involvement in Vietnam include: Joseph A. Fry, *Dixie Looks Abroad: The South and U.S. Foreign Relations, 1789–1973* (2002); Tennant S. McWilliams, *The New South Faces the World: Foreign Affairs and the Southern Sense of Self, 1877–1950* (1988); Alfred O. Hero Jr., *The Southerner and World Affairs* (1965); Edward W. Chester, *Sectionalism, Politics, and American Diplomacy* (1975); and Bertram Wyatt-Brown, "The Ethic of Honor in National Crises: The Civil War, Vietnam, Iraq, and the Southern Factor," *Journal of the Historical Society* 5 (2005).

For the general cultural and political contexts nationally and especially in the South, I have employed James C. Cobb, *Redefining Southern Culture: Mind and Identity in the Modern South* (1999); Cobb, *Away*

Down South: A History of Southern Identity (2005); Cobb, *The South and America since World War II* (2011); Michael Perman, *Pursuit of Unity: A Political History of the American South* (2009); Jeff Woods, *Black Struggle, Red Scare: Segregation and Anti-Communism in the South, 1948–1968* (2004); David Goldfield, *Still Fighting the Civil War: The American South and Southern History* (2002); Bertram Wyatt-Brown, *Southern Honor: Ethics and Behavior in the Old South* (1982) and the Wyatt-Brown article cited above; Terry H. Anderson, *The Movement and the Sixties: Protest in America from Greensboro to Wounded Knee* (1995); Mark H. Lytle, *America's Uncivil Wars in the Sixties Era: From Elvis to the Fall of Richard Nixon* (2005); Stephen J. Whitfield, *The Culture of the Cold War* (1996); and Tom Engelhardt, *The End of Victory Culture: Cold War America and the Disillusioning of a Generation,* rev. ed. (2007).

In a model article that does not fit neatly into any of the categories of this essay, John Ernst and Yvonne Baldwin, in "The Not So Silent Minority: Louisville's Antiwar Movement, 1966–1975," *Journal of Southern History* 73 (February 2007), address the motivations of antiwar activists, students, women, race, religion, antiwar GI coffeehouses, conscientious objectors, and expatriates and in so doing affords multiple insights into the South and the war. Reynolds Stewart Kiefer, "Dissent in the Desert: The Vietnam Era Antiwar Movement in El Paso (MA thesis, University of Texas, El Paso, 1997), provides similar coverage, especially for college students, Mexican Americans, key community members, and antiwar soldiers at Fort Bliss. In "The Big Muddy and the Bayou State: Louisiana's Political and Public Reaction to the Vietnam War" (MA thesis, University of Louisiana at Lafayette, 2005), Thomas N. Naquin focuses on Louisiana's primary political figures, college students, and newspapers.

The most comprehensive and exceedingly helpful overview of southern congressmen and senators and Vietnam is Mark David Carson's excellent dissertation, "Beyond the Solid South: Southern Members of Congress and the Vietnam War" (Louisiana State University, 2003). See also Carson's "F. Edward Hebert and the Congressional Investigation of the My Lai Massacre," *Louisiana History* 37 (Winter 1996). In addition to Carson, the following have informed my understanding of Congress, American politics, congressional-executive relations, and the war: Robert David Johnson, *Congress and the Cold War* (2006); Gary Stone, *Elites for Peace: The Senate and the Vietnam War, 1964–1968* (2007); and Sandra Scanlon, *The Pro-War Movement: Support for the Vietnam War and the Making of Modern American Conservatism* (2013). William Conrad Gibbons, *The U.S. Government and the Vietnam War: Executive and Legislative Roles and Relationships*, 4 vols. (1986–1995), includes a broad and highly informative array of interviews, materials from the *Congressional Record*, and excerpts from congressional hearings, reports, and documents. Andrew L. Johns, *Vietnam's Second Front: Domestic Politics, the Republican Party, and the War* (2010), provides a stellar analysis of the GOP and the conflict, as well as important insights on Congress and the war. Robert Mann, *A Grand Delusion: America's Descent into Vietnam* (2001), is an excellent narrative account of congressional-executive relations from the early 1950s through the end of the war. Both George C. Herring, "The Executive, Congress, and the Vietnam War, 1965–1975," in Michael Barnhart, ed., *Congress and Foreign Policy: Controlling the Use of Force in the Nuclear Age* (1987), and Robert D. Schulzinger, "Richard Nixon, Congress, and the War in Vietnam, 1969–1974," in Randall B. Woods, ed., *Vietnam and the American Political Tradition: The Politics of Dissent* (2003), contribute important insights.

Numerous biographies, autobiographies, and more specific studies of prominent southerners and the war have been essential to my efforts. For Lyndon Johnson, I have relied primarily on Randall B. Woods, *LBJ: Architect of American Ambition* (2006); George C. Herring, *LBJ and Vietnam: A Different Kind of War* (1994); Robert Dallek, *Lone Star Rising: Lyndon Johnson and His Times, 1908–1960* (1991); Dallek, *Flawed Giant: Lyndon Johnson and His Times, 1961–1973* (1998); Lloyd C. Gardner, *Pay Any Price: Lyndon Johnson and the Wars for Vietnam* (1995); and Doris Kearns Goodwin, *Lyndon Johnson and the American Dream* (1991). Dean Rusk has left his version of events in *As I Saw It* (1990) and has received perceptive treatment in Thomas W. Zeiler, *Dean Rusk: Defending the American Mission Abroad* (2000), and Thomas J. Schoenbaum, *Waging Peace and War: Dean Rusk in the Truman, Kennedy, and Johnson Years* (1988).

For Richard B. Russell, see Jeff Woods, *Richard B. Russell: Southern Nationalism and American Foreign Policy* (2007); Gilbert C. Fite, *Richard B. Russell, Jr., Senator from Georgia* (1991); and Caroline F. Ziemke, "Senator Richard B. Russell and the 'Lost Cause' in Vietnam," *Georgia Historical Quarterly* 72 (Spring 1988). Michael S. Downs has assessed John C. Stennis and the war in "A Matter of Conscience: John C. Stennis and the Vietnam War" (PhD dissertation, Mississippi State University, 1989), and "Advise and Consent: John Stennis and the Vietnam War, 1954–1973," *Journal of Mississippi History* 55 (May 1993). For other conservative southern Democrats, see Ronald L. Heinemann, *Harry Byrd of Virginia* (1996); Thomas A. Becnel, *Senator Allen Ellender of Louisiana: A Biography* (1995); Karl E. Campbell, *Senator Sam Ervin: Last of the Founding Fathers* (2007); Brian Lewis Crispell, *Testing the Limits: George Armistead Smathers and Cold War America* (1999); Ben F. Bulla, *Textiles and Politics: The Life of B. Everett Jordan: From Saxapahaw to the United States Senate* (1992); Robert Mann, *Legacy to Power: Senator Russell Long of Louisiana* (1992); Will F. Huntley, "Mighty Rivers of Charleston" (PhD dissertation, University of South Carolina, 1993); and Herman E. Talmadge, with Mark Royden Winchell, *Talmadge: A Political Legacy, a Politician's Life: A Memoir* (1987).

To understand the principal southern antiwar political figures, Randall B. Woods's *Fulbright: A Biography* (1995) is essential for both Fulbright and the more general antiwar movement in Congress. See also Woods, "Dixie's Dove: J. William Fulbright, the Vietnam War, and the American South," *Journal of Southern History* 60 (August 1994). William C. Berman, *William Fulbright and the Vietnam War: The Dissent of a Political Realist* (1988), is also quite useful. Albert Gore Sr. has been examined carefully in Kyle Longley, *Senator Albert Gore, Sr.: Tennessee Maverick* (2004), and Robert C. Hodges, "The Cooing of a Dove: Senator Albert Gore Sr.'s Opposition to the Vietnam War," *Peace and Change* 22 (April 1997). The most helpful works for John Sherman Cooper are: Robert Schulman, *John Sherman Cooper: The Global Kentuckian* (1976); Robert F. Maddox, "John Sherman Cooper and the Vietnam War," *Journal of the West Virginia Historical Association* 11 (1987); Fredrik Logevall, "A Delicate Balance: John Sherman Cooper and the Republican Opposition to the Vietnam War," in R. B. Woods, *Vietnam and the American Political Tradition* (2003); and Johns, *Vietnam's Second Front*. The views of other antiwar southerners have been assessed in Patrick L. Cox, *Ralph Yarborough, the People's Senator* (2002); Gary A. Keith, *Eckhardt: There Once Was a Congressman from Texas* (2007); and Claude Dennison Pepper, with Hayes Gorey, *Pepper: Eyewitness to a Century* (1987).

In addition to many of the materials cited above, I have relied more specifically on the following for the Nixon years: Johns, *Vietnam's Second*

Front; Walter LaFeber, *The Deadly Bet: LBJ, Vietnam and the 1968 Election* (2005); Dan T. Carter, *The Politics of Rage: George Wallace, the Origins of the New Conservatism, and the Transformation of American Politics* (1995); Carter, *From George Wallace to Newt Gingrich: Race in the Conservative Counterrevolution* (1996); Kenneth Heineman, "The Silent Majority Speaks: Antiwar Protest and Backlash, 1965–1972," *Peace and Change* 17 (October 1992); Jeffrey Kimball, *Nixon's Vietnam War* (1998); Melvin Small, *The Presidency of Richard Nixon* (1999); and Small, *Johnson, Nixon, and the Doves* (1988). For the South's response to My Lai and Calley's prosecution, see the Mark David Carson article cited above; Michael R. Belknap, *The Vietnam War on Trial: The My Lai Massacre and the Court-Martial of Lieutenant Calley* (2002); and David Frum, *How We Got Here: The 70's: The Decade That Brought You Modern Life (for Better or Worse)* (2000).

My coverage of African American views of the war and the intersection of the Civil Rights Movement and Vietnam is derived primarily from an excellent body of existing work. Informative and highly perceptive overviews of African Americans and US foreign relations are available in Brenda Gayle Plummer, *Rising Wind: Black Americans and U.S. Foreign Affairs, 1935–1960* (1996); Plummer, *In Search of Power: African Americans in the Era of Decolonization* (2013); Thomas Borstelmann, *The Cold War and the Color Line: American Race Relations in the Global Arena* (2001); and Mary L. Dudziak, *Cold War Civil Rights: Race and the Image of American Democracy* (2002). Among the focused works on Vietnam and the Civil Rights Movement, the most recent and most useful study is Daniel S. Lucks, *Selma to Saigon: The Civil Rights Movement and the Vietnam War* (2014). Lawrence Allen Eldridge's *Chronicles of a Two-Front War: Civil Rights and Vietnam in the African American Press* (2011) adds a comprehensive analysis of black papers. I also gleaned useful materials from Andrew J. DeRoche, *Andrew Young: Civil Rights Ambassador* (2003); Herman Graham III, *The Brothers' Vietnam War: Black Power, Manhood, and the Military Experience* (1997); Adam Fairclough, "Martin Luther King, Jr. and the War in Vietnam," *Phylon* 45 (March 1984); Henry E. Darby and Margaret N. Rowley, "King on Vietnam and Beyond," *Phylon* 17 (September 1986); Herbert Shapiro, "The Vietnam War and the American Civil Rights Movement," *Journal of Ethnic Studies* 16 (Winter 1989); and Thomas J. Noer, "Martin Luther King, Jr. and the Cold War,"

Peace and Change 22 (April 1997). I have supplemented these studies by working selectively in the microfilm copies of the Records of the National Association for the Advancement of Colored People, the Records of the Southern Christian Leadership Conference, and the Student Nonviolent Coordinating Committee Papers (all in the Manuscripts Division of the Library of Congress) and examining available copies of the *Atlanta Daily World*, the *Birmingham World*, the *Jackson Advocate*, and the *Norfolk Journal and Guide* (both online and at the Moorland-Spingarn Research Center at Howard University).

For Mexican American soldiers and students, I have utilized Ralph Guzman, "Mexican American Casualties in Vietnam," *La Raza* 1 (2012); Lea Ybarra, ed., *Vietnam Veteranos: Chicanos Recall the War* (2004); George Mariscol, ed., *Aztlan and Viet Nam: Chicano and Chicana Experiences of the War* (1999); Charley Trujillo, ed., *Soldados: Chicanos in Viet Nam* (1990); and Lorena Oropeza, *Rasa Si Guerra No! Chicano Protest during the Viet Nam War Era* (2005).

The South and defense spending are examined by Bruce J. Schulman, *From Cotton Belt to Sunbelt: Federal Policy, Economic Development, and the Transformation of the South, 1938–1980* (1994); "Southern Militarism," *Southern Exposure* 1 (1973); David L. Carlton, "The American South and the U.S. Defense Economy: A Historical View," in Carlton and Peter A. Coclanis, eds., *The South, the Nation, and the World: Perspectives on Southern Economic Development* (2003); Kari Frederickson, "Confronting the Garrison State: South Carolina in the Early Cold War Era," *Journal of Southern History* 72 (May 2006); Frederickson, *Cold War Dixie: Militarization and Modernization in the American South* (2013); Catherine A. Lutz, *Home Front: A Military City and the American Twentieth Century* (2001); Ann Markusen, Peter Hall, Scott Campbell, and Sabina Deitrick, *The Rise of the Gunbelt: The Military Remapping of Industrial America* (1991); and Thomas Borstelmann, "The Cold War and the American South," in Jeffrey A. Engel, ed., *Local Consequences of the Global Cold War* (2008).

In assessing the crucial religious dimension of the South's responses to the Cold War and Vietnam, see Andrew Preston, *Sword of the Spirit, Shield of Faith: Religion in American War and Diplomacy* (2012), and William Inboden, *Religion and American Foreign Policy, 1945–1960: The Soul of Containment* (2008), for path-breaking overviews. David J. Settje, *Faith and War: How Christians Debated the Cold and Vietnam Wars* (2011), devotes more extensive attention to Vietnam. For more specifically southern studies, see Richard L. Nutt, *Toward Peacemaking: Presbyterians in the South and National Security, 1945–1983* (1994), and Gregory D. Tomlin, "Hawks and Doves: Southern Baptist Responses to Military Intervention in Southeast Asia, 1965–1973" (PhD dissertation, Southwestern Baptist Theological Seminary, 2003).

Christian G. Appy, *Working-Class War: American Combat Soldiers and Vietnam* (1993); Kyle Longley, *Grunts: The American Combat Soldier in Vietnam* (2008); and Yvonne Honeycutt Baldwin and John Ernst, "In the Valley: The Combat Infantryman and the Vietnam War," in David L. Anderson and John Ernst, eds., *The War That Never Ends: New Perspectives on the Vietnam War* (2007), provide excellent overviews of American ground soldiers' experiences in Vietnam. Baldwin and Ernst include revealing materials from their work on Kentucky soldiers and veterans. Heather Marie Stur, *Beyond Combat: Women and Gender in the Vietnam Era* (2011), adds important coverage of women soldiers and volunteer NGO workers who served in the war zone. James E. Westheider, *Fighting on Two Fronts: African Americans and the Vietnam War* (1997); Westheider, *The African American Experience in Vietnam: Brothers in Arms* (2008); and Graham, *The Brothers' Vietnam War*, concentrate on African American soldiers. Nick Turse, *Kill Anything That Moves: The Real American War in Vietnam* (2013), complements these works and devotes special attention to the war's devastating impact on Vietnamese civilians.

In addressing southern soldiers I have consulted twenty oral interviews in the Vietnam Oral History Project at the US Army History and Education Center, Carlisle, PA, and read selectively in the massive oral history section of Texas Tech University's online Vietnam Archive. Southerners are emphasized in James R. Wilson, ed., *Landing Zones: Southern Veterans Remember Vietnam* (1990); William J. Brinker, ed., *A Time for Looking Back: Putnam County* [Tennessee] *Veterans, Their Families, and the Vietnam War* (1990); and Jim Wilson, *The Sons of Bardstown: 25 Years of Vietnam in an American Town* (1994). Biographies, autobiographies, and southerners' oral histories included in other published collections supplement these works. See Gregory Daddis, *Westmoreland's War: Reassessing American Strategy in Vietnam* (2014); H. R. McMaster, "Adaptive Leadership: Harold G. 'Hal' Moore," in Harry S. Laver and Jeffrey J. Matthews, eds., *The Art of Command: Military Leadership from George Washington to Colin Powell* (2008); Trent Angers, *The Forgotten Hero of My Lai: The Hugh Thompson Story* (1999); Wallace Terry, ed., *Bloods: Black Veterans of the Vietnam War: An Oral History* (1985); Kathryn Marshall, ed., *In the Combat Zone: An Oral History of American Women in Vietnam, 1966–1975* (1987); Keith Walker, ed., *A Piece of My Heart: The Stories of 26 Women Who Served in Vietnam* (1986); Ron Steinman, ed., *The Soldiers' Story: Vietnam in Their Own Words* (2000); Bernard Edelman, ed., *Dear America: Letters Home from Vietnam* (1985); Christian G. Appy, *Patriots: The Vietnam War Remembered from All Sides* (2003); Ybarra, *Vietnam Veteranos;* William C. Westmoreland, *A Soldier Reports* (1976); Larry Gwin, *Baptism: A Vietnam Memoir* (1999); Max Cleland, *Heart of a Patriot: How I Found the Courage to Survive Vietnam, Walter Reed and Karl Rove* (2009); Terry Whitmore, as told to Richard Weber, *Memphis Nam Sweden* (1971); Harold G. Moore and Joseph L. Galloway, *We Were Soldiers Once . . . and Young: Ia Drang—The Battle that Changed the War in Vietnam* (1993); and Moore and Galloway, *We Are Soldiers Still: A Journey Back to the Battlefields of Vietnam* (2008). For more perspective on Jim Webb, Gustav Hasford, and their novels, see Owen W. Gilman Jr., *Vietnam and the Southern Imagination* (1992); Myra MacPherson, *Long Time Passing: Vietnam and the Haunted Generation* (1984); Matthew Samuel Ross, "An Examination of the Life and Work of Gustav Hasford" (MA thesis, University of Nevada, Las Vegas, 2010); and Ross, "Haunted by the Ghosts of Pickett's Charge: Echoes of the Civil War in Two Novels by Unreconstructed Veterans of the Vietnam War" (forthcoming in *Southern Cultures*).

For southern students, I have read student newspapers from the University of Georgia, Louisiana State University, the University of South Carolina, the University of Texas at Austin, and the University of Virginia and drawn extensively on materials in the Nixon Project for the unprecedented student protests in May and June 1970. Surveys of student opinions and campus incidents, commissioned by the Nixon administration and carried out by the Urban Institute and the Urban Research Corporation, provided important insights into the attitudes and actions of southern students compared to those in other regions. National student protests are examined by Charles DeBenedetti, with Charles Chatfield, *An American Ordeal: The Antiwar Movement of the Vietnam Era* (1990); Kenneth J. Heineman, *Campus Wars: The Peace Movement at American State Univer-*

sities in the Vietnam Era (1993); Melvin Small, *Antiwarriors: The Vietnam War and the Battle for America's Hearts and Minds* (2002); and Rhodri Jeffreys-Jones, *Peace Now! American Society and the Ending of the Vietnam War* (1999). In addition to a number of excellent university histories and individual studies of southern students, such as Mitchell K. Hall, "'A Crack in Time': The Response of Students at the University of Kentucky to the Tragedy at Kent State, May 1970," *Register of the Kentucky Historical Society* 83 (Winter 1985); Ruth Anne Thompson, "'A Taste of Student Power': Protest at the University of Tennessee, 1964–1970," *Tennessee Historical Quarterly* 57 (Spring–Summer 1998); and Stephen H. Wheeler, "'Hell No—We Won't Go, Ya'll': Southern Student Opposition to the Vietnam War," in Marc Jason Gilbert, ed., *The Vietnam War on Campus: Other Voices, More Distant Drums* (2001), I have drawn on several important books and dissertations: Gregg L. Michel, *Struggle for a Better South: The Southern Student Organizing Committee, 1964–1969* (2004); Doug Rossinow, *The Politics of Authenticity: Liberalism, Christianity, and the New Left in America* (1998); Jeffrey A. Turner, *Sitting In and Speaking Out: Student Movements in the American South, 1960–1970* (2010); and Stephen Eugene Parr, "The Forgotten Radicals: The New Left in the Deep South: Florida State University, 1960–1972" (PhD dissertation, Florida State University, 2000). Martha Biondi, *The Black Revolution on Campus* (2012); Ibram H. Rogers, *The Black Campus Movement: Black Students and the Racial Reconstruction of Higher Education* (2012); and Tim Spofford, *Lynch Street: The May 1970 Slayings at Jackson State College* (1988) provided essential information for black students.

The revealing relationship of southerners, country music, and the war can be examined in Milton McLaurin, "Country Music and the Vietnam War," in James C. Cobb and Charles R. Wilson, eds., *Perspectives on the American South: An Annual Review of Society, Politics, and Culture* 3 (1985); Ray Pratt, "'There Must Be Some Way Outta Here!': The Vietnam War in American Popular Music," in Kenton J. Clymer, ed., *The Vietnam War: Its History, Literature, and Music* (1998); Lee Andresen, *Battle Notes: Music of the Vietnam War* (2000); and Jens Lund, "Country Music Goes to War: Songs for the Red-Blooded American," *Popular Music and Society* 1, no. 4 (1972).

Michael J. Allen, *Until the Last Man Comes Home: POWs, MIAs, and the Unending Vietnam War* (2009), provides essential context for examining Jerry McCuistion's experience as a POW wife and her role in bringing the POW issue to national attention.

In considering the South, the end of the war, and the conflict's meaning, I drew upon Gaines M. Foster, "Coming to Terms with Defeat: Post-Vietnam America and the Post–Civil War South," *Virginia Quarterly Review* 66 (Winter 1990); C. Vann Woodward, *The Burden of Southern History* (1968); Cobb, *Redefining Southern Culture;* Jeffrey P. Kimball, "The Stab-in-the-Back Legend and the Vietnam War," *Armed Forces and Society* 14 (Spring 1988); Robert J. McMahon, "Contested Memory: The Vietnam War and American Society, 1975–2001," *Diplomatic History* 26 (Spring 2002); and George C. Herring, "The War That Never Seems to Go Away," in Anderson and Ernst, eds., *The War That Never Ends* (2007).

Index

under Nixon and, 253; on Nixon's
Vietnam options in 1971, 324;
Nixon's Vietnam strategies and,
253, 255; peace negotiations and,
348, 349, 350, 354
Knowles, Richard T., 174
Korean War, 45–46, 47
Kunstler, William, 313
Ky, Nguyen Cao, 72

Laird, Melvin, 115, 253, 254, 302–3,
323
Lam Son 719, 325, 326
Landrum, Phillip M., 324, 329
Laotian invasion, 325, 326
Larsen, W. W., 29
Lausche, Frank L., 129
League of Nations, 32
Lee, Robert E., 151
Le May, Curtis, 251
Lend-Lease Bill, 33
Lerner, Mitchell, 65–66
Leuchtenburg, William E., 72–73
Lexington (KY) Herald Leader, 275–76,
287, 311
Limited Test Ban Treaty (1963), 45
Lincoln, Abraham, 20
Linebacker campaigns, 349, 350, 352,
353–54
linkage, 254, 255
Little Rock School integration crisis,
48–49
Lockley, Timothy, 149
Lodge, Henry Cabot, 32
Long, Russell B.: 1966 SFRC hearings
and, 129–30, 140; assessment of
the war, 360–61, 362; early views
of US intervention in Vietnam,
56, 63; Gulf of Tonkin Resolution
and, 88; influence over defense
spending during the Vietnam War,
70, 71; on Johnson's intervention
in the Dominican Republic, 46;

response to the Formosa Resolution,
61; support for the war under
Johnson, 110, 112, 126, 200, 242;
support for the war under Nixon,
260; unwillingness to accept
responsibility for the war's outcome,
361; women constituents' views on
the war, 337
Louisiana Purchase, 17, 21
Louisiana State University, 294–95,
298, 303, 304, 309–10, 318
Louisville (KY) Courier-Journal: on
the 1973 peace settlement and
assessment of the war, 356–57; on
the Gulf of Tonkin Resolution,
91–92; response to the Julian
Bond–SNCC controversy, 210;
response to the Cambodian
invasion, 274–75; response to the
Laotian invasion, 326; views of the
war in 1968, 248; views of the war
under Johnson, 116, 121, 138
Lowe, Lewis, II, 156, 162
Loyola University (New Orleans), 304
Lucks, Daniel, 365
Lynchburg News, 25
Lynn, Loretta, 336
LZ X-ray, battle of, 174–77. *See also* Ia
Drang, battle of

Maddox (USS), 82
Maddox, Lester, 265
Madison, James, 14, 15, 18
mad-man strategy, 254, 255, 268, 349,
350
Mahon, George H., 2, 45, 69–70, 126,
259, 364
Mann, Robert, 7, 352
Mansfield, Mike, 103, 107, 332
Mansfield Resolution, 332, 348
Mao Zedong, 39–40
March on the Pentagon, 195
Marshall, George C., 77

race and racism: Anglo-Saxonism,
34–35; discrimination in the
drafting of African Americans, 154–
55; experiences of African American
soldiers in Vietnam, 163–66, 192;
impact on southern response to US
foreign relations, 23; opposition to
the Civil Rights Movement and,
48–49; southern attitudes during
the Cold War years, 37, 42–44,
48–49. *See also* slavery
Radford, Arthur, 57
Raisor, Tom, 178
Randolph, Nancy, 153
Rankin, Cheri, 153–54
Rankin, Jeanette, 303
Rarick, John R., 265
Rayburn, Sam, 34, 40
Red Cross Supplemental Recreation
Activities Overseas, 154, 161
Reddan, John T. M., 266
"Redeemers," 22
regionalism: defined, 8–9; US foreign
relations and, 1. *See also* southern
regionalism
religion: Muhammad Ali's opposition
to the war and, 212–13; antiwar
southerners and, 122, 203, 204,
206–7, 351–52; Johnson's belief
in Christian internationalism,
74–75; Presbyterians, 203–4; as a
response of southern soldiers to war
experiences, 163; role in southern
response to the war, 119–20,
202–7, 351–52; southern African
Americans and opposition to the
war, 6, 207; Southern Baptists,
204–7; southern evangelical
Protestantism, 31–32; southern
views of the Cold War and,
39–40; John Tower's defense of the
morality of US actions in Vietnam,
202; Woodrow Wilson and, 31

republicanism, 14
Republic of South Vietnam. *See* South
Vietnam
Reston, James, 195, 226, 350
Richardson, Charles, 149–50
Richmond News Leader, 92
Richmond Planet, 26
Richmond Times Dispatch, 314
Riddick, Ida, 337–38
Riels, George D. "Danny," 152, 162,
167, 168
Rivers, L. Mendel: on the Bay of Pigs
invasion, 46; defense of William
Calley, 184; defense spending in the
South and, 40, 41; hostility toward
antiwar students, 286; influence
over defense spending during the
Vietnam War, 69–70, 71; response
to the Formosa Resolution, 61–62;
response to the My Lai massacre,
265; significance to the Vietnam
War, 2; views of the war under
Johnson, 112–13, 126, 200
Robbins, John, 161
Robertson, A. Willis: constituents'
views of the war, 119, 141; early
views of US intervention in
Vietnam, 63, 80; Gulf of Tonkin
Resolution and, 51, 88–89;
influence over defense spending
during the Vietnam War, 69; views
of the war under Johnson, 113
Robinson, Jackie, 215
Rolling Thunder campaign: 1967 SPIS
hearings and reactions, 225–32;
escalation in 1967, 195; extent
of, 97; Johnson resumes in 1966,
134; Johnson's 1968 decision
for de-escalation, 241; Johnson's
dissimulation regarding, 99–100,
104; Johnson's pursuit of a limited
war and, 98–99; March 1967 SPIS
report on, 198; southern legislators

supporting, 126, 200; views of Presbyterians on, 204
Roosevelt, Franklin Delano, 34
Rostow, Walt Whitman, 124
ROTC, 299–300
Rubin, Jerry, 313
"Ruby Don't Take Your Love to Town" (Tillis), 336
Rusk, Dean: 1966 SFRC hearings and reactions, 127, 128, 129, 130–34, 137; 1968 SFRC hearings, 245–46; assessment of Vietnam in 1963, 78; biographical overview, 76–77; defense of the war in 1967, 237; exchanges with Fulbright, 104, 125–26, 130–34; foreign policy perspectives, 77–78; Gulf of Tonkin Resolution and, 51, 82, 83; Johnson's 1968 decision for de-escalation and, 240, 241; in Johnson's strategy for controlling congressional responses to the war, 100–101; movement toward war in Vietnam in 1964, 78–79; objectives for peace negotiations in 1968, 241–42; pursuit of a limited war in Vietnam, 98–99; on racial discrimination in the United States, 48; rejects the 1967 Ashmore-Baggs peace efforts, 197, 198; relationship with Johnson, 77; significance to the Vietnam War, 2; unwillingness to accept responsibility for the war's outcome, 361; Frazier Woolard's accusations against, 124
Russell, Richard B.: antiwar southerners and, 6; assessment of Asians, 5; constituents' views of the war, 118, 120, 141, 142, 224, 258; defense spending during the Cold War years and, 40, 41; early views of US commitment to Vietnam, 51, 54–55, 57–58, 63, 67; Gulf of

Tonkin Resolution and, 51, 83, 84, 85, 88; influence over defense spending during the war, 69, 70; Johnson's personal agony over the war and, 219; opposition to foreign aid, 43; opposition to Hawaii's admission as a state, 42; opposition to the Civil Rights Movement, 48; relationship with Johnson, 106; response to the Middle East Resolution, 62; significance to the Vietnam War, 2; support for military spending and strength, 44, 45; support for the Korean War, 45–46; support for the reassertion of congressional powers in foreign relations, 220; support for the war under Nixon, 242, 259–60, 359–60; views of US involvement in Vietnam under Johnson, 79–80, 95, 96, 106–8, 126, 144, 199–200
Rustin, Bayard, 215

Sadler, Barry, 335
Saint-Marie, Buffy, 334
Salisbury, Harrison, 196
Sanchez, S. B., 157
Santo Domingo, 18
Savannah River Plant, 40
Scott, C. A., 257
Scott, Gary, 165
Scott, Hugh, 262, 269, 323
segregationists: during the Cold War years, 42
Senate Appropriations Committee, 69
Senate Armed Services Committee (SASC), 40, 41, 69, 111, 229, 260, 261
Senate Foreign Relations Committee (SFRC): 1966 public hearings on the war and reactions, 8, 98, 125–35, 137, 138, 139–40, 144; 1968 hearings, 243–46;

STUDIES IN CONFLICT, DIPLOMACY, AND PEACE

SERIES EDITORS: George C. Herring, Andrew L. Johns, and Kathryn C. Statler

This series focuses on key moments of conflict, diplomacy, and peace from the eighteenth century to the present to explore their wider significance in the development of U.S. foreign relations. The series editors welcome new research in the form of original monographs, interpretive studies, biographies, and anthologies from historians, political scientists, journalists, and policymakers. A primary goal of the series is to examine the United States' engagement with the world, its evolving role in the international arena, and the ways in which the state, nonstate actors, individuals, and ideas have shaped and continue to influence history, both at home and abroad.

ADVISORY BOARD MEMBERS

David Anderson, California State University, Monterey Bay
Laura Belmonte, Oklahoma State University
Robert Brigham, Vassar College
Paul Chamberlin, University of Kentucky
Jessica Chapman, Williams College
Frank Costigliola, University of Connecticut
Michael C. Desch, University of Notre Dame
Kurk Dorsey, University of New Hampshire
John Ernst, Morehead State University
Joseph A. Fry, University of Nevada, Las Vegas
Ann Heiss, Kent State University
Sheyda Jahanbani, University of Kansas
Mark Lawrence, University of Texas
Mitchell Lerner, Ohio State University
Kyle Longley, Arizona State University
Robert McMahon, Ohio State University
Michaela Hoenicke Moore, University of Iowa
Lien-Hang T. Nguyen, University of Kentucky
Jason Parker, Texas A&M University
Andrew Preston, Cambridge University
Thomas Schwartz, Vanderbilt University
Salim Yaqub, University of California, Santa Barbara

BOOKS IN THE SERIES

The Gulf: The Bush Presidencies and the Middle East
Michael F. Cairo

Diplomatic Games: Sport, Statecraft, and International Relations since 1945
Edited by Heather L. Dichter and Andrew L. Johns

Nothing Less Than War: A New History of America's Entry into World War I
Justus D. Doenecke

Grounded: The Case for Abolishing the United States Air Force
Robert M. Farley

The American South and the Vietnam War: Belligerence, Protest, and Agony in Dixie
Joseph A. Fry

Obama at War: Congress and the Imperial Presidency
Ryan C. Hendrickson

The Conversion of Senator Arthur H. Vandenberg: From Isolation to International Engagement
Lawrence S. Kaplan

The Currents of War: A New History of American-Japanese Relations, 1899–1941
Sidney Pash

So Much to Lose: John F. Kennedy and American Policy in Laos
William J. Rust

Lincoln Gordon: Architect of Cold War Foreign Policy
Bruce L. R. Smith

www.ingramcontent.com/pod-product-compliance
Lightning Source LLC
Chambersburg PA
CBHW020340100426
42812CB00029B/3193/J